PRESIDENTS

EVERY

QUESTION

ANSWERED

SMITHSONIAN INSTITUTION

HYLAS
PUBLISHING

PRESIDENTS

EVERY QUESTION ANSWERED

Everything you could possibly want to know
about the Nation's Chief Executives

Carter Smith
Introduction by Allen Weinstein

HYLAS
PUBLISHING

Hylas Publishing
Publisher: Sean Moore
Creative Director: Karen Prince
Design: Matt Collins, Cyber Media (India) Limited
Editor: Hannah Choi
Production Consultant: Madeleine Day
www.hylaspublishing.com

Editorial Consultants: Media Projects

First Published by
Hylas Publishing
129 Main Street, Irvington,
New York 10533

Text Copyright: Hylas Publishing
Compilation Copyright: Hylas Publishing 2004
The moral right of the author has been asserted.

First American Edition Published in 2004
02 03 04 05 10 9 8 7 6 5 4 3 2 1

ISBN 1-59258-066-1

Cyber Media (India) Limited
Project Manager: Taru Agarwal
Team Leader: Vatsala Arora
Visualizer: Divya Topa
Designer: Sheetal Gambhir
Text & Research: Laldinmoi Pangamte
Copyeditor: Moushumi Mohanty
www.cmil.com

Set in Univers, aGaramond and Centaure MT
Printed and bound in England by Butler and
Tanner Color origination by Radstock
Reproductions Ltd, Midsomer Norton

Distributed by National Book Network

Contents

Presents of a Young Nation

Presidents of the Gilded Age

Presidents of the Early 20th Century

Presidents of A Global Power

Foreword

by Allen Weinstein

Carter Smith's compendium, *Presidents: Every Question Answered*, provides readers with an entertaining and informative overview of the fascinating history of America's Chief Executives. To clarify matters at the outset concerning the book's tongue-in-cheek subtitle, "every" question concerning the U.S. Presidency is obviously not answered in this engaging volume—though a great many are. Those seeking historical background should find *Presidents* an extremely helpful introduction to the office and its occupants, from George Washington to George W. Bush. Even the buffs and professional historians who scan the book may discover either some long-forgotten information or unfamiliar facts.

The book's format lends itself to leisurely browsing. Each President is introduced in a brief essay followed by basic biographical facts, chronological summaries of major events in that President's administration, a timeline, profiles of the First Lady (when there was one), boxed discussions of major events, and relevant quotations concerning the incumbent.

Alert readers will recognize that Carter Smith has given certain presidents whose period in office most historians consider especially significant—among them Washington, Lincoln, Franklin Roosevelt, and Ronald Reagan—more detailed attention than others whose term or terms in office were arguably of lesser importance. Readers' judgments may or may not agree with those of the author; this writer, for example, has his own occasional divergences from Mr. Smith's allocations. But that should not detract from enjoyment of the volume overall.

Readers may find of special interest in a book such as this the evolution of the Presidency in power and purpose among the three branches of government, especially in the second half of the twentieth century. Still, the Constitution's

GRAND, NATIONAL UNION BANNER FOR 1864.
LIBERTY, UNION AND VICTORY.

delegation of authority to holders of the office—virtually everyone at the time expected trustworthy George Washington to be its initial occupant—prefigured its later development. Even some of the Founders expected this. Thus, the British historian Marcus Cunliffe reminded us that Alexander Hamilton "predicted that a time would come 'when every vital question of state will be merged in the question, Who will be the next President?' " This prediction, Cunliffe noted, "was borne out, in large part because the Presidency became the apex of the contest between excited and organized political parties [in the United States]."

In our time, the American public has come to expect—indeed, demand— vigorous leadership from its Presidents in both foreign and domestic affairs. Only on occasion in the 19th century—the Civil War years under Lincoln being the most notable exception—was this the case. The modern pursuit of a powerful Chief Executive began with Theodore Roosevelt's assumption of the office after William McKinley's assassination. It was "TR," as he was known, who wrote of his almost-seven years in office that he had developed "a very definite philosophy about the Presidency. I think it should be a very powerful office, and I think the President should be a very strong man who uses without hesitation every power that the position yields; but...he should be sharply watched by the people [and] held to a strict accountability by them."

Only a few of the subsequent occupants of the American Presidency have disputed TR's expansive vision of the office and its authority. Even earlier, however, some American presidents rarely hesitated to define the powers of their office as broadly as their specific actions required.

Readers who browse the pages of this book can discover for themselves the varied uses (and occasional abuses) of presidential power as each Chief Executive experiences the achievements and failures, dramas and melodramas, tumult and occasional tragedy of his historic moment as President of the United States.

NOTE: The collection of facts and other material for every presidential essay in the book, as well as the opinions it offers on specific Presidents, are entirely those of Carter Smith, the book's author, to whom all reader comments should be addressed.

THE FOUNDING

PRESIDENTS

George Washington

"I long ago despaired of any other reward for my services than the satisfaction arising from a consciousness of doing my duty, and from the esteem of my friends".

According to historian Gordon Wood, George Washington "was an extraordinary man who made it possible for ordinary men to rule". Certainly, few men of his time were held in such high regard by their countrymen. The hero of the Revolution had held together his ragtag continental army through harsh winters and repeated retreats and defeats to finally outlast the British and prevail at Yorktown. Thus by the time Washington reluctantly came out of brief retirement from national service to act as presiding officer at the Constitutional Convention in 1787, he was not merely the favored choice to be elected president, but the only choice. The drafters of the Constitution—Alexander Hamilton, James Madison, Gouverneur Morris and others—would write the Constitution and create a strong presidency with Washington in mind. He remains the only American president to receive all electoral votes cast—not once, but twice.

Nonetheless, when Washington assumed the office, both the presidency and the American system itself were still very much unformed. It would be the precedents Washington set that would give practical substance to the theories set down in Philadelphia. His decision to summon his administration's department heads to meet regularly firmly established Cabinet meetings as a standard practice for all presidents to follow. It was Washington who decided that the president should live in the same place where he worked, and he helped to choose the site and design of the future capital city that would bear his name.

Washington was not without his critics. Jefferson criticized him for being overly reliant on the advice of Treasury Secretary Alexander Hamilton, who favored a strong federal government and improved relations with Great Britain. Nevertheless, Washington skillfully balanced the opposing interests in the country. Despite his deep regret that political parties grew out of the opposing camps within his own administration, he worked hard to instill in his contemporaries a sense of the national union, bearing in mind what he saw as the best interests of future Americans, or the "unborn millions" as he called them. For this then, it is no wonder that he is remembered as "Father of His Country".

Biographical Facts

Born: February 22, 1732 in Pope's Creek, Westmoreland County, Virginia

Ancestry: English

Father: Augustine Washington; born 1694 in Westmoreland County, Virginia; died April 12, 1743 in King George County, Virginia

Father's Occupations: Planter; iron manufacturer

Mother: Mary Ball Washington; born 1708 in Lancaster County, Virginia; died August 25, 1789 near Fredericksburg, Virginia

Wife: Martha Dandridge Custis; born June 21,1731 in New Kent County, Virginia; died May 22, 1802 in Mount Vernon, Virginia

Marriage: January 6, 1759 in New Kent County, Virginia

Children: None; two adopted from his wife's first marriage

Home: Mount Vernon, Virginia

Education: Private tutoring by family

Religious Affiliation: Episcopalian

Occupations before Presidency: Surveyor; soldier; planter

Military Service: Virginia Militia; Commander in Chief of Continental Army

Political Offices before Presidency: Member of Virginia House of Burgesses; Justice of Fairfax County; Delegate to First and Second Continental Congresses; President of Constitutional Convention

Political Party: None, but favored Federalists

Age at Inauguration: 57

Occupation after Presidency: Planter

Death: December 14, 1799 at Mount Vernon, Virginia

Place of Burial: Mount Vernon, Virginia

Nickname: Old Man; Father of His Country

Writings: *The Writings of George Washington from the Original Manuscript Sources*

Election of 1789

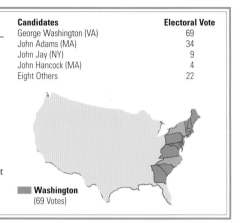

Candidates	Electoral Vote
George Washington (VA)	69
John Adams (MA)	34
John Jay (NY)	9
John Hancock (MA)	4
Eight Others	22

About the Election: After the new Constitution was ratified, the Electoral College met in January 1789. Each elector voted for two candidates, with the person garnering the most votes becoming president, and the runner-up becoming vice president. Although George Washington had initially been hesitant to run for the office, he was the unanimous first choice of the electors. John Adams of Massachusetts was the second choice of most Federalists. However, Alexander Hamilton feared that if Adams was the unanimous choice for vice president, he would actually tie Washington. To prevent embarrassment to Washington, Hamilton arranged that a number of other candidates enter the race to pull votes away from Adams. Thus, Adams won the second highest total, and was elected vice president.

■ **Washington**
(69 Votes)

Washington's First Term 1789-1793

April 30, 1789: GEORGE WASHINGTON IS INAUGURATED as the first president of the United States in New York City, the nation's first capital.

July 4, 1789: Congress, led by Representative James Madison, enacts the FIRST PROTECTIVE TARIFF, after he consults with President Washington about the need for the measure.

March 26, 1790: Congress passes the United States' first NATURALIZATION LAW, which establishes terms of citizenship.

May 29, 1790: RHODE ISLAND RATIFIES THE CONSTITUTION, becoming the last of the original thirteen states under the Articles of Confederation to join the newly formed Union.

May 31, 1790: President Washington signs the FIRST UNITED STATES COPYRIGHT LAW.

July 16, 1790: President Washington signs a bill into law that permanently placed the nation's capital along the Potomac River, in an area to be called the DISTRICT OF COLUMBIA.

August 4, 1790: President Washington signs a bill into law that directs the federal government to assume the REVOLUTIONARY WAR DEBTS of the states.

December 6, 1790: THE UNITED STATES CAPITOL MOVES from New York to Philadelphia, where it remains until the District of Columbia is completed in 1800.

December 13, 1790: Secretary of the Treasury Alexander Hamilton, with President Washington's support, calls for the House of Representatives to create an official BANK OF THE UNITED STATES. Before submitting a bill to the House, however, Washington asks that members of his Cabinet give him their opinions of the proposal.

February 15, 1791: Secretary of State Thomas Jefferson challenges the constitutionality of Hamilton's proposal for a Bank of the United States. Adhering to a STRICT CONSTRUCTION of the Tenth Amendment, which reserves powers not delegated to the federal government to the states, Jefferson argues that the incorporation of a national bank is not a power specifically granted by the Constitution.

George and Martha Washington with two of Martha's grandchildren, Eleanor (Nelly) Custis, and George Washington Parke Custis.

	1732	1733	1740	1746
■ Washington's Life				
■ U.S. & World Events	George Washington is born on February 22, in Westmoreland County, Virginia.	Georgia, the last of the original 13 British colonies in North America, is founded.	Frederick the Great begins his reign in Russia.	At age 15, Washington begins work as a surveyor.

First Lady: Martha Custis Washington

Martha Washington, said one of her contemporaries, was "simple, easy and dignified". Although she had grown up as the daughter of a wealthy Virginia planter, she did not shy from difficult work. After her first husband, Colonel Daniel Parke Custis died, leaving her alone at age 25 with two small children, she managed the Custis estate on her own. During the Revolutionary War, she often followed her second husband from camp to camp, putting herself in danger as she knit stockings for the soldiers.

When her husband became president, Mrs. Washington was initially wary about living such a public life, but in time took to her role. She hosted weekly state dinners, as well as co-hosting informal receptions with Vice President John Adams' wife, Abigail. A warm, gracious and sensible woman, Martha Washington acted as hostess for her husband but took no part in public affairs.

Washington (from right), Hamilton and Jefferson

February 23, 1791: In the DOCTRINE OF IMPLIED POWERS, HAMILTON USES A LOOSE CONSTRUCTION of the Constitution to defend his proposal for a national bank. He argues that the bank was a means by which Congress would exercise its constitutional power to collect taxes and regulate trade. According to Hamilton, because that power was specifically approved in the Constitution, the creation of the bank as a means towards that end was also constitutional.

February 25, 1791: Although Washington is not fully convinced by either Jefferson's or Hamilton's argument, he signs the bill for the creation of the Bank of the United States. He bases his decision on his belief that in cases in which neither opposing argument has swayed him, his support should go to the Cabinet officer whose department is directly involved.

March 3, 1791: At Hamilton's urging, Congress approves its FIRST INTERNAL REVENUE LAW, creating 14 revenue districts and placing a tax on all distilled spirits. The tax is strongly opposed by small farmers in the West, who rely on distilling whisky in order to use up surplus rye and corn crops. The federal law allows agents to enter

Washington's First Administration

First Inauguration: April 30, 1789 at Federal Hall, in New York City, New York
Second Inauguration: March 4, 1793 at Federal Hall, Philadelphia, Pennsylvania
Vice President: John Adams
Secretary of State : Thomas Jefferson
Secretary of the Treasury: Alexander Hamilton
Secretary of War: Henry Knox
Attorney General: Edmund Randolph
Postmaster General: Samuel Osgood (1789-1791); Timothy Pickering (1791-1793)
Supreme Court Appointments: John Jay, Chief Justice (1789); John Rutledge (1789);

William Cushing (1789); Robert H. Harrison (1789); James Wilson (1789); John Blair (1789); James Iredell (1790); Thomas Johnson (1791)
1st Congress: (March 4, 1789-March 4, 1791)
Senate: 17 Federalists; 9 Antifederalists
House: 38 Federalists; 26 Antifederalists
2nd Congress: (March 4, 1791-March 4, 1793)
Senate: 16 Federalists;
13 Democratic-Republicans
House: 37 Federalists;
33 Democratic-Republicans
States Admitted During Term:
North Carolina (1789); Rhode Island (1790); Vermont (1791); Kentucky (1792)

1752	1754-63	1755-58	1759	1762
Washington inherits his brother's estate at Mount Vernon, as well as 18 slaves.	France and Britain fight for control of North America in the French and Indian War.	Washington is commissioned as a colonel, commanding all Virginia forces in the Ohio Territory during the French and Indian War.	Washington marries widow Martha Custis.	French philosopher Jean-Jacques Rousseau publishes *The Social Contract*, imagining a society in which every individual has responsibility for every other.

The U.S. Constitution was written with the understanding that Washington would serve as the first President. He is seen here presiding over the opening of the Constitutional Convention in Philadelphia in 1787.

homes and collect taxes from whisky producers.

May–June, 1791: Thomas Jefferson and James Madison travel through New York and New England to build a national **ANTI-FEDERALIST** coalition. They find support among leading New York politicians such as Governor George Clinton, Robert R. Livingston, and Aaron Burr.

September 9, 1791: Appointed commissioners name the site of the new capital after George Washington. The larger area is called District of Columbia.

October 31, 1791: An anti-Washington newspaper, the *National Gazette*, is formed by poet and journalist, Philip Freneau.

November 4, 1791: The **MIAMI INDIANS** soundly defeat an American military force of 1400 men led by General Arthur St. Clair at the cost of 900 American lives. The Washington Administration had sent

Washington's first Cabinet included Secretary of War, Henry Knox; Secretary of State, Thomas Jefferson; Attorney General Edmund Randolph; and Secretary of the Treasury, Alexander Hamilton.

	1765	1759-74	1773	1775
■ Washington's Life				
■ U.S. & World Events	Great Britain adopts the Stamp Act to raise revenues from American colonies.	Washington serves in the Virginia House of Burgesses, supporting the Patriot cause.	American Patriots dump British tea in Boston Harbor to protest high tariffs on imported goods.	Washington is selected to serve as Commander in Chief of the Continental Army.

Election of 1792

About the Election: In 1792, George Washington was once again reluctant to run for election as president. In addition to old age and illness, Washington also had grown tired with attacks on his administration by the Democratic-Republican controlled press. These attacks highlighted the bitter split within his administration between the Federalists, led by Secretary of the Treasury Alexander Hamilton and the Democratic-Republicans, led by Secretary of State Thomas Jefferson. James Madison, among others, convinced Washington to stand for a second term, arguing that only he could hold the nation together.

For vice president, Hamilton and the Federalists backed John Adams for a second term. The Democratic-Republicans backed New York Governor George Clinton. Federalists strongly opposed Clinton, believing that he had stolen the New York governor's race through fraud. In addition, because it was believed that Clinton intended to remain as governor of New York while also serving as vice president, the federal government would be weakened. In the end, Adams won reelection as vice president by a solid margin.

Candidates	Electoral Vote
George Washington (VA)	132
John Adams (MA)	77
George Clinton (NY)	50
Thomas Jefferson (VA)	5
Aaron Burr (NY)	1

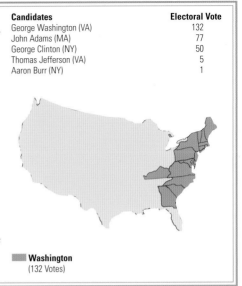

■ **Washington**
(132 Votes)

St. Clair to the Ohio country with the hope that his presence would clear the way for American settlers.

November 26, 1791: Washington convenes all of his administration's department heads to discuss foreign and military affairs. Although he had consulted with individual Cabinet members throughout his administration, this marked the **FIRST FULL CABINET MEETING** in history.

December 15, 1791: The first ten amendments to the U.S. Constitution, known as the **BILL OF RIGHTS**, which guarantees specific individual rights, are ratified by a two-thirds majority of the states, thus becoming part of the U.S. Constitution.

January 12, 1792: President Washington appoints Thomas Pinckney as the **FIRST UNITED STATES MINISTER TO ENGLAND.** Washington instructs him to convey a spirit of "sincere friendship" and to seek the liberation of American commerce from British regulations.

February 2, 1792: The **PRESIDENTIAL SUCCESSION ACT** is passed. The law states that if both the president and vice president die, become disabled, or are otherwise removed from office, the president pro tempore of the Senate would succeed him. If there were no Senate president, the Speaker of the House of Representatives would assume the presidency. Although Thomas Jefferson proposed that the Secretary of State be placed next in line, Federalists stopped his proposal. (In 1886,

Jefferson's proposal would be passed.)

May 8, 1792: Because of growing resistance from Native Americans in the Northwest, Congress passes **THE MILITIA ACT.** The act commissions General Anthony Wayne as Commander in Chief of the Army and authorizes that all white males between the ages of 18 and 45 be enrolled for military service.

September 9, 1792: In a letter to Washington, Jefferson discloses that he intends to resign as Secretary of State when Washington's first term ends because of Jefferson's increasingly hostile personal relationship with Alexander Hamilton.

October 13, 1792: The cornerstone for the Executive Mansion is laid in Washington, D.C.

Washington's Second Term 1793-1797

April 22, 1793: **FRANCE DECLARES WAR ON GREAT BRITAIN, SPAIN, AUSTRIA AND PRUSSIA** after the proclamation of the French Republic in September 1792, and the execution of King Louis XVI on January 21. U.S. public opinion divides between supporters of France and Great Britain. Within Washington's own administration, Hamilton supports Great Britain, while Jefferson favors France. Although the U.S. and France are allies, according to the treaty signed in 1778, Washington seeks to maintain "strict neutrality" and issues the **NEUTRALITY PROCLAMATION**, stating that the United States was at peace with

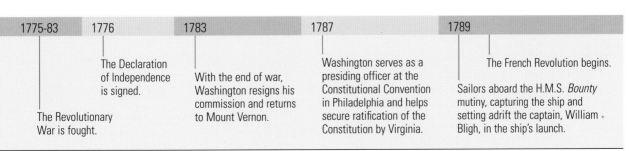

1775-83	1776	1783	1787	1789
	The Declaration of Independence is signed.	With the end of war, Washington resigns his commission and returns to Mount Vernon.	Washington serves as a presiding officer at the Constitutional Convention in Philadelphia and helps secure ratification of the Constitution by Virginia.	The French Revolution begins.
The Revolutionary War is fought.				Sailors aboard the H.M.S. *Bounty* mutiny, capturing the ship and setting adrift the captain, William Bligh, in the ship's launch.

Washington's Second Administration

Second Inauguration: March 4, 1793
at Federal Hall, Philadelphia, Pennsylvania
Vice President: John Adams
Secretary of State: Thomas Jefferson
(1793-1794); Edmund Randolph (1794-1795);
Timothy Pickering (1795-1797)
Secretary of the Treasury: Alexander Hamilton
(1793-1795); Alexander Wolcott (1795-1797)
Secretary of War : Henry Knox (1793-1795);
Timothy Pickering (1795-1796);
James McHenry (1796-1797)
Attorney General: Edmund Randolph
(1793-1794); William Bradford (1794-1795)
Postmaster General:
Timothy Pickering (1793-1795)

Supreme Court Appointments:
William Patterson (1793); John Rutledge,
Chief Justice (1795); Samuel Chase (1796);
Oliver Ellsworth, Chief Justice (1796)
3rd Congress: (March 4, 1793-March 4, 1795)
Senate: 17 Federalists;
13 Democratic-Republicans
House: 48 Federalists
57 Democratic-Republicans;
2nd Congress: (March 4, 1795-March 4, 1797)
Senate: 19 Federalists;
13 Democratic-Republicans
House: 54 Federalists;
52 Democratic-Republicans
States Admitted: Tennessee (1796)

both France and England, and warning American citizens not to commit hostile acts against either side.

July 31, 1793: THOMAS JEFFERSON SUBMITS his resignation as Secretary of State after President Washington begins to heed Hamilton's advice on foreign affairs. The resignation does not become effective until December 31.

November 6, 1793: Great Britain issues Orders in Council that allow for the SEIZURE OF AMERICAN SHIPS carrying French goods in the West Indies and the IMPRESSMENTS OF AMERICAN SAILORS. As a result, tension between the United States and Great Britain rises to the verge of war.

April 19, 1794: The U.S. Senate confirms Washington's choice of JOHN JAY, the Chief Justice of the U.S. Supreme Court, as special envoy to Britain. Jay's assignment is to seek British withdrawal from the Northwest Territory, reparations for American ships seized by Britain, an end to the impressments of American sailors, compensation for slaves seized during the American Revolution, and restoration of trade rights in the West Indies.

June 5, 1794: Congress passes the NEUTRALITY ACT, which forbids U.S. citizens from enlisting in the service of a foreign government and bans the outfitting of armed foreign vessels in U.S. ports.

John Jay, first Chief Justice of the Supreme Court.

July–November, 1794: In the WHISKY REBELLION, small farmers in western Pennsylvania break into an open revolt against a 1791 U.S. FEDERAL TAX ON WHISKY PRODUCERS, comparing the tax to the Stamp Act of 1765, which helped fuel the American Revolution. In response, Washington calls up 15,000 militia from Virginia, Maryland, New Jersey and Pennsylvania. After attempts to reach a negotiated settlement fail, he follows Hamilton's advice and orders the militia to forcibly put down the rebellion, displaying the use of federal power to enforce a federal law within a state.

November 19, 1794: In JAY'S TREATY, Great Britain agrees to withdraw its troops from the Northwest Territory by 1796, to pay the United States $10 million in reparations for seized ships, and to open ports in the British West Indies to very limited U.S. trade. In return, the United States agrees to establish commissions to settle pre-Revolutionary War debts owed to British creditors, and to allow British subjects to continue trading fur on U.S. soil.

January 29, 1795: Congress passes the NATURALIZATION ACT. The law requires non-citizens to live in the United States for at least five years before they are permitted to apply for naturalized citizenship.

January 31, 1795: ALEXANDER HAMILTON RESIGNS as Secretary as of the Treasury, but he remains active in public life and continues to greatly influence Washington.

March 1795: OPPOSITION TO JAY'S TREATY arises after the terms are made public. Democratic-Republicans insist that better terms could have been won by threatening to cut off trade with Great Britain. Southern planters are outraged for the treaty's failure to compensate them for the loss of their slaves. Northern merchants complain that the trade provisions

	1789	1790	1792	1793
■ Washington's Life				
■ U.S. & World Events	Washington is elected the first president of the United States.	The U.S. Capitol relocates temporarily to Philadelphia while planning for a new site on the banks of the Potomac River begins.	Washington is reelected to a second term.	French King Louis XVI is guillotined. The Reign of Terror begins.

George Washington ordered that the slaves on his Mount Vernon estate be freed after his wife's death.

were unsatisfactory. On June 24, after heated debate, the Senate ratifies the agreement, despite Democratic-Republican attempts to block it by withholding the money to enforce it. Washington reluctantly signs the treaty.

October 27, 1795: In PINCKNEY'S TREATY (known officially as the Treaty of San Lorenzo), the United States and Spain settle their dispute over the southern and western borders of the United States. Spain recognizes the Mississippi River to be the border to the west and the 31st parallel as the border to the south. Spain also grants the United States the right to deposit goods at the port of New Orleans. The treaty helps the United States gain control over its vast western lands.

September 19, 1796: WASHINGTON'S FAREWELL address, which he drafted with the help of James Madison, Alexander Hamilton and John Jay, is published in the *Daily American Advertiser* of Philadelphia. In it, Washington announces that he will not run for a third term. He condemns the growth of political parties, especially along regional lines, and warns about protecting the nation's public credit. He also advises the country to stay clear of permanent political alliances with other nations.

Scandal! The Citizen Genêt Affair

In April 1793, at the height of the most radical phase of the French Revolution, the French government sent Edmond Charles Genêt (popularly known as Citizen Genêt) to the United States to win support for France. Immediately after arriving in Charleston, South Carolina, and before presenting his credentials to the U.S. government, Genêt began to commission American seaman to serve as mercenary privateers against British shipping in the West Indies. Enthusiastic pro-French crowds met Genêt wherever he went as he toured the United States. However, when he publicly urged Americans to ignore President Washington's Neutrality Proclamation, Washington, supported by both pro-British Federalists and pro-French Democratic-Republicans, demanded that France recall the envoy. By this time, the new Jacobin government of France had come to power. When Genêt's successor arrived in America in 1794 to arrest Genêt, Washington refused to permit his extradition, recognizing that Genêt would face execution in France. Thus, Genêt remained in America, became an American citizen and married one of the daughters of New York's governor, George Clinton.

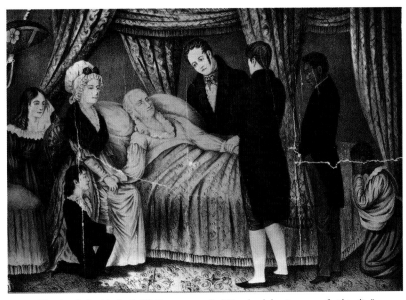

Two days before his death, Washington remarked "I go hard, but I am not afraid to die."

1794	1796	1798	1799
Eli Whitney invents the cotton gin, making short-staple cotton profitable and increasing the demand for slaves in the American South.	British poet and illustrator William Blake publishes *Songs of Experience*. Washington declines to seek a third term and retires to Mount Vernon.	Ireland, led by the revolutionary Wolfe Tone, rises against British rule. The revolt fails.	Washington dies on December 14, in Mount Vernon, Virginia.

John Adams

2nd President (1797–1801)

*"There are two types of education...One should teach us how to make a living,
And the other how to live."*

John Adams once said of himself, "I do not say when I became a politician, for that I never was". Nonetheless, political maneuvering between the nascent Federalist and Democratic-Republican political parties marked Adams' single term as president. While the two parties were born during the Washington administration, it was not until the Adams presidency that their rivalry reached full flower; even though both Washington and Adams distrusted political parties. Adams believed that it was critical that the federal government use its powers to unite the young nation and its people with a common sense of identity and purpose. Although his superior intelligence and unscrupulous morality had helped make him one of the greatest of the founding fathers, Adams was temperamentally unsuited to the task of balancing competing political forces. By his own admission, he was "puffy, vain, and conceited"—traits that made it difficult for him to win the loyalty of many members of his own Federalist party, much less the country as a whole.

The threat of war with France brought Adams into conflict with Alexander Hamilton, who, with many other Federalists, supported war against France. However, Adams believed, like Washington, that the United States should remain neutral in the ongoing war in Europe. Later, he maintained that sustaining this neutrality throughout his term was one of his chief accomplishments as president. Unfortunately, the means that Adams used in achieving this success only deepened the divisions in the country. The Alien and Sedition laws, passed in 1798, granted Adams broad new powers to arrest virtually anyone who criticized his policies. Historians have argued that his mistake was to confuse uniform public opinion with a united nation. Moreover, when Adams signed the peace treaty with France in 1800, he further angered anti-French forces in his own party. Defeated by Thomas Jefferson in 1800, Adams left Washington without attending Jefferson's inaugural. Years later when his son, John Quincy, was elected to the presidency, Adams communicated to him, "No man who ever held the office of president would congratulate a friend on obtaining it".

Biographical Facts

Born: October 30, 1735 in Braintree (Quincy), Massachusetts

Ancestry: English

Father: John Adams; born January 28, 1691 in Braintree (Quincy), Massachusetts; died May 25, 1761 in Braintree (Quincy), Massachusetts

Father's Occupations: Farmer; cordwainer

Mother: Susanna Boylston Adams; born March 5, 1699 in Brookline, Massachusetts; died April 17, 1797 in Quincy, Massachusetts

Wife: Abigail Smith; born November 22, 1744 in Weymouth, Massachusetts; died October 28, 1818 in Quincy, Massachusetts

Marriage: October 25, 1764 in Weymouth, Massachusetts

Children: Abigail Amelia (1765-1813); John Quincy (1767-1848); Susanna (1768-1770); Charles (1770-1800); Thomas Boylston (1772-1832)

Home: Peacefield, Quincy, Massachusetts

Education: Attended private schools in Braintree; received B. A. (1755) and M.A. from Harvard (1758)

Occupations before Presidency: Teacher; farmer; lawyer; surveyor; selectman

Religious Affiliation: Unitarian

Military Service: None

Political Offices before Presidency: Representative to Massachusetts General Court; Delegate to First and Second Continental Congresses; Member of Provincial Congress of Massachusetts; Delegate to Massachusetts Constitutional Convention; Commissioner to France; Minister to Netherlands and Britain; U.S. Vice President

Political Party: Federalist

Age at Inauguration: 61

Occupation after Presidency: Writer

Death: July 4, 1826 at Quincy, Massachusetts

Place of Burial: First Unitarian Church, Quincy, Massachusetts

Nickname: Duke of Braintree; His Rotundity

Writings: *The Works of John Adams; The Adams-Jefferson Letters; Diary and Autobiography of John Adams; The Papers of John Adams; The Political Writings of John Adams*

Election of 1796

Candidates	Party	Electoral Vote
John Adams (MA)	Federalist	71
Thomas Jefferson (VA)	Democratic-Republican	68
Thomas Pinckney (SC)	Federalist	59
Aaron Burr (NY)	Democratic-Republican	30
Samuel Adams (MA)	Democratic-Republican	15
Oliver Ellsworth (CT)	Federalist	11
Seven others		22

About the Election: George Washington declined to run for a third term, and for the first time, the presidential election was a fierce contest. As in the previous two elections, the candidate with the highest electoral vote count became president while the runner-up became vice president. The Democratic-Republicans chose Thomas Jefferson as their candidate. John Adams was the favored candidate for the Federalists, but Alexander Hamilton rallied Southern electors to support the presumed Federalist vice-presidential candidate, Thomas Pinckney of South Carolina. When word of Hamilton's plan leaked out, Adams' supporters convinced New England electors not to vote for Pinckney. Washington himself personally endorsed Adams, and the fate of Hamilton's plan was sealed. Following a bitter campaign in which Jefferson's supporters accused Adams of wishing to be king, and Adams' supporters charged Jefferson with demagoguery, Adams squeaked out a victory by the slimmest of margins, receiving only three more electoral votes than Jefferson. Adams was elected president, and Jefferson became vice president. It was the only time the country had a president and vice president from rival political parties.

Adams (71 Votes)
Jefferson

Adams' Term 1797-1801

April 30, 1797: The French become enraged when the U.S.-BRITISH JAY TREATY takes effect because it does not guarantee U.S. trade rights with France. They begin seizing Amercian ships and cargoes, and they refuse to receive U.S. minister, Charles Cotesworth Pinkney, who President John Adams has sent to Paris to secure friendly relations.

January 8, 1798: The ELEVENTH AMENDMENT to the Constitution of the United States is passed. It declares that federal courts cannot decide cases involving individuals from different states.

May 3, 1798: Separating naval forces from land forces, Congress establishes the DEPARTMENT OF THE NAVY in preparation for a possible war with France.

May 28, 1798: PREPARING FOR WAR, Congress empowers Adams to enlist 10,000 men for service. It also authorizes Adams to instruct commanders of ships-of-war to seize armed French vessels attacking American merchants along the coast.

June 18, 1798: The NATURALIZATION ACT is passed. It requires foreign-born residents of the United States to have lived in the United States for at least 14 years before becoming naturalized citizens. They also have to declare their intent to become citizens at least five years before they are legally granted citizenship.

June 25, 1798: The ALIEN ACT, passed by Congress, grants Adams the power to deport any foreigner he deems potentially dangerous to the country's safety.

July 2, 1798: ADAMS APPOINTS GEORGE WASHINGTON commanding general of the U.S. military.

July 6, 1798: THE ALIEN ENEMIES ACT is passed. The law allows the U.S. government to arrest any citizen of an enemy power who resides in, or visits the United States in times of declared war.

July 14, 1798: Virtually nullifying the First Amendment freedoms of speech and press, the SEDITION ACT is enacted. It makes all American citizens subject to fines or prison should they be

Quote By Adams:

"The divinity of Jesus is made a convenient cover for absurdity. Nowhere in the Gospels do we find a precept for creeds, confessions, oaths, doctrines, and whole carloads of other foolish trumpery that we find in Christianity."

Quote About Adams:

"He is distrustful, obstinate, excessively vain, and takes no counsel from anyone."
-*Thomas Jefferson*

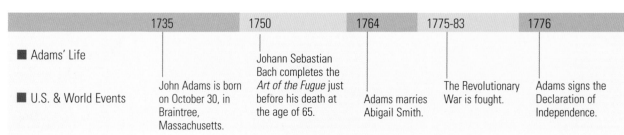

	1735	1750	1764	1775-83	1776
■ Adams' Life					
■ U.S. & World Events	John Adams is born on October 30, in Braintree, Massachusetts.	Johann Sebastian Bach completes the *Art of the Fugue* just before his death at the age of 65.	Adams marries Abigail Smith.	The Revolutionary War is fought.	Adams signs the Declaration of Independence.

First Lady: Abigail Smith Adams

Born in the Massachusetts village of Weymouth, Abigail Smith received no formal education like most women of her time. Instead, she was taught at home by her grandmother. Throughout her life, she was known for her deep intelligence.

After she married John Adams in 1764, she worked as his close partner, traveling with him on diplomatic missions to Europe. On occasions that she remained at home, she corresponded with him frequently. Her letters speak volumes about a woman who stayed at home to struggle with wartime shortages and inflation. She ran the farm with almost no help and taught four children when formal education was interrupted. Her grandson Charles Francis Adams published a nearly complete collection of her letters in 1841, and again in 1876.

She handled the role of the First Lady with dignity and tact. One of her best known pieces of advice to her husband was to "remember the ladies". So forceful was Mrs. Adams that after her husband became president, his political rivals took to calling her "Mrs. President".

found "obstructing the implementation of federal law, or for publishing malicious or false writings against Congress, the president, or the government".

November 16, 1798: The Kentucky legislature adopts the KENTUCKY RESOLUTION, written by Thomas Jefferson. The resolution argues that states have the right to override federal powers not outlined in the U.S. Constitution.

February 9, 1799: The United States 38-gun frigate *Constellation* captures the French ship of *L'Insurgente* near the island of St. Kitts in the first American victory in the undeclared war known as the QUASI-WAR.

March 30, 1799: Adams selects William Vans Murray, Chief Justice Oliver Ellsworth, and North Carolina Governor Davie to serve as U.S. ENVOYS TO FRANCE after Talleyrand assures the United States that France will receive them with respect.

February 1, 1800: The U.S. *Constellation* defeats the French ship *La Vengeance* on the high seas.

May 7, 1800: CONGRESS DIVIDES THE NORTHWEST TERRITORY into two parts, with the border being a line drawn at the junction of the Ohio and Kentucky Rivers.

September 30, 1800: The Quasi-War ends as French and American diplomats sign the TREATY OF MORTFONTAINE in Paris.

November, 1800: CONGRESS MEETS IN WASHINGTON for the first time and Adams moves into the new Executive Mansion.

November 11, 1800: ADAMS IS DEFEATED BY THOMAS JEFFERSON in the presidential election.

January 20, 1801: Adams appoints JOHN MARSHALL as chief justice of the Supreme Court.

February 27, 1801: The JUDICIARY ACT reduces the number of Supreme Court justices to five, and creates 16 circuit courts. Determined to ensure Federalist control over the judiciary, Adams uses the law to make more than 200 MIDNIGHT APPOINTMENTS of federal judges and other officials. He makes his last appointment at 9 p.m. on March 2—the night before Jefferson's inauguration.

March 3, 1801: Adams leaves Washington, D.C. alone, without attending Jefferson's inauguration.

Adams' Administration

Inauguration: March 4, 1797 at Federal Hall, Philadelphia, Pennsylvania
Vice President: Thomas Jefferson
Secretary of State: Timothy Pickering; John Marshall (from June 6, 1800)
Secretary of the Treasury: Oliver Wolcott, Jr.; Samuel Dexter (from January 1, 1801)
Secretary of War: James McHenry; Samuel Dexter (from June 12, 1800)
Attorney General: Charles Lee
Postmaster General: Joseph Habersham
Supreme Court Appointments: Bushrod Washington (1798); Alfred Moore (1799);

John Marshall, Chief Justice (1801)
Secretary of the Navy: Benjamin Stoddert
5th Congress: (March 4, 1797-March 4, 1799)
Senate: 20 Federalists;
12 Democratic-Republicans
House: 58 Federalists;
48 Democratic-Republicans
6th Congress: (March 4, 1799-March 4, 1801)
Senate: 19 Federalists;
13 Democratic-Republicans
House: 64 Federalists;
42 Democratic-Republicans

1796	1801	1805	1812-14	1824	1826
Adams is elected president.	Thomas Jefferson takes office after defeating Adams for the presidency.	Lord Nelson defeats the French Navy at Trafalgar.	The War of 1812 is fought.	Adams' son, John Quincy Adams, is elected president.	Adams dies on July 4, in Braintree, Massachusetts.

Thomas Jefferson

3rd President (1801–1809)

"We hold these truths to be self-evident, that all men are created equal…"

When Thomas Jefferson entered office in 1801, his reputation as a Renaissance man was already in place. An inventor, archeologist, naturalist, architect, and violinist who spoke six languages, he was also the greatest American political thinker of his age. In 1776, he had crafted the Declaration of Independence as a leading member of the Second Continental Congress. As governor of Virginia, he had shaped Virginia's Statute on Religious Freedom. He had also served as secretary of state under Washington and vice president under Adams. Throughout his political career, he advocated the need for individual liberty, separation of church and state, strict interpretation of the U.S. Constitution, and limited federal government with strictly limited powers. One of his first acts in office was to sharply reduce the size of the federal budget.

Ironically, during his two terms in office, Jefferson is best remembered for vastly increasing the power of the federal government. In 1803, he doubled the size of the United States when he authorized the Louisiana Purchase for $15 million—even though the Constitution made no provision that empowered the president to purchase territory from a foreign power. What is more, once the purchase was made, Jefferson made the federal government the sole governing authority for Louisiana.

During his stormy second term in office, Jefferson again wielded the power of the federal government forcefully—though much less successfully. Frustrated by ongoing interference with American shipping by both Great Britain and France, Jefferson pushed through the Embargo Act, which closed American ports to international trade. His attempts to enforce the act only strengthened his Federalist opposition, who advocated secession from the Union. By the time Jefferson left office in 1809, he made it clear that his presidency had been a "splendid misery." When he died on July 4, 1826, fifty years to the day after the signing of his Declaration of Independence, he had already composed his tombstone. On it, he cites his authorship of the Declaration of Independence, his founding of the University of Virginia and his responsibility for Virginia's Statute of Religious Freedom. No mention is made of his service as president for eight years.

Biographical Facts

Born: April 13, 1743 in Goochland (now Albemarle) County, Virginia

Ancestry: Welsh

Father: Peter Jefferson; born February 29, 1708 in Chesterfield County, Virginia; died August 17, 1757 in Albemarle County, Virginia

Father's Occupations: Planter; surveyor

Mother: Jane Randolph Jefferson; born February 9, 1720 in London, England; died March 31, 1776 in Albemarle County, Virginia

Wife: Martha Wayles Skelton; born October 19, 1748 in Charles City County, Virginia; died September 6, 1782 in Monticello, Virginia

Marriage: January 1, 1772 in Charles City County, Virginia

Children: Martha (1772-1836); Maria (1778-1804); Lucy Elizabeth (1782-1785); (two daughters and a son died in infancy)

Home: Monticello, Charlottesville, Virginia

Education: Private tutoring; attended country school in Albemarle County, Virginia; received B.A. from College of William and Mary (1762)

Religious Affiliation: None

Occupations before Presidency: Planter; lawyer; writer; philosopher; scientist; architect

Military Service: None

Political Offices before Presidency: Member of Virginia House of Burgesses; County Lieutenant; County Surveyor; Deputy Delegate to Second Continental Congress; Member of Virginia House of Delegates; Governor of Virginia; Commissioner to France; Minister to France; Secretary of State; U.S. Vice President

Age at Inauguration: 57

Occupations after Presidency: Planter; writer; educator

Death: July 4, 1826 at Monticello, Charlottesville, Virginia,

Place of Burial: Monticello, Charlottesville, Virginia

Nickname: Red Fox

Writings: *Autobiography; Notes on the State of Virginia; Public and Private Papers; Addresses; Letters (Library of America)*

Election of 1800

Candidates	Party	Electoral Vote
Thomas Jefferson (VA)	Democratic-Republican	73
Aaron Burr (NY)	Democratic-Republican	73
John Adams (MA)	Federalist	65
Charles C. Pinckney (SC)	Federalist	64
John Jay (NY)	Federalist	1

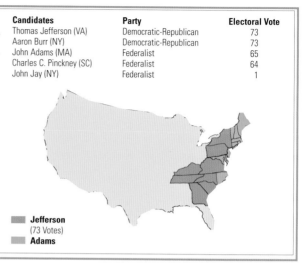

■ **Jefferson**
(73 Votes)
■ **Adams**

About the Election: By 1800, President John Adams had lost the support of his own party and had angered the opposition Democratic-Republicans (led by Thomas Jefferson) by passing the Alien and Sedition acts. Due to the efforts of Aaron Burr, the primary Democratic-Republican candidate for vice president, the Democratic-Republicans easily carried the South and also won New York. As in the previous elections, in the election of 1800, each elector voted for two men. This time, however, it ended in a tie between Jefferson and Burr, and the election was decided in the Federalist-dominated House of Representatives. On the 36th ballot, the House chose Jefferson, whom Alexander Hamilton essentially viewed as the lesser of two evils. In future elections, electors would cast separate ballots for president and vice president.

Jefferson's First Term 1801-1805

March 4, 1801: THOMAS JEFFERSON'S INAUGURATION is the first to be held in Washington, D.C. In his inaugural address, he advocates limited federal government, the rights of states, and a foreign policy that seeks peace with all nations and "entangling alliances with none." He also promises a "frugal government" that would be dedicated to fiscal economy.

May 14, 1801: The *pasha* (ruler) of TRIPOLI DECLARES WAR on the United States after Jefferson refuses his demand for tribute money exceeding the $80,000 agreed to by treaty. The U.S., under its first two presidents, had paid nearly $2 million to the states of Morocco, Algiers, Tunis and Tripoli to enable its ships to conduct commerce and trade through the Mediterranean Sea. Although the U.S. never officially declares war on Tripoli, Jefferson sends a naval squadron to the Mediterranean Sea on May 20. The conflict does not end until 1805, when the pasha signs a peace treaty, relinquishing claims on tribute money and giving the U.S. free navigation and trade rights in the Mediterranean.

December 8, 1801: In JEFFERSON'S FIRST ANNUAL MESSAGE TO CONGRESS, he sends a written letter rather than addressing

A paperweight bearing Jefferson's image.

the Congress in person, as Washington and Adams had done previously. All future presidents until Woodrow Wilson in 1913 will follow Jefferson's precedent.

February 6, 1802: Congress passes a bill establishing the U.S. Military Academy. The academy formally opens at West Point, New York on July 4.

March 8, 1802: At Jefferson's insistence, CONGRESS REPEALS THE JUDICIARY ACT OF 1801. On April 29, a new Judiciary Act restores the number of Supreme Court justices to six, schedules one term per year for the high court, and establishes six circuit courts, each one headed by a Supreme Court justice.

May 3, 1802: Congress passes an act incorporating Washington, D.C. as a city. The mayor of the city is to be appointed by the president.

October 16, 1802: The Spanish administrator of New Orleans bans American vessels from depositing goods in the port of New Orleans, ending a long established practice. This action causes Jefferson great alarm. Louisiana had been French territory until 1762, when it had ceded the territory to Spain. However, Jefferson is aware that Spain had secretly returned the Louisiana Territory to France. He also knows that France, unlike Spain is an

	1743	1755	1769
■ Jefferson's Life			
	George Frideric Handel's *Messiah* is performed for the first time, in Dublin, Ireland.		Spanish missionaries form the Mission of San Diego de Alcala in California. It is the first in a series of Spanish missions in California.
■ U.S. & World Events		The Seven Years' War begins in Europe when Prussia invades Saxony.	
	Thomas Jefferson is born on April 13 in Albemarle County, Virginia.		

First Lady: Martha Wayles Skelton Jefferson

Martha Jefferson never had the opportunity to serve as First Lady. The physical strain of frequent pregnancies seriously weakened her health, and she died 19 years before her husband's election. Of their marriage, Jefferson was often quoted as saying that it was "ten years of uncheckered happiness."

Jefferson became president in 1801 and since he had never remarried, asked his daughter Martha Jefferson Randolph (above) and Dolley Madison, a family friend and the wife of Secretary of State James Madison, to act as official hostesses. The job of hostess held great social importance, as it went against the mores of the day for women to attend social events hosted by a single male host.

expansionist power, and France may use its control of the mouth of the Mississippi to hinder the American westward expansion. Such an act would draw the United States into European conflicts. Jefferson thus instructs Robert Livingston, U.S. minister to France, to negotiate either for land on the lower Mississippi River or an irrevocable guarantee of free navigation and trade rights in New Orleans.

January 12, 1803: Jefferson names James Monroe minister plenipotentiary to France, and instructs him to purchase New Orleans and West Florida for $2 million, authorizing him to negotiate up to $10 million if necessary. That same month, Jefferson asks Congress to finance a westward expedition aimed at improving relations with Native Americans and collecting information about the plants and animals of the region in order to increase interstate commerce. Congress approves the mission and Jefferson's personal secretary, Meriwether Lewis, is selected to lead it. Lewis chooses Captain William Clark, brother of Revolutionary War hero George Rogers Clark, to serve as his fellow expedition leader.

February 24, 1803: The Supreme Court establishes the power of the judiciary to overrule congressional law in the case of *MARBURY V. MADISON.* After Jefferson orders Secretary of State James Madison to withhold the signed and sealed appointment of William Marbury as Justice of the Peace for the district of Columbia, Marbury sues for a writ ordering his appointment by President Adams be enforced. The Court dismisses Marbury's suit, arguing that it has no jurisdiction in the case. Chief Justice John Marshall goes further, arguing that Section 13 of the Judiciary Act of 1789, which empowered the Court to issue such a writ, was unconstitutional. Thus, the decision becomes the first Supreme Court ruling to strike down a Congressional law as unconstitutional. The decision establishes the right of the Supreme Court to review laws passed by Congress or state legislatures.

April 11, 1803: Before Monroe even arrives in Paris to negotiate with France, French foreign minister Talleyrand asks Robert Livingston how much the United States will pay not just for New Orleans but for the entire Louisiana Territory. By

Jefferson's First Administration

Inauguration: March 4, 1801 in Senate Chamber, Washington, D.C.
Vice President: Aaron Burr
Secretary of State: James Madison
Secretary of the Treasury: Samuel Dexter; Albert Gallatin (from May 14, 1801)
Secretary of War: Henry Dearborn
Attorney General: Levi Lincoln
Postmaster General: Joseph Habersham: Gideon Granger (from November 28, 1801)
Secretary of the Navy: Benjamin Stoddert; Robert Smith (from July 27, 1801)
Supreme Court Appointment:
William Johnson (1804)

7th Congress
(March 4, 1801-March 4, 1803)
Senate: 18 Democratic-Republicans; 14 Federalists
House: 69 Democratic-Republicans; 36 Federalists
8th Congress
(March 4, 1803-March 4, 1805)
Senate: 25 Democratic-Republicans; 9 Federalists
House: 102 Democratic-Republicans; 39 Federalists
State Admitted: Ohio (1803)
End of Presidential Term: March 4, 1805

1772	1775-83	1776	1777	1779-81
	The Revolutionary War is fought.		As a member of the Virginia House of Delegates, he drafts Virginia's Statute for Religious Freedom.	
Jefferson marries Martha Wayles Skelton. Their daughter Martha is born.		Jefferson writes the Declaration of Independence.		Jefferson serves as Governor of Virginia.

In 1804, Jefferson negotiated a purchase of West Florida from Spain, but failed to keep the deal secret from France. In this cartoon, Jefferson, a prairie dog, coughs up $2 million, while being stung by Napoleon, a hornet. A French diplomat waves maps of Florida. Jefferson never completed the purchase.

this time, France's failure to prevent a revolt by African slaves in its territory of Haiti (1794-1804) had convinced Napoleon to focus his empire in Europe. By the end of April, the **LOUISIANA PURCHASE** is completed, and the treaty is signed officially on May 2. The United States agrees to purchase the Louisiana Territory for 60 million francs, or approximately $15 million. The purchase of 828,000 square miles stretching from the Mississippi River to the Rocky Mountains effectively doubles the size of the United States. However, the agreement does not clearly define boundaries, leaving ambiguity over the position of west Florida and Texas. In addition, normally loose-constructionist Federalists condemn Jefferson's purchase of Louisiana, since the Constitution does not expressly cover the right of presidents to purchase and govern foreign territory. They were concerned that any new states carved out of the new territory would change the balance of power between the North and the South, allowing pro-agrarian, pro-slavery, and pro-frontier interests to outweigh Northern industrial and mercantile interests. For Jefferson's part, the typically-strict constructionist argues that the right of the federal government to govern the territory stems from its right to acquire it. By October, Congress approves the treaty and the United States formally takes control of Louisiana Territory in December.

August 31, 1803: The **LEWIS AND CLARK EXPEDITION** sets out on the Ohio River. The following May, they begin their journey up the Missouri River with 32 soldiers and 10 civilians. The winter of 1804 is spent with the Mandan people of present-day North Dakota. While with the Mandan, the party meets Sacagawea, a young Shoshone woman, and her husband, a French fur trapper named Toussaint Charbonneau. The couple serve as Lewis and Clark's interpreters as they cross the Bitteroot Mountains of Idaho and continue on to the Pacific coast. Sacagawea is also carrying her

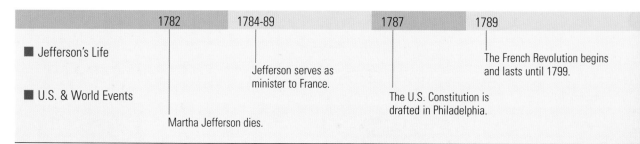

	1782	1784-89	1787	1789
■ Jefferson's Life				The French Revolution begins and lasts until 1799.
■ U.S. & World Events		Jefferson serves as minister to France.	The U.S. Constitution is drafted in Philadelphia.	
	Martha Jefferson dies.			

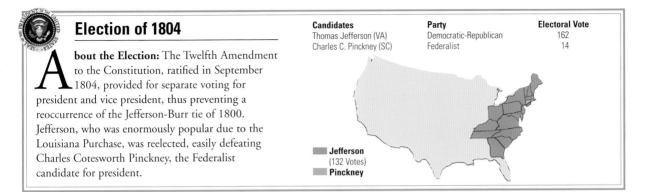

Election of 1804

About the Election: The Twelfth Amendment to the Constitution, ratified in September 1804, provided for separate voting for president and vice president, thus preventing a reoccurrence of the Jefferson-Burr tie of 1800. Jefferson, who was enormously popular due to the Louisiana Purchase, was reelected, easily defeating Charles Cotesworth Pinckney, the Federalist candidate for president.

Candidates	Party	Electoral Vote
Thomas Jefferson (VA)	Democratic-Republican	162
Charles C. Pinckney (SC)	Federalist	14

Jefferson (132 Votes)
Pinckney

son Jean Baptiste, who is born on February 11, 1805. On November 7, 1805, the expedition sights the Pacific Ocean for the first time and builds Fort Clatsop at the mouth of the Columbia River. By the time Lewis and Clark return to St. Louis on September 23, 1806, they have collected vast amounts of new scientific information. Their journey soon leads to a rapid growth in Western settlement and expansion.

December 12, 1803: Congress passes the Twelfth Amendment, which establishes the system of casting separate votes for president and vice president. Prior to the amendment, electors could cast two votes and the candidate winning the majority was elected president while the candidate with the second highest majority of votes was elected vice president. Congress ratifies the amendment on September 25, 1804.

February 16, 1804: Lieutenant **STEPHEN DECATUR** destroys the American frigate *Philadelphia*, which had been captured by Tripolitan pirates and converted into a warship.

February 25, 1804: Jefferson is unanimously nominated for reelection, while George Clinton, governor of New York, is nominated for vice president. The Federalist Party selects Charles Cotesworth Pinckney as its presidential candidate.

Jefferson's Second Term 1805-1809

July 23, 1805: In the **ESSEX DECISION**, a British judge rules that British naval ships have the right to seize American merchant ships unless the owner of the ship can prove that the final destination of the ship is a U.S. port. The British also claim the right to search the ships for British deserters, and to *impress* or force them back into British naval service. The decision allows the British Navy to impede U.S. trade

with France or Spain, which are both at war with Britain.

August 9, 1805: Lieutenant Zebulon Pike begins an expedition to seek the sources of the Mississippi River. In the second **PIKE EXPEDITION**, he explores Colorado and New Mexico. On November 15, 1807, he sights the mountain, which

Lewis and Clark were aided by a Shoshone woman named Sacagawea. In this image, Sacagawea translates for the Corp of Discovery, as the expedition was sometimes called, on the Columbia River in present-day Washington.

1790-93	1797-1801	1801-09	1801
Jefferson serves as the first U.S. Secretary of State during the Washington Administration.	He serves as vice president, during the Adams Administration.	Jefferson serves as president of the United States.	The U.S. Military Academy at West Point, New York is founded.

Jefferson's Second Administration

Inauguration: March 4, 1805 at Senate
Chamber, Washington, D.C.
Vice President: George Clinton
Secretary of State: James Madison
Secretary of the Treasury: Albert Gallatin
Secretary of War: Henry Dearborn
Attorney General: John Breckinridge; Caesar
A. Rodney (from January 20, 1807)
Postmaster General: Gideon Granger
Secretary of the Navy: Robert Smith
Supreme Court Appointments: Brockholst
Livingston (1806); Thomas Todd (1807)

9th Congress
(March 4, 1805-March 4, 1807)
Senate: 27 Democratic-Republicans;
7 Federalists
House: 116 Democratic-Republicans;
25 Federalists
10th Congress
(March 4, 1807-March 4, 1809)
Senate: 28 Democratic-Republicans;
6 Federalists
House: 118 Democratic-Republicans;
24 Federalists

is later named in his honor – Pike's Peak in Colorado.

January 23, 1806: Secretary of State James Madison reports that the British are infringing on American rights to conduct commerce and violating American rights as a neutral nation. He also reports that American sailors are being taken prisoner on British ships and impressed to serve under the British flag. In response, the Senate passes a resolution condemning the **BRITISH IMPRESSMENT OF AMERICAN SEAMEN** on February 12.

April 18, 1806:
After Britain ignores complaints about the seizure of American ships and the impressment of American sailors, Congress passes a **NON-IMPORTATION ACT,** banning a large number of British goods from the American market, including hemp, flax, brass, and tin.

November 21,1806:
Napoleon issues the **BERLIN DECREE,** responding to a British blockade of the European coast from the city of Brest, France, to the mouth of the Elbe River in present-day Germany. Under the decree, France begins a total blockade of the British Isles and forbids any commerce or communication with them. The decree also authorizes the seizure of all ships and cargo headed for Britain, including all American ships.

December 31, 1806: In the spring of 1806, Jefferson had instructed William Pinkney and James Monroe to negotiate a treaty with Britain that provides an end to the impressment of American sailors, restoration of U.S. trade rights in the Caribbean, and payment for all American ships seized after the Essex Decision. However, Britain offers only a slight compromise on Caribbean trade but nothing else. Monroe and Pinkney agree to the treaty, but Jefferson, embarrassed by its weak terms, does not submit it to Congress. The **MONROE-PINKNEY TREATY** is never ratified.

June 22, 1807: The British frigate *Leopard* halts the U.S. frigate *Chesapeake,* claiming that four sailors aboard the American ship are British deserters. When the commander of the American ship refuses to surrender the men, the *Leopard* opens fire, killing three and wounding eighteen before taking the four accused deserters. On July 2, in response to the **CHESAPEAKE–LEOPARD INCIDENT,** Jefferson orders all British warships to leave American waters. In turn, the British order increased

Jefferson's home at Monticello is one of his crowning achievements as an architect. The domed mansion on a hill above Charlottesville, Virginia featured 18-foot ceilings.

	1809	1812-14	1815
■ Jefferson's Life			
		The War of 1812 is fought.	Following the burning of Washington, D.C. during the War of 1812, Jefferson sells his 6,700-volume library to Congress, thus restoring the Library of Congress.
■ U.S. & World Events			
	Jefferson retires to his home at Monticello.		

impressments of British seamen from American and other neutral ships.

December 18-21, 1807: Jefferson recommends that Congress issue an embargo against Great Britain and France. Despite Federalist opposition, Congress passes the EMBARGO ACT, halting virtually all trade with foreign nations and banning American ships from sailing into foreign ports. It also requires domestic coastal traffic to post bonds worth twice the value of their cargo to ensure that they do not land anywhere other than a U.S. port. The Embargo Act proves to be a disaster. Upon its passage, a vast smuggling network is established, with goods often being carried by land and sea to and from Canada. American ships that are at sea when the act takes effect stay at sea, and continue to trade with cooperation from the British government. The embargo only benefits the British, as its merchants no longer have to compete with those from the United States. The act is also useful to France: Napoleon issues the BAYONNE DECREE, ordering the seizure of all U.S. ships entering ports in France, Italy and the Hanseatic towns in present-day Germany. Napoleon reasons that, with the Embargo Act in effect, any U.S. ships found in European ports must be British vessels with false documents. His savvy strategy costs U.S. ships about $10 million in cargo.

January 1, 1808: CONGRESS BANS AFRICAN SLAVE TRADE and orders that slave ships be seized. The fate of slaves onboard those ships is to be left to the state in which the ship is captured. Despite the law, an illegal slave trade will continue up until the U.S. Civil War in 1861.

March 1808: Secretary of State JAMES MADISON easily wins the presidency after Jefferson declines to run for reelection. Following George Washington's example, Jefferson leaves the office after serving two terms.

January 9, 1809: Jefferson pushes the ENFORCEMENT ACT through Congress. The act authorizes severe penalties for anyone not obeying the Embargo Act. The Enforcement Act only serves to anger Northern interests further. Jonathan Trumbull, governor of Connecticut, asserts that whenever Congress exceeds its constitutional powers, state legislatures have a duty to protect the people against such unlawful powers. Other state governments refuse to supply the federal government with the militia needed to carry out enforcement.

February 20, 1809: In the Supreme Court case of *U.S. v. Peters*, Chief Justice John Marshall reasserts the power of the federal government over individual states.

Scandal! Aaron Burr, Scoundrel

After Jefferson dropped Aaron Burr as his running mate for the election of 1804, Burr decided to run for governor of New York. He lost the battle when fellow New Yorker and former Treasury Secretary Alexander Hamilton used his influence to deny him victory. Hamilton suspected that Burr had allied himself with a group of New Englanders known as the Essex Junto. Members of the Essex Junto were pushing a plan for New England to secede from the United States. They offered Burr their support in his governor's race if he promised that New York would secede as well. When Hamilton declared Burr "a dangerous man, and one who ought not to be trusted with the reins of government," Burr challenged him to a duel. On July 11, 1804, Burr shot and killed Hamilton.

Although Hamilton's death disgraced Burr, his ambition remained unchecked. Immediately after Hamilton's death, Burr contacted the British ambassador to the United States, asking for financial support of a plot for the Western territories to secede from the United States. Burr wanted to be made the emperor of the new western nation; but Britain never supplied Burr with any funds. The plot was discovered, and Burr was charged with treason. Although he and several associates were acquitted of the charge, Burr was forced into European exile to avoid prosecution for Hamilton's death and other crimes. He eventually returned to the United States where he spent his final years practicing law in New York City.

March 15, 1809: Reversing course, Congress repeals the Embargo Act after it has been in effect for 14 months. It becomes clear to Jefferson that the act will not force compliance from either Britain or France. In addition, public outcry over the Embargo Act becomes overwhelming. A milder law is passed called the NON–INTERCOURSE ACT, which allows unfettered trade with all nations other than Great Britain and France. Three years later, the United States will be at war with Britain.

1817

The construction of the University of Virginia (originally Central College) begins. The college is designed by Jefferson.

1820

The Missouri Compromise, which admits Maine into the Union as a free state and Missouri as a slave state is passed. The law also abolishes slavery in the remainder of the Louisiana Territory.

1826

Jefferson dies on July 4, at Monticello, Virginia.

James Madison

4th President (1809–1817)

"In framing a government, which is to be administered by men over men, the great difficulty lies in this: you must first enable the government to control the governed, and in the next place, oblige it to control itself."

James Madison is known for two of his nicknames: "Father of the Constitution" and "Little Jemmy." He was called the latter because at five feet four inches, he was one of the shortest presidents, and the former because he stands as one of the towering figures in U.S. history.

Like Jefferson, Madison is best known for his achievements before reaching the presidency. In 1787, he helped shape the debate at the Constitutional Convention in Philadelphia and the notes he volunteered to record at the Convention remain one of the greatest sources of insight into the proceedings. Later, supporters would even dub him "Father of the Constitution," which Madison dismissed, arguing that the document was not "the off-spring of a single brain," but "the work of many heads and many hands." In addition to the Constitution, he also co-authored, with Alexander Hamilton and John Jay, the essays that collectively became known as *The Federalist*. The essays stressed the need for a strong central government, and promoted the U.S. Constitution as the best model for that government.

Despite Madison's role in *The Federalist* papers, he shared Thomas Jefferson's distrust of centralized federal power. He believed Hamilton's policies would mostly benefit Northern merchants and bankers over the interests of the South.

During Madison's first term as president, he found himself buffeted by both domestic and international crises. By the time of his reelection in 1812, he had reluctantly declared war on Britain. Not only were the British refusing to reverse policy oppressive to American shipping, but ambitious American expansionists, who wanted to claim British-held territories in the West, were also urging Madison to declare war.

While his opponents would refer to the War of 1812 as "Mr. Madison's War," the conflict helped restore Madison's reputation with the public. Even though the war did not change the status quo, the fact that "Little Jemmy" had battled the greatest power on earth to a draw burnished his legacy. His popularity grew, and his final months in office produced the "Era of Good Feelings" that would last for several years.

Biographical Facts

Born: March 16, 1751 in Port Conway, Virginia

Ancestry: English

Father: James Madison; born March 27, 1723 in Port Conway, Virginia; died February 27, 1801 in Montpelier, Virginia,

Father's Occupations: Justice of the peace; vestryman; farmer

Mother: Eleanor Conway Madison; born January 1732 in Port Conway, Virginia; died February 11, 1829 in Montpelier, Virginia

Wife: Dorothea (Dolley) Payne Todd; born May 20, 1768 in Guilford County, North Carolina; died July 12, 1849 in Washington, D.C.

Marriage: September 15, 1794 in Harewood, Virginia

Home: Montpelier, Virginia

Education: Early education at Donald Robertson's school and from private tutor; B.A. from the College of New Jersey (Princeton) in 1771

Religious Affiliation: Episcopalian

Occupation before Presidency: Politician

Military Service: Colonel, Virginia Militia

Political Offices before Presidency: Member of Orange County Committee of Safety; Delegate to the Virginia Convention;

Member of Virginia Legislature: Member of Virginia Executive Council; Delegate to Continental Congress; Delegate to Annapolis Convention; Delegate to Constitutional Convention; Member of the Virginia Ratification Convention; U.S. Congressman; Secretary of State

Party: Democratic-Republican

Age at Inauguration: 57

Death: June 28, 1836 at Montpelier, Virginia

Place of Burial: Montpelier, Virginia

Nickname: Father of the Constitution, Little Jemmy

Writings: *The Writings of James Madison; The Papers of James Madison*

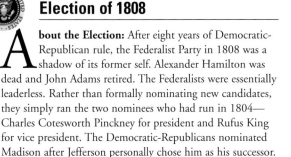

Election of 1808

About the Election: After eight years of Democratic-Republican rule, the Federalist Party in 1808 was a shadow of its former self. Alexander Hamilton was dead and John Adams retired. The Federalists were essentially leaderless. Rather than formally nominating new candidates, they simply ran the two nominees who had run in 1804—Charles Cotesworth Pinckney for president and Rufus King for vice president. The Democratic-Republicans nominated Madison after Jefferson personally chose him as his successor. George Clinton, governor of New York, was nominated for vice president. Although anger over the Embargo Act helped Pinckney win most of the electoral votes in New England, he was still handily defeated by Madison.

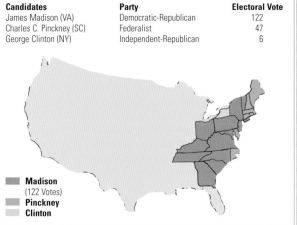

Candidates	Party	Electoral Vote
James Madison (VA)	Democratic-Republican	122
Charles C. Pinckney (SC)	Federalist	47
George Clinton (NY)	Independent-Republican	6

Madison (122 Votes)
Pinckney
Clinton

Madison's First Term 1809-1813

March 4, 1809: MADISON IS SWORN INTO OFFICE by Chief Justice John Marshall, and his inaugural ball is a lavish celebration. Madison's inaugural address makes clear that he will not tolerate foreign interference, foreshadowing the course of action he will take while in office, namely his declaration of war against Britain in 1812.

April 19, 1809: After the British ambassador assures that some restrictions on American merchant ships would be lifted, MADISON LEGALIZES TRADE WITH GREAT BRITAIN. When it is later learned that the ambassador's assurances are not official British policy, Madison revives the Non-Intercourse Act.

May 1, 1810: Replacing the Non-Intercourse Act, MACON'S BILL NO. 2 authorizes Madison to reopen trade with Britain and France, with the stipulation that if one of them drops its restrictions on American shipping by March 3, 1811, the U.S. would again prohibit trade with the other.

August 5, 1810: Napoleon learns of Macon's Bill No. 2 and instructs his foreign minister to inform the U.S. that restrictions on U.S. vessels will be loosened if the U.S. declares non-intercourse with Britain, and lifted only when Britain lifts its restrictions on shipping. When the French minister implies restrictions had already been lifted, MADISON REOPENS TRADE WITH FRANCE.

October 27, 1810: The UNITED STATES ANNEXES WEST FLORIDA when Madison proclaims West Florida territory and authorizes its military occupation.

November 1810: Under the assumption that Napoleon has lifted restrictions on American shipping, MADISON PROHIBITS TRADE WITH BRITAIN—ending any hopes for peace negotiations with the foreign power.

February 20, 1811: Congress allows the CHARTER FOR THE FIRST BANK OF THE U.S. TO EXPIRE; a renewal of the charter faces severe opposition. Democratic-Republicans, since the bank's inception, have questioned its constitutionality, and many are wary of the significant role British investors have in the bank. In addition to this, the federal bank is also opposed by advocates for the growing number of state-chartered banks.

February 28, 1811: Madison vetoes a bill that would provide land grants to a Mississippi church.

April 6, 1811: Madison appoints JAMES MONROE as his secretary of state and employs him to negotiate with Britain about ending restrictions on American shipping.

May 16, 1811: After the British warship Guerrière detains the American ship Spitfire off New York harbor and impresses an American-born sailor into service, the American gunboat President is ordered to protect American ships. En route, the President mistakes the British LITTLE BELT for the Guerrière, and when the British ship fails to identify itself, fires on it, killing 9 and wounding 23.

September 19, 1811: The U.S. learns that Napoleon had never issued a decree loosening restrictions on American vessels.

November 4, 1811: In the Congressional elections of 1811, a group of Southern and Western Democratic-Republicans,

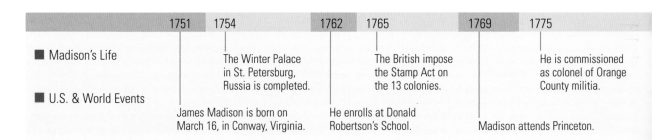

	1751	1754	1762	1765	1769	1775
■ Madison's Life						He is commissioned as colonel of Orange County militia.
		The Winter Palace in St. Petersburg, Russia is completed.		The British impose the Stamp Act on the 13 colonies.		
■ U.S. & World Events		James Madison is born on March 16, in Conway, Virginia.	He enrolls at Donald Robertson's School.		Madison attends Princeton.	

First Lady: Dolley Payne Todd Madison

Raised as a Quaker, Dolley Payne Todd was a young widow living in Philadelphia when she first formally met James Madison in the spring of 1794; they married that September. They had no children of their own, but raised Payne Todd, Dolley's son from her previous marriage.

Mrs. Madison's long career at the center of society started when her husband was appointed as Jefferson's secretary of state in 1801. Her warm personality appealed to most people. During her husband's eight-year tenure in the Cabinet, Mrs. Madison occasionally assisted with formal functions at the White House. She later became the nation's most famous First Lady. She was known for her grace, tact and welcoming spirit—the ideal hostess who continued to skillfully entertain even in temporary quarters after the burning of the White House during the War of 1812.

known as "**WAR HAWKS**" are elected to Congress. Among them are Henry Clay of Kentucky, who becomes Speaker of the House, and John C. Calhoun of South Carolina, who will chair the Senate Foreign Relations Committee. Clay, Calhoun and other militant expansionists press for war against Great Britain, who they accuse of orchestrating Native American attacks on American frontier settlements.

November 7-8, 1811: Warriors from the Shawnee nation raid American troops under **GENERAL WILLIAM HENRY HARRISON**, governor of Indiana Territory. Harrison and his men overcome the Shawnee and destroy their village at Tippecanoe. His victory at the **BATTLE OF TIPPECANOE**, celebrated as a heroic legend, will eventually propel Harrison to the presidency in 1841.

April 1, 1812: Congress agrees to Madison's proposal for an **EMBARGO AGAINST BRITAIN**. The embargo comes at a time of economic hardship in Britain, and its businesses call for the repeal of the **ORDERS IN COUNCIL**, which prohibits foreign commerce in forbidden European ports.

April 20, 1812: Vice President George Clinton dies, after serving in that office since 1805 under two different presidents, Jefferson and Madison.

April 30, 1812: LOUISIANA IS ADMITTED as the 18th state.

June 1, 1812: Madison sends a message to Congress. giving four reasons for declaration of war with Britain: the impressments of American sailors; violation of American neutrality; the blockade of American ports; and Britain's refusal to repeal the Orders in Council.

June 4, 1812: The U.S. House of Representatives votes 79-49 in favor of war with Britain

June 16, 1812: BRITAIN REVOKES THE ORDERS IN COUNCIL, but the news does not reach the U.S. Congress until after war is declared. The British repeal comes after France officially repeals its own decrees restricting American trade.

June 18, 1812: The Senate votes 19-13 in favor of war.

June 19, 1812: MADISON DECLARES WAR on Britain.

June 30, 1812: Following

Madison's First Administration

Inauguration: March 4, 1809 at House of Representatives, in Washington, D.C.
Vice President: George Clinton
Secretary of State: Robert Smith; James Monroe (from April 6, 1811)
Secretary of the Treasury: Albert Gallatin
Secretary of War: William Eustis; James Monroe (from January 1, 1813); John Armstrong (from February 5, 1813)
Attorney General: Caesar Augustus Rodney; William Pinkney (from January 6, 1812)
Postmaster General: Gideon Granger
Secretary of the Navy: Robert Smith; Paul Hamilton (from May 15, 1809); William Jones (from January 19, 1813)

Supreme Court Appointments:
Joseph Story (1811); Gabriel Duvall (1811)
11th Congress
(March 4, 1809-March 4, 1811)
Senate: 28 Democratic-Republicans; 6 Federalists
House: 94 Democratic-Republicans; 48 Federalists
12th Congress
(March 4, 1811-March 4, 1813)
Senate: 30 Democratic-Republicans; 6 Federalists
House: 108 Democratic-Republicans; 36 Federalists
State Admitted: Louisiana (1812)

1776	1776-83	1777	1783	1784	1787
	The Revolutionary War is fought.		The Montgolfier brothers demonstrate the first ascension balloon in Annonay, France.		He attends the Constitutional Convention.
Madison attends the Virginia Convention.		He is elected member of the Governor's Council of States.		Madison becomes a member of the Virginia House of Delegates.	

the outbreak of war, Congress issues interest-bearing treasury notes—the first circulating currency.

July 1, 1812: The BRITISH DISCOVER AMERICAN PLANS to launch an attack on Upper Canada from Detroit when they capture the personal baggage of American General William Hull.

July 12, 1812: Hull and 2,200 men cross the Detroit River into Canada and occupy Sandwich.

July 17, 1812: The British capture an American post on Michilimackinac Island, in the strait of Mackinaw between Lakes Huron and Michigan. Following the British victory, Shawnee leader TECUMSEH ALLIES WITH THE BRITISH.

August 8, 1812: Hull and his men retreat from Sandwich to Detroit, concerned that Tecumseh will cut American lines of communication.

August 15, 1812: In the FORT DEARBORN MASSACRE. Native Americans kill 86 adults and 12 children at the garrison at Fort Dearborn (present-day Chicago).

August 16, 1812: Fearing another massacre of women, GENERAL HULL SURRENDERS DETROIT to the British. With Detroit under their command, the British control Michigan territory and the Lake Erie region. Hull will later be court-martialed for cowardice and neglect of duty.

August 19, 1812: The 44-gun U.S.S. *CONSTITUTION*, commanded by Isaac Hull, defeats the 38-gun British warship *Guerrière* off the coast of Nova Scotia.

September 17, 1812: William Henry Harrison is made brigadier general and receives orders to retake Detroit. Ten thousand men are placed under his command.

October 13–November 28, 1812: THE NIAGARA CAMPAIGN FAILS when British forces crush an American attack on Canada from across the Niagara River. Reinforcements from the New York militia had refused to leave New York.

October 17, 1812: The *Wasp*, a 18-gun sloop commanded by American Captain Jacob Jones, defeats the British 18-gun brig *Frolic* 600 miles off the Virginia coast.

October 25, 1812: The *United States*, commanded by STEPHEN DECATUR, the hero of the Barbary Wars, captures British frigate *Macedonian* off the Madeira Islands.

November 5, 1812: Madison vetoes a naturalization bill because he believes it would be subjected "to abuse by aliens having no real purpose of effectuating naturalization."

December 2, 1812: MADISON IS REELECTED, defeating the anti-war candidate DeWitt Clinton, governor of New York.

December 29, 1812: The *Constitution* destroys the 38-gun British frigate *Java* off the coast of Brazil. The victory earns the American ship the nickname "OLD IRONSIDES."

Madison's Second Term 1813-1817

January 13, 1813: Madison replaces Secretary of War William Eustis with John Armstrong.

January 22, 1813: AMERICANS ARE DEFEATED AT FRENCHTOWN at the western end of Lake Erie, and 500

*The **Constitution** defeats the British warship **Guerriere** August 19,1812.*

	1788	1789	1794	1795
■ Madison's Life		Madison is elected to the U.S. House of Representatives.		
	He is defeated in the election to the Senate.			Napoleon invades Italy.
■ U.S. & World Events	Madison writes 29 of *The Federalist* papers.	George Washington becomes the first U.S. president.	Madison marries Dolley Todd.	

Election of 1812

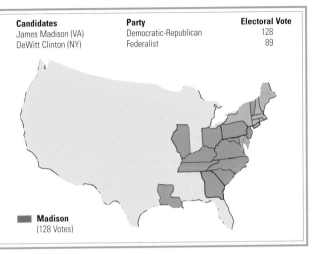

Candidates	Party	Electoral Vote
James Madison (VA)	Democratic-Republican	128
DeWitt Clinton (NY)	Federalist	89

■ **Madison**
(128 Votes)

About the Election: The election of 1812 was essentially a referendum on Madison's war policy. Elbridge Gerry, the governor of Massachusetts, replaced George Clinton as Madison's vice president, following Clinton's death. Opposing Madison was Dewitt Clinton, George Clinton's nephew, and the Democratic-Republican mayor of New York City. Running as an independent candidate with New England Federalist support, Clinton ran a campaign both condemning and supporting the war, depending on the audience that he was addressing. Most of New England and the mid-Atlantic states favored Clinton, but the Southern and Western states voted for Madison, giving him enough votes to win the reelection.

Americans are taken prisoners and 400 are killed in action.

March 25, 1813: *Essex*, sailing around the Cape Horn, engages in the first U.S. naval encounter in the Pacific Ocean.

April 15, 1813: GENERAL JAMES WILKINSON TAKES THE SPANISH FORT AT MOBILE in Alabama and occupies the region from Mobile to the Perdido River.

April 27, 1813: AMERICANS CAPTURE YORK (present-day Toronto), the capital of Upper Canada. However, casualties are high: 320 Americans, including General Zebulon Pike, are killed in a gunpowder explosion. The Americans torch York's government buildings, and in turn, British troops set fire to Washington, D.C. in 1814.

May 1-9, 1813: GENERAL HARRISON SUCCESSFULLY DEFENDS FORT MEIGS at the mouth of the Maumee River against a combined force of the Shawnee and the British.

May 26, 1813: The British blockade is extended to the mouth of the Mississippi River, affecting ports in New York, Charleston, Port Royal and Savannah.

June 1, 1813: The British 38-gun frigate *Shannon* captures the American 38-gun frigate *Chesapeake* off the coast of Massachusetts. Among the 146 American casualties is Captain James Lawrence, whose final order, "**DON'T GIVE UP THE SHIP!**" becomes a rallying cry for the U.S. Navy.

July 27, 1813: The CREEK WAR BEGINS when a group of American settlers skirmished with a faction of the Creek nation known as the Red Sticks.

August 2, 1813: The AMERICANS SUCCESSFULLY DEFEND FORT

STEPHENSON on the Sandusky River against a British attack. But, Harrison's forces are unable to launch their planned offensive to recapture Detroit since the British still control Lake Erie.

August 30, 1813: In the FORT MIMS MASSACRE. Creek warriors burn Fort Mims in Alabama. In response, ANDREW JACKSON, a major general in the Tennessee militia, organizes a force of 2,000 volunteers.

September 10, 1813: Ten vessels under Captain Oliver Hazard Perry defeat a squadron of six British vessels in the BATTLE OF LAKE ERIE, the bloodiest of the war. Perry loses 80 percent of the men onboard his flagship *Lawrence*, named after the martyred captain of the *Chesapeake*. Despite the loss of life, Perry prevails and communicates to General Harrison, "We have met the enemy and they are ours."

September 18, 1813: Having lost control of Lake Erie, the BRITISH EVACUATE DETROIT, despite Tecumseh's objections, and begin a retreat northwards.

October 5, 1813: Now free to move his forces, General Harrison catches retreating British and Native American forces at Moravian Town on the Thames River. During the BATTLE OF THE THAMES, Tecumseh is killed. His Native American Confederacy collapses and the U.S. secures the Northwest.

November 3-9, 1813: Tennessee volunteers, under Andrew Jackson, destroy Creek settlements at Talishatchee and Talledega.

November 4, 1813: British Prime Minister Lord Castlereagh offers to negotiate a PEACE TREATY with Madison. The president accepts immediately.

November 11, 1813: An American plan to capture Montreal

1798	1801	1802	1803	1804

Madison composes the Virginia Resolutions, arguing that individual states have the right to overturn federal laws that are deemed unconstitutional.

Jefferson appoints Madison secretary of state.

His father, James Madison, Sr., dies.

Beethoven's *Moonlight Sonata* is composed.

The United States purchases the Louisiana Territory from France.

Napoleon becomes Emperor of France.

in a two-pronged attack fails as General James Wilkinson's force is defeated, which leads to the retreat of the second force, under General Wade Hampton, back across the U.S. border.

November 16, 1813: BRITISH SHIPS BLOCKADE LONG ISLAND SOUND, closing all American ports south of New London, Connecticut.

December 17, 1813: Congress orders an EMBARGO ON TRADE WITH BRITISH TROOPS, prohibiting New England and New York

---

Madison's Second Administration

Inauguration: March 4, 1813 at the House of Representatives in Washington, D.C.
Vice President: Elbridge Gerry
Secretary of State: James Monroe
Secretary of the Treasury: Albert Gallatin; George W. Campbell (from February 9, 1814); Alexander J. Dallas (from October 14, 1814); William H. Crawford (from October 22, 1816)
Secretary of War: John Armstrong; James Monroe (from October 1, 1814); William H. Crawford (from August 8, 1815); George Graham (from October 22, 1816)
Attorney General: William Pinkney; Richard Rush (from February 11, 1814)

Postmaster General: Gideon Granger; Return J. Meigs, Jr. (from April 11, 1814)
Secretary of the Navy: William Jones; Benjamin W. Crowninshield (from January 16, 1815)
13th Congress: (March 4, 1813-March 4, 1815) Senate: 27 Democratic-Republicans; 9 Federalists
House: 112 Democratic-Republicans; 68 Federalists
14th Congress: (March 4, 1815-March 4, 1817) Senate: 25 Democratic-Republicans; 11 Federalists
House: 117 Democratic-Republicans; 65 Federalists

---

merchants from supplying British troops in Canada. The ban is modified in January 1814 when the citizens of Nantucket Island off the coast of Massachusetts nearly starve to death.

December 29-30, 1813: BRITISH RETALIATE for the burning of the Canadian villages of Newark and Queensland, by capturing Fort Niagara, burning the American settlements of Buffalo and Black Rock, and encouraging Native American raids on the surrounding countryside.

January 22-27, 1814: Tennessee volunteers are defeated at Emuckfaw, Enotachopco Creek, and Calibee Creek.

March 27, 1814: In the decisive battle of the Creek War, Andrew Jackson's forces defeat the Creek at the BATTLE OF HORSESHOE BEND, killing roughly 900 warriors and taking 500 women and children prisoner. In August, one faction of the Creek nation cedes two-thirds of its lands to the U.S., agreeing to relocate from southern and western Alabama.

March 31, 1814: In a special message to Congress, Madison recommends the repeal of the Embargo and Non-Importation Acts. The House of Representatives passes this bill on April 7 and the Senate on April 12.

April 14, 1814: Madison signs a bill authorizing the REPEAL OF THE EMBARGO AND NON-IMPORTATION ACTS.

July 22, 1814: By signing the TREATY OF GREENVILLE, representatives of the Miami, Seneca, Shawnee and Wyandot nations agree to end the conflict with the United States and to declare war on the British.

August 19-24, 1814: In late August, the British devise a plan to divert American forces from Canada by attacking American naval

and military sites along the mid-Atlantic coast. The plan calls for forces under British General Robert Ross to destroy a flotilla of American gunboats under Commodore Joshua Barney and to attack both Baltimore and Washington. On August 22, Barney destroys his flotilla rather than surrendering to the enemy. Two days later, American General William Winder gathers up a rag-tag force of militia from surrounding states in order to meet the advancing British army of 4,000 soldiers outside Bladensburg, where Madison and some members of his Cabinet have gone for protection. Winder's men are quickly routed and withdraw to Georgetown, leaving Barney's naval forces to ward off the BRITISH ADVANCE ON WASHINGTON.

August 24-25, 1814: BRITISH TROOPS MARCH INTO WASHINGTON, and set fire to the Capitol, the White House, most government offices, several homes, and the office of the *National Intelligencer* newspaper. U.S. Secretary of the Navy William Jones orders the destruction of the Washington Navy yard to prevent it from falling into British hands. Within days, Secretary of War John Armstrong resigns his post and Secretary of State James Monroe assumes the duty.

September 11, 1814: American naval forces defeat a British fleet at the BATTLE OF LAKE CHAMPLAIN. The victory gives the Americans undisputed control of the crucial Lake Champlain waterway.

September 12-14, 1814: On September 12, the British army disembarks about 14 miles from Baltimore, while a British fleet moves on Fort McHenry in Baltimore Harbor. A force of 1,000 guards Fort McHenry. Due to the strong opposition from

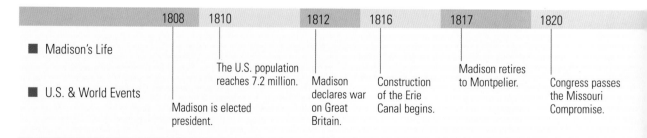

	1808	1810	1812	1816	1817	1820
■ Madison's Life						
		The U.S. population reaches 7.2 million.	Madison declares war on Great Britain.	Construction of the Erie Canal begins.	Madison retires to Montpelier.	Congress passes the Missouri Compromise.
■ U.S. & World Events	Madison is elected president.					

American troops, the land assault is slowed before reaching the heights of Baltimore. American witness Francis Scott Key is inspired to write the words to "**THE STAR SPANGLED BANNER.**"

October 17, 1814: With the disarray of American currency during the war, Secretary of the Treasury Alexander Dallas recommends the creation of a **SECOND BANK OF THE UNITED STATES.** When Congress passes a diluted version of Dallas's proposal, President Madison vetoes it.

November 7, 1814: General Andrew Jackson disobeys orders and seizes the Florida settlement of Pensacola.

December 15–January 5, 1814: Organized by anti-war New England Federalists, the **HARTFORD CONVENTION** seeks to revise the U.S. Constitution. Using language similar to that of the Kentucky and Virginia Resolutions (written by Jefferson and Madison, respectively), the delegates threaten to secede New England from the Union. However, when the Treaty of Ghent ends the war, the convention collapses, and its delegates are discredited in the wave of patriotic support for Madison.

December 24, 1814: The **TREATY OF GHENT** ends the war and restores the U.S.-Canada border to what it had been before the war. The treaty does not deal with the issues that started the war: impressments, blockades, and other naval rights. The Senate ratifies the treaty unanimously on February 15, 1815.

January 1, 1815: Two weeks after the signing of the Treaty of Ghent, Andrew Jackson and a group of expert Tennessee and Kentucky riflemen decimate a larger force of British troops at the **BATTLE OF NEW ORLEANS.** The British casualties amount to a total of 2,036. Americans suffer only 8 deaths and 13 wounded. Jackson's victory makes him a national hero.

January 8, 1815: Jackson and his men inflict heavy losses on the British at the Battle of New Orleans.

January 30, 1815: Thomas Jefferson's library is purchased to restore the Library of Congress, which was destroyed in the fire set by British troops in 1814.

June 17-30, 1815: The Barbary Coast state of Algiers renews demands for tribute money from American ships in the Mediterranean. Stephen Decatur captures two Algerian ships and forces the government of Algiers to release American prisoners and to sign a treaty ending the harassment of American vessels in the Mediterranean.

July 3, 1815: Great Britain agrees to allow American vessels to trade in the East Indies.

July 4, 1815: The cornerstone of the first monument to honor George Washington is laid at Baltimore, Maryland.

April 10, 1816: **CONGRESS CREATES THE SECOND BANK OF THE UNITED STATES** as a depository for the government's money. The bank does not charge interest, however, for its use, and pays the federal government a $1.5 billion bonus.

December 4, 1816: Named as Madison's chosen successor, **JAMES MONROE IS ELECTED PRESIDENT.** He defeats Federalist candidate Rufus King of New York in a landslide victory.

December 12, 1815: Madison orders the removal of all persons who have illegally appropriated or settled upon United States public lands.

December 3, 1816: In his last State of the Union Address, Madison suggests that Congress should consider the establishment of a national bank.

December 11, 1816: **INDIANA IS ADMITTED** as the 19th state.

February 7, 1817: The Gas Light Company of Baltimore is the first commercial gas light company in the United States. It lights its first gas light at Market and Lemon Streets in Baltimore, Maryland.

March 3, 1817: In his final days in office, Madison signs a bill establishing Alabama territory, and he **VETOES THE BONUS BILL.** John C. Calhoun had proposed that the bonus paid to the federal government by the Second Bank of the United States be used to create a permanent fund to finance internal improvements, such as roads connecting the Western states and territories to the Eastern seaboard. Monroe argues that a constitutional amendment is needed to give Congress the power to fund such projects.

The Battle of Lake Erie, September 10, 1813

1826	1828	1829	1836	1836
He becomes a member of the Board of Rectors, University of Virginia.				Madison dies on June 28 in Montpelier, Virginia.
	Andrew Jackson signs the Indian Removal Act.	Madison's mother, Eleanor Conway Madison, dies.		
Madison becomes rector of University of Virginia.			The siege of the Alamo takes place in Texas.	

James Monroe

"The earth was given to mankind to support the greatest number of which it is capable, and no tribe or people have a right to withhold from the wants of others more than is necessary for their own support and comfort."

James Monroe, the last of the "Virginia Dynasty," became president by paying his dues. During the Revolution, he fought under the command of George Washington at Valley Forge, and after the war, he became an aide to Thomas Jefferson, then governor of Virginia. Throughout his political career, Monroe had a close friendship and professional rivalry with James Madison. Unlike Jefferson and Madison, however, Monroe was no political philosopher or scholar. Instead, he was a career politician who had risen from the ranks as an efficient administrator.

Politically, Monroe inherited the Jeffersonian belief in restraining the power of the federal government. He was a member of the Democratic-Republican Party, and he supported states' rights and a pro-French foreign policy. Following a strict construction of the Constitution, Monroe vetoed a federal bill to pay for the construction of roads and canals that would connect the West with the commercial centers of the East because he believed the Constitution did not authorize such spending.

Like the younger generation of Democratic-Republicans who came to power during the War of 1812, Monroe was a nationalist. He helped negotiate the treaty for the Louisiana Purchase, and lent his name to the Monroe Doctrine, which championed the right of the U.S and the Americas to be free from European interference. He authorized the building of a permanent military and oversaw the acquisition of Florida from Spain.

Monroe's presidency came at a time of transition. The opposing Federalist Party was collapsing, and Monroe presided over an "Era of Good Feelings" that was free of inter-party political strife. Despite this, deep divisions were developing in American society. Slavery was becoming a national issue that could no longer be ignored. Nevertheless, just as the U.S. Constitution, written when James Monroe was a young man, had avoided coming to terms with the issue, the Missouri Compromise, passed at the end of Monroe's first term as president, merely patched together a framework for dividing the nation between free and slave states.

Biographical Facts

Born: April 28, 1758 in Westmoreland County, Virginia
Ancestry: Scotch
Father: Spence Monroe; born Westmoreland County, Virginia; died 1774 in Westmoreland County, Virginia
Father's Occupations: Carpenter; farmer
Mother: Elizabeth Jones Monroe; born King Geoge Country, Virginia
Wife: Elizabeth Kortright; born June 30, 1768 in New York; died September 23, 1830 in Oak Hill, Virginia
Marriage: February 16, 1786 in New York, New York
Children: Eliza Kortright Monroe (1786-1835); James Spence Monroe (1799-1800); Maria Hester Monroe (1803-50)
Homes: Ash Lawn, Charlottesville, Virginia; Oak Hill, Loudoun County, Virginia
Education: Parson Campbell's school; College of William and Mary
Religious Affiliation: Episcopalian

Occupation before Presidency: Lawyer
Military Service: Lieutenant Colonel in Third Virginia Regiment and Continental Army
Political Offices before Presidency: Military Commissioner for Southern Army; Representative to Virginia Legislature, Virginia Assembly; Member of Governor Jefferson's Council; Representative to Virginia House of Delegates, Continental Congress, U.S. Senate; Minister to France, England; Governor of Virginia; Secretary of State; Secretary of War
Political Party: Democratic-Republican
Age at Inauguration: 58
Occupation after Presidency: Writer
Death: July 4, 1831 in New York, New York
Place of Burial: Hollywood Cemetery, Richmond, Virginia
Nicknames: The Last Cocked Hat; Era-of-Good-Feeling President
Writings: *The Political Writings of James Monroe*

43

Election of 1816

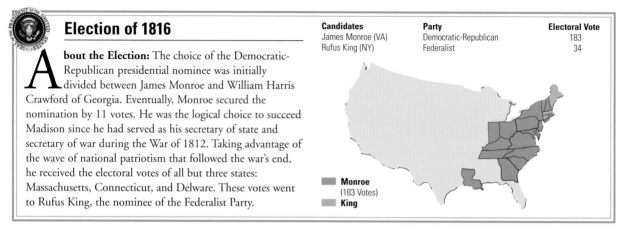

Candidates	Party	Electoral Vote
James Monroe (VA)	Democratic-Republican	183
Rufus King (NY)	Federalist	34

About the Election: The choice of the Democratic-Republican presidential nominee was initially divided between James Monroe and William Harris Crawford of Georgia. Eventually, Monroe secured the nomination by 11 votes. He was the logical choice to succeed Madison since he had served as his secretary of state and secretary of war during the War of 1812. Taking advantage of the wave of national patriotism that followed the war's end, he received the electoral votes of all but three states: Massachusetts, Connecticut, and Delaware. These votes went to Rufus King, the nominee of the Federalist Party.

■ **Monroe** (183 Votes)
■ **King**

Monroe's First Term 1817-1821

March 4, 1817: MONROE'S INAUGURAL ADDRESS reflects the nation's present state of transition. A new generation of Democratic-Republicans has emerged since the war—one that is conducive to the principles of the dying Federalist Party—and Monroe also adapts his beliefs to incorporate Federalist principles. With the War of 1812 fresh on his mind, he proposes the establishment of an adequate federal military, funding for national improvements, such as interstate roads and a stable national banking system.

April 28-29, 1817: In signing the RUSH-BAGOT AGREEMENT, Britain and the United States agree to disarm their forces on the Great Lakes.

July 12, 1817: After Monroe visits Boston on a national goodwill tour, a Boston newspaper, the *Columbian Centinal*, proclaims the present time to be an "Era of Good Feelings." The the term gains national popularity.

December 26, 1817: Members of the Seminole tribe in Spanish-held Florida attack American settlements along the Georgia border in response to U.S. raids seeking out runaway slaves. Monroe orders GENERAL ANDREW JACKSON to pursue the hostile Seminole across the border into Florida. After Jackson accomplishes this, he writes to Monroe that he plans to take possession of Florida. The president does not respond.

April 7–May 24, 1818: ANDREW JACKSON INVADES FLORIDA, seizing St. Marks in April and Pensacola in May, just as Secretary of State John Quincy Adams is negotiating with Spain for the purchase of Florida. Jackson captures and executes two British traders, igniting popular outrage in Britain. However, the British government fails to respond to the situation, and Monroe makes no move to punish Jackson because his exploits are praised by the general population.

October 20, 1818: In the CONVENTION OF 1818, the border between the United States and Canada is fixed along the 49th parallel from the Lake of the Woods in present-day Minnesota to the Rocky Mountains. No border is set for the Oregon territory west of the Rockies, placing this area under joint occupancy between the U.S. and Britain. Both American and British subjects freely settle in Oregon for the next ten years.

November 18, 1818: During his NEGOTIATIONS WITH SPAIN over the purchase of Florida, Secretary of State John Quincy Adams defends Jackson's invasion as self-defense and accuses Spain of aiding and abetting the Seminole attacks on Americans. He suggests that if Spain is unable to stop the Seminole attacks on American settlements, it should cede the Florida territory to the United States.

February 2, 1819: In the case of *TRUSTEES OF DARTMOUTH COLLEGE V. WOODWARD*, Supreme Court Chief Justice John Marshall rules that a charter given to a private corporation is protected from interference by state legislatures by the contract clause of the Constitution. In 1816, the New Hampshire legislature had attempted to change the college into a state institution by transferring the control of trustee appointments to the governor. The New Hampshire court had ruled in favor of the state, but this decision is overturned by the federal court, which emphasizes the term "contract" as a transaction between private parties, and not between the government and its citizens.

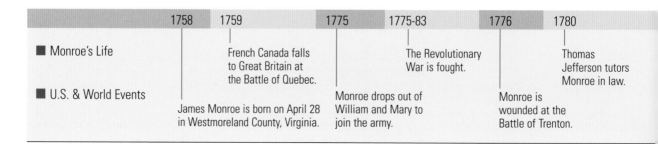

	1758	1759	1775	1775-83	1776	1780
■ Monroe's Life		French Canada falls to Great Britain at the Battle of Quebec.		The Revolutionary War is fought.		Thomas Jefferson tutors Monroe in law.
■ U.S. & World Events		James Monroe is born on April 28 in Westmoreland County, Virginia.	Monroe drops out of William and Mary to join the army.		Monroe is wounded at the Battle of Trenton.	

First Lady: Elizabeth Kortright Monroe

Elizabeth Kortright was an unlikely match for James Monroe; her father, Captain Lawrence Kortright, had made a fortune privateering during the French and Indian War and took no active role in the War for Independence. Monroe, on the other hand, was a patriot veteran with little money. But the couple fell in love after meeting in 1785 in New York City.

As First Lady, Mrs. Monroe came under criticism for her absence at formal functions and for her lack of interest in paying social calls upon her neighbors. She and her daughter Eliza also offended certain circles by creating a formal atmosphere common to European courts, in contrast to Dolly Madison's expansive social style. Mrs. Monroe is also remembered for saving the life of Madame de Lafayette, made possible by a prison visit that saved the Frenchwoman from certain beheading in 1794, while Monroe was serving as ambassador to France.

February 22, 1819: Under pressure, Spain signs the **ADAMS-ONIS TREATY**, withdrawing its claims on west Florida and ceding all of east Florida to the United States. In return, the United States renounces its claim to Texas. The treaty also set the western borders of the Louisiana Territory at the mouth of the Sabine River on the Gulf of Mexico along the Red and Arkansas Rivers and the 42nd parallel to the Pacific Ocean. The treaty is ratified by the U.S. Senate two years later.

March 6, 1819: In *MCCULLOCH V. MARYLAND*, the Supreme Court rules that Congress has the power to incorporate a national bank. Chief Justice Marshall uses Alexander Hamilton's doctrine of implied powers to rule that the bank's creation was constitutional. Declaring "the power to tax involves the power to destroy," Marshall also denies Maryland the right to tax the Baltimore branch of the bank.

January 31, 1820: The merchant ship *Elizabeth*, chartered by the **AMERICAN COLONIZATION SOCIETY (ACS)**, leaves New York for west Africa in order to establish a colony of free African Americans. One of the founders of the ACS, Monroe had advocated sending black Americans to Africa ever since his tenure as Virginia's governor. As president, he convinces Congress to appropriate $100,000 for the mission and offers the ACS federal aid in gaining territory. When the colony of Liberia is founded, the capital is named Monrovia in Monroe's honor.

March 6, 1820: Monroe signs the **MISSOURI COMPROMISE**, which admits Maine as a free state, and Missouri as a slave state. It also bans slavery from the remainder of the Louisiana Territory north of the line 36° 30′. By 1819, both Missouri and Maine had sought admission to the Union—at a time when states were divided equally between slave and free. Northerners opposed the admission of Missouri as a slave state, fearing that it would allow other slave territories to join the Union. Southerners, however, would not support any legislation banning slavery in Missouri.

April 20, 1820: Congress passes the **LAND ACT**, abolishing the credit system and requiring cash payments for all public land purchases.

Monroe's First Administration

Inauguration: March 4, 1817 at the Capitol in Washington, D.C.
Vice President: Daniel D. Tompkins
Secretary of State: John Quincy Adams
Secretary of the Treasury: William Harris Crawford
Secretary of War: John C. Calhoun
Attorney General: Richard Rush; William Wirt (from November 15, 1817)
Postmaster General: Return Jonathan Meigs, Jr.
Secretary of the Navy: Benjamin Crowninshield; Smith Thompson (from January 1, 1819)

Fifteenth Congress
(March 4, 1817-March 4, 1819)
Senate: 34 Democratic-Republicans; 10 Federalists
House: 141 Democratic-Republicans; 42 Federalists
Sixteenth Congress
(March 4, 1819-March 4, 1821)
Senate: 35 Democratic-Republicans; 7 Federalists
House: 156 Democratic-Republicans: 27 Federalists
States Admitted: Mississippi (1817); Illinois (1818); Alabama (1819); Maine (1820)

1783	1785	1786	1787	1789	1793	1794
		Monroe marries Elizabeth Kortwright.		George Washington becomes the first president of the United States.		Washington appoints Monroe as minister to France.
Monroe is elected to the Continental Congress.	Congress establishes the dollar as the official currency of the United States.		The Constitutional Convention is held.		King Louis XVI of France is beheaded.	

Monroe's Second Administration

Inauguration: March 5, 1821 at House of Representatives, Washington, D.C.
Vice President: Daniel D. Tompkins
Secretary of State: John Quincy Adams
Secretary of the Treasury: William H. Crawford
Secretary of War: John C. Calhoun
Attorney General: William Wirt
Postmaster General: Return Jonathan Meigs, Jr.; John McLean (from July 1, 1823)
Secretary of the Navy: Smith Thompson; Samuel L. Southard (from September 16, 1823)
Supreme Court Appointment: Smith Thompson (1823)

Seventeenth Congress
(March 4, 1821-March 4, 1823)
Senate: 44 Democratic-Republicans; 4 Federalists
House: 158 Democratic-Republicans; 25 Federalists
Eighteenth Congress
(March 4, 1823-March 4, 1825)
Senate: 44 Democratic-Republicans; 4 Federalists
House: 187 Democratic-Republicans; 26 Federalists
State Admitted: Missouri (1821)

The new law is a response to the credit inflation created by the Panic of 1819, the nation's first significant financial crisis, when the nation's banks began recalling loans, foreclosing mortgages and forcing people from their homes and farms. The Land Act of 1820 makes land more affordable and allows new opportunities to the American population.

May 15, 1820: To combat the continuing illegal slave trade, Congress agrees to reward $50 to anyone informing authorities about an illegally-imported African slave.

December 6, 1820: In an uncontested election, JAMES MONROE WINS A SECOND TERM.

Monroe's Second Term 1821-1825

March 5, 1821: Since March 4, the assigned day for a president's inauguration, falls on a Sunday, President Monroe sets a precedent by ordering that his INAUGURATION DAY be delayed until the following day.

September 4, 1821: Alexander I, Czar of Russia, extends RUSSIAN TERRITORIAL CLAIMS to south of the 51st parallel in Oregon Territory. He also orders that the waters surrounding these territories be placed off limits to other nations.

December 21, 1821: Secretary of War John C. Calhoun announces his intent to run for president in 1824. He eventually withdraws his name and runs for vice-president. The collapse of the Federalist Party, and popular opposition to Congress choosing candidates, results in the presidential nominating process falling to state legislatures.

March 8, 1822: President Monroe calls for U.S. RECOGNITION OF NEW LATIN AMERICAN REPUBLICS.

March 22, 1822: The Tennessee legislature nominates GENERAL ANDREW JACKSON to run for president in 1824.

June 19, 1822: The United States recognizes the former Spanish colony of Columbia.

November, 1822: At the CONGRESS OF VERONA, European leaders discuss Spain and its American colonies. Despite protests from Great Britain, members of the Holy Alliance of France, Austria, Russia, and Prussia agree to allow a French intervention in Spain. France also requests that its allies invade Spain's colonies in South America, but the issue is not decided. The following year, when Britain attempts to secure a promise from France that it will not intervene in the Americas, France refuses.

November 18, 1822: The Kentucky legislature nominates HENRY CLAY to run for president in 1824.

December 12, 1822: The United States recognizes the former Spanish colony of Mexico.

January 27, 1823: The United States recognizes the former Spanish colony of Argentina.

July 17, 1823: Secretary of State John Quincy Adams strongly protests Russians claims on lands in the Oregon territory, stating that all parties "should assume distinctly the principle that the American continents are no longer subjects for any new European colonial establishments."

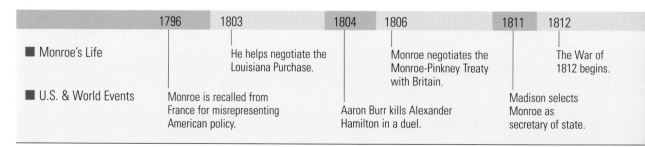

	1796	1803	1804	1806	1811	1812
■ Monroe's Life		He helps negotiate the Louisiana Purchase.		Monroe negotiates the Monroe-Pinkney Treaty with Britain.		The War of 1812 begins.
■ U.S. & World Events	Monroe is recalled from France for misrepresenting American policy.		Aaron Burr kills Alexander Hamilton in a duel.		Madison selects Monroe as secretary of state.	

Election of 1820

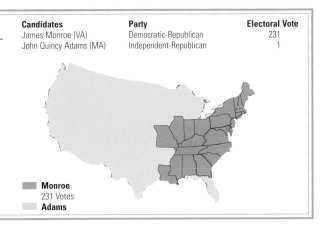

Candidates	Party	Electoral Vote
James Monroe (VA)	Democratic-Republican	231
John Quincy Adams (MA)	Independent-Republican	1

About the Election: Since the Federalist Party had disintegrated by the 1820 election, Monroe ran unopposed for reelection. His secretary of state, John Quincy Adams, received one electoral vote from New England to allow George Washington to remain the only president elected unanimously. Some sources maintain that the solitary vote cast by William Plumer of North Hampshire was to show his opposition to the "Virginia dynasty of presidents." The full amount of 235 electoral votes for the president and vice president were not cast due to the death of three electors.

Monroe
231 Votes
Adams

August 20, 1823: BRITAIN PROPOSES A JOINT ANGLO-U.S. ALLIANCE against European intervention in the Americas. American Ambassador Richard Rush says that President Monroe might favor the agreement if Britain recognizes the new Latin American republics. Monroe discusses the matter with both Thomas Jefferson and James Madison, who support the British plan. Secretary of State Adams proposes that the United States announce its own policy rather than act in the shadow of Great Britain.

October 9, 1823: France finally agrees to disavow any claims on former Spanish colonies in the Americas.

December 2, 1823: President Monroe adopts Adams' advice on foreign intervention, but rejects his plan to convey the new U.S. policy in a series of communications to other nations. Instead, he announces it to Congress in his annual message. The statement, known as the MONROE DOCTRINE, contains the following key points: 1) that the Americas are a unique and separate political system from the European system; 2) that the Americas will no longer be considered subjects of European colonization; 3) that the United States will consider any European attempt to colonize American territory a direct threat to the safety of the United States; and 4) that the United States will not interfere with existing European colonies in the Americas, intervene in the internal affairs of European

Speaker of the House, Henry Clay

nations, or take part in any European wars that do not directly impact the Americas.

February 14, 1824: Congress nominates a presidential candidate for the last time—Secretary of the Treasury William H. Crawford.

February 15, 1824: The Massachusetts legislature nominates Secretary of State John Quincy Adams as a candidate for president.

March 30, 1824: Promoting the TARIFF OF 1824, Speaker of the House Henry Clay describes the U.S. economic policy of tariffs and internal improvements as the "AMERICAN SYSTEM" of expanding domestic trade and lowering dependence on foreign goods.

April 14, 1824: Russia agrees to withdraw claims to a portion of the Oregon Territory, and to pull back to the 54°40′ line. It also promises to lift restrictions on waters surrounding American territories. In return, the United States withdraws its claims to land north of the 54°40′ line.

April 30, 1824: Congress passes a bill authorizing the president to order surveys for INTERNAL IMPROVEMENTS, such as the building of roads and canals.

December 1, 1824: The election of 1824 is thrown into the House of Representatives after none of the candidates wins the 131 electoral votes required for victory. On February 9, 1825 the House decides the election in favor of John Quincy Adams.

1814	1816	1818	1820	1829	1831

Monroe is elected president.

Monroe becomes secretary of war.

English novelist Mary Shelley's *Frankenstein,* **or the** *Modern Prometheus,* **is published.**

Monroe is reelected.

French photographer Louis Daguerre accidentally discovers that an iodized silver plate exposed to light can produce images when the plate is fumed with mercury vapor.

Monroe dies on July 4 in New York City.

John Quincy Adams

6th President (1825–1829)

"Courage and perseverance have a magical talisman, before which difficulties disappear and obstacles vanish into air."

John Quincy Adams had a grand vision for America. The United States he saw was a bustling web of commerce, linked together by an expanding network of canals and national highways. It was a world's leader in science and other intellectual pursuits—a nation where a grand network of government observatories would study the universe, where a national university would instill in citizens a love of arts and literature and where the base maneuvering of political parties would be set aside for the national good.

If vast experience, unassailable ethics and deep intelligence was what was required of a great president, John Quincy Adams might have been one of the greatest in American history. Educated in Europe and at Harvard College, Adams spoke several languages. He began a long career at the age of 27, serving as minister to the Netherlands, followed by postings to Prussia, Russia, and Great Britain. He negotiated the end of the War of 1812 for James Madison, the cessation of Florida to the United States by Spain for James Monroe. He was also responsible for the Monroe Doctrine.

Even so, Adams was a failure as president. The circumstances behind the election of 1824, in which the House chose him over Jackson—despite Jackson winning more popular votes—guaranteed him difficulties. A sober personality, lack of social skill, and his refusal to replace pro-Jackson men within his own administration only made things worse, and he never built his own network of loyal supporters. By the time Jackson defeated him in 1828, Adams had already proclaimed that he could "scarcely conceive a more harassing, wearying, teasing existence" than being president.

Adams continued to serve the public after the presidency. In 1830, he became the only ex-president to be a member of the House of Representatives. A leading anti-slavery voice in Congress, he argued a case in front of the U.S. Supreme Court in 1841, and won freedom for enslaved Africans who had mutinied onboard the ship *Amistad* and killed the captain.

Adams continued to serve his country until the end of his life—suffering a stroke on the House floor in 1846. He died two years later at the age of 81.

Biographical Facts

Born: July 11, 1767 in Braintree (Quincy), Massachusetts

Ancestry: English

Father: John Adams; born October 19, 1735 in Braintree (Quincy), Massachusetts; died July 4, 1826 in Quincy, Massachusetts

Father's Occupations: Lawyer; U.S. Vice President; U.S. President

Mother: Abigail Smith Adams; born November 11, 1744 in Weymouth, Massachusetts; died October 28, 1818 in Quincy, Massachusetts

Wife: Louisa Catherine Johnson; born February 12, 1775 in London, England; died May 14, 1852 in Washington, D.C.

Marriage: July 26, 1797 in London, England

Children: George Washington (1801-1829); John (1803-1834); Charles Francis (1807-1886); Louisa Catherine (1811-1812)

Home: Peacefield, Quincy, Massachusetts

Education: Studied in Paris, Amsterdam, Leyden and The Hague; received B. A. from Harvard (1787); studied law with Theophilus Parsons (1788-90)

Religious Affiliation: Unitarian

Occupations before Presidency: Lawyer; professor

Military Service: None

Political Offices before Presidency: Minister to the Netherlands; Minister to Prussia; Member of Massachusetts Senate; Member of U.S. Senate; Minister to Russia; Minister to Great Britain; Secretary of State

Political Party: Federalist until 1808; Democratic-Republican until 1825; National Republican (Whig) thereafter

Age at Inauguration: 57

Occupations after Presidency: Congressman; writer

Death: February 23, 1848 in Washington, D.C.

Place of Burial: First Unitarian Church, Quincy, Massachusetts

Nickname: Old Man Eloquent

Writings: *Memoirs; Writings of John Quincy Adams*

Election of 1824

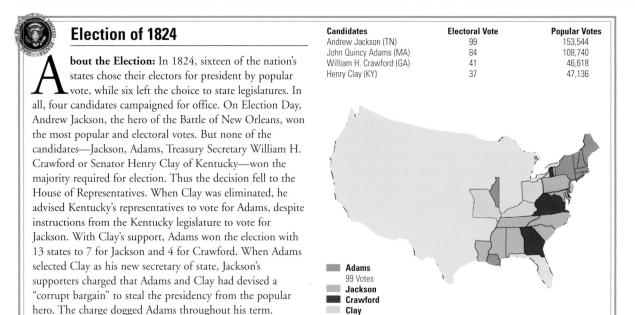

Candidates	Electoral Vote	Popular Votes
Andrew Jackson (TN)	99	153,544
John Quincy Adams (MA)	84	108,740
William H. Crawford (GA)	41	46,618
Henry Clay (KY)	37	47,136

About the Election: In 1824, sixteen of the nation's states chose their electors for president by popular vote, while six left the choice to state legislatures. In all, four candidates campaigned for office. On Election Day, Andrew Jackson, the hero of the Battle of New Orleans, won the most popular and electoral votes. But none of the candidates—Jackson, Adams, Treasury Secretary William H. Crawford or Senator Henry Clay of Kentucky—won the majority required for election. Thus the decision fell to the House of Representatives. When Clay was eliminated, he advised Kentucky's representatives to vote for Adams, despite instructions from the Kentucky legislature to vote for Jackson. With Clay's support, Adams won the election with 13 states to 7 for Jackson and 4 for Crawford. When Adams selected Clay as his new secretary of state, Jackson's supporters charged that Adams and Clay had devised a "corrupt bargain" to steal the presidency from the popular hero. The charge dogged Adams throughout his term.

Adams
99 Votes
Jackson
Crawford
Clay

Adams' Term 1825-1829

March 5, 1825: ADAMS APPOINTS OPPONENTS TO FILL FEDERAL POSTS, in an effort to place his administration above political divisions. He renominates all political appointees from the Monroe Administration, as long as they prove themselves competent and have not committed official misconduct. Included among these nominees are many of Adams' political opponents, virtually ensuring that Adams will never build a strong base of support for his policies. Adams' situation is made more difficult when Vice President John C. Calhoun uses his power to appoint Senate committees in order to fill key posts with anti-Adams senators.

December 6, 1825: In his first annual message to Congress, Adams recommends an ambitious program that includes the construction of roads and canals, the founding of a national university, the exploration of the west, a national astronomical observatory, the standardization of weights and measures, and a variety of new laws to promote agriculture, manufacturing, commerce, arts, literature and science. Virtually all of ADAMS' PROPOSALS MEET WITH RESISTANCE from both Southern advocates of states' rights, who oppose such expansive new federal programs and from supporters of Andrew Jackson, who remain bitter about the 1824 election.

December 26, 1825: After the governments of Mexico and Columbia invite the United States to participate in the PANAMA CONGRESS, a meeting intended to create a union of new Latin American republics, Adams accepts the invitation and nominates delegates to attend it. However, Congress objects because attending the meeting will constitute U.S. interference in the affairs of a foreign government. Congress also criticizes Adams for accepting the invitation without first consulting it. Congress ultimately sends two delegates. They do not attend the conference because one delegate dies en route and the other does not arrive in time.

Quote by Adams:

"Always vote for principle, though you may vote alone and you may cherish the sweetest reflection that your vote is never lost."

Quote about Adams:

"Of all the men whom it was ever my lot to accost and to waste civilities upon, he was the most doggedly and systematically repulsive. With a vinegar aspect, cotton in his leathern ears and hatred in his heart, he sat…like a bulldog among spaniels."
– W. H. Lyttleton

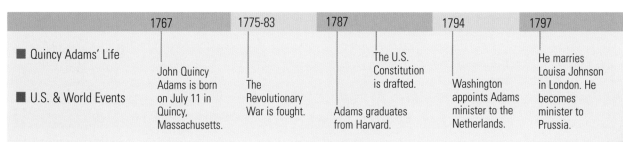

	1767	1775-83	1787	1794	1797
■ Quincy Adams' Life	John Quincy Adams is born on July 11 in Quincy, Massachusetts.	The Revolutionary War is fought.	The U.S. Constitution is drafted. Adams graduates from Harvard.	Washington appoints Adams minister to the Netherlands.	He marries Louisa Johnson in London. He becomes minister to Prussia.
■ U.S. & World Events					

First Lady: Louisa Catherine Johnson Adams

Born to a British mother and an American father, and raised in London, Louisa Catherine Johnson's upbringing ensured that she had highly refined social skills. The only First Lady born outside the United States, she did not come to the U.S until four years after she had married John Quincy Adams. The young couple traveled widely as Adams' appointment as United States minister took them to Berlin, St. Petersburg, and London. Mrs. Adams' health weakened while abroad, but as First Lady, she pressed on to become a leader in Washington society.

Although Mrs. Adams privately suffered from bouts of depression, her reputation as an outstanding hostess remained strong. An accomplished harpist and singer, her music served as a source of solace for herself and entertainment for others.

January 6, 1826: The *United States Telegraph*, an ANTI-ADAMS NEWSPAPER, begins publishing in Washington, D.C. Editor Duff Green of Kentucky is a friend of Vice President Calhoun. He edits the paper in the interest of Calhoun's views.

January 10, 1827: A bill to increase TARIFFS ON WOOL is introduced by New England textile merchants seeking protection from British competition. The bill is ultimately rejected by the Senate with the deciding vote cast by Calhoun.

July 30–August 30, 1827: Delegates from 13 states convene in Harrisburg, Pennsylvania to call again for higher tariffs on not only wool but also hemp, flax, iron and steel, and other goods. The recommendations of the HARRISBURG CONVENTION are presented to Congress in December, where Southern representatives oppose them, since the agricultural economy in the South is highly dependent on international markets and protective tariffs will raise prices on imported goods.

May 19, 1828: With the 1828 election in mind, supporters of Andrew Jackson decide to use the tariffs issue to weaken Adams further. Jacksonians on the House Committee on Manufactures submit a bill that contains such high tariffs that no region of the country would vote for it. The expectation of Jacksonians is that when the bill fails to pass, voters in the contested mid-Atlantic states will blame Adams for its defeat. Jacksonians would then work to win these voters by assuring the passage of new steel tariffs. However, after the committee submits the bill to the House, both the House and Senate pass the bill in May. Nicknamed the TARIFF OF ABOMINATIONS, the bill gains the support of New Englanders who favor the principles of tariffs, and Western and mid-Atlantic followers of Jackson, who vote for it primarily to deprive Adams of a campaign issue.

December 3, 1828: Democratic candidate ANDREW JACKSON EASILY DEFEATS ADAMS in the presidential election.

December 19, 1828: The state legislature of South Carolina adopts eight resolutions calling the Tariff of Abominations unconstitutional. Vice President John C. Calhoun writes an anonymous essay, titled *South Carolina Exposition and Protest*, asserting the right of the states to nullify federal laws. This right is again affirmed by Calhoun in 1832, in the DOCTRINE OF NULLIFICATION.

Quincy Adams' Administration

Inauguration: March 4, 1825 at the Capitol in Washington, D.C.
Vice President: John C. Calhoun
Secretary of State: Henry Clay
Secretary of the Treasury: Richard Rush
Secretary of War: James Barbour; Peter Buell Porter (from June 21, 1828)
Attorney General: William Wirt
Postmaster General: John McLean
Secretary of the Navy: Samuel Lewis Southard
Supreme Court Appointment:
Robert Trimble (1826)

19th Congress
(March 4, 1825-March 4, 1827)
Senate: 26 National Republicans;
20 Democratic-Republicans
House: 105 National Republicans;
97 Democratic-Republicans
20th Congress
(March 4, 1827-March 4, 1829)
Senate: 28 Democratic-Republicans;
20 National Republicans
House: 119 Democratic-Republicans;
94 National Republicans

1798	1809	1814	1817	1825	1828	1830	1848
	James Madison appoints Adams minister to Russia.	Adams signs the Treaty of Ghent, ending the War of 1812.	He begins serving as secretary of state in James Monroe's administration.	The House of Representatives elects Adams president.	Adams loses reelection to Andrew Jackson.		Adams dies on February 23, in Washington, D.C.
Napoleon Bonaparte occupies Rome.						He is elected to the House of Representatives.	

Andrew Jackson

"The people are the sovereigns, they can alter and amend."

Born in the Waxhaws, a backwoods settlement in the Carolinas, Andrew Jackson was the first president who did not come from the elite class of society. His claim to fame was as a military hero. In 1815, he became a national figure when he led a vastly outnumbered group of volunteers to victory over an experienced British force at the Battle of New Orleans. Soon thereafter, his name surfaced as a possible presidential candidate. Jackson felt differently though: "I know what I am fit for," he said, "I can command a body of men in a rough way; but I am not fit to be president."

By 1824, he had reconsidered his decision. In the first popular presidential election, he won more popular votes and electoral votes than the other three candidates. However, he did not win an outright majority of electoral votes as constitutionally required. As a result, the election fell to the House of Representatives, who chose John Quincy Adams.

The thought that Jackson had nearly become president triggered deep anxiety among his opponents who genuinely feared that he could become an American Napoleon. But his defeat in 1824 only rallied his supporters. They formed the Democratic Party for the express purpose of electing Jackson president, and in 1828, he won an easy victory.

Jackson's exercise of presidential powers was unprecedented; he vetoed bills more frequently than all of his predecessors combined. Although he often claimed to do so on constitutional grounds, he ruled largely by instinct – if he felt Congress was wrong, he used his powers to block it.

At the same time, Jackson was a fierce defender of the Union. In the most dramatic confrontation of his two terms, he came close to marching troops into South Carolina when states' rights advocates argued that they had the right to nullify federal laws. He was also a strong advocate of expansion, ordering the brutal relocation of thousands of Native Americans from their homelands in the southeast to clear the land for white settlers. At the close of Jackson's eight-year tenure, the presidency had been transformed. Although the pendulum of power would swing back in the direction of Congress upon his retirement, it would do so in reaction to his controversial rule. His vice president, Martin Van Buren, succeeded to the presidency.

Biographical Facts

Born: March 15, 1767 in the Waxhaws, South Carolina

Ancestry: Scotch-Irish

Father: Andrew Jackson; born in Ireland; died March 1, 1767 in Waxhaws, South Carolina

Father's Occupations: Linen weaver; farmer

Mother: Elizabeth Hutchinson Jackson; born Ireland; died 1781 in Charleston, South Carolina

Wife: Rachel Donelson Robards; born June 15, 1767 in Halifax County, Virginia; died December 22, 1828 in Nashville, Tennessee

Marriage: August 1, 1791 in Natchez, Mississippi second ceremony: January 17, 1794 in Nashville, Tennessee

Child: Andrew Jackson, Jr. (adopted) (1808-1865)

Home: The Hermitage, Nashville, Tennessee

Education: Attended public schools; studied law in Salisbury, South Carolina

Religious Affiliation: Presbyterian

Occupations before Presidency: Lawyer; soldier; politician

Military Service: Judge advocate of Davison County Militia; Major General of Tennessee Militia; Major General of U.S. Army

Political Offices before Presidency: Attorney General of Western District of North Carolina; Delegate to Tennessee State Constitutional Convention; Member of U.S. House of Representatives; Member of U.S. Senate; Tennessee Supreme Court Judge; Governor of Florida Territory

Political Party: Democratic

Age at Inauguration: 61

Death: June 8, 1845 in Nashville, Tennessee

Place of Burial: The Hermitage, Nashville, Tennessee

Nickname: Old Hickory

Writings: *Correspondence of Andrew Jackson*

Election of 1828

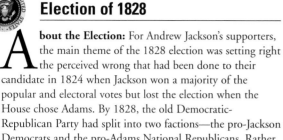

Candidates	Party	Electoral Vote	Popular Vote
Andrew Jackson (TN)	Democratic	178	647,286
John Quincy Adams (MA)	National Republican	83	508,064

About the Election: For Andrew Jackson's supporters, the main theme of the 1828 election was setting right the perceived wrong that had been done to their candidate in 1824 when Jackson won a majority of the popular and electoral votes but lost the election when the House chose Adams. By 1828, the old Democratic-Republican Party had split into two factions—the pro-Jackson Democrats and the pro-Adams National Republicans. Rather than focus on issues, the campaign was bitterly personal. Henry Clay, Adams' most powerful supporter, orchestrated an attack on Rachel Jackson in a Cincinnati newspaper that read, "Ought a convicted adultress and her paramour husband be placed in the highest offices of this free and Christian land?" Adams' support was limited to New England, New Jersey, Maryland and Delaware, while Jackson's coalition swept the rest of the nation, ensuring him an easy victory.

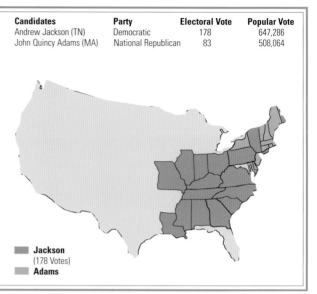

Jackson
(178 Votes)
Adams

Jackson's First Term 1829-1833

March 4, 1829: On **INAUGURATION DAY**, Jackson promises a restrained federal government, the protection of states' rights, fair treatment of Native Americans, and a reform of civil service laws. However, in his speech, delivered at the Capitol, he does not address several contentious issues—tariffs, internal improvements, or the Second Bank of the United States. Following the speech, Jackson rides solemnly on horseback to the White House, trailed by boisterous backwoods supporters. At the White House, the crowd barges into the mansion, hooting and hollering, pushing and shoving all the way. As the mob descends on the refreshment table, women faint, crystal and china are smashed and fistfights break out. Jackson, dressed in black and still in mourning for his wife who had died recently, is forced to escape from the back door, ushered by a phalanx of arm-locked bodyguards.

January 18-27, 1830: In December 1829, Senator Samuel Foot of Connecticut proposed that the Congress consider temporarily restricting the sale of public lands. A few weeks later, Thomas Hart Benton of Missouri denounces the idea, saying that Northeasterners like Foot are attempting to prevent the settlement of the West in fear of the economic competition it would bring to the East and South. States' rights advocate,

Robert Hayne of South Carolina, supporting Benton, goes further. Using a strict-constructionist, states' rights argument, he argues that "the very life of our system is the independence of the states . . ." In response, Daniel Webster of Massachusetts condemns Hayne and others who "habitually speak of the Union in terms of indifference, or even of disparagement". For the next week, the **WEBSTER–HAYNE DEBATES** transfixes the Senate as the two men discuss the nature of the U.S. Constitution and the United States itself.

April 8, 1830: The government of Mexico bans slavery as well as further settlement in its northern territory of Tejas. This law irks the colony of American settlers who had begun migrating to the territory with their slaves after Mexico won its independence from Spain in 1821.

April 13, 1830: Senators Benton and Hayne invite Jackson to a dinner honoring Thomas Jefferson, hoping to cement the political alliance between the Western and Southern states. The dinner is also intended as a means of sounding out the president for his views on the nullification issue. During dinner, they raise toasts praising South Carolina's nullification stance. At last Jackson, raises his glass, and staring down at Vice President John C. Calhoun delivers the following toast: "**OUR UNION: IT MUST BE PRESERVED.**" The startled vice president counters, "The Union, next to liberty, most dear. May we always remember that

	1767	1775-83	1781	1787
■ Jackson's Life		The American Revolution is fought.	During the Revolution, the 14-year old Jackson is captured by the British. After he refuses to shine a British officer's boots, the Redcoat slashes him across the hand and head, leaving his face permanently scarred.	
■ U.S. & World Events		Andrew Jackson is born on March 15, in the Waxhaws, South Carolina.		The U.S. Constitution is drafted.

First Lady: Rachel Donelson Robards Jackson

Rachel Donelson Robards married Andrew Jackson in 1791 after what she thought was a legal divorce from her abusive first husband. Her legal mistake, though eventually corrected, came back to haunt the couple throughout Jackson's political career. Although she preferred Jackson to stay away from politics, she eventually accepted his decision. Known to be a kind and welcoming person, the childless Mrs Jackson raised several relatives' children and formally adopted one nephew, Andrew Jackson, Jr. in 1809.

Mrs Jackson was plagued by bronchial and heart trouble. When she died of a heart attack five days after her husband won election, her niece, Emily Donelson, stepped in to serve as a skillful and tactful White House hostess. During the Peggy Eaton Affair, Mrs. Donelson was replaced temporarily by Sarah Yorke Jackson, the president's daughter-in-law. Sarah Jackson later assumed the role of the White House hostess when Emily Donelson died of tuberculosis in 1836.

Jackson's First Administration

Inauguration: March 4, 1829 at the Capitol, Washington, D.C.
Vice President: John C. Calhoun (resigned December, 1832)
Secretary of State: Martin Van Buren; Edward Livingston (from May 24, 1831)
Secretary of the Treasury: Samuel D. Ingham; Louis McLane (from August 8, 1831)
Secretary of War: John H. Eaton; Lewis Cass (from August 8. 1831)
Attorney General: John M. Berrien; Roger B. Taney (from July 20, 1831)
Postmaster General: John McLean; William T. Barry (from April 6, 1829)

Secretary of the Navy: John Branch; Levi Woodbury (from May 23, 1831)
Supreme Court Appointments: John McLean (1829); Henry Baldwin (1830)
21st Congress: (March 4, 1829-March 4, 1831)
Senate: 26 Democrats;
22 National Republicans
House: 139 Democrats;
74 National Republicans
22nd Congress: (March 4, 1831-March 4, 1833)
Senate: 25 Democrats,
21 National Republicans; 2 Others
House: 141 Democrats;
58 National Republicans; 14 Others

it can only be preserved by distributing equally the benefits and burdens of the Union."

May 28, 1830: Jackson signs the INDIAN REMOVAL ACT, which orders that all Native American peoples living in the southeastern part of the country be relocated to a newly designated "Indian Territory" west of the Mississippi River. Over the next eight years, each of the "five civilized tribes" are forced west to present-day Oklahoma—the Choctaw of Alabama and Mississippi in 1831, the Creek of Alabama and Georgia in 1836, the Chickasaw of Mississippi in 1836 and 1837, the Cherokee in 1838 and 1839, and many of the Seminole by 1842. During these forced migrations, tens of thousands of Native Americans die of exposure, hunger or disease.

May 30, 1830: Earlier in 1830, several of Calhoun's opponents informed Jackson that the vice president had favored punishing him for invading Florida during the Seminole War in 1819. In late May, Jackson writes the following to Calhoun: "Understanding you now, no further communication with you on this subject is necessary." It is the start of a break between the two men.

May 31, 1830: Jackson signs a bill for funding new construction on the Cumberland Road. It will be the only large internal improvement bill he signs in his entire tenure.

December 8, 1830: Jackson vetoes a federal funding of a 60-mile road in Kentucky. His veto signals a setback for the National Republican Party, led by Kentuckian Henry Clay.

February 15, 1831: The SPLIT BETWEEN JACKSON AND CALHOUN deepens when the latter orders that a pamphlet containing correspondence about Jackson's actions in the First Seminole War be published.

April 7, 1831: Secretary of War John Eaton resigns. Jackson ends the EATON AFFAIR (see feature) by appointing Eaton as the governor of Florida.

April 11, 1831: Secretary of State Martin Van Buren resigns, helping JACKSON REORGANIZE HIS CABINET. Jackson then appoints anti-Calhoun men as successors to Ingham, Berrien, and Branch.

September 26, 1831: THE ANTI-MASONIC PARTY becomes the first political party to hold

1791	1796	1797	1812	1814
	Tennessee is admitted into the Union and Jackson serves as its first Representative in the House.	Jackson is elected to the Senate.	Jackson commands a group of Tennessee volunteers in the Creek War.	He defeats the Creek at Horseshow Bend.
Jackson marries Rachel Robards.				

Quotes By Jackson:

"There are no necessary evils in government. Its evils exist only in its abuses".
—To Congress, July 10, 1832

"I have only two regrets: that I have not shot Henry Clay or hanged John C. Calhoun".

Quotes About Jackson:

"I never knew a man more free from conceit, or one to whom it was a greater extent a pleasure, as well as a recognized duty, to listen patiently to what might be said to him upon any subject under consideration . . .Neither, I need scarcely say, was [Jackson] in the habit of talking, much less boasting, of his own achievements".
— Martin Van Buren

"General Jackson is the majority's slave; he yields to its intentions, desires, and half revealed instincts, or rather he anticipates and forestalls them".
— Alexis de Tocqueville

"I feel much alarmed at the prospect of seeing General Jackson President. He is one of the most unfit men I know for such a place".
— Thomas Jefferson

a presidential nominating convention and also the first third party to field a presidential candidate. The party, based on opposition to the Masons and other secret societies, is also opposed to Jackson's policies.

December 12, 1831: The NATIONAL REPUBLICAN CONVENTION nominates for president former Speaker of the House, Henry Clay of Kentucky.

March 3, 1832: In the case *WORCESTER V. GEORGIA*, the Supreme Court rules that only the federal government, and not the state of Georgia, has jurisdiction over lands occupied by the Cherokee Nation. The ruling declares that a Georgia state law requiring all whites living in Cherokee Territory to pledge allegiance to the state is unconstitutional. Georgia ignores the court decision with Jackson's approval to do so.

April 6–August 2, 1832: Seeking to reclaim lands lost to the United States in Wisconsin Territory and Illinois following the War of 1812, warriors of the Sac and Fox Nation, led by Black Hawk, begin a guerilla war, known as BLACK HAWK'S WAR. The charismatic Black Hawk is taken prisoner, and in 1833, is presented to President Jackson. According to some, Jackson felt so threatened by the warrior's popularity that he released him and sent him back to the West.

May 21-22, 1832: The DEMOCRATIC PARTY CONVENTION nominates Jackson for reelection, and endorses Martin Van Buren for vice president.

July 10, 1832: After both the House and Senate vote to reauthorize it, Jackson vetoes the charter for the Second Bank of the United States. Although the bank had successfully kept inflation in check and benefited business, many political factions continued to oppose it. In announcing the BANK VETO, Jackson says, "It is to be regretted that the rich and powerful too often bend the acts of government to their selfish purposes . . .When the laws undertake . . . to make the rich richer and the potent more powerful, the humble members of society, the farmers, mechanics and laborers, who have neither the time nor the means of securing like favors for themselves, have a right to complain of the injustice of their government."

July 13, 1832: Jackson's veto of the bank draws fierce criticism from Nicholas Biddle, the bank's president. His supporters in the Senate attempt but fail to override the veto.

July 14, 1832: After Jackson recommends that Congress lower the high tariffs in the 1828 Tariff of Abominations, Congress passes the less severe TARIFF OF 1832. Rather than appeasing the nullifiers in South Carolina, the new tariff inflames them further.

August 28, 1832: In a letter to South Carolina Governor James Hamilton, John C. Calhoun reaffirms the DOCTRINE OF NULLIFICATION, defending it as a constitutional means of redressing federal acts that are harmful to a state's interests.

October 22, 1832: Governor Hamilton of South Carolina calls for a special state convention to discuss the issue of nullification.

October 29, 1832: U.S. FORTS ARE PLACED ON ALERT in response to the threat of nullification by South Carolina. President Jackson orders for heightened military presence at the U.S. forts in the harbor of Charleston, South Carolina, and places General Winfield Scott in command of the U.S. armed forces in South Carolina.

November 19-27, 1832: At a special state convention, SOUTH CAROLINA ADOPTS THE ORDINANCE OF NULLIFICATION that overturns the tariffs of 1828 and 1832 within the borders of South Carolina. The ordinance also rules that all state office holders swear allegiance to South Carolina and prohibits any appeals involving the ordinance from being made to the federal court.

December 4, 1832: In his ANNUAL MESSAGE TO CONGRESS, Jackson recommends the lowering of tariff rates again to help mollify Southern dissenters.

	1815	1818	1819
■ Jackson's Life			
■ U.S. & World Events	Jackson becomes a national hero after the Battle of New Orleans.	He invades Florida during the First Seminole War.	At the Peterloo Massacre, British troops in Manchester, England attack a crowd of unarmed protesters killing several and injuring hundreds. The crowds had been protesting English Corn Laws, which had led to falling wheat prices and unemployment.

Election of 1832

About the Election: The 1832 election featured the appearance of the Anti-Masonic Party, the first third party to join the presidential race. The main issue of the campaign was the lightning-rod personality of Andrew Jackson himself. Although the Anti-Masonic Party began as a group based on opposition to the Masons and other secret societies, it was essentially an anti-Jackson party. As such, it split the anti-Jackson vote with Henry Clay, the nominee of the National Republicans. South Carolina, where the state legislature still chose the candidate, casted its electoral votes for John Floyd, a pro-nullification candidate. During the campaign, the Anti-Masons set a precedent by holding the first national nominating convention, a practice that has been followed by all political parties ever since.

Candidates	Party	Electoral Vote	Popular Vote
Andrew Jackson (TN)	Democratic	219	701,780
Henry Clay (KY)	National Republican	49	484,205
John Floyd (VA)	Nullifier	11	100,715
William Wirt (MD)	Anti-Masonic	7	---
Others	---	---	7,273

Jackson (219 Votes)
Clay
Floyd
Wirt

December 5, 1832: JACKSON WINS REELECTION in the first popular election in U.S. history, where national political conventions vote for presidential candidates. Jackson defeats Henry Clay of Kentucky and Anti-Masonic Party nominee William Wirt of Maryland.

December 10, 1832: Jackson issues the PROCLAMATION TO THE PEOPLE OF SOUTH CAROLINA, calling Vice President Calhoun's doctrine of nullification an "impractical absurdity." The proclamation argues that no state can refuse to obey federal law, nor can any state chose to leave the Union. He warns the nullifiers: "Disunion by armed force is treason. Are you ready to incur its guilt?"

December 20, 1832: Having been elected to the Senate, CALHOUN RESIGNS AS VICE PRESIDENT.

January 16, 1833: Jackson asks Congress to grant him authority to use military force in South Carolina if necessary.

January 21, 1833: South Carolina suspends the Ordinance of Nullification, which declares the tariff laws of 1828 and 1832 "null and void."

February 20, 1833: Congress passes the FORCE BILL, sometimes called the "Bloody Bill", authorizing the use of military power to enforce federal law. If necessary, Jackson is allowed to use military force in South Carolina. He vows to try Calhoun for treason and "hang him high as Hamen."

March 1, 1833: After the bill has already won passage in the House, the Senate passes the COMPROMISE TARIFF BILL authored by Henry Clay. The bill reduces all tariffs for ten years.

Jackson's Second Term 1833-1837

March 15, 1833: SOUTH CAROLINA REVOKES THE ORDINANCE OF NULLIFICATION after Congress passes the compromise tariff bill. The state, however, declares the force bill "null and void."

April 1-13, 1833: American settlers, known as TEXIANS, in the Mexican territory of Tejas, convene in the town of San Felipe and decide to declare their independence from Mexico.

April 3, 1833: Although the Bank of the United States had lost its charter, it was still a solvent bank as long as it had money deposited in it. After Jackson seeks his Cabinet's advice on how to handle the issue, Attorney General Roger Taney suggests REMOVING THE FEDERAL DEPOSITS from the bank and distributing them to a number of state banks.

September 10, 1833: Jackson announces to his divided Cabinet that the United States government would no longer use the Bank of the United States for federal deposits—a decision that takes effect on October 1.

September 23, 1833: When Treasury Secretary William J. Duane refuses to withdraw federal funds from the bank, Jackson replaces him with Taney, who begins to shift federal funds to state banks, known later as Jackson's "PET BANKS."

December 26, 1833: Henry Clay introduces two bills in the Senate to censure President Jackson for withdrawing the deposits from the federal bank.

January 3, 1834: The Mexican government arrests and holds STEPHEN AUSTIN, the leader of the American Texian colony, for

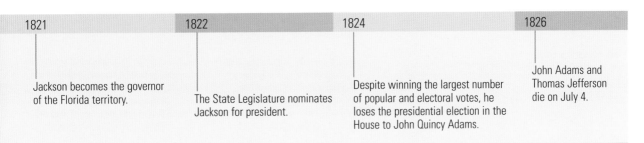

1821 — Jackson becomes the governor of the Florida territory.

1822 — The State Legislature nominates Jackson for president.

1824 — Despite winning the largest number of popular and electoral votes, he loses the presidential election in the House to John Quincy Adams.

1826 — John Adams and Thomas Jefferson die on July 4.

eight months after Austin arrives in Mexico City to inform the government of his colony's declaration of independence.

March 26, 1834: The SENATE CENSURES JACKSON for exceeding his constitutional powers. His opponents dub him "King Andrew."

April 4, 1834: The House issues resolutions supporting Jackson's bank policy.

April 14, 1834: Henry Clay uses the term "Whig" to describe the coalition of anti-Jackson forces. The new WHIG PARTY includes supporters of Clay and John Quincy Adams; states' rights advocates aligned with John C. Calhoun; former Jacksonians miffed over the bank policy; Southern planters, Northern merchants; and members of the Anti-Masonic Party.

June 24, 1834: The Senate declines to confirm Roger B. Taney as secretary of the treasury, becoming the first time ever a Cabinet nominee is rejected.

January 30, 1835: Richard Lawrence, who is later judged insane, makes the FIRST ATTEMPT ON THE LIFE OF A U.S. PRESIDENT as Jackson is leaving a funeral service in the Capitol. Lawrence, shooting at point-blank range, misfires twice. Jackson is unharmed.

June 30, 1835: A group of American Texians under William Travis seize the Mexican fort in Anahuac.

July 29, 1835: A boatload of abolitionist literature from New York is seized and burned in the harbor of Charleston, South Carolina. A crowd of nearly two thousand, about one-seventh of the white population of the city, witness the spectacle.

November, 1835: The SECOND SEMINOLE WAR begins, led by Seminole Chief Oceola, who refuses to relocate his people west of the Mississippi River as agreed to by treaty in 1832. The war lasts until August 14, 1843.

December 2, 1835: Reacting to the seizure of abolitionist literature at Charleston, Jackson proposes a BAN ON MAILING ANTI-SLAVERY LITERATURE in his annual message to Congress.

December 15, 1835: To clamp down on the American Texian independence movement, Mexican President Santa Anna abolishes all local laws in Texas and places the federal government of Mexico in charge of the territory.

December 29, 1835: A small group of Cherokee signs a treaty with the U.S. government ceding all Cherokee lands east of the Mississippi in exchange for $5 million as compensation for "transportation costs" and land in Indian Territory. Most other Cherokee denounce the agreement.

February 4, 1836: Agreeing with Jackson about the need to ban the mailing of abolitionist literature, but not accepting the right of the federal government to order it, John C. Calhoun presents a revised bill that allows the seizure of abolitionist literaure only when it violates the laws of an individual state. This bill is defeated in June.

February 23–March 6, 1836: With 3,000 men in his command, Mexican General Santa Anna lays siege on the garrison at THE ALAMO in Texas. A group of 188 Texians hold off the Mexicans until March 6. The battle cry "Remember the Alamo!" is first used six weeks later at the Battle of San Jacinto.

March 1, 1836: The charter for the Bank of the United States expires. The bank obtains a state charter and becomes the Bank of the United States of Pennsylvania.

March 2, 1836: At the Brazos River town of Washington, 59 representatives voted into existence the REPUBLIC OF TEXAS, adopting a new declaration of independence and crafting a constitution based on the U.S. Constitution.

March 9, 1836: After two anti-slavery petitions are submitted to the Senate, John C. Calhoun of South Carolina proposes banning the Senate from accepting future anti-slavery petitions.

Jackson's Second Administration

Inauguration: March 4, 1833 at the House of Representatives, Washington, D.C.
Vice President: Martin Van Buren
Secretary of State: Edward Livingston; Louis McLane (from May 29, 1833); John Forsyth (from July 1, 1834)
Secretary of the Treasury: Louis McLane; William J. Duane (from June 1, 1833); Roger B. Taney (from September 23, 1833); Levi Woodbury (from July 1, 1834)
Secretary of War: Lewis Cass
Attorney General: Roger B. Taney; Benjamin F. Butler (from November 18, 1833)
Postmaster General: William T. Barry; Amos Kendall (from May 1, 1835)

Secretary of the Navy: Levi Woodbury; Mahlon Dickerson (from June 30, 1834)
Supreme Court Appointments: James M. Wayne (1835); Roger B. Taney, Chief Justice (1836); Philip P. Barbour (1836)
23rd Congress: (March 4, 1833-March 4, 1835) Senate: 20 Democrats; 20 National-Republicans; 8 Others House: 147 Democrats; 53 Anti-Masons; 60 Others
24th Congress: (March 4, 1835-March 4, 1837) Senate: 27 Democrats; 25 Whigs House: 145 Democrats; 98 Whigs
States Admitted: Arkansas (1836); Michigan (1837)

	1828	1829	1831
■ Jackson's Life			
■ U.S. & World Events	Rachel Jackson dies. Two weeks later, Jackson defeats Adams to become President.	A cholera pandemic begins in Russia before spreading throughout Europe and elsewhere. By the time it ends in 1840, it will have killed several million people worldwide.	Nat Turner, an escaped slave leads a bloody slave rebellion in Virginia. He and his followers kill about 70 white men, women and children. In retaliation, the whites respond by killing about 100 African Americans.

His proposal is defeated in the Senate, but still under consideration in the House.

March 11, 1836: SENATOR JAMES BUCHANAN of Pennsylvania submits a motion to reject Calhoun's anti-slavery petitions.

March 27, 1836: Santa Anna's forces massacre 300 Texians at the BATTLE OF GOLIAD.

April 21, 1836: Sam Houston leads Texian forces to victory at the BATTLE OF SAN JACINTO in which Santa Anna is captured. Although Santa Anna is forced to sign a pledge stating that he will ensure that the Mexican Congress recognize the new Republic of Texas, the Mexican Congress will refuse.

May 18, 1836: Representative Henry Pinckney of South Carolina proposes a GAG RULE that bans "all petitions, memorials, resolutions, propositions. or papers relating to the subject of slavery."

May 25, 1836: Former President John Quincy Adams, presently serving in the House, becomes the leading voice of opposition against the gag rule. While he never argues in favor of abolishing slavery where it already exists, Adams does view the gag rule as unconstitutional, violating the right to petition.

May 26, 1836: The House votes to pass the gag rule, as well as a resolution stating that Congress has no power to interfere with slavery in the states.

June 23, 1836: Congress passes the DEPOSIT ACT, requiring the Secretary of State to choose one bank in each state and territory for federal deposits, and for those banks to assume the former powers of the Bank of the United States.

July 1-4, 1836: The House and Senate recognize the new REPUBLIC OF TEXAS. Initially Jackson hesitates to do so since he is concerned that it might violate U.S. pledges of neutrality and lead to war with Mexico. Later, after he reluctantly recognizes Texan independence, he becomes a strong advocate for Texas' admission to the Union as a state.

July 11, 1836: Jackson issues the SPECIE CIRCULAR. During his second term, land speculation in the West increases dramatically, encouraged by the growing use of paper money as legal tender and by the loose money policies of the "pet banks." Jackson's *SPECIE CIRCULAR*, drafted by Thomas Hart Benton, states that after August 15, the federal government will only accept gold, silver and in some cases, Virginia land scrip as payment for federal lands. The goal of the *Specie Circular* is to prevent fraud and speculation. Instead, it leads to financial panic as the reserves of Western "pet banks" become strained and people begin hoarding gold and silver. Although Jackson will defend the *Circular*, both houses of Congress will attempt to

---

Scandal! The Eaton Affair

In 1831, a scandal broke out concerning Peggy Eaton, the wife of Secretary of War John Eaton. Rumor circulated around Washington's social circles that Mrs. Eaton, a former barmaid, had a promiscuous past, that she had begun living with Secretary Eaton before they were married and had even given birth to two of Eaton's children out of wedlock. The capital's social elite, including the wives of Jackson's other Cabinet members, snubbed Mrs. Eaton. Even Jackson's own White House hostess, his niece Emily Donelson resigned over the matter.

Defending Eaton, Jackson, who clearly remembered the attacks his wife Rachel had suffered, even called a special Cabinet meeting to demand an end to the snub. Only Secretary of State Martin Van Buren, a bachelor, sided with Mrs. Eaton. Van Buren then decided to use the episode to his advantage. He submitted his resignation, knowing that would force a reorganization of the Cabinet. Rather than allow Van Buren to resign alone, John Eaton resigned himself, ending the scandal.

---

repeal it. They will not succeed until after Jackson leaves office.

December 7, 1836: MARTIN VAN BUREN defeats three Whig candidates in the presidential election.

December 19, 1836: Senator Benjamin Swift of Vermont presents resolutions opposing the admission of Texas or any other territory into the Union as a slave state. Swift's petitions also assert the right of Congress to ban slavery in the District of Columbia and to end interstate slave trading.

December 27, 1836: In response the Swift, Calhoun argues that states reserve the right to ban abolitionist petitions in order to prevent the federal government from becoming a vehicle for anti-slavery activity. According to Calhoun, the attempt to ban slavery from the District of Columbia is a "direct and dangerous attack on the institutions of slave-holding states."

February 12, 1837: In one of the early signs of the PANIC OF 1837, an unemployed mob breaks into New York flour warehouses and steals the inventory.

March 3, 1837: Jackson recognizes the Republic of Texas.

March 4, 1837: In his FAREWELL ADDRESS, Jackson appeals for loyalty to the Union and sound fiscal management. After seeing his friend Martin Van Buren sworn in as president, Jackson retires to the Hermitage in Nashville, Tennessee after serving two terms.

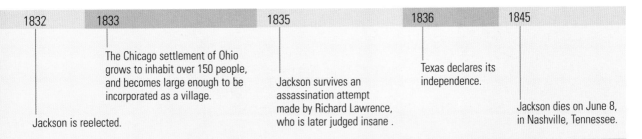

| 1832 | 1833 | 1835 | 1836 | 1845 |

The Chicago settlement of Ohio grows to inhabit over 150 people, and becomes large enough to be incorporated as a village.

Jackson survives an assassination attempt made by Richard Lawrence, who is later judged insane .

Texas declares its independence.

Jackson dies on June 8, in Nashville, Tennessee.

Jackson is reelected.

Martin Van Buren

8th President (1837–1841)

"I tread in the footsteps of illustrious men… in receiving from the people the sacred trust confided to my illustrious predecessor."

Martin Van Buren, who rose from obscurity as an upstate New York politician to become Andrew Jackson's powerful right-hand man as vice president, was one of the savviest political strategists of his time. Backed by his powerful political machine known as the Albany Regency of New York, Van Buren helped General Andrew Jackson win the election of 1828. He landed himself a Cabinet position as secretary of state in the process. During Jackson's first term, Van Buren deftly outmaneuvered Vice President John C. Calhoun in winning the allegiance of the president. By Jackson's second term, Van Buren had replaced Calhoun as vice president.

When Van Buren won the 1836 election, largely on Jackson's popularity, he pledged to follow the course set by his predecessor. He had no moral qualms about supporting the right of slave-holding states to ban the discussion of slavery in Congress, nor did he hesitate to order the eviction of thousands of Cherokee from their homelands. Van Buren saw his popularity plummet as the nation suffered through its first serious economic depression, the Panic of 1837, during which

detractors dubbed him" Martin Van Ruin." His unwillingness to address the problem of rising unemployment, as well as his stuffy appearance and obvious taste for expensive clothes, cost him the support of the "common man" that had swept Jackson into office. Van Buren also refused to extend federal aid to distressed banks and state governments. In 1840, he was easily defeated by the 67-year-old Whig candidate, General William Henry Harrison.

However, Van Buren was not without his achievements. A devoted Jeffersonian Democrat, he played a signicant role in the creaton of the Democratic Party. He also helped to establish the Independent Treasury Act, which restored stability to financial markets. In addition to this, during his term as president, Van Buren avoided potential war with Great Britain over Canada. He maintained a strong stance of neutrality despite widespread anti-British sentiment. Ultimately though, Van Buren is best known as a political operator whose only real agenda was his own rise to power. He served only one term, and despite attempts to win back the presidency in 1844 and 1848, he was never reelected.

Biographical Facts

Born: December 5, 1782 in Kinderhook, New York
Ancestry: Dutch
Father: Abraham Van Buren; born February 17, 1737 in Albany, New York; died April 8, 1817 in Kinderhook, New York
Father's Occupation: Farmer; tavern owner
Mother: Maria Hoes Van Alen Van Buren; born January 16, 1747 in Claverack, New York; died February 16, 1817 in Kinderhook, New York
Wife: Hannah Hoes; born March 8, 1783 in Kinderhook, New York; died February 5, 1819 in Albany, New York
Marriage: February 21, 1807 in Kinderhook, New York
Children: Abraham (1807-1873); John (1810-1866); Martin (1812-1855); Smith Thompson (1817-1876)
Home: Lindenwald, Kinderhook, New York
Education: Attended village school; Kinderhook Academy; studied law
Religious Affiliation: Dutch Reformed

Occupations before Presidency: Lawyer; politician
Military Service: None
Political Offices before Presidency: Surrogate of Columbia County, New York; New York State Senator; Attorney General of New York; Delegate to Third New York State Constitutional Convention; U.S. Senator; Governor of New York; Secretary of State; U.S. Vice President
Political Party: Democratic (during Presidency); Free Soil (from 1848)
Age at Inauguration: 54
Occupation after Presidency: Politician
Death: July 24, 1862 in Kinderhook, New York
Place of Burial: Kinderhook Cemetery, Kinderhook, New York
Nicknames: Little Magician; Red Fox of Kinderhook; Martin Van Ruin
Writings: *Inquiry into the Origin and Course of Political Parties in the United States; The Autobiography of Martin Van Buren*

"I had rather be right than be president."

February 12, 1839: Canadian lumberjacks capture Maine land agent Rufus McIntire as he attempts to expel them from the Aroostook Valley, setting off the **AROOSTOOK WAR**. In response, both Maine and New Brunswick call up their militia. When Nova Scotia appropriates money for war preparations, the United States Congress authorizes President Van Buren to call up 50,000 troops.

March 1839: U.S. General Winfield arranges a truce between the governments of Maine and New Brunswick, ending the Aroostook War. The Maine border is determined in 1842.

November 13, 1839: The anti-slavery Liberty Party is founded in New York by Gerrit Smith and other moderate abolitionists. Unlike more radical abolitionists like William Lloyd Garrison, the founders of the Liberty Party do not advocate secession from the Union over slavery. Instead, the party pledges its loyalty to the Union.

After failing to win the Democratic Party's nomination in 1844, Van Buren ran as the nominee of the anti-slavery Free Soil Party in 1848. His running mate, Charles Francis Adams, was the son of John Quincy Adams.

	1831	1832	1836	1838	1840
■ Van Buren's Life					
■ U.S. & World Events	In an adept political maneuver, Van Buren resigns over the Peggy Eaton Affair.	After his nomination as minister to Great Britain is rejected by the Senate, he becomes vice president.	Van Buren is elected president.	The first installments of Charles Dickens's *Oliver Twist* are published.	Van Buren loses his bid for reelection.

In this cartoon, Van Buren leaves Washington in a wagon pulled by his political allies. The new president, William Henry Harrison, stands on the steps to the right behind Whig senator Henry Clay, who holds an eviction notice and a key to the White House.

December 4, 1839: The Whig Party nominates **GENERAL WILLIAM HENRY HARRISON** as its candidate in the 1840 election. Harrison, famous for his success in the Battle of Tippecanoe, has no strong opinions about any of the issues, nor does he possess any political experience, other than his unsuccessful 1836 run for the presidency. **JOHN TYLER**, a staunch states' rights conservative from Virginia, is nominated as his vice president. Rather than focusing on any issues, the Whigs highlight Harrison's personal image.

March 23, 1840: The *Baltimore Republican* writes that "upon condition of his receiving a pension of $2000 and a barrel of cider, General Harrison would no doubt consent to withdraw his pretensions and spend his days in a log cabin on the banks of the Ohio." The Whigs seize upon this comment to portray Harrison as a rugged frontiersman of honest values. They also use the log cabin and cider as symbols during the campaign, contrasting them with the image of Van Buren as a career politician overly concerned with fine clothing and wealthy affectations. The "Log Cabin and Hard Cider" campaign becomes a model for presidential campaigns in the future,

incorporating slogans, banner-waving rallies, campaign paraphernalia, such as hats, coon skin caps and campaign songs, including "Tippecanoe and Tyler, Too!"

March 31, 1840: Van Buren passes an executive order limiting the work of federal employees to ten hours a day,

May 5, 1840: The Democratic Party unanimously renominates Van Buren as its presidential candidate.

July 4, 1840: Van Buren signs the **INDEPENDENT TREASURY ACT** passed by Congress the previous month. The act calls for setting up federal depositories independent of state banks.

December 2, 1840: **WILLIAM HENRY HARRISON DEFEATS VAN BUREN** in the presidential election.

December 13, 1840: Alexander McLeod, a Canadian sheriff, is arrested in New York State for the murder of an American seaman during the *Caroline* incident. The British government demands his immediate release.

December 26, 1840: Secretary of State John Forsyth declares that jurisdiction in the McLeod case belongs to New York State and not the U.S. federal government. When McLeod is brought to trial the following year, he is acquitted.

1844	1848	1848	1861	1862
Van Buren loses an attempt to win the Democratic presidential nomination.	Karl Marx and Friedrich Engels publish *The Communist Manifesto*.	Running as the nominee of the Free Soil Party, he fails to win back the presidency again.	The U.S. Civil War begins and lasts until 1865.	Van Buren dies on July 24 in Kinderhook, New York.

William Henry Harrison

9th President (1841)

"There is nothing more corrupting, nothing more destructive of the noblest and finest feelings of our nature, than the exercise of unlimited power."

As the nation headed towards the Election of 1840, the country's weak economy presented the Whigs with an opportunity to take control of the presidency. As a result of the Panic of 1837, the unpopular Democratic incumbent, Martin Van Buren, had derisively been given the nickname "Martin Van Ruin."

The logical Whig nominee seemed to be the powerful Senator of Kentucky, Henry Clay. However, Southern planters, who made up an influential faction of the early Whig Party, were angered when Clay had supported unpopular tariffs during the Jackson administration. The Whigs eventually agreed on William Henry Harrison, whose heroism at the Battle of Tippecanoe and the Battle of the Thames had given him an appeal similar to that of Andrew Jackson. Harrison had held a few political offices before the presidency, but had shown little leadership off the battlefield. At the time of his nomination in 1840, he was serving as a county clerk in Indiana Territory.

The Whigs had learned from Jackson's presidency that, in politics, military heroics often trumped political experience. Virtually ignoring the issues of the day, such as the failing economy and increasing conflicts over slavery, the Whigs focused their campaign on Harrison's public image as a rough-hewn "Log Cabin and Hard Cider" frontiersman. In truth, Harrison was a well-educated man, from an established Virgina family. He also enjoyed living luxuriously to the point where he was in constant debt.

The sort of president Harrison would have been is conjecture, as he did not live long enough after his election to make any major decisions. It may have been chaos, since it became clear that he had often promised the same government posts to more than one person. At his March 4, 1841 inauguration, dressed without a hat or overcoat, the 67-year-old president gave the longest inauguration speech ever given. Sick throughout most of the next month, he developed pneumonia in late March and died on April 4, serving just one month in office. The first president to die in office, Harrison was succeeded by Vice President John Tyler.

Biographical Facts

Born: February 9, 1773 in Charles City County, Virginia

Ancestry: English

Father: Benjamin Harrison; born April 5, 1726 in Charles City County, Virginia; died April 24, 1791 in Charles City County, Virginia

Father's Occupations: Planter; politician

Mother: Elizabeth Bassett Harrison; born December 13, 1730 in Charles City County, Virginia; died 1792 in Charles City County, Virginia

Wife: Anna Tuthill Symmes; born July 25, 1775 in Morristown, New Jersey; died February 25, 1864 in North Bend, Ohio

Marriage: November 25, 1795 in North Bend, Ohio

Children: Elizabeth Bassett (1796-1846); John Cleves Symmes (1798-1830); Lucy Singleton (1800-1826); William Henry (1802-1838); John Scott (1804-1878); Benjamin (1806-1840); Mary Symmes (1809-1842); Carter Bassett (1811-1839); Anna Tuthill (1813-1845); James Findlay (1814-1817)

Home: Grouseland, Vincennes, Indiana

Education: Private tutoring; attended Hampden-Sidney College

Religious Affiliation: Episcopalian

Occupations before Presidency: Soldier; politician

Military Service: Major General of Kentucky Militia; Brigadier General of U.S. Army; Major General in command of the Northwest, U.S. Army

Political Offices before Presidency: Secretary of Northwest Territory; U.S. Congressman; Governor of Indiana Territory and Superintendent of Indian Affairs; Ohio State Senator; U.S. Senator; Minister to Colombia

Political Party: Whig

Age at Inauguration: 68

Death: April 4, 1841 in Washington, D.C.

Place of Burial: William Henry Harrison State Park, North Bend, Ohio

Nicknames: Old Tippecanoe; Old Tip

Election of 1840

About the Election: The Whigs nominated Harrison and promoted his image as a Southern war hero to counteract with the public's perception of Van Buren as a stiff aristocrat. Harrison's "Log Cabin and Hard Cider" campaign is often called the first modern presidential campaign because it consisted of large rallies, sign-waving crowds, campaign songs and slogans. One group of Whigs would roll a ten-foot tall paper and tin ball emblazoned with pro-Harrison slogans from town to town—thus inaugurating the phrase "keep the ball rolling." Others handed out whisky in log cabin-shaped bottles supplied by the E.C. Booz distillery, originating the slang term "booze."

For its part, the Van Buren campaign may have also contributed to the lexicon of slang. The Van Buren camp popularized the term "O.K." to stand for "Old Kinderhook," in reference to Van Buren's small upstate New York hometown. In the end though, Van Buren only won seven states, including one outside of the Northeast. The selection of the conservative Virginian John Tyler as Vice President helped secure the South for the Whigs, while Harrison's own popularity in the West sealed the victory. Liberty Party candidate James Birney received only 7,000 popular votes.

Candidates	Party	Electoral Vote	Popular Vote
William Henry Harrison (OH)	Whig	234	1,274,624
Martin Van Buren (NY)	Democratic	60	1,127,781
James Birney (NY)	Liberty	7,069	

Harrison (73 Votes)
Cleveland

Harrison's Term 1841

March 4, 1841: HARRISON IS INAUGURATED, and he gives the longest inaugural address ever delivered. His speech, which he had written himself, makes clear that he pledges to reform the civil service, denies any intent to abolish slavery, and vows to use his veto power sparingly. His lengthy and highly academic speech, which includes several classical allusions, takes Harrison two hours to deliver, even after it has been edited by Henry Clay. Refusing to wear a hat and coat in the cold March air, the 67-year-old Harrison attends three different inaugural balls.

March 5, 1841: Harrison nominates DANIEL WEBSTER as secretary of state. Henry Clay, Harrison's first choice for the position, turns down the offer, believing that he will have more influence in Congress.

April 4, 1841: PRESIDENT HARRISON DIES of pneumonia. He becomes the first president to die in office. JOHN TYLER arrives in Washington the next day to be sworn in as president.

March 9, 1841: In the case *U.S V. THE AMISTAD*, the Supreme Court rules in favor of the Africans onboard the Spanish schooner *Amistad*. A group of kidnapped Africans had been sold and boarded onto the *Amistad* in Havana harbor. The Africans, led by a Mende prince named Cinque, rebelled and killed the members of the ship's crew, as well as the ship's captain. Two were spared after they promised the Africans safe passage back to Africa. For the next two months, the ship sailed toward

Quote by Harrison:

"The plea of necessity, that eternal argument of all conspirators."

Quote about Harrison:

"Let Van from his cooler of silver drink wine; And lounge on his cushioned settee; Our man on his buckeye bench can recline; Content with hard cider is he!"
– *Whig campaign song*

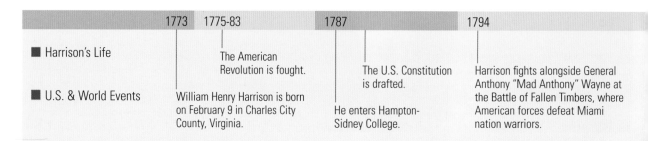

	1773	1775-83	1787	1794
■ Harrison's Life				
		The American Revolution is fought.		
			The U.S. Constitution is drafted.	
■ U.S. & World Events		William Henry Harrison is born on February 9 in Charles City County, Virginia.	He enters Hampton-Sidney College.	Harrison fights alongside General Anthony "Mad Anthony" Wayne at the Battle of Fallen Timbers, where American forces defeat Miami nation warriors.

First Lady: Anna Tuthill Symmes Harrison

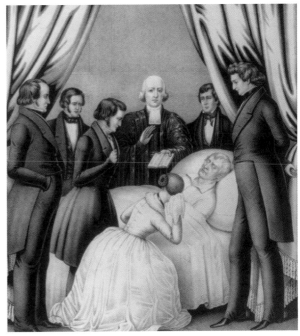

Anna Symmes father, Judge Symmes, did not want his gentle and educated daughter subjected to the harsh conditions faced by military families living on the frontier and initially opposed the union of his daughter to Lt. William Henry Harrison. However, after the couple married, Mrs. Harrison braved the frontier admirably, even as the family moved farther into the wilderness when Harrison became governor of Indiana Territory. As the couple advanced in age, Anna grew more opposed to her husband's presidential ambitions; Harrison was 67 years old when he took office. Upon his victory, Mrs. Harrison delayed going to Washington. Their widowed daughter-in-law, Jane Findlay Irwin Harrison, served as White House hostess. President Harrison died before Mrs. Harrison could embark on her journey to Washington.

Harrison dies on April 4, 1841, and his last known words, spoken on his deathbed, are: "I wish you to understand the true principles of government. I wish them carried out. I ask nothing more."

Africa by day, and back toward North America at night. Finally the ship came ashore on Long Island, New York and was seized by the U.S. Coast Guard. Cinque and the other Africans were charged with murder, mutiny, and piracy. Connecticut lawyer Roger Baldwin came to their defense, and won a decision in district court that because the revolt had taken place in international waters, no U.S. laws had been broken. The district court also ruled that since slavery did not exist in Connecticut, the Africans could not be returned to slavery. In early 1841, the Spanish government asked the Van Buren administration to appeal the lower court decision to the Supreme Court. In the Supreme Court case, former President John Quincy Adams joins the defense team, restating the argument that because neither New York or Connecticut law protected slavery, it was illegal to return the Africans to be enslaved by the Spanish government.

April 1, 1841: BROOK FARM, a utopian community near Boston, Massachusetts, and inspired by AMERICAN TRANSCENDENT-ALISM, seeks to combine manual labor and intellectual pursuits.

Harrison's Administration

Inauguration: March 4, 1841 at the Capitol, Washington, D.C.
Vice President: John Tyler
Secretary of State: Daniel Webster
Secretary of the Treasury: Thomas Ewing
Secretary of War: John Bell
Attorney General: John J. Crittenden
Postmaster General: Francis Granger

Secretary of the Navy:
George E. Badger
27th Congress
(March 4, 1841-March 4, 1843)
Senate: 28 Whigs;
22 Democrats; 2 Others
House: 133 Whigs;
102 Democrats; 6 Others

1798	1804	1822	1823	1828	1836	1840	1840
	Napoleon becomes Emperor of France.			Harrison becomes minister to Colombia.		He is elected president.	Harrison dies on April 4 in Washington, D.C.
Harrison is appointed Secretary of the Northwest Territory.		Liberia is founded in West Africa as a colony for former U.S. slaves.	Harrison is elected to the U.S. Senate.		He runs unsuccessfully for president.		

John Tyler

10th President (1841–1845)

"Wealth can only be accumulated by the earnings of industry and the savings of frugality."

John Tyler was the first man to become president without being elected to the post. A states' rights conservative, he had been selected as William Henry Harrison's running mate to curry support from the Southern wing of the Whig party. The Whigs won the presidency in 1840 not on issues, but on Harrison's reputation as a military hero. Their campaign slogan, "Tippecanoe and Tyler Too," shows that John Tyler was a political afterthought that no one dreamed would become president.

When Harrison died, Whig leaders assumed Tyler would follow their lead in implementing the party's agenda. In the spring of 1841, Henry Clay pushed forward his plans to create a new Bank of the United States. However, Tyler, who had no intention of serving only as their figurehead, vetoed the bills to create a new Bank of the United States.

In September, his entire Cabinet, with the exception of Secretary of State Daniel Webster, resigned in protest. Fellow Whigs derided him as "His Accidency." Opposed by both

Whigs and Democrats, virtually all of Tyler's proposals were dismissed by Congress. He was instrumental in the annexation of Texas, however. And his brand of nationalism reached not only Texas but farther afield—the Tyler Doctrine extended the scope of American interests to include the Hawaiian Islands. He also oversaw the opening of the first American trading ports in China.

John Tyler was never really comfortable as a Whig. He was a throwback to the Jeffersonian Democrats in the 1840 election, advocating states' rights and decentralized federal power. Tyler was a slave-holding member of the Virginia aristocracy, who at the very end of his life was elected to the Confederate House of Representatives.

Although some openly referred to him as "Acting President" after President Harrison's death, Tyler refused to merely keep the seat warm for the next-elected president. With this attitude, Tyler set a precedent for future presidents thrust into a similar position.

Biographical Facts

Born: March 29, 1790 in Charles City County, Virginia

Ancestry: English

Father: John Tyler; born February 28, 1747 in James City County, Virginia; died January 6, 1813 in Charles City County, Virginia

Father's Occupations: Judge; governor of Virginia

Mother: Mary Marot Armistead Tyler; born 1761 in York County, Virginia; died April 5, 1797 in Charles City County, Virginia

First Wife: Letitia Christian; born November 12, 1790 in New Kent County, Virginia; died September 10, 1842 in Washington, D.C.

First Marriage: March 29, 1813 in New Kent County, Virginia

Second Wife: Julia Gardiner; born May 4, 1820 in Gardiner's Island, New York; died July 10, 1889 in Richmond, Virginia

Second Marriage: June 26, 1844 in New York

Children (by first wife): Mary (1815-1848); Robert (1816-1877); John (1819-1896); Letitia (1821-1907); Elizabeth (1823-1850); Alice (1827-1854); Tazewell (1830-1874);

(by second wife): David Gardiner (1846-1927); John Alexander (1848-

1883); Julia (1849-1871); Lachlan (1851-1902); Lyon Gardiner (1853-1935); Robert Fitzwalter (1856-1927); Pearl (1860-1947)

Home: Sherwood Forest, Charles City County, Virginia

Education: Attended local Virginia schools; graduated from College of William and Mary (1807)

Religious Affiliation: Episcopalian

Occupation before Presidency: Lawyer

Military Service: Captain of Volunteer Company in Richmond, Virginia

Political Offices before Presidency: Member of Virginia House of Delegates; U.S. Representative; Governor of Virginia; U.S. Senator; U.S. Vice President

Political Party: Whig

Age at Inauguration: 51

Occupation after Presidency: Lawyer

Death: January 18, 1862 in Richmond, Virginia

Place of Burial: Hollywood Cemetery, Richmond

Nicknames: Accidental President; His Accidency

Tyler's Term 1841-1845

April 4, 1841: After the **DEATH OF HARRISON**, Vice President John Tyler assumes the presidency. He is the first ever to do so, setting the precedent for presidential succession.

April 9, 1841: **DISAGREEMENTS BETWEEN TYLER AND THE WHIG PARTY** become immediately apparent as Tyler announces his intention to restructure the government's fiscal system in keeping with Jeffersonian principles.

June 12, 1841: Henry Clay proposes a new **BANK OF THE UNITED STATES** that will have $30 million in capital and the authority to establish state branches. President Tyler asks for an additional clause stipulating that state branches can be formed only upon approval by individual states. The clause is initially added, but then replaced in the final bill with another that requires individual states to register their disapproval explicitly.

July 28–August 6, 1841: A final bill to create the Bank of the United States is passed by Congress.

August 13, 1841: Congress repeals the Independent Treasury Act, which had created a subtreasury system.

August 16, 1841: **TYLER VETOES THE BANK BILL** on constitutional grounds, angering Henry Clay and other members of the Whig Party.

August 19, 1841: The Senate fails to override Tyler's veto.

August 23–September 3, 1841: The bank bill is revised, lowering the proposed bank's capitalization to $21 million. But the new bill does not include a provision requiring state approval for the establishment of state branches.

September 9, 1841: Tyler vetoes the second bank bill, again on constitutional grounds. The Senate fails to override his veto.

September 11, 1841: **TYLER'S CABINET RESIGNS**, with the exception of Secretary of State Daniel Webster, who is in the midst of delicate negotiations with Great Britain regarding U.S.–Canadian borders. Webster resigns in 1843.

October 27, 1841: Enslaved Africans onboard the U.S. brig *Creole* mutiny and take command of the vessel. The ship

then stops in the Bahamas, where the mutineers are arrested. Webster works for the release of the mutineers to the U.S., arguing that since the slaves were on a U.S. vessel, they are subject to U.S. law.

October 29, 1841: Bishop John Joseph Hughes of New York calls for state funds for parochial schools, and he asks Catholics to vote for those candidates that support state funding. His action stirs widespread anger among anti-Catholic Protestants.

March 3, 1842: Massachusetts passes the first **CHILD LABOR LAW**, limiting the workday to ten hours for children under 12. That same month, the Massachusetts Supreme Court rules in the case of **COMMONWEALTH V. *Hunt*** that labor unions are legal and that workers have a right to strike.

March 21-23, 1842: Whig Representative **JOSHUA GIDDINGS** of Ohio submits a series of resolutions in the House against the federal sanction of slavery and against coastal slave trade. After the House votes to censure him, he resigns. The following month, his constituents reelect him and he returns to Congress.

March 31, 1842: **HENRY CLAY RESIGNS** from the Senate, after the Democratic Party takes control of the House of Representatives in the mid-term elections. Clay, the architect of the Whig Party's policy, intends to run for president in 1844.

June 25, 1842: Congress passes a **CONGRESSIONAL REAPPORTIONMENT ACT**, which provides that all Congressmen are to be elected by districts equal in number to each states' quota of representatives.

August 9, 1842: Secretary of State Daniel Webster concludes the **WEBSTER-ASHBURTON TREATY.** He normalizes U.S.-British relations by settling the disputed Maine-New Brunswick border that had led to the Aroostook War in 1839. The treaty settles boundary issues around western Lake Superior and resurveys some of the smaller borders.

December 1842: In response to fears that either Britain or France might annex the Hawaiian Islands, Tyler declares that the United States opposes "any attempt by another power . . . to take

Daniel Webster, former senator from Massachusetts, served as Tyler's Secretary of State.

	1790	1792		1801	1803
■ John Tyler's Life					
		Denmark becomes the first nation to abolish slave trade.			The Louisiana Purchase doubles the size of the United States.
■ U.S. & World Events					
	John Tyler is born on March 29, in Charles City County, Virginia.			Robert Fulton builds the first submarine, the *Nautilus,* in France.	

First Lady: Julia Gardiner Tyler

Julia Gardiner Tyler, a descendant of a prominent New York family, exhibited a graceful and practiced charm since an early age. Tyler became the first president to marry in office and though the couple was criticized for their 30-year age difference, Mrs. Tyler enjoyed her eight-month role as White House Hostess with relish. She was an active supporter of her husband, who had lost favor with his own party, as well as the opposition Democrats. She also possessed a good sense of humor. Following one lavish White House affair, she remarked to her husband, "They can no longer call you a man without a party!"

The Tylers retired to their plantation in Virginia, where five of their seven children were born. The defeat of the Confederacy left the widowed Mrs. Tyler impoverished until Congress voted in 1880 to award pensions to widowed First Ladies.

John Tyler's Administration

Inauguration: April 6, 1841 at Indian Queen Hotel, Washington, D.C.
Vice President: None
Secretary of State: Daniel Webster; Abel P. Upshur (from July 24, 1843); John C. Calhoun (from April 1, 1844)
Secretary of the Treasury: Thomas Ewing; Walter Forward (from September 13, 1841); John C. Spencer (from March 8, 1843); George M. Bibb (from July 4, 1844)
Secretary of War: John Bell; John C. Spencer (from October 12, 1841); James M. Porter (from March 8, 1843); William Wilkins (from February 20, 1844)
Attorney General: John J. Crittenden; Hugh S. Legare (from September 20, 1841); John Nelson (from July 1, 1843)
Postmaster General: Francis Granger;

Charles A. Wickliffe (from October 13, 1841);
Secretary of the Navy: George E. Badger; Abel P. Upshur (from October 11, 1841); David Henshaw (from July 24, 1843); Thomas W. Gilmer (from February 19, 1844); John Y. Mason (from March 26, 1844)
Supreme Court Appointment: Samuel Nelson (1845)
27th Congress (March 4, 1841-March 4, 1843)
Senate: 28 Whigs; 22 Democrats; 2 Others
House: 133 Whigs; 102 Democrats; 6 Others
28th Congress (March 4, 1843-March 4, 1845)
Senate: 28 Whigs; 25 Democrats; 1 Other
House: 142 Democrats; 79 Whigs; 1 Other
State Admitted: Florida (1845)
End of Presidential Term: March 4, 1845

possession of the islands, colonize them and subvert the native government." This speech, addressed to Congress, will become known as the TYLER DOCTRINE; it incorporates a broad interpretation of the Monroe Doctrine, extending it to include the Hawaiian Islands. Since arriving in the islands in 1820, American missionaries had grown increasingly influential in both Hawaiian social and political affairs. By 1840, Americans help the Hawaiian monarch rewrite the Kingdom's Constitution, to model it on the American government. Despite Tyler's vows to respect Hawaiian independence, by the end of the 1840s, American planters will own one third of Hawaii's land.

March 1843: Dr. Marcus Whitman, a missionary who had settled in OREGON TERRITORY in 1836, returns East to resolve rumors that the United States was prepared to abandon the territory. He first meets with Secretary of State Daniel Webster, who had many years before said of the territory, "What do we want with . . . this region of savages and wild beasts, of deserts and shifting sand and whirlwinds of dust, of cactus and prairie dogs?" Although Webster does nothing to dispell the rumors, President Tyler assures Whitman that the U.S. will not abandon the Oregon Territory.

May 8, 1843: SECRETARY OF STATE DANIEL WEBSTER RESIGNS over the issue of Texas' annexation. With his Northen anti-slavery constituents to consider, Webster is unable to support annexation of the slave territory.

May 29, 1843: John C. Frémont begins an expedition to Oregon Territory. The FRÉMONT EXPEDITION's goal is to survey the route to Oregon. On their return, Frémont and his men are able to resurvey the geography of northern California. They also explore the Great Basin between the Rockies and Sierra Nevada. Fremont is the first American to identify it as an independent system of rivers and lakes separated from the oceans by mountains.

June 1843: The AMERICAN REPUBLICAN PARTY is founded

1807	1812	1815	1817	1824	1827

Tyler marries Letitia Christian.

German brothers Jacob and Wilhelm Grimm publish the first edition of their *Fairy Tales*.

Tyler is elected to the House of Representatives.

Tyler enters the U.S. Senate.

Tyler graduates from Collage of William and Mary.

England legalizes trade unions.

in New York by anti-Irish Catholics. It proposes banning Catholics and foreigners from voting or holding office. The following year, one of its candidates, James Harper, is elected mayor of New York City after forming a coalition with New York Whigs.

August 23, 1843: MEXICAN PRESIDENT SANTA ANNA WARNS THE UNITED STATES that his government would consider any American attempt to annex Texas a declaration of war against Mexico. Popular pressure to annex the Republic of Texas had increased in the United States after Mexico invaded Texas in 1842.

October 1843: The Tyler administration informs the Republic of Texas that it would like to reopen the discussion of annexation to the U.S. Texas President Sam Houston initially rejects the offer, fearing the loss of British support.

February 18, 1844: Tyler, with his fiance Julia Gardiner, attends a ceremony on board the steamer U.S.S. PRINCETON to witness a demonstration of the ship's enormous cannon. During the ceremony, the cannon backfires, killing Secretary of State Abel P. Upshur, Secretary of the Navy Thomas Gilmer, David Gardiner (Julia Gardiner's father), and five others. Tyler, who had paused briefly below the deck to listen to his son-in-law sing, was unharmed.

March 22, 1844: The *Richmond Enquirer* publishes a letter from former President Andrew Jackson expressing support for Texas annexation.

April 12, 1844: After the U.S. assures Texas President Houston that a two-thirds majority of the Senate approves of Texas' admission to the Union, HOUSTON AGREES TO ANNEXATION, on the condition that the United States sends army and naval protection to guard against a Mexican invasion. The United States and the Republic of Texas sign the TEXAS ANNEXATION TREATY.

Missionaries Marcus and Narcissa Whitman were among the first American settlers in Oregon. In 1847, the Whitman mission, seen here, was attacked by a group of Cayuse and the Whitmans were killed.

	1825	1827	1828	1833	1836
■ John Tyler's Life					
		The first Negro newspaper, *Freedom's Journal*, begins publication in New York.		Oberlin College in Ohio becomes the first coeducational college.	Tyler renounces the Democratic Party over Andrew Jackson's use of federal powers.
■ U.S. & World Events					
	Tyler is elected governor of Virginia.		Andrew Jackson is elected president.		

April 17, 1844: Whig leader Henry Clay states that Texas annexation will lead to war with Mexico and would thus be "dangerous to the integrity of the Union." After Clay wins the presidential nomination of the Whig Party, he will qualify his stance, first saying that although he was in favor of annexation, the growing split over slavery made preserving the Union more important. Later, he supports annexation, on the condition that slavery be left out of the decision. Opponents will use **CLAY'S SHIFTING POSITION ON TEXAS** against him in the election.

April 22, 1844: In a letter to Congress, **PRESIDENT TYLER SUPPORTS TEXAS ANNEXATION.**

April 27, 1844: Former President Martin Van Buren opposes the annexation of Texas. For Van Buren, the choice is a difficult one, as it means breaking with Andrew Jackson over the issue. But as the expected Democratic nominee for president, Van Buren decides not to risk losing support of anti-slavery Democrats in New York and New England.

May 1, 1844: The **WHIG PARTY NOMINATES HENRY CLAY** for president.

May 3, 1844: In a sign of **RISING ANTI-CATHOLIC SENTIMENT**, several thousand anti-Catholic, "Native" Americans hold a rally in Kensington, Philadelphia—an Irish Catholic neighborhood. Violence erupts at the rally, and five days later, a Nativist mob sets fire to Irish Catholic churches, homes, a schoolhouse and a rectory in Kensington.

May 29, 1844: The Democratic Party rejects Martin Van Buren as its nominee for president. On the ninth ballot, the **DEMOCRATS NOMINATE JAMES K. POLK** of Tennessee. Polk, who favors Texas annexation, becomes the first "dark horse" candidate in American history.

June 8, 1844: Led by anti-slavery representatives from the North, the **U.S. SENATE REJECTS TEXAS ANNEXATION.** Tyler then attempts to gain approval through a congressional joint resolution, but Congress fails to act before adjourning.

June 26, 1844: Tyler marries Julia Gardiner in New Yock City. This is his second marriage.

July 3, 1844: The United States and China sign the **TREATY OF WANGHIA**, which allows the United States to open its first trading post in China. The treaty follows the First Opium War in 1839 between China and Great Britain. When Chinese government attempted to ban the sale of opium, the British bombarded Canton and forced China to allow the

John C. Fremont earned the nickname "the Pathfinder" for his three important expeditions in the American frontier.

drug trade to resume. Britain also demanded that additional Chinese ports be opened to British trade. As a result, merchants from other countries, including the United States, also began negotiating trade agreements with China.

July 4, 1844: **CATHOLIC AND NATIVIST FIGHTING IN PHILADELPHIA** comes to a climax. Armed with cannons, Nativists face off against the U.S. Army, and are eventually defeated.

August 30, 1844: The **LIBERTY PARTY**, formed by moderate abolitionists, nominates former slaveowner James G. Birney of Alabama as its nominee for president. The party had been founded in 1840 by Birney and other abolitionists who disagreed with William Lloyd Garrison's radical actions.

December 4, 1844: **JAMES K. POLK IS ELECTED PRESIDENT** on his promises to "reannex" Texas and "reoccupy" Oregon.

February 28, 1845: Congress passes a joint resolution to admit Texas to the Union. Texas accepts on June 23.

March 3, 1845: **FLORIDA IS ADMITTED AS A SLAVE STATE**, making it the 27th state in the Union. Also on that day—the last day of Tyler's term—Congress overrides Tyler's veto of a bill prohibiting payment for ships that he had ordered built. This is the first time in the nation's history that Congress successfully overrides a presidential veto.

1841	1842	1844	1846-48	1861	1862
			The U.S.–Mexican War is fought.	After presiding over a failed peace conference to prevent the Civil War, Tyler is elected to the Confederate House of Representatives.	The U.S. Civil War begins and lasts until 1865.
Tyler becomes president when William Henry Harrison dies.	Tyler's first wife, Letitia Tyler, dies.	Tyler marries Julia Gardiner.			Tyler dies on January 18, in Richmond Virginia.

James Knox Polk

11th President (1845–1849)

"I prefer to supervise the whole operations of the Government myself rather than entrust the public business to subordinates and this makes my duties very great."

Who is James K. Polk? asked a Whig slogan during the 1844 election. Polk may have been the nation's first "dark horse" candidate, but he was not an unknown. Andrew Jackson had been a friend of Polk's father, and the younger Polk's early political career had been boosted by the association. Polk entered the U.S. House of Representatives in 1824, when Jackson first ran for president against John Quincy Adams. Although Jackson lost that election, Polk became an aggressive pro-Jackson partisan in the House. He played a significant role in the four-year election campaign for Jackson who was elected president in 1829. His faithfulness to "Old Hickory," as Jackson was called, would pay dividends; Polk rose to Speaker of the House during Jackson's second term. He later served as Tennessee's governor. Throughout his life, Polk remained a firm believer in Jeffersonian democracy, skeptical of banks and paper credit. He also called for an end to the existing electoral system, declaring the people's right to elect the president directly.

A strong proponent of American expansion, Polk did not hesitate to back the annexation of Texas, even if it meant war with Mexico. Upon entering office, he promised to only serve one term. He also proclaimed four goals for his term: 1) a reduction in tariffs; 2) the creation of an independent treasury; 3) a settlement of disputes with Great Britain over Oregon; and 4) the acquisition of California. Hardworking and effective, Polk achieved all four goals during his single term.

These accomplishments came at a cost, however. California's acquisition was achieved only through war with Mexico—a war justified by Polk's assertion that Mexico had shed blood on American soil; but *that soil* was disputed territory. While most Americans approved of the war, a vocal minority did not. A young Abraham Lincoln, serving as a freshman in the House, declared Polk's claim the "sheerest deception" and challenged him to show the exact spot on American soil that blood had been shed.

Although, the victory over Mexico added more territory to the US than any other acquisition since the Louisiana Purchase, it also reignited the conflict over slavery. By the time Polk left office in 1849, his own party was bitterly divided over the question. Polk, physically drained by long hours of hard work, died just a few months after returning home.

Biographical Facts

Born: November 2, 1795 in Mecklenburg County, North Carolina

Ancestry: Scotch-Irish

Father: Samuel Polk; born July 5, 1772 in Tryon, North Carolina; died November 5, 1827 in Maury County, Tennessee

Father's Occupation: Farmer

Mother: Jane Knox Polk; born November 15, 1776 in Iredell County, North Carolina; died January 11, 1852 in Maury County, Tennessee

Wife: Sarah Childress; born September 4, 1803 in Murfreesboro, Tennessee; died August 14, 1891 in Nashville, Tennessee

Marriage: January 1, 1824 in Murfreesboro, Tennessee

Children: None

Home: Polk House, Columbia, Tennessee

Education: Private school; received B.A. from the University of North Carolina (1818); studied law

Religious Affiliation: Presbyterian

Occupation before Presidency: Lawyer

Political Offices before Presidency: Member of Tennessee Legislature; U.S. Representative; Speaker of the House of Representatives; Governor of Tennessee

Military Service: None

Political Party: Democratic

Age at Inauguration: 49

Occupation after Presidency: Retired

Death: June 15, 1849 in Nashville, Tennessee,

Place of Burial: State Capitol Grounds, Nashville, Tennessee

Nickname: Young Hickory; Napoleon of the Stump

Writings: *The Diary of James K. Polk*
Correspondence of James K. Polk

Quote by Polk:

"Public opinion: May it always perform one of its appropriate offices, by teaching the public functionaries of the state and of the federal government, that neither shall assume the exercise of powers entrusted by the Constitution to the other."

Quotes about Polk:

"[Polk] has no wit, no literature, no point of argument, no gracefulness of delivery, no eloquence of language, no philosophy, no pathos, no felicitous impromptus."
– John Quincy Adams

"To extraordinary powers of labor, both mental and physical, [Polk] unites the tact and judgment which are requisite to the successful direction of such an office as that of Chief Magistrate of a free people."
– Andrew Jackson

authorizes a volunteer army of 50,000 men.

May 15, 1846: COLONEL STEPHEN KEARNEY is ordered to take possession of New Mexico. Two weeks later, his orders are revised to include an invasion of California.

June 10–July 5, 1846: Launching what will become known as the BEAR FLAG REVOLT, American settlers attack General Castro's troops as they march toward Los Angeles. A second group captures Sonoma and proclaims California to be independent of Mexican rule. Captain John C. Frémont then arrives in Sonoma and is proclaimed leader of the Republic of California.

June 15, 1846: When the British resend their proposal to split the Oregan Territory at the 49th parallel, Polk submits it for Senate approval. The SENATE VOTES TO RATIFY THE OREGON TREATY, and some of his constituents accuse Polk of betraying the cause.

July 7-9, 1846: Warships led by U.S. Commodore John Sloat sail up the California coast to Monterey. There, a military force raises the American flag, claiming California for the United States. Sloat then orders the capture of Sonoma and San Francisco. The Bear Flag is replaced by the U.S. flag.

July 30, 1846: The WALKER TARIFF is passed. Named after the Secretary of Treasury, Robert J. Walker, it lowers tariffs and provides a base for further reductions in later years.

August 8, 1846: Anti-slavery forces in the U.S. House of Representatives help pass the WILMOT PROVISO, named after David Wilmot of Pennsylvania. It states that slavery will be banned from any new U.S. territory incorporated from

California. Polk proposes to weaken the proviso by limiting the ban to territory north of the Missouri Compromise line, but the Senate fails to pass it.

August 8, 1846: Polk signs a bill for authorizing the reeestablishmnet of the INDEPENDENT TREASURY SYSTEM.

August 13, 1846: Commodore Robert Stockton occupies Santa Barbara and Los Angeles. Several days later, he announces that CALIFORNIA IS ANNEXED TO THE UNITED STATES. Stockton names himself governor of the new U.S. territory.

August 15, 1846: As 4,000 Mexican troops depart without a fight, STEPHEN KEARNEY CLAIMS NEW MEXICO for the U.S.

September 23-30, 1846: Mexicans temporarily drive the Americans out of Los Angeles, Santa Barbara, San Diego and other parts of Southern California.

September 25, 1846: U.S. forces under Zachary Taylor capture the Mexican city of Monterey. Following the American victory at the BATTLE OF MONTEREY, Taylor agrees to an eight-week cease fire, during which his forces will not move further into Mexico unless either the United States or the Mexican government disavow the treaty.

October 13, 1846: Polk disavows the ceasefire. Taylor suspects that Polk's Democratic administration is trying to undercut him since the Whig Party had already begun discussing Taylor as a possible presidential candidate in 1848.

December 25, 1846: U.S. troops under Alexander Doniphan defeat a Mexican force at the BATTLE OF EL BRAZITO near present-day El Paso, Texas.

December 26, 1846: IOWA IS ADMITTED TO THE UNION as the 29th state.

January 3, 1847: With Polk's permission, General Winfield Scott orders that 9,000 troops be transferred out from under Taylor and into his command. He also orders that Taylor remain in Monterey to defend it against Mexican recapture.

January 10, 1847: Kearney takes Los Angeles again, ending the fighting in California. Three days later, the remaining Mexican forces in California surrender to Captain Frémont in the San Fernando Valley.

January 22, 1847: A letter by General Zachary Taylor defending the eight-week ceasefire and criticizing Polk is published in a New York newspaper.

February 15, 1847: Anti-slavery forces in the House once again help pass a measure to ban slavery in California.

February 19, 1847: CALHOUN WARNS OF CIVIL WAR and argues that Congress has no constitutional right to limit slavery

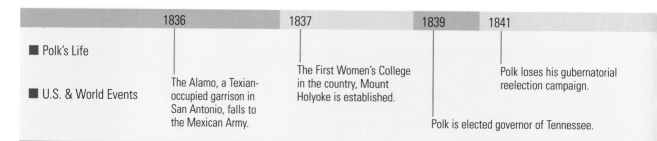

	1836	1837	1839	1841
■ Polk's Life				
■ U.S. & World Events	The Alamo, a Texian-occupied garrison in San Antonio, falls to the Mexican Army.	The First Women's College in the country, Mount Holyoke is established.	Polk is elected governor of Tennessee.	Polk loses his gubernatorial reelection campaign.

in California. He asserts that any attempt to destroy the balance of power between slave and free states would lead to civil war.

February 21–March 29, 1847: General Winfield Scott leads a force of 10,000 and captures Vera Cruz, a Mexican fortress that was known as the strongest military fortress in the western hemisphere. The **VERA CRUZ EXPEDITION**, the first large scale amphibious military operation undertaken by U.S. forces on foreign soil, is a success.

February 22-23, 1847: Disobeying orders to remain in Monterey, Zachary Taylor defeats 15,000 poorly trained Mexicans at the **BATTLE OF BUENA VISTA**. Following his victory, Taylor is reprimanded for his letter criticizing the administration. He requests that he be relieved of his command. The following fall, he returns to the United States a hero.

April 18, 1847: American forces under General Scott defeat the Mexican forces at the **BATTLE OF CERRO GORDO**.

August 18-19, 1847: About 3,300 Americans led by Scott defeat Mexican forces under Santa Anna at the **BATTLE OF CONTRERAS**. The following day, Scott's men win another victory, at the **BATTLE OF CHURUBUSCO** but suffer many casualities.

September 8, 1847: After Mexican officials reject the terms of a peace settlement, U.S. forces under Scott press toward Mexico City. On September 8, the Americans defeat a Mexican force after a long struggle at the **BATTLE OF MOLINO DEL REY**.

September 12-13, 1847: In the final approach to Mexico City, Scott's troops successfully storm the fortified hill at Chapultepec. Although the Americans are met by 100 brave young military students (immortalized as "**LOS NIÑOS**" in Mexican history), the United States captures the two main gates leading into Mexico City by approximately 6 p.m.

September 13-14, 1847: General Winfield Scott leads U.S. troops into Mexico City.

September 14–October 12, 1847: Mexican forces lay siege to a U.S. garrison at Puebla. The siege ends when the U.S. sends reinforcements from Vera Cruz.

January 24, 1848: The **CALIFORNIA GOLD RUSH** begins when James W. Marshall, who is building a sawmill on the property of Johann Augustus Sutter in the Sacramento Valley, spots gold in the American River.

February 2, 1848: United States representative Nicholas P. Trist and Mexican commissioners sign the **TREATY OF GUADALUPE HIDALGO**, ending the U.S.-Mexican War. Mexico cedes lands north of the Rio Grande, including New Mexico and California, to the United States. In return, the United States pays Mexico $15 million in gold and assumes territorial debts.

May 22, 1848: As Polk had sworn that he would only serve one term, a divided **DEMOCRATIC PARTY NOMINATES LEWIS CASS** of Michigan for president. Cass runs on a pro-expansion platform, advocating the annexation of all of Mexico.

May 29, 1848: **WISCONSIN IS ADMITTED TO THE UNION** as the 30th U.S. state.

June 7, 1848: At their national convention, the **WHIGS NOMINATE ZACHARY TAYLOR** as their presidential candidate.

August 9, 1848: A new national anti-slavery coalition takes shape. Anti-slavery Democrats ("the Barnburners") unite with the remnants of the old Liberty Party and with anti-slavery Whigs from New England ("Conscience Whigs") to form the **FREE SOIL PARTY**. At its August convention, the new party nominates **MARTIN VAN BUREN** for president.

August 14, 1848: Polk signs into law a bill authorizing the **FORMATION OF OREGON** as free territory, closed to slavery.

November 7, 1848: **ZACHARY TAYLOR IS ELECTED PRESIDENT**, defeating a divided opposition. Van Buren fails to win a state but costs Cass New York electoral votes, and thus the election.

December 5, 1848: In his last annual message to Congress, Polk announces that gold has been discovered in California. He receives specimens of the newly-found gold.

March 3, 1849: A new Cabinet department, known as the Home Department is created to unite a number of independent agencies such as the Bureau of Indian Affairs, and the Office of the Census. The Home Department's name will later be changed to the **DEPARTMENT OF THE INTERIOR**.

March 5, 1849: Eager to leave the White House, Polk attends **TAYLOR'S INAUGURATION**. He judges his successor to be "exceedingly ignorant of public affairs, and...of ordinary capacity." Polk retires to his home in Tennessee.

The Battle of Churubusco, August 19, 1847

1842	1843	1844	1848	1849
	English novelist Charles Dickens writes *A Christmas Carol*.		Liberia is proclaimed an independent Republic.	
The Opium War that had broken out in 1839 ends and opens China to trade.		Polk is elected president.	The first Women's Rights Convention is held at Seneca Falls, New York.	Polk dies on June 15, in Nashville, Tennessee.

Zachary Taylor

12th President (1849–1850)

"The idea that I should become President seems to me too visionary to require a serious answer. It has never entered my head, nor is it likely to enter the head of any sane person."

Zachary Taylor had never held elected office prior to running for president. He had never even voted. But his exploits in the U.S.-Mexican War had made him a national hero and the Whig Party saw him as an ideal nominee. By running a campaign that carefully avoided expressing opinions on any issues, Taylor narrowly defeated Democrat Lewis Cass of Michigan and former President Martin Van Buren, who was running under the banner of the anti-slavery Free Soil Party.

Taylor entered the White House at a time of severe crisis. Victory in the Mexican War had added to the Union vast new territories stretching from New Mexico to California. The decision on whether these new states should enter the Union as free or slave had tremendous significance, as it could dramatically change the balance of power that had kept the North and South from civil war for thirty years.

Whig leaders, such as Henry Clay of Kentucky, expected Taylor to follow their lead in resolving the conflict, but they were soon disappointed. To the furor of Whigs and Democrats alike, Taylor encouraged settlers in California and New Mexico to forgo territorial status and immediately hold statehood conventions. At these conventions, Taylor urged that they should decide the slavery issue for themselves, without Congressional interference.

Taylor owned more than 100 slaves and he was one of the larger slaveholders in the South. However, his long career in the military had made him a strong nationalist. In February 1850, as the great debates over the Compromise of 1850 were getting underway in Congress, President Taylor threatened Southern lawmakers that he would personally lead an invasion of the South should any of its states secede from the Union. He also made clear that he had no taste for compromise, vowing to veto any congressionally-imposed solution to the slavery crisis.

Taylor's sudden death in 1850 changed history. When Vice President Millard Fillmore took office, he quickly signed the the Compromise of 1850. Some have argued that had Taylor lived, the Civil War would have been avoided. More likely than not, however, war would have come sooner. Although Taylor is credited for his decisiveness and quick action, his attempt to remove Congress from the slavery discussion was naive at best. While snap judgments may have served Taylor well on the battlefield, the political conflict over slavery was a different sort of war altogether.

Biographical Facts

Born: November 24, 1784 in Orange County, Virginia

Ancestry: English

Father: Lt. Col. Richard Taylor; born April 3, 1744 in Orange County, Virginia; died January 19, 1829 near Louisville, Kentucky

Father's Occupations: Soldier; landowner; civil servant

Mother: Sarah Dabney Strother Taylor; born December 14, 1760; died December 13, 1822

Wife: Margaret Mackall Smith; born September 21, 1788 in Maryland; died August 18, 1852

Marriage: June 21, 1810 in Jefferson County, Kentucky

Children: Anne Mackall (1811-1875); Sarah Knox (1814-1835); Octavia Pannill (1816-1820); Margaret Smith (1819-1820); Mary Elizabeth (1824-1909); Richard (1826-1879)

Home: Baton Rouge, Louisiana

Education: Some tutoring

Religious Affiliation: Episcopalian

Occupations before Presidency: Soldier; farmer

Military Service: Volunteer in Kentucky militia; rose from First Lieutenant to Major General in the U.S. Army

Political Offices before Presidency: None

Political Party: Whig

Age at Inauguration: 64

Death: July 9, 1850 in Washington, D.C.

Place of Burial: Jefferson County, Kentucky

Nickname: Old Rough and Ready

Writings: *Letters of Zachary Taylor*

Millard Fillmore

13th President (1850–1853)

"God knows that I detest slavery, but it is an existing evil, for which we are not responsible, and we must endure it...till we can get rid of it without destroying the last hope of free government in the world."

When Zachary Taylor died suddenly in July 1850, many felt that his death, though tragic, would save the nation. "Old Rough and Ready" had been an enormously popular president, but his unyielding opposition to federal involvement in the slavery debate had helped push the nation to the brink of war.

Fillmore succeeded Taylor at a critical moment in the nation's history. The Mexican War had added new territories to the United States, causing uproar over whether these territories should be admitted as free or slave states. He proved to be very compliant as president. A few days before Taylor's death, Fillmore had reportedly told him that he would vote in favor of the Compromise of 1850 should the need arise to break tie votes in the Senate. When Fillmore later signed the five bills that made up the Compromise, one newspaper declared "the country saved." Proposed by Henry Clay of Kentucky, the Compromise admitted one territory as a free state and allowed slave owners to settle in the others. This hardly solved the problem, but it did preserve peace for nearly eleven years.

Pro-slavery groups opposed the provisions that admitted California as a free state and banned the slave trade in Washington, D.C. Abolitionists detested the Fugitive Slave Law that threatened those who aided runaway slaves with fines and prison. This law proved costly to Fillmore—and the Whig Party. Northern anti-slavery Whigs, angry at Fillmore for signing the bill, denied him their party's nomination in 1852. They chose aging military hero General Winfield Scott, who was soundly trounced. The Whig Party virtually collapsed after the loss. In the wake of the Whig defeat, two new parties were formed: the anti-slavery Republican Party and the anti-foreigner Know-Nothing party. Fillmore chose the latter and in 1856, won just one state as its nominee for president.

Biographical Facts

Born: January 7, 1800 in Locke, Cayuga County, New York

Ancestry: English

Father: Nathaniel Fillmore; born April 19, 1771 in Bennington, Vermont; died March 28, 1863

Father's Occupation: Farmer

Mother: Phoebe Millard Fillmore; born 1780 in Pittsfield, Massachusetts; died May 2, 1831

First Wife: Abigail Powers; born March 13, 1798 in Stillwater, New York; died March 30, 1853 in Washington, D.C.

First Marriage: February 5, 1826 in Moravia, New York

Second Wife: Caroline Carmichael McIntosh; born October 21, 1813 in Morristown, New Jersey; died August 11, 1881 in Buffalo, New York,

Second Marriage: Albany, New York, February 10, 1858

Children (by first wife): Millard Powers (1828-1889); Mary Abigail (1832-1854)

Home: East Aurora, New York

Religious Affiliation: Unitarian

Education: Attended public schools; studied law in Cayuga County and Buffalo, New York

Occupations before Presidency: Apprentice to cloth dresser; apprentice to wool carder; lawyer

Military Service: Major

Political Offices before Presidency: Member of New York Legislature; Member of U.S. House of Representatives; U.S. Vice President

Political Party: Whig (during Presidency); American (Know-Nothing) (from 1854)

Age at Inauguration: 50

Occupations after Presidency: Politician; chancellor of the University of Buffalo

Death: March 8, 1874 in Buffalo, New York

Place of Burial: Forest Lawn Cemetery, Buffalo, New York

Nickname: The American Louis Philippe

Writings: *Millard Fillmore Papers*

Read and Ponder
THE
FUGITIVE SLAVE LAW!

Which disregards all the ordinary securities of PERSONAL LIBERTY, which tramples on the Constitution, by its denial
of the sacred rights of Trial by Jury, *Habeas Corpus*, and Appeal, and which enacts, that the Cardinal Virtues of Christianity shall be considered, in the eye of the law, as CRIMES, punishable with the severest penalties,— *Fines and Imprisonment.*

Freemen of Massachusetts, R E M E M B E R , That Samuel A. Elliott of Boston, voted for this law, that Millard Filmore, our whig President *approved* it and the Whig Journals of Massachusetts sustain them in this iniquity.

This broadside against the Fugitive Slave Act was printed in Massachusetts—a stronghold of anti-slavery sentiment. The act, included in the Compromise of 1850, required that runaway slaves be returned to their owners, and provided severe penalities for nonenforcment.

Fillmore's Term 1850-1853

July 10, 1850: FILLMORE IS SWORN IN AS PRESIDENT, one day after Zachary Taylor's death. After all members of Taylor's Cabinet resign, Fillmore appoints to his Cabinet pro-Union, pro-Compromise Whigs, including Daniel Webster of Massachusetts as secretary of state.

August 6, 1850: FILLMORE AFFIRMS HIS SUPPORT FOR THE COMPROMISE OF 1850, and recommends that the Texas-New Mexico border dispute be resolved with a federal payment of $10 million to Texas in exchange for the state's abandonment of its claims to New Mexican land. Fillmore seeks to repeal the Wilmot Proviso, which closed all land won from Mexico to slavery.

September 9, 1850: Congress passes three of the five separate acts making up the Compromise of 1850. CALIFORNIA IS ADMITTED INTO THE UNION AS A FREE STATE. Congress also passes the TEXAS AND NEW MEXICO ACT, which settles the border dispute between the two states, organizes New Mexico's territorial government, and opens the state to slavery. The UTAH ACT is passed as well, establishing the Utah Territory as open to slavery. Shortly thereafter, Fillmore appoints Brigham Young, president of the Church of Latter Day Saints, governor of Utah Territory. Young's tenure will be marked by clashes with federal authorities who oppose many Mormon teachings.

September 18, 1850: Congress passes the controversial FUGITIVE SLAVE ACT. The new law threatens individuals who help runaway slaves with fines and imprisonment. It also requires that escaped slaves be returned to their owners without the right of a jury trial or the ability to testify on their own behalf. Southerners had criticized the 1793 Fugitive slave law because Northerners would not enforce it. This new law has severe penalties for nonenformcent. While moderate Northern Whigs and Democrats accept the Fugitive Slavery Act as a necessary compromise, abolitionists vow to interfere with its enforcement despite the harsh consequences.

September 20, 1850: CONGRESS BANS SLAVE TRADE IN THE DISTRICT OF COLUMBIA—passing the last of the five bills that make up the Compromise of 1850.

January 2, 1851: Congress ratifies the first COMMERCIAL TREATY BETWEEN THE UNITED STATES

Quote by Fillmore:

"Where is the true-hearted American whose cheek does not tingle with shame to see our highest and most courted foreign missions filled by men of foreign birth to the exclusion of the native-born?"
– during his unsuccessful "Know-Nothing" campaign for the Presidency, 1856

Quote about Fillmore:

"Whether to the nation or to the State, no service can or ever will be rendered by a more able or a more faithful public servant."

– John Quincy Adams

	1800	1826	1831	1831-1836	1850
■ Fillmore's Life		He marries Abigail Powers.		Charles Darwin serves as the naturalist on *HMS Beagle*, which surveys the waters around South America.	
■ U.S. & World Events	Millard Fillmore is born on January 7, in Cayuga County, New York.		Fillmore is elected to the U.S. House.		Taylor dies and Fillmore becomes president.

First Lady: Abigail Powers Fillmore

Abigail Powers Fillmore held a paying job before and during her marriage —a first for a First Lady. Married in 1826, the couple struggled financially, but eventually reached a point where she could quit work as a schoolteacher to devote herself to family life.

After Zachary Taylor's death on July 9, 1850, Fillmore and his wife moved into the White House. A graceful, but socially subdued and physically weak First Lady, Abigail Fillmore often relied on her daughter Abby to fill in as hostess. She did make a substantial lasting contribution as First Lady, however, as she was the first to create a White House library. After the death of Mrs. Fillmore, President Fillmore married Caroline McIntosh.

AND EL SALVADOR. The Latin American country had declared the first Central American Constitution in June 1824

July 25, 1851: Gold is discovered in Oregon.

August 11-12, 1851: The unauthorized **LOPEZ EXPEDITION**, aimed at invading and annexing Cuba to the United States, lands about 60 miles from Havana. The expedition, headed by

Cuban exile Narciso Lopez, includes volunteers from the South who want to expand slavery. Although Lopez had counted on anti-Spanish protests to erupt among the Cuban populace with his arrival, no such protests occur. When about 50 American volunteers are captured, tried, and executed, anti-Spanish riots break out, not in Havana, but at the Spanish Consulate in New Orleans. Consequently, Southerners condemn Fillmore for failing to support the invasion; while Northern Democrats criticize his subsequent apology to the Spanish.

June 1, 1852: The **DEMOCRATS NOMINATE FRANKLIN PIERCE** of New Hampshire for president.

June 16-21, 1852: The **WHIGS NOMINATE GENERAL WINFIELD SCOTT**, a significant figure of the Mexican War, for president. William R. King of Alabama is chosen as his running mate.

August 11, 1852: The **FREE SOIL PARTY NOMINATES SENATOR JOHN P. HALE** of New Hampshire for president on an anti-slavery platform that opposes the Compromise of 1850 and the further spread of slavery. George W. Julien of Indiana is nominated for vice president.

November 2, 1852: **FRANKLIN PIERCE IS ELECTED PRESIDENT** of the United States with William R. King as his vice president.

November 24, 1852: Fillmore authorizes **COMMODORE MATTHEW PERRY** to seek diplomatic and trade relations with Japan, a country that has been virtually shut off from the outside world for centuries. Fillmore wants to establish trade routes with Japan through San Francisco, Hawaii and Shanghai. Perry leaves Norfolk, Virginia for Edo Bay in Japan, with a fleet of four U.S. warships.

March 2, 1853: **WASHINGTON TERRITORY IS FORMED**; it had previously been the northern section of the Oregon Territory.

March 4, 1853: Pierce appoints James Campbell as the postmaster general. Thus Campbell becomes the first Catholic to serve in the Cabinet. Anger over the appointment gives rise to the American Party, or the **KNOW-NOTHING PARTY** (so named because members used the secret code "I know nothing" when outsiders asked about their views). In 1856, Fillmore is the presidential nominee of the Know-Nothing Party.

Fillmore's Administration

Inauguration: July 10, 1850 at the Hall of the House of Representatives, Washington, D.C.
Vice President: None
Secretary of State: Daniel Webster; Edward Everett (from November 6, 1852)
Secretary of the Treasury: Thomas Corwin
Secretary of War: Charles M. Conrad
Attorney General: John J. Crittenden
Postmaster General: Nathan K. Hall; Samuel D. Hubbard (from September. 14, 1852)
Secretary of the Navy: William A. Graham; John P. Kennedy (from July 26, 1852)

Secretary of the Interior: Thomas M. T. McKennan; Alexander H. H. Stuart (from September 16, 1850)
Supreme Court Appointment:
Benjamin R. Curtis (1851)
31st Congress (March 4, 1849-March 4, 1851)
Senate: 35 Democrats; 25 Whigs; 2 Others
House: 112 Democrats; 109 Whigs; 9 Others
32nd Congress (March 4, 1851-March 4, 1853)
Senate: 35 Democrats; 24 Whigs; 3 Others
House: 140 Democrats; 88 Whigs; 5 Others
State Admitted: California (1850)

1851	1852	1853	1856	1857-58	1858	1874
The first American edition of Melville Herman's *Moby Dick* is published.	Harriet Beecher Stowe's *Uncle Tom's Cabin* is issued in book form. Previously, it had been featured in abolitionist paper the *National Era* as a series.	Abigail Fillmore dies.	Fillmore runs unsuccessfully for president as the nominee of the Know-Nothing Party.	The Sepoy Mutiny takes place in India, when Indian nationals in the British colonial army rebel.	Fillmore marries Caroline McIntosh.	Fillmore dies on March 8, in Buffalo, New York.

Franklin Pierce

"I believe that involuntary servitude, as it exists in different States of this Confederacy, is recognized by the Constitution. I believe that it stands like any other admitted right, and that the States where it exists are entitled to efficient remedies to enforce the constitutional provisions."

In January 1853, the train carrying President-elect Franklin Pierce, his wife Jane, and their 11-year old son Bennie from Boston to Concord, New Hampshire, derailed. Young Bennie was killed before his parents' eyes. Mrs. Pierce, who had already suffered the deaths of her two other sons, interpreted this latest tragedy as a sign from God that her husband should not be preoccupied with thoughts of family, while he carried out the responsibilities of the presidency. From then on, Jane Pierce withdrew almost entirely from public view. This sense of tragedy brought by forces beyond Franklin Pierce's control haunted his presidency.

Franklin Pierce's early life did little to prepare him for leading a nation on the brink of war. Although Pierce's father had been the governor of New Hampshire, and Pierce had begun serving in the U.S. Congress by the age of 29, he did little to distinguish himself. As a young man in Washington's social circuit, Pierce was known as a handsome, charming bon vivant who enjoyed his drink. His charm, family connections, and deep desire to please helped to make him a leading figure in New Hampshire. But as a politician on the national stage, Pierce was more than content to follow the lead of others.

In 1852, pro-slavery Southern Democrats took notice after Pierce helped replace a Free Soil Democratic candidate for governor with a candidate more willing to compromise. As a pro-Southern politician from the North, he seemed like an ideal choice to unite the Democratic Party, if not the nation.

During his presidency, however, Pierce faced a series of troubles. He sincerely believed that the Compromise of 1850 had settled the issue of slavery. Nevertheless, Senator Stephen Douglas of Illinois reopened the issue by proposing that Kansas and Nebraska be allowed to settle the slavery question for themselves. Pierce quickly caved in to pressure from the pro-slavery forces, and this willingness to sign the Kansas-Nebraska Act led to virtual anarchy in Kansas, where armed pro-slave and free soil mobs faced off against each other.

By the time the Democratic Party held its convention to choose a nominee for president in 1856, Pierce had fallen out of favor. He became the first sitting president to be denied the nomination of his own party for reelection. James Buchanan was nominated instead.

In 1857, Pierce retired from public life and went back to New Hampshire to practice law.

Biographical Facts

Born: November 23, 1804 in Hillsboro, New Hampshire

Ancestry: English

Father: Benjamin Pierce; born December 25, 1757 in Chelmsford, Massachusetts; died April 1, 1839

Father's Occupations: Soldier; farmer; governor of New Hampshire

Mother: Anna Kendrick Pierce; born 1768; died December 1838

Wife: Jane Means Appleton; born March 12, 1806 in Hampton, New Hampshire; died December 2, 1863 in Andover, Massachusetts

Marriage: November 19, 1834 in Amherst, New Hampshire

Children: Franklin (February 2-5, 1836); Frank Robert (1839-1843); Benjamin (1841-1853)

Home: Pierce Homestead, Hillsboro Upper Village, New Hampshire

Education: Attended public school and Hancock Academy; graduated from Bowdoin College (1824)

Religious Affiliation: Episcopalian

Occupations before Presidency: Lawyer; politician; soldier

Military Service: Brigadier general in U.S. Army (1847-1848)

Political Offices before Presidency: Speaker of New Hampshire Legislature; Member of U.S. House of Representatives; Member of U.S. Senate; President of New Hampshire Constitutional Convention

Political Party: Democratic

Age at Inauguration: 48

Occupation after Presidency: Retired

Death: October 8, 1869 in Concord, New Hampshire

Place of Burial: Old North Cemetery, Concord, New Hampshire

Nickname: Young Hickory of the Granite Hills; Handsome Frank

Election of 1852

About the Election: The central issue in this election was the Compromise of 1850—in which California was admitted as a free state, New Mexico and Arizona were organized as territories open to slavery, New Mexico's border dispute with Texas was settled, the District of Columbia was closed to the slave trade, and the Fugitive Slave Act was toughened. Pierce backed the compromise strongly. Aging General Winfield Scott, supported by Northern anti-slavery Whigs, received the nomination of the bitterly divided Whig Party. Pierce won a huge victory, taking 27 states to only 4 for Scott.

Candidates	Party	Electoral Vote	Popular Vote
Franklin Pierce (NH)	Democratic	254	1,601,117
Winfield Scott (VA)	Whig	42	1,385,453
John P. Hale (NH)	Free-Soil	---	155, 825

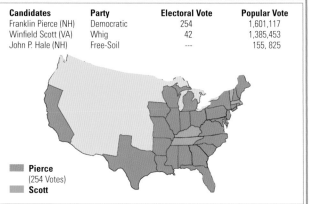

■ **Pierce**
(254 Votes)
■ **Scott**

Pierce's Term 1853-1857

March 4, 1853: Franklin PIERCE IS INAUGURATED. In his speech, he argues in favor of territorial expansion, and for the constitutional rights of the Southern states to maintain the slavery system.

December 30, 1853: The United States and Mexico sign the GADSDEN PURCHASE. Named after James Gadsden, the U.S. minister to Mexico, it allows for the purchase of almost 30,000 square miles in southern New Mexico and Arizona, to provide a route for a transcontinental railroad.

January 23, 1854: Illinois Senator Stephen Douglas, a Democrat, submits a bill in the Senate for the organization of Kansas and Nebraska into territories. He proposes that the two territories be admitted on the basis of "**POPULAR SOVEREIGNTY**," by which they are open to slavery according to the will of the people of those territories. In effect, the proposal, known as the "Kansas-Nebraska Act," repeals the Missouri Compromise by ending geographical limits on slavery's extension.

March 31, 1854: American Commodore Matthew Perry signs the **TREATY OF KANAGAWA** with Japan, thereby opening the island nation to contact and trade with the outside world, for the first time in centuries. The Japanese government allows the United States to create a consulate in Japan.

May 30, 1854: Although concerned that the bill will deepen the sectional conflict over slavery, Pierce signs the **KANSAS-NEBRASKA ACT** into law, after threats from pro-slavery forces.

June 5, 1854: Canada and the United States sign the **RECIPROCITY TREATY**, which allows U.S. fishermen to fish along the Canadian coast, New Brunswick, Nova Scotia, Prince Edward Island, and several other islands that were not yet united with Canada.

October 18, 1854: Pierce orders Pierre Soulé, the U.S. minister to Spain, James Buchanan, the U.S. minister to Great Britain, and John Y. Mason, the U.S. minister to France, to design a strategy to purchase Cuba from Spain. In a letter known as the **OSTEND MANIFESTO**, written largely by Soulé, the three ministers propose that should Spain refuse to sell the island, "then by every law, human and divine, we shall be justified in wresting it from Spain, if we possess the power." When U.S. Secretary of State William Marcy rejects the suggestion, Soulé resigns his post.

November 29, 1854: In an election marked by violence from pro-slavery mobs from Missouri (known as "**BORDER RUFFIANS**"), John W. Whitfield is elected territorial delegate from Kansas.

February 10, 1855: Nationality laws are reformed to guarantee U.S. citizenship to alien wives of U.S. citizens, and any children born to them overseas.

Quotes by Pierce:

"A Republic without parties is a complete anomaly. The history of all popular governments show how absurd is the idea of their attempting to exist without parties."

"You have summoned me in my weakness; you must sustain me by your strength."
– Inaugural Address

Quotes about Pierce:

"Whoever may be elected, we cannot get a poorer cuss than now disgraces the Presidential Chair!"
– B.B. French, Pierce's former Secretary

"Frank, I pity you—indeed I do, from the bottom of my heart!"
– Nathaniel Hawthorne

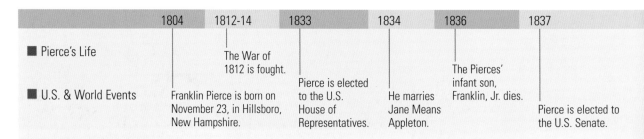

	1804	1812-14	1833	1834	1836	1837
■ Pierce's Life		The War of 1812 is fought.			The Pierces' infant son, Franklin, Jr. dies.	
■ U.S. & World Events	Franklin Pierce is born on November 23, in Hillsboro, New Hampshire.		Pierce is elected to the U.S. House of Representatives.	He marries Jane Means Appleton.		Pierce is elected to the U.S. Senate.

First Lady: Jane Means Appleton Pierce

Jane Appleton Pierce was the shy and sensitive daughter of Reverend Jesse Appleton, the former president of Bowdoin College. Initially, she supported her husband's interest in politics, but her dislike of Washington and the successive deaths of her sons affected her ability to function well as First Lady. Their third son, Benjamin, was killed in a train accident at age 11, just a few months before Franklin Pierce's inauguration. Although Mrs. Pierce did not attend the simple inauguration ceremony on March 4, 1853, she joined her husband later. She believed that her family's misfortunes were caused by her husband's involvement with "dirty" politics.

March 30, 1855: With help from armed Border Ruffians, a pro-slavery territorial legislature is elected in Kansas, to pass laws banning public protest against slavery.

June–October 1855: Initially backed by American business interests seeking a canal through Nicaragua, American filibuster WILLIAM WALKER takes advantage of a civil war to install himself as the dictator of Nicaragua. He rules as the country's president until May 1857. He is forced to leave Nicaragua after American businessman Cornelius Vanderbilt helps to organize a coalition of Nicaraguans and other Central Americans to oust Walker.

September–November 1855: Settlers in Kansas, opposed to opening the territory to slavery, hold their own conventions. Most Kansas "free state" settlers in Kansas were not abolitionists. However, by early November, the TOPEKA CONSTITUTION is drawn up. It prohibits slavery but also excludes free blacks from the territory. At the same time, weapons begin arriving in Kansas from abolitionist forces in the Northern states.

November 26, 1855: Fifteen hundred Border Ruffians attack Lawrence, Kansas, where they clash with Free State forces in what becomes known as the WAKARUSA WAR.

February 22, 1856: The Republican Party holds its first national convention in Pittsburgh, Pennsylvania. The American Party, or KNOW-NOTHING PARTY NOMINATES FORMER PRESIDENT MILLARD FILLMORE.

May 14, 1856: Although he had previously condemned William Walker's actions in Nicaragua, President Pierce receives one of Walker's emissaries.

June 2-5, 1856: For the first time in history, a major party refuses to nominate a sitting president for reelection when the Democrats bypass Franklin Pierce and nominate JAMES BUCHANAN for president.

June 17-19, 1856: The REPUBLICANS NOMINATE JOHN C. FRÉMONT for president.

September 17, 1856: In their final national convention, the Whigs nominate Millard Fillmore for president and Andrew J. Donelson for vice president.

November 4, 1856: JAMES BUCHANAN IS ELECTED PRESIDENT.

May 24, 1856: A gang of radical abolitionists gun down five pro-slavery Kansans along the POTTAWATOMIE CREEK.

January 15, 1857: Northern abolitionists hold a "STATE OF DISUNION" CONVENTION in Worcester, Massachusetts to consider steps for the peaceful separation of free states from the slave states. William Lloyd Garrison, publisher of *the liberator*, delivers a speech supporting separation.

Pierce's Administration

Inauguration: March 4, 1853 at the Capitol, Washington, D.C.
Vice President: William R. King (died April 18, 1853)
Secretary of State: William L. Marcy
Secretary of the Treasury: James Guthrie
Secretary of War: Jefferson Davis
Attorney General: Caleb Cushing
Postmaster General: James Campbell
Secretary of the Navy: James C. Dobbin
Secretary of the Interior: Robert McClelland

Supreme Court Appointment:
John A. Campbell (1853)
33rd Congress: (March 4, 1853-March 4, 1855)
Senate: 38 Democrats; 22 Whigs; 2 Others
House: 159 Democrats; 71 Whigs; 4 Others
34th Congress: (March 4, 1855-March 4, 1857)
Senate: 40 Democrats; 15 Republicans; 5 Others
House: 108 Republicans: 83 Democrats; 43 Others
End of Presidential Term: March 4, 1857

1843	1846	1848	1852	1853	1861-65	1869
The Pierces' second child, Frank Robert, dies of typhoid at age 4.	Pierce serves in the U.S.-Mexican War under Zachary Taylor.	Karl Marx and Freidrich Engels publish *The Communist Manifesto*.	Pierce wins the Democratic nomination for President.	Pierce's youngest son Bennie dies in a train wreck at age 11.	The U.S. Civil War is fought.	Pierce dies on October 8, in Concord, New Hampshire.

James Buchanan

15th President (1857–1861)

"Whatever the result may be, I shall carry to my grave the consciousness that I at least meant well for my country."

The last president to have served during the War of 1812, James Buchanan was older than three of the four presidents who had held office before him. During his forty years in politics, he had been in both houses of Congress. His long diplomatic career began in Andrew Jackson's administration when Buchanan served as minister to Russia. Following that appointment, he acted as James Polk's secretary of state and Franklin Pierce's minister to Great Britain. To Democrats, his long service out of the country made him an ideal nominee—not because of any particular diplomatic skill, but because his overseas duties had helped Buchanan to avoid most of the controversy at home, namely the issue over slavery.

As president, Buchanan proved to be a well-meaning but indecisive leader who avoided any situation that required decisive action. As a Pennsylvanian, Buchanan had no personal interest in maintaining slavery. But like Pierce and Fillmore before him, he believed it was better to yield to pro-slavery forces than to risk civil war. In truth, he had little understanding of the bitter forces at work that was tearing the country apart. In his inauguration address, Buchanan went so far as to describe the debate over slavery in the territories as

"happily, a matter of but little practical importance." When the Supreme Court ruled in *Dred Scott v. Sandford*, just days after Buchanan took office, that the federal government had no constitutional right to ban slavery from the territories— thereby overturning the Missouri Compromise that had kept blood from spilling for more than three decades—Buchanan believed the slavery issue had been resolved "speedily and finally."

President Buchanan soon realized, however, that the Supreme Court's Dred Scott decision had made things much worse. Then Buchanan miscalculated again by supporting Kansas' entry into the Union as a slave state, though Kansas had already voted against slavery in their territory. When South Carolina left the Union in 1860, Buchanan pleaded that the Union was a "sacred trust" that must be preserved; while at the same time, he trumpeted his conviction that the Constitution made the federal government powerless to prevent secession. When Abraham Lincoln was elected president in 1860, Buchanan was happy to cede his authority to his successor. "My dear, sir," he told Lincoln, "If you are as happy on entering the White House as I shall feel on returning to Wheatland, you are a very happy man indeed."

Biographical Facts

Born: April 23, 1791 in Cove Gap, Pennsylvania

Ancestry: Scotch-Irish

Father: James Buchanan; born 1761 in County Donegal, Ireland; died June 11, 1821 in Mercersburg, Pennsylvania

Father's Occupations: Businessman; justice of the peace

Mother: Elizabeth Speer Buchanan; born 1767 in Lancaster County, Pennsylvania; died 1833 in Greensburg, Pennsylvania

Wife: None

Children: None

Home: Wheatland, Lancaster, Pennsylvania

Education: Attended Old Stone Academy; graduated from Dickinson College (1809)

Religious Affiliation: Presbyterian

Occupation before Presidency: Lawyer

Military Service: None

Political Offices before Presidency: Member of Pennsylvania Legislature; Member of U.S. House of Representatives; Minister to Russia; Member of U.S. Senate; Secretary of State; Minister to Great Britain

Political Party: Democratic

Age at Inauguration: 65

Occupation after Presidency: Retired

Death: June 1, 1868 in Lancaster, Pennsylvania

Place of Burial: Woodward Hill Cemetery, Lancaster, Pennsylvania

Nickname: Ten Cent Jimmy; Old Buck

Writings: *Mr. Buchanan's Administration on the Eve of the Rebellion; Works of James Buchanan*

97

Election of 1856

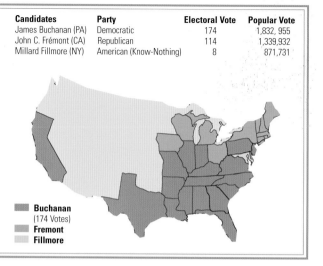

Candidates	Party	Electoral Vote	Popular Vote
James Buchanan (PA)	Democratic	174	1,832, 955
John C. Frémont (CA)	Republican	114	1,339,932
Millard Fillmore (NY)	American (Know-Nothing)	8	871,731

About the Election: Support for the controversial Compromise of 1850 formed the lynchpin of the Democratic Party's platform in 1856, despite the bloodshed that it had caused in Kansas. The Democrats chose James Buchanan as their nominee, largely because as a foreign minister to Great Britain, he had been overseas during the Compromise debate. The new Republican Party, a coalition of Northern Whigs and anti-slavery Democrats chose John C. Frémont, the hero of California's Bear Flag Rebellion. Former President Millard Fillmore ran as the nominee of the anti-immigrant, anti-Catholic American Party (also called the Know-Nothing Party). Frémont carried most of the free states, but Buchanan swept the South. Fillmore took only Maryland.

- **Buchanan** (174 Votes)
- **Fremont**
- **Fillmore**

Buchanan's Term 1857-1861

March 4, 1857: BUCHANAN IS INAUGURATED, and in his inaugural speech, he pushes for changes in import tariffs. Tariffs had been lowered by 20 percent during the Pierce administration—benefiting the South. However, the tariff decrease greatly harms Northern industry and the nation suffers an economic depression known as the Panic of 1857.

March 6, 1857: The Supreme Court announces its decision in the ***DRED SCOTT V. JOHN F. SANDFORD*** case. Scott, an enslaved African American, had sued for his freedom after his master had taken him from Missouri, where slavery was legal, to Illinois and Wisconsin, where it was not. The Supreme Court, led by Chief Justice Roger B. Taney, a conservative Southerner, rules that because African Americans are not citizens, they are not permitted to sue. In addition, the Court also states that the Constitution does not permit the federal government to ban slavery in the territories, thereby making the 1820 Missouri Compromise unconstitutional.

September 7-11, 1857: When Buchanan orders that Mormon leader Brigham Young be replaced as territorial governor of Utah, the Mormon militia, aided by a group of Native Americans from the Paiute Nation, attack and kill 140 unarmed non-Mormon emigrés who are passing through Utah en route to California. The attack becomes known as the MOUNTAIN MEADOWS MASSACRE.

October 5, 1857: Despite widespread violence and fraud by pro-slavery mobs, KANSAS ELECTS AN ANTI-SLAVERY LEGISLATURE.

December 21, 1857: Kansas votes on the LECOMPTON CONSTITUTION that had been drafted by an illegal pro-slavery legislature. President Buchanan urges Congress to admit Kansas to the Union as a slave state under the Lecompton Constitution.

March 23, 1858: Despite opposition from Stephen Douglas, the architect of "popular sovereignty," and from Republicans, the SENATE VOTES TO ACCEPT KANSAS

The Supreme Court's Dred Scott decision, covered here on the front page of "Frank Leslie's Illustrated Newspaper," ended forty years of uneasy peace by ruling the Missouri Compromise unconstitutional.

	1791	1802	1804	1811	1812
■ Buchanan's Life					
■ U.S. and World Events					

1802: Madame Tussaud's wax museum opens in London.

1791: James Buchanan is born on April 23 in Cove Gap, Pennsylvania.

1804: Napoleon becomes Emperor of France.

1811: Britain adopts paper money as currency.

1812: The War of 1812 begins between the United States and Great Britain.

Buchanan is admitted to the bar and begins practice at Lan Caster Pannsylvania.

Presidential Hostess:
Harriet Lane (Johnston)

Buchanan was the nation's only president who never married. Harriet Lane served as hostess for Buchanan, her uncle and legal guardian. She had lost both her parents by the age of 11. Only 26, Lane, nicknamed the "Democratic Queen," soon won popularity for her poise and enthusiasm. However, due to the rising tension in the nation over slavery, light entertainment and dinner parties at the presidential mansion became difficult to hold during the Buchanan years. At the age of 36, Lane married Baltimore banker Henry Elliott Johnston. The next eighteen years were marked by the deaths of her uncle, her two young sons, and her husband. Upon her death, Lane bequeathed to the nation her sizable art collection to the Smithsonian Institution. She also left a generous endowment to fund the Harriet Lane Outpatient Clinics.

AS A SLAVE STATE. The Senate's decision also contradicts the will of the majority of Kansans, who had voted against slavery. Rather than approve Kansas' admission as a slave state, the U.S. HOUSE OF REPRESENTATIVES ASKS KANSANS TO VOTE AGAIN on the state constitution.

May 4, 1858: In a compromise measure on Kansas, Congress agrees to ask Kansans to vote once more on the pro-slavery Lecompton Constitution. In a concession to pro-slavery representatives, Congress also promises to grant land to Kansas voters if they ratify the pro-slavery constitution.

May 11, 1858: MINNESOTA IS ADMITTED as a free state.

July 29, 1858: Townsend Harris completes commercial TREATY WITH JAPAN declaring peace and friendship with the United States. The treaty opens U.S. trade rights in Japanese ports and allows American citizens to permanently reside in ports and towns. Americans also have the right to lease ground, purchase buildings, and erect dwellings and warehouses. China had also signed a similar agreement with the U.S. on June 18.

August 2, 1858: Kansans once again reject the Lecompton Constitution by an overwhelming margin of 11,300 to 1,788. KANSAS IS ADMITTED TO THE UNION AS A FREE STATE in 1861.

August 21–October 15, 1858: Senator Stephen Douglas of Illinois and Abraham Lincoln, the Republican challenger for his Senate seat, hold a series of seven debates. During the LINCOLN-DOUGLAS DEBATES, Douglas refuses to state his personal view on slavery's morality. Instead, he argues that territorial governments can write laws to restrict slavery, despite the Dred Scott ruling that prohibits federal bans on slavery in the territories. Lincoln proclaims slavery as a moral issue and denounces the Dred Scott decision. Douglas wins the election, but Lincoln gains national prominence as an anti-slavery spokesman.

February 14, 1859: OREGON IS ADMITTED TO THE UNION as a free state.

March 12, 1859: At a meeting in Vicksburg, Mississippi, known as the SOUTHERN COMMERCIAL CONVENTION, Southern slave

Buchanan's Administration

Inauguration: March 4, 1857 at the Capitol, Washington, D.C.
Vice President: John C. Breckinridge
Secretary of State: Lewis Cass; Jeremiah S. Black (from Dec. 17, 1860)
Secretary of the Treasury: Howell Cobb; Philip F. Thomas (from December. 12, 1860); John A. Dix (from January 15, 1861)
Secretary of War: John B. Floyd; Joseph Holt (from January 18, 1861)
Attorney General: Jeremiah S. Black; Edwin M. Stanton (from December 22, 1860)
Postmaster General: Aaron V. Brown; Joseph Holt (from March 14, 1859); Horatio King (from February 12, 1861)
Secretary of the Navy: Isaac Toucey

Secretary of the Interior: Jacob Thompson
Supreme Court Appointment: Nathan Clifford
35th Congress: (March 4, 1857-March 4, 1859) Senate: 36 Democrats; 20 Republicans; 8 Others House: 118 Democrats; 92 Republicans; 26 Others
36th Congress: (March 4, 1859-March 4, 1861) Senate: 36 Democrats; 26 Republicans; 4 Others House: 114 Republicans; 92 Democrats; 31 Others
States Admitted: Minnesota (1858); Oregon (1859); Kansas (1861)

1814	1818	1820	1821	1829	1832
	France declares slave trade illegal.		The first U.S. natural gas well is tapped at Fredonia, New York.		Buchanan is appointed minister to Russia.
	Chile gains independence from Spain.		Buchanan is elected to the House of Representatives.		First French railway line opens.
Kingdom of Netherland is created.					

owners argue in favor of re-opening the African slave trade. The trade had been banned by Congress in 1808.

June 11, 1859: The COMSTOCK LODE, the biggest silver deposit found in U.S. history, is discovered in western Nevada.

July 5, 1859: Yet another constitutional convention is held in Kansas to resolve the debate over whether the state should be slave or free. Delegates draft a constitution that not only prohibits slavery but also protects women's rights regarding child custody cases, married women's property rights, and equality in public education.

October 4, 1859: The Kansas constitution, which defines Kansas a free state, is ratified by popular vote.

October 16, 1859: JOHN BROWN and a group of white and black men raid HARPER'S FERRY in Virginia as the first step in a plan to establish an abolitionist republic in the Appalachians. Brown, a violent, radical abolitionist, had previously led a murderous attack on four pro-slavery Kansans several years earlier. The Harper's Ferry plot fails and Brown is captured and hanged for murder, conspiracy, and treason against the state of Virginia. JOHN BROWN'S RAID alarms the South, while it rallies Northern abolitionists who proclaim him as a martyr.

February 27, 1860: Encouraged to run for the presidency, ABRAHAM LINCOLN travels to the Northeast on a speaking tour in early 1860. At Cooper Union in New York City, Lincoln outlines the Republican Party's strong opposition to slavery. The speech is printed in the *New York Tribune* and serves to push Lincoln to the front of the pack among those pursuing the Republican nomination.

April 23, 1860: The Democratic Party holds its nominating convention in Charleston, South Carolina. However, Southern delegates abandon Stephen Douglas because of his continued defense of "popular sovereignty." In Douglas' mind, territories should decide for themselves whether to permit slavery. Territories also have every right to ban slavery if they choose to

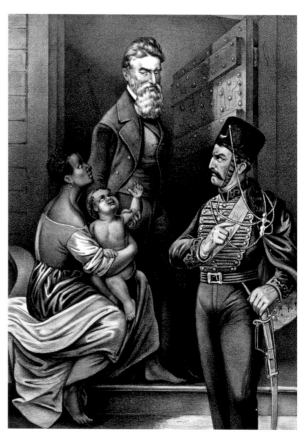

The radical abolitionist John Brown is taken to his execution in this idealized contemporary image.

	1834		1835	1836		1845	1847
■ Buchanan's Life		Slavery is abolished in all British territories.		Samuel Morse invents the telegraph.			Emily Bronte writes *Wuthering Heights*.
■ U.S. & World Events		Buchanan is elected to the Senate.		First Canadian railway opens.		Buchanan serves as secretary of state in the Polk administration.	

do so. After delegates from Alabama, Georgia, South Carolina, Arkansas, Delaware, and several other states walk out in protest, the **DEMOCRATIC CONVENTION ENDS WITHOUT A NOMINEE.**

May 9, 1860: The **CONSTITUTIONAL UNION PARTY**, made up of former Whig and Know-Nothing Party members, nominates John Bell for president.

May 18, 1860: The **REPUBLICANS NOMINATE ABRAHAM LINCOLN** for president

June 18, 1860: **NORTHERN DEMOCRATS NOMINATE STEPHEN DOUGLAS** for president.

June 28, 1860: **SOUTHERN DEMOCRATS NOMINATE JOHN C. BRECKINRIDGE** for president.

November 6, 1860: **ABRAHAM LINCOLN IS ELECTED PRESIDENT**, winning just 39 percent of the popular vote.

December 3, 1860: In his annual message to Congress, President Buchanan says that the South has no legal right to secede from the Union. But he also concedes that the federal government has no power to prevent a state's secession. Buchanan recommends an "explanatory" amendment to the Constitution on the issue of slavery.

December 18, 1860: In a final effort at compromise between the North and the South, Senator John Crittenden of Kentucky proposes that a constitutional amendment be passed to extend the Missouri Compromise line west to the Pacific. Although Buchanan supports it, President-elect Lincoln opposes the **CRITTENDEN COMPROMISE** and restates that he will not compromise on the extension of slavery.

December 20, 1860: **SOUTH CAROLINA SECEDES** from the Union, becoming the first state to do so.

January 8, 1861: Buchanan delivers his final message to Congress, referring to the Union as a "sacred trust." However, as he has done throughout his presidency, Buchanan fails to accept or recommend any action to preserve the Union.

January 9, 1861: **MISSISSIPPI SECEDES** from the Union.

January 10, 1861: **FLORIDA SECEDES** from the Union

January 11, 1861: **ALABAMA SECEDES** from the Union.

January 19, 1861: **GEORGIA SECEDES** from the Union.

January 26, 1861: **LOUISIANA SECEDES** from the Union

January 29, 1861: **KANSAS IS ADMITTED** as a free state.

February 4, 1861: The **CONFEDERATE STATES OF AMERICA (CSA) IS FORMED** in Montgomery, Alabama. Within a week, it adopts a provisional constitution and elects former Secretary of War **JEFFERSON DAVIS** as its president.

February 23, 1861: **TEXAS SECEDES** from the Union.

March 2, 1861: Congress creates **NEVADA TERRITORY** out of the western portion of Utah Territory. **DAKOTA TERRITORY** is created out of the northern portion of the Nebraska Territory.

March 4, 1861: **BUCHANAN ESCORTS PRESIDENT-ELECT ABRAHAM LINCOLN** to the inauguration ceremonies, and then to the presidential mansion. After leaving office, Buchanan retires to Wheatland, Pennsylvania.

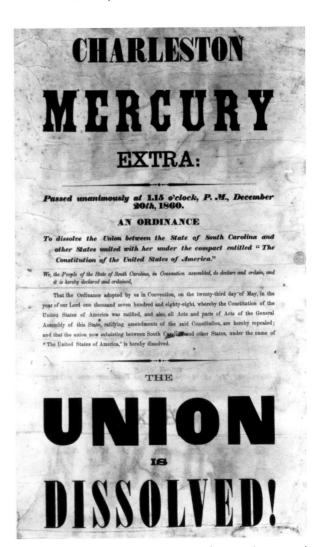

South Carolina seceded from the Union on December 20, 1860, announced here on the front page of the "Charleston Mercury."

1853	1858	1856	1861	1862
As Minister to Great Britain, Buchanan helps draft the controversial Ostend Manifesto, which urges the United States to seize Cuba by force from Spain.	The Atlantic cable is completed.	Buchanan is elected president. Austrian psychoanalyst Sigmund Freud is born.	The U.S. Civil War begins and lasts until 1965.	Buchanan dies June 1 in Lancaster, Pennsylvania.

Abraham Lincoln

16th President (1861–1865)

"Fourscore and seven years ago our fathers brought forth on this continent, a new nation, conceived in Liberty, and dedicated to the proposition that all men are created equal."

Although he had been born in obscurity in a log cabin, by the time Abraham Lincoln won the Republican Party's nomination for president in 1860, he had become a household name. His vocal opposition to the expansion of slavery had placed him at the forefront of the new Republican Party. And his election—won with less than 40 percent of the popular vote—triggered the secession of 11 Southern slave states from the Union.

Despite his opposition to slavery, Lincoln was no abolitionist. As he said himself, "My paramount object in this struggle is to save the Union, and it is not either to save or destroy slavery." At the same time, Lincoln was adamant that secession was a gross violation of the Constitution that had to be prevented by any means necessary.

Lincoln was well aware that he would be tested as no president had ever been before—not even Washington. His forbearance under such weight has made him one of the nation's most beloved heroes. But during his presidency, he was anything but this. Southerners saw him as a despotic tyrant, while members of his own party viewed him as a backwoods fool without the courage to take on the slavery issue directly. Many in the North were begining to question the president's ability to conduct the war effectively. Even after he issued the Emancipation Proclamation, freeing slaves in the Confederate states, Lincoln himself was convinced that he would lose his bid for reelection. However, when Vicksburg fell on July 4, 1863, the Union gained control of Mississippi River, cutting the Confederacy in two. And when Lee's forces were turned back at Gettysburg, the last Confederate offense in the North, Southern momentum for winning the war was finally broken. As the Union moved closer to victory, public perception of Lincoln changed. Politicians came to respect his skillful maneuvering, as the public rallied behind his straightforward yet eloquent defense of the nation's ideals.

At the end of the Civil War, Lincoln promoted peace and charity, hoping to bind the war-torn nation by embracing the Confederate rebels rather than punishing them. Lincoln spoke of caring for all of the wounded. His assassination just five days after Lee's surrender at Appomattox sealed his reputation as one of the nation's greatest martyrs.

Biographical Facts

Born: February 12, 1809 in Hardin County, Kentucky

Ancestry: English

Father: Thomas Lincoln; born January 6, 1778 in Rockingham County, Virginia; died January 15, 1851 in Coles County, Illinois

Father's Occupations: Farmer; carpenter

Mother: Nancy Hanks Lincoln; born February 5, 1784 in Virginia; died October 5, 1818 in Spencer County, Indiana

Stepmother: Sarah Bush Johnston; born December 12, 1788 in Hardin County, Kentucky; died April 10, 1869 in Charleston, Illinois

Wife: Mary Todd; born December 13, 1818 in Lexington, Kentucky; died July 16, 1882 in Springfield, Illinois

Marriage: November 4, 1842 in Springfield, Illinois

Children: Robert Todd (1843-1926); Edward Baker (1846-1850); William Wallace (1850-1862); Thomas ("Tad") (1853-1871)

Home: Eighth and Jackson streets, Springfield, Illinois

Education: Local tutors; self-educated

Religious Affiliation: None

Occupations before Presidency: Store clerk; storeowner; ferry pilot; surveyor; postmaster; lawyer

Political Party: Whig Republican (from 1856)

Military Service: Served in volunteer company for three months during Black Hawk War

Political Offices before Presidency: Member of Illinois General Assembly; Member of U.S. House of Representatives

Age at Inauguration: 52

Death: April 15, 1865 in Washington, D.C.

Place of Burial: Oak Ridge Cemetery, Springfield, Illinois

Nickname: Abe; Honest Abe; Illinois Rail-Splitter

Writings: *Collected Works of Abraham Lincoln*

Election of 1860

Candidates	Party	Electoral Vote	Popular Vote
Abraham Lincoln (IL)	Republican	180	1,865,593
Stephen Douglas (IL)	Democratic	12	1,382,713
John C. Breckinridge (KY)	Southern Democratic	72	848,356
John Bell (TN)	Constitutional Union	39	592,906

About the Election: The split in the Democratic Party virtually assured a Republican victory in the presidential election. The leading Democratic candidate, Stephen A. Douglas, had alienated the Southern wing of his party by arguing that, in keeping with his idea of popular sovereignty, territorial legislatures should be allowed to close their territories to slavery if they saw fit to do so. Southern Democrats held a separate convention and nominated John C. Breckinridge. Meanwhile, the Republican Party chose Abraham Lincoln, who had gained national recognition for his condemnation of slavery. Also running was John Bell of the Constitutional Union Party, which was made up of former members of the Whig and Know-Nothing parties. Bell promoted compromise as a means of preserving the Union. Lincoln won only 39 percent of the popular vote, but received a majority of the electoral votes. He swept all states in the North except New Jersey. In the South, the contest was between Bell and Breckinridge; Lincoln's name did not appear on the ballot in ten of the Southern states. With Lincoln's election, disunion was inevitable.

Lincoln (180 Votes)
Breckinridge
Bell
Douglas

Lincoln's First Term 1861-1864

March 4, 1861: In his INAUGURAL ADDRESS, Lincoln declares that he has no desire to interfere with slavery where it exists, but that secession from the Union is illegal, and that he will use force if necessary to prevent it. His tone is moderate, however, when addressing the Southern rebels. "The government will not assail you," Lincoln asserts, "You can have no conflict, without yourselves the aggressors."

March 11, 1861: The Confederate Congress unanimously adopts the CONFEDERATE CONSTITUTION, which is largely modeled on the U.S. Constitution. It even incorporates most of the Bill of Rights. However, in addition to prohibiting any law that outlaws slavery, the new constitution codifies the sovereignty of the individual Confederate states over the central government.

April 3, 1861: The first PONY EXPRESS run arrives in Sacramento, California. The mail

During his term in the U.S. House of Representatives, Lincoln opposed the U.S.-Mexican War.

service lasts for just six months, and by October, it is replaced by the transcontinental telegraph service.

April 12-13, 1861: Although South Carolina had seceded from the Union in December 1860, federal troops continue to occupy FORT SUMTER, a federal fort in Charleston's harbor commanded by Major Robert Anderson. Confederate president Jefferson Davis demands the fort's surrender, and at 4:30 a.m. on April 12, Confederate batteries under Lt. General P.T. Beauregard open fire on the fort, beginning the U.S. CIVIL WAR. Union forces at Fort Sumter do not return fire until later that morning, when Captain Abner Doubleday fires a volley at the rebel position at Cummings Point. Short on supplies, Anderson surrenders Fort Sumter after 34 hours of Confederate bombardment.

April 15, 1861: Declaring a state of insurrection, Lincoln issues a proclamation calling for 75,000 troops to repossess all federal facilities that have been seized by the Confederacy as the first step in putting down the rebellion. He also calls a

	1808	1809	1816	1821
■ Lincoln's Life		Abraham Lincoln is born on February 12 in Hardin County, Kentucky.		Emma Willard establishes Troy Female Seminary, the first college-level educational institution for women in the United States.
■ U.S. & World Events	Congress bans U.S. involvement in international slave trade.		James Monroe is elected president. Lincoln and his family move to Indiana.	

First Lady: Mary Todd Lincoln

Mary Ann Todd was born to a Southern family where she enjoyed the benefits of a private education and an aristocratic social life.

As First Lady, Mrs. Lincoln generated controversy. Southern relatives regarded her as a traitor to the Confederate cause. Many Northerners also viewed her with suspicion despite her pro-Union stance and support for Northern-bound blacks through the Contraband Relief Association. Her debilitating migraine headaches and long-standing emotional instability also led to public criticism, especially when she spent extravagantly on entertaining during war-time. At the same time, Mrs. Lincoln undertook the task of redecorating the public rooms of the White House and won admiration as an elegant hostess at social gatherings. The assassination of her husband, along with the death of three of her sons, contributed to the deterioration of her mental health until her death.

special session of Congress to meet on July 4: the **CIVIL WAR HAS OFFICIALLY BEGUN.**

April 17, 1861: In response to Lincoln's proclamation, **VIRGINIA SECEDES** from the Union.

April 19, 1861: Follwing General Winfield Scott's advice, **LINCOLN ORDERS A BLOCKADE OF CONFEDERATE PORTS.** which disrupts the import of supplies.

May 6, 1861: **ARKANSAS SECEDES** from the Union.

May 10, 1861: **RIOTS ERUPT IN ST. LOUIS** when 3,000 Union soldiers parade captured Missouri militiamen through the streets. A pro-Confederate mob attacks the Union soldiers with bricks and gunfire. The violence escalates when the Home Guard, a group of pro-Union German immigrants serving with the Union forces, return fire into the crowd. By nightfall, 28 civilians are dead or dying. Although the Union commander attempts to dismiss the Home Guard to restore peace, rebel mobs continue to rampage, burning buildings throughout the night. The Home Guard are called out once more to end the riots. Although Missouri remains under Union control, it continues to be a hotbed of unrest throughout the war. Meanwhile in Washington, the House of Representatives raises tariffs and taxes to pay for the war.

May 20, 1861: **NORTH CAROLINA SECEDES** from the Union.

May 21, 1861: The **CONFEDERATE CAPITAL MOVES TO RICHMOND, VIRGINIA** from Montgomery, Alabama.

June 8, 1861: **TENNESSEE SECEDES** from the Union.

July 21, 1861: At the **FIRST BATTLE OF BULL RUN** near Manassas, Virginia, Confederate General P.T. Beauregard defeats Union forces under General Irvin McDowell. In the battle, Confederate General Thomas J. Jackson earns his nickname "Stonewall" because of his unyielding ability to hold his position on the battlefield.

July 25, 1861: **CONGRESS AUTHORIZES RECRUITMENT** of a volunteer military and offers soldiers a $100 bonus for at least two years of service.

September 14, 1861: The **USS *COLORADO* BATTLES THE STEAMER *JUDAH*** off the coast

Lincoln's First Administration

Inauguration: March 4, 1861 at the Capitol, Washington, D.C.
Vice President: Hannibal Hamlin
Secretary of State: William H. Seward
Secretary of the Treasury: Salmon P. Chase; William P. Fessenden (from July 5, 1864)
Secretary of War: Simon Cameron; Edwin M. Stanton (from January 20, 1862)
Attorney General: Edward Bates; James Speed (from December 5, 1864)
Postmaster General: Montgomery Blair; William Dennison (from October 1, 1864)
Secretary of the Navy: Gideon Welles
Secretary of the Interior: Caleb B. Smith; John P. Usher (from January 1, 1863)

Supreme Court Appointments:
Noah H. Swayne (1862); Samuel F. Miller (1862); David Davis (1862); Stephen J. Field (1863); Salmon P. Chase, Chief Justice (1864)
37th Congress (March 4, 1861-March 4, 1863)
Senate: 31 Republicans; 10 Democrats; 8 Others
House: 105 Republicans; 43 Democrats, 30 Others
38th Congress (March 4, 1863-March 4, 1865)
Senate: 36 Republicans; 9 Democrats; 5 Others
House: 102 Republicans; 75 Democrats; 9 Others
States Admitted: West Virginia (1863); Nevada (1864)

1828	1830	1831	1832	1833
	Lincoln moves to Illinois.	Theodore Roosevelt is born.	Sauk chief Black Hawk is captured, ending Black Hawk's War.	Lincoln becomes postmaster of New Salem, Illinois.
Andrew Jackson is elected president.		Lincoln begins working as a clerk in a general store.	Lincoln briefly serves as a captain in a volunteer regiment during Black Hawk's War.	

Quotes by Lincoln:

"My paramount object in this struggle is to save the Union, and it is not either to save or destroy slavery. If I could save the Union without freeing any slave I would do it, if I could save it by freeing all the slaves I would do it; and if I could save it by freeing some and leaving others alone I would also do that."

"With malice toward none, with charity for all; with firmness in the right, as God gives us to see the right, let us strive on to finish the work we are in; to bind up the nation's wounds...to do all which may achieve and cherish a just, and a lasting peace, among ourselves, and with all nations."

Quotes about Lincoln:

"Executive force and vigor are rare qualities. The President is the best of us."
– *Secretary of State William H. Seward, to his wife*

"Our country owes all her troubles to him, and God simply made me the instrument of his punishment."
– *John Wilkes Booth*

of Pensacola, Florida. Navy Lt. John H. Russell and his crew arrive at the navy yard at 2 a.m. and set fire to the *Judah*. The Union suffers three deaths and four wounded.

October 31, 1861: GENERAL WINFIELD SCOTT RETIRES as commander in chief of the Union Army at the age of 75.

November 1, 1861: Lincoln appoints GEORGE B. MCCLELLAN COMMANDER OF THE UNION ARMY. After the Union defeat at Bull Run in July 1861, Lincoln had removed General McDowell.

February 20, 1862: Lincoln's son, Willie, dies of typhoid.

March 9, 1862: Union and Confederate warships, the *MONITOR* and the *MERRIMACK,* battle off the coast of Virginia. The Confederacy had converted the wooden steamship *Merrimack* into an ironclad gunship in order to run the Union blockade of Southern ports. The Union builds a similar warship, named the *Monitor*. Neither ship suffers any significant damage in the confrontation, and the *Merrimack* withdraws after hours of fighting. Confederates destroy the ship, fearing its capture by Union naval forces, while the *Monitor* sinks in a storm.

April 16, 1862: President Lincoln signs a bill that ABOLISHES SLAVERY IN THE DISTRICT OF COLUMBIA.

May 15, 1862: The Department of Agriculture is established without Cabinet status. On June 30, Isaac Newton is appointed commissioner of agriculture to oversee the dissemination of information about farming and planting.

May 20, 1862: The HOMESTEAD ACT OF 1862 is passed, enabling any American citizen or applicant for citizenship to obtain ownership of land (up to 160 acres), after having lived on it for five years.

June 1, 1862: Confederate president JEFFERSON DAVIS APPOINTS ROBERT E. LEE COMMANDER of the Confederate Army of Northern Virginia.

July 1862: After capturing Fort Pulaski on Tybee Island, Georgia, Union Major General David Hunter organizes the FIRST AFRICAN AMERICAN REGIMENT, by impressing slaves from plantations in nearby South Carolina Sea Islands.

July 2, 1862: The MORRILL LAND-GRANT COLLEGE ACT is passed. It provides federal land grants to state colleges that teach agriculture and the mechanical arts.

July 22, 1862: Lincoln announces to his

Lincoln appointed George McClellan Commander of the Army of the Potomac. McClellan later opposed Lincoln in the 1864 election.

	1834	1836	1837	
■ Lincoln's Life		He is receives his law license.	Queen Victoria ascends the throne in Great Britain.	
■ U.S. & World Events	Lincoln is elected to the Illinois Assembly as an anti-Jackson Whig.		Lincoln moves to Springfield, Illinois.	Lincoln marries Mary Todd.

Election of 1864

Candidates	Party	Electoral Vote	Popular Vote
Abraham Lincoln (IL)	National Union	212	2,206,938
George McClellan (NY)	Democratic	21	1,803,787

About the Election: Abraham Lincoln was not certain that he would win his party's nomination for reelection. Radical Republicans mocked Lincoln for what they saw as his extreme caution in executing the war, as well as for his lenient attitude towards the rebels. But moderate Republicans remained loyal to the president, and he was unanimously nominated for president.

While the Democratic Party's platform stated that the war was hopeless, and pledged to bring an immediate end to it, their nominee, former Army of the Potomac Commander George McClellan, argued against his party's vows. McClellan also declared that the emancipation of enslaved African Americans was not one of the goals of the war. For much of the campaign, McClellan seemed to have an edge over Lincoln until Union victories turned the tide of the election. Lincoln won a clear majority of both popular and electoral votes. McClellan won only three states: Kentucky, Delaware, and New Jersey.

■ **Lincoln** (212 Votes)
■ **McClellan**

Cabinet that he plans to free the slaves in the Confederacy. However, following Secretary of State William Seward's advice, Lincoln decides to wait until after a Union victory to publically announce the **EMANCIPATION PROCLAMATION**.

September 17, 1862: The Union defeats Confederate forces in one of the bloodiest days of the Civil War—the **BATTLE OF ANTIETAM** in Maryland. Lee's army retreats back into Virginia. Lincoln orders General McClellan to pursue and "destroy the rebel army if possible", but the cautious general fails to do so.

September 22, 1862: With the recent Union victory at Antietam, President Lincoln announces that on January 1, 1863 his Emancipation Proclamation will be in effect. Rebellious states are given 100 days to rejoin the Union, after which they would not necessarily lose ownership of their slaves.

November 1862: In the **MIDTERM CONGRESSIONAL ELECTIONS**, the Republican Party maintains control of both houses of Congress.

January 1, 1863: The Emancipation Proclamation goes into effect, freeing slaves in rebel areas.

February 24, 1863: New Mexico Territory is divided, with the western portion becoming the **TERRITORY OF ARIZONA**.

February 25, 1863: The **NATIONAL BANK ACT** is passed, and its main objective is to promote the sale of war bonds. It also establishes a national paper currency.

March 3, 1863: Congress passes a military draft law, but inserts a provision that allows draftees to avoid military service by hiring "substitutes" for $300.

March 3, 1863: Lincoln approves the establishment of the National Academy of Sciences.

At Shiloh in April 1862, Confederates surprised Union forces under Ulysses S. Grant (on horseback, right). Despite high casualties, the Union line held.

1839
The First Opium War begins in China.

1846
The U.S.-Mexican War begins.

1846
Lincoln is elected to the House of Representatives, where he speaks out against the U.S.-Mexican War.

1848
With the defeat of its troops, the Mexican government signs the Treaty of Guadalupe Hidalgo on February 2, ending the U.S.-Mexican War.

1850
Lincoln's son Eddie dies at the age of three.

Lincoln's Second Administration

Inauguration: March 4, 1865 at the Capitol, Washington, D.C.
Vice President: Andrew Johnson
Secretary of State: William H. Seward
Secretary of the Treasury: Hugh McCulloch
Secretary of War: Edwin M. Stanton
Attorney General: James Speed

Postmaster General: William Dennison
Secretary of the Navy: Gideon Welles
Secretary of the Interior: John P. Usher
39th Congress
(March 4, 1865-March 4, 1867)
Senate: 42 Unionists; 10 Democrats
House: 149 Unionists; 42 Democrats

March 3, 1863: Lincoln signs the Judiciary Act of 1863 that increases the number of Supreme Court justice appointments from nine to ten.

May 1-4, 1863: In one of his greatest victories, Robert E. Lee leads Confederate troops over a Union force under Joseph Hooker at the **BATTLE OF CHANCELLORSVILLE.** Lee seizes the initiative from Hooker when he orders Stonewall Jackson to take 26,000 men 16 miles to attack Hooker's right flank. Jackson's maneuver forces Hooker into retreat and inflicts heavy casualties on the federal force. Jackson is accidentally shot by his own troops during the battle, and his left arm is amputated. He dies from pneumonia on May 10.

May 3, 1863: IDAHO TERRITORY is established, and later becomes the states of Idaho, Montana and Wyoming.

June 20, 1863: WEST VIRGINIA JOINS THE UNION as the thirty-fifth state.

July 1-5, 1863: Following the victory at Chancellorsville, Jefferson Davis and Lee decide to launch an invasion with 75,000 men deep into Northern territory, in order to provoke anti-war sentiment among Northerners who are beginning to have doubts about the cost of the war. The **BATTLE OF GETTYSBURG** begins after Confederate troops advance into Pennsylvania, and Union General George Meade moves his army into place to block Lee's path. On July 1, Confederate forces under A.P. Hill meet Union advance scouts under John Buford in the small town of Gettysburg, Pennsylvania. In this first engagement, the Union scouts are driven back until Meade's main force reaches Gettysburg. The following day, Lee orders a massive attack against the Union lines, and the Confederates almost take the unprotected high ground at Little Round Top. On July 3, Lee commits his greatest mistake: he orders his 15,000-man infantry, led by George Pickett, to charge a half-mile across an open field. **PICKETT'S CHARGE** is a disaster. The following day, Lee's forces begin their long retreat back to

Virginia. Although Meade pursues them, he fails to destroy Lee's weakened army. Over the course of the bloody engagement, the Confederate Army has suffered nearly 30,000 casualties, and the Union, 23,000. For the rest of the war, Lee is outnumbered and forced to fight a defensive battle.

April–July, 1863: During a long siege, UNION GENERAL ULYSSES S. GRANT chokes off all supplies from Vicksburg, Mississippi, the important Confederate fort on the Mississippi River. Grant's strategy, which includes blocking food from reaching the city, eventually starves the Confederate forces holding the city. On July 4, Confederate General John Pemberton surrenders Vicksburg. Grant's aggressive approach in the **SEIGE OF VICKSBURG** impresses Lincoln greatly, and the president appoints him as his lieutenant general.

July 13, 1863: In the NEW YORK DRAFT RIOTS, angry working-

Photographer Timothy O'Sullivan took this photograph of Confederate dead— killed on July 1, at Gettysburg.

	1854	1855	1857	1858
■ Lincoln's Life				
■ U.S. & World Events	Lincoln gains national attention with a speech in Peoria, Illinois, denouncing slavery.	He runs for the Senate for the first time, but fails to win his party's nomination.	The Dred Scott Decision invalidates the Missouri Compromise.	Although he loses once again, Lincoln becomes a national figure during his second race for the U.S. Senate.

class New Yorkers, many of them Irish immigrants, riot in protest over the military draft. They are especially enraged by the provision that allows wealthier Americans to buy their way out of the service by paying a replacement $300 to serve in their stead. Nonetheless, the rioters take their anger out on African Americans, and several lynchings and beatings occurred. A black orphanage is looted and burned, and more than 200 children are forced to escape out the rear of the building. As many as 100 innocent bystanders, many of them African American, are murdered by the mobs. The riots do not end until President Lincoln sends in federal units returning from Gettysburg.

November 19, 1863: During a dedication ceremony for a new national cemetery at Gettysburg, Lincoln delivers his famous GETTYSBURG ADDRESS.

December 8, 1863: LINCOLN OFFERS PARDONS to Southerners who take oaths of loyalty to the Union. However, pardons are not offered to members of the Confederate government; former U.S. judges who left their posts to aid the Confederacy; members of the Confederate military with ranks higher than Army colonel or Navy lieutenant; members of the U.S. Congress who left their posts to serve the Confederacy; members of the U.S. Armed forces who resigned their commissions to serve in the Confederacy; or any person who treated African American prisoners of war or their white officers unlawfully. Few Southerners take advantage of the offer.

May 7-20, 1864: In one of the fiercest prolonged campaigns of the war, Lee and Grant battle to a bloody draw after two weeks of fighting at SPOTSLVANIA, Virginia.

June 7, 1864: The REPUBLICAN PARTY NOMINATES LINCOLN for a second term. Senator Andrew Johnson of Tennessee, a Democrat, is nominated as his vice president. Johnson is the only congressman from a rebel state to remain loyal to the Union. The Republican Party campaigns for a constitutional amendment abolishing slavery.

June 28, 1864: The Fugitive Slave Act of 1850 is repealed.

August 29, 1864: The DEMOCRATS NOMINATE GENERAL GEORGE MCCLELLAN, the former Union commander, as its nominee for president. Although McClellan himself is opposed to "peace at any cost," the Democratic platform describes the war effort a failure and calls for a ceasefire and peace conference.

September 1-2, 1864: When the Confederate Army evacuates the city, UNION GENERAL WILLIAM TECUMSEH SHERMAN CAPTURES ATLANTA. Beginning a campaign of "total war," he burns the city to the ground.

October 31, 1864: NEVADA IS ADMITTED to the Union.

November 8, 1864: Despite McClellan's peace platform, Union victories at Mobile, Alabama and Atlanta help turn the tide in Lincoln's favor by election day. LINCOLN IS REELECTED president, and the Republican Party increases its majority in both houses of Congress.

November 16, 1864: Leaving Atlanta, 62,000 troops under Sherman's command begin a 300-mile MARCH TO THE SEA. Cutting a swath of destruction from Atlanta to Savannah before turning north toward South Carolina, they destroy all supplies and facilities that are of any use to the Confederacy, including factories, cotton gins, warehouses, bridges, railroads and many public buildings.

January 31, 1865: With Lincoln's support, the House of Representatives approves the THIRTEENTH AMENDMENT, which calls for the end to slavery in all territories and states. By December 1865, the amendment is ratified by a two-thirds majority of the states and becomes law.

March 13, 1865: The CONFEDERACY RECRUITS SLAVES into the military as a last-ditch effort to obtain additional manpower for the war effort. The Confederate Congress offers slaves their freedom in return for voluntary service in the military.

March 3, 1865: CONGRESS CREATES THE FREEDMEN'S BUREAU to help freed African Americans in the South. The Bureau supplies blacks with food, clothing and medical care. In time, it also gives abandoned land to freed blacks.

Lincoln's Second Term
March 4–April 15, 1865

March 4, 1865: ABRAHAM LINCOLN IS INAUGURATED for a second term as president. With the Civil War reaching its end, Lincoln adopts a conciliatory approach to Reconstruction, and this is expressed in his inaugural address. The president calls for peace and ending the divisions that have torn apart the nation.

April 2, 1865: The Confederate government evacuates its capital, Richmond, Virginia.

April 9, 1865: After superior Union forces capture General Lee's army and essential Confederate supplies at Appomattox Courthouse in Virginia, LEE SURRENDERS TO GRANT.

April 14, 1865: Actor and Confederate sympathizer JOHN WILKES BOOTH SHOOTS LINCOLN at Ford's Theater in Washington, D.C., at approximately 10:15 p.m.

April 15, 1865: ABRAHAM LINCOLN DIES at 7:22 a.m. in the home of William Petersen. Vice President Andrew Johnson is sworn in as the seventeenth president of the United States.

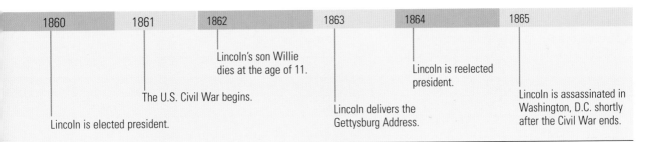

1860	1861	1862	1863	1864	1865

Lincoln's son Willie dies at the age of 11.

The U.S. Civil War begins.

Lincoln is reelected president.

Lincoln delivers the Gettysburg Address.

Lincoln is assassinated in Washington, D.C. shortly after the Civil War ends.

Lincoln is elected president.

Andrew Johnson

"Our government sprang from and was made for the people—not the people for the government. To them it owes an allegiance; from them it must derive its courage, strength, and wisdom."

Andrew Johnson was a hard-drinking, racist, self-made man from Tennessee who was snatched from obscurity by Abraham Lincoln only to become the first president in American history to be impeached. At the outbreak of the Civil War, Johnson found himself in a precarious position: he opposed the anti-slavery Republican Party, but also condemned secessionists as traitors. Because Johnson had been the only Southerner senator to remain loyal to the Union during the Civil War, Lincoln chose him as his running mate when he ran for reelection in 1864. This choice was a show of unity on Lincoln's part, who recognized that healing the wounds that had torn the nation apart would be the chief task of his second term.

Johnson's unpreparedness for the role was clear from the start. Upon Lincoln's death, only six weeks after inauguration, Johnson found himself without a party and without any powers. From the outset, Johnson's actions brought him into conflict with Radical Republicans in Congress, who saw Johnson as an inept leader too lenient with Southerners. Believing that Reconstruction was the responsibility of the executive, Johnson issued a series of proclamations, putting into effect Lincoln's Reconstruction policies. Republicans in Congress, however, were determined to punish Southern whites and to grant newly freed African Americans full rights of citizenship, including the right to vote. Johnson vetoed Congressional Reconstruction bills only to have Congress quickly override his vetoes. Another bill passed by Congress, which Johnson failed to defeat, was the Tenure of Office Act, which required Senate approval before the president could replace Cabinet members.

Throughout his presidency, the Radical Republicans in Congress continued to seize power from the executive office. When Johnson violated the Tenure of Office Act by firing Secretary of War Edwin Stanton, the Congressional trap was set. Impeached by the House, Johnson managed to survive conviction and removal from office by a single vote in the Senate. His acquital saved the office of the presidency, ensuring that political opposition in Congress was not enough to remove a president from office. After his term in office, Johnson remained active in politics. In 1875, Johnson was elected to the Senate and thus became the only former president to serve as a senator.

Biographical Facts

Born: December 29, 1808 in Raleigh, North Carolina
Ancestry: Scotch-Irish and English
Father: Jacob Johnson; born April 17, 1778 in South of Neuse River, North Carolina; died January 11, 1812 in Raleigh, North Carolina
Father's Occupations: Handyman and sexton
Mother: Mary McDonough Johnson; born July 17, 1782 in North Carolina; died February 13, 1856 in Greene County, Tennessee
Wife: Eliza McCardle; born October 4, 1810 in Leesburg, Tennessee; died January 15, 1876 in Greene County, Tennessee
Marriage: December 17, 1827 in Greenville, Tennessee
Children: Martha (1828-1901); Charles (1830-1863); Mary (1832-1883); Robert (1834-1869); Andrew (1852-1879)
Home: Greenville, Tennessee
Education: Self-taught and tutored by wife

Religious Affiliation: None
Occupations before Presidency: Tailor; legislator
Political Offices before Presidency: Alderman; Mayor; Member of Tennessee Legislature; Member of U.S. House of Representatives; Governor of Tennessee; Member of U.S. Senate; U.S. Vice President
Political Party: Democratic
Age at Inauguration: 56
Occupation after the Presidency: U.S. Senator
Death: July 31, 1875 in Carter County, Tennessee
Place of Burial: Andrew Johnson National Cemetery, Greenville, Tennessee
Nickname: Tennessee Tailor
Writings: *Papers of Andrew Johnson*

Johnson's Term 1865-1869

April 15, 1865: Following Abraham Lincoln's death, six weeks after inauguration, **JOHNSON TAKES THE OATH OF OFFICE.** He was the first vice president to succeed to the office upon the assassination of a president.

April 18, 1865: Union General William Tecumseh Sherman accepts the surrender of 37,000 men under the Confederate General Joseph E. Johnston. Sherman offers Johnston lenient terms, including some that have not been authorized by President Johnson. After the president demands that Sherman's terms be revised, General Johnston surrenders a second time.

May 26, 1865: General Edmund Kirby Smith, Commander of the Trans-Mississippi Department, surrenders at New Orleans, Louisiana to Major General E.S Canby. His unit is the last major Confederate unit to surrender.

May 29, 1865: **JOHNSON GRANTS AMNESTY** to all white Southerners who take an oath of loyalty to the Union. He allows those taking the oath to reclaim their property, excluding only senior Confederate officials or owners of large estates worth more than $20,000. Johnson also proposes appointing a provisional governor for former Confederate states who will condemn secession, oversee the end of slavery in that state, and usher through a new state constitution. According to Johnson's plan, once these conditions are met by a state, it will be accepted back into the Union.

December 2, 1865: Mississippi passes a series of **BLACK CODES** to deprive newly freed African Americans of their rights. The laws forbid an employed African American from leaving his job, or renting and owning land.Soon thereafter, other former Confederate states follow Mississippi's example.

December 4, 1865: In his **FIRST ANNUAL MESSAGE TO CONGRESS**, Johnson announces that the Union has been restored.

December 12, 1865: President Johnson begins to order that provisional governors of Confederate states turn over their offices to newly elected governors, many of which are former Confederate officials.

December 14, 1865: Congress reconvenes and creates a joint committee on Reconstruction. Congress refuses to accept Southern representatives and congressmen from restored states.

December 18, 1865: The **THIRTEENTH AMENDMENT**, ending slavery, goes into effect after it is ratified by 27 states.

February 12, 1866: **SECRETARY OF STATE WILLIAM H. SEWARD** demands that France withdraw from Mexico and sends General Philip Sheridan and 50,000 troops to the Mexican border. In 1863, France had installed the Austrian **ARCHDUKE MAXIMILIAN** as Emperor of Mexico. France eventually agrees to comply and withdraws its forces in the spring of 1867.

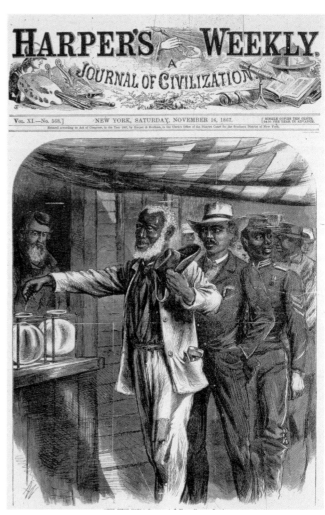

"Harpers Weekly" reports on African Americans casting their first votes.

	1801	1804	1812-14	1827
■ Johnson's Life				
	Thomas Jefferson is inaugurated as the third U.S. president.	New Jersey becomes the last Northern state to abolish slavery.		Johnson opens his own tailor shop in Greeneville, Tennessee, and marries Eliza McCardle.
■ U.S. & World Events	Andrew Johnson is born on December 29 in Raleigh, North Carolina.		The War of 1812 is fought.	

First Lady: Eliza McCardle Johnson

Eliza McCardle, daughter of a Scottish shoemaker, has the distinction of having taught her husband, Andrew Johnson, how to read, write, and do arithmetic. The couple wed as teenagers and lived on his tailor's income in Greenville, Tennessee. While her husband focused on his political career, she raised their five children: Martha, Charles, Mary, Robert, and Andrew.

After Lincoln's assassination, the White House became a hub for Johnson's large family, including daughter Martha and her husband, Senator David T. Patterson. Mrs. Johnson, an invalid for many years, rarely left her room, and Martha Patterson served graciously as official hostess, even during her father's impeachment proceedings.

February 19, 1866: Congress passes a bill to increase the power of the **FREEDMEN'S BUREAU** to include holding military trials for anyone found depriving African Americans of their civil rights. **JOHNSON VETOES THE FREEDMAN'S BUREAU RENEWAL BILL** on constitutional grounds.

February 22, 1866: Johnson condemns Representative

Thaddeus Stevens, Senator Charles Sumner, and reformer Wendell Phillips—the most visible members of the so-called **RADICAL REPUBLICANS**—as traitors.

March 27, 1866: Johnson vetoes the bill for the **CIVIL RIGHTS ACT OF 1866**, which grants citizenship to freed African Americans. The act bestows full citizenship rights to all persons born in the United States except for the untaxed Native Americans. The Civil Rights Act leads to the drafting of the Fourteen Amendment.

April 6, 1866: The Senate overrides Johnson's veto of the Civil Rights Act of 1866. Shortly thereafter, the House does the same.

June 1-3, 1866: The **FENIAN BROTHERHOOD**, a secret Irish-American faction of the Irish Republican Army (IRA), cross the Niagara River into Canada with the goal of capturing Canada and using it as a bargaining tool in negotiations for Irish independence. After they capture Fort Erie, the Fenians clash with Canadian militiamen at the Battle of Limestone Ridge. The Canadians force them to retreat back into New York. By this time, Johnson has declared that neutrality laws will be enforced.

June 13, 1866: Despite opposition from Johnson and most Southern representatives, Congress passes the **FOURTEENTH AMENDMENT** and sends it to the states for ratification. The amendment defines citizenship for the first time, explicitly declaring African Americans as legal citizens. It offers federal protection to African Americans against state or local laws that deny their rights, and repeals the three-fifths clause of the Constitution, which had counted a slave as three-fifths of a person in census counts. When the amendmentis ratified in July 1868, each African American is counted as a full person. As a result, Southern states gain 12 seats in the House.

June 20, 1866: A Radical Republican committee, known as the **JOINT COMMITTEE OF FIFTEEN**, declares that former Confederate states should not be entitled to representation in Congress. In addition, it also states that Congress will determine the Reconstruction policy, not President Johnson.

July 1866: Three Radical Republican members of

Johnson's Administration

Inauguration: April 15, 1865 at Kirkwood House, Washington, D.C.
Vice President: None
Secretary of State: William H. Seward
Secretary of the Treasury: Hugh McCulloch
Secretary of War: Edwin M. Stanton; John M. Schofield (from June 1, 1868)
Attorney General: James Speed; Henry Stanberry (from July, 1866); William M. Evarts (from July 20, 1868)
Postmaster General: William Dennison; Alexander W. Randall (from July, 1866)

Secretary of the Navy: Gideon Welles
Secretary of the Interior: James Harlan; Orville H. Browning (from September 1, 1866)
39th Congress
(March 4, 1865-March 4, 1867)
Senate: 42 Republicans; 10 Democrats
House: 149 Republicans; 42 Democrats
40th Congress
(March 4, 1867-March 4, 1869)
Senate: 42 Republicans; 11 Democrats
House: 143 Republicans; 49 Democrats
State Admitted: Nebraska (1867)

1831	1835	1834	1855
Johnson is elected mayor of Greenville, Tennessee.	Nat Turner leads a major slave uprising in Virginia.	Johnson is elected to the state legislature for the first time.	Johnson is elected to Congress.	A wave of republican and democratic uprisings take place throughout Europe.

Quotes by Johnson:

"I voted against him; I spoke against him; I spent my money to defeat him; but still I love my country; I love the Constitution; I intend to insist upon its guarantees."
—about Abraham Lincoln after he is elected president

"Of all the dangers which our nation has yet encountered, none are equal to those which must result from success of the current effort to Africanize the southern half of the country."
—commenting on proposals to grant blacks the right to vote

"Personal Freedom, property and life, if assailed by the passion, the prejudice, or the rapacity of the ruler, have no security whatsoever."
—Third annual message to congress - December 3, 1867.

"It's a damn poor mind that can only think of one way to spell a word."

Quote about Johnson:

"He is surrounded, hampered, tangled in the meshes of his own wickedness. Unfortunate, unhappy man, behold your doom!"
— Congressman Thaddeus Stevens, during Impeachment proceedings

JOHNSON'S CABINET RESIGNS: Postmaster General William Dennison, Attorney General James Speed, and Secretary of the Interior James Harlan. President Johnson replaces them with moderate Republicans.

July 16, 1866: Congress overrides President Johnson's veto of the Freedmen's Bureau Renewal Bill.

July 24, 1866: Congress **READMITS TENNESSEE TO THE UNION** after its Republican-controlled government ratifies the Fourteenth Amendment.

July 30, 1866: **RACE RIOTS** break out in New Orleans. White mobs, encouraged and aided by city police, murder dozens of blacks and pro-Union whites in New Orleans. Many Northerners believe the incident is an outcome of Johnson's lenient policies towards the South.

August 14, 1866: Queen Emma of the Sandwich Islands (present-day Hawaii) arrives in New York City and is officially received by Johnson; he is the first president to be visited by a queen.

August 28, 1866: In a failed attempt to prevent Radical-Republican gains in upcoming Congressional elections, Johnson begins a poorly-received campaign tour of the East and Midwest.

November 1866: In the midterm elections, Radical Republicans win sweeping victories across the North, gaining wide majorities in both houses of Congress.

December 3, 1866: In his second annual message, Johnson requests Congress to recognize restored states and to allow their representatives to occupy their seats in the House.

March 1, 1867: **NEBRASKA JOINS THE UNION** as the 37th state.

March 2, 1867: Overriding Johnson's veto, Congress passes the **FIRST RECONSTRUCTION ACT**, dividing the South into five military districts to be overseen by a military commander. Congress also passes the **ARMY APPROPRIATIONS ACT**, requiring the president to transmit his orders to the military through the commanding general of the Army in Washington. In addition to this, Congress also passes the **TENURE OF OFFICE ACT**, forbidding Johnson from firing Cabinet officers without Senate's approval.

March 23, 1867: Congress overrides Johnson's veto of the **SECOND RECONSTRUCTION ACT**. The act authorizes military commanders to call elections in the South for the purpose of electing delegates to new constitutional conventions. Congress intends for these new state governments to guarantee African American males suffrage and to ratify the Fourteenth Amendment.

March 30, 1867: Secretary of State William H. Seward agrees to purchase Alaska from Russia for $7.2 million. Critics of the purchase refer to Alaska as "**SEWARD'S FOLLY.**"

July 19, 1867: Congress overrides Johnson's veto of the **THIRD RECONSTRUCTION ACT**, which sets up voting rules in the South and specifically authorizes military commanders to remove any state or local official impairing the Reconstruction process

August 5, 1867: President Johnson asks **SECRETARY OF WAR EDWIN STANTON** to resign. Stanton, the sole Radical Republican in Johnson's Cabinet, refuses.

August 12, 1867: During congressional recess, **JOHNSON SUSPENDS STANTON** and replaces him with war hero **ULYSSES S. GRANT**.

August 28, 1867: The United States annexes the Midway Islands (present-day Hawaii).

September 3, 1867: President Johnson issues a proclamation that orders all civil and military officials to abide by judicial laws and decisions.

December 12, 1867: Johnson informs the Senate of his reasons for suspending Stanton.

January 13, 1868: The Senate refuses to support Johnson's removal of Stanton.

January 14, 1868: Influenced by congressional pressure, Ulysses S. Grant informs President Johnson that he will leave his temporary Cabinet post and return it to Edwin Stanton.

	1853	1855	1857	1860
■ Johnson's Life				
■ U.S. & World Events	Johnson is elected as governor of Tennessee	Walt Whitman's *Leaves of Grass* is published	Johnson enters the U.S. Senate	Johnson supports Stephen A. Douglas over Lincoln for president

February 21, 1868: Johnson fires Stanton and appoints General Lorenzo Thomas as the new secretary of war. In response, Stanton barricades himself in his office for almost two months.

February 24, 1868: The HOUSE VOTES TO IMPEACH JOHNSON for violating the Tenure of Office Act. Within two weeks, the House appoints seven managers to argue for Johnson's removal from office in front of the Senate.

May 16, 1868: The SENATE FALLS ONE VOTE SHORT OF CONVICTING JOHNSON after Senator James Grimes of Iowa votes in favor of the president.

May 20-21, 1868: REPUBLICANS NOMINATE ULYSSES S. GRANT for president.

May 26, 1868: The Senate votes to acquit President Johnson.

June 22-25, 1868: Congress overrides Johnson's vetoes of bills to readmit seven former Confederate states to the Union.

June 25, 1868: Congress passes an act that sets an eight-hour workday for laborers and mechanics who are employed by the federal government.

July 4, 1868: DEMOCRATS NOMINATE HORATIO SEYMOUR, governor of New York, for president.

July 4, 1868: Johnson grants full pardon to all former Confederates except for those accused of treason or felony.

July 9, 1868: Johnson submits the BURLINGAME TREATY between the U.S. and China to the Senate for approval. The treaty grants Chinese the right to unrestricted immigration to the U.S., in order to ensure that a steady supply of cheap labor is available to complete the Transcontinental Railroad—the Union Pacific Railroad's section of the railway.

July 28, 1868: The FOURTEENTH AMENDMENT to the Constitution is adopted, which is comprised of: Rights Guaranteed Privileges and Immunities of Citizenship, Due Process and Equal Protection

October 10, 1868: Johnson issues an order to the army calling for noninterference in any general or local election.

November 3, 1868: GRANT IS ELECTED PRESIDENT after winning roughly 450,000 votes from African Americans. He receives 300,000 more votes than Seymour.

Andrew Johnson takes the oath of office from Chief Justice Salmon P. Chase in the parlor of Kirkwood House in Washington, D.C. after Abraham Lincoln is assassinated by Charles Wilkes Booth.

1861
The Civil War begins and lasts until 1865.

1862
With Union forces in control of central Tennessee, Lincoln appoints Johnson as military governor of Tennessee.

1864
Johnson is elected vice president after Lincoln chooses him as his running mate on a National Unity Party ticket.

1865
Abraham Lincoln is assassinated by Charles Wilkes Booth. Vice President Johnson becomes president.

1875
Johnson suffers a paralytic stroke and dies on July 31 in Carter County, Tennessee.

Ulysses S. Grant

18th President (1869–1877)

"I shall have no policy of my own to interfere against the will of the people."

When the U.S. Civil War began in 1861, Ulysses S. Grant was scraping by as a clerk in his family's Illinois leather shop. No one would have imagined that by the end of the decade, he would be hailed as a national hero, much less become president of the United States.

Grant, a graduate of West Point who had served in the U.S.-Mexican War, had resigned his commission in 1854. After failed attempts at farming and selling real estate, he was eager to find a job in which he could be successful. When civil war erupted, he hoped to receive a new commission in the U.S. Army, but had to settle for command of a regiment of Illinois volunteers. But Grant proved his commanding skills when his men captured Forts Henry and Donelson. Although losses at Shiloh drew harsh criticism, Lincoln defended him, claiming that Grant could not be spared. With Grant's victories at Vicksburgh and Chattanooga, Lincoln promoted him to Lieutenant General in March 1864, giving him command of the Union Army. By the time Grant accepted Robert E. Lee's surrender at Appomattox Courthouse in Virginia, he was one of the most admired men in the nation.

Despite his complete lack of political experience, Grant's popularity made him the obvious choice for the Republican nomination in 1868. He effortlessly defeated former New York governor Horatio Seymour, who had criticized him during the Civil War and supported a negotiated peace with the Confederacy. Unfortunately, Grant's success as a military leader did not extend to his role as president. Although he was scrupulously honest, the selection of former military friends and politicians ultimately resulted in a Cabinet consisting of members who proved to be inept and unqualified.

Grant's administration was among the most corrupt in American history. His political inexperience nearly allowed speculators Jay Gould and James Fisk to corner the gold market. Both of his vice presidents, his secretary of treasury, and even his personal secretary were all implicated in major scandals. However, these scandals were not exposed until his second term, and Grant, still the popular war hero, won an overwhelming victory in his bid for reelection in 1872.

During his two terms as president, the Senate achieved its peak of power, a trend that began after the Civil War. Congress, and not the president, would take the lead in running the country. For much of the remaining 19th century, this pattern continued as the country elected weak presidents who only served single terms.

Biographical Facts

Born: April 27, 1822 in Point Pleasant, Ohio

Ancestry: English-Scotch

Father: Jesse Root Grant; born January 23, 1794 in Westmoreland County, Pennsylvania; died June 29, 1873 in Covington, Kentucky,

Father's Occupation: Leather tanner

Mother: Hannah Simpson Grant; born November 23, 1798 in Montgomery County, Pennsylvania; died May 11, 1883 in Jersey City, New Jersey

Wife: Julia Boggs Dent; born January, 26, 1826 in St. Louis, Missouri; died December 14, 1902 in Washington D. C.

Marriage: August 22, 1848 in St. Louis, Missouri

Children: Frederick Dent (1850-1912); Ulysses Simpson (1852-1929); Ellen Wrenshall (1855-1922); Jesse Root (1858-1934)

Education: Local schools; U.S. Military Academy, West Point (1843)

Religious Affiliation: Methodist

Occupations before Presidency: Soldier; farmer; real estate agent; custom house clerk; leather store clerk

Military Service: Second Lieutenant in 4th U.S. Infantry; Captain in 4th Infantry; Brigadier General; General in Chief of Union Army

Political Offices before Presidency: None

Political Party: Republican

Age at Inauguration: 46

Occupations after Presidency: Businessman; writer

Death: July 23, 1885 in Mount McGregor, New York

Place of Burial: Grant's Tomb, New York.

Nickname: Hero of Appomattox; Unconditional Surrender

Writings: *Personal Memoirs; Papers*

Election of 1868

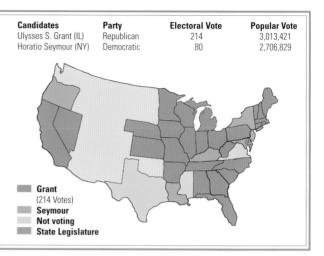

Candidates	Party	Electoral Vote	Popular Vote
Ulysses S. Grant (IL)	Republican	214	3,013,421
Horatio Seymour (NY)	Democratic	80	2,706,829

About the Election: Prior to the 1868 election, Grant allied himself with the Radical faction of the Republican Party. As the most famous hero of the Civil War, Grant became the obvious choice for the Republican nomination. The Democrats chose Horatio Seymour of New York, who ran on an anti-Reconstruction platform, arguing that voting rights for African Americans should be decided on a state-by-state basis.

Despite Grant's popularity, the popular vote was close. If not for African American votes in the South, Grant would have lost the popular vote. Votes from Texas, Mississippi, and Virginia were not counted since those three former Confederate states had not yet been readmitted to the Union.

- **Grant** (214 Votes)
- **Seymour**
- **Not voting**
- **State Legislature**

Grant's First Term 1869-1873

March 4, 1869: ULYSSES S. GRANT IS INAUGURATED as the 18th president of the United States.

March 18, 1869: Upon taking office, Grant backs a return to "hard money," or money backed by gold. Supporters in Congress help pass the **PUBLIC CREDIT ACT**, which requires that the government pay its debts in gold. Prior to this, the Treasury Department circulated paper money, or "Greenbacks," which were first issued during the start of the Civil War in 1861.

May 10, 1869: The first **TRANSCONTINENTAL RAILROAD IS COMPLETED** as the eastbound Union Pacific and the westbound Central Pacific meet at Promontory Summit in Utah.

September 24, 1869: On a day known as **BLACK FRIDAY,** the U.S. gold market collapses. Investors Jay Gould and James Fisk had planned to corner the gold market by buying large quantities of gold and selling everything at a greater profit. They conspired with Abel Rathbone Corbin, Grant's brother-in-law, who pledged to prevent Grant from selling government-owned gold. However, acting on public sentiment, Grant orders the immediate sale of $4 million in government gold, and its value on the market plunges, ruining thousands of investors.

November 29, 1869: Grant's private secretary, Orville Babcock, signs a **TREATY TO ANNEX SANTO DOMINGO** (present-day Dominican Republic). The following summer, the Senate rejects the annexation plan.

December 6, 1869: In his annual message to Congress, Grant calls for speedy action to stabilize the currency.

January 26, 1870: VIRGINIA IS READMITTED to the Union.

February 3, 1870: The **FIFTEENTH AMENDMENT**, granting African American men the right to vote, is ratified with President Grant's support.

February 23, 1870: MISSISSIPPI IS READMITTED to the Union.

March 30, 1870: TEXAS IS READMITTED to the Union.

May 24, 1870: Grant condemns the **FENIAN BROTHERHOOD**, the radical Irish-American nationalist group that has launched invasions of Canada in order to pressure Great Britain to grant Ireland independence. The next day, on May 25, the Fenians

A cartoon showing Grant "tanning the hides" of Confederate Generals. His opponents, Horatio Seymour and Frank Blair are next in line. The man wearing the headdress represents William 'Boss' Tweed of Tammany Hall in New York.

	1822	1825	1838	1839-42
■ Grant's Life		Tea from China is first introduced in Europe.	Thousands of Cherokee are forced to walk the "Trail of Tears" from the southeast to Indian Territory in present day Oklahoma. Many die	Grant attends West Point. When he arrives there, he finds that he is mistakenly enrolled as Ulysses Simpson Grant. He drops Hiram from
■ U.S. & World Events		Hiram Ulysses Grant is born on April 22 in Point Pleasant, Ohio.	during the journey of exhaustion, starvation and exposure.	his name.

First Lady: Julia Dent Grant

Julia Dent loved outdoor acitivities such as fishing and horseback riding. The daughter of a Southern plantation owner, she enjoyed the relaxed summers at home in between the years at boarding school.

However, her marriage to Ulysses S. Grant was filled with adversity and hardship. Her husband's military service made for difficult living conditions and a business failure near the end of his life caused the couple financial ruin.

Mrs. Grant later described her years as First Lady as "the happiest period" of her life, marked by high popularity and lavish entertaining. After her husband's death, her widow's pension, coupled with money from the sale of Grant's personal memoirs enabled her to live comfortably until her death.

interfere with the right to vote. The law is aimed at protecting the rights of African American men.

June 22, 1870: Congress creates the **DEPARTMENT OF JUSTICE** in order to accomodate the increasing responsibilities of the attorney general. The new attorney general, Amos T. Akerman, begins his office as head of the department two weeks later.

July 14, 1870: Grant expands the interpretation of the Monroe Doctrine, stating that a European power may not transfer its territory in the western hemisphere to another European power. This leaves former Spanish territory Santo Domingo free for American rule.

July 15, 1870: GEORGIA IS READMITTED to the Union.

December 5, 1870: In his second annual message to Congress, Grant emphasizes the importance of the Santo Domingo issue and relations with Spain and England. He also calls for civil service reform. Congress convenes with the representatives of all states present for the first time since 1860.

February 28, 1871: A second enforcement act, known as the **FEDERAL ELECTION LAW**, is passed in Congress. The new law orders that elections in all cities with populations greater than 20,000 be federally supervised. The law is aimed to protect African American voting rights.

March 3, 1871: NATIVE AMERICANS ARE DECLARED WARDS OF THE STATE after Congress decides to no longer recognize their tribes as legitimate powers. This ends the negotiation of treaties with Native Americans. Instead, all Native Americans are to be managed as the U.S. government sees fit.

invade Canada again, but are quickly defeated.

May 31, 1870: With Grant's urging, Congress passes the **FIRST ENFORCEMENT ACT**, which makes it a federal crime to

March 4, 1871: Grant appoints George William Curtis to lead the first **CIVIL SERVICE COMMISSION**, which is aimed at reforming the corrupt civil service. But Congress refuses to comply, forcing Curtis to resign.

May 8, 1871: United States signs the **TREATY OF WASHINGTON** with Great Britain. The treaty settles differences over damages inflicted on Union shipping by British-built Confederate cruisers, such as the *Alabama*. Disputes over fishing rights in

Grant's First Administration

Inauguration: March 4, 1869 at the Capitol, Washington, D.C.
Vice President: Schuyler Colfax
Secretary of State: Elihu B. Washburne; Hamilton Fish (from March 17, 1869)
Secretary of the Treasury: George S. Boutwell
Secretary of War: John A. Rawlins; William T. Sherman (from September 11, 1869); William W. Belknap (from November 1, 1869)
Attorney General: Ebenezer R. Hoar; Amos T. Akerman (from July 8, 1870); George H. Williams (from January 10, 1872)
Postmaster General: John A. J. Creswell
Secretary of the Navy: Adolph E. Borie; George M. Robeson (from June 25, 1869)

Secretary of the Interior: Jacob D. Cox; Columbus Delano (from November 1, 1870)
Supreme Court Appointments:
William Strong (1870); Joseph P. Bradley (1870); Ward Hunt (1872)
41st Congress
(March 4, 1869-March 4, 1871)
Senate: 56 Republicans; 11 Democrats
House: 149 Republicans; 63 Democrats
42nd Congress
(March 4, 1871-March 4, 1873)
Senate: 52 Republicans; 17 Democrats; 5 Others
House: 134 Republicans; 104 Democrats; 5 Others

1846-48	1847	1848	1851	1854	1858-60
Grant serves in the U.S.-Mexican War, working under both Zachary Taylor and Winfield Scott. He remains in the Army after the war.	The Mormons establish Salt Lake City.	He marries Julia Dent.	American novelist Herman Melville writes *Moby Dick*.	Grant resigns his commission and settles with his family on 80 acres of uncultivated land in Missouri. He nicknames his farm Hardscrabble.	Grant abandons farming and attempts real estate sales in St. Louis. His business fails.

the North Atlantic and access to Canadian-American waterways are also resolved. The treaty provides for an international tribunal comprising of Great Britain, Italy, Switzerland, and the U.S.

April 20, 1871: A THIRD ENFORCEMENT ACT, passed in April 1871, forbids wearing disguises, planning conspiracies, and intimidating officials. The enforcement acts, often called the KU KLUX KLAN ACTS, are specifically aimed at curbing the activities of the Ku Klux Klan, the Order of the White Camelia, and other secret racist terror groups that had sprung up throughout the South.

July 8, 1871: A *New York Times* investigation exposes the TWEED RING in which "Boss" William Marcy Tweed, head of New York City's Tammany Hall, along with his high-ranking friends, gained control of the city's spending budget. Through bribes, kickbacks, and outright theft, the group made as much as $200 million. In 1873, Tweed is convicted on 204 charges of fraud and sentenced to 12 years in prison.

March 1, 1872: Congress passes an act establishing the Yellowstone National Park in Wyoming, It is the world's first national park.

March 2, 1872: Commander Meade, of the USS *Narragansett,* is granted permission by Samoan High Chief Margua of Pago Pago to establish a naval station. The Senate fails to ratify the treaty.

March 10, 1872: Planning continues for a canal connecting the Caribbean to the Pacific Ocean and Grant names a special INTEROCEANIC CANAL COMMISSION to choose the best route across Central America. Four years later, the Commission recommends a route through Nicaragua.

May 22, 1872: Congress passes the AMNESTY ACT restoring political rights to all Southerners, except for a few former Confederate leaders.

June 5-6, 1872: The REPUBLICAN PARTY NOMINATES GRANT for reelection.

June 6, 1872: The TARIFF ACT OF 1872 is adopted, abolishing the income and excise taxes imposed during the CIVIL WAR. The act also cuts the duty on manufactured goods by ten percent.

July 9, 1872: DEMOCRATS NOMINATE HORACE GREELEY, a liberal reformer and editor of the *New York Tribune,* for president.

September 4, 1872: Vice President Schuyler Colfax, and several Republican senators and congressmen, are implicated in the CRÉDIT MOBILIER scandal. They are accused of accepting bribes in exchange for legislation that would favor the newly-created railroad construction company, the Crédit Mobilier of America. Representative Oakes Ames, head of the Credit Mobilier, had sold company stock at a nominal price to members of Congress. Ames, along with New York Representative James Brooks, are censured by Congress, but there are no prosecutions.

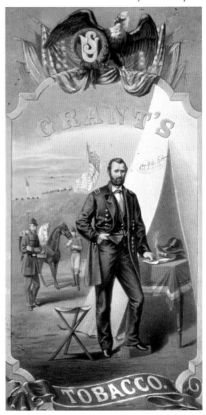

Grant, known for his heavy smoking, appears on this cigar advertisement.

	1860	1862	1863
■ Grant's Life			
■ U.S. & World Events	Grant and his family move to Galena, Illinois, where he works in his father's leather shop.	After serving in the Illinois militia the previous year, Grant gains national attention by taking key Confederate positions, Forts Henry and Donelson.	In a major victory, Grant captures Vicksburg, Mississippi. Later the same year, Lincoln names him commander of the U.S. Army.

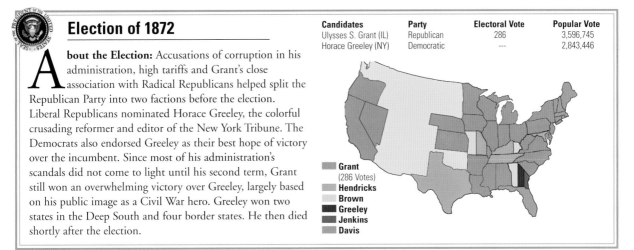

Election of 1872

About the Election: Accusations of corruption in his administration, high tariffs and Grant's close association with Radical Republicans helped split the Republican Party into two factions before the election. Liberal Republicans nominated Horace Greeley, the colorful crusading reformer and editor of the New York Tribune. The Democrats also endorsed Greeley as their best hope of victory over the incumbent. Since most of his administration's scandals did not come to light until his second term, Grant still won an overwhelming victory over Greeley, largely based on his public image as a Civil War hero. Greeley won two states in the Deep South and four border states. He then died shortly after the election.

Candidates	Party	Electoral Vote	Popular Vote
Ulysses S. Grant (IL)	Republican	286	3,596,745
Horace Greeley (NY)	Democratic	---	2,843,446

Grant (286 Votes)
Hendricks
Brown
Greeley
Jenkins
Davis

September 14, 1872: The tribunal established to settle the *Alabama* claims concludes its sessions. The commission orders Britain to pay the U.S. $15.5 million.

October 21, 1872: On the dispute over the British Columbia-Washington territory boundary, Emperor William I, as arbitrator, awards San Juan Islands to the U.S.

November 5, 1872: GRANT IS REELECTED in a landslide.

February 12, 1873: Congress passes the **COINAGE ACT,** which makes gold the only monetary standard. The act, called the **CRIME OF '73** by its critics, angers silver investors since rich silver deposits have recently been discovered in Nevada.

March 3, 1873: Congress grants salary increases of two years' retroactive pay for its members, the president, Supreme Court justices and other federal officials. It also authorizes federal postage stamps. On the same day, a bill banning the circulation of obscene literature is passed—a decision that has been urged by the **SOCIETY FOR THE SUPPRESSION OF VICE.**

Grant's Second Term 1873-1877

March 4, 1873: GRANT IS INAUGURATED for his second term.

September 18, 1873: The **PANIC OF 1873** is triggered by the failure of Jay Cooke & Company, a major banking firm and financier of the Northern Pacific Railroad. The failure causes a rippling effect in which the U.S. economy collapses. The New York Stock Exchange is closed for ten days and the Grant administration prints $26 million in paper money to stabilize the economy. The underlying causes of the crisis—industrial and agricultural overexpansion, as well as a railroad construction boom that produced massive land and stock speculation—lead to a six-year depression.

October 31, 1873: An American steamship, *VIRGINIUS,* is captured by the Spanish cruiser *Tornado* while carrying arms to Cuban revolutionaries. Fifty-three men, including eight American citizens, are executed by Spanish colonial authorities. In a conciliatory response, Spain returns the remaining American prisoners and pays damages.

January 13, 1874: The **TOMPKINS SQUARE RIOT** occurs when police charge into a demonstration of unemployed workers in New York's Tompkins Square Park, clubbing men, women, and children. The riot results in hundreds of casualties.

January 20, 1874: Due to widespread criticism, Congress repeals the pay raise it had voted for its members in the previous year. However, raises for the president, Supreme Court justices and other federal officials are left in place.

April 22, 1874: Grant vetoes a congressional bill to increase the amount of greenbacks in circulation to $400 million, arguing that the increase will only weaken the economy. On June 20, Congress adopts a new bill that increases the amount temporarily to $383 million.

September 15, 1874: Grant sends 5,000 troops and 3 gunboats to New Orleans to put down a rebellion by the **WHITE LEAGUE,** a racist organization comprised of former Confederate soldiers and New Orleans' business elite. Defeating the state militia, the White League reseizes state government offices,

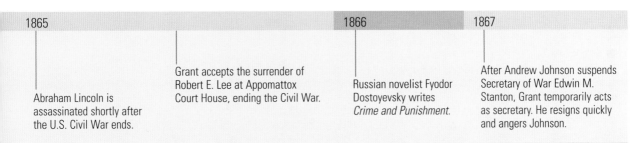

1865

Abraham Lincoln is assassinated shortly after the U.S. Civil War ends.

Grant accepts the surrender of Robert E. Lee at Appomattox Court House, ending the Civil War.

1866

Russian novelist Fyodor Dostoyevsky writes *Crime and Punishment.*

1867

After Andrew Johnson suspends Secretary of War Edwin M. Stanton, Grant temporarily acts as secretary. He resigns quickly and angers Johnson.

Grant's Second Administration

Inauguration: March 4, 1873 at the Capitol, Washington, D.C.
Vice President: Henry Wilson
Secretary of State: Hamilton Fish
Secretary of the Treasury:
William A. Richardson;
Benjamin H. Bristow (from June 4, 1874);
Lot M. Morrill (from July 7, 1876)
Secretary of War: William W. Belknap;
Alphonso Taft (from March 11, 1876);
James D. Cameron (from June 1, 1876)
Attorney General: George H. Williams;
Edwards Pierrepont (from May 15, 1875);
Alphonso Taft (from June 1, 1876)
Postmaster General: John A. J. Creswell;
James W. Marshall (from July 7, 1884);
Marshall Jewell (from September. 1, 1874);

James N. Tyner (from July 12, 1876)
Secretary of the Navy: George M. Robeson
Secretary of the Interior: Columbus Delano;
Zachariah Chandler (from October 19, 1875)
Supreme Court Appointment:
Morrison R. Waite, Chief Justice (1874)
43rd Congress: (March 4, 1873-March 4, 1875)
Senate: 49 Republicans; 19 Democrats;
5 Others
House: 194 Republicans; 92 Democrats;
14 Others
44th Congress: (March 4, 1875-March 4, 1877)
Senate: 45 Republicans; 29 Democrats;
2 Others
House: 169 Democrats; 109 Republicans;
14 Others
State Admitted: Colorado (1876)

May 10, 1875: The WHISKY RING scandal uncovers a conspiracy between U.S. Treasury officials and liquor distillers to steal millions in liquor taxes from the government. Grant's personal secretary Orville Babcock is later implicated in the scandal, but is acquitted when President Grant intervenes on his behalf.

November 22, 1875: VICE PRESIDENT HENRY WILSON DIES after suffering a stroke.

December 7, 1875: In his annual message to Congress, President Grant pushes for mandatory public education. He also calls for the separation

killing 24 black and 3 white supporters of the Republican Party in the process. When the federal troops force the White League to surrender, Grant is criticized for overreacting.

November 1874: Strengthened by anger over the many scandals involving Grant's administration, Democrats win a majority in the House of Representatives for the first time since 1857, and gain ten seats in the Senate.

January 10, 1875: The HAWAIIAN RECIPROCITY TREATY is signed, giving the United States exclusive trading rights with Hawaii. The treaty also prevents the Kingdom of Hawaii from ceding any of its territory to any other power.

January 14, 1875: With Grant's support, Congress passes the SPECIE RESUMPTION ACT, which restores the gold standard and limits the amount of paper money in circulation to $300 million. The act allows paper money to be redeemed for coin, beginning in 1879, and increases the number of national banks throughout the country.

March 1, 1875: Grant signs the CIVIL RIGHTS ACT, which guarantees equal rights for all Americans regardless of race in public places, such as inns and theaters. The new law also bans the exclusion of African Americans from juries. The law is never enforced and is declared unconstitutional in 1883.

of church and the state, elimination of polygamy, and enactment of stable currency laws.

December 15, 1875: The House overwhelmingly passes a resolution asking Grant not to seek a third term. Although Grant has already sworn off any intention to run for a third term in 1876, the issue is raised again in 1880.

April 4, 1876: Impeachment charges are brought against

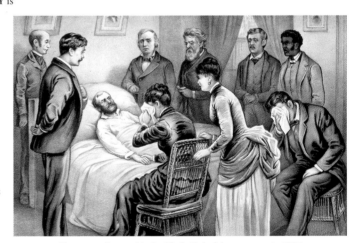

Grant, seen here on his deathbed, died of throat cancer in 1885.

	1868	1870	1872	1874
■ Grant's Life	After allying himself with the Radical Republicans, Grant wins the Republican nomination for president and then defeats Democrat Horatio Seymour to become president.		Grant defeats Horace Greeley to win reelection.	
■ U.S. & World Events		Construction of the Brooklyn Bridge begins.		The Women's Christian Temperance Union (WCTU) is established in Cleveland, Ohio.

Secretary of War **WILLIAM W. BELKNAP**. Belknap and his wife are charged with accepting bribes from businessmen seeking the rights to Native American trading posts in the West. Belknap resigns from his post, and he is acquitted of the charges.

May 10, 1876: The International Centennial Exposition commemorating the 100th anniversary of American independence is opened in Philadelphia.

May 18, 1876: The **NATIONAL GREENBACK PARTY**, formed to advocate expanded use of greenbacks, nominates New York manufacturer and philanthropist **PETER COOPER** for president. According to the party's platform, paper money backed by gold and silver only benefits the rich, while a free supply of paper money helps the working class.

June 14-16, 1876: Republicans nominate **RUTHERFORD B. HAYES** of Ohio for president.

June 25, 1876: Warriors of the Sioux and northern Cheyenne nations defeat General George A. Custer and 265 of his men at **LITTLE BIG HORN** in Montana. The battle will be commonly known as "Custer's Last Stand."

June 27-29, 1876: The Democrats nominate **SAMUEL J. TILDEN**, the governor of New York, for president. Tilden has risen to fame as a crusading reformer best known for prosecuting the Tweed Ring.

August 1, 1876: **COLORADO IS ADMITTED TO THE UNION** as the 38th state of the United States.

November 7, 1876: Tilden wins 250,000 more votes than Hayes. However, claiming that returns from Florida, Louisiana, South Carolina, and Oregon are in dispute, the Republican Party refuses to concede the election.

December 6, 1876: Two **COMPETING SETS OF ELECTORAL RETURNS** are submitted from Florida, Louisiana, South Carolina, and Oregon.

January 29, 1877: To sort out the election, Congress establishes an **ELECTORAL COMMISSION**, made up of five members from each house of Congress and five members from the Supreme Court. The Commission consists of eight Republicans and seven Democrats.

Feburary 9, 1877: Supreme Court Justice Joseph Bradley, a Republican member of the Electoral Commission, writes a legal opinion favoring the election of Tilden. However, influenced by pressures from fellow Republicans, he reverses his decision. The Commission votes not to examine the individual state returns, and eventually awards Florida's electoral votes to Hayes. On February 16, 23, and 28, the Commission awards electoral votes from the other disputed states to Hayes as well, and

Scandals! Crédit Mobilier and the Whisky Ring

Although Grant was never personally accused of corruption, many of his associates and appointees would be involved in scandals during his eight-year term. In September 1872, the New York Sun accused Vice President Schuyler Colfax, vice-presidential nominee William Wilson, Ohio Representative (and future U.S. president) James A. Garfield, and other politicians of making large illegal profits off of under-priced stock from a railroad construction company called Crédit Mobilier. The politician at the center of the scandal was Representative Oakes Ames of Massachusetts, who was responsible for distributing the Crédit Mobilier stock to willing government officials. Ultimately the House censured Ames and Representative James Brooks of New York for their role in the scandal.

In the Whisky Ring scandal, Grant's personal secretary Orville Elias Babcock is indicted for complicity in revenue frauds. The scandal was uncovered by an exposé in the St. Louis Democrat, in May 1875. As a result, 238 U.S. Treasury officials, along with Babcock, were indicted for conspiring with liquor distillers to steal millions of dollars in liquor taxes from the federal government. Babcock is acquitted after Grant personally intervenes on his behalf.

declares Hayes as president.

February 26, 1877: Republicans from Ohio, Hayes' home state, meet with Democrats from the South. Southerners agree to elect Hayes with the condition that he remove federal troops from Louisiana and South Carolina, appoint at least one Southerner to his Cabinet, and submit a bill funding internal improvement projects in the South.

March 2, 1877: Based on the Electoral Commission's recommendation, **CONGRESS DECLARES HAYES PRESIDENT**. Federal troops are immediately withdrawn from the South, bringing the end of Reconstruction.

1876-78	1879	1880	1884	1885
	The British defeat the Zulus in South Africa.			
After leaving office, Grant goes on a world tour with his wife and youngest son.		Grant seeks the Republican nomination for a third term, but on the 36th ballot, he loses the nomination to James A. Garfield.	After his brokerage firm fails, Grant is forced to file for bankruptcy.	Grant dies of throat cancer on July 23 in Mount McGregor, New York.

Rutherford B. Hayes

19th President (1877–1881)

"He serves his party best who serves the country best."

Rutherford Birchard Hayes entered office in the spring of 1877 with a dark cloud over his head. In the election of 1876, he received fewer popular votes than the corruption-fighting Democratic governor of New York, Samuel Tilden. Yet when some of his representatives met secretly with Southern Democrats and promised that Hayes would remove federal troops from the South in exchange for their support, Congress agreed to select Hayes as president. The Compromise of 1877, as this back-room bargain was called, would earn the new president the nicknames "Rutherfraud" and "His Fraudulency."

Once in office, however, Hayes proved to be scrupulously honest. As he had forsworn any intention of running for a second term, Hayes was free to do what was right for the country, rather than simply what was right for his career. For instance, he clashed with one of the most powerful leaders in his party by ordering civil servants not to participate directly in any political activity and then fired Chester A. Arthur, a future president, when Arthur violated that order. He vetoed a popular bill that banned immigration from China because he considered it racist. He stood firm against wasteful spending projects and for sound monetary policy. He criticized society's growing domination by corporations, was one of the first presidents to speak out in favor of protecting the environment and, with the strong support of his wife Lucy, backed the temperence movement by banning alcohol in the White House. Hayes inherited a presidency whose powers had greatly diminished during the Grant administration. He was determined to free the government from congessional domination and for four years he diligently worked at restoring the respectability and dignity of the president's office. Hayes steadfastedly worked at fulfilling his two primary goals of promoting national reconciliation and reforming the civil service. His administration ushered in a period of sectional harmony and political integrity.

Hayes' independence and honesty made him popular with the general public. But he was largely unable to regain control of the nation's agenda from Congress, especially after the Democrats took control of both the Senate and House in the midterm electons. When the end of his term came, he and Lucy happily retired to their home in Ohio, where he left politics and devoted himself to numerous social causes, such as public education, promotion of the rights of African Americans, and prison reform.

Biographical Facts

Born: October 4, 1822 in Delaware, Ohio

Ancestry: English

Father: Rutherford Hayes; born January 4, 1787 in Brattleboro, Vermont; died July 20, 1822 in Delaware, Ohio

Father's Occupation: Storeowner

Mother: Sophia Birchard Hayes; born April 15, 1792 in Wilmington, Vermont; died October 30, 1866 in Columbus, Ohio

Wife: Lucy Ware Webb; born August 28, 1831 in Chillicothe, Ohio died June 25, 1889 in Fremont, Ohio

Marriage: December 30, 1852 in Cincinnati, Ohio

Children: Birchard Austin (1853-1926); Webb Cook (1856-1934); Rutherford Platt (1858-1927); Joseph (1861-1863); George Crook (1864-1866); Fanny (1867-1950);

Scott (1871-1923); Manning (1873-1874)

Education: Academy at Norwalk, Ohio; Isaac Webb's school at Middletown, Connecticut; Kenyon College, Gambier, Ohio; Harvard Law School

Home: Spiegel Grove, Fremont, Ohio

Religious Affiliation: Methodist

Political Party: Republican

Age at Inauguration: 54

Occupations after the Presidency: Philanthropist; president of the National Prison Association

Death: Jan. 17, 1893 in Fremont, Ohio

Place of Burial: Spiegel Grove State Park, Fremont, Ohio

Nickname: Dark-Horse President; His Fraudulency; Rutherfraud

Writings: *Diary and Letters*

Election of 1876

Candidates	Party	Electoral Vote	Popular Vote
Rutherford B. Hayes (OH)	Republican	185	4,036,572
Samuel J. Tilden (NY)	Democratic	184	4,284,020
Peter Cooper (NY)	Greenback	---	81,737

About the Election: Heading into the 1876 election, a weak economy and rampant corruption within the Grant Administration had cost the Republican Party popular support. A call for reform dominated the election campaigns of the parties. The three main presidential candidates were favorite Democratic Samuel Tilden, relatively unknown Republican Rutherford Hayes, and Peter Cooper of the Greenback Party. On election day, Tilden won a majority of the popular votes but failed to get a majority of the electoral votes by one vote. The electoral commission voted for Hayes. Congress confirmed Hayes' election only after the Southern Democrats agreed to back Hayes if he promised to withdraw federal troops from the South, appoint a Southerner to his Cabinet, and look into demands for railroad subsidies. Hayes thus became the first president after John Quincy Adams to win the election without winning the popular vote.

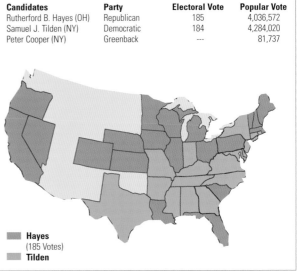

Hayes
(185 Votes)
Tilden

Hayes' Term 1877-1880

March 5, 1877: RUTHERFORD B. HAYES IS SWORN IN as the 19th president of the United States. The same day, he appoints David Key of Tennessee as the postmaster general, thereby fulfilling the promise made to Southern Democrats to include at least one Southerner in his Cabinet in exchange for their support over Tilden.

March 20, 1877: Hayes sends a commission to Louisiana to report on the conditions in the Southern state. The report provides him the political cover he needs to withdraw federal troops from Louisiana, another promise made to win the support of Southerners during the election.

April 10, 1877: HAYES WITHDRAWS FEDERAL TROOPS FROM SOUTH CAROLINA, and former Confederate General Wade Hampton becomes South Carolina's new governor.

April 24, 1877: HAYES WITHDRAWS SOLDIERS FROM LOUISIANA, and with their departure, Reconstruction comes to an end.

June 1, 1877: To stop Mexican bandits from crossing the international border into Texas, HAYES SENDS TROOPS TO PATROL THE TEXAS BORDER region, giving them the power to pursue Mexicans on both sides of the border. In protest, the president of Mexico also sends troops to the border.

June 22, 1877: In an effort at CIVIL SERVICE REFORM, President Hayes issues an executive order banning federal employees from participating in political activities, and making it illegal to fire civil servants for political reasons.

July 16, 1877: The GREAT RAILROAD STRIKE OF 1877 begins after workers on the Baltimore and Ohio (B&O) line are issued pay cuts.

September 6, 1877: HAYES FIRES CHESTER A. ARTHUR, the collector of the Port of New York (and future president), for violating his executive order against political activity by federal employees. The move angers Arthur's chief supporter, Senator Roscoe Conkling, who in response,

Quote by Hayes

"The vast wealth and power is in the hands of the few . . . who represent or control capital . . . This is a government of the people, by the people and for the people no longer. It is a government of corporations, by corporations and for corporations."

Quotes about Hayes

"Hayes is a modest man, but a very able one."
– John Sherman

"He is a third rate nonentity, whose only recommendation is that he is obnoxious to no one."
– Henry Adams

	1822	1828	1836	1840	1842
■ Hayes' Life					Hayes graduates from Kenyon College in Ohio.
		Andrew Jackson is elected president.	P.T. Barnum begins his career by buying and displaying a slave woman who he claims is George Washington's 160-year-old nurse. The woman will later be proven to be not older than 70 years.		
■ U.S. & World Events		Rutherford Birchard Hayes is born on October 4 in Delaware, Ohio.		The World's Anti-Slavery Convention is held in London.	

First Lady: Lucy Ware Webb Hayes

Lucy Ware Webb became the first college graduate to be the First Lady, and she consistently played an active role in public life. While her husband served as a Union general, Mrs. Hayes traveled to Civil War camps to tend to wounded and dying soldiers. After her husband became Ohio's governor, she often accompanied him on visits to prisons, asylums, and state reform schools. Mrs. Hayes entered the White House with confidence and expressed strong opinions on religion, morality, and women's rights. She remained a popular hostess despite her ban on alcohol at the White House, which earned her the nickname, "Lemonade Lucy."

blocks Hayes' choice, Theodore Roosevelt, Sr. (father of the future president) from getting the job. Roosevelt, and other Hayes appointees, finally win confirmation to the posts in 1879.

January 17, 1878: The UNITED STATES AND SAMOA SIGN A TREATY of friendship and nonexclusive rights to a naval station in the capital city, Pago Pago.

February 22, 1878: The GREENBACK PARTY convenes to adopt a platform calling for the free coinage of silver at the same rate as gold, legal limits to work hours, and a halt to Chinese immigration.

February 28, 1878: Overriding Hayes' veto, Congress passes the BLAND-ALLISON ACT, which remonitizes silver and allows for its coinage at a rate of 20 to 1 against gold. The law reverses the "Crime of '73", which had demonitized silver. It requires the Treasury to purchase between $2 million and $4 million in silver a month at market prices.

March 1, 1878: HAYES VETOES A BILL that would ban immigration from China.

March 23, 1878: To ease tensions along the border, Hayes recognizes the government of Porfirio Diaz in Mexico.

November 1878: DEMOCRATS GAIN CONTROL OF BOTH HOUSES OF CONGRESS, weakening Hayes' ability to govern.

January 1, 1879: In accordance with the Specie Act of 1875, the government begins to allow greenbacks to be redeemed for gold. Within the next few months, all CIVIL WAR-ERA GREENBACKS ARE RETIRED from circulation.

April 29, 1879: When Congress passes an Army Appropriations Bill that includes a ban on the use of FEDERAL TROOPS AT VOTING POLLS, Hayes vetoes the bill. The bill is an attempt to reverse the Reconstruction-era Enforcement Acts enacted to protect African-American rights, including the right to vote. By vetoing the Appropriations Bill, Hayes wins wide support from members of the Republican Party.

June 7, 1880: As Hayes had declared in 1876 that he would only serve one term, the Republican Party nominates James A. Garfield for president and Chester A. Arthur for vice president.

June 24, 1880: The DEMOCRATS NOMINATE WINFIELD SCOTT HANCOCK for president and William H. English for vice president.

November 2, 1880: GARFIELD IS ELECTED PRESIDENT.

November 17, 1880: The United States and China sign a treaty that repeals a section of the 1868 Burlingame Treaty. The U.S. has the power to "regulate, limit or suspend," but not completely prohibit Chinese immigration. The treaty also includes a clause banning the opium trade. In return, China is granted trading privileges.

Hayes' Administration

Inauguration: March 3, 1877 at the White House during a private ceremony and on March 5, 1877 at the Capitol, Washington, D. C.

Vice President: William A. Wheeler

Secretary of State: William M. Evarts

Secretary of the Treasury: John Sherman

Secretary of War: George W. McCrary; Alexander Ramsey (from December 12, 1879)

Attorney General: Charles Devens

Postmaster General: David M. Key; Horace Maynard (from August 25, 1880)

Secretary of the Navy: Richard W. Thompson; Nathan Goff, Jr. (from January 6, 1881)

Secretary of the Interior: Carl Schurz

Supreme Court Appointments:
John Marshall Harlan (1877);
William Burnham Woods (1880)

45th Congress: (March 4, 1877-March 4, 1879)
Senate: 39 Republicans; 36 Democrats; 1 Other
House: 153 Democrats; 140 Republicans

46th Congress: (March 4, 1879-March 4, 1881)
Senate: 42 Democrats; 33 Republicans; 1 Other
House: 149 Democrats; 130 Republicans; 14 Others

1761-65	1768-72	1870	1876	1881	1893
	He serves as governor of Ohio.		Despite losing the popular vote, Hayes is awarded the presidency by a special Electoral Commision.		Hayes dies on January 17 in Fremont, Ohio.
During the Civil War, Hayes serves with the 23rd Ohio volunteers.		Italy is united into a single nation after troops defeat French forces in Rome.		After leaving the White House, Hayes retires from politics, but continuees to promote numerous social causes.	

James A. Garfield

20th President (March–September 1881)

"I love agitation and investigation and glory in defending unpopular truth against popular error."

Born in a log cabin, James Abram Garfield rose from humble origins to become one of the most scholarly men to serve in the office. Once a classics professor at Hiram College, Garfield could write Greek with one hand and Latin with the other to entertain guests.

During the Civil War, Garfield fought bravely and he was elected to Congress while still on the battlefield. He advanced to become Speaker of the House and the "dark horse" presidential nominee of the Republican party in 1880.

His selection was made possible by a split in the Republican Party: one faction, the Stalwarts, were loyal to New York Senator Roscoe Conkling; the other, known as the Half-Breeds, supported Maine's senator, James G. Blaine. The two groups disagreed over the specific method of appointments to federal positions known as "patronage" or the "spoils system." The Stalwarts defended the spoils system, wanting control of all federal appointments to offices in New York; the Half-Breeds advocated reform. At the National Republican convention, the Stalwarts supported a third term for Ulysses S. Grant. Garfield was chosen as a compromise candidate after he promised to appoint the Stalwarts in civil service positions. To unite the party, Chester A. Arthur, a Stalwart, was chosen as vice president.

In July, an insane Stalwart job seeker shot Garfield as he and Blaine walked through a Washington train station. After being shot, Garfield lived for two and a half months, conducting the business of the presidency in agonizing pain from his bed. Meanwhile, doctors searched in vain for the bullet in his body, using unwashed fingers and dirty tools. The trauma to his body helped cause a fatal heart attack, which was misdiagnosed by his doctors. At his autopsy, the bullet was found four inches away from Garfield's spine, lodged in a protective cyst. It is likely that the president would have lived if his doctors had left him alone.

With his death, Garfield became a martyred symbol of civil service reform. Chester A. Arthur, who took office after Garfield's untimely death, signed the Pendleton Act in 1883, the first major civil service reform law ever passed.

Biographical Facts

Born: November 19, 1831 in Orange Township, Ohio

Ancestry: English and French

Father: Abram Garfield; born 1799 in Worcester, New York; died 1833 in Orange Township, Ohio

Father's Occupation: Farmer

Mother: Eliza Ballou Garfield; born 1801 in Richmond, New Hampshire; died 1888 in Mentor, Ohio

Wife: Lucretia Rudolph; born April 19, 1832 in Hiram, Ohio; died March 14, 1918 in Pasadena, California

Marriage: November 11, 1858 in Hiram, Ohio

Children: Eliza Arabella (1860-1863); Harry Augustus (1863-1942); James Rudolph (1865-1950); Mary (1867-1947); Irvin McDowell (1870-1951); Abram (1872-1958); Edward (1874-1876)

Education: Attended Geauga Academy and Western Reserve Eclectic Institute; graduated from Williams College (1856)

Home: Lawnfield, Mentor, Ohio

Religious Affiliation: Disciples of Christ

Occupations before Presidency: Schoolteacher; college professor; preacher; canal worker; soldier; president of Hiram College

Military Service: Commissioned Lieutenant Colonel of 42nd Ohio Volunteers in August (1861); Brigadier General of Volunteers (1862); Major General of Volunteers (1863)

Political Offices before Presidency: Member of Ohio Senate: Member of U.S. House of Representatives; Chairman of House Committee on Appropriations; Minority Leader in U.S. House of Representatives

Political Party: Republican

Age at Inauguration: 49

Death: September 19, 1881 in Elberon, New Jersey

Place of Burial: Lake View Cemetery, Cleveland, Ohio

Nickname: None

Writings: *Diary*

Chester A. Arthur

21st President (1881–1885)

"I may be president of the United States, but my private life is nobody's damned business."

Two years before becoming president, Chester A. Arthur was a little-known cog in the political machine of New York's powerful Senator Roscoe Conkling. As collector of the Customs House of New York, he controlled a thousand jobs and large sums of federal money. He allowed employees to profit from their positions. He is said to have personally garnered $40,000 by using his influence to get political appointments for his allies. In 1878, President Hayes fired him for failing to obey an executive order banning civil service workers from participating in politics.

Two years later, Chester Arthur found himself back in the spotlight as the vice-presidential nominee of the Republican Party. The Republican presidential nominee was James A. Garfield. To placate Conkling and his allies after they failed to secure Ulysses Grant a nomination for a third term, the Republicans chose Arthur as Garfield's running mate. Yet, few observers believed that Arthur might actually rise to the presidency. When Charles Guiteau, an unstable jobseeker shot Garfield and shouted, "I am a stalwart. Arthur is now president of the United States," even Arthur's supporters were stunned. One of his allies in New York proclaimed, "Chet Arthur? President of the United States? Good God!"

As president, Arthur surprised his political supporters even more—by largely ignoring them. He prosecuted Republicans for mail fraud and vetoed popular pork-barrel spending projects, such as the Rivers and Harbors Act of 1882. His most significant move may have been signing the Pendleton Civil Service Reform Act, which set up a system through which government jobs were assigned on merit and not political favoritism. He was also an environmentalist who "took interest in the natural resources of the West and was concerned about the reckless destruction of forests."

Arthur's surprisingly honest administration was short. In 1884, his fellow Republicans chose Conkling's chief rival, James G. Blaine, as their nominee. Like Conkling, Blaine had been tainted by charges of corruption. Yet, as one of the founding figures of the Republican Party, he was enormously popular with his party's faithful.

Throughout his presidency, Chester Arthur had suffered from Bright's Disease, a fatal illness of the kidney, but kept his poor health a secret. In 1886, two years after leaving office, Arthur died. He was just fifty-six years old.

Biographical Facts

Born: October 5, 1830 in North Fairfield, Vermont

Ancestry: Scotch-Irish and English

Father: William Arthur; born 1796 in County Antrim, Ireland; died October 27, 1875 in Newtonville, New York

Father's Occupation: Baptist minister

Mother: Malvina Stone Arthur; born April 24, 1802 in Berkshire, Vermont, died January 16, 1869 in Newtonville, New York

Wife: Ellen Lewis Herndon; born August 30, 1837 in Fredericksburg, Virginia; died January 12. 1880 in New York, New York

Marriage: October 25, 1859 in New York, New York

Children: William Lewis Herndon (1860-1863); Chester Alan, Jr. (1864-1937); Ellen (1871-1915)

Home: 123 Lexington Avenue, New York, New York

Religious Affiliation: Episcopalian

Education: Attended public schools and Lyceum School; graduated with honors from Union College (1848)

Occupations before Presidency: Teacher; school principal; lawyer

Political Offices before Presidency: Quartermaster General of New York State; New York Collector of Customs; U.S. Vice President

Military Service: None

Political Party: Republican

Age at Inauguration: 50

Occupation after Presidency: Lawyer

Death: November 18, 1886 in New York, New York

Place of Burial: Rural Cemetery, Albany, New York

Nickname: The Gentleman Boss; Elegant Arthur

Writings: *Papers*

135

Quote by Arthur:

"Men may die, but the fabrics of free institutions remains unshaken."

"The office of vice-president is a greater honor than I ever dreamed of attaining."

Quotes about Arthur:

"I can hardly imagine how he could have done better."
– Henry Ward Beecher

"Nothing like it ever before in the Executive mansion —liquor, snobbery and worse."
– Rutherford B. Hayes, comment on Chester Arthur's White House

Arthur's Term 1881-1885

September 20, 1881: **ARTHUR IS SWORN IN AS PRESIDENT** of the United States following the death of James Garfield, who had only served six months in office.

September 22, 1881: Arthur formally takes the oath of office in Washington, D.C.

November 14, 1881: The **TRIAL OF CHARLES GUITEAU,** Garfield's assassin, begins. During the trial, it is learned that Guiteau had stolen White House stationary and had repeatedly tried to get an appointment as a diplomat to France. Guiteau is convicted in January 1882 and hanged the following June. His skeleton is given to the Army Medical Museum.

December 15, 1881: Secretary of State **JAMES G. BLAINE RESIGNS FROM ARTHUR'S CABINET,** reinforcing the Republican Party's continued division. Blaine is the leader of the Republican Party's "Half-Breed" faction, and most Half-Breeds leave Arthur's Cabinet as well. Although Arthur rose to power as one of Roscoe Conkling's "Stalwart" supporters, he surprises many with his distance from the Stalwarts during his presidency.

February 28, 1882: Congress passes a bill tying Congressional representation to the national population census for the first time. The new law increases the number of Congressmen in the House of Representatives to 325.

March 16, 1882: Two weeks after Arthur declares his support for the treaty, the Senate ratifies the **GENEVA CONVENTION OF 1864** for the care of wounded war personnel. Among other rules, the treaty—also known as the Red Cross Treaty—stipulates that ambulances, hospitals, medical staff and chaplains are to be considered neutral.

March 22, 1882: In a response to the then-widespread practices of bigamy and polygamy among Mormons in Utah Territory, Congress passes the **EDMUNDS ACT.** The law forbids bigamists and polygamists from voting or holding office. The controversy over bigamy and polygamy delays Utah's admittance as a state until 1896.

May 6, 1882: After President Arthur angers labor groups with his veto of a bill that bans the immigration of Chinese workers, he signs a second version of the **CHINESE EXCLUSION ACT,** which includes a 10 year ban. The final bill, which bans immigration by "lunatics," "idiots," and Chinese laborers, and denies citizenship rights to Chinese already in the United States, is the only American immigration law to ban a group of people from entering the United States because of race or nationality. Despite Arthur's veto of the earlier ban, which prohibited Chinese immigration for 20 years, the law is renewed regularly until 1943.

May 15, 1882: Congress authorizes President Arthur to appoint a nine-man **TARIFF COMMISSION.** In December, the commission recommends that tariffs be lowered.

May 22, 1882: The **UNITED STATES RECOGNIZES THE KINGDOM OF KOREA,** although Korea has major Japanese and Chinese presence. Japan forcibly stations troops on Korean soil. To counter Japanese moves, China advises Korea to agree to trade agreements with the United States or other Western nations. The following year, Arthur receives Korean diplomats in New York City.

August 1, 1882: Arthur vetoes the **RIVERS AND HARBORS ACT,** a bill appropriating $19 million for improving various river and harbor facilities. The president sees the bill as pork-barrel spending. However, due to the bill's internal popularity, Congress gains the two-thirds votes to override his veto the next day.

September 11, 1882: Early in James Garfield's presidency, Postmaster Thomas James discovered that some employees of the U.S. Postal Service had been taking bribes in exchange for "**STAR ROUTE**" contracts in the West. Star Routes were mail routes that were subcontracted to private companies since they were inaccessible by stagecoach or riverboat. Although the jury finds that only two minor figures among the nine defendants in the **STAR ROUTE SCANDAL** are guilty, the jury foreman alleges that government agents had attempted to bribe him. The trial judge orders a retrial. In June 1883, all nine defendants are found not guilty.

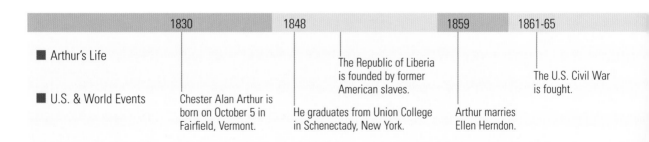

	1830	1848	1859	1861-65
■ Arthur's Life				
■ U.S. & World Events	Chester Alan Arthur is born on October 5 in Fairfield, Vermont.	He graduates from Union College in Schenectady, New York. / The Republic of Liberia is founded by former American slaves.	Arthur marries Ellen Herndon.	The U.S. Civil War is fought.

First Lady: Ellen Lewis Herndon Arthur

Ellen Herndon was an only child and born to a well-connected Virginia family. Her father, William Lewis Herndon, helped establish the Naval Observatory in Washington, D.C. At an early age, "Nell" became known for her singing voice, a gift that she continued to develop as a vocation throughout her life. Ellen Arthur, however, never served as the First Lady. She died suddenly of pneumonia a year before Arthur's election as vice president. President Arthur took it upon himself to completely refurbish the White House and installed the building's first elevator. His sister Mary McElroy served as official hostess and helped care for his daughter Ellen.

November 7, 1882: In the midterm elections, Democrats win control of the House.

January 16, 1883: In the wake of Garfield's death, Congress passes the **PENDLETON CIVIL SERVICE REFORM ACT** under public pressure. The first major attempt at reforming the corrupt civil-service system, the bill sets up a three-person commission and mandates that government positions be awarded according to merit rather than as political gifts. Arthur, who had entered office with a reputation for corruption, signs the bill and names the author of the bill, attorney Dorman B. Eaton, as chairman of the first Civil Service Commission.

March 3, 1883: Congress passes the "MONGREL" TARIFF ACT. Although Arthur's tariff commission had sought 20 to 25 percent reductions in tariffs, the law lowers tariffs on a select list of items by less than two percent.

May 13, 1884: CONGRESS REPEALS THE 1862 TEST OATH, which requires all office holders to swear they have never participated in illegal or disloyal conduct. The oath had been widely ignored following the end of Reconstruction. The removal of federal troops from the South had allowed many former Confederate soliders and politicians to ignore the oath and win election to office.

May 17, 1884: A territorial government is established in Alaska.

May 28, 1884: The Greenback Party nominates Benjamin Butler for president. Butler served in the Union army at New Orleans and was a former Radical Republican..

June 6, 1884: The Republican Party nominates James G. Blaine, leader of the Half-Breeds, as its nominee in the upcoming presidential election.

June 27, 1884: The UNITED STATES BUREAU OF LABOR is created as a division of the Department of the Interior. It becomes the Department of Labor in 1888.

July 11, 1884: The Democratic Party nominates GROVER CLEVELAND, governor of New York, for president.

November 4, 1884: CLEVELAND DEFEATS BLAINE in the presidential election.

February 25, 1885: CONGRESS BANS THE FENCING OF PUBLIC LANDS in the West.

February 26, 1885: Congress passes the CONTRACT LABOR LAW, or Foran Act, which prohibits American companies from employing low-paid foreign workers in order to break strikes by native workers.

Arthur's Administration

Inauguration: September 20, 1881 in New York

Vice President: None

Secretary of State: James G. Blaine; Frederick T. Frelinghusen (from December. 19, 1881)

Secretary of the Treasury: William Windom; Charles J. Folger (from November 14, 1881); Walter Q. Gresham (from September 24, 1884); Hugh McCulloch (from October 31, 1884)

Secretary of War: Robert T. Lincoln

Attorney General: Wayne MacVeagh: Benjamin H. Brewster (from January 3,1882)

Postmaster General: Thomas L. James; Timothy O. Howe (from January 5, 1882);
Walter Q. Gresham (from April 11, 1883); Frank Hatton (from October 14, 1884)

Secretary of the Navy: William H. Hunt; William E. Chandler (from April 17, 1882)
Secretary of the Interior: Samuel J. Kirkwood; Henry M. Teller (from April 17, 1882)

Supreme Court Appointments: Horace Gray (1881); Samuel Blatchford (1882)

47th Congress: (March 4, 1881-March 4, 1883) Senate: 37 Republicans; 37 Democrats; 1 Other House: 147 Republicans; 135 Democrats; 11 Others

48th Congress: (March 4, 1883-March 4, 1885) Senate:38 Republicans; 36 Democrats; 2 Others House: 197 Democrats; 118 Republicans; 10 Others

1878	1880	1881	1885	1886
President Rutherford Hayes fires Arthur from his job as collector of the Customs House of New York.	Ellen Arthur dies of tuberculosis.	Arthur becomes president when President James Garfield dies.	The Washington Monument is dedicated in Washington, D.C.	Arthur dies on November 18 in New York City, New York.

Grover Cleveland

22nd and 24th President (1885–1889, 1893–1897)

"I am honest and sincere in my desire to do well, but the question is whether I know enough to accomplish what I desire."

In 1881, Grover Cleveland was elected the mayor of Buffalo. Within a year, he was the governor of New York, and two years after that, the president of the United States. Cleveland's steady rise was due to his reputation as an honest New York Democratic reformer. As such, he stood in contrast to the corruption-ridden Democrats associated with New York City's Tammany machine.

Seen as a courageous and hardworking man, the Democrats considered him an ideal choice to be president. As president, he insisted upon honesty and efficiency regardless of party affiliations. In an age marked by rampant corruption and political patronage, he was able to restore a certain level of dignity to the presidential office. Cleveland's reform efforts lay in blocking harmful legislation rather than implementing new legislation through government activism. He blocked Civil War pensions that he suspected were fraudulent, vetoed spending that ran counter to his vision of limited federal government, condemned Republican spending and supported the gold standard as the single basis for American money. Cleveland also favored lowering tariffs, which the Republicans vehemently opposed. The issue of tariffs cost him reelection in 1888.

By 1892, many Americans were dissatisfied with both the Democratic and Republican parties, viewing them as captives of corporate interests. The new People's Party (or Populist Party) began to campaign for an eight-hour workday, public ownership of railroads, and free coinage of silver. Although Cleveland was reelected to a second term, his views on the gold standard put him at odds not only with the People's Party, but also with the emerging populist wing of the Democratic Party, led by William Jennings Bryan.

Cleveland's innate conservatism made him generally unsympathetic to the causes of working people. His veto of a bill to send a mere $10,000 in aid to drought-stricken farmers and his heavy-handed response to the Pullman Strike of 1894 made him quite unpopular by the end of his second term. Nonetheless, he was probably the most influential president of the period between Abraham Lincoln and Theodore Roosevelt. During an era when real power lay with the pro-business factions of Congress, Cleveland was not afraid to use the power of the presidency. During his two terms, he vetoed more bills than all of the presidents combined that had served before him. In doing so, he set an example for the activist presidents of the early 20th century.

Biographical Facts

Born: March 18, 1837 in Caldwell, New Jersey
Ancestry: Irish-English
Father: Richard Falley Cleveland; born June 19, 1804 in Norwich, Connecticut; died October 1, 1853 in Holland Patent, New York
Father's Occupation: Minister
Mother: Ann Neal Cleveland; born February 4, 1806 in Baltimore, Maryland; died July 19, 1882 in Holland Patent, New York
Wife: Frances Folsom; born July 21, 1864 in Buffalo, New York; died October 29, 1947
Marriage: June 2, 1886 in Washington, D.C.
Children: Ruth Cleveland (1891-1904); Esther Cleveland (1893-1980); Marion Cleveland (1895-1977); Richard Folsom Cleveland (1897-1974); Francis Grover Cleveland (1903-1995)

Education: Public schools
Religious Affiliation: Presbyterian
Occupation before Presidency: Clerk; teacher; lawyer
Political Offices before Presidency: Erie County Assistant District Attorney; Sheriff of Erie County; Mayor of Buffalo; Governor of New York
Political Party: Democratic
Age at Inauguration: 47
Occupation after Presidency: Princeton University Trustee
Death: June 24, 1908 in Princeton, New Jersey
Place of Burial: Princeton, New Jersey
Nickname: Big Steve; Uncle Jumbo
Writings: *Presidential Problems*

Election of 1884

Candidates	Party	Electoral Vote	Popular Vote
Grover Cleveland (NY)	Democratic	219	4,879,507
James G. Blaine (ME)	Republican	182	4,850,293
Benjamin F. Butler (MA)	Greenback-Labor	---	175,370
John P. St. John (KS)	Prohibition	---	150,369

About the Election: In the campaign of 1884, the private lives and morals of candidates took center stage, while political issues were pushed to the background. Republican nominee, James G. Blaine, was accused of accepting bribes, while Cleveland was criticized for fathering a child out of wedlock. On Election Day, Cleveland carried the entire South and the swing states of New Jersey, Connecticut, and Indiana. But his home state of New York decided the election. When Reverend Samuel Burchard, a Blaine supporter, accused the Democrats of being the party of "rum, Romanism and rebellion," angry Irish-Americans turned out in force for Cleveland, giving him a razor-thin 1,200-vote margin of victory in New York, and the majority of the nation's electoral votes.

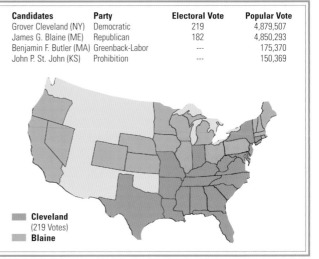

Cleveland (219 Votes)
Blaine

Cleveland's First Term 1885-1889

March 4, 1885: Former New York governor **GROVER CLEVELAND IS SWORN IN** as the 22nd president.

November 25, 1885: Vice President Thomas Hendricks dies.

January 19, 1886: Cleveland signs the **PRESIDENTIAL SUCCESSION ACT**, which specifies that if both the president and vice president are removed from office, die, resign, or are otherwise unable to complete their terms, they are to be succeeded by the heads of executive departments in the order in which the departments were created. The law remains in effect until 1947. Congress later changes the order of presidential succesion by replacing the president pro tempore and the Speaker of the House with Cabinet officers.

February 8, 1886: Cleveland signs the **DAWES GENERAL ALLOTMENT (SEVERALTY) ACT**, which dissolves Native American tribes as legal entities and orders that all Native American reservations be broken into smaller plots of land owned by individuals and families. The new law has a devastating impact on traditional Native American culture, which has previously not known any concept of individual property ownership.

May 1, 1886: Demanding an eight-hour work day, 340,000 union members begin a **NATIONWIDE WORK STOPPAGE**. Chicago is the center of the movement.

May 3, 1886: CHICAGO POLICE FIRE INTO A CROWD of workers at the McCormick Harvester plant, killing one man and wounding many others.

May 4, 1886: The **HAYMARKET MASSACRE** occurs at a mass protest in Chicago's Haymarket Square. Violence erupts when 180 police officers storm the demonstration to break it up. An unknown assailant throws a bomb at the front lines of the police advance, killing 8 policemen and injuring 67 more. The police respond by shooting and clubbing members of the crowd, killing and wounding many more. As a result, 4 labor leaders, none of whom have anything to do with the bomb, are hanged.

May 10, 1886: In the landmark case of *SANTA CLARA COUNTY V. SOUTHERN PACIFIC RAILROAD*, the Supreme Court rules that corporations are entitled to the same rights as accorded to individuals under the equal protection clause of the Constitution. Chief Justice Morrison R. Waite states, "The court does not wish to hear arguments on the question whether the provision in the Fourteenth Amendment to the Constitution, which forbids a state to deny to any person within its jurisdiction the equal protection of its laws, applies to these corporations. We are all of the opinion that it does."

May 11, 1886: Cleveland asks Congress to accept the **STATUE OF LIBERTY** as a gift from France, commemorating the centenary of the American-French alliance during the Revolutionary War. The statue is be placed on Beloe Island in New York Harbor, which is later renamed Liberty Island. It takes six months to mount the statue to her base.

August 3, 1886: Congress authorizes the building of additional ships for the United States Navy.

November 2, 1886: Although Republicans lose 4 Senate seats

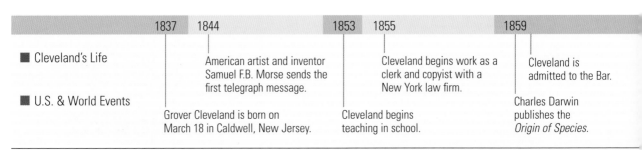

	1837	1844		1853	1855		1859

■ Cleveland's Life

American artist and inventor Samuel F.B. Morse sends the first telegraph message.

Cleveland begins work as a clerk and copyist with a New York law firm.

Cleveland is admitted to the Bar.

■ U.S. & World Events

Grover Cleveland is born on March 18 in Caldwell, New Jersey.

Cleveland begins teaching in school.

Charles Darwin publishes the *Origin of Species*.

First Lady: Frances Folsom Cleveland

Grover Cleveland was a family friend, law partner, and estate administrator of Frances Folsom's father, and he had always known and advised the young girl, who he fondly called "Frank." Despite the age difference of 27 years, romance eventually grew between the two and the couple became the first in the nation's history to be married in the White House. As official hostess, Mrs. Cleveland replaced her sister-in-law, Rose Elizabeth Cleveland, and became one of the nation's most popular First Ladies. Mrs. Cleveland maintained her place in the public eye even through her husband's stormy second term. President Cleveland, however, grew increasingly annoyed at the public's obsession with the First Lady. He tried to stop businessmen from using his wife's image to sell products, but his attempts were unsuccessful.

Five years after the death of her husband, she married Princeton archeology professor, Thomas J. Preston, Jr.

in the **MIDTERM ELECTIONS**, they maintain a 39-37 seat majority. In the House of Representatives, Democrats lose 14 seats, but maintain their majority.

December 8, 1886: Samuel Gompers founds the **AMERICAN FEDERATION OF LABOR (AFL)**.

January 20, 1887: The Senate approves the renewal of the 1875 commercial treaty with Hawaii that gave the U.S. sole authority to build a naval base at Pearl Harbor, Oahu.

February 3, 1887: Congress passes the **ELECTORAL COUNT ACT** to avoid disputed national elections. Rather than have the contentious results settled in Congress, as was the case in 1876, the new law makes each state responsible for its own electoral returns and forces Congress to accept those results, unless there is evidence of irregularities.

February 4, 1887: THE INTERSTATE COMMERCE COMMISSION (ICC) is created to manage interstate railroads. In time, the ICC's power extends beyond railroads to include all forms of common carriers. In March, Cleveland appoints Thomas Cooley as the first commissioner of the ICC.

February 11, 1887: CLEVELAND VETOES THE DEPENDENT PENSION BILL, which grants a pension to anyone serving 90 or more days in the military. By the mid-1880s, pension payments to Union Army veterans had become a major expense for the U.S. Treasury. Although he approves more pension requests than any president before him, Cleveland angers veteran groups by vetoing many that appear fraudulent.

February 16, 1887: CLEVELAND VETOES THE TEXAS SEED BILL, which aims to provide $10,000 to drought-stricken farmers. He argues that federal aid in such a case "encourages the expectation of paternal care on the part of the government and weakens the sturdiness of our national character." Despite this belief, Cleveland uses surplus government funds to pay off wealthy bondholders at $28 above the $100 value of each bond, at a cost of $45 million.

March 2, 1887: Congress passes the **HATCH ACT**, which subsidizes the creation of agricultural science stations within every state with a land-grant college.

Cleveland's First Administration

Inauguration: March 4, 1885 at the Capitol, Washington, D.C.
Vice President: Thomas A. Hendricks
Secretary of State: Thomas F. Bayard
Secretary of the Treasury: Daniel Manning; Charles S. Fairchild (from April 1, 1887)
Secretary of War: William C. Endicott
Attorney General: Augustus H. Garland
Postmaster General: William F. Vilas: Don M. Dickinson (from January 16, 1888)
Secretary of the Navy: William C. Whitney
Secretary of the Interior: Lucius Q.C. Lamar; William F. Vilas (from January 16, 1888)

Secretary of Agriculture: Norman J. Colman
Supreme Court Appointments:
Lucius Q.C. Lamar (1888):
Melville W. Fuller, Chief Justice (1888)
49th Congress: (March 4, 1885-March 4, 1887)
Senate: 43 Republicans; 34 Democrats
House: 183 Democrats; 140 Republicans;
2 Others
50th Congress: (March 4, 1887-March 4, 1889)
Senate: 39 Republicans; 37 Democrats
House: 169 Democrats; 152 Republicans;
4 Others
End of Presidential Term: March 4, 1889

1861	1863	1867	1871	1879	1881
	Cleveland is appointed Assistant District Attorney of Erie County, New York.		The German Empire is founded following the Franco-Prussian War.		Cleveland is elected mayor of Buffalo, New York.
The U.S. Civil War begins and lasts until 1865.		The Dominion of Canada is founded.	Cleveland is elected the Sheriff of Erie County, New York.	Physicist Albert Einstein is born in Ulm, Germany.	

March 3, 1887: After Cleveland challenges its constitutionality, the **TENURE OF OFFICE ACT IS REPEALED**. The act, which had led to Andrew Johnson's impeachment in 1868, had required Senate approval of any attempt by the president to remove a member of his Cabinet.

June 7-15, 1887: By the end of the Civil War, there were at least 500 Confederate flags in the possession of the federal government. After Cleveland orders that confiscated **CONFEDERATE BATTLE FLAGS** be returned to the South, angry Union veteran groups and Republicans protest so fiercely that the president revokes the order. The captured flags are eventually returned in 1905.

December 6, 1887: In his annual address to Congress, **CLEVELAND ARGUES AGAINST HIGH TARIFFS**, stating that they had encouraged the formation of trusts and artificially high prices. The tariffs had also led to large federal surpluses since their adoption during the Civil War. Although originally intended as temporary measures to protect American industry during the war, Northern business interests had lobbied successfully to not only keep tariffs after the war, but to raise them. Although Southern Democrats in the House pass a bill to reduce tariff rates moderately, Republicans in the Senate reject the bill.

March 12, 1888: A 36-hour blizzard hits the New York City region, resulting in the loss of 400 lives and millions of dollars in property damage.

April 30, 1888: Conservative judge Melville W. Fuller is appointed Supreme Court chief justice.

May 28, 1888: The **NATIONAL GREENBACK PARTY NOMINATES BENJAMIN BUTLER** for president.

May 30, 1888: The **PROHIBITION PARTY** nominates Clinton B. Fisk for president.

Rioters throw a dynamite bomb into a crowd of policemen during a violent strike rally in Haymarket Square, Chicago.

	1882	1883	1884	1885
■ Cleveland's Life				
■ U.S. & World Events		German philosopher Karl Marx dies.	Cleveland is elected president.	
	Cleveland is elected governor of New York.		Mark Twain writes *The Adventures of Huckleberry Finn.*	The Indian National Congress is founded.

Election of 1892

About the Election: In a rematch election, fought largely over huge Republican tariff increases passed in 1890, Cleveland won the most decisive electoral victory in 20 years. At the same time, the election marked the emergence of major agrarian and populist discontent in the country, as People's Party candidate, James B. Weaver became the first third party candidate to win electoral votes since 1860. The People's Party called for the expansion of silver coinage, increase in agricultural prices, federal control of railroads, restrictions on immigration, and the direct election of U.S. senators. The party aimed at restricting the influence of large corporations and reducing the gross disparities of wealth in the country. The People's Party, whose appeal was limited mainly to the Western states, had hoped to expand its national base but virtually disappeared by the next presidential election in 1896.

Candidates	Party	Electoral Vote	Popular Vote
Grover Cleveland (NY)	Democratic	277	5,555,426
Benjamin Harrison (IN)	Republican	145	5,182,690
James B. Weaver (IA)	People's (Populist)	22	1,029,846
John Bidwell (CA)	Prohibition	---	264,133
Simon Wing (MA)	Socialist Labor	---	21,164

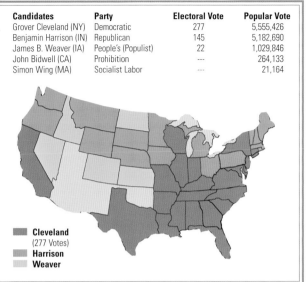

■ **Cleveland**
(277 Votes)
■ **Harrison**
☐ **Weaver**

June 13, 1888: The **DEPARTMENT OF LABOR** is established.

June 25, 1888: **REPUBLICANS NOMINATE BENJAMIN HARRISON**, grandson of William Henry Harrison, for president.

July 29, 1888: A yellow fever epidemic strikes Jacksonville, Florida, and lasts for much of the remainder of the year. Over 400 people die and 4,500 people fall ill.

September 8, 1888: The **DEMOCRATS NOMINATE CLEVELAND** for a second term. **ADLAI E. STEVENSON**, a former Illinois congressman, is chosen as his running mate.

October 8, 1888: Cleveland extends the **CHINESE EXCLUSION ACT**, which prohibits the immigration of Chinese laborers.

November 6, 1888: Although Cleveland wins the popular vote, **HARRISON DEFEATS CLEVELAND** in the electoral vote, 233 to 168. Votes in Indiana assure Harrison's victory after Republican Party managers send thousands of out-of-state voters to Indiana to cast votes for Harrison.

January 15, 1889: After Germany sends troops to the Samoan Islands, Cleveland warns that the U.S. insists on Samoan independence. Outright war is averted in March, however, when a hurricane hits the islands. In the months that follow, the U.S., Britain, and Germany negotiate a treaty. In the deal, Great Britain relinquishes claims to Samoa in return for other South Pacific territory. The Samoan islands are then split between Germany and the United States.

February 11, 1889: The **DEPARTMENT OF AGRICULTURE** is established with Cabinet status. Its purpose is to develop and execute policy on farming and food, as well as to meet the needs of farmers and ranchers throughout America.

February 22, 1889: **NORTH DAKOTA, SOUTH DAKOTA, MONTANA AND WASHINGTON ENTER THE UNION** as states.

Cleveland's Second Term 1893-1897

March 4, 1893: **CLEVELAND IS INAUGURATED**, and he becomes the only president to serve two nonconsecutive terms.

March 9, 1893: Although Benjamin Harrison had agreed to annex the islands following the overthrow of Hawaiian Queen Liliokalani, **CLEVELAND WITHDRAWS FROM THE TREATY TO ANNEX HAWAII**. He then sends James H. Blount to Hawaii to investigate the question of its annexation further. Four months later, Blount reports that most Hawaiians oppose annexation, noting that only wealthy American sugar planters on the islands favor it. What is more, he also informs President Cleveland that the American ambassador to Hawaii, John L. Stevens, had directly participated in overthrowing Queen Liliokalani.

April 22, 1893: The **PANIC OF 1893** begins when the U.S. Treasury gold reserve falls below $100 million for the first time. Over the next several weeks, stock prices drop dramatically. Railroads plunge into bankruptcy and the banking system is strained. Cleveland instructs the U.S. Treasury to sell

1886		1888	1892		1893

Cleveland marries 22-year-old Francis Folsom in the first wedding at the White House.

Apache warrior Geronimo is captured.

Cleveland wins reelection, becoming the only president elected to two non-consecutive terms.

Cleveland loses his bid for reelection.

After a cancerous growth is found on the roof of Cleveland's mouth, part of his jaw is removed in a secret operation. The same year, his daughter Esther becomes the first child born in the White House.

Cleveland's Second Administration

Inauguration: March 4, 1893 at the Capitol, Washington, D.C.
Vice President: Adlai E. Stevenson
Secretary of State: Walter Q. Gresham; Richard Olney (from June 10, 1895)
Secretary of the Treasury: John G. Carlisle
Secretary of War: Daniel S. Lamont
Attorney General: Richard Olney; Judson Harmon (from June 11, 1895)
Postmaster General: Wilson S. Bissell; William L. Wilson (from April 4, 1895)
Secretary of the Navy: Hilary A. Herbert
Secretary of the Interior: Hoke Smith; David R. Francis (from September 4, 1896)

Secretary of Agriculture: Julius Sterling Morton
Supreme Court Appointments: Edward D. White (1894); Rufus W. Peckham (1895)
53rd Congress: (March 4, 1893-March 4, 1895)
Senate: 44 Democrats; 38 Republicans; 3 Others
House: 218 Democrats; 127 Republicans; 11 Others
54th Congress: (March 4, 1895-March 4, 1897)
Senate: 43 Republicans; 39 Democrats; 6 Others
House: 244 Republicans; 105 Democrats; 7 Others
State Admitted: Utah (1896)
End of Presidential Term: March 4, 1897

government bonds in exchange for gold and the sale raises $293 million. Even so, 600 banks fail within a year, 194 railroads file for bankruptcy, and 2,500,000 people are unemployed. Democrats blame high tariffs and Republican-spending in Congress for the crisis. Free silver and gold standard supporters blame each other. Although, the economy gradually begins to improve, it is not until the end of Cleveland's second term.

June 30, 1893: As the gold reserve continues to drop, President Cleveland demands that Congress repeal the SHERMAN SILVER PURCHASE ACT so that silver notes can no longer be redeemed in gold. On August 28, the House votes to repeal the Sherman Silver Purchase Act. Though many Westerners favor free silver, the Senate also votes for the repeal.

August 24, 1893: A tornado strikes Savannah, Georgia and Charleston, South Carolina, killing 1,000 people.

September 16, 1893: The CHEROKEE STRIP, a stretch of land between Kansas and Oklahoma, opens for settlement. Over 100,000 Americans rush to purchase six million acres of land that had been purchased by the U.S. government from the Cherokee nation in 1891.

September 17, 1893: A yellow fever epidemic strikes the population of Brunswick, Georgia.

November 7, 1893: WOMEN'S SUFFRAGE is adopted in Colorado. Wyoming was the first state to grant women suffrage in 1869, while it was still a territory.

December 18, 1893: After Cleveland recommends that Queen Liliokalani return to the throne, the HAWAIIAN PROVISIONAL GOVERNMENT REFUSES TO CEDE POWER. Although

he condemns the provisional government, Cleveland decides not to use military force to remove it.

January 4, 1894: President Cleveland grants amnesty to elderly Mormons, who have violated the Anti-Polygamy Act of 1882 on the condition that they observe the law hereafter.

January 8, 1894: A major FIRE AT THE CHICAGO WORLD'S COLUMBIAN EXHIBITION destroys almost all exhibits, causing over $2 million in damage.

March 25, 1894: JACOB COXEY and his 400-member "Army of the Commonwealth of Christ" leave Ohio for Washington, D.C. to demand relief for the unemployed. Although "COXEY'S ARMY" gains national attention, Coxey and two others are arrested for trespassing when they reach Capitol Hill.

April 20, 1894: Over 100,000 COAL WORKERS STRIKE for higher wages in Columbus, Ohio.

May 11-July 20, 1894: EUGENE DEBS, president of the American Railway Union, organizes the PULLMAN STRIKE to protest the high cost of living in the company-run town on the outskirts of Chicago. Before long, the strike halts rail service in 27 states and territories. When violence breaks out, Cleveland sends in troops to restore order and force trains back into service. Debs is arrested when he fails to obey an injunction against interfering with the mail and interstate commerce.

July 4, 1894: Hawaii's provisional government declares the REPUBLIC OF HAWAII. The U.S. government recognizes the republic the following month.

August 27, 1894: Democrats in Congress push through the FIRST GRADUATED INCOME TAX. In a bitter debate, Republican Senator John Sherman attacks the new tax as "socialism, communism, devilism." The following year, the U.S. Supreme Court declares the law unconstitutional.

September 4, 1894: Twelve thousand New York City GARMENT WORKERS GO ON STRIKE in order to protest sweatshop conditions and piecework wages

November 6, 1894: In MIDTERM ELECTIONS, Republicans win control of both the Senate and House of Representatives.

	1893	1896		1897	1898		1899
■ Cleveland's Life		Ethiopians defeat the Italian Army at Adowa.			U.S. declares war on Spain.		
■ U.S. & World Events		Frederick Jackson delivers lectures on "The Significance of the Frontier in American History."		Cleveland leaves Washington for Princeton, New Jersey.			U.S. signs the Treaty of Paris, ending the war with Spain.

December 24, 1894: American automobile manufacturer, HENRY FORD, finishes construction of the first working gasoline engine. He builds his first motor car in 1896.

February 20, 1895: Congress gives President Cleveland the authority to try to negotiate a settlement between Venezuela and Great Britain over the border of British Guiana.

November 5, 1895: Utah's new constitution grants women suffrage. It also outlaws polygamy and prevents control of the state government by a church.

January 4, 1896: UTAH IS ADMITTED TO THE UNION as the 44th state after its government bans bigamy and polygamy.

February 24, 1895: Cuban nationals rebel against Spanish rule. Spanish military commander General Valeriano Weyler begins confining rebels, as well as neutral Cuban men, women and children in disease-ridden concentration camps. While many Americans send financial support to the rebels, President Cleveland maintains a position of U.S. neutrality.

May 18, 1896: In *PLESSY V. FERGUSON*, the Supreme Court rules that segregation is constitutional as long as African Americans are given facilities that are "SEPARATE BUT EQUAL" to those of white citizens.

May 27, 1896: The PROHIBITION PARTY nominates Joshua Levering for president. The National Party, a free silver party, nominates Charles E. Bentley.

June 16-18, 1896: The REPUBLICAN PARTY CHOOSES WILLIAM MCKINLEY as their nominee for president. McKinley campaigns for a single gold standard, high tariffs, and an expansionist foreign policy.

July 4, 1896: The Socialist Labor Party nominates Charles H. Matchett for president.

July 8, 1896: Democratic Party presidential nominee WILLIAM JENNINGS BRYAN delivers an eloquent speech in favor of free silver at the Democratic Convention. In closing, he declares, "You shall not press down upon the brow of labor this crown of thorns, you shall not crucify mankind upon a CROSS OF GOLD!"

July 20, 1896: Great Britain refuses to accept U.S. arbitration in its border dispute with Venezuela. In response, President Cleveland argues that British pressure on Venezuela violates the Monroe Doctrine, which forbids European colonization or interference in the Americas. After Cleveland threatens to intervene, Britain eventually agrees in 1897 to allow an international tribunal arbitrate the boundary dispute.

August 16, 1896: Gold is discovered on the Klondike River near Dawson in Yukon Territory, Canada. The discovery launches the KLONDIKE GOLD RUSH, as thousands of fortune seekers head for northwestern Canada.

November 3, 1896: WILLIAM MCKINLEY is elected president, defeating Democratic nominee William Jennings Bryan.

This cartoon, titled "The Chasm of Defeat Awaits His Uncertain Tread," illustrates how Chinese labor was still a contentious issue as Cleveland headed into the 1888 election. The Chinese Exclusion Act of 1882 had banned Chinese immigration for ten years, and the pressure to extend it was strong.

1901	1902	1904	1905	1908
	Britain wins the Boer War, which had begun in 1899.	Cleveland's eldest daughter Ruth dies.	A domestic cook on Long Island, New York, named Mary Mallon, causes a deadly epidemic of typhoid. "Typhoid Mary" continues to take jobs as a cook even after learning she is a contagious carrier of the fatal disease.	Cleveland dies on June 24 in Princeton, New Jersey.
Cleveland becomes a trustee of Princeton University, where he befriends university president, and future U.S. president, Woodrow Wilson.				

Benjamin Harrison

23rd President (1889–1893)

"When I came into power, I found that the party managers had taken it all to themselves. I could not name my own Cabinet. They had sold out every place to pay the election expenses."

Benjamin Harrison was a former soldier and a lifelong loyalist of the Republican Party. His only apparent qualification for the presidency was that he happened to be the grandson of William Henry Harrison, an equally nondescript soldier who had served a month as the nation's president in 1841 before dying in office.

Although the younger Harrison had been appointed to the U.S. Senate by the Indiana legislature in 1881, he did little in office to distinguish himself. For the most part, he limited himself to promoting federal pensions for Civil War veterans and following the instructions of party leaders. A former Presbyterian minister, Harrison did manage to stay out of scandals—a rare feat for any Gilded Age politician. And in the eyes of Republican Party managers, this clean record made Harrison the perfect candidate for the presidency. Harrison campaigned almost entirely from his front porch in Indianapolis, and party leaders poured millions of dollars in contributions from big businesses into key swing states. Corporate America, which detested President Grover Cleveland for his promotion of lower tariffs, was only too happy to comply.

If Harrison had been inclined to exercise the powers of the presidency once he arrived in office, he would have found himself disappointed rather quickly. While Cleveland had left office with a huge surplus in the Treasury, the House of Representatives, with a thin Republican majority, went about spending that surplus as quickly as possible. Cleveland had vetoed bills that awarded Civil War pensions to veterans because the risk of fraudulent claims ran too high. Congress resubmitted these bills to Harrison, who only too willingly signed them into law. Civil War pension costs soon became one of the largest expenses in the federal budget.

In 1890, Congress paid off much of its debts to the business community by passing the McKinley Tariff, a dramatic increase in import fee. The tariff angered Americans by increasing the prices of many consumer goods. The American public soon responded in the 1890 midterm elections by giving Democrats control of both houses of Congress. Lingering anger over the tarriff helped Grover Cleveland win back the presidency in 1892. Harrison returned to Indianapolis and resumed his law practice. In 1897, he helped Venezuela in the settlement of its border dispute with Great Britain. Three years later, he died at his home and was buried in Indianapolis.

Biographical Facts

Born: August 20, 1833 in North Bend, Ohio

Ancestry: English-Scotch

Father: John Scott Harrison; born October 4, 1804 in Vincennes, Indiana; died May 25, 1878 in North Bend, Ohio

Father's Occupations: Farmer; U.S. congressman

Mother: Elizabeth Irwin Harrison; born July 18, 1810 in Mercersburg, Pennsylvania; died August 15, 1850

First Wife: Caroline (Carrie) Scott; born October 1, 1832 in Oxford, Ohio; died October 25, 1892 in Washington, D.C.

First Marriage: October 20, 1853 in Oxford, Ohio

Second Wife: Mary Scott Lord Dimmick; born April 30, 1858 in Honesdale, Pennsylvania; died January 5, 1948 in New York City

Second Marriage: New York City in April 6, 1896

Children: Russell Benjamin (1854-1936); Mary Scott (1858-1930); Elizabeth (1898-1955)

Education: Private tutoring; attended Farmers' College; received B.A. from Miami University (1852)

Home: Indianapolis, Indiana

Religious Affiliation: Presbyterian

Occupations before Presidency: Lawyer; notary public; soldier

Military Service: Colonel in 70th Indiana Volunteers; Brevet Brigadier General, Union Army

Political Offices before Presidency: Commissioner for the Court of Claims; City Attorney; Secretary of Indiana Republican Central Committee; State Supreme Court Reporter; Member of U.S. Senate

Political Party: Republican

Age at Inauguration: 55

Occupation after Presidency: Lawyer

Death: March 13, 1901 in Indianapolis, Indiana

Place of Burial: Crown Hill Cemetery, Indianapolis, Indiana

William McKinley

25th President (1897–1901)

"It is sometimes sneeringly said by those who do not like free government, that here we count heads. True, heads are counted, but brains also . . ."

In 1890, the U.S. Census Department declared that the period of Western expansion was over—that the American frontier had closed. A decade later, the U.S. flag flew halfway around the globe, over an empire stretching from Puerto Rico to Hawaii and Philippines. Overseeing this expansion was the 25th president, William McKinley.

McKinley began his career as a protégé of another Republican president from Ohio, Rutherford B. Hayes. After McKinley served under Hayes during the Civil War, Hayes helped him build his career. In 1876, when Hayes won his controversial presidential election, McKinley was elected to the House of Representatives.

In Congress, his main interest was high tariffs, believing they would protect farmers and laborers from cheap foreign competition. In 1890, he sponsored the McKinley Tariff, which raised tariffs dramatically.

Tariffs benefited corporate America, who used the high rates to keep prices artificially steep. When the Panic of 1893 struck, many blamed McKinley and his high tariff. Even so, he had caught the eye of a wealthy Ohio industrialist, Marcus Hanna. With Hanna's assistance, McKinley won election to two terms as Ohio's governor, and in 1896, the Republican nomination for president. McKinley then defeated the free-silver Democrat, William Jennings Bryan, to become president.

In 1898, when the U.S.S. *Maine* exploded in Havana's harbor, everything changed. A media frenzy pushed a reluctant McKinley to declare war on Spain, which ruled over colonial Cuba. In a matter of months, U.S. forces had destroyed the Spanish Navy—both in the Caribbean and in the Philippines. Far from accepting a closed frontier, the United States had dramatically expanded its power overseas, signaling the beginning of a new era.

Following the Spanish-American War, McKinley reversed course on the issue of high tariffs. He started to believe that if overseas markets were to be opened to American goods, commercial barriers had to fall at home. Moving away from the tariff protectionism of his own Republican party, McKinley promoted the gradual and steady implementation of his "tariff reciprocity" policy. His sweeping reelection at the turn of the century renewed his determination to push through his proposals for reciprocal tariff treaties. In addition to this, President McKinley's ability to negotiate trade agreements with other nations helped end the Gilded Age of protectionism and Congressional control.

Even so, the fundamandally conservative McKinley refrained from using the full powers of his office. However, Theodore Roosevelt, who succeeded McKinley after he was assassinated in 1901, had no such hesitation.

Biographical Facts

Born: January 29, 1843 in Niles, Ohio

Ancestry: Scotch-Irish and English

Father: William McKinley; born November 15, 1807 in Pine Township, Pennsylvania; died November 24, 1892 in Canton, Ohio

Father's Occupation: Iron-founder

Mother: Nancy Allison McKinley; born April 22, 1809 in New Lisbon, Ohio; died December 12, 1897 in Canton, Ohio

Wife: Ida Saxton; born June 8, 1847 in Canton, Ohio; died May 26, 1907 in Canton, Ohio

Marriage: January 25, 1871 in Canton, Ohio

Children: Katherine (1871-1875); Ida (1873-1873)

Home: Market Avenue, Canton, Ohio

Education: Poland Academy; Allegheny College; Albany Law School

Religious Affiliation: Methodist

Occupations before Presidency: Teacher; soldier; lawyer

Military Service: Ohio 23rd Volunteers; Major, U.S. Army

Political Offices before Presidency: Member of U.S. House of Representatives; Governor of Ohio

Political Party: Republican

Age at Inauguration: 54

Death: September 14, 1901 in Buffalo, New York

Place of Burial: Canton, Ohio

Nickname: Idol of Ohio

Writings: *The Tariff in the Days of Henry Clay and Since*

Election of 1896

Candidates	Party	Electoral Vote	Popular Vote
William McKinley (OH)	Republican	271	7,102,246
William J. Bryan (NE)	Democratic	176	6,492,559
John M. Palmer (IL)	National Democratic	---	133,148
Joshua Levering (MD)	Prohibition	---	132,007

About the Election: In 1896, the populist, free-silver faction of the Democratic Party won over the more conservative wing. After his dramatic "Cross of Gold Speech" at the Democratic Convention, Kansas newspaperman William Jennings Bryan crisscrossed the nation as both the Democratic and Populist presidential nominee. Taking advantage of Bryan's distrust in the business community, the Republicans nominated pro-tariff, pro-gold standard William McKinley. McKinley's campaign manager Marcus Hanna raised millions of dollars from corporate America to outspend the Democrats 12 to 1. Hanna and McKinley were also able to take labor votes away from Bryan by warning that a free-silver policy would lead to job losses and economic instability. McKinley won every state north of Virginia and east of Missouri.

■ **McKinley**
233 (Votes)
■ **Bryan**

McKinley's First Term 1897-1901

March 4, 1897: MCKINLEY IS INAUGURATED as the twenty-fifth president of the United States.

March 15, 1897: McKinley calls a special session of Congress to revise tariff laws. In July, he signs the DINGLEY TARIFF LAW, hiking the tariffs by about 57 percent. As a result, Democrats and Progressives blame McKinley and the Republicans for the dramatic price increases that follow.

May 24, 1897: Congress appropriates $50,000 to assist Americans living in Cuba.

September 10, 1897: Miners in Luzerne County, Pennsylvania win an eight-hour workday after miners in Ohio, West Virginia, and the Lehigh Valley of Pennsylvania walk off their jobs in protest. The multiple demonstrations occur after police open fire on striking coal workers in Pennsylvania.

December 6, 1897: In his first annual message to Congress, McKinley argues that Spain must reform its policies in Cuba.

January 25, 1898: The U.S. battleship *MAINE* arrives in Havana to protect American lives and property in case of riots.

February 9, 1898: WILLIAM RANDOLPH HEARST, publisher of the *New York Journal*, prints a letter by the Spanish minister to the United States which contains insults to McKinley.

February 15, 1898: THE *MAINE* EXPLODES AND SINKS IN HAVANA HARBOR, killing 266 Americans. Although Hearst and others charge that Spanish espionage caused the disaster, there is little evidence of this theory. Nonetheless, the sinking of the *Maine* becomes a major impetus for war, and the majority of Americans rally in support of American invervention in Cuba's fight for independence from Spain.

March 9, 1898: Congress appropriates $50 million for national defense.

March 17, 1898: The U.S. Navy reports that the *Maine* explosion was the result of external factors. Several days later, the Spanish Navy rebuts the report with its own contention that the explosion occurred onboard the ship (Less than a century later, in 1976, researchers confirm that heat from a fire in a coalbin exploded near a supply of ammunition.)

April 11, 1898: In a failed effort to avoid war, Spain's prime minister offers Cuba limited autonomy.

April 19, 1898: While declaring that the United States has no intention of annexing the island, CONGRESS AUTHORIZES MCKINLEY TO INTERVENE IN CUBA in order to force Spanish withdrawal. Spain severs relations with the United States.

April 21, 1898: McKinley orders a blockade of Cuban ports.

April 22, 1898: Congress passes the VOLUNTEER ARMY ACT. The act authorizes the formation of a volunteer unit known as the First Volunteer Cavalry, or the "Rough Riders." The Rough Riders are commanded by Colonel Leonard Wood and future president, Lt. Colonel THEODORE ROOSEVELT.

	1843	1846-48	1848	1850	1855
■ McKinley's Life					
■ U.S. & World Events		The U.S.-Mexican War is fought.		Nathamiel Hawthorne writes the *Scarlet Letter*.	Scottish explorer David Livingstone finds and names Victoria Falls on the Zambezi River in Southern Africa.
		William McKinley is born on January 29 in Niles, Ohio.	The California Gold Rush begins.		

First Lady: Ida Saxton McKinley

As a young woman, Ida Saxton lived a life of ease and opportunity. Well-educated, she even worked as a cashier in her father's bank. Mrs. McKinley suffered from phlebitis and epileptic seizures brought on during the difficult births of her two daughters, both of whom died. By the time she arrived at the White House, Mrs. McKinley was a declared invalid.

The McKinleys behaved in as traditional a manner as possible, and Mrs. McKinley formally received guests while seated in a blue velvet chair. If she experienced an epileptic seizure in public, her husband, ever at her side, would place a large handkerchief over her face until the "spell" passed. After her husband's death, Mrs. McKinley was cared for by her younger sister.

April 23, 1898: SPAIN DECLARES WAR on the United States.

April 25, 1898: Congress declares war on Spain, launching the SPANISH-AMERICAN WAR.

May 1, 1898: Commodore George Dewey, leading a six-ship squadron easily outguns a larger Spanish fleet at MANILA BAY in the Philippines. By August, U.S. troops occupy Manila.

June 1, 1898: In a short-lived victory for labor groups, Congress passes the ERDMAN ARBITRATION ACT, which authorizes federal mediation between interstate carriers and their employees. In 1908, the Supreme Court will rule against the law that bans interstate carriers from discriminating against or blacklisting Union members.

June 10, 1898: To raise money for the war, Congress passes the WAR REVENUE ACT. The act also raises taxes on beer, tobacco, amusements, and specified business transactions.

June 12-14, 1898: Seventeen thousand Americans led by General William Shafter leave Key West, Florida, for Cuba.

June 21, 1898: American naval forces seize the Spanish island of Guam and claim the island as U.S. territory.

June 24, 1898: American ground troops defeat the Spanish at the BATTLE OF LAS GUASIMAS, the first major land battle of the Spanish-American War.

July 1, 1898: After heavy fighting, U.S. forces capture the Spanish garrisons at El Caney and SAN JUAN HILL. Future president Theodore Roosevelt leads his group of "Rough Riders" in the charge at San Juan Hill, earning himself national fame.

July 3, 1898: American naval forces destroy the Spanish fleet off the coast from the city of SANTIAGO.

July 7, 1898: McKinley signs a Congressional resolution to annex the Hawaiian islands.

July 17, 1898: U.S. General William Shafter captures Santiago and 24,000 Spanish troops.

July 25, 1898: U.S. troops invade and quickly seize control of PUERTO RICO.

August 12, 1898: Spain agrees to grant Cuba its independence and cede Puerto Rico and Guam to the United States. The status of the Philippines is left to be determined at a postwar conference between the United States and Spain.

August 14, 1898: SPAIN SURRENDERS to the United States in the Philippines.

September 9, 1898: McKinley asks Secretary of State William R. Day to resign so that he may lead a

McKinley's First Administration

Inauguration: March 4, 1897 at the Capitol, Washington, D.C.
Vice President: Garret A. Hobart
Secretary of State: John Sherman; William R. Day (from April 28, 1898); John Hay (from September 30, 1898)
Secretary of the Treasury: Lyman J. Gage
Secretary of War: Russell A. Alger; Elihu Root (from August 1, 1899)
Attorney General: Joseph McKenna; John W. Griggs (from February 1, 1898)
Postmaster General: James A. Gary; Charles Emory Smith (from April 21, 1898)
Secretary of the Navy: John D. Long

Secretary of the Interior: Cornelius N. Bliss; Ethan A. Hitchcock (from February 20, 1899)
Secretary of Agriculture: James Wilson
Supreme Court Appointment:
Joseph McKenna (1898)
55th Congress: (March 4, 1897-March 4, 1899)
Senate: 47 Republicans; 34 Democrats; 7 Others
House: 204 Republicans; 113 Democrats; 40 Others
56th Congress: (March 4, 1899-March 4, 1901)
Senate: 53 Republicans; 26 Democrats; 8 Others
House: 185 Republicans; 163 Democrats; 9 Others

1861	1865	1867	1869

After heroic service in the Civil War McKinley rises to the rank of brevet major.

Abraham Lincoln is assassinated.

The Ku Klux Klan is formally formed in Nashmille.

McKinley becomes a prosecuting attorney at Stark County, Ohio.

The U.S. Civil War begins.

McKinley is admitted to the bar.

McKinley's Second Administration

Inauguration: March 4, 1901 at the Capitol, Washington, D.C.
Vice President: Theodore Roosevelt
Secretary of State: John Hay
Secretary of the Treasury: Lyman J. Gage
Secretary of War: Elihu Root
Attorney General: John W. Griggs; Philander C. Knox (from April 10, 1901)

Postmaster General: Charles Emory Smith
Secretary of the Navy: John D. Long
Secretary of the Interior: Ethan A. Hitchcock
Secretary of Agriculture: James Wilson
57th Congress: (March 4, 1901-March 4, 1903)
Senate: 55 Republicans; 31 Democrats; 4 Others
House: 197 Republicans; 151 Democrats; 9 Others

PEACE TREATY COMMISSION. John Hay replaces Day as secretary of state.

September 26, 1898: McKinley appoints the DODGE COMMISSION to investigate the conduct of the War Department.

November 8, 1898: In the MIDTERM ELECTIONS, Republicans maintain control of both houses of Congress.

December 5, 1898: In his message to Congress, President McKinley affirms his desire to build a Central American canal.

December 10, 1898: The United States and Spain sign the TREATY OF PARIS, which requires Spain to cede Puerto Rico and Guam to the United States. The U.S also takes temporary control of Cuba and pays Spain $20 million for its holdings in the Philippines. Many take this payment to be an outright purchase of the Philippines from Spain and oppose the annexations. These anti-imperialists do not want to run the risk of becoming involved in further wars, and because of their opposition, the Senate barely ratifies the peace treaty in 1899— the difference being a single vote.

January 1, 1899: The United States takes official control of Cuba and establishes a military government in Cuba.

February 4, 1899: Philippine freedom fighters, led by EMILIO AGUINALDO, attack U.S. forces in Manila, beginning the PHILIPPINE-AMERICAN WAR.

May 29, 1899: McKinley orders that 3,000 to 4,000 civil service jobs be exempt from examinations.

July 19, 1899: SECRETARY OF WAR RUSSELL A. ALGER RESIGNS, effective August 1, after the Dodge Commission criticizes his handling of the war. Elihu Root replaces Alger.

September 6, 1899: Secretary of State John Hay informs Japan, Great Britain, and Russia about America's OPEN DOOR POLICY toward China. Hay calls for open access to China's trade markets and warns that the United States desires that Chinese sovereignty be maintained.

December 5, 1899: In his annual address to Congress, McKinley calls for expanding the U.S. Navy. He also affirms America's intent to hold the Philippines as a U.S. territory.

February 5, 1900: Great Britain and the United States sign the HAY-PAUNCEFOTE TREATY, which allows the United States to build a canal in Central America. The Senate ratifies a slightly modified version of the treaty on December 20.

March 7, 1900: McKinley signs the GOLD STANDARD ACT, which sets gold as the standard of value for all American money. The act effectively ends the long debate over gold and silver-backed monetary policies.

April 30, 1900: Congress passes the ORGANIC ACT, making Hawaii a U.S. territory. With the act's passage, U.S. laws go into effect in Hawaii, ending its era of Asian contract labor. Thousands of Chinese and Japanese laborers are free to leave Hawaii. Many settle in California, Washington, and Oregon.

June 19-21, 1900: THE REPUBLICAN PARTY RENOMINATES MCKINLEY for the presidency and chooses Spanish-American War hero and New York governor Theodore Roosevelt as their nominee for vice president.

June 21, 1900: The American military governor of the Philippines offers amnesty to Filipino rebels.

July 3, 1900: Secretary of State John Hay issues the second OPEN DOOR declaration, stating the goal of the United States in keeping China intact despite Western intervention.

July 5, 1900: The DEMOCRATS NOMINATE WILLIAM JENNINGS

	1870	1873	1876
■ McKinley's Life			
■ U.S. & World Events	Standard Oil of Ohio is incorporated, launching the career of John D. Rockefeller.	McKinley marries Ida Saxton. Following the deaths of two of their children, Mrs. McKinley will sink into lifelong mental and physical illness.	McKinley is elected to Congress.

Election of 1900

Candidates	Party	Electoral Vote	Popular Vote
William McKinley (OH)	Republican	292	7,218,491
William J. Bryan (NE)	Democratic	155	6,356,734
John C. Wooley (IL)	Prohibition	---	208,914
Eugene V. Debs (IN)	Socialist	---	87,814

About the Election: In the aftermath of the Spanish-American War, McKinley's political fortunes skyrocketed. Facing William Jennings Bryan for the second time, free silver was again an issue and Bryan did his best to use corporate, pro-gold standard forces for an attack on American imperialism. However, with the economy now strong, most Americans were not inclined to replace McKinley. Bryan was again shut out of the Northeast and Midwest, and although he won most of the South, he lost some of the Western states that he had won in 1896. He even lost in his home state of Nebraska. Republicans also made major gains in both the House and the Senate.

McKinley
233 (Votes)
Bryan

BRYAN for president for the second time.

November 6 , 1900: MCKINLEY IS REELECTED. Republicans also increase their majorities in both houses of Congress.

December 29, 1900: The Netherlands agrees to sell the Dutch West Indies to the United States. However, the purchase does not occur until 1917, when Congress authorizes payment for the islands. They are then renamed the **U.S. VIRGIN ISLANDS**.

January 10, 1901: Oil is found in Beaumont, Texas.

March 1, 1901: Congress passes the **PLATT AMENDMENT**, allowing the United States to send troops to Cuba to protect it from foreign intervention. Although Cuba is nominally independent, the amendment signals its complete domination by the United States after the Spanish-American War.

McKinley's Second Term 1901

March 4, 1901: MCKINLEY IS INAUGURATED for a second term. Theodore Roosevelt is sworn in as vice president. On the same day, African American representative George H. White of North Carolinas leaves Congress. There will not be another African in Congress for more than 25 years.

March 11, 1901: Britain informs the United States that it will not accept amendments made by the Senate to the Hay-Pauncefote Treaty regarding a Central American canal.

March 23, 1901: Filipino rebel leader **EMILIO AGUINALDO IS CAPTURED**, effectively ending the Philppine-American War. Scattered fighting lasts for at least another year.

June 11, 1901: President McKinley announces that he will not run for a third term.

September 6, 1901: Polish-American anarchist **LEON CZOLGOSZ SHOOTS MCKINLEY** in the stomach when the president is touring the Pan-American Exposition in Buffalo, NY. McKinley dies over a week later, and Vice President Theodore Roosevelt is sworn in as president.

A cartoon showing Mckinley serving up an expansionist bill of fare to Uncle Sam. On the menu are "Cuba Steak, Porto Rico Pig, Philippine Floating Islands or the Sandwich Islands" (present-day Hawaii).

1882	1885	1896	1900	1901

German scientist Robert Koch isolated an organism he called "tubercle bacillus," identifying it as the cause of tuberculosis.

McKinley is reelected to the House of Representatives.

Turkish authorities massacre hundreds of thousands of Armenians.

McKinley is elected president.

He is reelected.

McKinley is assassinated by Leon Czolgosz on September 14 in Buffalo, New York.

PRESIDENTS

OF THE EARLY 20TH CENTURY

Theodore Roosevelt

26th President (1901–1909)

"No President has ever enjoyed himself as much as I."

Theodore Roosevelt, a sickly child, was picked on as a youngster. But by the time he became president, he had transformed himself into a robust man of action. Having spent time as a boxer, a ranch hand, a police commissioner, and a military hero, he was a living example of "The Strenuous Life"—the very name of a book he published in 1900 after being nominated for the vice presidency.

Roosevelt was unsuited to be any man's Number Two. But his fame made him a vote-getter. New York political boss Tom Platt figured that kicking Roosevelt up to the vice presidency was worth the risk. Marcus Hanna, William McKinley's campaign manager wasn't convinced. Because his wing of the Republican party was loyal to the interests of big business, he did not trust the reform-minded Roosevelt. "Don't you realize," he argued, "there's only one life between that madman and the White House?" On September 14, 1901, Hanna's worst nightmare came true. McKinley, shot by an assassin a week earlier, had died. Roosevelt was president.

Over the next seven years, Roosevelt reshaped the presidency. He believed in using his full powers to ensure justice for all, regardless of wealth or connections. He wielded the rarely used Sherman Anti-Trust Act to break up monopolies he thought harmed the national interest. In one of his most far-reaching achievements, he launched widespread conservation efforts that brought state and federal governments together to protect the nation's natural resources.

Roosevelt was also a committed imperialist who viewed expansion as a testament to what he saw as America's intellectual and racial superiority. He approved U.S. support of Panama's revolt against Columbia and made Panama surrender the canal to the U.S.

Elected in his own right in 1904, he declined to run again in 1908. However, when he felt that his friend William Howard Taft was abandoning his agenda, he entered the 1912 election race on the Progressive Party ticket. Despite his defeat to Woodrow Wilson, he stayed active in politics until his death.

Biographical Facts

Born: October 27, 1858 in New York City

Ancestry: Dutch, Scotch, English, and Huguenot

Father: Theodore Roosevelt; born September 22, 1831 in New York City; died February 9, 1878 in New York City

Father's Occupations: Glass importer; merchant; banker

Mother: Martha Bulloch Roosevelt; born July 8, 1834 in Roswell, Georgia; died February 14, 1884 in New York City

First Wife: Alice Hathaway Lee; born July 29, 1861 in Chestnut Hill, Massachusetts; died February 14, 1884 in New York City

First Marriage: October 27, 1880 in Brookline, Massachusetts

Second Wife: Edith Kermit Carow; born August 6, 1861 in Norwich, Connecticut; died September 30, 1948 in Oyster Bay, New York

Second Marriage: December 2, 1886 in London, England

Children: Alice Lee Roosevelt (1884-1980); Theodore Roosevelt Jr. (1887-1944); Kermit Roosevelt (1889-1943); Ethel Carow Roosevelt (1891-1977); Archibald Bulloch Roosevelt (1894-1979); Quentin Roosevelt (1897-1918)

Education: Private tutoring; received B.A. from Harvard (1880); studied law at Columbia Law School

Homes: 20th Street, New York City; Sagamore Hill, Oyster Bay, New York

Religious Affiliation: Dutch Reformed; Episcopalian

Occupations before Presidency: Writer; historian; politician

Military Service: Lieutenant Colonel, Colonel, First U.S. Volunteer Cavalry Regiment ("Rough Riders")

Political Offices before Presidency: New York State Assemblyman; U.S. Civil Service Commissioner; President of New York Board of Police Commissioners; Assistant Secretary of the Navy; Governor of New York; U.S. Vice President

Political Party: Republican; Progressive Party (1912)

Age at Inauguration: 42

Occupations after Presidency: Writer; politician

Death: January 6, 1919 in Oyster Bay, New York

Nickname: TR; Trust-Buster; Teddy

Writings: *The Naval War of 1812; The Winning of the West; African Game Trails; Autobiography; America and the World War*

by the Panama Canal Company and the Roosevelt administration, **PANAMA DECLARES INDEPENDENCE FROM COLUMBIA**. Three days later, the U.S. recognizes the Republic of Panama

November 18, 1903: U.S. and Panama sign the **HAY-BUNEAU-VARILLA TREATY**, giving the U.S. control of a ten-mile-wide canal zone in exchange for $10 million and an annual fee of $250,000.

December 12, 1903: Acting on a request made by the Venezuelan government, Roosevelt proposes to mediate the conflict over unsettled debts that prompted Great Britain, Germany, and Italy to attack Venezuelan warships and impose blockades on Venezuelan ports. The countries approve the proposal on December 19.

January 4, 1904: Although the Supreme Court rules that the inhabitants of Puerto Rico are not aliens and cannot be denied entry to the continental United States. But the Supreme Court refuses to declare Puerto Ricans as full citizens.

February 29, 1904: President Roosevelt appoints the **PANAMA CANAL COMMISSION** to oversee the construction of the Panama Canal.

March 14, 1904: In the case of ***NORTHERN SECURITIES V. UNITED STATES***, the Supreme Court rules that the railroad holding company violated the Sherman Anti-Trust Act of 1890. The act had rarely been enforced since its passage, but President Roosevelt uses it as a major tool in his effort to break up unfair monopolies.

May 5, 1904: The Socialist Party nominates **EUGENE V. DEBS** for president.

June 21-23, 1904: **REPUBLICANS NOMINATE ROOSEVELT** for reelection.

July 6-9, 1904: Rather than choose William Jennings Bryan as their standard-bearer, the Democratic Party abandons its populist wing. Instead **DEMOCRATS NOMINATE ALTON B. PARKER**, a conservative New York judge. The nomination is an attempt to appeal to commercial interests who are opposed to Roosevelt's trust-busting activism.

November 8, 1904: In a **LANDSLIDE VICTORY**, Roosevelt trounces Parker.

December 6, 1904: In his annual message to Congress, the "**ROOSEVELT COROLLARY**" to the Monroe Doctrine is outlined. Roosevelt argues that "in flagrant cases of wrongdoing or impotence" in the western hemisphere, the U.S. has the right to "the exercise of an international police power."

January 21, 1905: The **DOMINICAN REPUBLIC** agrees to allow the Roosevelt administration to administer its customs and manage its international debt payments. In 1907, the two nations formalize the arrangement in a treaty that the Senate eventually ratifies.

February 1, 1905: Roosevelt establishes the **NATIONAL FOREST SERVICE** in the Department of Agriculture. Gifford Pinchot becomes the first head of the service.

Roosevelt's Second Term 1905-1909

February 20, 1905: In the case of ***JACOBSON V. MASSACHUSETTS***, the Supreme Court rules that the Massachusetts law ordering mandatory smallpox vaccinations is a legitimate exercise of the state's police power to protect the public health of its citizens.

March 4, 1905: **ROOSEVELT IS INAUGURATED** for his first full-term as president.

April 17, 1905: In ***LOCHNER V. NEW YORK***, the Supreme Court rules that a New York law limiting the number of workhours for bakers is illegal since it interferes with the right of free contracts. Overall, the Supreme Court rules that it is an excessive use of state powers.

July 7, 1905: The **INDUSTRIAL WORKERS OF THE WORLD (IWW)** is established. It is a more radical union than the cautious **AMERICAN FEDERATION OF LABOR**, popularly known as the "Wobblies."

July 11-13, 1905: A group of African American intellectuals, launch the **NIAGARA MOVEMENT**,

	1897	1898	1899-1902	1900
■ Roosevelt's life	Roosevelt serves as McKinley's assistant secretary of the Navy during the Spanish-American War, and becomes famous for leading the U.S. Volunteer Cavalry (Rough Riders) up Kettle Hill at the Battle of San Juan.	Roosevelt is elected governor of New York.	The British Army defeats Dutch Afrikaaners in South Africa's Boer War.	Roosevelt is elected vice president.
■ U.S. & World Events				

Election of 1904

Candidates	Party	Electoral Vote	Popular Vote
Theodore Roosevelt (NY)	Republican	336	7,628,461
Alton B. Parker (NY)	Democratic	140	5,084,223
Eugene V. Debs (IN)	Socialist	---	402,283
Silas C. Swallow (PA)	Prohibition	---	258,536
Thomas E. Watson (GA)	People's	---	117,183

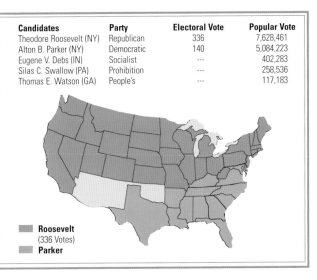

■ **Roosevelt**
(336 Votes)
■ **Parker**

About the Election: As Theodore Roosevelt had siezed the reform agenda from the Democratic Party, the Democrats bypassed William Jennings Bryan and nominated a pro-Wall Street, conservative judge from upstate New York named Alton B. Parker. Parker, a firm advocate of the gold standard, reversed the course of the Democratic Party platform by denouncing free silver.

Even so, the election campaign was relatively issueless, since the colorless Parker was no match for the wildly popular Roosevelt, who swept all but the South. At the same time, the Socialist candidate, Eugene V. Debs, increased his vote total from about 86,000 votes in 1900 to over 400,000. His vote totals would continue to increase in each of the next two elections, reaching close to a million votes in 1912.

Roosevelt rides to his 1904 inauguration in a carriage. He was the last president to do so, since subsequent presidents rode in an automobile.

at a meeting in Niagara Falls, New York to lobby for civil rights and equality for African Americans.

September 2, 1905: Roosevelt arranges the **PORTSMOUTH TREATY** and helps orchestrate an end to the war between Russia and Japan at a conference in Portsmouth, New Hampshire. In 1906, President Roosevelt wins the **NOBEL PEACE PRIZE** for his role in arranging the peace treaty.

January 16, 1906: Roosevelt attends the **ALGECIRAS CONFERENCE**, in the hope of mediating a solution to the conflict between France and Germany over Morocco.

April 13, 1906: A RACE RIOT in Brownsville, Texas occurs, after white civilians taunt a group of African American soldiers. Three whites are killed in the riot.

April 18, 1906: A MAJOR EARTHQUAKE STRIKES SAN FRANCISCO, CALIFORNIA, killing 452 people and destroying 490 city blocks. Immigration records are also destroyed, ushering in a period of illegal immigration from China. Because family members are not excluded from joining their relatives in the U.S., many illegal Chinese immigrants in San Francisco claim to be related to legal immigrants. These men are known as "**PAPER SONS,**" since their status as relatives existed only on paper.

May 21, 1906: The U.S and Mexico agree to share the Rio Grande water for irrigation purposes.

June 8, 1906: Roosevelt signs the **NATIONAL MONUMENTS ACT** and establishes the first 18 national monuments, including Devils Tower, Muir Woods, and Mount Olympus.

June 29, 1906: Roosevelt directs the passage of the **HEPBURN ACT**, which revitalizes the **INTERSTATE COMMERCE COMMISSION** and authorizes greater governmental authority over railroads.

June 30, 1906: Upton Sinclair's novel *The Jungle*, a behind-the-scenes look at a Chicago meatpacking plant, influences Roosevelt to sign the **MEAT INSPECTION ACT** and the **PURE FOOD AND DRUG ACT**. The laws require that the contents of foods be clearly labeled and that all plants involved in interstate commerce be subject to federal inspections.

August 23, 1906: Following a disputed election, the president

1901	1903		1904
When McKinley is assassinated, Roosevelt becomes the youngest president to take office.	The first World Series is played. The Boston Red Stockings of the American League defeat the Pittsburgh Pirates, 5 games to 3.	Orville and Wilbur Wright successfully fly the first powered flight of a heavier-than-air machine, at Kitty Hawk, North Carolina.	Roosevelt is reelected.

Roosevelt's Second Administration

Inauguration: March 4, 1905 at the Capitol, Washington, D.C.
Vice President: Charles Warren Fairbanks
Secretary of State: John Hay;
Elihu Root (from July 19, 1905);
Robert Bacon (from January 27, 1909)
Secretary of the Treasury: Leslie M. Shaw;
George B. Cortelyou (from March 4, 1907)
Secretary of War: William H. Taft;
Luke E. Wright (from July 1, 1908)
Attorney General: William H . Moody;
Charles J. Bonaparte (from December 17, 1906)
Postmaster General: George B. Cortelyou;
George von L. Meyer (from March 4, 1907)
Secretary of the Navy: Paul Morton;
Charles J. Bonaparte (from July 1, 1905);
Victor H. Metcalf (from December 17, 1906);

Truman H. Newbery (from December 1, 1908)
Secretary of the Interior:
Ethan A. Hitchcock;
James R. Garfield (from March 4, 1907)
Secretary of Agriculture: James Wilson
Secretary of Commerce and Labor:
Victor H. Metcalf;
Oscar S. Straus (from December 17, 1906)
Supreme Court Appointment:
William H. Moody (1906)
59th Congress: (March 4, 1905-March 4, 1907)
Senate: 57 Republicans; 33 Democrats
House: 250 Republicans; 136 Democrats
60th Congress: (March 4, 1907-March 4, 1909)
Senate: 61 Republicans; 31 Democrats
House: 222 Republicans; 164 Democrats
State Admitted: Oklahoma (1907)

Roosevelt (left), with conservationist John Muir,
on Glacier Point in Yosemite, California.

of Cuba asks the U.S. to intervene in a rebellion. After Congress invokes the **PLATT AMENDMENT**, which authorizes the United States to occupy Cuba, Roosevelt sends troops to the island.

September 22-24, 1906: In a **RACE RIOT IN ATLANTA**, 21 people die. Among the number of casualties, 18 of them are African Americans.

September 29, 1906: Under the authority of the **PLATT AMENDMENT**, the U.S. intervenes in Cuba and Roosevelt appoints Secretary of War (and future president) **WILLIAM HOWARD TAFT** military governor of Cuba.

November 6, 1906: In the **MIDTERM ELECTIONS**, the Republicans add 4 seats to their Senate majority. However, the party loses 28 seats in the House when its members refuse to endorse the "Labor's Bill of Rights," drafted by the American Federation of Labor.

November 9-26, 1906: In the **FIRST OVERSEAS JOURNEY BY AN AMERICAN PRESIDENT**, Roosevelt and his wife Edith travel to Panama to inspect the building of the Panama Canal.

December 12, 1906: President Roosevelt appoints Oscar S. Straus secretary of commerce and labor. Straus is the **FIRST JEWISH CABINET MEMBER**.

January 26, 1907: **CONGRESS BANS CAMPAIGN CONTRIBUTIONS** to candidates for national office.

February 20, 1907: Roosevelt signs the **IMMIGRATION ACT OF 1907**. The act includes a provision, known as the "**GENTLEMEN'S AGREEMENT**," allowing the president to restrict Japanese immigration. Roosevelt also signs the Executive Order 589, which bans Japanese people with passports from Hawaii, Mexico, or Canada from reemigrating to the U.S. mainland.

March 2, 1907: Roosevelt issues a presidential proclamation and establishes forest reserves in six Western states.

March 14, 1907: Roosevelt appoints an **INLAND WATERWAYS COMMISSION** to study the relationship between forest preservation and commercial waterways.

March 21, 1907: **U.S. MARINES LAND IN HONDURAS** amid

	1906	1908	1910	1912
■ Roosevelt's Life			The Mexican Revolution begins.	Accusing Taft of abandoning his progressive policies, Roosevelt runs for president as the nominee of the Progressive (Bull Moose) Party. He loses to Democrat Woodrow Wilson during the election campaign.
■ U.S. & World Events	Roosevelt receives the Nobel Peace Prize for his role in the settlement of the Russo-Japanese war.	Declining to accept renomination, Roosevelt promotes William Howard Taft's candidacy.		

violent political clashes.

June 15, 1907: U.S. representatives promote the establishment of a **WORLD COURT** at the Second International Peace Conference in The Hague.

October 22, 1907: After the stock market plummets in March and numerous businesses begin to fail, the **PANIC OF 1907** is triggered by a run on the Knickerbocker Trust Company in October. The panic ends in December after the intervention of the federal government and the J.P. Morgan and Co.

In 1907, Roosevelt sent the U.S. Navy's "Great White Fleet" on a global goodwill tour to display U.S. strength.

October 23, 1907: Roosevelt returns to Washington from a hunting trip to address the economy. The president allows the J.P. Morgan's U.S. Steel Company to purchase the Tennessee Coal and Iron Company without risking an anti-trust lawsuit from the federal government.

November 16, 1907: OKLAHOMA IS ADMITTED TO THE UNION and it becomes the 46th state.

December 16, 1907: The U.S. Navy, nicknamed "THE GREAT WHITE FLEET," begins a 14-month worldwide voyage to display American naval strength.

February 3, 1908: In *LOEWE V. LAWLOR*, the Supreme Court rules that the anti-trust law applies to labor unions.

May 10, 1908: The SOCIALIST PARTY NOMINATES EUGENE V. DEBS for a second time.

May 13-15, 1908: Roosevelt organizes a **WHITE HOUSE CONSERVATION CONFERENCE**. It is attended by members of the Cabinet, Supreme Court, Congress, and governors from 34 states. A National Conservation Commission is founded to study conservation of the nation's natural resources.

May 30, 1908: Congress passes the **ALDRICH–VREELAND ACT**, allowing banks to issue money based on commercial paper and government bonds. The act also establishes the **NATIONAL MONETARY COUNCIL** to monitor and investigate the American banking system. The commission's recommendations eventually lead to the formation of the **FEDERAL RESERVE SYSTEM** in 1913.

June 16-20, 1908: Although many delegates support another term for Roosevelt, he had previously announced that he would not run. As a result, the **REPUBLICANS NOMINATE WILLIAM HOWARD TAFT**, Roosevelt's personal choice as sucessor. Taft had served as Roosevelt's Secretary of War, and was appointed military governor in both the Philippines and Cuba.

July 7-10, 1908: For the third time, the **DEMOCRATS NOMINATE WILLIAM JENNINGS BRYAN** as their presidential nominee.

July 15, 1908: The **PROHIBITION PARTY** nominates Eugene Chaflin for president.

July 24, 1908: The **SOCIALIST LABOR PARTY**, founded in 1874 as the Workingman's Party, nominates August Gilhous for president. Unlike the Socialist Party, the Socialist Labor Party advocates revolution rather than reform. The radical party, dominated by German-immigrant followers of Karl Marx, is less successful than Debs' party, whose membership is more widespread.

November 3, 1908: TAFT IS ELECTED after he defeats William Jennings Bryan in the presidential election.

February 12, 1909: A group of black and white intellectuals form the **NATIONAL ASSOCIATION FOR THE ADVANCEMENT OF COLORED PEOPLE (NAACP)**.

February 18, 1909: The North American Conservation Conference convenes at the White House.

1914	1916	1917	1918	1919
	After failing to win the Republican nomination, Roosevelt supports Charles E. Hughes.	U.S. declares war on Germany and thereby enters World War I.	President Woodrow Wilson announces his Fourteen Points as the basis for peace. Germany signs armistice ending World War I.	Roosevelt dies on January 6 in Oyster Bay, New York.
The First World War begins.				

William Howard Taft

"The President cannot make clouds to rain and cannot make corn to grow, he cannot make business good; although when these things occur, political parties do claim some credit for the good things that have happened in this way."

Even during his own lifetime, the public perception of William Howard Taft was defined less by who he was than by who he was not. Simply put, he was not Theodore Roosevelt, and Taft was destined to remain in the former president's shadow throughout his presidency.

Had Roosevelt not personally selected Taft as the man who might best fulfill his Progressive vision, Taft's single term in office may have been a smoother one. But where Roosevelt's spirit of crusading zeal had won him daily headlines and massive popularity, the plodding, legalistic Taft moved at a lumbering pace and was never able to inspire the kind of passion that Roosevelt had.

That is not to say that Taft did not further the Progressive cause. In fact, as a trust-buster fighting against corporate monopolies, Taft achieved more during his term than Roosevelt had in his. But when Roosevelt called for a "New Nationalism" that would increase conservation efforts, protect labor, begin a graduated income tax, and enlist the federal government in efforts to help women, chidren, and the poor,

Taft parted with his friend. In his view, such federal government action was unconstitutional. He had a moderate view of presidential power and believed that the president should not exercise powers beyond those explicitly authorized by the Constitution.

Though Taft, a Republican, had been one of Roosevelt's closest advisors, in some ways he was closer in philosophy to the more conservative and cautious Grover Cleveland, a Democrat. Like former President Cleveland, Taft was a reformer, but he too had grave concerns about the expansion of federal powers that Roosevelt and his supporters advocated. In 1912, many Republican Party regulars agreed that Taft won the Republican presidential nomination over Roosevelt with a clear majority. But when Roosevelt jumped to the Progressive line, Taft finished a distant third to him and the winner, Woodrow Wilson. In 1921, Taft became the first and only former president to be appointed chief justice of the United States. His deliberative and cautious approach made him a natural choice for the position.

Biographical Facts

Born: September 15, 1857 in Cincinnati, Ohio

Ancestry: English and Scotch-Irish

Father: Alphonso Taft; born November 5, 1810 in Townshend, Vermont; died May 21, 1891 in San Diego, California

Father's Occupations: Lawyer; Secretary of War; Attorney General; U.S. Diplomat

Mother: Louise Torrey Taft; born September 11, 1827 in Boston, Massachusetts; died December 7, 1907 in Cincinnati, Ohio

Wife: Helen (Nellie) Herron; born 1861 in Cincinnati, Ohio; died 1943 in Washington, D.C.

Marriage: June 19, 1886 in Cincinnati, Ohio

Children: Robert Alphonso Taft (1889-1953), Helen Herron Taft (1891-1987), Charles Phelps Taft (1897-1983)

Education: Woodward High School, Cincinnati, Ohio; received B.A. from Yale University (1878); Cincinnati Law School (1880)

Religious Affiliation: Unitarian

Occupations before Presidency: Lawyer; reporter; professor; Dean of University of Cincinnati Law School

Political Offices before Presidency: Assistant Prosecuting Attorney, Hamilton County, Ohio; Ohio Superior Court Judge; U.S. Solicitor General; Federal Circuit Court Judge; Civil Governor of Philippines; Secretary of War

Political Party: Republican

Age at Inauguration: 51

Occupations after Presidency: Kent professor of constitutional law, Yale University; joint chairman of National War Labor Board; chief justice of U.S. Supreme Court

Death: March 8, 1930 in Washington, D.C.

Place of Burial: Arlington National Cemetery, Washington, D.C.

Nicknames: Bill; Big Bill; Big Lub

Writings: *The Anti-Trust and the Supreme Court; The United States and Peace; Our Chief Magistrate and His Powers*

Quotes by Taft:

"Don't sit up nights thinking about making me the president for that will never come and I have no ambition in that direction. Any party which would nominate me would make a great mistake."

"Politics, when I am in it, makes me sick."

Quotes about Taft:

"It's very difficult for me to understand how a man who is so good as chief justice could have been so bad as president."
– *Justice Louis Brandeis*

"Taft meant well, but he meant well feebly."
– *Theodore Roosevelt*

Sherman Anti-Trust Act and orders it to dissolve. Two weeks later, the Supreme Court orders the **AMERICAN TOBACCO COMPANY** to do the same.

May 16, 1911: PRESIDENT PORFIRIO DIAZ OF MEXICO RESIGNS as a result of a popular revolution led by a wealthy reformer named **FRANCISCO MADERO**. During the revolution, American property owners are forced to abandon their holdings and flee the country.

June 6, 1911: The United States signs the **KNOX-CASTRILLO CONVENTION** with Nicaragua. Under the treaty's terms, Nicaragua grants the U.S. the right to intervene and to assume control of Nicaragua's customs in order to pay off the national debt. Secreaty of State Knox arranges for a $1.5 million bank loan to Nicaragua. In return, the lenders are granted control of the National Bank of Nicaragua and the government-owned railway. The Senate later rejects the treaty.

July 26, 1911: Alarmed by concerns that trade with Canada has been harmed by the 1909 Payne-Aldrich Treaty, Taft signs a **CANADIAN TARIFF RECIPROCITY AGREEMENT**. The agrement reduces tariffs on many farm imports in exchange for lower rates on American goods. After the House and Senate approve of the agreement, Taft and several members of Congress describe the treaty as the first step toward U.S. annexation of Canada.

August 17, 1911: TAFT VETOES TARIFF REDUCTIONS on wool and woolen goods, arguing that the Tariff Board has not completed its investigation. The Progressives criticize the president again for abandoning their movement.

October 26, 1911: TAFT SUES U.S. STEEL for violating the Sherman Anti-Trust Act. The president alleges that Roosevelt in

Taft, with wife Helen seated beside him in an open carriage, tipping his top hat to the crowd on Inauguration Day in March 1909.

1907 had mistakenly allowed U.S. Steel to purchase the Tennessee Coal and Iron Company. The charge infuriates Roosevelt and ends his friendship with Taft.

November 6, 1911: Mexican revolutionary Francisco Madero takes office as president of Mexico.

January 6, 1912: NEW MEXICO IS ADMITTED to the Union.

January 17, 1912: Taft recommends that the federal government begin adopting an **ANNUAL FEDERAL BUDGET**.

February 14, 1912: When the Arizona legislature strikes the clause from its constitution that allows recall of judges, Taft agrees to admit the territory as the 48th state in the union. Once **ARIZONA ACHIEVES STATEHOOD**, it reinserts the recall clause.

February 22, 1912: Former President Theodore Roosevelt announces his plan to run for the Republican nomination.

March 14, 1912: The Justice Department sues to stop the merger of the Southern Pacific and Union Pacific Railroads.

April 9, 1912: Taft authorizes the creation of the **CHILDREN'S BUREAU** in the Department of Commerce. **JULIA LATHROP** is

	1901	1904	1908
■ Taft's Life			Taft is elected president.
■ U.S. & World Events	After the Spanish-American and Philippine-American Wars, Taft becomes the first civil governor of the Philippines.	Taft joins Theodore Roosevelt's Cabinet as secretary of war.	Mother's Day is formally observed for the first time in Grafton, West Virginia and Philadelphia.

appointed director of the new agency, making her the highest-ranking woman in the federal government.

June 5, 1912: AMERICAN MARINES LAND IN CUBA to ensure order under the 1903 PLATT AMENDMENT, which barred Cuba from relinquishing control to a foreign power.

June 19, 1912: Congress passes a labor law authorizing an EIGHT-HOUR WORK DAY for all workers with federal contracts.

June 18-22, 1912: TAFT WINS THE REPUBLICAN NOMINATION, defeating former President Theodore Roosevelt.

June 25–July 2, 1912: DEMOCRATS NOMINATE WOODROW WILSON, governor of New Jersey, for president.

August 2, 1912: A group of Japanese investors attempt to purchase land in Magdalena Bay in the Gulf of California. In response, Congress warns that the United States would see the purchase of any strategically important areas of North America by any private foreign company with a close relationship to its government as "a grave concern." This statement becomes known as the LODGE COROLLARY to the Monroe Doctrine, after Henry Cabot Lodge of Massachusetts.

August 5, 1912: The PROGRESSIVE (BULL MOOSE) PARTY NOMINATES THEODORE ROOSEVELT for president.

August 20, 1912: After popular anger over the Knox-Castrillo Convention erupts into a full-scale revolt in Nicaragua, Taft sends battleships to the country to protect American interests.

August 24, 1912: The PANAMA CANAL ACT exempts American shipping from paying tolls when passing through the Panama Canal. Many Americans, along with Britons, consider this a violation of the Hay-Pauncefote Treaty of 1901.

October 30, 1912: VICE PRESIDENT JOHN SHERMAN DIES and Taft selects Nicholas Butler, the president of Columbia University, as his new running mate.

November 5, 1912: WOODROW WILSON DEFEATS TAFT AND ROOSEVELT in the presidential election.

February 18, 1913: GENERAL VICTORIANO HUERTA OVERTHROWS MADERO in Mexico. Taft refuses to intervene, despite the urging for action by the American public.

February 25, 1913: THE SIXTEENTH AMENDMENT, which authorizes the collection of income taxes is ratified by the states.

March 1, 1913: The WEBB-KENYON INTERSTATE LIQUOR ACT is passed, prohibiting the shipment of liquor into "dry" states.

March 4, 1913: Congress divides the DEPARTMENT OF LABOR AND COMMERCE into two separate Cabinet-level departments.

President-elect Woodrow Wilson and Taft in open carriage arriving at the U.S. Capitol for Wilson's first inauguration on March 4, 1913.

1910	1912	1914	1914-18	1921	1930
	Taft is defeated in his bid for reelection.		World War I is fought.		Taft dies on March 8 in Washington, D.C.
The U.S. population reaches 91.9 million.		He joins the faculty of Yale as a law professor.		President Harding selects Taft as chief justice of the Supreme Court.	

Thomas Woodrow Wilson

28th President (1913–1921)

"It is only by working with an energy which is almost superhuman and which looks to uninterested spectators like insanity that we can accomplish anything worth the achievement."

Woodrow Wilson may well have witnessed more dramatic changes in national and global affairs than any president since Washington. In many instances, his policies were the catalysts for those changes. In others, he found himself powerless to effect forces that were beyond his control.

Wilson held only one public office prior to becoming president, but he possessed incredible political skill, deftly utilizing his exceptional talent for words to push through his proposals. He entered office as a highly regarded reformer, who had taken on entrenched business interests in his state of New Jersey to win national attention. In his first two years as president, he ushered in an array of legislation. He lowered tariffs, established a graduated income tax, the Federal Reserve System, and the Federal Trade Commission. Later, he signed laws banning child labor and limiting workdays to eight hours.

In foreign affairs, he promised that the United States would no longer seek to expand its territories. At the same time, he used U.S. military strength to maintain stability in countries thoughout the Americas, sending troops to the Dominican Republic, Mexico, Nicaragua, and Haiti. As Wilson campaigned for reelection in 1916, his campaign slogan proclaimed that he had succeeded in keeping the country out of the war in Europe.

However, as he began his second term, Wilson realized that he could not avoid the war, and Congress declared war on Germany in April 1917 with his urging. Despite this, Wilson worked diligently to convince the combatants to accept a war without winners—"a war to end all wars." To ensure his vision of lasting peace, Wilson proposed a League of Nations, "affording mutual guarantees of political independence and territorial integrity to great and small states alike." Although the final treaty departed from most of what he proposed, the idealistic Wilson presented the treaty to the U.S. Senate, asking, "Dare we reject it and break the heart of the world?" Rather than compromise with the Republicans, who controlled Congress, an exhausted Wilson toured the nation trying to mobilize popular support for the treaty's ratification. During the tour, he suffered a stroke and nearly died.

Despite the failure of the League of Nations, Wilson's vision ultimately led to the creation of the United Nations. For his work, which radically increased U.S. participation in world affairs, Wilson was awarded the Nobel Peace Prize in 1919.

Biographical Facts

Born: December 28, 1856 in Staunton, Virginia

Ancestry: Scotch-Irish

Father: Joseph Ruggles Wilson; born February 28, 1822 in Steubenville, Ohio; died January 21, 1903 in Princeton, New Jersey

Father's Occupation: Presbyterian minister

Mother: Janet (Jessie) Woodrow Wilson; born 1836 in Carlisle, England; died April 15, 1888 in Clarksville, Tennessee

First Wife: Ellen Louise Axson; born May 15, 1860 in Rome, Georgia; died August 6, 1914 in Washington, D.C.

First Marriage: June 24, 1885 in Savannah, Georgia

Second Wife: Edith Bolling Galt; born October 15, 1872 in Wytheville, Virginia ; died December 28, 1961in Washington, D.C.

Second Marriage: Washington, D.C. December 18, 1915

Children (by first wife): Margaret Woodrow (1886-1944);

Jessie Woodrow (1887-1932); Eleanor Randolph (1889-1967)

Home: Woodrow Wilson House, Washington, D.C.

Education: Private tutors; Davidson College; Princeton University; University of Virginia Law School; Johns Hopkins University

Religious Affiliation: Presbyterian

Occupations before Presidency: Lawyer; teacher; college president; author

Political Party: Democratic

Death: February 3, 1924 in Washington, D.C.

Place of Burial: Washington Cathedral, Washington, D.C.

Nickname: Schoolmaster in Politics

Writings: *George Washington; A History of the American People; Constitutional Government in the United States; Papers of Woodrow Wilson*

173

Election of 1912

Candidates	Party	Electoral Vote	Popular Vote
Woodrow Wilson (NJ)	Democratic	435	6,296,547
Theodore Roosevelt (NY)	Progressive	88	4,118,571
William H. Taft (OH)	Republican	8	3,486,720
Eugene V. Debs (IN)	Socialist	---	900,672
Eugene W. Chafin (IL)	Prohibition	---	206,275

About the Election: Although Taft had been Theodore Roosevelt's hand-picked successor, his cautious conservatism convinced Roosevelt to enter the race as the nominee of the Progressive, or Bull Moose, Party. Roosevelt called for a "New Nationalism," led by an interventionist government working to protect the environment and the interests of workers and consumers. This split in the Republican Party, caused by Roosevelt's Bull Moose Party, led to the election of Governor Woodrow Wilson of New Jersey, the Democratic nominee. Wilson's version of progressive reform, called "New Freedom," advocated a return to small businesses, emphasizing the "man on the make," rather than the man who had already succeeded. His emphasis on small business played well in Democratic strongholds, like the South, but he also found support in traditionally Republican states as well.

Wilson (435 Votes)
T. Roosevelt
Taft

Wilson's First Term 1913-1917

March 4, 1913: WILSON IS INAUGURATED as the twenty-eighth president of the United States. The same day, Congress divides the Department of Commerce and Labor into two separate Cabinet level departments.

April 8, 1913: Wilson becomes the first president since John Adams to address Congress in person when he makes a speech proposing a revision of tariffs.

May 19, 1913: In California, the WEBB ALIEN LAND-HOLDING ACT is passed, despite protests from President Wilson and the government of Japan. The new state law bans ownership of land by Japanese immigrants.

May 31, 1913: The SEVENTEETH AMENDMENT, authorizing the direct election of U.S. senators, goes into effect. Prior to the amendment, senators were chosen by state legislatures.

October 3, 1913: Wilson signs the UNDERWOOD-SIMMONS TARIFF ACT, which dramatically reduces tariffs.

October 10, 1913: To mark the COMPLETION OF THE PANAMA CANAL, Wilson sets off an explosion that destroys the Gamboa Dike in Panama, by pressing a button at the White House. After 36 years of labor, the bankruptcy of thousands of investors, and the deaths of more than 25,000 men, the Panama Canal is finished, cutting the sailing distance from the East Coast to the West by more than 8,000 miles. The canal, which connects the Pacific Ocean and the Caribbean Sea with a single waterway, opens for barge business the following May and all other traffic the following August.

December 23, 1913: Wilson signs the FEDERAL RESERVE ACT, which creates the Federal Reserve System, made up of a Federal Reserve Board and twelve regional banks. The new system provides protections for the U.S. banking and monetary systems that have not existed since 1830, when Andrew Jackson dismantled the Second Bank of the United States.

April 9, 1914: Mexican authorities in Tampico mistakenly detain U.S. Marines who have come ashore for supplies. The Mexican commander apologizes and Mexico's president Victoriano Huerta sends his regret over the incident. However, when the U.S. commander Henry T. Mayo demands that Mexican troops salute the U.S. flag, Huerta refuses. In response, WILSON ORDERS THE U.S. FLEET TO TAMPICO BAY.

April 21, 1914: U.S. FORCES SEIZE THE MEXICAN CUSTOM HOUSE AT VERA CRUZ and take control of the city. Rather than apologize for detaining marines at Tampico, President Huerta severs relations with the U.S. the following day. American troops remain in Vera Cruz until November.

April 25, 1914: The governments of Argentina, Brazil, and Chile, referred to as the "ABC Powers," offer to mediate a

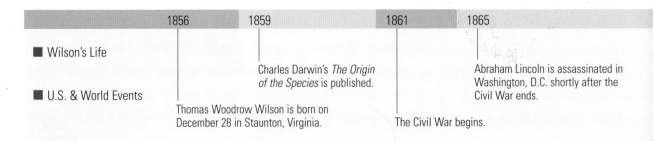

	1856	1859	1861	1865
■ Wilson's Life				
■ U.S. & World Events		Charles Darwin's *The Origin of the Species* is published.		Abraham Lincoln is assassinated in Washington, D.C. shortly after the Civil War ends.

Thomas Woodrow Wilson is born on December 28 in Staunton, Virginia.

The Civil War begins.

First Ladies: Ellen Louise Axson Wilson, first wife; Edith Bolling Galt Wilson, second wife

Ellen Louise Axson Wilson

Edith Bolling Galt Wilson

The first Mrs. Wilson held her post as First Lady with Southern grace and dignity. An accomplished painter, she pursued her interest in art and entertained at formal parties. Throughout Wilson's career, Mrs. Wilson helped her husband work on speeches and advised him on various issues. Echoing the strong beliefs of many women of her day, Mrs. Wilson used her influence to help improve living conditions among the nation's urban poor and she worked for a remedial bill for housing. Her death on August 6, 1914, from a liver condition, once called Bright's disease, spurred passage of the housing bill in Congress.

Wilson remarried in 1915, to a young widow named Edith Boling Galt. The second Mrs. Wilson was considered one of the nation's most influential First Ladies. After her husband suffered a stroke in 1919 that left him partially paralyzed, her behavior as Wilson's constant companion earned her the nickname of "Secret President". Though she did not make major decisions or initiate policies, she screened Wilson's visitors and mail and selected matters she found deserving of his attention.

Wilson's First Administration

Inauguration: March 4, 1913 at the Capitol, Washington, D.C.
Vice President: Thomas R. Marshall
Secretary of State: William Jennings Bryan; Robert Lansing (from June 23, 1915)
Secretary of the Treasury: William G. McAdoo
Secretary of War: Lindley M. Garrison; Newton D. Baker (from March 9, 1916)
Attorney General: James C. McReynolds; Thomas W. Gregory (from September 3, 1914)
Postmaster General: Albert S. Burleson
Secretary of the Navy: Josephus Daniels
Secretary of the Interior: Franklin K. Lane
Secretary of Agriculture: David F. Houston

Secretary of Commerce: William C. Redfield
Secretary of Labor: William B. Wilson
Supreme Court Appointments:
James C. McReynolds (1914);
Louis D. Brandeis (1916); John H. Clarke (1916)
63rd Congress: (March 4, 1913-March 4, 1915)
Senate: 51 Democrats; 44 Republicans; 1 Other
House: 291 Democrats; 127 Republicans; 17 Others
64th Congress: (March 4, 1915-March 4, 1917)
Senate: 56 Democrats; 40 Republicans
House: 230 Democrats; 196 Republicans; 9 Others
End of Presidential Term: March 4, 1917

settlement in the Mexican crisis. Wilson accepts, but the offer becomes unnecessary after Mexico's President Huerta resigns in July.

August 1-4, 1914: Following the assassination of Austrian Archduke Ferdinand in Serbia, **WORLD WAR I BEGINS** in Europe. Austria declares war on Serbia, and when Russians come to the defense of Serbians, Germany joins the conflict on the side of Austria, invading Russia and France, which was allied to Russia. Great Britain declares war on Germany after Belgium is invaded, which is neutral and protected by a treaty with Great Britain.

November 3, 1914: In the midterm elections, the Democrats gain five seats in the Senate, and despite losing 61 seats in the House, continue to hold a majority.

October 14, 1914: Wilson signs the **CLAYTON ANTI-TRUST ACT**. It strengthens the Sherman Anti-Trust Act of 1890 by prohibiting exclusive sales contracts, discriminatory pricing, rebates, inter-corporate stock holdings, and interlocking directorates in corporations capitalized at $1 million or more in the same area of business. The act also restricts the use of the federal injunction against labor disputes and legalizes peaceful strikes, picketing and boycotts.

February 8, 1915: D.W.

1866	1869	1879	1881	1885
Fyodor Dostoevsky writes *Crime and Punishment*.	Rail lines Central Pacific and Union Pacific meet in Promontory, Utah. North America becomes the first continent to have a rail line running from coast to coast.	Wilson graduates from Princeton University.	He graduates from University of Virginia aw school.	Wilson marries Ellen Louise Axson.

Griffith's releases his landmark film *BIRTH OF A NATION*, which portrays members of the Ku Klux Klan as heroic figures who rescue the South from the savagery of freed blacks. Wilson praises the film as "history written on lighting." The president had previously told a group of African American visitors to the White House that "segregation is not humiliating but a benefit, and ought to be so regarded by you gentlemen."

May 7, 1915: A GERMAN U-BOAT SINKS THE *LUSITANIA*, a British passenger liner, off the coast of Ireland, killing 1,198 passengers, including 63 infants and 114 Americans. Wilson accuses Germany of violating American neutrality and pledges to hold it responsible. While Germany apologizes, it also argues that the action was justified, claiming that the ship was smuggling weapons. The affair incites many Americans against Germany.

July 29, 1915: The U.S. SENDS MARINES TO HAITI, following the assassination of the nation's president. In September, the U.S. will make Haiti a U.S. protectorate.

December 4, 1915: The KU KLUX KLAN receives a state charter from Georgia. Unlike the original Klan, the new group will target religious minorities, such as Catholics and Jews, as well as ethnic minorities. The new Klan attracts many members outside of the South.

January 24, 1916: In *BRUSHABER V. UNION PACIFIC RAILROAD*, the Supreme Court overturns the federal income tax, stating that the 16th Amendment does not amend the Constitution to allow the income tax, but merely clarifies federal law.

January 28, 1916: WILSON APPOINTS LOUIS B. BRANDEIS to the Supreme Court. When confirmed, Brandeis becomes the first Jewish judge in American history.

March 9, 1916: Seventeen Americans die when Mexican revolutionary Francisco "PANCHO" VILLA leads a group of 1,500 guerillas on a cross-border raid on the New Mexico village of Columbus. The Mexicans attack the 13th Cavalry, bringing back more than a hundred of its horses, along with a large load of machine guns across the border. In retaliation, Wilson orders Brigadier General John "Black Jack" Pershing to pursue Villa and his men. American troops kill 50 Mexican guerillas in the U.S. and after crossing the border, kill another 70 in Mexico.

April 24, 1916: A GERMAN U-BOAT TORPEDOES THE SUSSEX, a French passenger steamship. Several Americans are drowned. President Wilson issues an ultimatum to Germany concerning German policy on unrestricted submarine warfare, which allows German U-boats to sink merchant vessels without warning should they be suspected of trading with the Allies.

May 1916: U.S. MARINES LAND IN THE DOMINICAN REPUBLIC to restore political stability to the country after its president steps down from office. American troops remain there until 1924.

June 21, 1916: MEXICAN FORCES FIRE UPON AMERICAN TROOPS at Carrizal, Mexico, after the U.S. ignores an ultimatum to leave the country. Seventeen Americans are killed or wounded. Thirty-eight Mexicans are killed.

July 17, 1916: Wilson signs the FEDERAL FARM LOAN ACT. The new law creates a loan-term credit system for farmers, similar to those that are already in existence for industry and commerce. The act divides the country into 12 districts, overseen by a Federal Farm Loan Board.

July 22, 1916: During a Preparedness Day Parade in San Francisco, a BOMB KILLS 10 PEOPLE and wounds 40. Two labor leaders, Tom Mooney and Warren K. Billings, are convicted for the crime during a controversial trial. Mooney is sentenced to hang and Billings to spend life in jail. However, after it is discovered that key testimony at the trial was false, Wilson commutes Mooney's sentence to life in prison. Mooney and Billings are eventually released in 1939.

July 30, 1916: In a case of possible sabotage by German spies, an ammunition depot explodes at Toms River Island near Jersey City, New Jersey.

	1901	1902	1904
■ Wilson's Life			
■ U.S. & World Events	Italian inventor Guglielmo Marconi sends the first wireless transatlantic communication.	Wilson's *A History of the American People* is published in five volumes. The same year he is named president of Princeton University.	Susan B. Anthony and Carrie Chapman Catt establish the International Women Suffrage Alliance.

Election of 1916

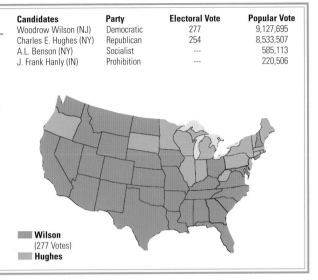

Candidates	Party	Electoral Vote	Popular Vote
Woodrow Wilson (NJ)	Democratic	277	9,127,695
Charles E. Hughes (NY)	Republican	254	8,533,507
A.L. Benson (NY)	Socialist	---	585,113
J. Frank Hanly (IN)	Prohibition	---	220,506

About the Election: The Democrats renominated Woodrow Wilson, adopting an anti-war platform that praised Wilson for preserving national honor, while keeping the country out of war. Wilson himself was doubtful about his ability to maintain peace and his program of neutrality emphasized preparedness. Supreme Court Justice Charles Evans Hughes won the Republican nomination, defeating Theodore Roosevelt, who robustly promoted joining the war. Hughes was favored because he could appeal to both conservatives and progressives. On election night, the outcome was confused because of delays in receiving the election returns from California. Many believed that Hughes had won and newspapers carried the story of Wilson's "defeat." But the final count in California gave the state to Wilson and he won the reelection.

Wilson (277 Votes)
Hughes

August 4, 1916: The U.S. agrees to purchase the **DANISH WEST INDIES**, or Virgin Islands, from Denmark for $25 million.
September 3, 1916: To avoid a railroad strike from occurring as the nation prepares for possible war, Wilson signs the **ADAMSON ACT**, which sets the workday for most railroad workers at eight hours. The new law paves the way for later acceptance of an eight-hour workday in other industries.
January 17, 1917: In another explosion deemed the work of German saboteurs, a munitions plant in Kingsland, New Jersey, is destroyed. The German government, upon hearings in 1939, is ultimately ordered to pay $50 million in damages.
January 28, 1917: The **WAR DEPARTMENT RECALLS GENERAL PERSHING'S TROOPS** from Mexico after they fail to capture Mexican revolutionary Pancho Villa.
January 31, 1917: **GERMANY ANNOUNCES THAT IT WILL RESTART SUBMARINE WARFARE** against both belligerent and neutral ships in the Atlantic Ocean.
Februrary 3, 1917: The **UNITED STATES BREAKS OFF DIPLOMATIC RELATIONS WITH GERMANY.**
February 5, 1917: Congress passes the **IMMIGRATION ACT OF 1917** over Wilson's veto. The new law requires that all immigrants pass a literacy test. It also creates an "Asiatic Barred Zone," affecting many immigrants from India.
February 24, 1917: Britain intercepts a memo from German

foreign minister Arthur Zimmermann to the German ambassador of Mexico. The **ZIMMERMAN NOTE** proposes an alliance between Germany and Mexico and suggests that Germany help Mexico win back the land it had lost in the U.S.-Mexican War. In response, President Wilson asks Congress permission to arm merchant ships.

Wilson's Second Term 1917-1921

March 4, 1917: **WILSON IS INAUGURATED FOR HIS SECOND TERM**, and in his inaugural address, Wilson prepares the American public for the likelihood of war.
March 12, 1917: The **RUSSIAN REVOLUTION** begins when Czar Nicholas II is forced to resign. The Bolshevik Party comes into power by autumn.
April 4-6, 1917: The Senate and House both vote for a **DECLARATION OF WAR AGAINST GERMANY**. Among the members of the House who vote against the resolution is **JEANETTE RANKIN** of Montana, the first woman to serve in Congress.
April 14, 1917: Wilson creates the **COMMITTEE ON PUBLIC INFORMATION (CPI)** to manage wartime propaganda and censorship activities.
April 24, 1917: Wilson signs a bill launching the first **LIBERTY LOAN** drive, allowing the Treasury Department to offer $3 billion in interest-bearing war bonds to the public.

1905	1907	1910	1912

Russian troops open fire on unarmed striking workers on January 22, later known as "Bloody Sunday".

Pablo Picasso paints one of his first Cubist works, *Les Demoiselles d'Avignon.*

Wilson is elected governor of New Jersey.

British passenger ship, *Titanic*, hits an iceberg and sinks in the North Atlantic Ocean.

Wilson's Second Administration

Inauguration: March 5, 1917 at the Capitol, Washington, D.C.

Vice President: Thomas R. Marshall

Secretary of State: Robert Lansing; Bainbridge Colby (from March 23, 1920)

Secretary of the Treasury:
William G. McAdoo;
Carter Glass (from December 16, 1918);
David F. Houston (from February 2, 1920)

Secretary of War: Newton D. Baker

Attorney General: Thomas W. Gregory; A. Mitchell Palmer (from March 5, 1919)

Postmaster General: Albert S. Burleson

Secretary of the Navy: Josephus Daniels

Secretary of the Interior: Franklin K. Lane;

John B. Payne (from March 13, 1920)

Secretary of Agriculture: David F. Houston; Edwin T. Meredith (from February 2, 1920)

Secretary of Commerce: William C. Redfield; Joshua W. Alexander (from December 16, 1919)

Secretary of Labor: William B. Wilson

65th Congress: (March 4, 1917-March 4, 1919)
Senate: 53 Democrats; 42 Republicans
House: 216 Democrats; 210 Republicans;
6 Others

66th Congress: (March 4, 1919-March 4, 1921)
Senate: 49 Republicans; 47 Democrats
House: 240 Republicans; 190 Democrats;
3 Others

End of Presidential Term: March 4, 1921

May 18, 1917: Congress passes the SELECTIVE SERVICE ACT, which requires all men between the ages of 21 and 30 to register for military service. The law will be supplanted in August 1918 by the Man Power Act, which broadens the age range to all men between ages 18 and 45.

June 15, 1917: At President Wilson's urging, Congress passes the ESPIONAGE ACT, which makes public criticism of the government or military punishable by up to $10,000 in fines or 20 years in prison. It is the harshest federal limitation on free speech since John Adams signed the Alien and Sedition Acts in 1798, during the nation's conflict with France.

July 28, 1917: The WAR INDUSTRIES BOARD is established to coordinate the nation's war industry production. In March 1918, the War Industries Board will be reorganized and Bernard Baruch will be appointed to head it.

August 10, 1917: Congress passes the Lever Food and Fuel Control Act, allowing Wilson to manage the production, conservation, and pricing policies for food, coal, and other commodities during the war. Future president HERBERT HOOVER IS APPOINTED FOOD ADMINISTRATOR. Hoover later proposes that Americans conserve food by having one meatless day, two wheatless days and two porkless days each week.

September 5, 1917: Federal agents RAID THE INDUSTRIAL WORKERS OF THE WORLD (IWW) in 24 cities nationwide, confiscating books and other literature. They also arrest 10 people, including William "Big Bill" Haywood, the union's

leader.

October 24, 1917: Launching the "OCTOBER REVOLUTION," Russian Bolsheviks seize power in Petrograd, Russia and set up a provisional committee to govern Russia. A RUSSIAN CIVIL WAR between the Bolsheviks ("Reds") and all other Russians ("Whites") continue until 1922.

December 18, 1917: Congress passes the Eighteenth Amendment to the Constitution and sends it to the states for ratification. The amendment marks the BEGINNING OF THE PROHIBITION ERA by outlawing the sale, manufacture, or transport of alcohol nationwide.

January 8, 1918: Addressing Congress, Wilson proposes his famous "FOURTEEN POINTS" for a just and lasting peace. One of his proposals is for a "LEAGUE OF NATIONS" that will prevent future world wars. Wilson's speech is distributed worldwide through the Office of Public Information.

March 3, 1918: The Russian Bolshevik government signs the TREATY OF BREST-LITOVSK with Germany, ending hostilities between the two nations.

May 16, 1918: Congress passes the SEDITION ACT, giving the postmaster general the authority to ban the mailing of "subversive" publications.

June 23, 1918: A British force lands in Murmansk, Russia in order to protect Allied supplies from falling into German or Bolshevik hands and to force Germany to fight a two-front war. In August, a joint British-French force lands in Archangel. On September 4, an American force joins the British in Murmansk to seize a railroad. The Allied involvement in northern Russia leads to a virtual WAR BETWEEN THE ALLIES AND BOLSHEVIKS.

June 4, 1918: The U.S. Second Division halts a German offensive at the BATTLE OF CHATEAU-THIERRY.

June 6-25, 1918: In bitter fighting at the BATTLE OF BELLEAU WOOD, the U.S. Second Division and Fourth Marine Brigade retake territory previously lost to Germany.

July 15, 1918: In the SECOND BATTLE OF THE MARNE, 85,000 American troops help the Allies hold off a two-pronged attack

	1914	1915	1916
■ Wilson's Life		Wilson marries Edith Bolling Galt.	
■ U.S. & World Events	Ellen Wilson dies from Bright's disease.	One million Armenians die after the Ottoman government deports them to the deserts of present-day Syria.	Wilson is reelected.

on the French city of Reims.

July 18–August 6, 1918: More than 250,000 U.S. troops join French forces in the AISNE-MARNE counterattack against the Germans. The offensive helps change the course of the war.

August 8, 1918: Allied forces attack the Germans at AMIENS.

September 12, 1918: U.S. troops take 15,000 German prisoners at the BATTLE OF ST. MIHIEL.

September 14, 1918: Socialist EUGENE V. DEBS IS SENTENCED TO TEN YEARS IN PRISON for making an anti-war speech, thus violating the Espionage Act.

September 26–November 11, 1918: Over 1.2 million American troops participate in the BATTLE OF THE MEUSE–ARGONNE. The Allies cut off German rail supply lines.

November 5, 1918: In the midterm elections, the Republicans win majorities in both houses of Congress.

November 9, 1918: WORLD WAR I ENDS as Germany's Kaiser Wilhelm II abdicates the throne. The German government appeals for a peace treaty based upon President Wilson's "Fourteen Points" speech.

January 18, 1919: The PARIS PEACE CONFERENCE opens, with Wilson in attendance. In February, Wilson presents his plan for a LEAGUE OF NATIONS to the conference.

January 29, 1919: The EIGHTEENTH AMENDMENT is ratified by the states, making into law the prohibition of alcohol.

March 3, 1919: In the case of *SCHENCK V. UNITED STATES*, the Supreme Court rules that American civil liberties may be curtailed by the federal government if there is a "CLEAR AND PRESENT DANGER" to law and order.

May 19, 1919: Congress approves the NINETEENTH AMENDMENT to the Constitution, which guarantees women the right to vote. The amendment is then submitted to the states for ratification.

July 10, 1919: Due to the demands of other allies, Wilson fails to secure his vision of peace, which is based on his Fourteen Points. However, he submits the Treaty of Versailles and his proposal for the League of Nations to the Senate for ratification.

August 31, 1919: The COMMUNIST LABOR PARTY OF AMERICA is founded in Chicago. Attorney General A. Mitchell Palmer begins a series of nationwide mass arrests of those suspected of political agitation. All those arrested in the PALMER RAIDS who are foreign-born are deported. The following January, Attorney General Palmer expands the raids dramatically, arresting almost 2,700 people in 33 cities nationwide.

September 4, 1919: Wilson begins an exhausting tour to promote the Treaty of Versailles and the League of Nations. On September 26, WILSON SUFFERS A STROKE while on this tour.

October 28, 1919: Overiding Wilson's veto, Congress passes the VOLSTEAD ACT to enforce the Eighteenth Amendment.

November 19, 1919: In a major defeat for Wilson, the SENATE VOTES AGAINST RATIFYING THE TREATY OF VERSAILLES.

April 1, 1920: The last AMERICAN FORCES WITHDRAW FROM NORTHERN RUSSIA, where they have been supporting the "White" Russian Army against the Communist Bolsheviks in the Russian Civil War.

April 15, 1920: Two factory workers in South Braintree, Massachusetts, are murdered. Three weeks later, Italian immigrants NICOLA SACCO and BARTOLOMEO VANZETTI are charged with the crime and eventually found guilty. They are executed following one of the most controversial court cases in American history.

June 8-12, 1920: The REPUBLICANS SELECT WARREN G. HARDING, an Ohio senator, as their nominee for president and Massachusetts governor CALVIN COOLIDGE for vice president.

June 28, 1920: The DEMOCRATS NOMINATE JAMES M. COX, Governor of Ohio, for president and former Assistant Secretary of the Navy, FRANKLIN DELANO ROOSEVELT, for vice president.

August 26, 1920: The NINETEENTH AMENDMENT, granting women's suffrage, becomes law.

November 2, 1920: HARDING IS ELECTED PRESIDENT in one of the largest landslide victories in American history.

Wilson, at right, at the Paris Peace Conference, with (left to right) Georges Clemenceau of France, Vittorio Orlando of Italy, and David Lloyd George of Great Britain.

1918	1919	1922	1924
Influenza epidemic kills more than 20 million people worldwide in a single year.	Wilson suffers a paralytic stroke that leaves him an invalid for the rest of his life. The same year he is awarded the Nobel Peace Prize.	Civil war breaks out between Northern and Southern Ireland.	Wilson dies in his sleep on February 3, in Washington, D.C.

Warren Gamaliel Harding

29th President (1921–1923)

"My God, this is a hell of a job! I have no trouble with my enemies. . .But my damn friends, they're the ones that keep me walking the floor nights."

When Woodrow Wilson suffered a stroke in 1919 that left him an invalid, the Progressive Era of presidential activism and international engagement came to an end.

For most Americans, that was very good news. Having survived a horrific world war, most yearned for simpler times free of conflict at home or entanglements overseas. Warren G. Harding, an inconsequential backbench senator from the small town of Marion, Ohio, seemed to many to be just the man for the times. Prior to the election, he summed up the national mood by declaring, "America's present need is not heroics, but healing; not nostrums, but normalcy; not revolution, but restoration; not agitation, but adjustment; not surgery, but serenity …" The term, "normalcy," invented by Harding referred to a return to the political and economic isolation that had characterized the U.S. before World War I. Harding handily defeated the Democratic Party's progressive nominee, James M. Cox.

Harding's call for simpler times didn't make the job of president any simpler. In fact, he was among the first to admit that he was overmatched by the job. "I don't know what to do or where to go," he wrote to a friend. "Somewhere there must be a book that talks all about it." Ultimately, Harding was content to look to the Republican Congress for direction. Wartime controls were eliminated, taxes cut, tariffs raised, and immigration tightened. His administration also fulfilled its campaign promise of economy in government.

By 1923, Harding remained immensely popular. What the public didn't know was that his administration was rife with corruption. Among the most dishonest members of his Cabinet was Interior Secretary Albert Fall, who accepted bribes from private oil interests for naval petroleum reserves at Teapot Dome, Wyoming, and Elk Hills, California. Although Harding did not participate in Fall's scheme, he knew about it and did nothing because he feared it would damage his reputation.

Although additional scandals, involving the chief of the Bureau of Veteran's Affairs and Attorney General Harry Dougherty surfaced during Harding's administration, Teapot Dome did not become public until after Harding's death. On a national tour with his wife in 1923, Harding died of heart failure in San Francisco, California. By the time a sensational book by a woman alleging to have been his former mistress—and mother of his illegitimate child—surfaced in 1930, Harding's reputation was already sullied.

Biographical Facts

Born: November 2, 1865 in Blooming Grove, Ohio

Ancestry: English and Scotch-Irish

Father: George Tryon Harding; born June 12 1843 in Blooming Grove, Ohio; died November 19, 1928 in Santa Ana, California

Father's Occupations: Farmer; physician

Mother: Phoebe Dickerson; born December 21, 1843 in Blooming Grove, Ohio; died May 20, 1910

Wife: Florence Kling De Wolfe; born August 15, 1860 in Marion, Ohio; died November. 21, 1924 in Marion, Ohio

Marriage: July 8, 1891 in Marion, Ohio

Children: None

Education: Local schools; Ohio Central College

Home: Harding Home and Museum, 380 Mt. Vernon Ave, Marion, Ohio

Religious Affiliaton: Baptist

Occupation before Presidency: Newspaper editor; teacher; insurance salesman; reporter; publisher

Military Service: None

Political Offices before Presidency: Member of Ohio Senate; Lieutenant Governor of Ohio; U.S. Senator

Political Party: Republican

Age at Inauguration: 55

Death: August 2, 1923 in San Francisco, California

Place of Burial: Hillside Cemetery, Marion, Ohio

Nickname: None

Writings: *Rededicating America; Our Common Country*

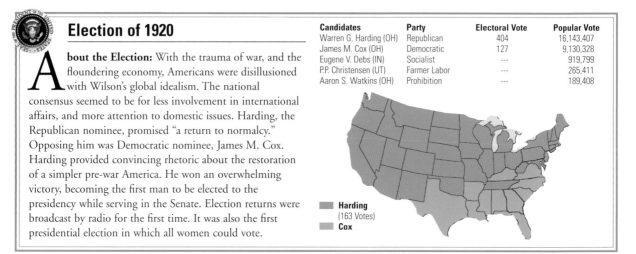

Election of 1920

About the Election: With the trauma of war, and the floundering economy, Americans were disillusioned with Wilson's global idealism. The national consensus seemed to be for less involvement in international affairs, and more attention to domestic issues. Harding, the Republican nominee, promised "a return to normalcy." Opposing him was Democratic nominee, James M. Cox. Harding provided convincing rhetoric about the restoration of a simpler pre-war America. He won an overwhelming victory, becoming the first man to be elected to the presidency while serving in the Senate. Election returns were broadcast by radio for the first time. It was also the first presidential election in which all women could vote.

Candidates	Party	Electoral Vote	Popular Vote
Warren G. Harding (OH)	Republican	404	16,143,407
James M. Cox (OH)	Democratic	127	9,130,328
Eugene V. Debs (IN)	Socialist	---	919,799
P.P. Christensen (UT)	Farmer Labor	---	265,411
Aaron S. Watkins (OH)	Prohibition	---	189,408

Harding (163 Votes)
Cox

Harding's Term 1921-1923

March 4, 1921: **HARDING IS INAUGURATED** as the 29th president of the United States.

April 20, 1921: The Senate ratifies the **THOMPSON-URRUTIA TREATY** with Colombia, paying the South American nation $25 million for the loss of Panama in 1903.

May 19, 1921: Harding signs the **EMERGENCY QUOTA ACT**, tightening immigration quotas by cutting the number of immigrants from any single nation to three percent of the number of persons from that country living in the United States in 1910.

May 27, 1921: Harding signs the protectionist **EMERGENCY TARIFF ACT**, which raises tariffs on farm products. Tariffs will be raised even higher a year later by the **FORDNEY-MCCUMBER TARIFF ACT**. Intended to protect American farmers from overseas competition, the rising tariffs weaken international commerce as other nations respond by raising their tariff rates as well.

June 10, 1921: Harding signs the **BUDGET AND ACCOUNTING ACT**, which establishes the Bureau of the Budget and the General Accounting Office as part of the Treasury Department.

June 30, 1921: Harding nominates former president **WILLIAM HOWARD TAFT** to replace Edward D. White as chief justice of the Supreme Court. Taft is sworn in on July 11.

September 26, 1921: Harding's Secretary of Commerce (and future president) **HERBERT HOOVER** leads a conference in Washington to examine the rising unemployment rate.

November 12, 1921–February 6, 1922: At the **WASHINGTON NAVAL ARMAMENT CONFERENCE**, Great Britain, France, Italy, Japan, and the United States agree to limit their respective naval armament, including battleships. The treaty is later ratified by the Senate.

November 23, 1921: The **SHEPPARD-TOWNER MATERNITY AND INFANCY ACT** is passed, which awards funds to state governments for maternal and child care, specifically clinics specializing in prenatal care. The passage of this act signals that women voters are gaining greater political power. The act also provides for the education and regulation of midwives.

February 18, 1922: President Harding signs the **CAPPER-VOLSTEAD ACT**, also known as the Cooperative Marketing Act. The act allows farmers to buy and sell through cooperatives without being prosecuted for violations of federal anti-trust laws.

September 19, 1922: Harding vetoes the **SOLDIERS' BONUS BILL**, arguing that balancing the budget takes precedence over the nation's debt to veterans of the Great War.

Quotes by Harding:

"I am not fit for this office and never should have been here."

"American business is not a monster, but an expression of God-given impulse to create, and the savior of our happiness."

Quote about Harding:

"If you were a girl, Warren, you'd be in the family way all the time. You can't say no."

– Harding's father

	1865	1873	1884	1891
■ Harding's Life				
■ U.S. & World Events	Warren Gamaliel Harding is born on November 2 in Blooming Grove, Ohio.	Christopher Latham Sholes invents the typewriter. One of the first works to be produced on a typewriter is Mark Twain's *Adventures of Tom Sawyer*.	Harding buys a bankrupt newspaper, the *Marion Star*, for $300.	Harding marries a wealthy divorcee, Florence Kling DeWolfe, who helps him transform the *Marion Star* into a successful newspaper.

First Lady: Florence "Fossie" Mabel Kling Harding

Florence Kling spent her childhood surrounded by wealth and privilege. She was the daughter of the richest man in smalltown Marion, Ohio. While studying classical piano at the Cincinnati Conservatory, she eloped at the age of 19. Her first marriage produced one son. After her first husband abandoned her, she supported her son and herself by giving piano lessons to children of the neighborhood. Her self-reliant and strong-willed nature continued to characterize her personality as she threw herself into promoting her second husband's political career. As First Lady, Mrs. Harding reignited the social arm of the White House, throwing garden parties for veterans and poker parties for friends, where, despite Prohibition, liquor flowed freely.

Scandal! Teapot Dome Scandal

The Teapot Dome Scandal, which became public in 1924 after Harding's death, began in 1922 when Interior Secretary Albert B. Fall secretly took control of naval oil reserves contained on public lands in California and Wyoming. The reserve program, launched in 1915, had grown out of the federal conservation movement that had been supported by the three preceding administrations. As a senator, Fall believed that the control of oil reserves were best left to private industry and while serving as the interior secretary, he set about opening the government reserves to private business. The investigations by the Senate Committee on public lands and surveys revealed that after taking control of the reserves, Fall had leased the Wyoming reserve known as Teapot Dome and California's Elk Hills reserve to private oil interests. In return, Fall received over $400,000 in gifts and "loans" from the businesses involved. When the scandal became public, President Coolidge was forced to appoint special prosecutors to investigate the case. Investigations of the scandal lasted throughout most of the 1920s. In 1927, the Supreme Court returned the oil reserves to the federal government. In 1929, Fall was convicted of bribery, fined $100,000, and served one year in prison.

September 22, 1922: Harding signs the CABLE ACT, which stipulates that an American woman does not necessarily lose her U.S. citizenship if she marries a foreigner.

June 5, 1922: The Supreme Court rules in the case of *UNITED MINE WORKERS V. CORONADO COAL CO.* that striking miners are liable for damages to company property.

April 9, 1923: In the case of *ADKINS V. CHILDREN'S HOSPITAL*, the Supreme Court rules that fixed minimum wage laws for women and children are unconstitutional.

August 2, 1923: While on a tour of the country, President Harding falls ill with ptomaine poisoning, which progresses into pneumonia. On August 2, HARDING DIES in his hotel room in San Francisco, California.

Harding's Administration

Inauguration: March 4, 1921 at the Capitol, Washington, D.C.
Vice President: Calvin Coolidge
Secretary of State: Charles Evans Hughes
Secretary of the Treasury: Andrew W. Mellon
Secretary of War: John W. Weeks
Attorney General: Harry M. Daughterty
Postmaster General: Will H. Hays; Hubert Work (from March 4, 1922); Harry S. New (from March 5, 1923)
Secretary of the Navy: Edwin Denby
Secretary of the Interior: Albert B. Fall; Hubert Work (from March 5, 1923)
Secretary of Agriculture: Henry C. Wallace

Secretary of Commerce: Herbert C. Hoover
Secretary of Labor: James J. Davis
Supreme Court Appointments: William H. Taft; Chief Justice (1921); George Sutherland (1922); Pierce Butler (1922); Edward T. Sanford (1923)
67th Congress: (March 4, 1921-March 4, 1923) Senate: 59 Republicans; 37 Democrats House: 301 Republicans; 131 Democrats: 1 Other
68th Congress: (March 4, 1923-March 4, 1925) Senate: 51 Republicans; 43 Democrats; 2 Others House: 225 Republicans; 205 Democrats; 5 Others
End of Presidential Term: August 2, 1923

1903	1904	1914	1917	1918	1920	1823
	Victory in Russo-Japanese war establishes Japan as a world power.		U.S. declares war on Germany and joins the Allies.			Harding dies on August 2 in San Francisco, California.
Harding is elected lieutenant governor of Ohio.		Harding is elected to the United States Senate.		President Woodrow Wilson announces his Fourteen Points as the basis for peace.	Harding is elected president.	

John Calvin Coolidge

30th President (1923–1929)

"Government should not assume for the people the inevitable burdens of existence."

Calvin Coolidge is generally considered one of America's lesser presidents. Reaching the presidency upon the death of Warren G. Harding, Coolidge, who advocated minimal government intervention, spent his six years in office doing as little as possible. As Wall Street stock speculation reached new heights, Coolidge stayed hands off, saying that, "The chief business of America is business." But he had little understanding of the country's growing farm and labor problems. As farms nationwide suffered financial crises, he vetoed bills to send them aid. He also opposed a bill that provided World War I veterans with bonuses, and he cut taxes dramatically to shrink the size of government coffers. But despite his generally poor reputation among historians, he remained consistently popular with the American public throughout his term.

At first glance, Coolidge's popularity seems at odds with his dour, taciturn personality. Nicknamed "Silent Cal," he was known for being a shy man of very few words and was rarely photographed with much of a smile. Yet in a time when Americans had tired of the professorial pontification of Woodrow Wilson and the disheartening and sordid corruption of the Harding administration, Coolidge's straightforward New

England reserve seemed refreshing.

In spite of his aversion to government interference, the federal government did pass several pieces of practical legislation to deal with the growth of rapidly growing new industries. The Air Commerce Act, for instance, required that all airplane pilots and aircraft be registered. In addition to this, the Federal Radio Commission was founded to regulate the radio industry.

However, Coolidge failed to take any steps to rein in the massive stock speculation that helped bring on the Great Depression. Although he was warned about the danger of this sort of speculation, Coolidge scrupulously noted that as president, he had no direct authority over Wall Street. Although, he could have used his influence to request the Federal Reserve Board to tighten regulations, he chose not to do so. In fact, his reliance on Andrew Mellon, the nation's third richest man, as treasury secretary, only assured the least amount of government interference.

Despite these criticisms, President Coolidge remained true to the principles of small government to the end. When Ronald Reagan took office almost 50 years later, he restored Coolidge's portrait to the walls of the presidential mansion.

Biographical Facts

Born: July 4, 1872 in Plymouth Notch, Vermont

Ancestry: English

Father: John Calvin Coolidge; born March 31, 1845 in Plymouth, Vermont; died March 18, 1926 in Plymouth Notch, Vermont

Father's Occupations: Storekeeper; farmer

Mother: Victoria Josephine Moor Coolidge; born March 14, 1846 in Plymouth, Vermont; died March 14, 1885 in Plymouth Notch, Vermont

Wife: Grace Anna Goodhue; born January 3, 1879 in Burlington, Vermont; died July 8, 1957 in Northampton, Massachusetts

Marriage: October 4, 1905 in Burlington, Vermont

Children: John (1906-2000); Calvin (1908-1924)

Education: Plymouth district school; Black River Academy; St. Johnsbury Academy; received B.A. from Amherst College (1895)

Home: Coolidge Homestead, Plymouth Notch, Vermont

Religious Affiliation: Congregationalist

Occupation before Presidency: Lawyer

Political Offices before Presidency: Member of House of Representatives, Massachusetts; Mayor of Northampton, Massachusetts; Member and President of Massachusetts Senate; Lieutenant Governor of Massachusetts; Governor of Massachusetts; U.S. Vice President

Political Party: Republican

Age at Inauguration: 51

Occupation after Presidency: Writer

Death: January 5, 1933 in Northampton, Massachusetts

Place of Burial: Hillside Cemetery, Plymouth, Vermont

Nickname: Silent Cal

Writings: *The Autobiography of Calvin Coolidge*

Original by Cartotto 1929
Copy by Burgess Bell 1972

Herbert Clark Hoover

31st President (1929–1933)

"Prosperity cannot be restored by raids upon the public treasury."

In May 1932, thousands of World War I veterans and their families descended on Washington, D.C. to lobby the goverment. They wanted President Hoover to allow them to borrow against military bonuses they had been given six years earlier. For two months, Hoover refused to meet them. Then in July, he ordered the Army to disperse them. The military then burned the makeshift camps of the "Bonus Army" to the ground and rounded up the protesters using armored tanks and tear gas. Remarking on the events, Hoover said, "Thank God we still have a government . . . that knows how to deal with a mob."

Herbert Hoover was born in 1874 to Quaker parents. Orphaned at a young age, he was raised by his aunt and uncle, who taught him to honor hard work and thriftiness. In school, Hoover had studied mining engineering and later earned a personal fortune as an international engineer. By 1914, he had amassed a fortune worth $4 million.

Hoover's Quaker background had also taught him the importance of service to others. He led humanitarian food programs for those displaced by World War I. In 1917, Woodrow Wilson asked him to manage the nation's wartime food conservation programs. His reputation as a humanitarian became such that future president Franklin Roosevelt would declare, "He certainly is a wonder, and I wish we could make him president of the United States."

And yet, President Hoover held such disdain for the Bonus Army Marchers in 1932 because he viewed personal responsibility as the key to progress. While individuals and private institutions were responsible for serving humanity, the federal government was not. Hoover felt that the Constitution did not permit direct federal relief to individuals. As the economic crisis that began in 1929 worsened, and pressure on him mounted, he did take some action, but those steps were either the wrong ones, such as the disastrous Smoot-Hawley Tariff that set off a virtual international trade war, or too modest, such as his plan to forgive debt payments from European nations (that couldn't afford to pay them anyway). What Hoover didn't seem to understand was that, in addition to federal programs to end the hard times, the American public wanted a president who could give them hope and inspiration. Unable to provide that, Hoover left office under one of the darkest clouds ever to shadow a presidency.

Biographical Facts

Born: August 10, 1874 in West Branch, Iowa

Ancestry: Swiss-German

Father: Jesse Clark Hoover; born September 2, 1846 in Miami Country, Ohio; died December 14, 1880 in West Branch, Iowa

Father's Occupation: Blacksmith

Mother: Hulda Randall Minthorn Hoover; born May 4, 1849 in Norwich, Oxford County, Canada; died February 22, 1883 in West Branch, Iowa

Wife: Lou Henry; born March 29, 1875 in Waterloo, Iowa; died January 7, 1944 in New York City

Marriage: February 10, 1899 in Monterey, California

Children: Herbert Clark (1903-1969), Allan Henry (1907-1993)

Education: Local schools; Newberg Academy; received B.A. from Stanford University (1895)

Home: West Branch, Iowa

Religious Affiliation: Society of Friends (Quaker)

Occupation before Presidency: Mining Engineer

Political Offices before Presidency: Chairman of Commission for Relief in Belgium; U.S. Food Administrator; Chairman of Supreme Economic Council; Secretary of Commerce

Political Party: Republican

Age at Inauguration: 54

Occupations after Presidency: Chairman of Commission for Polish Relief; Chairman of Finnish Relief Fund; Coordinator of Food Supply for World Famine; Chairman of Commissions on Organization of the Executive Branch of the Government (Hoover Commission); writer

Death: October 20, 1964 in New York

Place of Burial: Hoover Presidential Library, West Branch, Iowa

Nickname: None

Writings: *The Challenge of Liberty; America's First Crusade; Memoirs; The Ordeal of Woodrow Wilson*

Election of 1928

Candidates	Party	Electoral Vote	Popular Vote
Herbert C. Hoover (CA)	Republican	444	21,391,993
Alfred E. Smith (NY)	Democratic	87	15,016,169
Norman Thomas (NY)	Socialist	---	267,835

About the Election: When Coolidge announced that he would not run for reelection, the country was still enjoying a period of national prosperity. Hoover—presented as a poor boy who worked his way to wealth and fame—was a fitting candidate. His successful career embodied the nation's technological and economic progress to millions of Americans and he was nominated on the first ballot at the Republican Party's national convention. Opposing him was Democratic candidate Governor Alfred E. Smith of New York. A Roman Catholic and strongly opposed to Prohibition, Smith was perceived as an Eastern urbanite. His religion also made him the target of prejudice and insinuation during the campaign, as some charged that his loyalty to the Pope superceded his loyalty to the United States. No major political party would nominate another Catholic until 1960, when John F. Kennedy defeated Richard Nixon.

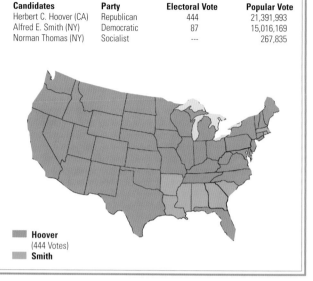

Hoover
(444 Votes)
Smith

Hoover's Term 1929-1933

March 4, 1929: HERBERT HOOVER IS INAUGURATED as the 31st president of the United States.

March 28, 1929: The Hoover Administration helps Standard Oil of California (SOCAL) obtain OIL RIGHTS IN THE SHEIKHDOM OF BAHRAIN. A British protectorate, Bahrain previously sold its oil only to British companies.

April 6, 1929: HOOVER SENDS WARPLANES TO THE ARIZONA-MEXICO BORDER where American troops are killed in a crossfire between the Mexican government and rebel forces.

June 15, 1929: Hoover signs the AGRICULTURAL MARKETING ACT, creating a Federal Farm Board to promote agricultural commodity marketing by extending loans to cooperatives.

September 3, 1929: Although statistics reveal that about 60 percent of the American public live below the official poverty line, stock prices reach an all-time high. The soaring stock market leads Hoover to state that Americans had won "THE FINAL TRIUMPH OVER POVERTY."

October 24, 1929: On a day remembered as "BLACK THURSDAY," prices on the New York Stock Exchange (NYSE) tumble as 13 million shares are sold. Four days later on "BLACK TUESDAY," investors dump over 16 million more shares on the NYSE, and thousands of people are ruined.

December 2, 1929: Secretary of State Henry Stimson cites the Kellogg-Briand Pact, which had symbolically outlawed war, to calm HOSTILITIES BETWEEN CHINA AND THE SOVIET UNION. Earlier in the year, the Chinese had seized control of a Soviet-controlled railroad in Manchuria.

April 22, 1930: The U.S., Great Britain, and Japan sign the LONDON NAVAL TREATY, agreeing to limit the number of warships in each navy.

June 17, 1930: Hoover signs the SMOOT-HAWLEY TARIFF ACT, which raises tariffs dramatically in order to limit competition for domestic products. The law launches an international trade war as other nations immediately pass similar laws increasing their tariffs.

December 2, 1930: Hoover asks Congress to fund several PUBLIC WORKS PROJECTS, though the

Quotes by Hoover:

"True Liberalism is found not in striving to spread bureaucracy but in striving to set bounds to it."

"The sole function of Government is to bring about a condition of affairs favorable to the beneficial development of private enterprise."

Quote about Hoover

"A private meeting with Hoover is like sitting in a bath of ink."
– Secretary of State Henry Stimson

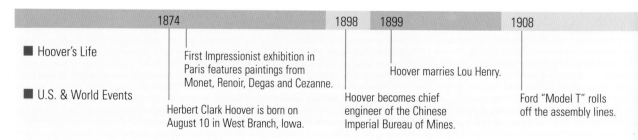

	1874		1898	1899		1908
■ Hoover's Life		First Impressionist exhibition in Paris features paintings from Monet, Renoir, Degas and Cezanne.		Hoover marries Lou Henry.		
■ U.S. & World Events		Herbert Clark Hoover is born on August 10 in West Branch, Iowa.	Hoover becomes chief engineer of the Chinese Imperial Bureau of Mines.			Ford "Model T" rolls off the assembly lines.

First Lady: Lou Henry Hoover

Lou Henry was the first woman, and the only First Lady, to earn a geology degree from Stanford University. She met Hoover at Stanford, and they married after graduating. Mrs. Hoover shared her husband's scientific and academic interests, and also loved the outdoors.

At the White House, Mrs. Hoover entertained elegantly, funding social events and redecorating projects with family money as the country plunged further into economic depression. Mrs. Hoover was known for treating guests, old and young, titled or not, with equal fanfare and attention. Her generosity continued throughout her life and she played a significant role in establishing the Girl Scout movement in the country.

president remains philosophically hesitant about the federal government providing direct aid to the unemployed. Congress allocates over $100 million to employ some of the 4.5 million Americans who are out of work.

December 11, 1930: One of the nation's largest banks, the BANK OF THE UNITED STATES, which is based in New York City, closes. It is one of over 1,300 banks to close.

February 27, 1931: Congress overrides Hoover's veto to pass the BONUS LOAN BILL, allowing veterans to receive loans at half the value of the bonus certificates issued to them in 1924.

June 20–September 21, 1931: In an effort to ease the worldwide depression, Hoover proposes a one-year MORATORIUM ON DEBT payments owed to the U.S. by European nations in exchange for a halt to loan payments by the U.S. However, France delays accepting the idea, and causes the collapse of all German banks in mid-July. Great Britain responds by detaching its currency from the gold standard. Americans, in turn, start hoarding gold and withdrawing money from banks for fear that the U.S. will follow Britain's example. The run on banks causes over 800 more banks to fail in the U.S.

September 18, 1931: JAPAN INVADES MANCHURIA and installs a puppet government sparking undeclared war with China. In January, Secretary of State Henry L. Stimson condemns the action and presents what becomes known as the STIMSON DOCTRINE, declaring that the United States refuses to recognize any territory that is seized by force.

December 7, 1931: Protesting the lack of jobs, hundreds of "HUNGER MARCHERS" arrive in Washington to present a petition to Hoover. They are turned back at the White House.

January 22, 1932: The RECONSTRUCTION FINANCE CORPORATION is created for lending money to banks, insurance companies and other institutions.

July 2, 1932: DEMOCRATS NOMINATE FRANKLIN ROOSEVELT for president. In his acceptance speech, he promises "a new deal for the American people."

November 8, 1932: ROOSEVELT DEFEATS HOOVER in a landslide election victory.

March 4, 1933: Hoover escorts President-elect Roosevelt to his inauguration, making for an awkward day since the two men do not trust each other. During

the ri
Roos

Hoover's Administration

Inauguration: March 4, 1929 at the Capitol, Washington, D.C.
Vice President: Charles Curtis
Secretary of State: Henry L. Stimson
Secretary of the Treasury:
Andrew W. Mellon;
Ogden L. Mills (from February 13, 1932)
Secretary of War: James W. Good;
Patrick J. Hurley (from December 9, 1929)
Attorney General: James DeWitt Mitchell
Postmaster General: Walter F. Brown
Secretary of the Navy: Charles F. Adams
Secretary of the Interior: Ray L. Wilbur
Secretary of Agriculture: Arthur M. Hyde

Secretary of Commerce: Robert P. Lamont; Roy D. Chapin (from December 14, 1932)
Secretary of Labor: James J. Davis;
William N. Doak (from December 9, 1930)
Supreme Court Appointments:
Charles Evans Hughes, Chief Justice (1930);
Owen J. Roberts (1930);
Benjamin N. Cardozo (1932)
71st Congress: (March 4, 1929-March 4, 1931)
Senate: 56 Republicans; 39 Democrats; 1 Other
House: 267 Republicans; 167 Democrats; 1 Other
72nd Congress: (March 4, 1931-March 4, 1933)
Senate: 48 Republicans; 47 Democrats; 1 Other
House: 220 Democrats; 214 Republicans; 1 Other

1917	1928	1931	1944	1964

Hoover is named United States Food Administrator.

The U.S. Congress makes the "Star Spangled Banner" the official national anthem.

Hoover dies on October 20 in New York City.

U.S. declares war on Germany and joins the Allies. The war ends the following year.

Hoover is elected president.

Lou Hoover dies.

Franklin Delano Roosevelt

32nd President (1933–1945)

"The only thing we have to fear is fear itself."

Dear Mr. President. This is just to tell you that everything is all right now. The man you sent found our house all right, and we went down to the bank with him and the mortgage can go on for a while longer. You remember I wrote you about losing the furniture too. Well, your man got it back for us. I never heard of a president like you.

This letter was from an average, Depression-weary citizen, one out of millions who were directly affected by Franklin Delano Roosevelt's vision of America. Roosevelt saw his role in office as far greater than simply to be the chief administrator of government policy; but a president's job was also to lift the nation's spirit, to educate, and to provide vision. Putting theory into practice, despite enormous pain from polio, the president learned to "walk" with steel braces, supported by aides, so that he might project a strong image to the nation and lead them out of economic turmoil.

Roosevelt also believed it was his duty to act. Through his famous New Deal, he created programs to put America back to work, stabilize the economy, and increase the money supply. Some New Deal program goals were contradictory, and the critics condemned Roosevelt for expanding the federal government in an alarming manner.

Once Germany attacked Poland in September 1939, Roosevelt worked to prepare an isolationist American public for the threat of probable U.S. involvement in the war. He helped American industry transform into "an arsenal of democracy" that produced ships, planes, and supplies faster than ever before. After Japan's attack of Pearl Harbor in 1941, he formed a close partnership with British Prime Minister Winston Churchill to lead the fight against the Axis powers.

Certainly, Roosevelt had his critics. In 1937, he tried to pack the Supreme Court with liberal judges, costing him support even from some of his closest allies. During the war, he ordered over 112,000 Japanese Americans to be detained in internment camps throughout the West, stripping them of their rights. He also chose to ignore Nazi concentration camps, arguing that the sooner the Allies won the war, the sooner the Holocaust would end. When Roosevelt died in 1945, he had been president for so long that many Americans couldn't imagine that there had ever been another president. More than half a century after his death, his legacy continues to be honored and debated.

Biographical Facts

Born: January 30, 1882 in Hyde Park, New York
Ancestry: Dutch
Father: James Roosevelt; born July 16, 1828 in Hyde Park, New York; died December 8, 1900 in New York.
Father's Occupations: Lawyer; financier; railroad vice president
Mother: Sara Delano Roosevelt; born September 21, 1854 in Newburgh, New York; died September 7, 1941 in Hyde Park, New York
Wife: Anna Eleanor Roosevelt; born October 11, 1884 in New York; died November 7, 1962 in New York
Marriage: March 17, 1905 in New York
Children: Anna Eleanor Roosevelt (1906-1975); James Roosevelt (1907-1991); Franklin Delano Roosevelt Jr. (1909); Elliott Roosevelt (1910-1990); Franklin Delano Roosevelt Jr. (1914-1988); John Aspinwall Roosevelt (1916-1981)

Education: Private tutor; Groton School; received BA from Harvard University (1903); studied law at Columbia University
Home: Hyde Park, New York
Religious Affiliation: Episcopalian
Occupations before Presidency: Lawyer; politician
Military Service: None
Political Offices before Presidency: Member New York State Senate; Assistant Secretary of the Navy; Governor of New York
Political Party: Democratic
Age at Inauguration: 51
Death: April 12, 1945, in Warm Springs, Georgia
Place of Burial: Hyde Park, New York
Nickname: FDR
Writings: *The Happy Warrior, Alfred E. Smith; FDR: His Personal Letters*

AD FAMILIAM GENTIVM COMEM CONTEND

STUDY OF
SIDENT ROOSEVELT
FOR PAINTING
THREE AT YALTA
NVAS SIZE 92" x 92"
N OUTLINE SKETCH

CHANDOR   MARCH: 1945.   THE WHITE HOUSE, WASHINGTON.

Election of 1932

Candidates	Party	Electoral Vote	Popular Vote
Franklin D. Roosevelt (NY)	Democratic	472	22,809,638
Herbert C. Hoover (CA)	Republican	59	15,758,901
Norman Thomas (NY)	Socialist	---	881,951
William Z. Foster (NY)	Communist	---	102,785
William D. Upshaw (GA)	Prohibition	---	81,869

About the Election: The nation entered the 1932 election season mired deep in economic depression. Because many Americans blamed incumbent Herbert Hoover for the financial crisis, Democrats knew they had an opportunity to recapture the presidency. Roosevelt, the governor of New York, won the nomination after selecting Speaker of the House John Nance Garner of Texas, the favorite of Southern Democrats, as his vice-presidential candidate. After winning the nomination on the fourth ballot, Roosevelt gave the first acceptance speech ever delivered to a presidential nominating convention, pledging "a new deal for the American people." He promised to provide relief for the unemployed and farmers, to balance the budget, and to end Prohibition. Roosevelt carried all but six states with 472 electoral votes to Hoover's 59, and Democrats took control of Congress.

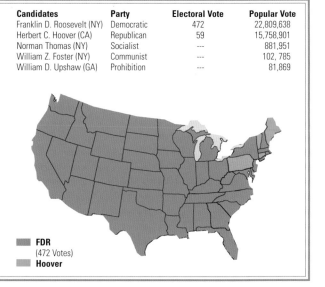

■ **FDR**
(472 Votes)
■ **Hoover**

Roosevelt's First Term 1933-1937

March 4, 1933: ROOSEVELT IS INAUGURATED, and in his address, he promises active government intervention to revive the economy. During the first 100 days of his term, Congress passes an array of new programs.

March 5, 1933: ROOSEVELT ORDERS A BANK HOLIDAY to halt a Depression-induced run on the nation's banks.

March 6, 1933: ELEANOR ROOSEVELT holds a press conference to which she only invites female members of the press. The press conference signals the First Lady's intent to take a very active role in the administration.

March 9, 1933: At Roosevelt's urging, Congress passes the EMERGENCY BANKING ACT. The law requires that all banks prove that they are solvent before they reopen after the bank holiday. By March 12, over 1,000 banks reopen.

March 12, 1933: Roosevelt gives his first "FIRESIDE CHAT" radio address to the nation. The regular addresses add enormously to the president's popularity and help reassure the nation during its time of struggle.

March 31, 1933: Congress creates the CIVILIAN CONSERVATION CORPS (CCC), putting a 250,000 young men between the ages of 18 and 25 to work on a new national reforestation program. By the time the program ends in 1941, it provides work for 2,000,000 men.

April 19, 1933: Roosevelt takes the UNITED STATES OFF THE GOLD STANDARD in order to stimulate the economy.

May 12, 1933: Congress passes the FEDERAL EMERGENCY RELIEF ACT (FERA) to provide grants, rather than loans, to the states. In turn, states provide relief to the American public. Congress also creates the AGRICULTURAL ADJUSTMENT ADMINISTRATION (AAA), which restricts the production of certain crops and pays farmers not to till their land. Roosevelt hopes that the AAA will reduce agricultural production, raise prices, and aid suffering farmers.

May 27, 1933: Congress passes the FEDERAL SECURITIES ACT, requiring all issues of stocks and bonds to be registered and approved by the federal government.

June 16, 1933: In a flurry of activity, Congress creates several major programs that will be the cornerstones of Roosevelt's New Deal. In passing the NATIONAL INDUSTRY RECOVERY ACT (NIRA), Congress launches the PUBLIC WORKS ADMINISTRATION (PWA) to provide construction work on highways, public buildings, and other federal infrastructure projects. The NIRA also creates the NATIONAL RECOVERY ADMINISTRATION (NRA), which formalizes the fair competition codes that had been established by industry and trade associations since the end of World War I. The NRA gives Roosevelt the power to mandate and enforce these codes. On the same day, Congress also passes the Farm Credit Act and the Banking Act of 1933, which establishes the FEDERAL BANK

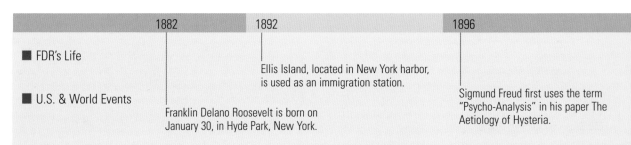

■ FDR's Life

■ U.S. & World Events

1882

Franklin Delano Roosevelt is born on January 30, in Hyde Park, New York.

1892

Ellis Island, located in New York harbor, is used as an immigration station.

1896

Sigmund Freud first uses the term "Psycho-Analysis" in his paper The Aetiology of Hysteria.

First Lady: Anna Eleanor Roosevelt

Eleanor Roosevelt is considered one of the greatest humanitarians of the modern age, and is remembered for her tireless devotion to improving the lives of those in need. After Franklin Delano Roosevelt was stricken with polio in 1921, Mrs. Roosevelt became politically active in order to help her husband continue his career. At the White House, Mrs. Roosevelt radically transformed the role of the First Lady. In addition to entertaining thousands of guests, she traveled across the country bringing hope to the millions who suffered during the Great Depression. She also held press conferences, gave radio broadcasts, and wrote a daily syndicated newspaper column, "My Day"—all unprecedented activities for a First Lady.

After being widowed in 1945, Mrs. Roosevelt continued her socially conscious work as U.S. delegate to the United Nations, as well as advocate for civil rights. She died of tuberculosis at the age of 74.

DEPOSIT INSURANCE CORPORATION (FDIC).

August 5, 1933: Roosevelt creates the **NATIONAL LABOR BOARD** to enforce labor's collective bargaining rights. The action is a major victory for the labor movement.

November 8, 1933: Roosevelt appoints Harry Hopkins to lead the **CIVIL WORKS ADMINISTRATION**, a federal jobs program.

December 5, 1933: The **21st AMENDMENT**, which ends Prohibition, is ratified and becomes law. Enforcement of the alcohol ban had grown lax and many argued that the ban had led to an increase in organized crime.

February 2, 1934: Roosevelt establishes the **EXPORT-IMPORT BANK** to stimulate international trade.

March 24, 1934: The **TYDINGS-MCDUFFIE ACT** sets a timetable for Philippine independence. The islands, held by the United States since the Spanish-American War, become independent in 1946.

April 12, 1934: Isolationist Senator Joseph Nye of North Dakota launches an investigation into "war profiteering" by arms manufacturers during World War I. The **NYE HEARINGS** give impetus to those who believe that American involvement in European wars is driven by corporate-profit motives rather than for national security or morality.

May 10-11, 1934: A major drought-driven dust storm sweeps across Texas, Oklahoma, Arkansas, Kansas and Colorado, blowing dust as far east as the Atlantic Ocean. The region becomes known as a "**DUST BOWL**." The storms convince thousands of unemployed farmers and laborers to leave the plains for California in search of work.

June 6, 1934: Roosevelt signs the Securities Exchange Act, creating the **SECURITIES EXCHANGE COMMISSION** (**SEC**). The SEC is charged with licensing stock exchanges in an attempt to clamp down on illegal speculation.

June 19, 1934: Congress replaces the Federal Radio Commission, created by President Calvin Coolidge, with the **FEDERAL COMMUNICATIONS COMMISSION** (**FCC**). The expanded body regulates not only radio, but telegraph and telephone services as well.

FDR's First Administration

Inauguration: March 4, 1933, at the Capitol, Washington, D.C.
Vice President: John Nance Garner
Secretary of State: Cordell Hull
Secretary of the Treasury:
William H. Woodin;
Henry Morgenthau, Jr. (from January 8, 1934)
Secretary of War: George H. Dern
Attorney General: Homer S. Cummings
Postmaster General: James A. Farley
Secretary of the Navy: Claude A. Swanson
Secretary of the Interior: Harold L. Ickes
Secretary of Agriculture: Henry A. Wallace

Secretary of Commerce: Daniel C. Roper
Secretary of Labor: Frances Perkins
73rd Congress
(March 4, 1933-January 3, 1935)
Senate: 60 Democrats; 35 Republicans; 1 Other
House: 310 Democrats; 117 Republicans; 5 Others
74th Congress
(January 3, 1935-January 3, 1937)
Senate: 69 Democrats; 25 Republicans;
2 Others
House: 319 Democrats; 103 Republicans;
10 Others
End of Presidential Term: January 20, 1937

1898	1900	1901
The Spanish-American War is fought.	Franklin Roosevelt enrolls at Harvard University.	President William McKinley is assassinated in September, and Theodore Roosevelt, FDR's distant cousin, takes office.

July 5, 1934: Coastal strikes by the **INTERNATIONAL LONGSHOREMAN ASSOCIATION** (ILA) escalate on **BLACK THURSDAY**, when seven workers—including strike leader Shelvy Daffron—die at the hands of police in Seattle, Washington. Although numerous arrests of "Reds" take place, the government meets most of ILA's demands in October, ending the strike.

November 6, 1934: The Democrats increase their majorities in both the House of Representatives and the Senate in **MIDTERM ELECTIONS**.

January 4, 1935: In his annual **STATE OF THE UNION ADDRESS**, Roosevelt introduces a **SECOND PHASE OF NEW DEAL PROGRAMS**. While the aim of many of the first New Deal programs is to quickly shore up the nation's economy, the aim of the second is to provide long-term security to the elderly, unemployed, and others who may be in need.

May 6, 1935: Roosevelt creates the **WORKS PROGRESS ADMINISTRATION (WPA)** with his closest advisor, Harry Hopkins, as its head. The WPA puts millions of Americans to work on construction projects and also employs artists and writers to bring their talents to small communities. Republicans condemn the project as a wasteful allocation of government resources.

May 11, 1935: Roosevelt establishes the **RURAL ELECTRIFICATION ADMINISTRATION** to finance power-plant construction and install electrical lines in regions that private companies do not serve.

May 27, 1935: In the case *A.L.A. Schecter Poultry Corporation v. United States*, the **SUPREME COURT RULES THAT THE NIRA IS UNCONSTITUTIONAL**—a major blow to Roosevelt's administration. The NRA, which was established under the NIRA, is officially terminated at the end of the year.

July 5, 1935: In a major victory for organized labor, Roosevelt signs the **NATIONAL LABOR RELATIONS ACT**, creating the **NATIONAL LABOR RELATIONS BOARD (NLRB)**. The NLRB ensures the right of labor unions to organize and bargain collectively.

August 14, 1935: Roosevelt signs the **SOCIAL SECURITY ACT**. The landmark law provides generations of Americans over the age of 65 with guaranteed pensions, sets up an unemployment insurance system, and assists states in providing aid to dependent children, the blind, and senior citizens who do not qualify for Social Security payments.

August 30, 1935: Congress passes the **REVENUE ACT**, which raises taxes on inheritances and gifts, as well as taxes on higher incomes and corporations.

This poster designed by Charles Colner was published by the National Recovery Administration during the Great Depression.

	1903	1905	1907
■ FDR's Life			
■ U.S. & World Events	Roosevelt is appointed editor of the Harvard Crimson, the school's newspaper.	He marries President Theodore Roosevelt's niece and his own distant cousin, Eleanor Roosevelt.	Russia joins Great Britain and France, and forms the Triple Entente. Austria-Hungary, Germany and Italy make up the Triple Alliance.

Election of 1936

About the Election: The Democratic National Convention renominated Roosevelt and Garner. The Republicans chose Alfred M. Landon of Kansas for president and Frank Knox, Chicago Daily News publisher, for vice president. Radical populist groups also campaigned for a Union Party presidential ticket with inconsequential results. The Republicans charged that Roosevelt had not followed through with balancing the budget, but the president was confident and pointed to the progress that had been made against unemployment since 1933. Roosevelt had a significant following in the African-American population, as well as in the ethnic, working-class communities of the big industrial cities. He won by a landslide, receiving 523 electoral votes to Landon's 8. He carried every state except Maine and Vermont, scoring the largest victory margin in the Electoral College since James Monroe in 1820.

Candidates	Party	Electoral Vote	Popular Vote
Franklin D. Roosevelt (NY)	Democratic	523	27,752,869
Alfred M. Landon (KS)	Republican	8	16,674,665
William Lemke (NY)	Union	---	882, 479
Norman Thomas (NY)	Socialist	---	187,720
Earl Browder (KS)	Communist	---	80,159

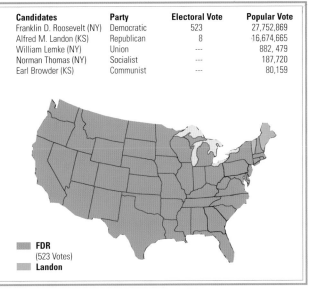

■ **FDR**
(523 Votes)
■ **Landon**

August 31, 1935: Roosevelt signs the **NEUTRALITY ACT**, which prevents American corporations from shipping weapons to belligerents during wartime.

January 6, 1936: The **SUPREME COURT DECLARES THE AGRICULTURAL ADJUSTMENT ACT UNCONSTITUTIONAL** because federal aid to suffering farmers went against the rights given to states by the Constitution. According to the ruling, such aid should be at the state level, not the federal.

March 2, 1936: Congress responds to the Supreme Court's decision on the AAA by passing the **SOIL CONSERVATION AND DOMESTIC ALLOTMENT ACT**, which provides services that are similar to those provided by the AAA.

November 3, 1936: **ROOSEVELT WINS REELECTION** in a major landslide, winning 523 electoral votes to 8 for Landon.

Roosevelt's Second Term 1937-1941

January 20, 1937: In his **SECOND INAUGURAL ADDRESS**, President Roosevelt declares, "I see one-third of a nation ill-housed, ill-clad, ill-nourished."

February 5, 1937: In the wake of the Supreme Court's recent rulings against his New Deal programs, Roosevelt proposes that as many as six justices be added to the Supreme Court if any justice over the age of 70 refuses to retire. As the older justices on the court are the ones that oppose his programs, Roosevelt's proposal is actually an effort to **PACK THE SUPREME COURT** with

his supporters. Although Congress later passes a bill to allow justices to retire at 70 with full pay, Roosevelt's attempt to remove justices who oppose him costs him support.

March 1, 1937: U.S. Steel agrees to recognize the United Steel Workers Union. Over the next several years, other major American steel companies follow suit.

May 1, 1937: Roosevelt signs a third **NEUTRALITY ACT**, requiring belligerents to pay for any non-military items in cash and to transport the goods in their own ships. The laws becomes known as the "cash-and-carry" law.

July 22, 1937: In an attempt to alleviate some of the financial strain in the agricultural sector of the country, Congress creates the **FARM SECURITIES ADMINISTRATION (FSA)**, which gives low-interest loans to small farmers.

September 2, 1937: Congress passes the **NATIONAL HOUSING ACT**, which creates the U.S. Housing Authority to administer home-construction loans.

December 12, 1937: Japan attacks the U.S. gunboat **PANAY** on China's Yangtze River, despite Roosevelt's declaration of neutrality in the war between China and Japan. Japan apologizes, citing a case of mistaken identity.

January 3, 1938: In his State of the Union address, Roosevelt asks Congress for **INCREASED MILITARY FUNDING**, particularly for the U.S. Navy. Later in the year, Congress agrees to spend $1 billion over ten years to upgrade naval readiness.

1910

1913

1914

Roosevelt is appointed assistant secretary of the Navy.

Roosevelt is elected to the New York Senate.

Archduke Franz Ferdinand is assassinated on June 28, sparking the outbreak of World War I. Austria-Hungary declares war on Serbia exactly one month later.

Roosevelt's Second Administration

Inauguration: January 20, 1937 at the Capitol, Washington, D. C.
Vice President: John Nance Garner
Secretary of State: Cordell Hull
Secretary of the Treasury: Henry Morgenthau, Jr.
Secretary of War: Harry H. Woodring; Henry L. Stimson (from July 10, 1940)
Attorney General: Homer S. Cummings; Frank Murphy (from January 17, 1939); Robert H. Jackson (from January 18, 1940)
Postmaster General: James A. Farley; Frank C. Walker (from September 10, 1940)
Secretary of the Navy: Claude A. Swanson; Frank Knox (from July 10, 1940)
Secretary of the Interior: Harold L. Ickes
Secretary of Agriculture: Henry A. Wallace; Claude R. Wickard (from September 5, 1940)
Secretary of Labor: Frances Perkins

Secretary of Commerce: Daniel C. Roper; Harry L. Hopkins (from January 23, 1939); Jesse H. Jones (from September 19, 1940)
Supreme Court Appointments:
Hugo L. Black (1937); Stanley F. Reed (1938); Felix Frankfurter (1939); William O. Douglas (1939); Frank Murphy (1940)
75th Congress
(January 3, 1937-January 3, 1939)
Senate: 76 Democrats; 16 Republicans; 4 Others
House: 331 Democrats; 89 Republicans; 13 Others
76th Congress
(January 3, 1939-January 3, 1941)
Senate 69 Democrats; 23 Republicans; 4 Others
House: 261 Democrats; 164 Republicans; 4 Others
End of Presidential Term: January 20, 1941

February 16, 1938: President Roosevelt signs a second AGRICULTURAL ADJUSTMENT ACT, which in turn creates the Federal Crop Insurance Corporation.

March 13, 1938: NAZI GERMANY ANNEXES AUSTRIA and Adolf Hitler claims it is in order to bring order to Austria.

May 26, 1938: THE HOUSE OF UN-AMERICAN ACTIVITIES COMMITTEE (HUAC) is founded to investigate both right-wing and left-wing groups in the United States. In time, the committee takes a leading role in the anti-Communist investigations of the 1940s and 1950s.

May 27, 1938: Congress overrides President Roosevelt's veto to pass a CORPORATE INCOME TAX CUT.

June 25, 1938: The FAIR LABOR STANDARDS ACT is passed, which raises the minimum wage and sets a 40-hour workweek for all workers in companies involved in interstate commerce.

March 15, 1939: GERMANY INVADES CZECHOSLOVAKIA and controls the entire country within two weeks.

April 1, 1939: The SPANISH CIVIL WAR ENDS, and the United States recognizes General Franco's government.

April 7, 1939: ITALY INVADES ALBANIA. King Zog is exiled.

August 23, 1939: Germany and the U.S.S.R. sign a NON-AGGRESSION PACT, which Germany later breaks.

September 1, 1939: GERMANY INVADES POLAND and Warsaw

surrenders a week later. The invasion begins World War II.

September 3, 1939: FRANCE AND ENGLAND DECLARE WAR on Germany. The United States continues to maintain its neutrality.

October 18, 1939: The United States closes all ports and waters to warring submarines.

November 4, 1939: In order to assist Britain and France, Roosevelt signs the NEUTRALITY ACT OF 1939. The revised law ends the "cash-and-carry" sale of arms.

November 30, 1939: The U.S.S.R. INVADES FINLAND, and after fierce resistance, Finland surrenders in March.

April 9, 1940: The NAZIS INVADE NORWAY AND DENMARK. Denmark surrenders immediately. Norway resists but falls as well.

May 10, 1940: WINSTON CHURCHILL becomes the prime minister of Great Britain, replacing the discredited Neville Chamberlain. On the same day, Germany captures the low countries of Luxembourg, the Netherlands, and Belgium.

May 26–June 4, 1940: Over 300,000 French and British troops successfully evacuate from the coastal town of DUNKIRK in France before they can be struck by the advancing Nazis. Although Paris falls to Hitler within two weeks, the Allied army survives to defend its home shores.

June 20, 1940: Roosevelt appoints Henry L. Stimson secretary of war and Frank Knox as secretary of the Navy. Both men are Republicans and are chosen in order to unite the nation under a semblance of a "coalition government."

June-July 1940: The Republicans nominate Wendell L. Willkie for president. The Democrats nominate Roosevelt in an unprecedented bid for a third term.

June 28, 1940: Congress passes the ALIEN REGISTRATION ACT, requiring all foreigners to register with the government and to be fingerprinted. The law also makes it a crime to advocate the forceful overthrow of the U.S. government.

July 10, 1940: The BATTLE OF BRITAIN BEGINS when

	1914	1915	1917
■ FDR's Life			
■ U.S. & World Events	The Panama Canal, which cuts the sailing distance from the East Coast to the West Coast by more than 8,000 miles, is finished.	Albert Einstein announces his general theory of relativity.	Bolsheviks, led by Vladimir Lenin, storm Petrograd's Winter Palace, the headquarters of the Provisional Government, and proclaim Soviet power.

Election of 1940

About the Election: Breaking precedent, the Democratic Party renominated Franklin Roosevelt for a third consecutive term. The Republicans nominated Wendell L. Willkie of Indiana, a liberally inclined businessman. Willkie supported Roosevelt's foreign policy and many of the New Deal programs, but opposed the restrictions the Roosevelt administration had imposed on business. The Republicans also argued that no president had ever sought three terms in succession. Roosevelt defended his administration's programs, and despite the growing crisis, promised to keep the nation out of war.

Candidates	Party	Electoral Vote	Popular Vote
Franklin D. Roosevelt (NY)	Democratic	449	27,307,819
Wendell L. Willkie (NY)	Republican	82	22,321,018
Norman Thomas (NY)	Socialist	---	99,557

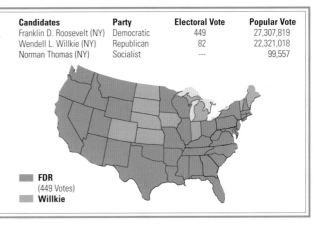

■ **FDR**
(449 Votes)
■ **Willkie**

Frances Perkins, the first female Cabinet member, worked to develop an "old-age" insurance program. The result was the 1935 Social Security Act designed to provide elderly retired workers with pensions.

Germany attacks Great Britain. Despite repeated German bombing raids, Britain maintains control of its skies and the Nazis are forced to call off the operation in October and to abandon plans of invading Britain.

September 3, 1940: The U.S. trades 50 destroyers in exchange for the right to construct air and naval bases on British lands in the Americas.

September 16, 1940: Roosevelt signs the **SELECTIVE TRAINING AND SERVICE ACT**, authorizing the first peace-time military draft in U.S. history and requiring all men between the ages of 21 and 35 to register for military training.

November 5, 1940: **ROOSEVELT IS REELECTED**, winning an unprecedented third term and defeating Republican candidate Wendell L. Willkie.

December 29, 1940: With Great Britain desperate for American military supplies, President Roosevelt declares in a fireside chat that the United States must become the "**ARSENAL OF DEMOCRACY.**"

January 6, 1941: In his State of the Union Address, Roosevelt argues that Congress must support his plan to send aid to Britain and the other allies. He argues that only by doing so can the United States protect the "**FOUR ESSENTIAL FREEDOMS**" that he names as freedom of speech and expression, freedom of worship, freedom from want, and freedom from fear.

Roosevelt's Third Term 1941-1945

January 20, 1941: **ROOSEVELT IS INAUGURATED** for the third time.

February 4, 1941: The **UNITED SERVICE ORGANIZATIONS (USO)** is formed to provide social, educational, welfare, and religious services to the armed forces and defense industries.

March 11, 1941: Roosevelt signs the **LEND-LEASE ACT**, which allows the president to lend arms and other war materials to any nation if it is in U.S. interest to do so. The purpose of the act is to ensure support to Great Britain without formally declaring war on Nazi Germany or Italy.

May 27, 1941: The Germans overrun **GREECE** and **YUGOSLAVIA.**

1918
Roosevelt tours European battlefields and meets with military leaders.

U.S. declares war on Germany, and joins the Allies.

1919
The Treaty of Versailles reorganizes European boundaries and creates new international organizations, including the League of Nations.

1920
Roosevelt runs unsuccessfully for Vice President of the United States.

Roosevelt's Third Administration

Inauguration: January 20, 1941 at the Capitol, Washington, D.C.
Vice President: Henry Agard Wallace
Secretary of State: Cordell Hull; Edward R. Stettinius (from December 1, 1944)
Secretary of the Treasury: Henry Morgenthau, Jr.
Secretary of War: Henry L. Stimson
Attorney General: Robert H. Jackson; Francis Biddle (from September 5, 1941)
Postmaster General: Frank C. Walker
Secretary of the Navy: Frank Knox; James V. Forrestal (from May 18, 1944)
Secretary of the Interior: Harold L. Ickes
Secretary of Agriculture: Claude R. Wickard
Secretary of Comemrce: Jesse H. Jones

Secretary of Labor: Frances Perkins
Supreme Court Appointments: Harlan Fiske Stone, Chief Justice (1941); James F. Byrnes (1941); Robert H. Jackson (1941); Wiley B. Rutledge (1943)
77th Congress
(January 3, 1941-January 3, 1943)
Senate: 66 Democrats; 28 Republicans; 2 Others
House: 268 Democrats; 162 Republicans; 5 Others
78th Congress
(January 3, 1943-January 3, 1945)
Senate: 58 Democrats; 37 Republicans; 1 Other
House: 218 Democrats; 208 Republicans; 4 Others
End of Presidential Term: January 20, 1945

June 22, 1941: In a dramatic end to the NAZI-SOVIET NON-AGGRESSION PACT of 1939, GERMANY INVADES THE SOVIET UNION.
June 25, 1941: Under pressure from African-American labor leader ASA PHILIP RANDOLPH, who has threatened to lead one million black men in a protest march to Washington, Roosevelt creates the FAIR EMPLOYMENT PRACTICES COMMITTEE (FEPC) to end discrimination in the defense industry.
July 26, 1941: Roosevelt appoints GENERAL DOUGLAS MACARTHUR commander in chief of U.S. forces in the Far East.
August 14, 1941: Roosevelt and British Prime

During the Great Depression, millions were unemployed, few jobs were available, and almost every bank was closed.

Minister Winston Churchill issue the ATLANTIC CHARTER after meeting secretly on battleships off the coast of Newfoundland, Canada.
October 27, 1941: When a GERMAN U-BOAT ATTACKS THE U.S. DESTROYER *KEARNEY*, Roosevelt announces that "America has been attacked." But the president does not declare war on Germany.
October 30, 1941: One hundred Americans die when the U.S. destroyer *REUBEN JAMES* IS SUNK BY A U-BOAT.
December 7, 1941: JAPAN LAUNCHES A SURPRISE ATTACK ON U.S. MILITARY BASE IN PEARL HARBOR in Hawaii. At approximately 7:55 a.m, the first Japanese warplanes strike Hickham Field, an army base south of Pearl Harbor. The raid lasts less than two hours. Approximately 2,400 people are killed and 1,200 are wounded. The Japanese attack costs the United States Navy 6 battleships and 150 planes.
December 8, 1941: After the Pearl Harbor attack, the UNITED STATES DECLARES WAR ON JAPAN.
December 11, 1941: GERMANY AND ITALY DECLARE WAR ON THE UNITED STATES.
December 10, 1941: JAPAN INVADES THE PHILIPPINES.
December 25, 1941: JAPAN CAPTURES HONG KONG.
January 2, 1942: JAPAN CAPTURES MANILA, the capital city of the Philippines. This forces American troops to retreat to the Bataan Peninsula.
January 14, 1942: Roosevelt orders all foreigners in the United States to register with the federal government. Italian, German, and Japanese immigrants, as well as Korean and Chinese immigrants who are mistaken for Japanese, face harassment as they are suspected of disloyalty to the U.S. because of their ethnic backgrounds.
February 20, 1942: President Roosevelt orders Japanese-Americans on the West Coast to be forcibly removed to INTERNMENT CAMPS throughout the West.
March 11, 1942: General Douglas MacArthur is forced to leave the Philippines as Japanese troops advance on American forces. On leaving, MacArthur promises, "I shall return!"

	1921	1924	1925
■ FDR's Life			
■ U.S. & World Events	Roosevelt is stricken with polio.	In his first major public appearance since his polio attack, Roosevelt nominates New York Governor Alfred E. Smith for president at the Democratic National Convention.	F. Scott Fitzgerald writes *The Great Gatsby*.

Election of 1944

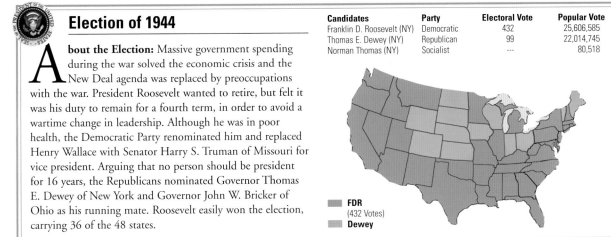

Candidates	Party	Electoral Vote	Popular Vote
Franklin D. Roosevelt (NY)	Democratic	432	25,606,585
Thomas E. Dewey (NY)	Republican	99	22,014,745
Norman Thomas (NY)	Socialist	---	80,518

■ FDR
(432 Votes)
■ Dewey

About the Election: Massive government spending during the war solved the economic crisis and the New Deal agenda was replaced by preoccupations with the war. President Roosevelt wanted to retire, but felt it was his duty to remain for a fourth term, in order to avoid a wartime change in leadership. Although he was in poor health, the Democratic Party renominated him and replaced Henry Wallace with Senator Harry S. Truman of Missouri for vice president. Arguing that no person should be president for 16 years, the Republicans nominated Governor Thomas E. Dewey of New York and Governor John W. Bricker of Ohio as his running mate. Roosevelt easily won the election, carrying 36 of the 48 states.

April 9-10, 1942: American and Filipino soldiers, captured on Bataan Peninsula, begin a forced 100-mile march through the jungle to a prison camp. In what becomes known as the **BATAAN DEATH MARCH**, thousands die from exhaustion, starvation, and poor treatment in Japanese hands.

April 18, 1942: Major General James Doolittle heads a surprise bombing raid on Tokyo.

May 4-8, 1942: American naval fighter planes inflict heavy damage on the Japanese at the **BATTLE OF THE CORAL SEA**. It is the first naval battle in history in which surface ships do not engage one another directly but attack eachother with firepower from the warplanes.

June 4-6, 1942: Although the U.S. loses the carrier *Yorktown*, the U.S wins a major victory at the **BATTLE OF MIDWAY**.

August 7, 1942: U.S. marines land on **GUADALCANAL** in the Solomon Islands.

August 22, 1942: Germany attacks the Russian city of **STALINGRAD** in order to quell Soviet resistance. However, as the assault lasts into winter, the Germans soon find themselves bogged down.

January 14-24, 1943: Roosevelt, Churchill, and other allied leaders meet at **CASABLANCA**, Morocco, and agree to demand unconditional surrender from the Axis powers. They also agree to invade Europe via Sicily and Italy, begin a bombing campaign in Germany, send more aid to Russia, and increase efforts to win submarine warfare in the Atlantic.

March 2-4, 1943: The United States and Australia issue a

major defeat to Japan in the **BATTLE OF THE BISMARCK SEA**.

May 7, 1943: Britain captures the Tunisian city of Bizerte from the Germans, while the U.S. takes the capital, Tunis.

May 12, 1943: As Germany and Italy retreat from North Africa, the Allies take control of the strategic Suez Canal.

May 16, 1943: Nazis put down a major uprising in the Jewish ghetto of Warsaw, Poland. The **WARSAW UPRISING**, which began in the previous month, ends with the leveling of the ghetto and the removal of the Jews to concentration camps.

June 14, 1943: In the case of *WEST VIRGINIA BOARD OF EDUCATION V. BARNETTE*, in which Jehovah's Witnesses sued to prevent the state from requiring school children to salute the American flag, the Supreme Court rules that such requirements are unconstitutional if they contradict religious beliefs.

June 20-22, 1943: Thirty-four people are killed when **RACE RIOTS** break out in Detroit after whites protest the employment of blacks in jobs that had previously been restricted to them.

July 10, 1943: The Allies begin an assault on Sicily. They succeed in capturing the island over the next five weeks.

July 19, 1943: Although they had previously avoided bombing Rome because of its religious and historical importance, the Allies launch an air raid on the Italian capital. Within a week, Italian Fascist dictator **BENITO MUSSOLINI IS FORCED TO RESIGN**. By early September, Italy offers its unconditional surrender to the Allies.

August 11-24, 1943: Roosevelt, Churchill, and others meet in Quebec, Canada, and agree to launch a major invasion of

1927

Charles Lindbergh flies the Spirit of St. Louis nonstop from New York to Paris.

1928

Roosevelt is elected governor of New York.

1929

On October 29, "Black Tuesday," the U.S. stock market collapses. For the next decade, the country is in extreme economic crisis, known as the Great Depression.

Roosevelt's Fourth Administration

Inauguration: January 20, 1945 at the White House, Washington, D.C.
Vice President: Harry S. Truman
Secretary of State: Edward R. Stettinius
Secretary of the Treasury: Henry Morgenthau, Jr.
Secretary of War: Henry L. Stimson
Attorney General: Francis Biddle
Postmaster General: Frank C. Walker
Secretary of the Navy: James V. Forrestal
Secretary of the Interior: Harold L. Ickes

Secretary of Agriculture: Claude R. Wickard
Secretary of Commerce: Jesse H. Jones; Henry A. Wallace (from March 2, 1945)
Secretary of Labor: Frances Perkins
79th Congress
(January 3, 1945-January 3, 1947)
Senate: 56 Democrats; 38 Republicans; 1 Other
House: 242 Democrats; 190 Republicans; 2 Others
End of Presidential Term: April 12, 1945

France in the spring of 1944. In late November, Churchill and Roosevelt meet again at the **TEHRAN CONFERENCE** in Iran, with Soviet dictator Josef Stalin in attendance. There, they finalize a date for the invasion of France.

December 17, 1943: Eighty years after its passage, the **CHINESE EXCLUSION ACT IS REPEALED.** Congress ends the restriction because China is its wartime ally.

December 24, 1943: Roosevelt announces that General

DWIGHT D. EISENHOWER will serve as supreme commander of the Allied invasion force.

June 6, 1944: The **D-DAY** invasion of Europe begins. Troops from the United States, Great Britain, and Canada land under heavy gunfire on a series of beaches in Normandy, France. Despite heavy casualties, the Allied forces are able to hold the beachheads. Known as **OPERATION OVERLORD**, the invasion involves 176,000 Allied troops and thousands of aircraft and ships.

June 13, 1944: The Germans begin launching unpiloted V-1 flying bombs, or "**BUZZ BOMBS**" across the English channel. Only one manages to reach London. In September, however, the Germans begin launching more powerful V-2 rockets.

June 19-20, 1944: The United States destroys over 400 Japanese planes and three aircraft carriers in a decisive victory at

The largest seaborne invasion in history, called Operation Overload, took place on June 6 (D-Day) when Allied troops stormed the shores of Normandy to take the Germans by surprise.

	1930	1932	1936
■ FDR's Life		Roosevelt is elected president, and wins reelection for four successive terms.	Benny Goodman racially integrates his band when he hires jazz pianist Teddy Wilson and vibraphonist Lionel Hampton.
■ U.S. & World Events	Mohandas Gandhi proclaims a new campaign of civil disobedience, and leads hundreds of Indians in a march to the sea to protest British Salt Acts.		

the **BATTLE OF THE PHILIPPINE SEA.**

June-July 1944: Although he had hoped to retire, **ROOSEVELT ACCEPTS A FOURTH NOMINATION** made by the Democratic Party. The president feels it is his duty to remain in office until the end of the war.

July 1-22, 1944: Diplomats from 44 nations meet at Bretton Woods, New Hampshire, to establish the **INTERNATIONAL MONEY FUND (IMF)** and an International Bank for Reconstruction and Development, otherwise known as the **WORLD BANK.**

July 25, 1944: **OPERATION COBRA**—an Allied effort to cut off German forces in Brittany, France —succeed in breaking through German defensive lines.

In this photgraph taken by Joe Rosenthal, U.S. marines raise American flag on top of Mt. Suribachi in Japan on February 23, 1945 in the Battle of Iwo Jima.

August 21-October 7, 1944: United States, Britain, China, and the U.S.S.R. meet at the **DUMBARTON OAKS CONFERENCE** in Washington, D.C. to begin planning for what will eventually become the **UNITED NATIONS.**

October 20-26, 1944: Led by General Douglas MacArthur, American forces invade Leyte Island in the Philippines. While attempting to defend the island, the Japanese Navy is devastated after losing 24 large ships.

November 7, 1944: **ROOSEVELT IS REELECTED**, winning a fourth term. **HARRY S. TRUMAN** is elected vice president.

December 16, 1944: Germany launches a surprise attack on Allied forces in the Ardennes forest. Although caught off guard in what becomes known as the **BATTLE OF THE BULGE**, the Allies launch a counterattack within two weeks.

Roosevelt's Fourth Term 1945

February 4-11, 1945: Roosevelt, Churchill, and Stalin meet at the **YALTA CONFERENCE** in the Russian Crimea. At the Conference, the three leaders agree to allow the liberated leaders of Europe to form independent, democratically-elected

governments—a pledge that the Soviets break after the war. Stalin agrees to enter the war against Japan in exchange for Soviet annexation of the Kurile Islands, half of Sahkilin Island, and portions of Korea. Stalin also receives privileged trade rights in the Chinese cities of Dairen and Port Arthur. What is more, the United States and Great Britian agree to recognize the independence of Outer Mongolia from China, and to allow Soviet annexation of eastern Poland. The United States and Great Britain secretly permit the Soviet states of Ukraine and Belorussia to enter the United Nations as full members with voting rights. Stalin also demands $20 billion in reparations from Germany, a demand that is referred to a postwar reparations committee.

February 4-24, 1945: The **U.S. FORCES RECAPTURE MANILA,** the capital of the Philippines.

April 1–June 21, 1945: In one of the bloodiest battles of the Pacific War, the U.S. captures the island of **OKINAWA.**

April 5, 1945: The Soviet Union enters the war against Japan.

April 12, 1945: **PRESIDENT ROOSEVELT DIES** after suffering a massive cerebral hemorrhage at Warm Springs, Georgia. Vice President Harry Truman is sworn in as president.

1939	1943	1945
Nazi Germany invades Poland, beginning World War II.	Jackson Pollack's first solo show is held at Peggy Guggenheim's Art of This Century gallery in New York. Pollock, part of the Abstract Expressionists, invented the drip method of splattering paint onto the canvas.	Roosevelt dies on April 12 in Warm Springs, Georgia.

Harry S Truman

33rd President (1945–1953)

"I never gave anybody hell—I just told the truth on these fellows and they thought it was hell."

When Harry Truman arrived at the White House after Franklin Roosevelt's death, the stunned vice president asked Eleanor Roosevelt if there was anything he could do for her. She replied, "Is there anything we can do for you? You're the one in trouble now."

Before Roosevelt died, Truman had only met with the president twice. He had never heard of the atomic weapons program that was nearing completion. One day after taking office, Truman told reporters that he felt as if "the moon, the stars and all the planets had fallen on [him]." By the end of his administraton, he had faced some of the most crucial decisions an American president has ever had to make. Confronted with the very real possibility that a land assault on the islands of Japan would take two years and cost hundreds of thousands of lives, Truman approved of the plan to drop atomic bombs on Hiroshima and Nagasaki.

Truman then faced a new challenge—from the Soviet Union. Under the Truman Doctrine, which defined "containment" as the nation's foreign policy, he promised to send aid to any nation under threat of foreign domination, namely that of Communism. The Marshall Plan, which had originally been a speech given by Secretary of State George C. Marshall, spurred economic recovery in western Europe and insulated it from Communist expansion. When Stalin blockaded West Berlin, Truman airlifted supplies into the city until the blockade ended.

On the domestic front, he found his path blocked by Republicans and Southern Democrats. He was widely expected to lose his bid for reelection in 1948, but shocked pundits by winning his first full term. When the Korean War began, he did not hesitate to send troops. But when he fired General MacArthur for insubordination, he was pelted with paper cups and other flying objects while throwing out the first ball at a season-opening baseball game in Washington, D.C. But by firing the war hero, he likely avoided an expanded war. While he left office with his popularity at an all-time low, his standing has increased in recent years. As Winston Churchill said to him, "I loathed your taking the place of Franklin Roosevelt. I misjudged you badly. Since that time, you, more than any other man, have saved Western Civilization."

Biographical Facts

Born: May 8, 1884 in Lamar, Missouri

Ancestry: Scotch-English

Father: John Anderson Truman; born December 5, 1851 in Jackson County, Missouri; died November 3, 1914 in Grandview, Missouri

Father's Occupation: Farmer

Mother: Martha Ellen Young Truman; born November 25, 1852 in Jackson County, Missouri; died July 26, 1947 in Grandview, Missouri

Wife: Elizabeth Virginia Wallace; born February 13, 1885 in Independence, Missouri; died October 18, 1982 in Independence, Missouri

Marriage: June 28, 1919 in Independence, Missouri

Child: Mary Margaret (1924-)

Home: Truman Farm Home, Grandview, Missouri

Education: Graduated from public high school; attended Kansas City School of Law

Religious Affiliation: Baptist

Occupations before Presidency: Railroad timekeeper; bank clerk; farmer; haberdasher

Military Service: Missouri National Guard; Captain in 129th Field Artillery

Political Offices before Presidency: County Judge for Eastern District of Jackson County, Missouri; Presiding Judge, County Court, Jackson County, Missouri; United States Senator; U.S. Vice President

Political Party: Democratic

Occupation after Presidency: Writer

Age at Inauguration: 60

Death: December 26, 1972 in Kansas City, Missouri

Place of Burial: Independence, Missouri

Nickname: Give 'Em Hell Harry

Writings: *Memoirs*

deemed as security risks and fired

June 5, 1947: In a speech at Harvard University, **SECRETARY OF STATE GEORGE C. MARSHALL** proposes an economic aid plan for Europe. Commonly referred to as the **MARSHALL PLAN**, the Economic Recovery Program is intended to prevent starvation in the areas that had been effected by the war, repair the damaged infrastructure as quickly as possible, and boost the European economy. By providing western Europe with immediate aid, Marshall argues, the United States will also prevent the spread of Communism into the West. Congress approves of the plan the following year.

June 23, 1947: Congress overrides

In this photograph, Truman signs the Foreign Aid Assistance Act, which provides a program of foreign aid to Greece and Turkey. The provision of economic support to any nation resisting Communist pressure came to be known as the Truman Doctrine.

Truman's veto of the **TAFT-HARTLEY ACT**, or Labor-Management Relations Act. The bill, which Truman derides as a "slave labor bill," is a major defeat for the labor movement. The act mandates that a company workforce can only unionize if the majority of the laborers vote in favor of the union. In addition, the new law gave employers the right not to bargain with unions if they chose not to do so and prohibits unions from contributing to political campaigns.

June 29, 1947: Truman becomes the first U.S. president to addresses the **NATIONAL ASSOCIATION OF COLORED PEOPLE** (NAACP).

July 26, 1947: By passing the **NATIONAL SECURITY ACT**, Congress creates the National Security Council, the Central Intelligence Agency, the United States Air Force and the Cabinet position of

	1929	1934	1939	1941
■ Truman's Life				Truman gains national attention as head of the Committee to Investigate the National Defense Program. The group exposes wasteful spending and saves the government about $15 billion.
■ U.S. & World Events	On October 29, referred to as "Black Tuesday," the U.S. stock market collapses. For the next decade, the country is in extreme economic crisis, known as the Great Depression.	Truman is elected to the United States Senate.	Hitler invades Poland, starting World War II.	

Election of 1948

Candidates	Party	Electoral Vote	Popular Vote
Harry S Truman (MO)	Democratic	303	24,105,812
Thomas E. Dewey (NY)	Republican	189	21,970,065
Strom Thurmond (SC)	States' Rights	39	1,169,063
Henry Wallace (IA)	Progressive	---	1,157,172
Norman Thomas (NY)	Socialist	---	139,414
Claude A. Watson (IN)	Prohibition	---	103,224

About the Election: The issue of civil rights splintered the Democratic Party in 1948. When the party nominated Truman for a full term, Southern Democrats founded their own party, the Dixiecrats, and nominated Governor Strom Thurmond of South Carolina. Liberal Democrats, who had already left the party to form the Progressive Party, picked Vice President Wallace as their candidate. The Republicans again nominated Thomas E. Dewey and polls predicted that Dewey would win by a landslide. But Truman had support from labor groups who were loyal to Franklin D. Roosevelt and after a "whistle-stop" campaign, which had the president traveling by train to make more than 350 speeches, Truman won the election in one of the biggest upsets in political history—with less than 50 percent of the popular vote.

Truman (303 Votes)
Dewey
Thurmond

secretary of defense.

February 2, 1948: As a follow-up to the release of a report called "TO SECURE THESE RIGHTS" by the president's Commission on Civil Rights, which argues for equal opportunity to education, decent housing, jobs, anti-lynching and anti-poll tax laws, Truman asks Congress to act on the Commission's recommendations.

April 3, 1948: Truman signs the FOREIGN ASSISTANCE ACT that provides $5.3 billion for the Marshall Plan. The act also authorizes $275 million in military aid to Greece and Turkey, $403 million for economic and military assistance to China, and $60 million for a U.N. Children's Fund.

May 14, 1948: The UNITED STATES RECOGNIZES ISRAEL.

June 24, 1948: In late 1947 and early 1948, the U.S., Britain, and France unite their three German military zones into one zone, and create a single currency that is used throughout the zone in order to reestablish economic stability. The Soviet Union, on the other hand, refuses to abandon its currency, the Soviet Reichsmark. The Soviets, who had hoped that economic destabilization in Europe would lead to the spread of Communism, are angered by the Marshall Plan and the Allied currency plans. In response, the Soviet Union orders that all Western convoys bound for Berlin through Soviet Germany be searched. When the Western officials refuse the Soviet demand, Soviet Premier Stalin orders a blockade of all overland access

routes to West Berlin, known as the BERLIN BLOCKADE.

June 25, 1948: Truman signs the DISPLACED PERSONS BILL that allows the admission of 205,000 displaced Europeans to the U.S. The act is amended in June 1950 to raise the number of displaced Europeans admissible from 205,000 to 415,000.

June 26, 1948: The U.S. and Great Britain begin airlifting supplies into West Berlin. The BERLIN AIRLIFT is in response to the Soviet blockade of land routes into the city.

July 15, 1948: The DEMOCRATIC PARTY NOMINATES TRUMAN for a second term, with Alben W. Barkley as his running mate.

July 17, 1948: Southern Democrats, also known as DIXIECRATS, angered by Truman's call for civil rights legislation, nominate STROM THURMOND, the segregationist governor of South Carolina, for president. The Republican party nominates Thomas E. Dewey of New York.

July 26, 1948: Truman calls a SPECIAL SESSION of the 80th Congress, demanding action on civil rights.

July 30, 1948: Truman issues an executive order, which ends segregation in the U.S. Armed Services.

September 6–October 30, 1948: Truman, a heavy underdog in the race for president, campaigns in all areas of the nation other than the South, attacking the Republican Congress.

November 2, 1948: In a surprise and major defeat to the Republican Party, TRUMAN DEFEATS DEWEY and the Democrats retake both the Senate and the House of Representatives.

1944

Truman is elected vice president.

1945

Roosevelt dies and Truman becomes president. The war in Europe ends in April, and the war in Asia, in August.

1948

Truman is elected to a full term as president.

1949

Mao Zedong declares the founding of the People's Republic of China in Tiananmen Square in Beijing.

1952

Truman decides not to run for reelection.

Truman's Second Administration

Inauguration: January 20, 1949 at the Capitol, Washington, D.C.
Vice President: Alben W. Barkley
Secretary of State: Dean G. Acheson
Secretary of the Treasury: John W. Snyder
Secretary of Defense: James V. Forrestal; Louis A. Johnson (from March 28, 1949); George C. Marshall (from September 21, 1950); Robert A. Lovett (from September 17, 1951)
Attorney General: Thomas C. Clark; J. Howard McGrath (from August 24, 1949); James P. McGranery (from May 27, 1952)
Postmaster General: Jesse M. Donaldson
Secretary of the Interior: Julius A. Krug; Oscar L. Chapman (from January 19, 1950)

Secretary of Agriculture: Charles F. Brannan
Secretary of Commerce: Charles Sawyer
Secretary of Labor: Maurice J. Tobin
Supreme Court Appointments:
Thomas C. Clark (1949);
Sherman Minton (1949)
81st Congress
(January 3, 1949-January 3, 1951):
Senate: 54 Democrats; 42 Republicans
House: 263 Democrats; 171 Republicans; 1 Other
82nd Congress
(January 3, 1951-January 3, 1953)
Senate: 49 Democrats; 47 Republicans
House: 234 Democrats; 199 Republicans; 1 Other
End of Presidential Term: January 20, 1953

January 5, 1949: In his State of the Union Address, Truman proposes domestic legislation he calls the "FAIR DEAL". This includes a repeal of the Taft-Hartley law, reinstatement of the Wagner Act, which guarantees the right to collective bargaining, a minimum wage, increased price supports for farm products, improvements in housing, and the protection of civil rights.

Truman's Second Term 1949-1953

April 4, 1949: The NORTH ATLANTIC TREATY ORGANIZATION (NATO) is created when 12 nations sign the North Atlantic Treaty. The original member states include Belgium, Canada, Denmark, France, Great Britain, Italy, Iceland, Luxembourg, the Netherlands, Norway, Portugal, and the United States.
May 12, 1949: Soviet Union lifts the Berlin blockade.
May 31, 1949: Former State Department official ALGER HISS goes on trial in New York. He is accused of lying to a grand jury that is investigating charges of espionage. Whittaker Chambers, a confessed messenger for a Communist spyring, has claimed that Hiss gave him official classified documents.
July 15, 1949: The HOUSING ACT is signed. It provides federal dollars for urban slums and builds low-cost housing.
September 22, 1949: Truman signs the MUTUAL DEFENSE ASSISTANCE BILL, which authorizes military assistance to NATO allies in the event of another war.
September 23, 1949: The American public learns that the Soviet Union has exploded its first atomic bomb at Semipalatinsk nuclear testing range. Americans are shocked

because they were not expecting the Soviet Union to possess knowledge of nuclear weapons so soon.
February 9, 1950: In a speech in Wheeling, West Virginia, Senator Joseph McCarthy of Wisconsin, announces that he possesses a list of 205 known Communists working in the State Department. Although McCarthy refuses to turn over his list, the speech marks the start of his prominence in the nation's affairs.
February 14, 1950: MAO ZEDONG of the People's Republic of China meets with JOSEF STALIN of the Soviet Union to sign a Sino-Soviet alliance. Despite the treaty, the two nations will be rivals rather than true allies.
April 7, 1950: The National Security Council produces an analysis of Soviet and Communist Chinese intentions and threats to President Truman. The document argues that the United States is unprepared for the military threat posed by Communism and calls for a large build-up in the U.S. military in order to contain the Soviet Union. This POLICY OF CONTAINMENT is the cornerstone of U.S. Cold War foreign policy for the next two decades.
June 25, 1950: Communist-controlled North Korea invades South Korea, beginning the KOREAN WAR.
June 27, 1950: Truman announces that he has ordered American ground forces to Korea. Three days later, he orders a blockade of the Korean coast. Despite the blockade, the South Korean capital of SEOUL FALLS the following day.
August 28, 1950: Truman signs the SOCIAL SECURITY ACT, extending Social Security coverage to an additional ten million citizens. Truman sends a message to Congress requesting it to authorize $134 million to finance the provisions of the new act.
September 15, 1950: United States forces drive inland from INCHON on the West Coast of Korea in an effort to retake Seoul. They succeed on September 26.
September 23, 1950: Congress passes the INTERNAL SECURITY ACT over Truman's veto. The act requires all Communist organizations to register with the federal

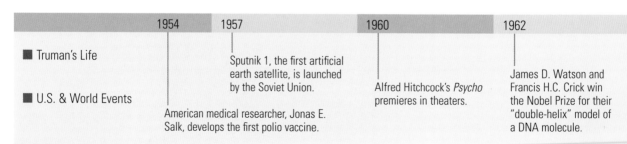

	1954	1957	1960	1962
■ Truman's Life				
		Sputnik 1, the first artificial earth satellite, is launched by the Soviet Union.	Alfred Hitchcock's *Psycho* premieres in theaters.	James D. Watson and Francis H.C. Crick win the Nobel Prize for their "double-helix" model of a DNA molecule.
■ U.S. & World Events	American medical researcher, Jonas E. Salk, develops the first polio vaccine.			

government. Members of these organizations are forbidden from becoming American citizens.

October 15, 1950: President Truman meets with **GENERAL DOUGLAS MACARTHUR** for the first time on Wake Island to discuss America's Far East policy.

November 20, 1950: American troops under Douglas MacArthur reach the Yalu River on the border of Manchuria. **MACARTHUR'S ADVANCE TO THE CHINESE BORDER** angers not only the Chinese, but also President Truman, since crossing the border amounts to a declaration of war on China. The advance also risks the Soviet Union's entry into the war since Mao and Stalin had earlier signed a military alliance.

November 25, 1950: China launches a massive counterattack against the U.S. troops in North Korea. Within four days, the Chinese force the Americans to retreat.

December 16, 1950: Truman declares a **STATE OF NATIONAL EMERGENCY** and imposes wage and price controls.

January 1, 1951: North Korean forces retake Seoul, South Korea. U.S. troops retake it for the second time in March.

February 22, 1951: The **TWENTY SECOND AMENDMENT** is adopted, limiting presidents to serving only two terms and vice presidents, who became president, to no more than half of a successor's term and one full term. The amendment is passed in reaction to Franklin D. Roosevelt's election to four terms.

April 11, 1951: After months of public bickering between the two men, **TRUMAN FIRES GENERAL MACARTHUR** from his command of both U.S. and U.N. forces in Korea. MacArthur returns home to a hero's welcome. He announces his retirement to a joint session of Congress just over a week later, declaring, "Old soldiers never die, they just fade away."

March 8, 1952: Chinese foreign minister Chou En-lai and the Soviet representative to the United Nations, Jacob Malik, accuse the United States of employing **GERM WARFARE IN KOREA**. However, when Malik refuses to allow the International Red Cross to investigate the charges, the crisis passes.

April 6, 1952: President Truman announces that the United States is developing a Hydrogen bomb.

April 8, 1952: To prevent a shutdown in American steel mills, **TRUMAN ORDERS THAT STEEL MILLS BE SEIZED** by the federal government. In June, the Supreme Court rules that Truman's action had been unconstitutional.

June 26–June 27, 1952: The House of Representatives and the Senate, respectively, override Truman's veto of the **MCCARRAN-WALTER ACT**. The immigration law ends racial restrictions on immigration, but maintains a quota system based

Truman's "Fair Deal" recommended that all Americans have health insurance, that the minimum wage be increased, and that all Americans be guaranteed equal rights.

on the 1920 census.

July 11, 1952: **REPUBLICANS NOMINATE GENERAL DWIGHT D. EISENHOWER** for president and **SENATOR RICHARD M. NIXON** of California for vice president.

July 26, 1952: **DEMOCRATS NOMINATE GOVERNOR ADLAI STEVENSON** of Illinois for president.

November 1, 1952: The United States detonates the first **HYDROGEN BOMB** at Enewetak Atoll in the Marshall Islands. The explosion is dramatically more powerful than the atomic bomb exploded at Nagasaki.

November 4, 1952: **EISENHOWER IS ELECTED** president.

1963	1965	1969	1972	1973
	President Johnson sends the first American ground troops to Vietnam.		Truman dies on December 26 in Kansas City, Missouri.	U.S., North and South Vietnam, and the Viet Cong sign a cease fire agreement.
President Kennedy is assassinated.		American astronaut Neil Armstrong becomes the first man on the moon.		

Dwight David Eisenhower

34th President (1953–1961)

"Every gun that is made, every warship launched, every rocket fired, signifies in the final sense a theft from those who hunger and are not fed, those who are cold and are not clothed."

During much of the 19th century, America's political parties frequently sought popular generals as their standard bearers. Yet by the early 20th century, this tradition had ended. With the exception of Theodore Roosevelt's dalliance as a Rough Rider and Harry Truman's service in the Missouri National Guard, no president in the first half of the century even served in the military.

Dwight D. Eisenhower, on the other hand, had known no career except the military when he became president in 1953. He had served in Panama and the Philippines before commanding the Allies during World War II. The last president born in the 19th century, Eisenhower's pre-presidential years mirrored his country's growing international influence in the 20th century.

Upon election, he endeavored to maintain the status that the U.S. had gained over the past decade. He fulfilled his promise of ending the Korean War by threatening to use atomic weapons if the Chinese Communists did not arrange a truce. He favored economy in government undertakings and throughout his tenure worked to reduce governmental expenditure. He believed in strategic efficiency rather than conventional military superiority and he managed to cut defense budgets. To meet Soviet aggression, he propounded a policy of "massive retaliation."

When Joseph McCarthy launched his hunt for domestic Communists, Eisenhower kept quiet, even when McCarthy attacked his good friend and former Secretary of State George C. Marshall. Eisenhower detested McCarthy, but declared, "I just won't get down in the gutter with that man." Nonetheless, when the law was at issue, Eisenhower acted, even if reluctantly. He was at heart a segregationist, but when Orville Faubus of Arkansas blocked the desegregation of Central High in Little Rock, Eisenhower sent in the 101st Airborne.

Eisenhower has been called a "do-nothing" president. Yet he is to be credited for keeping the nation out of war through times of prosperity. Just before leaving office, he warned that although a strong defense was necessary, the growing "Military-Industrial Complex" made the nation less secure rather than more. The life-long military man concluded his warning with a prayer for peace.

Biographical Facts

Born: October 14, 1890 in Denison, Texas

Ancestry: Swiss-German

Father: David Jacob Eisenhower; born September 23, 1863 in Elizabethville, Pennsylvania; died March 10, 1942 in Abilene, Kansas

Father's Occupation: Mechanic

Mother: Ida Elizabeth Stover Eisenhower; born May 1, 1862 in Mount Sidney, Virginia; died September 11, 1946 in Abilene, Kansas

Wife: Mamie Geneva Doud; born November 14, 1896 in Boone, Iowa

Marriage: July 1, 1916 in Denver, Colorado

Children: Doud Dwight (1917-1921); John Sheldon (1922-)

Home: Gettysburg, Pennslyvania

Education: Attended public schools; graduated from U.S. Military Academy, West Point, New York (1915)

Occupations before Presidency: Soldier, president of Columbia University

Religious Affiliation: Presbyterian

Military Service: Commissioned Second Lieutenant in U.S. Army; Commander of European Theater of Operations; Supreme Commander of Allied Expeditionary Force in Western Europe; General of the Army; Army Chief of Staff; Supreme Commander of Allied Powers in Europe

Political Party: Republican

Age at Inauguration: 62

Occupation after Presidency: Writer

Death: March 28, 1969 in Washington, D.C.

Place of Burial: Abilene, Kansas

Nickname: Ike

Writings: *Crusade in Europe; The White House Years: Mandate for Change, Waging Peace; At Ease: Stories I Tell to Friends*

Eisenhower's Second Administration

Inauguration: January 20, 1957 at the Capitol, Washington, D.C.
Vice President: Richard M. Nixon
Secretary of State: John Foster Dulles; Christian A. Herter (from April 22, 1959)
Secretary of the Treasury: George M. Humphrey; Robert B. Anderson (from July 29, 1957)
Secretary of Defense: Charles E. Wilson; Neil H. McElroy (from October 9, 1957); Thomas S. Gates, Jr. (from January 26, 1960)
Attorney General: Herbert Brownell, Jr.; William P. Rogers (from January 27, 1958)
Postmaster General: Arthur Ellsworth Summerfield
Secretary of the Interior: Frederick A. Seaton
Secretary of Agriculture: Ezra Taft Benson

Secretary of Commerce: Sinclair Weeks; Frederick H. Mueller (from August 6, 1959)
Secretary of Labor: James P. Mitchell
Secretary of Health, Education, and Welfare: Marion B. Folsom; Arthur S. Flemming (from August 1, 1958)
Supreme Court Appointments: Charles Whittaker (1957); Potter Stewart (1958)
85th Congress
(January 3, 1957-January 3, 1959)
Senate: 49 Democrats; 47 Republicans
House: 233 Democrats; 200 Republicans
86th Congress
(January 3, 1959-January 3, 1961)
Senate: 64 Democrats; 34 Republicans
House: 283 Democrats; 153 Republicans
States Admitted: Alaska (1959); Hawaii (1959)

order. When nine black children had attempted to join the Central High School, Governor Orville Faubus had ordered the National Guard to prevent their entry.

September 24, 1957: After the withdrawal of the National

Daisy Bates (back row, second from right), an organizer for the National Association for the Advancement of Colored People (NAACP), with the nine African-American students who desegregated Central High School in Little Rock in 1957.

Guard, violence erupts and Little Rock Central High remains closed. Eisenhower deploys federal troops to reopen the school and enable the black students to attend the school.

October 4, 1957: The SOVIET UNION LAUNCHES THE SPUTNIK, the first earth satellite. This event sets off demands for more intensive American efforts in defense and technology.

November 19, 1957: The U.S. and NATO agree to the development of missile bases in Western Europe.

December 17, 1957: The United States makes its first successful test firing of an intercontinental ballistic missile, the USAF *Atlas*, at Cape Canaveral, Florida.

January 31, 1958: EXPLORER I, the first American satellite is launched from Cape Canaveral, Florida.

March 31, 1958: The Soviet Union announces that it will stop nuclear tests and asks the U.S. and Britain to do the same. On October 3, the Soviet Union resumes testing.

April 1, 1958: Eisenhower signs the EMERGENCY HOUSING ACT. The act is expected to provide jobs by stimulating housing construction. It is also supposed to help reverse the current downturn in the national economy.

April 14, 1958: The Federal Reserve Board releases figures indicating the worst recession in the postwar period.

May 13, 1958: Vice President Richard M. Nixon sets off on a Latin American tour. He arrives to find many anti-U.S. demonstrations in the places he visits.

July 15, 1958: In a letter to Congress, Eisenhower explains his deployment of Marines to Lebanon as an attempt to prevent alleged threats by the Soviet Union and UAR to overthrow the Arab regime. He states that the Lebanese government had requested American help.

September 2, 1958: Eisenhower signs the NATIONAL DEFENSE EDUCATION ACT, which provides student loans and fellowships to stimulate education in the sciences, mathematics and modern foreign languages.

1957	1958	1961
■ Eisenhower's Life		Eisenhower retires to his farm in Gettysburg, Pennsylvania.
■ U.S. & World Events	Jack Kerouac writes *On the Road*, and identifies the Beat Generation.	Army officers overthrow the monarchy in Iraq and declares Iraq a republic.	The East German government builds Berlin Wall to prevent East Germans from emigrating to the West.

November 4, 1958: The Democrats win sweeping victories in the general elections and gain control of both the House and Senate by the largest margins since Franklin Roosevelt's landslide victory in 1936.

November 8, 1958: The U.S. signs an agreement with the EUROPEAN ATOMIC ENERGY COMMUNITY (Euratom) in Brussels to expedite nuclear power production in Europe.

January 1, 1959: Cuban President Fulgencio Batista abdicates after forces loyal to FIDEL CASTRO capture Havana.

January 3, 1959: ALASKA is proclaimed the 49th state.

March 18, 1959: HAWAII is admitted as the 50th state.

June 19, 1959: The Senate rejects Eisenhower's appointment of Lewis L. Strauss as secretary of commerce. The last time a presidential appointee was rejected was the appointment of Charles B. Warren as attorney general, made by President Calvin Coolidge in1925.

July 15, 1959: The STEEL STRIKE begins despite Eisenhower's offer of talks. It lasts for 116 days. Eisenhower invokes the TAFT HARLEY ACT, which declares strikes illegal.

December 1, 1959: The U.S. and 11 other nations sign a treaty to promote the peaceful development of Antarctica.

December 2, 1959: President Eisenhower goes on a 19-day tour of "PEACE AND GOODWILL" of 11 countries on 3 continents—Asia, North Africa, and Europe.

May 6, 1960: Eisenhower signs the CIVIL RIGHTS ACT OF 1960. This act is more comprehensive and forceful than the Civil Rights Act of 1957. It appoints federal referees to conduct inquiries into voting rights violations and provides for hefty fines and imprisonment of those who violate a person's voting rights or attempt to defy court orders.

May 7, 1960: The U.S. admits that the U-2 plane shot down in U.S.S.R. was on a spying mission. U-2 RECONNAISSANCE FLIGHTS had begun in 1956. On May 1, the Soviet Union had announced that a U-2 plane had been shot down and the American pilot had confessed to espionage. On May 11, Eisenhower, while defending such flights as "distasteful but vital," cancels all future U-2 flights.

May 16, 1960: The East-West summit conference in Paris collapses following the U-2 incident. The Soviet Union threatens retaliation against countries that provide bases for U-2 planes and demand that the U.S. punish the guilty.

June 8, 1960: President Eisenhower signs the MILITARY CONSTRUCTION AUTHORIZATION ACT.

July 11, 1960: DEMOCRATICS NOMINATE JOHN F. KENNEDY FOR PRESIDENT and Lyndon Johnson for vice president.

Scandal! Sherman Andrews

Eisenhower's first White House Chief of Staff, Sherman Adams, was an efficient administrator who oversaw the daily functioning of the White House. Adams was given full responsibility for fixing the President's daily schedule—determining who met the President and what matter the President needed to look into each morning.

In the beginning of 1958, investigations by Congress on federal regulatory commissions revealed that Adams had made enquiries from the Federal Trade Commission about several pending cases, which would affect Bernard Goldfine's company. The outcome of these cases would determine if Goldfine's company was labeling its products according to federal guidelines. Further investigations revealed that Adams had received several gifts from Goldfine, including a vicuna coat, free use of a Boston hotel suite, and a Persian rug. The families of Adams and Goldfine, a Boston industrialist, had become friendly during Adams' tenure as the governor of New Hampshire. Adams stated that the gifts were tokens of friendship between the two, and not illegal business transactions.

However, investigations further revealed that Goldfine declared the many gifts he gave to public officials as business expenses. The Republican candidates standing for reelection in the Congressional elections called for Adams' resignation. Adams resigned after the Republican national chairman Meade Alcorn informed him that the issue could damage the Party's electoral chances. Eisenhower later recollected that the Adams affair was the saddest event of his presidency.

July 25, 1960: REPUBLICANS NOMINATE RICHARD M. NIXON FOR PRESIDENT and Henry Cabot Lodge for vice president.

September 22, 1960: In his speech at the United Nations, Eisenhower proposes a broad peace program.

September 26, 1960: The debates between nominees Nixon and Kennedy are broadcasted on television for the first time in the nation's history.

November 8, 1960: KENNEDY IS ELECTED PRESIDENT of the United States. Democrats retain control of both the House of Representatives and the Senate.

January 3, 1961: THE UNITED STATES SEVERS DIPLOMATIC RELATIONS WITH CUBA, in response to Fidel Castro's demand for the reduction of U.S. state department personnel in Cuba.

1962

James D. Watson and Francis H.C. Crick win the Nobel Prize for their discovery that a DNA molecule forms a "double-helix", resembling a twisted ladder.

1963

President Kennedy is assassinated on November 22, in Dallas, Texas.

1965

President Johnson sends the first American troops to Vietnam.

1969

Eisenhower dies on March 28 in Washington, D.C.

John F. Kennedy

35th President (1961–1963)

"We stand for freedom. That is our conviction for ourselves; that is our only commitment to others."

John F. Kennedy, born to an ambitious and wealthy father, had no plans of joining politics in his early years. After graduating from Harvard, he went on a tour of Latin America and Europe with no specific career plans. His travels during this period would mold his understanding of world politics, such as the threat of Communism, which was spreading to developing countries. His display of courage during World War II earned him the Navy and Marine Corps Medal. However, injuries suffered during his military service worsened his already fragile physical health.

At the end of the war, he began developing an interest in politics. Kennedy attributed this change to the death of his older brother, Joe, who had planned to pursue a career in politics. Kennedy, who was initially aspiring to be a journalist, said, "Just as I went into politics because Joe died, if anything happens to me tomorrow, my brother Bobby would run for my seat in the Senate. And if Bobby died, Teddy would take over for him." Kennedy was elected to the House of Representatives, and after serving three terms, he was elected to the Senate. He and his brother, Robert, who would later become his attorney general, carefully planned his candidacy for the Democratic presidential nomination of 1960. In his nomination acceptance speech, he called for a New Frontier that was "not a set of promises" but a "set of challenges."

Less than four months into his presidency, he oversaw the disastrous invasion of Cuba. His belief that the Eisenhower administration had allowed a missile gap to develop between the U.S. and the Soviet Union was soon proved wrong as intelligence reports revealed that the Soviet Union's missile program was far behind that of the U.S. Kennedy, however, went on to expand the military strength of the country, thereby precipitating a spiraling arms race with the Soviet Union. His administration faced the most intense moments of the Cold War, be it the Cuban Missile Crisis or the building of the Berlin Wall. However, his deft handling of the crises paradoxically brought in a period of peace with the Soviet Union for the rest of his term, culminating with the signing of the Nuclear Test Ban Treaty.

Despite Kennedy's difficult success in international relations, he was less successful on the domestic front. Many of the Democratic Southern conservatives in Congress often joined the Republicans in opposing Kennedy's proposals for civil rights legislation, programs for the aged, Medicare and federal aid for education.

Biographical Facts

Born: May 29, 1917 in Brookline, Massachusetts

Ancestry: Irish

Father: Joseph Patrick Kennedy; born September 6, 1888 in East Boston, Massachusetts; died November 16, 1969 in Hyannis Port, Massachusetts

Father's Occupations: Financier; diplomat

Mother: Rose Fitzgerald Kennedy; born July 22, 1890 in Boston, Massachusetts; died January 22, 1995 in Hyannis Port, Massachusetts

Wife: Jacqueline Lee Bouvier; born July 28, 1929 in Southampton, New York; died May 19, 1994 in New York, New York,

Marriage: September 12, 1953 in Newport, Rhode Island,

Children: Caroline Bouvier (1957-); John Fitzgerald, Jr. (1960-1999); Patrick Bouvier (1963)

Religious Affiliation: Roman Catholic

Education: Choate School; London School of Economics; Princeton University; Harvard University; Stanford University

Occupations before Presidency: Author; politician; military officer; journalist

Military Service: Ensign, lieutenant (j.g.), lieutenant, U.S. Naval Reserve

Political Offices before Presidency: Member of U.S. House of Representatives; Member of U.S. Senate

Political Party: Democrat

Age at Inauguration: 43

Death: November 22, 1963 at Dallas, Texas

Place of Burial: Arlington National Cemetery, Arlington, Virginia

Nickname: JFK; Jack

Writings: *Why England Slept; Profiles in Courage*

Election of 1960

Candidates	Party	Electoral Vote	Popular Vote
John F. Kennedy (MA)	Democratic	303	34,226,731
Richard M. Nixon (CA)	Republican	219	34,108,157

About the Election: Setting precedent, Kennedy began methodically campaigning for the 1960 nomination right after the Democratic convention in 1956. After winning over seven primary states, Kennedy won the nomination, with Lyndon B. Johnson as his running mate. The Republicans nominated Richard M. Nixon. Kennedy's perceived disadvantages were his youth, his family's wealth, his inexperience in foreign affairs, and his religion, Roman Catholicism. Nixon had the advantage of having been vice president under Eisenhower, an extremely popular president. But Kennedy and his attractive wife were appealing to the public. The four televised debates with Nixon, which marked the first time that presidential candidates debated issues face to face, showed a charismatic and confident Kennedy to millions of viewers. He defeated Nixon by fewer than 115,000 popular votes, but won a clear majority in the Electoral College, receiving 303 votes to 219 for Nixon.

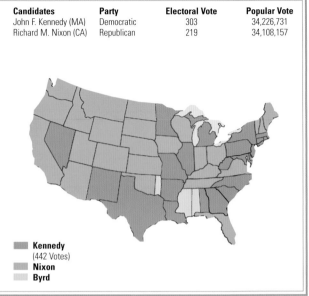

- **Kennedy** (442 Votes)
- **Nixon**
- **Byrd**

Kennedy's Term 1961-1963

January 20, 1961: PRESIDENT JOHN F. KENNEDY IS INAUGURATED, and in his inaugural address he calls for a renewed quest for peace.

January 25, 1961: In the first live television press conference given by a president, Kennedy announces the RELEASE OF RB-47 FLIERS BY RUSSIANS. Captain Freeman Olmstead and Captain John McKone were survivors of the jet reconnaissance plane shot down by the Russians over the Bering Sea.

February 3, 1961: Kennedy calls for the implementation of a $4-MILLION PROGRAM TO SUPPORT CUBAN REFUGEES in the U.S.

March 1, 1961: Kennedy creates the PEACE CORPS, which trains young volunteers to participate in various economic, educational, and welfare projects in developing countries. Congress passes the Peace Corps Act on September 22, 1961, assigning to the Corps a permanent status.

March 6, 1961: President Kennedy establishes a COMMITTEE ON EQUAL EMPLOYMENT OPPORTUNITY and appoints Vice President Lyndon B. Johnson as its chairman.

March 22, 1961: In a special message to Congress, Kennedy urges the institution of a single foreign aid agency. On September 4, the president signs the FOREIGN ASSISTANCE ACT OF 1961, which creates the AGENCY FOR INTERNATIONAL DEVELOPMENT as the chief United States aid agency.

April 12, 1961: The Soviet Union sends Yuri Gagarin to space. He becomes the first human space traveler.

April 17-20, 1961: Kennedy approves the BAY OF PIGS invasion. 1,400 CIA-trained, anti-Castro Cuban exiles land on the beaches of western Central Cuba, at Bahia de Cochinos (Bay of Pigs) in Las Villas province. With the cancellation of air reinforcements and the failure of expected local support, the men are defeated by Castro's troops by April 19. The next year, Cuba releases 1,173 prisoners in exchange for $55.5 million worth of food and medicine.

April 21, 1961: In a press conference, Kennedy accepts full responsibility for the Bay of Pigs fiasco, saying, "I am the responsible officer of the government."

May, 1961: The CONGRESS ON RACIAL EQUALITY (CORE) sends "Freedom Riders" to the South, in order to defy segregation in interstate bus facilities. The strategy is for an interracial group to board buses destined for the South. The whites sit in the back of the bus, while the blacks in the front. At rest stops, the whites would go into blacks-only areas.

May 5, 1961: Kennedy signs a bill raising the minimum wage under the FAIR LABOR STANDARDS ACT from $1 to $1.25.

May 25, 1961: Kennedy urges Congress to approve legislation for a moon project, as well as for the expansion of foreign aid.

	1917	1918	1922	1928
■ Kennedy's Life	U.S. declares war on Germany and joins the Allies.		American-born poet T.S. Eliot completes *The Waste Land*.	
■ U.S. & World Events	John Fitzgerald Kennedy is born on May 29 in Brookline, Massachusetts.	Germany signs armistice that ends World War I.		Joseph Stalin begins his five-year plan for economic development in the Soviet Union.

First Lady: Jacqueline Lee Bouvier Kennedy

As a young girl Jacqueline Bouvier wrote poems and stories, studied ballet, and loved to ride horses. She excelled academically and after graduating from George Washington University, met Senator John Kennedy while working as a journalist and photographer.

First Lady "Jackie" Kennedy was admired for her beauty, intelligence and style, as well as her public commitment to her primary role as wife and mother. Her love of the arts inspired a nationwide focus on culture, and she transformed the White House into a museum of American history and arts. Mrs. Kennedy's courage during her husband's assassination earned respect worldwide. She remained a public figure throughout her life despite her desire for privacy.

June 5, 1961: The Supreme Court orders the Communist Party to register itself as an agent of a foreign power.

June 30, 1961: Kennedy signs the HOUSING ACT OF 1961 that provides for public housing; college housing loans; housing for the aged; mortgage assistance; and urban development.space.

Kennedy's Administration

Inauguration: January 20, 1961 at the Capitol, Washington, D.C.
Vice President: Lyndon B. Johnson
Secretary of State: Dean Rusk
Secretary of the Treasury: C. Douglas Dillon
Secretary of Defense: Robert S. McNamara
Attorney General: Robert F. Kennedy
Postmaster General: J. Edward Day;
John A. Gronouski (from September 30, 1963)
Secretary of the Interior: Stewart L. Udall
Secretary of Agriculture: Orville L. Freeman
Secretary of Commerce: Luther H. Hodges
Secretary of Labor: Arthur J. Goldberg;
W. Willard Wirtz (from September 25, 1962)

Secretary of Health, Education, and Welfare: Abraham A. Ribicoff;
Anthony J. Celebrezze (from July 31, 1962)
Ambassador to United Nations: Adlai E. Stevenson
Supreme Court Appointments:
Byron R. White (1962);
Arthur J. Goldberg (1962)
87th Congress: (January 3, 1961-January 3, 1963)
Senate: 65 Democrats; 35 Republicans
House: 263 Democrats; 174 Republicans
88th Congress: (January 3, 1963-January 3, 1965)
Senate: 67 Democrats; 33 Republicans
House: 258 Democrats; 177 Republicans

July 1, 1961: President Kennedy proposes to Congress an economic program that includes an increase in Social Security benefits; the raising of minimum wages; an extension of unemployment insurance; and construction projects to stimulate the economy and lower unemployment.

July 25, 1961: The United States warns East Germany that interference with access routes to West Berlin would be considered an act of aggression.

August 5-17, 1961: The Inter-American Economic and Social Council meeting at Punta del Este, Uruguay, results in the signing of the CHARTER OF ALLIANCE FOR PROGRESS to provide economic aid and to promote political and social reform in Latin America. The U.S. promises $1 billion in aid, as a way to prevent the spread of Communism in the region.

August 12, 1961: Communist officials begin construction of the BERLIN WALL to stop people from moving to West Germany.

August 18, 1961: Kennedy announces that he has sent a 1,500-man battle group to West Berlin to strengthen its 5,000-man garrison. Vice President Johnson flies to Berlin and assures American support for West Germany.

September 1, 1961: The Soviet Union suddenly breaks the test ban that had been in force since November 3, 1958. It explodes 50 bombs over two months. On September 15, the U.S. and Britain also begin their underground tests, while test ban negotiations continue in Geneva.

October 18-25, 1961: Kennedy sends his military adviser, General Maxwell D. Taylor, to South Vietnam to assist its government against attacks by Communist Vietcong guerillas.

On December 11, TWO U.S. ARMY HELICOPTER UNITS REACH VIETNAM—the first direct U.S. military support for South Vietnam's fight against Communist guerrillas.

November 2, 1961: Kennedy declares that the U.S. will restart atmospheric nuclear testing. This is in response to the Soviet Union's large nuclear explosion in the Soviet Arctic, which took place on October 30. The U.S. test series begin in April, near Christmas Island, the largest atoll in the Pacific.

1935 — Irish Protestants riot against Catholics in Belfast.

1936 — Edward VIII abdicates the British throne to marry American divorcee Wallis Simpson. His brother George succeeds him and Edward becomes the Duke of Windsor.

1939 — Hitler invades Poland, starting World War II. Kennedy writes his senior thesis, *Why England Slept.* It later becomes a bestselling book.

1940 — Kennedy graduates from Harvard University.

January 11, 1962: In his second STATE OF THE UNION ADDRESS, Kennedy proposes a new department of urban affairs and housing; a trade expansion act; school aid legislation; tax issues; health insurance programs for the elderly; and federal aid for public fallout shelters. The House defeats the bill containing Kennedy's proposal for a new department of urban affairs and housing on February 21. And on July 17, the Senate defeats a bill for medical care for the elderly.

January 29, 1962: After thirty-nine months of negotiations led by the UNITED NATIONS DISARMAMENT COMMISSION, the East-West talks on nuclear test bans officially fail in Geneva.

February 6, 1962: Kennedy proposes a five-year $57 million program to aid public schools.

February 7, 1962: President Kennedy announces an embargo on all trade with Cuba, with the exception for certain medicines and foods.

February 20, 1962: Lieutenant Colonel John Herschel Glenn, Jr. becomes the first U.S. astronaut in orbit. Piloting the Mercury-Atlas 6 *FRIENDSHIP 7* spacecraft, he orbits the earth three times.

April 11, 1962: President Kennedy condemns the rise in steel prices, and he calls the price increase, "wholly unjustifiable." U.S. Steel, a leading American steel producer and manufacturer, had announced a $6-per-ton price increase on April 10 and seven other steel companies had followed suit. On April 12, after the president's speech, the steel companies cancel the price increase.

May 12, 1962: President Kennedy deploys American naval and ground forces to Laos after Communist rebels take over Northern Laos. On July 23, a series of accords are signed at the Geneva Conference under which Laos is to be ruled by a neutralist government under Prince Souvanna Phouma—whom the Eisenhower administration had seen as too accommodating to the Communists.

May 15, 1962: Kennedy sends 4,000 American troops to Thailand.

Kennedy and his brother, Robert, both seen here, carefully planned for the Democratic presidential nomination of 1960. Robert would later become Kennedy's attorney general.

June 25, 1962: In *Engel v. Vitale*, the Supreme Court rules that the reading of a prayer in New York public schools prepared by the New York Board of Regents is unconstitutional.

September 10, 1962: Supreme Court Justice Hugo Bleak orders that JAMES MEREDITH be admitted to the University of Mississippi, setting off a chain of events leading to violent outbreaks on the all-white University of Mississippi campus. Segregationists riot to prevent Meredith's enrollment, leaving 2 persons killed, and 375 injured, including 165 U.S. marshals. Order is restored upon the arrival of 3,000 federal troops.

October 16, 1962: President Kennedy receives conclusive proofs that the Soviet Union is installing offensive missile bases in Cuba.

October 22, 1962: Kennedy announces a naval "quarantine" on Cuba because of the construction of Soviet nuclear missile bases. A tanker and freighter are stopped but then allowed to proceed after being cleared. Eighteen Russian merchant ships heading towards Cuba suddenly reverse course on October 25. U.S. planes follow the ships all the way to Soviet ports.

October 28, 1962: Soviet Premier Khrushchev and President Kennedy come to an agreement whereby the

	1941	1943	
■ Kennedy's Life			
■ U.S. & World Events	Kennedy serves in the U.S. Navy during World War II.	Kennedy is assigned to a PT boat stationed off the Solomon Islands in the South Pacific. After a Japanese attack, Kennedy and his crew are shipwrecked for five days. Afterwards, He is awarded the Navy and Marine Corps Medal and the Purple Heart.	Winston Churchill, Joseph Stalin and Franklin Roosevelt, known together as the "Big Three," hold their first meeting in Tehran, Iran.

Soviet Union will stop construction of missile bases in Cuba and will remove its rockets under United Nations supervision if the U.S. will promise not to invade Cuba. On November 8, Kennedy receives information that all known missiles have been dismantled. On November 20, the **U.S. NAVAL BLOCKADE OF CUBA IS LIFTED**.

January 14, 1963: Kennedy proposes tax cuts to boost the economy; a domestic peace corps; the extension of Social Security benefits to retired workers; and civil rights legislation. The bill providing for an $11.1 billion cut in taxes is passed by the House on September 25.

February 8, 1963: The U.S. resumes conducting underground nuclear tests.

February 28, 1963: President Kennedy proposes a civil rights bill that focuses on voting rights, while avoiding controversial provisions for equal employment opportunities and desegregation in public utilities.

May 10, 1963: Five weeks of racial tension is resolved in **BIRMINGHAM, ALABAMA** through an agreement providing for **PARTIAL AND GRADUAL DESEGREGATION** of public facilities. Two days later, Kennedy announces the deployment of 3,000 troops near the city to keep the peace.

June 11, 1963: Governor Wallace of Alabama, in the presence of National Guards troops, allows two **AFRICAN AMERICAN STUDENTS TO ENTER THE UNIVERSITY OF ALABAMA**. On the same day, Kennedy, in a nationwide television address, states that the nation is "confronted primarily with a moral issue." Kennedy's determination to enforce desegregation eventually prompts Governor Wallace to declare the **INTEGRATION OF PUBLIC SCHOOLS** in his state of Alabama by September 11.

June 19, 1963: Kennedy urges for a strong civil rights legislation. His omnibus bill provides for equal access to restaurants, hotels, and retail establishments, as well as in interstate commerce. The president also empowers the attorney

In this meeting in the White House Cabinet Room, Kennedy and Martin Luther King, Jr., along with other community leaders, discuss Kennedy's civil rights bill. From left to right: Whitney Young, Jr. (Urban League); Martin Luther King, Jr. (SCLC); John Lewis (SNCC); Rabbi Joachim Prinz (American Jewish Congress); Dr. Eugene Carson Blake (National Council of Churches); A. Philip Randolph; President Kennedy; Walter Reuther (United Auto Workers); and Vice President Johnson (behind Reuther).

general to establish school integration suits when requested by those who are unable to do so.

July 25, 1963: The **U.S., GREAT BRITAIN, AND SOVIET UNION AGREE TO SIGN A LIMITED NUCLEAR TEST TREATY**, at the Kremlin, in Moscow, on August 5. The treaty is a product of nearly five years of talks. The three nations agree to halt nuclear tests in the atmosphere, outer space, and under water. The treaty however does not ban underground tests.

August 16, 1963: U.S. and Canada agree to arm Canadian air defense systems with nuclear warheads under U.S. supervision.

August 28, 1963: Approximately 200,000 persons, mostly African Americans, join a **CIVIL RIGHTS MARCH IN WASHINGTON D.C.** to demonstrate peacefully for "jobs and freedom."

October 9, 1963: President Kennedy approves the sale of 150 million bushels of wheat to the Soviet Union.

November 1, 1963: South Vietnamese president Ngo Dinh Diem and his brother are assassinated in Saigon during a coup d'état led by the **ARMY OF THE REPUBLIC OF VIETNAM (ARVN)**.

November 22, 1963: KENNEDY IS ASSASSINATED in Dallas, Texas by Lee Harvey Oswald. Vice President Lyndon B. Johnson is sworn in as president. Oswald is shot dead while in police custody by Jack Ruby on November 24.

1944	1946	1947	1952	1960	1963

Kennedy's older brother, Joe, who had planned to pursue a career in politics, dies in World War II. Kennedy decides to take his place and enters politics.

U.S. announces the Marshall Plan, officially named the European Recovery Program.

He is elected to the U.S. House of Representatives.

Kennedy is elected president.

Kennedy is elected to the U.S. Senate.

Kennedy is assassinated on November 22, in Dallas, Texas.

Lyndon Baines Johnson

36th President (1963–1969)

"For this is what America is all about. It is the uncrossed desert and the unclimbed ridge. It is the star that is not reached and the harvest that is sleeping in the unplowed ground."

Twenty-three-year-old Lyndon Baines Johnson came from rural Texas to Washington, D.C. as the private secretary of a newly-elected Texas Congressman, Richard M. Kleberg. Johnson diligently worked to understand the political process in Washington and soon built a reputation as a political operator with the expertise of a seasoned Washington insider.

In Washington, Johnson was a passionate supporter of President Franklin D. Roosevelt, who appointed him to the Naval Affairs Committee in 1937. The death of Roosevelt in April 1945 was a signficant personal loss for Johnson, who considered the president as a "second daddy."

During his tenure in the House of Representatives, Johnson went on active duty in World War II and received a Silver Star for "gallantry in action." After serving five terms in the House, he was elected to the Senate in 1949. In 1960, Johnson lost the Democratic presidential nomination to J.F. Kennedy, who later chose him as his running mate.

Assuming the presidency after Kennedy's death, Johnson endeavored to push through Kennedy's unfinished agenda and soon persuaded Congress to pass legislation on civil rights, tax cuts, and medical care. After winning the 1964 presidential election, he went on to achieve major breakthroughs in his Great Society programs by ensuring voting rights for African Americans, medical care for the poor and the elderly, and aid for education.

Johnson's conduct of foreign affairs was focused on the Vietnam War where he pursued a program of "phased escalation" of the Vietnam War believing that it would hasten the resolution of the conflict. Increasing numbers of American casualties and spiraling war expenditure by the end of 1967 resulted in inflation, wage price increases, and mounting anti-war riots. The war ultimately shaped the public perception of the president; by March 1968, his declining popularity forced Johnson to declare that he would not stand for reelection.

Although he may be remembered as a president who failed in the Vietnam War, it is to Johnson's credit that American society witnessed one of the most profound changes in history. He presided over a time of unusual turmoil in American life, a period of rebellion among the blacks, poor, and young. His Great Society may have had mixed results, but he will be remembered as the "president for the poor and Negroes." The ideal of a nation free of poverty and racial division remains his abiding legacy to America.

Biographical Facts

Born: August 27, 1908 near Stonewall, Gillespie County, Texas
Ancestry: English
Father: Samuel Ealy Johnson, Jr.; born October 11, 1877 in Buda, Texas; died October 11, 1937 in Austin, Texas
Father's Occupations: Schoolteacher; farmer; state legislator
Mother: Rebekah Baines Johnson; born June 26, 1881 in McKinney, Texas; died September 12, 1958 in Austin, Texas
Wife: Claudia Alta Taylor; born December 22, 1912 in Karnack, Texas
Marriage: November 17, 1934 in San Antonio, Texas
Children: Lynda Bird (1944-); Luci Baines (1947-)
Home: LBJ Ranch, Johnson City, Texas
Education: Johnson City High School; Southwest Texas State Teachers College (B.S.1930); attended Georgetown University Law School

Religious Affiliation: Disciples of Christ
Occupations before Presidency: Teacher; rancher; politician
Military Service: Lieutenant Commander, Commander, U.S. Naval Reserve
Political Offices before Presidency: Director, National Youth Administration Director, Texas; Member of U.S. House of Representatives; Member of U.S. Senate; U.S. Vice President
Political Party: Democratic
Age at Inauguration: 55
Death: January 22, 1973 at San Antonio, Texas
Place of Burial: Near Johnson City, Texas
Nickname: LBJ
Writings: *The Vantage Point: Perspectives of the Presidency, 1963-1969*

Johnson's First Term 1963-1964

November 22, 1963: JOHNSON IS SWORN IN on aboard Air Force One, which is carrying President Kennedy's slain body from Texas to Washington.

November 27, 1963: In his address to a joint session of Congress, Johnson promises to continue Kennedy's policies.

January 8, 1964: In his STATE OF THE UNION ADDRESS, Johnson urges Congress to enact legislation to eliminate racial prejudice. He calls for a national "WAR ON POVERTY."

January 9, 1964: American students in the Canal Zone display only the United States flag at their school, which incited a mob from Panama to enter the zone. Twenty-five people die when United States soldiers and Panamians exchange gunfire. On January 10 Panama cuts off diplomatic relations with the U.S. On April 3, Johnson signs an agreement with the Panama government to look for a peaceful solution.

January 23, 1964: The 24th Amendment to the Constitution is adopted. It outlaws poll taxes in federal elections.

February 26, 1964: Johnson signs a bill providing for an $11.5 billion cut in personal and corporate income taxes.

March 16, 1964: Johnson asks for the cooperation of Congress in the waging of "a nationwide war on the sources of" poverty. To meet this objective, he proposes the creation of a Job Corps for unemployed youths among other measures.

May 22, 1964: In a speech at the University of Michigan, Johnson expresses his plans for a GREAT SOCIETY. He states that "The Great Society rests on abundance and liberty for all. It demands an end of poverty and racial justice."

June 21, 1964: Three young civil rights volunteers participating in a voter-registration drive in Mississippi disappear. Their bullet-ridden bodies are found by the FBI on August 4. Other incidents of RACE-RELATED VIOLENCE occur in Mississippi throughout the summer.

July 2, 1964: The president signs the CIVIL RIGHTS ACT OF 1964, which protects voting rights, bans racial discrimination in employment and in public places, and encourages integration of educational facilities.

July 13, 1964: The Republican Party convenes in San Francisco. It nominates Barry M. Goldwater of Arizona for

President Johnson met with Civil Rights leader Martin Luther King, Jr. to discuss voting rights for African Americans. While King praised Johnson's policies on poverty and unemployment, he remained skeptical of the intentions and the apparent reluctance of the Johnson Administration to pursue civil rights legislation.

	1908	1917	1924	1928
■ Johnson's Life				
■ U.S. & World Events	Lyndon Baines Johnson is born on August 27 near Stonewewall, Texas.	U.S. declares war on Germany and joins the Allies.	Vladimir Lenin, leader of the Soviet Union, dies of a brain hemorrhage.	Johnson becomes principal of a school for Mexican children in Cotulla, Texas.

First Lady: Claudia Alta "Lady Bird" Taylor Johnson

Two years after graduating in the top ten percent of her class from the University of Texas, Claudia Taylor met Lyndon Johnson. Seven weeks later, she agreed to marry him. She then devoted herself to her husband's political career, stepping in to guide his staff while he served in World War II, and again after his heart attack in 1955.

Nicknamed from childhood, "Lady Bird" raised national awareness of the environment during her time as First Lady. She also took an active role in her husband's War on Poverty programs. Mrs. Johnson published her memoirs, *White House Diary*, in 1970, and continues to support the National Wildflower Research Center, which she founded in 1982.

President and William E. Miller of New York for vice president.

July–August 1964: RIOTS BREAK OUT IN HARLEM and in the African-American sections of Philadelphia.

August 5, 1964: U.S. Navy planes conduct AIR RAIDS ON NORTH VIETNAM in retaliation for alleged attacks on American destroyers in international waters in the Gulf of Tonkin. On August 7, Congress passes a joint resolution approving the bombing and empowers the president to implement the necessary actions required to prevent such attacks in the future. In 1954, Vietnam had been divided according to North and South, after the French defeat in the Battle of Dien Bien Phu. South Vietnam, whose capital became Saigon, was ruled by an anti-Communist government, and allied with the U.S. North Vietnam was Communist-ruled, controlled by the Viet Minh, and allied with the Soviet Union and China.

August 20, 1964: Johnson signs the ECONOMIC OPPORTUNITY ACT, which creates a Job Corps, a domestic Peace Corps (Volunteers in Service to America), training programs, loans, and assistance to poverty alleviation projects. The act allocates an initial expenditure of $1 billion.

September 3, 1964: President Johnson signs the NATIONAL WILDERNESS PRESERVATION ACT, introducing a system of preserving wilderness areas, and assigning nine million acres in national forests.

September 27, 1964: The WARREN COMMISSION created to probe the assassination of President Kennedy concludes that Lee Harvey Oswald was solely responsible for the murder. It also concludes that Jack Ruby acted alone in the killing of Oswald.

October 14, 1964: Dr. Martin Luther Jr., is awarded the NOBEL PEACE PRIZE. He announces that he would turn over the prize money of $54,123 to the cause of the civil rights movement. At the age of thirty-five, King is the youngest man to have received the Nobel Peace Prize.

November 4, 1964: JOHNSON IS ELECTED PRESIDENT, after receiving 486 electoral votes to 52 for Goldwater, his Republican opponent.

Johnson's Second Term 1965-1969

January 4, 1965: In his State of the Union message, President Johnson urges Congress to pass legislation to help fulfill his "Great Society" program.

January 20, 1965: JOHNSON IS INAUGURATED and he proposes a new program for the Great Society. His program includes a voting rights bill, federal assistance to public schools, and immigration law reform.

February 1, 1965: POLICE ARREST DR. MARTIN LUTHER KING, JR., and 770 other

Johnson's First Administration

Vice President: Hubert H. Humphrey
Secretary of State : Dean Rusk
Secretary of the Treasury: C. Douglas Dillon
Secretary of Defence: Robert S. McNamara
Attorney General: Robert F. Kennedy
Postmaster General: John A. Gronouski
Secretary of the Interior: Stewart L. Udall
Supreme Court Appointments: None
Secretary of Agriculture: Orville L. Freeman

Secretary of Commerce: Luther H. Hodges
Secretary of Labor: W. Willard Wirtz
Secretary of Health, Education, and Welfare: Anthony J. Celebrezze
Ambassador to United Nations: Adlai Stevenson
88th Congress: (January 9, 1963-October 3, 1965)
Senate: 67 Democrats; 33 Republicans
House: 258 Democrats; 176 Republicans

1930	1931	1934	1935	1937
Johnson graduates from Southwest Texas State Teachers College (now Southwest Texas State University).	Johnson goes to Washington, D.C. as a Congressional secretary.	He marries Claudia Alta "Lady Bird" Taylor.	He becomes national youth administrator for Texas.	Johnson is elected to the U.S. House of Representatives. He meets President Roosevelt, and is appointed to the Naval Affairs Committee.

Johnson's Second Administration

Vice President: Hubert H. Humphrey
Secretary of State: Dean Rusk
Secretary of the Treasury: Henry H. Fowler
Secretary of Defense: Robert S. McNamara;
Clark M. Clifford (from March 1, 1968)
Attorney General: Nicholas Katzenbach;
Ramsey Clark (from March 10, 1967)
Postmaster General: Lawrence F. O'Brien;
W. Marvin Watson (from April 26, 1968)
Secretary of the Interior: Stewart L. Udall
Secretary of Agriculture: Orville L. Freeman
Secretary of Commerce: John T. Connor;
Alexander B. Trowbridge
(from June 14, 1967);
Cyrus R. Smith (from March 6, 1968)
Secretary of Labor: W. Willard Wirtz
**Secretary of Health, Education, and
Welfare:** John W. Gardner;
Wilbur J. Cohen (from March 1, 1968)

Secretary of Housing and Urban Development:
Robert C. Weaver (from January 17, 1966);
Robert C. Wood (from January 2, 1969)
Secretary of Transportation:
Alan S. Boyd (from January 12, 1967)
Ambassador to United Nations;
Arthur J. Goldberg;
George W. Ball (from June 24, 1968);
James Russell Wiggins (from October 4, 1968)
Supreme Court Appointments:
Abe Fortas (1965); Thurgood Marshall (1968)
89th Congress
(from January 3, 1965-January 3, 1967)
Senate: 68 Democrats; 32 Republicans
House: 295 Democrats; 140 Republicans
90th Congress
(January 3, 1967-January 3, 1969)
Senate: 64 Democrats; 36 Republicans
House: 248 Democrats; 192 Republicans

December 21-24, 1967: President Johnson visits Australia, South Vietnam, Thailand, Pakistan and Italy.

January 23, 1968: The *U.S.S. Pueblo*, an electronic intelligence gathering ship is captured by North Korean patrol boats. It had been roaming the North Korean coast around Wonsan to survey the strength of North Korean radar installations. Claiming that the ship had trespassed into its territorial waters, the North Korean government refuses to free the ship and its 83 crewmembers. The crew is released on December 23 after the U.S. signs a North Korean-dictated admission that the ship had entered North Korean waters. The U.S., however, rejects the admission saying it is a false confession of espionage.

February 24, 1968: On February 13, President Johnson orders an additional 10,500 American ground troops to South Vietnam to meet the increased aggression. South Vietnamese confidence is badly shaken.

February 29, 1968: The NATIONAL ADVISORY COMMISSION ON CIVIL DISORDERS (KERNER COMMISSION) gives a report in which it concludes that African American unrest is caused by white racism and recommends measures to assist African Americans. The Commission was instituted by President Johnson on July 27, 1967, and headed by Governor Otto Kerner of Illinois, to look into the causes and events of unrest in black-dominated localities.

March 31, 1968: In a televised speech, Johnson announces that he has called for a stop to the bombing of 90 percent of North Vietnam and urges North Vietnam leaders to join him in taking steps towards peace. On April 7, North Vietnam agrees to make contacts with the U.S. as a beginning to peace talks.

April 4, 1968: DR. MARTIN LUTHER, JR., IS ASSASSINATED in Memphis, Tennessee. His death is followed by racial riots in 125 cities all over the country. The riots leave 46 persons dead and cause extensive property damage. King's assassin, James Earl Ray, is a high-school dropout, and a small-time thief. He is arrested in London on June 8.

April 11, 1968: President Johnson signs the CIVIL RIGHTS ACT OF 1968, forbidding racial discrimination in the selling or renting of housing. The act pertains to eighty percent of the nation's housing.

April 26, 1968: An anti-war rally culminates in a march to Central Park's Sheep Meadow by a total of 87,000 protesters.

May 10, 1968: The United States and North Vietnam begin talks in Paris to prepare for peace negotiations. W. Averell Harriman leads the U.S. delegation and Xuan Thuy leads the Vietnamese delegation.

June 6, 1968: After his win in the California primary, SENATOR ROBERT F. KENNEDY DIES of gunshot wounds from assassin, Palestinian immigrant Sirhan B. Sirhan. Sirhan shot Kennedy on June 5 in the Los Angeles Ambassador Hotel. Johnson, in a televised speech to the nation, calls upon Americans to renounce violence and asks Congress for legislation on stricter control on guns.

July 1, 1968: Sixty-two nations, including Great Britain, the U.S.S.R, and the United States, sign a treaty for the NONPROLIFERATION OF NUCLEAR WEAPONS. The U.S. ratifies

	1954	1955	1960	1963
■ Johnson's Life		Johnson becomes Senate majority leader.		
■ U.S. & World Events	U.S. Senate votes to condemn Senator Joseph McCarthy for contempt of various Senate proceedings.		Johnson is elected vice president of the United States.	Kennedy is assassinated and Johnson becomes president.

and adopts the treaty on March 13, 1969.

July 26, 1968: Johnson signs the **CONSERVATION AND BEAUTIFICATION BILL**, which becomes his 50th bill passed in the area of conservation and the preservation of natural beauty.

August 5, 1968: The Republican Party convenes in Miami Beach, Florida. It nominates former Vice President **RICHARD M. NIXON** of New York for president and Spiro T. Agnew of Maryland for vice president.

August 26, 1968: The Democratic Party convenes in Chicago. It nominates Vice President Humphrey for president and Senator Edmund S. Muskie of Maine for vice president.

September 17, 1968: The American Independent Party nominates George C. Wallace of Alabama for president. Curtis Le May is his running mate.

September 27, 1968: Johnson signs the **FEDERAL WATER SUPPLY BILL**, enabling the states to receive federal funds for improving their water supply networks.

October 31, 1968: Johnson announces that the **U.S. WILL STOP BOMBING NORTH VIETNAM** on November 1, thereby ending a deadlock in the Paris peace talks. However, he reassures South Vietnam that the U.S. will continue to oppose the imposition of a coalition government upon them. The National Liberation Front is allowed to join the negotiations and South Vietnam, which was initially reluctant to join the talks, agrees to do so on November 26.

November 5, 1968: Republican candidate **NIXON IS ELECTED PRESIDENT**. But Democrats maintain control of both the House of Representatives and the Senate.

January 14, 1969: In his **LAST STATE OF THE UNION ADDRESS**, Johnson calls upon the new administration to continue the program of the Great Society. He becomes the first outgoing president since John Adams to personally deliver his address.

January 20, 1969: Johnson establishes **MARBLE CANYON NATIONAL PARK** in Arizona and Colorado.

Ultimately, with the fall of Saigon, the Vietnam War is a defeat for the United States. Vietnam was reunified under Communist control, and officially became the Socialist Republic of Vietnam by 1976. During the war, 3.2 million Vietnamese were killed, in addition to 1.5 to 2 million Lao and Cambodians. Nearly 58,000 Americans lost their lives, and about 300,000 were wounded.

1964		1971	1973
Nelson Mandela, leader of the African National Congress, is sentenced to life imprisonment in South Africa.	Johnson is elected to a full term as president.	U.S. Supreme Court upholds measure to bus children in order to enforce integration in schools.	Johnson dies of a heart attack on January 22, at his ranch in Johnson City, Texas.

Richard Milhous Nixon

"Always remember others may hate you but those who hate you don't win unless you hate them. And then you destroy yourself."

The thirty-seventh president of the United States, who became the first in American history to resign from office, was born in a small-business family in the town of Yorba Linda, California. Young Nixon was above average in his studies. Before joining the United States Navy in 1942, he practiced law in California for five years. Relieved from active duty, he decided to join politics and pushed himself into national politics using his skills as a tactician.

Nixon's 23-year-old political career before he became the president was plagued by controversies. Elected to the 80th Congress in 1946 on the Republican ticket, he served two terms before his election to the U.S. Senate in 1950. Seen as a hard-line anti-Communist, Nixon shot to fame as a result of his successful attempts to expose the Communist connections of Alger Hiss. He became vice president to Eisenhower in 1952 and was reelected for another term in 1956. However, as a presidential candidate in 1960, he lost to Senator John F. Kennedy. Finally, having greatly improved his campaigning strategies and reoriented his positions on salient issues, he was elected president in 1968.

As president, Nixon chose to exercise political pragmatism on domestic issues. His civil rights policies, judicial appointments, and failed attempts to appoint Southerners to the Supreme Court were intended to pacify the conservative South. Upon assuming the presidency, he declared that the 1970s must become "a decade of government reform". To resolve the economy he inherited, he introduced a series of unorthodox and innovative measures. In foreign affairs, he believed in applying American power and diplomatic influences to regional and global problems.

In early 1973, the U.S. and North Vietnam signed an agreement, which led to U.S. withdrawal from Vietnam. With the Soviet Union, Nixon concluded agreements for grain sales, and most importantly, arms limitation, or SALT-I, in 1972. But his major foreign policy triumph was his 1972 state visit to Beijing which normalized U.S. relations with China.

Nixon's last months in office were rocked by disastrous scandals. In the face of certain impeachment after the "Watergate" scandal, Nixon resigned the presidency on August 9, 1974. Despite his achievements during his first term and abortive second term, his presidency is remembered mainly for the controversial Watergate scandal.

Biographical Facts

Born: January 9, 1913 in Yorba Linda, California

Ancestry: Scotch-Irish and German-English Irish

Father: Francis Anthony Nixon; born December 3, 1878 in McArthur, Ohio; died September 4, 1956 in Whittier, California

Father's Occupations: Gas station and general store owner

Mother: Hannah Milhous; born March 7, 1885 in Butlerville, Indiana; died September 30, 1967 in Whittier, California

Wife: Thelma (Pat) Catherine Ryan; born March 16, 1912 in Ely, Nevada; died June 22, 1993 in Park Ridge, New Jersey

Marriage: June 21, 1940 in Riverside, California

Children: Patricia (1946-); Julie (1948-)

Education: Attended public schools; received B.A. from Whittier College (1934), received LL.D. from Duke University Law School (1937)

Religious Affiliation: Society of Friends (Quaker)

Occupations before Presidency: Lawyer; businessman; public official

Military Service: Lieutenant Commander of U.S. Navy (1942-1946)

Political offices before Presidency: Member of the House of Representatives, California; Member of the Senate; U.S. Vice President

Political Party: Republican

Age at Inauguration: 56

Occupations after Presidency: Writer

Died: April 22, 1994 in New York

Place of Burial: Richard Nixon Library, Yorba Linda, California

Nickname: None

Writings: *Six Crises; RN; The Real War; Leaders; Real Peace; No More Vietnams; 1999:Victory without War; In the Arena Seize the Moment; Beyond Peace*

Gerald Rudolph Ford

38th President (1974–1977)

"I am acutely aware that you have not elected me as your president by your ballots, so I ask you to confirm me with your prayers."

Gerald R. Ford harbored no intentions of becoming the president of the United States made history by serving both as an unelected vice president and an unelected president. Ford grew up in the conservative environment of Grand Rapids, Michigan. A good student, he also exhibited exceptional skills in athletics. He graduated from Yale Law School in 1940 and with U.S. entry into World War II, he enrolled as an ensign in the U.S. Navy and trained recruits in North Carolina. After a year, he served on an aircraft carrier in the Pacific theatre. By the end of the war, he had risen to the rank of lieutenant commander. He then returned to Grand Rapids to practice law.

Ford joined local politics as a Republican reformer. He was elected to the House of Representatives in 1948, where he served for 25 years. Throughout his political career he remained a strong proponent of a conservative fiscal policy and a foreign policy that centered on containment. Ford was elected House minority leader in 1965. After the resignation of Vice President Spiro T. Agnew on October 10, 1973, Nixon appointed Ford as his vice president on December 6, 1973. Within a year, he was sworn in as president when Nixon resigned from office on August 9, 1974 in the wake of the Watergate scandal.

The fact that Ford entered the office without a transition period complicated his political situation. His Cabinet was initially composed of Nixon's appointees and he could not effectively command his administration. In addition to this, Ford also had to bear the burden of Watergate. He angered Americans when he granted unconditional pardon to Nixon. His inability to generate media appeal further alienated him from the American people. Nevertheless, Ford worked diligently to restore stability to the economy, which was in disarray. He tried to reduce federal interference in the economy and to maintain a balanced budget in the face of high inflation.

On the foreign policy front, Ford had an opportunity to strengthen his position. After the fall of Saigon, which was a military defeat for the U.S, Ford used force against Cambodian Khmer Rouge troops and bombed mainland Cambodia to restore the credibility of the U.S. military. He continued the Nixon policy of détente and made progress with the Soviets in negotiations for arms control. Amid criticism, Ford attended the Helsinki conference in 1975.

Ultimately, President Ford's inability to distance himself from Nixon and the Watergate scandal, and failure to control the economy, especially rising inflation led to his defeat in the presidential election of 1976.

Biographical Facts

Born: July 14, 1913 in Omaha, Nebraska

Ancestry: English

Father: Leslie Lynch King; born July 25, 1886 in Chadron, Nebraska; died February 18, 1941 in Tucson, Arizona

Father's Occupation: Wool merchant

Stepfather: Gerald Rudolph Ford; born December 19, 1890 in Grand Rapids, Michigan; died January 26, 1962 in Grand Rapids, Michigan

Stepfather's Occupation: President, Ford Paint & Varnish, Co.

Mother: Dorothy Ayer Gardner King Ford; born February 27, 1892 in Harvard, Illinois; died September 17, 1967 in Grand Rapids, Michigan

Wife: Elizabeth "Betty" Bloomer Warren; born April 8, 1918 in Chicago, Illinois

Marriage: October 15, 1948 in Rapids, Michigan

Children: Michael Gerald Ford (1950-); John Gardner Ford (1952-); Steven Meigs Ford (1956-); Susan Elizabeth Ford (1957-)

Education: University of Michigan (1935); Yale Law School (1941)

Religious Affiliation: Episcopalian

Occupations before Presidency: Lawyer

Military Service: Lieutenant Commander in the Navy, World War II

Political Offices before Presidency: Minority Leader, House of Representatives; U.S. Vice President

Political Party: Republican

Age at Inauguration: 61

Occupation after Presidency: Public Speaker; businessman

Writings: *A Time to Heal*

Ford's Term 1974-1977

August 9, 1974: VICE PRESIDENT FORD IS SWORN IN as the 38th president of the United States after President Nixon resigns in the wake of the Watergate scandal.

August 12, 1974: In his address to Congress, Ford calls for measures to curb inflation, the "public enemy number one." He also states that he will work to restore American "trust" in the federal government and the presidency.

August 20, 1974: Ford nominates Nelson A. Rockefeller, former governor of New York, for the post of vice president, saying "he is a good partner for me."

August 22, 1974: Ford announces his support for the EQUAL RIGHTS AMENDMENT.

September 2, 1974: Ford signs the EMPLOYEES RETIREMENT INCOME SECURITY ACT, which provides federal protection of pension plans for 23 million Americans.

September 4, 1974: The United States establishes diplomatic relations with East Germany. Ford appoints John Sherman as the first United States ambassador to East Germany.

September 8, 1974: FORD GRANTS UNCONDITIONAL PARDON TO FORMER PRESIDENT NIXON, and as a result, Gallup polls indicate a drastic drop in Ford's public approval rating to 49 percent from 71 percent. The president pardons Nixon of all criminal charges, relating to the Watergate scandal.

September 16, 1974: Ford makes a conditional amnesty proclamation, offering pardon to thousands of draft evaders and military deserters from the time of the Vietnam War.

October 1, 1974: The "Watergate Cover-Up" trial of seven former presidential aides begins.

October 15, 1974: Congress passes campaign reform legislation allowing the PUBLIC FUNDING OF PRESIDENTIAL CAMPAIGNS.

November 21, 1974: Congress overrides President Ford's veto to pass the FREEDOM OF INFORMATION ACT that increases public access to government files.

November 25-24, 1974: President Ford and Secretary Leonid Brezhnev confer at Vladivostok, U.S.S.R., and sign an agreement to limit the number of intercontinental ballistic missiles, heavy bombers, and submarine-launched missiles.

January 1, 1975: John N. Mitchell, H.R. Haldeman, John D.Ehrlichman, and Robert C. Mardian are convicted in the Watergate trial while Kenneth Parkinson is acquitted.

February 21, 1975: Former White House aides Haldeman and Ehrlichman and former Attorney General John Mitchell are sentenced to 30 months of imprisonment.

On December 1, 1975, President Ford arrives in Beijing for a five-day visit with Chinese leaders.

Quotes by Ford:

"Truth is the glue that holds government together. Compromise is the oil that makes governments go."

"It was very, very uncomfortable. . . If I was critical of Nixon, the press and the public would have said, well, he was trying to undercut Nixon so he will get the job. On the other hand, if I stayed too loyal it might appear that I was supporting somebody who was involved in this very unwise action."

Quotes about Ford:

"I could think of no public figure better able to lead us in national renewal than this man so quintessentially American, of unquestioned integrity, at peace with himself, thoughtful and knowledgeable of national affairs and international responsibilities, calm and unafraid."
– *Henry Kissinger, 1982*

"Jerry Ford is so dumb he can't walk and chew gum at the same time....He is a nice fellow, but he spent too much time playing football without a helmet."
–*Lyndon B. Johnson*

	1913	1916	1917	1935
■ Ford's Life		Ford's mother, Dorothy King, marries Gerald R. Ford. They begin calling Leslie King, Jr. by the name Gerald R. Ford, Jr.		Ford legally takes the name Gerald R. Ford, Jr. and graduates from the University of Michigan.
■ U.S. & World Events	[Ford] Leslie Lynch King, Jr. is born on July 14, in Omaha, Nebraska.		U.S. declares war on Germany and joins the Allies in World War I.	

First Lady: Elizabeth Anne Bloomer Ford

After studying modern dance at Bennington College in Vermont, Betty Bloomer joined Martha Graham's famous dance group in New York City. She worked as a fashion model, retail fashion coordinator, and dance teacher.

Betty Ford stepped into the challenging role of First Lady with humor and frankness, making known her support for the arts, rights of senior citizens, and the Equal Rights Amendment (ERA)—feminist legislation, which her husband opposed. Her public openness about her struggle with breast cancer and alcohol addiction provided inspiration to citizens with similar conditions. The Betty Ford Center, which she founded, runs a nationally-renowned drug and alcohol recovery program.

April 27, 1975: Communist forces carry out heavy shelling on Saigon and threaten to capture it. President Ford orders helicopter evacuation of Americans in Saigon.

May 1975: Unemployment rises to its highest rate since 1941.

May 14, 1975: U.S. forces rescue American merchant ship *Mayaguez*, which had been captured by a Cambodian vessel. The operation leaves 15 Americans dead and 50 wounded.

June 9, 1975: THE ROCKEFELLER COMMISSION confirms original allegations of domestic espionage by the CIA.

August 1, 1975: President Ford and leaders of 34 other nations sign the charter of the CONFERENCE ON SECURITY AND COOPERATION IN HELSINKI, FINLAND.

September 27, 1975: The global ORGANIZATION OF PETROLEUM EXPORTING COUNTRIES (OPEC) votes for a ten-percent increase of oil prices.

October 24, 1975: Rioting over school integration takes place in South Boston, Massachusetts.

November 3, 1975: In an administrative shuffle known as the Halloween Massacre, SECRETARY OF STATE HENRY KISSINGER RESIGNS his second post as head of the National Security Council. Secretary of Defense James A. Schlesinger and CIA director William E. Colby are dismissed by President Ford.

December 22, 1975: The ENERGY POLICY AND CONSERVATION ACT decreases crude oil prices, calls for greater efficiency of automobile technology, and sanctions a national petroleum reserve.

May 28, 1976: U.S. and the Soviet Union sign a treaty to curtail underground nuclear explosions and allow on-site inspections.

July 20, 1976: The FIRST NASA MISSION, VIKING I, lands on Mars and transmits pictures and data from outer space.

September 27, 1976: In the first presidential television debate between an incumbent and his opponent, President Ford and Democratic candidate Jimmy Carter debate domestic issues before a live audience.

Ford's Administration

Inauguration: August 9 1974, in Washington, D.C.
Vice President: Nelson Rockefeller
Secretary of State: Henry Kissinger
Secretary of the Treasury: William E. Simon
Secretary of Defense: James Schlesinger; Donald Rumsfeld (from November 20, 1975)
Attorney General: William Saxbe; Edward H. Levi (from February 7, 1975)
Secretary of the Interior: Rogers C.B. Morton; Stanley K. Hathaway (from June 12, 1975); Thomas S. Kleppe (from October 17, 1975)
Secretary of Agriculture: Earl Butz; John A. Knebel (from November 4, 1976)
Secretary of Transportation: Claude S. Brinegar; William T. Coleman Jr.
Secretary of Commerce: Frederick B. Dent; Rogers C. B. Morton (from May 1, 1975); Elliot L. Richardson (from February 2, 1976)
Secretary of Labor: Peter J. Brennan;

John T. Dunlop (from March 18, 1975); W. J. Usery Jr. (from February 10, 1976)
Secretary of Health, Education, and Welfare: Caspar W. Weinberger; F. David Matthews (from August 8, 1975)
Secretary of Housing and Urban Development: James T. Lynn; Carla Anderson Hills (from March 10, 1975)
Ambassador to United Nations: John P. Scali; Daniel P. Moynihan (from June, 1975); William W. Scranton (from March 1976)
Supreme Court Appointments: John Paul Stevens (1975)
93rd Congress (January 3, 1973-1975)
Senate: 56 Democrats; 42 Republicans, 2 other
House: 255 Democrats; 180 Republicans
94th Congress (January 3, 1975-1977)
Senate:60 Democrats, 37 Republicans, 2 other
House:291 Democrats, 144 Republicans, 1 other

1941	1948	1999	2003
Pearl Harbor is attacked, beginning U.S. involvement in World War II.		Ford is awarded the Presidential Medal of Freedom, the nation's highest civilian honor.	
Ford graduates from Yale Law School and opens a law firm in Grand Rapids.	Ford marries Elizabeth (Betty) Bloomer and is elected to the first of 13 successive terms in the U.S. House of Representatives.		U.S. invades Iraq to oust dictator Saddam Hussein, who is suspected to be hiding weapons of mass destruction.

James Earl Carter

39th President (1977–1981)

"War may sometimes be a necessary evil. But no matter how necessary, it is always an evil, never a good. We will not learn how to live together in peace by killing each other's children."

Jimmy Carter was perhaps the most "outsider" president to enter the White House in the 20th century. Born and raised in Plains, Georgia, Carter graduated from the U.S. Naval Academy, he worked for two years on battleships. Carter volunteered for submarine duty, serving on the USS *Pomfret* and *K-1*. He was transferred to the elite nuclear submarine program in 1952. Following his father's death in 1953, he returned to Plains, took charge of the family peanut farm, and quickly became a local leader. He was elected to the Georgia Senate in 1962 where he served for two terms. In 1970, Carter was elected the governor of Georgia.

Using his image as an outsider pitted against the Washington establishment, Carter won the presidency of the United States. He wisely exploited the popular distrust of and alienation from the government in the wake of Vietnam and Watergate. He established a peculiar governing style by bringing simplicity and integrity to his administration, which impressed many. His simple manner deflated the pretensions of the imperial presidency. He sought to open the government to the underrepresented groups through his appointment of African Americans to high posts.

In response to Carter's proposals, Congress created the Department of Education and deregulated the airline, trucking, and railroad industries . A billion-dollar "superfund" was established to clean up abandoned chemical waste sites, and a comprehensive national energy policy was formulated.

Carter's significant achievements came in the form of foreign policy initiatives, such as the Panama Canal treaty, the Camp David Accords, and human rights policies abroad. However, he could not handle the increasingly sour relations with the Soviet Union when it invaded Afghanistan in December 1979, and the hostage crisis in Iran, which dragged on for 444 days.

Carter's presidency is rated as one of the ten worst in U.S. history, and he is often described as an ineffective and miserable president, who alienated many Washington insiders and members of Congress. During his term, inflation and interest rates were at record highs, and the president was seen as ineffectual in domestic affairs and weak in foreign affairs. But, on the other hand, it can be said that Carter gave the country an administration that was marked by integrity and high-mindedness, despite severe constraints.

Biographical Facts

Born: October 1, 1924 in Plains, Georgia

Ancestry: English

Father: James Earl Carter; born September 12, 1894 in Arlington, Georgia; died July 23, 1953 in Plains, Georgia

Father's Occupations: Insurance broker; farmer; fertilizer dealer

Mother: Lillian Gordy Carter; born August 15, 1898 in Richland, Georgia; died April 30, 1983 in Plains, Georgia

Mother's occupaton: Nurse; Peace Corp volunteer

Wife: Eleanor Rosalynn Smith Carter; born August 18, 1927 in Plains, Georgia

Marriage: July 7, 1946 in Plains, Georgia

Children: John William ("Jack") (1947-); James Earl III ("Chip") (1950-); Donnel Jeffrey ("Jeff") (1952-); and Amy Lynn (1967-)

Education: Georgia Southwestern College (1941-42); Georgia Institute of Technology (1942-43);

United States Naval Academy, (1947); Union College (1952-53)

Religious Affiliation: Baptist

Occupations before the Presidency: Soldier; farmer; warehouseman

Military Service: Navy Lieutenant

Political Offices before the Presidency: Governor of Georgia; State Legislative Service, Georgia

Political Party: Democratic

Age at Inauguration: 53

Nickname: Jimmy

Writings: *Why Not the Best?; A Government as Good as Its People; The Wit and Wisdom of Jimmy Carter; Keeping Faith; Everything to Gain; An Outdoor Journal; Turning Point; The Blood of Abraham; Always a Reckoning; Living Faith; The Virtues of Aging; An Hour Before Daylight*

Ronald Reagan

40th President (1981–1989)

"It is not my intention to do away with government. It is rather to make it work—work with us, not over us; stand by our side, not ride on our back. Government can and must provide opportunity, not smother it; foster productivity, not stifle it."

Ronald Wilson Reagan's first political office as the governor of California was marked by his beliefs in lower taxes and reduced government spending. During his campaign in the 1980 presidential election, he attacked the Carter administration's failure to prevent the two-digit rise in prices and the high unemployment rate. He also criticized the incumbent for his inability to drive the Soviets out of Afghanistan and to resolve the Iranian-hostage crisis.

Upon assuming the presidency, Reagan proposed strong measures to curtail the severe recession and the ailing economy with his three-pronged economic policy dubbed "Reaganomics," which included the reduction of federal spending through cuts in social programs, a dramatic cut in taxes, and a reduction in federal regulation. By the end of his first term, inflation was brought under control, interest rates were lower, and employment had risen.

Reagan's administration saw the largest peacetime military expansion in world history. He adopted both covert and overt support to anti-Communist insurgencies in Third World countries, including El Salvador. He also sent troops to

Lebanon to help defend its Christian government against uprising Muslim groups. Reagan viewed various international problems as Cold War conflicts with moral significance and serious consequences. He referred to the Soviet Union as an "evil empire" and Soviet Communism as "the focus of evil in the modern world."

Reagan was at the peak of his popularity when he stood for reelection in 1984. His landslide victory over Walter Mondale was due in large part to his success in restructuring the American economy. However, the Iran-Contra Affair and the 1987 stock market crash, combined with continuing budget deficits, made his second term less popular.

Reagan's legacy remains a contested one. The oldest person to serve as president, he implemented a new style of leadership that downplayed his role as administrator and emphasized the use of news media to communicate with the public. He also forged a relationship with Soviet leader Gorbachev that greatly defused historic tensions, paving the way for the end of the Cold War. Finally, it is to his credit that the nation experienced profound changes in economic policy in half a century.

Biographical Facts

Born: February 6, 1911 in Tampico, Illinois
Ancestry: Irish and Scotch-English
Father: John "Jack" Edward Reagan; born August 13, 1883 in Fulton, Illinois; died May 18, 1941 in Hollywood, California
Father's Occupation: Shoe salesman
Mother: Nellie Clyde Wilson; born July 24, 1883 in Clyde Township, Illinois; died July 25, 1962 in Santa Monica, California
First Wife: Jane Wyman; born January 4, 1914 in St. Joseph, Missouri
First Marriage: January 26, 1940 in Los Angeles, California
Second Wife: Nancy Davis; born July 6, 1921 in New York City
Second Marriage: March 4, 1952 in San Fernando Valley, California
Children (by first wife): Maureen Elizabeth Reagan (1941-2001); Michael Edward Reagan (1945-)

(by second wife): Patricia Ann Reagan (1952-); Ronald Prescott Reagan (1958-)
Education: Received B.A. from Eureka College (1932)
Home: Los Angeles, California
Religious Affiliation: Episcopalian
Occupations before Presidency: Military; radio announcer; actor
Military Service: Second Lieutenant; First Lieutenant; Captain, Army
Political Offices before Presidency: Governor of California
Political Party: Republican
Age at Inauguration: 69
Nickname: The Great Communicator; Dutch
Writings: *Where's the Rest of Me?*; *The Creative Society*; *Abortion and the Conscience of the Nation*; *Speaking My Mind*; *An American Life*

253

Election of 1980

Candidates	Party	Electoral Vote	Popular Vote
Ronald Reagan (CA)	Republican	489	43,899,248
James Carter (GA)	Democrat	49	35,481,435
John Anderson (IL)	Independent	0	5,719,437

About the Election: Reagan won the Republican nomination, defeating John B. Anderson and George H.W. Bush. Anderson ran as an Independent, while Bush beat out former President Gerald Ford as Reagan's running mate. The Democrats renominated Jimmy Carter and Walter Mondale. Key issues in the election, all of which highlighted Carter's weaknesses, were the economy, national security, and the Iran hostage crisis. Reagan based his proposed policies on the "supply-side" theory and interpreted welfare policies, which are inevitably financed by excessive taxation, as leading causes to economic depression. In a campaign that emphasized growth rather than conservation, Reagan promised to cut taxes and reduce government interference in business, while increasing energy production and spending to achieve "military superiority". Reagan won by a large margin, with a popular vote of 43.9 million.

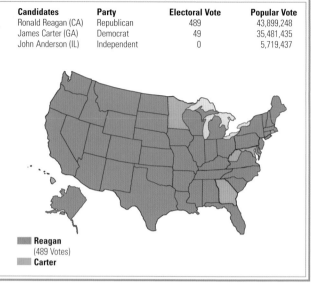

▓ **Reagan**
(489 Votes)
▓ **Carter**

Reagan's First Term 1981-1985

January 20, 1981: RONALD REAGAN IS INAUGURATED as the 40th president of the United States. On the day of Reagan's inauguration, soon after he delivers his presidential address, the Iranian government frees the 52 American hostages in Iran.

March 1, 1981: Reagan considers sending United States armaments to help rebels in Afghanistan. A month before Reagan assumed office, the Soviet Union had sent in tanks and troops into Afghanistan to protect the Soviet-controlled government from being overthrown by rebellious opposition groups. Former president Jimmy Carter had condemned the Soviet action, and had suspended the sale of wheat and advanced technology to the Soviet Union, postponing the second round of the strategic arms limitation talks. The grain embargo is eventually lifted on April 24 by President Reagan.

March 2, 1981: The Reagan administration increases its assistance to El Salvador's fight against leftist rebels.

March 3, 1981: REAGAN REJECTS THE SALT TREATY negotiated by a UN commission during Carter's presidency, arguing that certain provisions of the treaty would adversely affect American offshore fishing and deep-sea mining industries. The treaty defines the proper use of the sea for commercial purposes, and encourages the sharing of marine technology.

March 6, 1981: Before leaving for Canada, Reagan asks the Senate to approve a Canada-U.S. boundary treaty.

March 30, 1981: REAGAN IS SHOT in the chest by John Warnock Hinckley, Jr. The president is admitted to the hospital and recovers within a fortnight.

April 1, 1981: U.S. freezes aid to Nicaragua due to the new Sandinista government's covert support to Marxist rebels in neighboring El Salvador.

April 12, 1981: U.S. space shuttle *COLUMBIA*, the world's first reusable spacecraft, is launched on its maiden flight from Cape Canaveral, Florida.

July 1, 1981: Reagan's plan to stimulate the economy while fighting inflation—popularly dubbed "REAGANOMICS"—combines a three-phase tax cut with sharp reductions in federal spending for social programs, including funding for health, food, housing, and education. Reaganomics is based on the theory of "supply-side" economics, which focuses not on the demand for goods but on the supply of goods. It predicts that cutting taxes would leave more money for those who supplied goods for consumers—business owners and investors.

July 29, 1981: Congress approves the president's proposal providing for nearly **$750 BILLION IN TAX CUTS**. Unprecedented in the history of the U.S., this tax cut is one of the election campaign promises fulfilled by Reagan.

	1911	1917	1918	1932
■ Reagan's Life				
		U.S. declares war on Germany in World War I.	President Wilson's 14 Points for the basis of peace negotiations, is accepted by the new German chancellor Maximilian, Prince of Baden. Germany signs the armistice on November 11.	Reagan graduates from Eureka College.
■ U.S. & World Events		Ronald Reagan is born on February 6 in Tampico, Illinois.		

First Lady: Nancy Davis Reagan

After graduation from Smith College, Nancy Davis became a successful professional actress, a career she happily left upon marriage and motherhood. She was the second wife of Ronald Reagan; his first wife, Jane Wyman, was also an actress.

As First Lady, Nancy Reagan was protective of her husband and stood by his side through an assassination attempt and political scandal. She also acted as his informal advisor. Nancy Reagan favored formal White House social events, and during her first year, she was criticized for overspending on redecorating projects and official parties.

During her stay at the White House, she worked with numerous charitable groups and organizations, and took an active interest in supporting the emotionally and physically handicapped. Her focus later became drug abuse among America's youth and she launched a long term campaign that encouraged citizens to "Just Say No" to drugs. Now living with her husband in California after retirement, she continues to work for the cause of drug abuse among children. In her book, My Turn (1989),she gives a personal account of her life in the White House.

Reagan's First Administration

Inauguration: January 20, 1981 at the Capitol in Washington, D.C.
Vice President: George Herbert Walker Bush
Secretary of State:
Alexander Haig Jr. (1981-1982);
George Shultz (from July 16, 1982)
Secretary of the Treasury:
Donald T. Reagan;
James Baker (from February 4, 1985);
Nicholas F. Brady (from September 15, 1988)
Secretary of Defense: Caspar Weinberger;
Frank Carlucci (from November 23, 1987)
Attorney General: Edwin Meese;
Richard Thornburgh (from August 12, 1988)
Secretary of the Interior: Donald Hodel
Secretary of Agriculture: Richard E. Lyng
Secretary of Transportation:
Elizabeth Dole (1983-1987);
James Burnley (from December 3, 1987)
Secretary of Commerce: Malcolm Baldridge
Secretary of Labor: Raymond Donovan

Secretary of Health and Human Services:
Richard Schweiker; Margaret Heckler
(from March 9, 1983)
Secretary of Housing and Urban Development: Samuel Pierce
Secretary of Energy: James Edwards;
Donald Hodel (from November 5, 1982)
Secretary of Education: Terrell Bell
Ambassador to United Nations:
Jeane J. Kirkpatrick
Supreme Court Appointments:
Sandra Day O'Connor (1981)
97th Congress
(January 3, 1981-January 3, 1983)
Senate: 46 Democrats; 53 Republicans, 1 other
House: 242 Democrats; 192 Republicans, 1 other
98th Congress
(January 3, 1983-January 3, 1985)
Senate: 46 Democrats; 54 Republicans
House: 269 Democrats; 166 Republicans
End of Presidential Term: January 20, 1985

August 5, 1981: Reagan dismisses 13,000 air traffic controllers who violated federal law by going on strike. His deft handling of the situation by quickly recruiting new traffic controllers ensures the smooth functioning of air traffic with only a brief interruption.

September 25, 1981: The first woman justice of the United States Supreme Court SANDRA DAY O' CONNOR is sworn in.

October 2, 1981: REAGAN ANNOUNCES HIS DEFENSE PROGRAM, which includes the development of both stationary MX missiles in hardened silos and B-1 bombers. Congress authorizes $625 million on May 24, 1983 to fund MX missile research and development.

October 9, 1981: Reagan signs a bill recognizing the agreement between North and South Carolina, which establishes their lateral seaward boundary.

October 28, 1981: The Senate approves the sale of American Airborne Warning and Control System planes (AWACS) to Saudi Arabia.

November 2, 1981: In the Congressional elections, Republicans retain control of the Senate but Democrats gain a majority in the House of Representatives by winning an additional 20 seats.

November 14, 1981: U.S.-

1936	1937	1939	1940	1941
	Reagan moves to Hollywood and begins his acting career. He makes his film debut in *Love Is On the Air*.		Reagan marries Jane Wyman.	
Reagan is employed as a sportscaster for the WHO station in Des Moines, Iowa.		Hitler invades Poland, starting World War II.		Japanese attack U.S. Fleet in Pearl Harbor, Hawaii, killing approximately 3,000 people.

Egyptian forces conduct **OPERATION BRIGHT STAR MILITARY** exercises, the biggest U.S. war game in the Middle East since 1945.

December 4, 1981: President Reagan issues an executive order authorizing the CIA to carry out covert domestic surveillance.

December 15, 1981: Congress approves the largest peacetime military budget in the nation's history, providing $199.7 billion for military spending, with an additional construction grant of $ 7.1 billion, for the fiscal year of 1982.

January 26, 1982: In his **STATE OF THE UNION ADDRESS** to Congress, Reagan calls for a "new federalism" that will transfer federal social programs, including the welfare system and the food-stamp program, to individual state governments.

March 22, 1982: Reagan signs the joint resolution passed by Congress that the Soviet Union must respect the rights of its citizens to practice their religion, as well as allow them to emigrate from the U.S.S.R. The resolution demands that these issues be addressed at the 38th meeting of the United Nations Commission on Human Rights at Geneva in February 1982.

May 26, 1982: In Chicago, Secretary of State Alexander Haig delivers an address defining the direction of American foreign policy. Détente, which allowed for coexistence with the Soviet Union in the 1970s, is replaced with a stricter foreign policy that opposes governments under Soviet control, such as in the countries of Central America and the Caribbean.

June 5, 1982: **ISRAEL INVADES LEBANON** in an effort to drive out Palestine Liberation Organization (PLO) guerrillas who are attacking Israel from bases in Lebanon. The Reagan administration understands the continuing factional strife in Lebanon as a Cold War problem, and supports the invasion, believing that Israeli presence will help maintain Lebanese independence from radical Muslim groups. Israel agrees to stop shelling Beirut with the arrival of French, Italian, and American troops as UN observers to oversee the withdrawal of PLO forces from West Beirut to Jordan and Tunisia. But Israel soon reoccupies Beirut much to the disappointment of the Reagan administration which was working for an arrangement whereby Israel would recognize Palestinian independence on the West Bank of Jordan. Following the occupation, Lebanese Christian militia massacre hundreds of Palestinians in the refugee camps. The international community strongly condemns Israel for its direct role in the incident and the U.S. for its support of Israeli action. Disagreements in the Reagan administration over involvement in Lebanon lead to the resignation of Secretary of State Haig who is replaced by George Schultz.

June 6, 1982: Reagan addresses the combined Houses of the British Parliament, expressing his support of British action against Argentina in the British-controlled Falkland Islands, northeast of the southern tip of South America. Argentine forces had invaded the islands in April to claim the land as theirs. On June 14, they surrender to British forces.

June 30, 1982: The Senate fails to pass the **EQUAL RIGHTS AMENDMENT ACT** within the stipulated deadline. Only 35 states out of the required 38 have ratified it.

September 24, 1982: The U.S. and other NATO nations withdraw from the International Atomic Energy Commission following the denial of a seat to Israel. Secretary of State George Shultz states that the U.S. would leave any UN agency that excludes Israel from deliberations. He also says that it would withhold payment of $8.5 million assessed for the 1982 operation of the Atomic Energy Agency. U.S. rejoins the commission on May 6, 1983.

October 12, 1982: Reagan signs a bill making it a criminal offence to issue threats to former presidents, major presidential candidates, and other persons protected by the Secret Service.

	1942	1945	1947	1948
■ Reagan's Life			Reagan becomes president of the Screen Actors Guild and testifies before the U.S.	
■ U.S. & World Events	Reagan serves in the U.S. Air Force.	Germany surrenders to the Allies on May 8. Japan surrenders in August.	House Committee of Un-American Activities against Communists in Hollywood.	Reagan divorces Jane Wyman.

Reagan and his wife Nancy on the campaign trail with Senator Strom Thurmond of South Carolina.

November, 1982: Cold War tensions and the slow progress of arms-control programs lead to the rise of the "**NUCLEAR FREEZE**" movement, which calls for a pact between the United States and the Soviet Union to limit their nuclear arsenals. Approximately one million "nuclear freeze" advocates march to New York City's Central Park in the largest mass demonstration in U.S. history.

December 3, 1982: The Labor Department reports that the unemployment rate is 10.6 percent, the highest since 1940. Nearly 12 million people are out of work.

March 8, 1983: President Reagan refers to the Soviet Union as an "evil empire" and Soviet Communism as "the focus of evil in the modern world."

March 23, 1983: Reagan calls for research and development under the **STRATEGIC DEFENSE INITIATIVE (SDI)**, popularly known as **STAR WARS**. SDI, which incorporates a new, laser-beam operated defensive shield, would allow the U.S. to intercept enemy missiles before they reach their targets, as well as destroy enemy missiles and warheads in space.

March 24, 1983: Congress passes an act allocating funds to provide employment to thousands of jobless Americans.

October 23, 1983: A Muslim terrorist drives an explosive-laden truck into the U.S. Marine Corps' Headquarters in Beirut leaving 241 marines dead. Reagan had sent American marines to Lebanon with the intention of restoring peace to the war-torn nation after a number of Muslim groups revolted against the Christian government. The marines were soon subjected to attacks from warring Lebanese factions, many of which represented anti-American, pro-Iranian groups. In the face of increasing attacks from PLO snipers on American marine forces, the Reagan administration had authorized the marines to shell Muslim positions in the hills above Beirut. In spite of the subsequent escalation in attacks against U.S. forces, including a

1950	1951	1952	1954	1961
	J.D. Salinger writes *Catcher in the Rye.*		He agrees to work with General Electric to host a 30-minute television series and to promote the free-enterprise system to an audience of General Electric employees.	Soviet cosmonaut Yuri Gagarin is the first man to travel in space when he orbits the earth in *Vostok I.*
Communist-ruled North Korea invades South Korea.		Reagan marries Nancy Davis.		

Ronald Reagan and Soviet premier Mikhail Gorbachev in Geneva, Switzerland, in 1985.

car-bomb attack on the American embassy, the administration kept the marines in Beirut to demonstrate its commitment to resolving the conflict in Lebanon, while ensuring American influence in the area. The **BOMBING OF U.S. MARINE HEADQUARTERS IN BEIRUT** provokes widespread public outcry for the withdrawal of American forces from Lebanon. Congress even threatens to use the 1973 War Powers Act to force a withdrawal of all American forces from Beirut. On February 7, 1984, President Reagan agrees to transfer the marines to naval vessels in the Mediterranean.

October 25, 1983: At the beginning of October, Prime Minister Maurice Bishop of Grenada is assassinated in a military coup by pro-Marxist rebels. Citing security concerns for the 1,000 American students on the island, **REAGAN DEPLOYS FORCES TO GRENADA** on October 25. The forces defeat the initial resistance of over 700 Cuban soldiers and soon install a

pro-American establishment. The invasion is condemned by most of the Latin American governments. American citizens, however, show strong approval of the invasion. The U.S. vetoes a United Nations Security Council resolution that condemns the Grenada invasion as "precipitous and unnecessary." Britain's Prime Minister Margaret Thatcher strongly opposes Reagan's action charging that the British had not been consulted even though Grenada was a Commonwealth nation.

November 1, 1983: Over a two-day meeting in Washington D.C., 50 scientists discuss the findings by U.S. and Soviet Union teams on "The World after Nuclear War." The teams of the two rival nations conclude that nuclear war would drastically alter the climate of the Northern Hemisphere, causing a "**NUCLEAR WINTER**"—several months of darkness consisting of freezing weather conditions.

November 11, 1983: The first shipment of American cruise

	1964	1965	1966	1968
■ Reagan's Life				
■ U.S. & World Events	Reagan endorses Republican presidential candidate Barry Goldwater on television.	President Johnson sends the first ground troops to Vietnam.	Reagan is elected governor of California, and he serves two terms.	He is defeated by Nixon at the Republican National Convention for the presidential nomination.

Election of 1984

Candidates	Party	Electoral Vote	Popular Vote
Ronald Reagan (CA)	Republican	525	53,354,037
Walter Mondale (MN)	Democrat	13	36,884,260

About the Election: Reagan and Bush easily won renomination at the 1984 Republican National Convention in Dallas. The Democrats nominated former Vice President Walter F. Mondale for president and Representative Geraldine A. Ferraro of New York for vice president. Ferraro was the first woman to be nominated for either vice president or president by a major political party. In the campaign, Mondale argued that Reagan's foreign policies had increased tensions between the United States and the Soviet Union and that the president's economic reforms only favored the wealthy class. Reagan pointed to the fall in unemployment and inflation and the rise in economic growth. In the election, Reagan won in a landslide receiving 54.5 million popular votes to 37.6 million for Mondale.

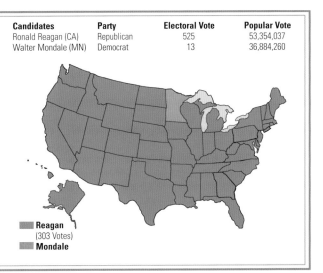

■ **Reagan** (303 Votes)
■ **Mondale**

missiles reaches Great Britain. Two weeks later, the Soviet Union withdraws from the arms-limitations talks for the reduction of nuclear missiles in Europe.

November 12, 1983: Congress votes to curb aid to El Salvador until its government convicts the murderers of four American missionaries.

November 29, 1983: Reagan and Israeli Prime Minister Yitzhak Shamir agree to form a joint committee to coordinate military plans.

December 12, 1983: Reagan signs into law the **BOLAN AMENDMENT**, prohibiting the use of funds "for the purpose of overthrowing the government of Nicaragua".

December 28, 1983: U.S. WITHDRAWS ITS MEMBERSHIP FROM UNESCO, after the White House charges the organization with displaying "endemic hostility" towards a free society and "those that protect a free press, free markets and above all, individual human rights." The U.S. states that it would renew its membership only if the agency returns to its original principles of free government and human rights.

April 23, 1984: Margaret Heckler, Secretary of Health and Human Services announces that a National Cancer Institute team headed by Dr. Robert Gallo has discovered the **HUMAN IMMUNODEFICIENCY VIRUS (HIV)** to be the viral cause for AIDS— acquired immune deficiency syndrome.

May 1, 1984: Reagan concludes a five-day visit to China, during which he signs accords on nuclear cooperation and

cultural relations with the Communist power.

July 18, 1984: Reagan signs the **DEFICIT REDUCTION ACT** that increases taxes by about $50 billion and reduces governmental expenses by about $30 billion. The provisions of the act are to be implemented over the next three years.

July 19, 1984: The Democratic Party Convention at San Francisco nominates Walter Fredrick Mondale of Minnesota as its presidential candidate on the first ballot.

August 23, 1984: The Republican Party Convention at Dallas nominates Reagan as its presidential candidate on the first ballot.

November 6, 1984: REAGAN IS REELECTED to the presidency, after carrying 49 states. In the Congressional elections, the Republicans maintain control of the Senate while the Democrats hold the majority in the House.

Reagan's Second Term 1985-1989

January 20, 1985: REAGAN IS INAUGURATED FOR HIS SECOND TERM by Chief Justice Burger. As the inauguration day falls on a Sunday, a second swearing-in ceremony is held on Monday. His inaugural parade is cancelled because of extremely cold weather.

February 6, 1985: To resolve the credit crisis in the agricultural sector, the greatest threat to U.S. agriculture since the Great Depression, the administration relaxes the rules of a $650-million loan guarantee program.

March 1, 1985: Reagan refers to the Contras as the "moral equal of our founding fathers" and says that Nicaragua has

1970	1973	1976	1980

U.S., South and North Vietnam, and the Viet Cong sign a cease fire agreement.

Reagan is defeated by Ford at the Republican National Convention for the presidential nomination.

Reagan is reelected governor of California.

In *Roe v. Wade*, U.S. Supreme Court rules that state laws cannot forbid a woman to have an abortion in the first trimester of pregnancy.

Iraq attacks Iran and the two countries are at war for eight years.

George Herbert Walker Bush

41st President (1989–1993)

"America is never wholly herself unless she is engaged in high moral principle. We as a people have such a purpose today. It is to make kinder the face of the nation and gentler the face of the world."

George H. W. Bush's election to the presidency was the consummation of a long and extensive public career, ranging from Congressman, ambassador to the U.N, chief liaison officer at the U.S. liaison office in China, CIA director, and two terms as vice president. Helped by the healthy state of the economy and the warm afterglow of President Ronald Reagan's personal popularity, Bush was able to garner the support of the moderates by promising a "kinder, gentler nation."

His presidency witnessed one of the most profound changes in international relations in the 20th century. During his tenure, the Cold War ended with the collapse of the Soviet Union, and relations with China became strained following the suppression of a student protest in Beijing. American troops overthrew Panamanian dictator Manuel Noriega and the U.S. led an international coalition to victory in the Persian Gulf War against Iraq. In Latin America, Bush's policy departed from Cold War concerns, and abandoning Reagan's military approach to problems of Central America, he encouraged regional diplomatic solutions and a greater role for the UN.

In domestic affairs, however, the president and Congress failed to arrive at a consensus on many issues. Bush inherited a large burden of debt and had to face the Democratic-controlled Congress throughout his four years. Nonetheless, the president was able to persuade Congress to pass two significant legislations—the Disabilities Act and the Clean Air Act. After the Iran-Contra scandal of the Reagan era, Bush worked to restore integrity to the government. The Americans with Disabilities Act mitigated both legal and physical obstacles that hindered the daily lives of individuals with disabilities. The Clean Air Act, which Bush signed in 1990, was a compromise between business and environment groups to update and impose stricter air pollution standards for the first time in 12 years.

The extraordinary growth of the American economy since 1983 came to an end in 1991. The signing of the NAFTA and the economy's recovery in late 1992 failed to reduce unemployment. Caught between the need to reduce the budget deficit and increase military commitments in the Persian Gulf, Bush compromised with Congress on the budget and agreed to raise taxes even though, during his 1980 campaign, Bush had promised to oppose new taxes.

Upon leaving office, Bush returned to Texas. He served on the board of the Episcopal Church Foundation. Eight years after leaving the presidency, he witnessed the election of his son, George W. Bush, to the presidency.

Biographical Facts

Born: June 12, 1924 in Milton, Massachusetts

Ancestry: English

Father: Prescott Bush; born May 15, 1895 in Columbus, Ohio; died October 8, 1972 in New York City.

Father's Occupations: Investment banker; U.S. Senator

Mother: Dorothy Walker Bush; born July 1, 1901 near Walker's Point, Maine; died November 19, 1992 near Walker's Point, Maine

Wife: Barbara Pierce Bush; born June 8, 1925 in New York, New York

Marriage: January 6, 1945 in Rye, New York

Children: George W. Bush (1946-); Robin Bush (1949-1953); John Ellis "Jeb" Bush (1953-); Neil Bush (1955-); Marvin Bush (1956-); Dorothy Bush (1959-)

Religious Affiliation: Episcopalian

Education: Attended private schools; Phillips Academy at Andover; received B.A. from Yale University (1945)

Occupations before Presidency: Military officer; businessman

Military Service: Lieutenant (junior), U.S. Navy

Political Offices before Presidency: United States House of Representatives, Texas; Ambassador to the United Nations; Chairman, Republican National Committee; United States Envoy to China; Director, Central Intelligence Agency; U.S. Vice President

Political Party: Republican

Age at Inauguration: 64

Occupations after Presidency: Writer; public speaker

Nickname: Poppy

Writings: *Looking Forward; A World Transformed; Heartbeat*

263

obstruction of congressional inquiries and proceedings, while attempting to cover up the Reagan administration's involvement in the Iran-Contra affair. Poindexter is convicted of criminal conspiracy with his assistant Lieutenant Colonel Oliver North, but it is overruled in November 1991.

April 24, 1990: Nicknamed the "junk bond king," **MICHAEL MILKEN** is fined $600 million and sentenced to serve time in prison in the largest securities fraud case in Wall Street history.

June 1, 1990: Bush and Soviet leader Mikhail Gorbachev sign agreements in Washington to limit nuclear arms, eliminate most chemical weapons, and resume normal economic relations.

June 21, 1990: Bush vetoes a bill requiring employers to grant employees up to twelve weeks of unpaid leave to care for newborn, recently-adopted, or ill children. Bush argues that such matters should be settled between workers and management, and that the bill would only bring about "rigid, federally imposed requirements."

July 26, 1990: Bush signs the **AMERICANS WITH DISABILITIES ACT**, an unprecedented legislation protecting the rights of disabled persons. The act prohibits discrimination in employment, public places and transportation on account of physical disability. It also requires businesses, schools, and public institutions to provide facilities for easy access to people in wheelchairs and with other disabilities.

November 5, 1990: Bush signs a budget law aimed at reducing the federal budget by $492 billion through five years. The law includes **$140 BILLION IN NEW TAXES** over a five-year period, thus reversing Bush's campaign promise in 1988 that he would oppose any new taxes.

November 15, 1990: Bush signs the **CLEAN AIR ACT** limiting the amount of pollutants in the air nationwide. The act restricts toxic emissions from automobiles, industry and utility

smokestacks, and implements a program that would phase out chlorofluorocarbon use. The act updates and imposes more stringent air pollution standards for the first time in 12 years. Its aim is to reduce acid rain pollutants, fight urban smog, and eliminate industrial toxic emissions by the end of the century. The estimated cost of enforcing the act is $25 billion per year.

November 29, 1990: Bush signs the **IMMIGRATION ACT OF 1990**, the most comprehensive revision of immigration rules in over fifty years. It limits the total number of immigrants to 700,000 persons per year.

January 12, 1991: Following an intensive debate for two days, Congress authorizes Bush to use force against Iraq. The United Nations imposes a January 16 deadline for the withdrawal of Iraqi troops from Kuwait, which Iraq has occupied since August 1990. After the deadline, a U.S.-led international coalition begins the offensive dubbed **OPERATION DESERT STORM** with heavy bombing and missile attacks on Baghdad and Iraqi positions in Kuwait. The ground assault begins on February 24, routing the Iraqis within three days. Iraq agrees to close down its facilities for manufacturing chemical, nuclear, and biological weapons, but will delay doing so.

February 27, 1991: The Senate Ethics Committee concludes its probe into the "**KEATING FIVE**" group of senators who have allegedly accepted hefty contributions from Charles Keating, owner of Lincoln Savings and Loan Association. Keating had been convicted of fraud, racketeering, and conspiracy t*o deceive investors, mostly elderly citizens, into buying junk bonds.

February 27, 1991: **BUSH DECLARES THE LIBERATION OF KUWAIT AND IRAQ'S DEFEAT** after offensive operations cease. The next day, Iraq accepts the ceasefire and agrees to abide by all the UN resolutions relating to its invasion.

March 27, 1991: Implementing the **1987 INTERMEDIATE RANGE NUCLEAR MISSILE TREATY (INF)** with the Soviet Union, the U.S. announces that it has completed the removal of its last medium-range nuclear missiles from the European continent.

July 31, 1991: Bush and Gorbachev sign the **NUCLEAR ARMS REDUCTION TREATY** in Moscow that reduces Soviet Union's nuclear warheads from 10,841 to 8,040 within seven years, and U.S. warheads from 12,081 to 10,395. In September, both sides announce further cuts in their nuclear stock.

October 20, 1991: Bush vetoes a bill providing for federal unemployment benefits to meet rising unemployment. The president argues that it will increase the budget deficit.

December 25, 1991: Leader of the Soviet Union for almost seven years, **MIKHAIL GORBACHEV RESIGNS**. The Soviet Union is

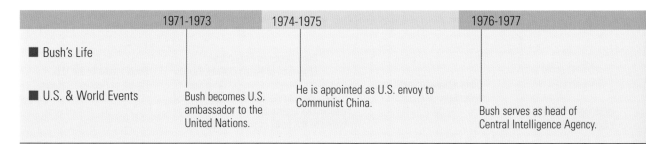

	1971-1973	1974-1975	1976-1977
■ Bush's Life			
■ U.S. & World Events	Bush becomes U.S. ambassador to the United Nations.	He is appointed as U.S. envoy to Communist China.	Bush serves as head of Central Intelligence Agency.

On November 22, 1990, President Bush visits U.S. troops in Saudi Arabia to celebrate Thanksgiving. The troops are deployed in Saudi Arabia during Operation Desert Storm.

dissolved and the Commonwealth of Independent States is created from 11 republics.

February 1, 1992: The newly-elected president of Russia, **BORIS YELTSIN**, meets with President Bush at Camp David.. They formally declare the end of the Cold War.

April 29, 1992: **RIOTS IN LOS ANGELES** erupt after the acquittal of four white police officers who had ruthlessly beaten a black motorist. Dozens die in the violence, while thousands are injured and arrested. Many Los Angeles businesses and homes are destroyed.

July 1, 1992: The Bush administration announces that the national unemployment level has reached 7.8 per cent, the highest level in eight years.

July 15-16, 1992: The Democratic Party convention nominates **BILL CLINTON** of Arkansas for president and **ALBERT GORE** of Tennessee for vice president.

July 29, 1992: The Supreme Court in *PLANNED PARENTHOOD V. CASEY* reaffirms the 1973 *ROE V. WADE* decision that gave women the right to abortion, but at the same time upholds states' right to regulate and restrict abortions.

August 8, 1992: Bush calls upon the United Nations to help protect relief supplies to war-torn Bosnia and Herzegovina.

November 3, 1992: **CLINTON IS ELECTED PRESIDENT**, and Democrats retain their majority in Congress.

December 9, 1992: Congress authorizes Bush to send 28,000 U.S. troops in an expeditionary force to Somalia to oversee the release of humanitarian aid to starving Somalians.

December 17, 1992: Bush signs the **NORTH AMERICAN FREE TRADE AGREEMENT** with Mexico and Canada, paving way for the creation of the world's biggest free trade zone.

December 24, 1992: Bush grants pardon to six former government officials convicted of perjury during the Congressional investigation of the Iran-contra scandal.

January 3, 1993: Bush and Yeltsin sign the **STRATEGIC ARMS REDUCTION TREATY (START II)**, which provides for a reduction of nuclear arsenals to about one-third of their present levels within ten years. The U.S. Senate ratifies the treaty on January 20, 1996. Russia's Duma ratifies the treaty on April 14, 2000.

January 13, 1993: Bush orders a series of **BOMBING RAIDS ON IRAQ**, following Hussein's refusal to allow inspections of Iraq's nuclear sites by U.N. inspectors. Bush is also angered by Iraqi incursions into Kuwait to recover materials from the 1991 war.

1979	1980	1984	1988	1992
	Bush is elected vice president of the United States.			Bush loses the presidency to Democratic opponent Bill Clinton.
Saddam Hussein becomes president of Iraq.	Iraq attacks Iran and the two countries are at war for eight years.	Bush is reelected vice president.	He is elected president.	

William Jefferson "Bill" Clinton

42nd President (1993–2001)

"There is nothing wrong with America that cannot be cured with what is right in America."

Inaugurated at the age of 47, Bill Clinton became the third youngest American president after Theodore Roosevelt and John F. Kennedy, and similar to them, Clinton also brought with him an idealistic spirit of change. He campaigned as a "different kind of Democrat," and promoted a "new covenant" that emphasized community service and individual responsibility. Early in his administration, he also worked to ensure corporate responsibility by promoting and signing the Family and Medical Leave Act, which guaranteed employees the right to take unpaid leave from work to care for a sick relative without losing their jobs.

Clinton devoted enormous energy in his first term to reforming the nation's health care system. In a controversial move, he appointed First Lady Hillary Rodham Clinton to head the reform efforts. An advocate for children and a skilled lawyer in her own right, Mrs. Clinton nonetheless became a lightning rod for opposition. Her commission's proposed overhaul went down in resounding defeat. To make matters worse, a 1993 peacekeeping expedition to Somalia and a federal assault on a Waco, Texas religious cult both ended in fiasco. What's more, accusations had surfaced that the Clintons illegally profited from a phony land deal known as Whitewater. By late 1994, Clinton's popularity had plummeted, and the

Democrats had lost control over Congress for the first time since the Truman administration.

It has been said that Bill Clinton possessed the sharpest political skills of his era. He outmaneuvered the new Republican-led Congress when they threatened to shut down the government unless he cut the Medicaid and Medicare programs. When he refused, the Republicans made good on their threat, and found the public blaming them instead of Clinton for the impasse.

President Clinton had regained the momentum. He promoted increasing the minimum wage and providing student loans in exchange for community service. He also approved a major overhaul of the federal welfare system.

In 1996, he became the first Democrat to be reelected since FDR. But the apparent turnaround was not to last. Allegations soon surfaced that Clinton had an inappropriate relationship with a young White House intern. When he denied it, the House began impeachment hearings against him. Clinton was eventually acquitted, but his reputation had been seriously damaged. Despite presiding over a period of peace and economic prosperity, he will also be remembered by many for the personal flaws that prevented him from achieving greater success.

Biographical Facts

Born: August 19, 1946 in Hope, Arkansas

Ancestry: English and French

Father: William Jefferson Blythe III; born February 27, 1918 in Sherman, Texas; died May 17, 1946 near Sikeston, Missouri

Father's Occupation: Traveling salesman

Stepfather: Roger Clinton; born July 25, 1909; died November 1967

Stepfather's Occupations: Car dealer

Mother: Virginia Dell Cassidy; born June 6, 1923 in Bodcaw, Arkansas; died January 6, 1994 in Hot Springs, Arkansas

Wife: Hillary Diane Rodham; born October 26, 1947 in Park Ridge, Illinois

Marriage: October 11, 1975 in Fayetteville, Arkansas

Child: Chelsea Victoria Clinton (1980-)

Education: Received B.S. from Georgetown University (1968); attended Oxford University; earned J.D. from Yale University Law School (1973)

Religious Affiliation: Baptist

Occupations before Presidency: Professor; lawyer

Military Service: None

Political Offices before Presidency: Attorney General of Arkansas; Governor of Arkansas

Political Party: Democrat

Age at Inauguration: 47

Occupation after Presidency: Writer; political adviser

Nickname: Slick Willie

Writings: *Putting People First; Between Hope and History*

Election of 1992

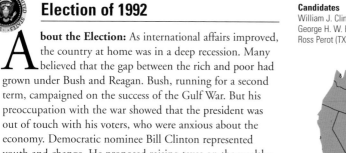

Candidates	Party	Electoral Vote	Popular Vote
William J. Clinton (AR)	Democrat	370	43,682,624
George H. W. Bush (TX)	Republican	168	38,117,331
Ross Perot (TX)	Independent	0	19,217,213

About the Election: As international affairs improved, the country at home was in a deep recession. Many believed that the gap between the rich and poor had grown under Bush and Reagan. Bush, running for a second term, campaigned on the success of the Gulf War. But his preoccupation with the war showed that the president was out of touch with his voters, who were anxious about the economy. Democratic nominee Bill Clinton represented youth and change. He proposed raising taxes on the wealthy to help reduce the federal budget deficit, increasing spending on education, and controlling costs of health care, which called for heavier involvement by the federal government. Bush blamed the recession on the Democratic-controlled Congress, which had refused to enact most of Bush's plans. Texas billionaire Ross Perot ran as an Independent with the federal deficit as his main concern.

Clinton
(370 Votes)
Bush
Perot

Clinton's First Term 1993-1997

January 20, 1993: WILLIAM JEFFERSON CLINTON IS INAUGURATED as the 42nd president of the United States.

January 25, 1993: Clinton appoints First Lady HILLARY RODHAM CLINTON to chair a task force for the revision of the health care system. The task force is to prepare health care reform legislation, which is to be submitted to Congress within one hundred days of Clinton's inauguration.

February 5, 1993: Clinton signs the FAMILY AND MEDICAL LEAVE ACT (FMLA). The act entitles eligible employees to take up to 12 workweeks of unpaid, job-protected leave during any 12-month period for specified family and medical reasons.

February 26, 1993: A TRUCK BOMB EXPLODES IN THE PARKING GARAGE OF THE WORLD TRADE CENTER in New York City leaving six people dead and hundreds injured. Radical Muslim fanatics Sheikh Omar Abdel Rahman and one of his accomplices are convicted for the crime in November 1997.

February 28, 1993: The United States begins sending humanitarian aid supplies to war-torn Bosnia.

March 11, 1993: JANET RENO is confirmed by the United States Senate, and sworn in the next day, becoming the first female attorney general of the United States.

June 27, 1993: Clinton orders a cruise missile attack on Iraqi intelligence headquarters in the Al-Mansur district of Baghdad, in response to the attempted assassination of former U.S. President George Bush during his visit to Kuwait in mid-April.

August 10, 1993: Clinton signs the OMNIBUS BUDGET RECONCILIATION ACT reducing the federal budget deficit by $496 billion through five years. To achieve this target, the act provides for a $255 billion reduction in government spending and an additional income of $241 billion through new taxes.

September 13, 1993: Clinton presides over the signing of the first PEACE ACCORD BETWEEN ISRAEL AND PALESTINE. Israeli Prime Minister Yitzhak Rabin and Palestinian Chairman Yasser Arafat sign the peace agreement at the White House in Washington, D.C. The accord grants Palestine limited self-government on the Gaza Strip and on the occupied West Bank.

September 21, 1993: Clinton signs the bill creating the NATIONAL SERVICE PROGRAM, which provides $1.5 billion over three years to enable students to repay federal educational aid through community service.

October 3, 1993: An encounter between U.S. forces and Somalian guerrillas leaves 18 American soldiers dead and over 50 wounded. Originally sent as part of a UN coalition of forces on a humanitarian mission in December 1992, the forces had become increasingly involved in clashes with Somalian rebels. Clinton announces that all the troops would be recalled by

	1946	1947	1950	1963
■ Clinton's Life				
			North Korea invades South Korea.	
■ U.S. & World Events	William Jefferson Blythe IV is born on August 19 in Hope, Arkansas. He later takes his stepfather's name.	The United Nations divides Palestine into a Jewish state and an Arab state.		As Arkansas' delegate to Boys Nation, Clinton attends the national conference in Washington, D.C., and shakes hands with President Kennedy.

First Lady: Hillary Rodham Clinton

Hillary Diane Rodham excelled academically and demonstrated leadership from an early age. She graduated from Wellesley College and Yale Law School and pursued a successful career in law and public service.

Hillary Rodham Clinton became the first First Lady to be appointed an official position (chair of her husband's Task Force on National Health Care Reform). She was also the first White House spouse to continue her own career (that of a well-respected lawyer). Elected to the Senate in 2000, Mrs. Clinton became the only First Lady to hold a national office after her husband's term ended. Though a lightning rod who is opposed by conservatives, many voters publicly support her ambitious achievements, as does her husband.

Clinton's First Administration

Inauguration: January 20, 1993 at the U.S. Capitol in Washington, D.C.
Vice President: Albert Gore, Jr.
Secretary of State: Warren M. Christopher
Secretary of the Treasury:
Lloyd Bentsen (1993-1994);
Robert Rubin (from January 11, 1995)
Secretary of Defense: Les Aspin;
William J. Perry (from February 3, 1994)
Attorney General: Janet Reno
Secretary of the Interior: Bruce Babbitt
Secretary of Agriculture: Michael Espy;
Dan Glickman (from March 30, 1995)
Secretary of Transportation: Federico Peña
Secretary of Commerce: Ronald Brown;
Michael Kantor (from April 12, 1996)
Secretary of Health and Human Services:
Donna Shalala

Secretary of Labor: Robert Reich
Secretary of Energy: Hazel O'Leary
Secretary of Education: Richard Riley
Secretary of Housing and Urban Development: Henry Cisneros
Secretary of Veterans' Affairs: Jesse Brown
Ambassador to United Nations:
Madeline Albright
Supreme Court Appointments:
Ruth Bader Ginsburg
103rd Congress
(January 3, 1993-January 3,1995)
Senate: 57 Democrats; 43 Republicans
House: 258 Democrats; 176 Republicans
104th Congress
(January 3, 1995-January 3,1997)
Senate: 48 Democrats; 52 Republicans
House: 204 Democrats; 230 Republicans

March 31, 1994. Defense Secretary Les Aspin resigns his post following the incident.

November 30, 1993: President Clinton signs into law the BRADY HANDGUN VIOLENCE PREVENTION ACT, which requires a five-day waiting period when purchasing a handgun and also establishes a national criminal background check system to be used by firearms dealers.

December 8, 1993: Clinton signs into law the NORTH AMERICAN FREE TRADE AGREEMENT in the face of opposition from labor groups. Bringing Mexico into the existing free-trade arrangement between the U.S. and Canada, the act creates the world's biggest free trade zone.

January 14, 1994: Clinton and Russia's president BORIS YELTSIN sign the KREMLIN ACCORDS that stop the preprogrammed aiming of nuclear missiles to specified targets and require the dismantling of nuclear arsenal in the Ukraine.

February 3, 1994: Clinton announces the lifting of the 19-year trade embargo against Vietnam, stating that the South East Asian nation is cooperating with the U.S. in helping to locate over 2,000 Americans still listed as missing since the Vietnam War. The two countries resume free trade in July 2000.

April 22, 1994: FORMER PRESIDENT RICHARD NIXON DIES after suffering from a stroke. Former presidents Bush, Reagan, Carter, and Ford, along with Clinton, attend Nixon's funeral.

May 6, 1994: PAULA CORBIN JONES FILES A LAWSUIT AGAINST CLINTON, alleging sexual harassment and defamation of character. Jones contends in 1991, while Clinton was governor of Arkansas, he had made unwanted sexual advances towards her and later helped to destroy her career because of her refusal.

May 26, 1994: Clinton signs the FREEDOM OF ACCESS TO CLINIC ENTRANCES ACT (FACE) in order to protect abortion clinics, and their staff and clients from violent threats, assault, vandalism and blockades. The act makes it a federal crime to prevent the

1965	1968	1973	
President Johnson sends the first American ground troops to Vietnam.	Civil rights leader Martin Luther King, Jr., is assassinated. Clinton graduates from Georgetown University and begins two years of study at Oxford University as a Rhodes scholar.	Clinton graduates from Yale Law School. He teaches law at University of Arkansas Law School.	U.S., North and South Vietnam, and the Vietcong sign a ceasefire agreement.

Quotes by Clinton:

"I ask you to join in a re-United States. We need to empower our people so they can take more responsibility for their own lives in a world that is ever smaller, where everyone counts... We need a new spirit of community, a sense that we are all in this together, or the American Dream will continue to wither. Our destiny is bound up with the destiny of every other American".

"If you live long enough, you'll make mistakes. But if you learn from them, you'll be a better person. It's how you handle adversity, not how it affects you. The main thing is never quit, never quit, never quit".

"When I was sixteen, I acted like a was forty and when I was forty, I acted like I was sixteen".

Quotes about Clinton:

"Mr. Clinton better watch out if he comes down here. He'd better have a bodyguard".
– *Senator Jesse Helms*

Bill Clinton is not my commander in chief.
– *Oliver North*

operation of abortion clinics.

September 12, 1994: Clinton threatens to use force in order to reinstate Haiti's ousted president Jean Bertrand Aristide to power. American troops land in Haiti to help restore the democratically-elected president to power after militant guerillas take control of the government. Aristide returns to power in October.

September 18, 1994: Clinton signs the **VIOLENT CRIME CONTROL AND LAW ENFORCEMENT ACT**, which extends the death penalty to cover over 50 federal crimes. The act also provides funds to communities for the purpose of hiring 100,000 new policemen and establishing various drug-treatment and educational programs.

November 8, 1994: In the midterm elections, the **REPUBLICAN PARTY GAINS CONTROL OF BOTH HOUSES OF CONGRESS** for the first time in four decades.

January 23, 1995: Clinton signs the **CONGRESSIONAL ACCOUNTABILITY ACT**, requiring Congress to follow the same laws governing the workplace that are being applied to the rest of the country, including laws forbidding discrimination based on gender and race.

June 12, 1995: The Supreme Court, in ***ADARAND CONSTRUCTORS, INC. V. PENA***, rules that all federal affirmative action programs must be "narrowly tailored" and permitted only if there is a "compelling governmental interest."

July 11, 1995: Full diplomatic relations begin between the U.S. and Vietnam after twenty years.

October 1, 1995: A New York Federal Court finds Muslim cleric Sheikh Omar Abdel-Rahman of Egypt, along with nine other Muslims, guilty of plotting to bomb the World Trade Center and the United Nations headquarters in New York City, as well as to assassinate Egypt's president, and to destroy vital New York highway tunnels.

October 2, 1995: Clinton asks Congress to authorize 100 FBI agents to investigate potential terrorist plans and permit the armed forces to probe crimes related to chemical, biological, or nuclear weapons. Congress rejects the proposal.

November 13, 1995: The Clinton administration and Republican-controlled Congress reach a deadlock in negotiations over balancing the budget for the fiscal year of 2002, leading to a **ONE-WEEK SHUTDOWN OF THE FEDERAL GOVERNMENT**.

December 17, 1995: The continuing failure of Clinton and Congress to agree on the budget leads to a second governmental shutdown until the first week of January 1996. Many services, including the issuance of passports, come to a halt. The deadlock in the negotiations centers around welfare programs, Medicare, Medicaid, and tax cuts.

Clinton congratulates Israeli Prime Minister Yitzak Rabin and Palestinian leader Yasser Arafat as they sign the Oslo Accords at the White House.

	1974	1975	1979		1980
■ Clinton's Life					
■ U.S. & World Events	Clinton is defeated by John Paul Hammerschmidt during the general election for the U.S. House of Representatives.	Clinton marries Hillary Rodham.	He is elected governor of Arkansas at 32. He becomes one of the youngest governors in the nation's history.		Clinton loses reelection to Republican rival Frank D. White.

Election of 1996

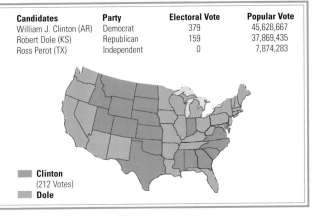

Candidates	Party	Electoral Vote	Popular Vote
William J. Clinton (AR)	Democrat	379	45,628,667
Robert Dole (KS)	Republican	159	37,869,435
Ross Perot (TX)	Independent	0	7,874,283

About the Election: President Clinton and Vice President Gore were renominated without serious opposition. The Republicans nominated Robert J. Dole of Kansas for president and Jack Kemp of New York for vice president. At 72 years of age, Dole was one of the oldest presidential candidates in history. Ross Perot also ran again on the Reform Party ticket. In the presidential campaign, Clinton emphasized improvements his administration had made in the economy, as well as preserving programs, such as Medicare and welfare. Despite questions about his ethics and moral character, Clinton was reelected for a second term.

Clinton (212 Votes)
Dole

January 26, 1996: First Lady **HILLARY CLINTON TESTIFIES BEFORE A FEDERAL GRAND JURY** concerning her investments in the **WHITEWATER** development deal. She is the first wife of a sitting president to be subpoenaed for testifying in a court case. **KENNETH STARR**, the independent federal prosecutor, issues the subpoena to investigate the allegation that the Clintons were involved in illegal real estate dealings in Arkansas.

April 24, 1996: Clinton signs into law an **ANTI-TERRORISM BILL** that provides for new punishments and strategies to fight terrorism. The law authorizes the United States government to deport any noncitizens suspected of terrorism links and bans fundraising in the U.S. by terrorist groups.

May 2, 1996: The House passes the bi-partisan **RYAN WHITE CARE ACT REAUTHORIZATION BILL**, which provides emergency financial relief to cities, states, and local community-based programs affected by the AIDS epidemic.

August 20, 1996: Clinton signs a bill that raises the minimum wage from $4.25 to $5.15 per hour, giving ten million Americans a salary increase just before the November presidential election.

November 5, 1996: **CLINTON IS REELECTED**, defeating the Republican candidate Robert Dole. Republicans retain their majority in both houses of Congress.

Clinton's Second Term 1997-2001

January 20, 1997: **CLINTON IS SWORN IN** for a second term.
March 21, 1997: Clinton and Russia's president Boris Yeltsin confer at Helsinki about European security, the future of arms limitation, and the importance of Russian economic growth for the Russian Federation.

May 27, 1997: The Supreme Court, in *JONES V. CLINTON*, allows the Paula Jones' sexual harassment suit against the president to proceed during his term in office.

October 22, 1997: In a speech before the National Geographic Society, Clinton proposes a $5 billion tax incentive package to encourage the conservation of energy and the development of technology that would steadily decrease American dependence on fossil fuel.

December 29, 1997: Clinton approves the opening of an Iranian gas pipeline from Turkmenistan. He gives his approval following Iran's agreement to pay for all construction costs within the border of Turkey.

February 2, 1998: President Clinton signs the first balanced budget in three decades.

March 6, 1998: The **SENATE GOVERNMENTAL AFFAIRS COMMITTEE**, probing political-party fundraising in the 1996 elections, reports that there were numerous abuses, the gravest being the attempt by the People's Republic of China to influence the election by illegally contributing to Clinton's campaign.

March 16, 1998: Democratic fundraiser Johnny Chung pleads guilty to charges of illegally channeling $20,000 to the Clinton-Gore campaign in 1995.

August 7, 1998: The U.S. embassies in Kenya and Tanzania are blown up by car bombs, leaving several hundred dead. Four men—a Tanzanian, a Jordanian, a Saudi Arabian, and an American citizen involved in the bombing are tried by a U.S. District Court on February 5, 2001, on charges of plotting with the Islamic terrorist **OSAMA BIN LADEN** to blow up the embassies.

August 20, 1998: Clinton orders cruise missile bombings on

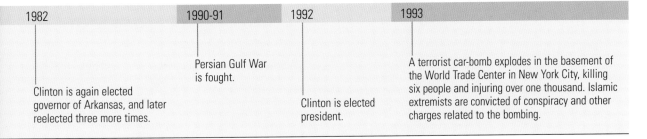

1982	1990-91	1992	1993

Persian Gulf War is fought.

Clinton is again elected governor of Arkansas, and later reelected three more times.

Clinton is elected president.

A terrorist car-bomb explodes in the basement of the World Trade Center in New York City, killing six people and injuring over one thousand. Islamic extremists are convicted of conspiracy and other charges related to the bombing.

Clinton's Second Administration

Inauguration: January 20, 1997 at the U.S. Capitol in Washington, D.C
Vice President: Albert Gore, Jr.
Secretary of State: Madeline Albright
Secretary of the Treasury: Robert Rubin; Lawrence Summers (from July 2, 1999)
Secretary of Defense: William Cohen
Attorney General: Janet Reno
Secretary of the Interior: Bruce Babbitt
Secretary of Agriculture: Dan Glickman
Secretary of Transportation: Rodney Slater
Secretary of Commerce: William Daley; Norman Y. Mineta (from July 21, 2000)
Secretary of Labor: Alexis Herman
Secretary of Health and Human Services: Donna Shalala
Secretary of Energy: Frederico Peña; Bill Richardson (August 18, 1998)

Secretary of Education: Richard Riley
Secretary of Housing and Urban Development: Andrew Cuomo
Secretary of Veterans' Affairs: Jesse Brown; Togo West (from May 5, 1998)
Ambassador to United Nations: Bill Richardson, Richard Holbrooke (from October, 1999)
Supreme Court Appointments: Stephen Breyer
105th Congress (January 3, 1997-January 3, 1999)
Senate: 57 Democrats; 43 Republicans
House: 258 Democrats; 176 Republicans
106th Congress (January 3, 1999-January 3, 2001)
Senate: 57 Democrats; 43 Republicans
House: 258 Democrats; 176 Republicans

November 12, 1998: CLINTON SIGNS THE 1997 KYOTO PROTOCOL adopted under the aegis of the United Nations to combat global warming.

November 13, 1998: CLINTON AGREES TO SETTLE THE PAULA JONES LAWSUIT by paying $850,000.

December 16, 1998: Clinton announces the commencement of OPERATION DESERT FOX. The U.S. and British begin air assaults against Iraq after Saddam Hussein's refusal to allow United Nation inspections for weapons of mass destruction.

March 24, 1999: NATO forces begin OPERATION ALLIED FORCE by conducting bombing raids on Belgrade to coerce Serbians to halt their assaults on Albanian Muslims in the Kosovo province. The bombing continues for another 72 days.

terrorist bases in Afghanistan and on a facility in the Sudan.

September 30, 1998: The Clinton administration attains a budget surplus for the first time since 1969.

April 12, 1999: Clinton is held in contempt of court for falsely testifying in January 1998 during his deposition in the Paula Jones' lawsuit.

September 10, 1999: Clinton pardons 11 members of the Puerto Rican terrorist group ARMED FORCES OF PUERTO RICAN NATIONAL LIBERATION (FALN), who were incarcerated for armed robberies. The House of Representatives condemns the act by a vote of 311 to 41, accusing the president of trying to court New York's Puerto Rican voters for First Lady Hillary Clinton's possible Senate campaign.

September 25, 1999: A Floridian fisherman rescues Elian Gonzalez, a six-year-old Cuban refugee, from a shipwreck. Following a prolonged custody battle between his father in Cuba and his Miami relatives, Gonzalez is taken by U.S. officials

Speaker of the House Newt Gingrich (right), a conservative Republican, looks on as Bill Clinton is inaugurated for the second time in 1997.

	1995	2000	
■ Clinton's Life			
■ U.S. & World Events	Israeli Prime Minister Yitzhak Rabin is assassinated by an Israeli law student with connections to right-wing extremists.	With the results of the 2000 election in dispute, the Supreme Court votes 5-4 to halt a vote recount. Texas governor George W. Bush is elected president.	Mrs. Hillary Rodham Clinton is elected to the Senate.

on April 22, 2000 and returned to his father in Cuba on June 28.

November 28–December 4, 1999: The Seattle summit meeting of the **WORLD TRADE ORGANIZATION (WTO)** is disrupted by thousands of activists protesting the economic policies of global business.

January 2000: The United States government announces a $184 billion surplus.

March 1, 2000: The House approves by a unanimous vote the resolution allowing Social Security recipients to earn unlimited income without losing benefits. The Senate also passes a unanimous vote on it on March 22.

March 22, 2000: A class-action suit filed against the federal government by female employees is settled by a payment of $508 million. Women employees of the U.S. Information Agency had filed the suit after being denied promotions.

April 24, 2000: The **STATE DEPARTMENT'S BUREAU OF INTELLIGENCE AND RESEARCH** is disciplined following the loss of sensitive information after the loss of a laptop computer.

June 4, 2000: Clinton and Russia's newly-elected president Vladimir Putin sign an agreement to build a Russian-U.S. center designed to detect missile launches, and to permanently dispose of 34 tons of weapons-grade plutonium from each of the countries' weapons' stock.

June 12, 2000: Former President Richard M. Nixon is awarded $18 million as a reward for documents and recordings seized by the Justice Department after Nixon's resignation.

June 26, 2000: The **HUMAN GENOME PROJECT** and Celera Genomics announce that they have finished the "first draft" (over 90 percent) of the **HUMAN GENOME SEQUENCE**. The project endeavoured to map the human genome down to the nucleotide level and to identify all present genes, which number approximately 30,000 to 35,000 genes.

July 8, 2000: The plans for the **$60 BILLION NATIONAL MISSILE DEFENSE SYSTEM** receives a setback after a new high-speed missile interceptor fails in testing.

August 16, 2000: The Democratic Convention nominates Vice President **AL GORE** for president.

August 23, 2000: Federal National Institutes of Health repeal the existing prohibition on medical research involving human embryonic stem cells.

August 31, 2000: President Clinton formally vetoes a Republican-backed repeal of the federal estate tax.

September 20, 2000: Special prosecutor Robert W. Ray concludes the Whitewater inquiry after failing to find any wrongdoing by the president and first lady.

Scandal! The Monica Lewinsky Affair

The Monica Lewinsky scandal erupted after Kenneth Starr, the independent prosecutor investigating Clinton's involvement in the Whitewater development deal in Arkansas, initiated an inquiry into whether Clinton had committed perjury in a sexual harassment case filed against him by a former Arkansas government employee. The lawsuit was filed by Paula Jones who alleged that Clinton had made unwanted advances towards her when he was Arkansas governor in 1991. Jones' lawyers who were seeking to establish Clinton's "pattern of behavior" in order to buttress their case against him had come across Monica Lewinsky's affair with Clinton.

Lewinsky, as a White House intern, had an affair with the president, the details of which she revealed to her 'friend' Linda Tripp. The secret tapes made by Tripp during her conversations with Lewinsky eventually fell in the hands of Jones' lawyers and Kenneth Starr. President Clinton was subpoenaed to testify in Jones' case, during which he denied his affair with Lewinsky. He also allegedly asked Lewinsky to make the same denial. The Whitewater prosecutor doubted Clinton's testimony and began collecting evidence to prove the president's guilt of lying and covering up his affair with Lewinsky.

By the beginning of 1998, the president's affair was exposed, and Clinton immediately denied it. After further revelations into the affair, he confessed that he had the affair and apologized for having misled people about it. Starr relentlessly collected 'proof' of Clinton's relationship with Lewinsky, and by the end of 1998, Congress had begun impeachment proceedings against President Clinton on two counts—lying under oath and obstruction of justice. The Senate eventually acquitted Clinton in February 1999.

October 10, 2000: Clinton signs into law legislation that creates normal trade relations with China.

October 12, 2000: Two Islamic suicide bombers ram an explosive-laden raft into USS destroyer *Cole* while it was refueling in Aden, Yemen. The bomb kills 17 Americans and injures 37. An inquiry into the incident concludes that the captain and crew did not take necessary security precautions.

November 7, 2000: **FIRST LADY HILLARY CLINTON IS ELECTED TO THE SENATE,** winning a seat from New York.

2001
Two hijacked 757 airliners speed into the twin towers of the World Trade Center in New York City, causing the collapse of both towers and killing almost 3,000 people. A third hijacked plane crashes into the Pentagon building in Washington, D.C, and a fourth plane in Pennsylvania.

2002
Energy giant Enron collapses—the largest bankruptcy in U.S. history—and the U.S. Justice department begins its criminal investigation of business practices at the company.

2003
North Korea's president Kim Jong II withdraws from the Nuclear Non-Proliferation Treaty, and the country reactivates its nuclear development program.

George Walker Bush

43rd President (2001–2005)

"Terrorist attacks can shake the foundations of our biggest buildings, but they cannot touch the foundation of America. These acts shatter steel, but they cannot dent the steel of American resolve."

In 2000, public opinion in the United States was bitterly divided. Although even many Democrats viewed Bill Clinton as personally flawed, many also still favored his policies. Yet Republicans and many independents were ready for change. George W. Bush, governor of Texas, and son of former President Bush, who Clinton had defeated in 1992, promised to bring about that change. Arguing that he was a "uniter, not a divider" and a "compassionate conservative" who would "change the tone" in Washington, Bush ran a close race with Clinton's vice president Al Gore.

On Election Day, Bush lost the popular vote to Gore. However, the electoral vote was contested due to irregularities in Florida. Ultimately, the Supreme Court ruled to stop the partial recount of the Florida vote, awarding the election to Bush. He became the first son of a president since John Quincy Adams to become president himself. And like the younger Adams, he had won in a disputed election.

When Bush took office, he persuaded Congress to approve the greatest tax cut since the Reagan administration. Two years later, faced with a lagging economic recession, he pushed through an even larger cut. He shaped the agenda on education reform by imposing annual standardized tests for students. In foreign affairs, Bush shifted policy away from the direction that Clinton had followed. Generally distrustful of international treaties that he viewed as counter to U.S. self-interest, Bush rejected a long-sought agreement on global warming known as the Kyoto Protocol.

The September 11, 2001 terrorist attacks on New York City and Washington, D.C. shifted the focus of the administration. In the weeks after the attacks, most Americans rallied to the president's side, as he vowed to wage a war on worldwide terrorism. That fall, American forces moved into Afghanistan and crushed the Taliban government that had supported the Al Qaeda terrorist forces.

Charging that Iraqi leader Saddam Hussein held weapons of mass destruction and was an imminent threat to the United States, Bush then convinced Congress to authorize an invasion of Iraq. In the spring of 2003, despite global opposition, Bush launched arguably the first preemptive war in American history. Although the Iraqi government collapsed, allowing Bush to proclaim "Mission Accomplished," the war continued to provoke domestic controversy and global anger, particularly when no weapons of mass destruction were found a full year after occupation. Heading into the 2004 election season, the nation remained at least as divided as it was four years before. Although a majority of Americans credited him for his strong response against terrorism, widespread job loss throughout his term threatened Bush's chances for a second term.

Biographical Facts

Born: July 6, 1946 in New Haven, Connecticut

Ancestry: English

Father: George Herbert Walker Bush; born June 12, 1924 in Milton, Massachusetts

Father's Occupations: Co-founder of Zapata Petroleum and Zapata Off-Shore; U.S. Congressman; CIA Director; Republican National Committee Chairman; U.S. Vice President; U.S. President;

Mother: Barbara Pierce Bush; born June 8, 1925 in NewYork, New York,

Wife: Laura Welch Bush; born November 4, 1946 in Midland, Texas,

Marriage: November 5, 1977 in Midland, Texas

Children: Barbara Bush (1981-); Jenna Bush (1981-)

Home: Bush ranch, Crawford, Texas

Education: Received B.A. from Yale University (1968), received M.B.A. from Harvard University (1975)

Religious Affiliation: Methodist

Occupations before Presidency: Board Member, Tom Brown, Inc.; Founder, CEO of Bush Exploration; General Partner, Texas Rangers Baseball Organization

Military Service: Texas Air National Guard

Political offices before Presidency: Governor of Texas

Political Party: Republican

Age at Inauguration: 55

Nickname: Dubya

Writings: *A Charge to Keep*

Election of 2000

Candidates	Party	Electoral Vote	Popular Vote
George W. Bush (TX)	Republican	271	50,459,211
Albert Gore (TN)	Democrat	267	51,003,894
Ralph Nader (CT)	Green Party	0	2,834,410
Patrick Buchanan (VA)	Reform Party	0	446,743

About the Election: During his campaign for presidency, Bush condemned the scandals of the Clinton administration and pledged to restore honor to the White House. Vice President Albert Gore, the Democratic nominee, argued that Bush's proposal to use a federal budget surplus to cut taxes was dangerous, and that programs, such as Social Security and Medicare, would be left without sufficient funds. In an effort to avoid being tied to Clinton scandals, Gore proved hesitant to discuss the Clinton administration's record of achievement, focusing instead on his own plans for the future.

The presidential race was the closest in American history. Although Gore won the popular vote, Bush appeared to have won the electoral vote by winning Florida by several hundred votes. However, because a number of votes were disputed, Florida election officials conducted a recount. An initial machine recount confirmed Bush's win. However, when it appeared that voting irregularities in certain counties had cost Gore votes, he demanded that manual recounts be done. In response, the Bush campaign sued to prevent those recounts.

Bush
233 (Votes)
Gore

While the Florida Supreme Court ruled that the recount should continue, the United States Supreme Court overruled the lower court, and on a 5-4 vote, ordered that the recount be halted, giving Bush Florida's electoral votes, and thus the presidency.

Bush's Term 2001-2005

January 20, 2001: Former Texas Governor **GEORGE BUSH IS SWORN IN** as the 43rd president of the United States.

January 22, 2001: **BUSH WARNS IRAQI PRESIDENT SADDAM HUSSEIN** to comply with the U.N. resolution against the development of biological, chemical, and nuclear weapons imposed on Iraq following the 1991 Persian Gulf War.

January 29, 2001: President Bush proposes a $48 million plan to extend prescription drug coverage to 9.5 million Medicare recipients.

February 8, 2001: Bush sends his **$1.6 TRILLION TAX-CUT PROPOSAL** to Congress. On March 8, the House passes the main part of the president's proposal.

February 9, 2001: While conducting its routine rapid-surfacing exercise, nuclear submarine U.S.S. *Greenville* sinks a Japanese fishing boat off the Hawaiian coast, killing nine people.

March 14, 2001: Bush, stressing the need to maintain low energy prices, announces that utility companies will not be enjoined to curb carbon dioxide emissions, thereby effectively

rejecting the U.S. commitment to the **KYOTO PROTOCOL**, a global pact to fight global warming. Bush is vehemently condemned for this announcement. A year later, the Bush administration releases an alternative plan to the Kyoto Protocol.

March 31, 2001: A U.S. Navy spy plane on a surveillance mission on the southern coast of China collides with a Chinese fighter and is forced to make an emergency landing on Hainan Island. The Chinese government detains both the crew and the plane, and eventually releases them after tense negotiations.

April 2, 2001: The Senate passes the **FINANCE REFORM BILL** prohibiting large, unlimited donations to political parties. The legislation also creates limits on special-interest promotion.

April 25, 2001: Bush confirms that the U.S. has been providing the Taiwanese government with new submarines.

April 29, 2001: The Bush administration announces its intention to build a **MISSILE DEFENSE SHIELD**, thereby rejecting the 1972 Anti-Ballistic Missile Treaty. Bush argues that the treaty, an obsolete contract from the Cold War, gives little protection against terrorist attacks. He states that the shield will allow for sharp reductions in America's nuclear stock.

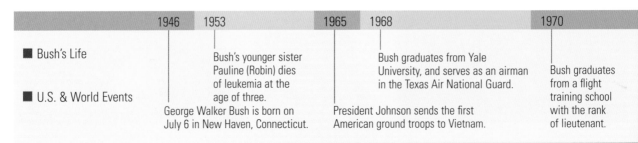

	1946	1953	1965	1968	1970
■ Bush's Life		Bush's younger sister Pauline (Robin) dies of leukemia at the age of three.		Bush graduates from Yale University, and serves as an airman in the Texas Air National Guard.	Bush graduates from a flight training school with the rank of lieutenant.
■ U.S. & World Events		George Walker Bush is born on July 6 in New Haven, Connecticut.		President Johnson sends the first American ground troops to Vietnam.	

First Lady: Laura Welch Bush

Laura Welch Bush holds a Bachelor's degree in education and a Masters in Library Science. She pursued both careers until the birth of her twins, Barbara and Jenna, in 1981.

As first lady of Texas and as the nation's First Lady, Mrs. Bush continues to focus on education, literacy and family issues. Her national initiative "Ready to Read, Ready to Learn," stresses a family literacy approach that begins long before school. Her annual National Book Festivals feature prominent authors and illustrators. Though often regarded as quiet, in November 2001, Mrs. Bush spoke out during her husband's radio address on behalf of the oppressed women and children of Afghanistan, and took an active role in his campaign for reelection in 2004.

June 7, 2001: Bush signs a $1.35 TRILLION TAX-CUT BILL that refunds all taxpayers and reduces tax rates particularly for the higher brackets over a ten-year period.

June 11, 2001: Bush makes his first overseas trip as president to Europe, visiting Belgium, Poland, Sweden, and Slovenia. In Belgium, Bush attends a meeting with the NORTH ATLANTIC COUNCIL, the most powerful subgroup of NATO, and disappoints many European allies with his strong opposition to the Kyoto Protocol and his plans for a missile defense shield.

June 14, 2001: The Senate approves legislation incorporating Bush's proposal to reform the education system through mandatory annual standardized tests. The program also penalizes schools whose students have not shown improvement.

June 28, 2001: The United States Court of Appeals for the District of Columbia overturns a lower court's ruling that approves the splitting of MICROSOFT CORPORATION into two competing companies.

July 25, 2001: U.S. rejects a draft agreement to implement the 1972 Biological Weapon Convention that prohibits countries from manufacturing or acquiring biological weapons.

August 2, 2001: The House passes an energy bill that includes legislation for drilling in the Arctic National Wildlife Refuge in Alaska. On March 19, the Senate will reject the proposal to open the Refuge for oil exploration.

August 9, 2001: EMBRYONIC STEM CELL RESEARCH is approved for federal funding after a controversial decision by the president. Bush announces that the federal government will fund limited research on already existing human embryonic stem cells.

September 11, 2001: HIJACKERS FLY TWO JETLINERS INTO THE TWIN TOWERS OF THE WORLD TRADE CENTER in New York City. Another plane slams into the Pentagon in Washington, D.C., and a fourth plane crashes in western Pennsylvania. The terrorist attack results in the death of 2,995 people,

Bush's Administration

Inauguration: January 20, 2001 at the U.S. Capitol in Washington D.C.
Vice President: Richard Cheney
Secretary of State: Colin L. Powell
Secretary of the Treasury: Paul H. O'Neill; John W. Snow (from February 3, 2003)
Secretary of Defense: Donald H. Rumsfeld
Attorney General: John Ashcroft
Secretary of the Interior: Gale Norton
Secretary of Agriculture: Ann M. Veneman
Secretary of Transportation: Norman Y. Mineta
Secretary of Commerce: Don Evans
Secretary of Labor: Elaine Chao
Secretary of Health and Human Services: Tommy G. Thompson
Secretary of Housing and Urban Development: Melquiades Martinez

Secretary of Energy: Spencer Abraham
Secretary of Education: Rod Paige
Secretary of Veterans' Affairs: Anthony Principi
Secretary of Homeland Security: Tom Ridge
Ambassador to United Nations: John Negroponte
Supreme Court Appointments: None through April 2004
108th Congress
(January 3, 2001-January 3, 2003)
Senate: 50 Democrats; 49 Republicans, 1 other
House: 212 Democrats, 221 Repubicans, 2 others
109th Congress
(January 3, 2003-January 3, 2005)
Senate: 48 Democrats; 51 Republicans, 1 other
House: 205 Democrats, 225 Republicans

1973	1975	1977	1975	1979	1980
U.S., North and South Vietnam and the Viet Cong sign a cease-fire agreement.		He marries Laura Welch, and makes a failed bid for a seat in the U.S. House of Representatives. Bush graduates from Harvard Business School and receives his M.B.A. degree.		Saddam Hussein becomes the president of Iraq. Bush incorporates his oil-exploration firm, Arbusto Energy, later called the Bush Exploration Company.	Iraq attacks Iran, and the two countries are at war for eight years.

Quotes by Bush:

"America has never been united by blood or birth or soil. We are bound by ideals that move us beyond our backgrounds, lift us above our interests and teach us what it means to be citizens. Every child must be taught these principles. Every citizen must uphold them. And every immigrant, by embracing these ideals, makes our country more, not less, American."

Quotes about Bush:

"Bush is unusually incurious, abnormally unintelligent, amazingly inarticulate, fantastically uncultured, extraordinarily uneducated, and apparently proud of all of these things."
– Christopher Hitchens

"When Bush talks you feel he is talking from his gut; you don't hear the sound of pollsters and consultants hovering in the background."
– Michael Beschloss

"George Bush was not elected by a majority of voters in the United States. He was appointed by God."
–General William Boykin,

including all 265 people aboard the four planes.

September 12, 2001: Bush in a speech to Cabinet members and congressional leaders in the White House condemns the "deliberate and deadly" attacks, which are more than acts of terror but "acts of war." The president travels to the site of the collapsed Twin Towers two days later to see the extent of devastation caused by the terrorist attacks.

September 14, 2001: All U.S. military forces throughout the world are placed on the highest level of alert, known as **FORCE PROTECTION CONDITION DELTA**.

September 19, 2001: The U.S. Defense Department deploys dozens of combat aircraft to the Persian Gulf, the Indian Ocean, and the former Soviet republics of Uzbekistan and Tajikistan.

September 20, 2001: Addressing a televised joint session of Congress, Bush orders the Taliban government of Afghanistan to hand over **OSAMA BIN LADEN**, the wealthy Saudi Arabian exile, to the United States. Bin Laden is the prime suspect in the September 11 attacks.

September 24, 2001: Bush by executive order calls upon U.S. financial institutions to freeze the assets of 27 groups and individuals suspected to have links with terrorists.

October 7, 2001: The U.S. and Britain conduct air strikes against **AL QAEDA AND TALIBAN MILITIA TERRORIST BASES IN AFGHANISTAN**. Bush announces that the raids are the beginning of a "sustained, comprehensive and relentless" campaign against terrorists responsible for September 11 attacks. Three days later, the president releases a most-wanted list of terrorists, which includes Bin Laden and 21 other terrorists wanted for the past 16 years.

October 26, 2001: President Bush signs the **PATRIOT ACT**, a controversial anti-terrorism bill authorizing law enforcement and intelligence agencies to investigate terrorist suspects, and carry out wiretapping and surveillance.

November 6, 2001: Bush addresses a 17-nation anti-terrorism summit in Warsaw in hopes of strengthening the U.S.-led coalition against global terrorism.

December 2, 2001: **ENRON CORPORATION**, the multi-billion dollar energy company, announces bankruptcy, adversely affecting financial markets worldwide.

January 8, 2002: President Bush signs the **NO CHILD LEFT BEHIND ACT**, which promises nearly $1 billion a year over the next five years to strengthen public schools.

January 29, 2002: In his first **STATE OF THE UNION ADDRESS** to Congress, Bush mainly discusses the fight against terrorism and the need for homeland security. He refers to North Korea, Iran, and Iraq as forming an "axis of evil."

March 18, 2002: General Tommy Franks, head of the U.S. Central Command, declares the successful end of the U.S.-led military operation in Afghanistan's Shahkot mountain range.

May 13, 2002: The United States and Russia announce their agreement to reduce their countries' stock of nuclear weapons by two-thirds over the next decade. President Bush and the Russia's president Vladimir Putin sign a **NUCLEAR ARMS REDUCTION TREATY** on May 24.

June 6, 2002: Bush proposes the creation of a new Cabinet department, the **DEPARTMENT OF HOMELAND SECURITY** that merges government agencies to better coordinate domestic protections against terrorism. Congress clears the **HOMELAND SECURITY DEPARTMENT BILL** on November 19.

July 15, 2002: The U.S. Senate approves the bill providing a comprehensive overhaul of laws governing corporate fraud, securities, and accounting. The new measure is in response to a wave of corporation accounting scandals.

September 12, 2002: Bush urges the U.N. to halt **IRAQ'S DEVELOPMENT OF WEAPONS OF MASS DESTRUCTION**, warning that inaction would make a military confrontation with Iraq "unavoidable."

September 12, 2002: Bush sends to Congress a draft resolution granting him the power to use all

	1984	1988	1990-91	1993
■ Bush's Life	Bush's company merges with another small oil firm, Spectrum 7 Energy Corporation, and Bush becomes Spectrums's chief executive officer.	His father, George Herbert Walker Bush, is elected president.	The Persian Gulf War is fought.	Bush is investigated by the Securities and Exchange Commission regarding his sale of Harken shares right before the company declares significant losses in 1990. No charges are brought against him.
■ U.S. & World Events				

necessary means "including force," to destroy Iraqi weapons of mass destruction.

November 5, 2002: In the Congressional elections, the REPUBLICAN PARTY GAINS CONTROL OF CONGRESS.

Januray 24, 2003: TOM RIDGE, former governor of Pennsylvania, becomes the first Secretary of Homeland Security.

January 28, 2003: U.S SPACE SHUTTLE COLUMBIA DISINTEGRATES IN THE SKY upon its reentry into the Earth's atmosphere after completing its 16-day scientific mission. All its seven crew members are killed and debris of the shuttle is scattered across the states of Texas and Louisiana.

March 7, 2003: The U.S., Britain, and Spain set a deadline of March 17 for the U.N. Security Council to prove that Iraq has fully complied with its disarmament obligations.

March 21, 2003: The U.S. military launches a major air campaign, dubbed "SHOCK AND AWE," against Iraq's capital as U.S. ground troops secure control of southern portions of the country. The attack is followed by worldwide protests around the world, including demonstrations in London, New York City, and other cities in Europe, across the U.S. and the Middle East.

March 25, 2003: The Bush administration asks Congress to authorize $74.7 billion for the war in Iraq. The House approves a $ 86.9-billion package on October 17 to fund American military operations in Iraq and Afghanistan, as well as the reconstruction of Iraq.

March 25, 2003: Bush issues an executive order delaying the public release of government documents for three years.

April 15, 2003: President Bush declares the COLLAPSE OF SADDAM'S HUSSEIN REGIME. On May 1, he announces the end of combat operations in Iraq.

May 28, 2003: Bush signs the bill providing for $330 BILLION IN TAX CUTS and $20 billion in federal assistance to the states.

July 24, 2003: The Joint Congressional Committee on Intelligence releases its reports after a ten-month long probe into intelligence failures leading up to the September 11 attacks.

November 6, 2003: In an address to the National Endowment for Democracy in Washington, D.C., Bush calls for an extensive democratic transformation of the Middle East.

December 13, 2003: U.S. FORCES CAPTURE SADDAM HUSSEIN, former Iraqi president, in a small underground hideout near the village of Ad Dawr, nine miles from the Iraqi city of Tikrit. The U.S. announces Hussein's arrest the next day.

January 7, 2004: Bush proposes to grant temporary legal status to illegal aliens working in the U.S. He proposes the granting of a six year permit to such workers.

January 14, 2004: Bush unveils his plan to create a human colony on the moon that will ultimately become a base for a manned EXPEDITION TO MARS.

January 15, 2004: NASA establishes the Office of Exploration Systems to develop technologies for the planned mission to the moon and Mars.

March 2, 2004: SENATOR JOHN KERRY wins the Democratic presidental nomination and prepares for his campaign against President Bush in November.

On September 11, 2001, two hijacked airliners struck the World Trade Center towers in New York City, destroying both buildings and killing almost 3,000 people. A third plane hit the Pentagon outside of Washington D.C. and a fourth, believed to be headed for the White House, crashed in Western Pennsylvania.

2000

After a contested election, the U.S. Supreme Court halts a recount of ballots in Florida and Bush is elected president.

2001

Two hijacked 757 airliners speed into the twin towers of the World Trade Center in New York City, causing the collapse of both towers. A third hijacked plane crashes into the Pentagon building in Washington, D.C., and a fourth plane in Pennsylvania. Al Qaeda, an Islamic fundamentalist terrorist group, is believed to be responsible.

2003

U.S. invades Iraq to oust dictator Saddam Hussein, who is suspected of hiding weapons of mass destruction.

INAUGURAL ADDRESSES

George Washington

First Inaugural Address In the City of New York

Thursday, April 30, 1789

Fellow-Citizens of the Senate and of the House of Representatives:

Among the vicissitudes incident to life no event could have filled me with greater anxieties than that of which the notification was transmitted by your order, and received on the 14th day of the present month. On the one hand, I was summoned by my country, whose voice I can never hear but with veneration and love, from a retreat which I had chosen with the fondest predilection, and, in my flattering hopes, with an immutable decision, as the asylum of my declining years—a retreat which was rendered every day more necessary as well as more dear to me by the addition of habit to inclination, and of frequent interruptions in my health to the gradual waste committed on it by time. On the other hand, the magnitude and difficulty of the trust to which the voice of my country called me, being sufficient to awaken in the wisest and most experienced of her citizens a distrustful scrutiny into his qualifications, could not but overwhelm with despondence one who (inheriting inferior endowments from nature and unpracticed in the duties of civil administration) ought to be peculiarly conscious of his own deficiencies. In this conflict of emotions all I dare aver is that it has been my faithful study to collect my duty from a just appreciation of every circumstance by which it might be affected. All I dare hope is that if, in executing this task, I have been too much swayed by a grateful remembrance of former instances, or by an affectionate sensibility to this transcendent proof of the confidence of my fellow-citizens, and have thence too little consulted my incapacity as well as disinclination for the weighty and untried cares before me, my error will be palliated by the motives which mislead me, and its consequences be judged by my country with some share of the partiality in which they originated.

Such being the impressions under which I have, in obedience to the public summons, repaired to the present station, it would be peculiarly improper to omit in this first official act my fervent supplications to that Almighty Being who rules over the universe, who presides in the councils of nations, and whose providential aids can supply every human defect, that His benediction may consecrate to the liberties and happiness of the people of the United States a Government instituted by themselves for these essential purposes, and may enable every instrument employed in its administration to execute with success the functions allotted to his charge. In tendering this homage to the Great Author of every public and private good, I assure myself that it expresses your sentiments not less than my own, nor those of my fellow-citizens at large less than either. No people can be bound to acknowledge and adore the Invisible Hand which conducts the affairs of men more than those of the United States. Every step by which they have advanced to the character of an independent nation seems to have been distinguished by some token of providential agency; and in the important revolution just accomplished in the system of their united government the tranquil deliberations and voluntary consent of so many distinct communities from which the event has resulted can not be compared with the means by which most governments have been established without some return of pious gratitude, along with an humble anticipation of the future blessings which the past seem to presage. These reflections, arising out of the present crisis, have forced themselves too strongly on my mind to be suppressed. You will join with me, I trust, in thinking that there are none under the influence of which the proceedings of a new and free government can more auspiciously commence.

By the article establishing the executive department it is made the duty of the President "to recommend to your consideration such measures as he shall judge necessary and expedient." The circumstances under which I now meet you will acquit me from entering into that subject further than to refer to the great constitutional charter under which you are assembled, and which, in defining your powers, designates the objects to which your attention is to be given. It will be more consistent with those circumstances, and far more congenial with the feelings which actuate me, to substitute, in place of a recommendation of particular measures, the tribute that is due to the talents, the rectitude, and the patriotism which adorn the characters selected to devise and adopt them. In these honorable qualifications I behold the surest pledges that as on one side no local prejudices or attachments, no separate views nor party animosities, will misdirect the comprehensive and equal eye which ought to watch over this great assemblage of communities and interests, so, on another, that the foundation of our national policy will be laid in the pure and immutable principles of private morality, and the preeminence of free government be exemplified by all the attributes which can win the affections of its citizens and command the respect of the world. I dwell on this prospect with every satisfaction which an ardent love for my country can inspire, since there is no truth more thoroughly established than that there exists in the economy and course of nature an indissoluble union between virtue and happiness; between duty and advantage; between the genuine maxims of an honest and magnanimous policy and the solid rewards of public prosperity and felicity; since we ought to be no less persuaded that the propitious smiles of Heaven can never be expected on a nation that disregards the eternal rules of order and right which Heaven itself has ordained; and since the preservation of the sacred fire of liberty and the destiny of the republican model of government are justly considered, perhaps, as deeply, as finally, staked on the experiment entrusted to the hands of the American people.

Besides the ordinary objects submitted to your care, it will remain with your judgment to decide how far an exercise of the occasional power delegated by the fifth article of the Constitution is rendered expedient at the present juncture by the nature of objections which have been urged against the system, or by the degree of inquietude which has given birth to them. Instead of undertaking particular recommendations on this subject, in which I could be guided by no lights derived from official opportunities, I shall again give way to my entire confidence in your discernment and pursuit of the public good; for I assure myself that whilst you carefully avoid every alteration which might endanger the benefits of an united and effective government, or which ought to await the future lessons of experience, a reverence for the characteristic rights of freemen and a regard for the public harmony will sufficiently influence your deliberations on the question how far the former can be impregnably fortified or the latter be safely and advantageously promoted.

To the foregoing observations I have one to add, which will be most properly addressed to the House of Representatives. It concerns myself, and will therefore be as brief as possible. When I was first honored with a call into the service of my country, then on the eve of an arduous struggle for its liberties, the light in which I contemplated my duty required that I should renounce every pecuniary compensation. From this resolution I have in no instance departed; and being still under the impressions which produced it, I must decline as inapplicable to myself any share in the personal emoluments which may be indispensably included in a permanent provision for the executive department, and must accordingly pray that the pecuniary estimates for the station in which I am placed may during my continuance in it be limited to such actual expenditures as the public good may be thought to require.

Having thus imparted to you my sentiments as they have been awakened by the occasion which brings us together, I shall take my present leave; but not without resorting once more to the benign Parent of the Human Race in humble supplication that, since He has been pleased to favor the American people with opportunities for deliberating in perfect tranquillity, and dispositions for deciding with unparalleled unanimity on a form of government for the security of their union and the advancement of their happiness, so His divine blessing may be equally conspicuous in the enlarged views, the temperate consultations, and the wise measures on which the success of this Government must depend.

Second Inaugural Address In the City of Philadelphia

Monday, March 4, 1793

Fellow Citizens:

I am again called upon by the voice of my country to execute the functions of its Chief Magistrate. When the occasion proper for it shall arrive, I shall endeavor to express the high sense I entertain of this distinguished honor, and of the confidence which has been reposed in me by the people of united America.

Previous to the execution of any official act of the President the Constitution requires an oath of office. This oath I am now about to take, and in your presence: That if it shall be found during my administration of the Government I have in any instance violated willingly or knowingly the injunctions thereof, I may (besides incurring constitutional punishment) be subject to the upbraidings of all who are now witnesses of the present solemn ceremony.

John Adams

Inaugural Address In the City of Philadelphia

Saturday, March 4, 1797

When it was first perceived, in early times, that no middle course for America remained between unlimited submission to a foreign legislature and a total independence of its claims, men of reflection were less apprehensive of danger from the formidable power of fleets and armies they must determine to resist than from those contests and dissensions which would certainly arise concerning the forms of government to be instituted over the whole and over the parts of this extensive country. Relying, however, on the purity of their intentions, the justice of their cause, and the integrity and intelligence of the people, under an overruling Providence which had so signally protected this country from the first, the representatives of this nation, then consisting of little more than half its present number, not only broke to pieces the chains which were forging and the rod of iron that was lifted up, but frankly cut asunder the ties which had bound them, and launched into an ocean of uncertainty.

The zeal and ardor of the people during the Revolutionary war, supplying the place of government, commanded a degree of order sufficient at least for the temporary preservation of society. The Confederation which was early felt to be necessary was prepared from the models of the Batavian and Helvetic confederacies, the only examples which remain with any detail and precision in history, and certainly the only ones which the people at large had ever considered. But reflecting on the striking difference in so many particulars between this country and those where a courier may go from the seat of government to the frontier in a single day, it was then certainly foreseen by some who assisted in Congress at the formation of it that it could not be durable.

Negligence of its regulations, inattention to its recommendations, if not disobedience to its authority, not only in individuals but in States, soon appeared with their melancholy consequences—universal languor, jealousies and rivalries of States, decline of navigation and commerce, discouragement of necessary manufactures, universal fall in the value of lands and their produce, contempt of public and private faith, loss of consideration and credit with foreign nations, and at length in discontents, animosities, combinations, partial conventions, and insurrection, threatening some great national calamity.

In this dangerous crisis the people of America were not abandoned by their usual good sense, presence of mind, resolution, or integrity. Measures were pursued to concert a plan to form a more perfect union, establish justice, insure domestic tranquillity, provide for the common defense, promote the general welfare, and secure the blessings of liberty. The public disquisitions, discussions, and deliberations issued in the present happy Constitution of Government.

Employed in the service of my country abroad during the whole course of these transactions, I first saw the Constitution of the United States in a foreign country. Irritated by no literary altercation, animated by no public debate, heated by no party animosity, I read it with great satisfaction, as the result of good heads prompted by good hearts, as an experiment better adapted to the genius, character, situation, and relations of this nation and country than any which had ever been proposed or suggested. In its general principles and great outlines it was conformable to such a system of government as I had ever most esteemed, and in some States, my own native State in particular, had contributed to establish. Claiming a right of suffrage, in common with my fellow-citizens, in the adoption or rejection of a constitution which was to rule me and my posterity, as well as them and theirs, I did not hesitate to express my approbation of it on all occasions, in public and in private. It was not then, nor has been since, any objection to it in my mind that the Executive and Senate were not more permanent. Nor have I ever entertained a thought of promoting any alteration in it but such as the people themselves, in the course of their experience, should see and feel to be necessary or expedient, and by their representatives in Congress and the State legislatures, according to the Constitution itself, adopt and ordain.

Returning to the bosom of my country after a painful separation from it for ten years, I had the honor to be elected to a station under the new order of things, and I have repeatedly laid myself under the most serious obligations to support the Constitution. The operation of it has equaled the most sanguine expectations of its friends, and from an habitual attention to it, satisfaction in its administration, and delight in its effects upon the peace, order, prosperity, and happiness of the nation I have acquired an habitual attachment to it and veneration for it.

What other form of government, indeed, can so well deserve our esteem and love?

There may be little solidity in an ancient idea that congregations of men into cities and nations are the most pleasing objects in the sight of superior intelligences, but this is very certain, that to a benevolent human mind there can be no spectacle presented by any nation more pleasing, more noble, majestic, or august, than an assembly like that which has so often been seen in this and the other Chamber of Congress, of a Government in which the Executive authority, as well as that of all the branches of the Legislature, are exercised by citizens selected at regular periods by their neighbors to make and execute laws for the general good. Can anything essential, anything more than mere ornament and decoration, be added to this by robes and diamonds? Can authority be more amiable and respectable when it descends from accidents or institutions established in remote antiquity than when it springs fresh from the hearts and judgments of an honest and enlightened people? For it is the people only that are represented. It is their power and majesty that is reflected, and only for their good, in every legitimate government, under whatever form it may appear. The existence of such a government as ours for any length of time is a full proof of a general dissemination of knowledge and virtue throughout the whole body of the people. And what object or consideration more pleasing than this can be presented to the human mind? If national pride is ever justifiable or excusable it is when it springs, not from power or riches, grandeur or glory, but from conviction of national innocence, information, and benevolence.

In the midst of these pleasing ideas we should be unfaithful to ourselves if we should ever lose sight of the danger to our liberties if anything partial or extraneous should infect the purity of our free, fair, virtuous, and independent elections. If an election is to be determined by a majority of a single vote, and that can be procured by a party through artifice or corruption, the Government may be the choice of a party for its own ends, not of the nation for the national good. If that solitary suffrage can be obtained by foreign nations by flattery or menaces, by fraud or violence, by terror, intrigue, or venality, the Government may not be the choice of the American people, but of foreign nations. It may be foreign nations who govern us, and not we, the people, who govern ourselves; and candid men will acknowledge that in such cases choice would have little advantage to boast of over lot or chance.

Such is the amiable and interesting system of government

(and such are some of the abuses to which it may be exposed) which the people of America have exhibited to the admiration and anxiety of the wise and virtuous of all nations for eight years under the administration of a citizen who, by a long course of great actions, regulated by prudence, justice, temperance, and fortitude, conducting a people inspired with the same virtues and animated with the same ardent patriotism and love of liberty to independence and peace, to increasing wealth and unexampled prosperity, has merited the gratitude of his fellow-citizens, commanded the highest praises of foreign nations, and secured immortal glory with posterity.

In that retirement which is his voluntary choice may he long live to enjoy the delicious recollection of his services, the gratitude of mankind, the happy fruits of them to himself and the world, which are daily increasing, and that splendid prospect of the future fortunes of this country which is opening from year to year. His name may be still a rampart, and the knowledge that he lives a bulwark, against all open or secret enemies of his country's peace. This example has been recommended to the imitation of his successors by both Houses of Congress and by the voice of the legislatures and the people throughout the nation.

On this subject it might become me better to be silent or to speak with diffidence; but as something may be expected, the occasion, I hope, will be admitted as an apology if I venture to say that if a preference, upon principle, of a free republican government, formed upon long and serious reflection, after a diligent and impartial inquiry after truth; if an attachment to the Constitution of the United States, and a conscientious determination to support it until it shall be altered by the judgments and wishes of the people, expressed in the mode prescribed in it; if a respectful attention to the constitutions of the individual States and a constant caution and delicacy toward the State governments; if an equal and impartial regard to the rights, interest, honor, and happiness of all the States in the Union, without preference or regard to a northern or southern, an eastern or western, position, their various political opinions on unessential points or their personal attachments; if a love of virtuous men of all parties and denominations; if a love of science and letters and a wish to patronize every rational effort to encourage schools, colleges, universities, academies, and every institution for propagating knowledge, virtue, and religion among all classes of the people, not only for their benign influence on the happiness of life in all its stages and classes, and of society in all its forms, but as the only means of preserving our Constitution from its natural enemies, the spirit of sophistry, the spirit of party, the spirit of intrigue, the profligacy of corruption, and the pestilence of foreign influence, which is the angel of destruction to elective governments; if a love of equal laws, of justice, and humanity in the interior administration; if an inclination to improve agriculture, commerce, and manufacturers for necessity, convenience, and defense; if a spirit of equity and humanity toward the aboriginal nations of America, and a disposition to meliorate their condition by inclining them to be more friendly to us, and our citizens to be more friendly to them; if an inflexible determination to maintain peace and inviolable faith with all nations, and that system of neutrality and impartiality among the belligerent powers of Europe which has been adopted by this Government and so solemnly sanctioned by both Houses of Congress and applauded by the legislatures of the States and the public opinion, until it shall be otherwise ordained by Congress; if a personal esteem for the French nation, formed in a residence of seven years chiefly among them, and a sincere desire to preserve the friendship which has been so much for the honor and interest of both nations; if, while the conscious honor and integrity of the people of America and the internal sentiment of their own power and energies must be preserved, an earnest endeavor to investigate every just cause and remove every colorable pretense of complaint; if an intention to pursue by amicable negotiation a reparation for the injuries that have been committed on the commerce of our fellow-citizens by whatever nation, and if success can not be obtained, to lay the facts before the Legislature, that they may consider what further measures the honor and interest of the Government and its constituents demand; if a resolution to do justice as far as may depend upon me, at all times and to all nations, and maintain peace, friendship, and benevolence with all the world; if an unshaken confidence in the honor, spirit, and resources of the American people, on which I have so often hazarded my all and never been deceived; if elevated ideas of the high destinies of this country and of my own duties toward it, founded on a knowledge of the moral principles and intellectual improvements of the people deeply engraven on my mind in early life, and not obscured but exalted by experience and age; and, with humble reverence, I feel it to be my duty to

add, if a veneration for the religion of a people who profess and call themselves Christians, and a fixed resolution to consider a decent respect for Christianity among the best recommendations for the public service, can enable me in any degree to comply with your wishes, it shall be my strenuous endeavor that this sagacious injunction of the two Houses shall not be without effect.

With this great example before me, with the sense and spirit, the faith and honor, the duty and interest, of the same American people pledged to support the Constitution of the United States, I entertain no doubt of its continuance in all its energy, and my mind is prepared without hesitation to lay myself under the most solemn obligations to support it to the utmost of my power.

And may that Being who is supreme over all, the Patron of Order, the Fountain of Justice, and the Protector in all ages of the world of virtuous liberty, continue His blessing upon this nation and its Government and give it all possible success and duration consistent with the ends of His providence.

Thomas Jefferson

First Inaugural Address In the Washington, D.C

Wednesday, March 4, 1801

Friends and Fellow-Citizens:

Called upon to undertake the duties of the first executive office of our country, I avail myself of the presence of that portion of my fellow-citizens which is here assembled to express my grateful thanks for the favor with which they have been pleased to look toward me, to declare a sincere consciousness that the task is above my talents, and that I approach it with those anxious and awful presentiments which the greatness of the charge and the weakness of my powers so justly inspire. A rising nation, spread over a wide and fruitful land, traversing all the seas with the rich productions of their industry, engaged in commerce with nations who feel power and forget right, advancing rapidly to destinies beyond the reach of mortal eye—when I contemplate these transcendent objects, and see the honor, the happiness, and the hopes of this beloved country committed to the issue, and the auspices of this day, I shrink from the contemplation, and humble myself before the magnitude of the undertaking. Utterly, indeed, should I despair did not the presence of many whom I here see remind me that in the other high authorities provided by our Constitution I shall find resources of wisdom, of virtue, and of zeal on which to rely under all difficulties. To you, then, gentlemen, who are charged with the sovereign functions of legislation, and to those associated with you, I look with encouragement for that guidance and support which may enable us to steer with safety the vessel in which we are all embarked amidst the conflicting elements of a troubled world.

During the contest of opinion through which we have passed the animation of discussions and of exertions has sometimes worn an aspect which might impose on strangers unused to think freely and to speak and to write what they think; but this being now decided by the voice of the nation, announced according to the rules of the Constitution, all will, of course, arrange themselves under the will of the law, and unite in common efforts for the common good. All, too, will bear in mind this sacred principle, that though the will of the majority is in all cases to prevail, that will to be rightful must be reasonable; that the minority possess their equal rights, which equal law must protect, and to violate

would be oppression. Let us, then, fellow-citizens, unite with one heart and one mind. Let us restore to social intercourse that harmony and affection without which liberty and even life itself are but dreary things. And let us reflect that, having banished from our land that religious intolerance under which mankind so long bled and suffered, we have yet gained little if we countenance a political intolerance as despotic, as wicked, and capable of as bitter and bloody persecutions. During the throes and convulsions of the ancient world, during the agonizing spasms of infuriated man, seeking through blood and slaughter his long-lost liberty, it was not wonderful that the agitation of the billows should reach even this distant and peaceful shore; that this should be more felt and feared by some and less by others, and should divide opinions as to measures of safety. But every difference of opinion is not a difference of principle. We have called by different names brethren of the same principle. We are all Republicans, we are all Federalists. If there be any among us who would wish to dissolve this Union or to change its republican form, let them stand undisturbed as monuments of the safety with which error of opinion may be tolerated where reason is left free to combat it. I know, indeed, that some honest men fear that a republican government can not be strong, that this Government is not strong enough; but would the honest patriot, in the full tide of successful experiment, abandon a government which has so far kept us free and firm on the theoretic and visionary fear that this Government, the world's best hope, may by possibility want energy to preserve itself? I trust not. I believe this, on the contrary, the strongest Government on earth. I believe it the only one where every man, at the call of the law, would fly to the standard of the law, and would meet invasions of the public order as his own personal concern. Sometimes it is said that man can not be trusted with the government of himself. Can he, then, be trusted with the government of others? Or have we found angels in the forms of kings to govern him? Let history answer this question.

Let us, then, with courage and confidence pursue our own Federal and Republican principles, our attachment to union and representative government. Kindly separated by nature and a wide ocean from the exterminating havoc of one quarter of the globe; too high-minded to endure the degradations of the others; possessing a chosen country, with room enough for our descendants to the thousandth and thousandth generation; entertaining a due sense of our equal right to the use of our own faculties, to the acquisitions of our own industry, to honor and confidence from our fellow-citizens, resulting not from birth, but from our actions and their sense of them; enlightened by a benign religion, professed, indeed, and practiced in various forms, yet all of them inculcating honesty, truth, temperance, gratitude, and the love of man; acknowledging and adoring an overruling Providence, which by all its dispensations proves that it delights in the happiness of man here and his greater happiness hereafter—with all these blessings, what more is necessary to make us a happy and a prosperous people? Still one thing more, fellow-citizens—a wise and frugal Government, which shall restrain men from injuring one another, shall leave them otherwise free to regulate their own pursuits of industry and improvement, and shall not take from the mouth of labor the bread it has earned. This is the sum of good government, and this is necessary to close the circle of our felicities.

About to enter, fellow-citizens, on the exercise of duties which comprehend everything dear and valuable to you, it is proper you should understand what I deem the essential principles of our Government, and consequently those which ought to shape its Administration. I will compress them within the narrowest compass they will bear, stating the general principle, but not all its limitations. Equal and exact justice to all men, of whatever state or persuasion, religious or political; peace, commerce, and honest friendship with all nations, entangling alliances with none; the support of the State governments in all their rights, as the most competent administrations for our domestic concerns and the surest bulwarks against antirepublican tendencies; the preservation of the General Government in its whole constitutional vigor, as the sheet anchor of our peace at home and safety abroad; a jealous care of the right of election by the people—a mild and safe corrective of abuses which are lopped by the sword of revolution where peaceable remedies are unprovided; absolute acquiescence in the decisions of the majority, the vital principle of republics, from which is no appeal but to force, the vital principle and immediate parent of despotism; a well disciplined militia, our best reliance in peace and for the first moments of war, till regulars may relieve them; the supremacy of the civil over the military authority; economy in

the public expense, that labor may be lightly burthened; the honest payment of our debts and sacred preservation of the public faith; encouragement of agriculture, and of commerce as its handmaid; the diffusion of information and arraignment of all abuses at the bar of the public reason; freedom of religion; freedom of the press, and freedom of person under the protection of the habeas corpus, and trial by juries impartially selected. These principles form the bright constellation which has gone before us and guided our steps through an age of revolution and reformation. The wisdom of our sages and blood of our heroes have been devoted to their attainment. They should be the creed of our political faith, the text of civic instruction, the touchstone by which to try the services of those we trust; and should we wander from them in moments of error or of alarm, let us hasten to retrace our steps and to regain the road which alone leads to peace, liberty, and safety.

I repair, then, fellow-citizens, to the post you have assigned me. With experience enough in subordinate offices to have seen the difficulties of this the greatest of all, I have learnt to expect that it will rarely fall to the lot of imperfect man to retire from this station with the reputation and the favor which bring him into it. Without pretensions to that high confidence you reposed in our first and greatest revolutionary character, whose preeminent services had entitled him to the first place in his country's love and destined for him the fairest page in the volume of faithful history, I ask so much confidence only as may give firmness and effect to the legal administration of your affairs. I shall often go wrong through defect of judgment. When right, I shall often be thought wrong by those whose positions will not command a view of the whole ground. I ask your indulgence for my own errors, which will never be intentional, and your support against the errors of others, who may condemn what they would not if seen in all its parts. The approbation implied by your suffrage is a great consolation to me for the past, and my future solicitude will be to retain the good opinion of those who have bestowed it in advance, to conciliate that of others by doing them all the good in my power, and to be instrumental to the happiness and freedom of all.

Relying, then, on the patronage of your good will, I advance with obedience to the work, ready to retire from it whenever you become sensible how much better choice it is in your power to make. And may that Infinite Power which rules the destinies of the universe lead our councils to what is best, and give them a favorable issue for your peace and prosperity.

Second Inaugural Address

Monday, March 4, 1805

Proceeding, fellow-citizens, to that qualification which the Constitution requires before my entrance on the charge again conferred on me, it is my duty to express the deep sense I entertain of this new proof of confidence from my fellow-citizens at large, and the zeal with which it inspires me so to conduct myself as may best satisfy their just expectations. On taking this station on a former occasion I declared the principles on which I believed it my duty to administer the affairs of our Commonwealth. My conscience tells me I have on every occasion acted up to that declaration according to its obvious import and to the understanding of every candid mind.

In the transaction of your foreign affairs we have endeavored to cultivate the friendship of all nations, and especially of those with which we have the most important relations. We have done them justice on all occasions, favored where favor was lawful,

and cherished mutual interests and intercourse on fair and equal terms. We are firmly convinced, and we act on that conviction, that with nations as with individuals our interests soundly calculated will ever be found inseparable from our moral duties, and history bears witness to the fact that a just nation is trusted on its word when recourse is had to armaments and wars to bridle others.

At home, fellow-citizens, you best know whether we have done well or ill. The suppression of unnecessary offices, of useless establishments and expenses, enabled us to discontinue our internal taxes. These, covering our land with officers and opening our doors to their intrusions, had already begun that process of domiciliary vexation which once entered is scarcely to be restrained from reaching successively every article of property and produce. If among these taxes some minor ones fell which had not been inconvenient, it was because their amount would not have paid the officers who collected them, and because, if they had any merit, the State authorities might adopt them instead of others less approved.

The remaining revenue on the consumption of foreign articles is paid chiefly by those who can afford to add foreign luxuries to domestic comforts, being collected on our seaboard and frontiers only, and incorporated with the transactions of our mercantile citizens, it may be the pleasure and the pride of an American to ask, What farmer, what mechanic, what laborer ever sees a taxgatherer of the United States? These contributions enable us to support the current expenses of the Government, to fulfill contracts with foreign nations, to extinguish the native right of soil within our limits, to extend those limits, and to apply such a surplus to our public debts as places at a short day their final redemption, and that redemption once effected the revenue thereby liberated may, by a just repartition of it among the States and a corresponding amendment of the Constitution, be applied in time of peace to rivers, canals, roads, arts, manufactures, education, and other great objects within each State. In time of war, if injustice by ourselves or others must sometimes produce war, increased as the same revenue will be by increased population and consumption, and aided by other resources reserved for that crisis, it may meet within the year all the expenses of the year without encroaching on the rights of future generations by burthening them with the debts of the past. War will then be but a suspension of useful works, and a return to a state of peace, a return to the progress of improvement.

I have said, fellow-citizens, that the income reserved had enabled us to extend our limits, but that extension may possibly pay for itself before we are called on, and in the meantime may keep down the accruing interest; in all events, it will replace the advances we shall have made. I know that the acquisition of Louisiana had been disapproved by some from a candid apprehension that the enlargement of our territory would endanger its union. But who can limit the extent to which the federative principle may operate effectively? The larger our association the less will it be shaken by local passions; and in any view is it not better that the opposite bank of the Mississippi should be settled by our own brethren and children than by strangers of another family? With which should we be most likely to live in harmony and friendly intercourse?

In matters of religion I have considered that its free exercise is placed by the Constitution independent of the powers of the General Government. I have therefore undertaken on no occasion to prescribe the religious exercises suited to it, but have left them, as the Constitution found them, under the direction and discipline of the church or state authorities acknowledged by the several religious societies.

The aboriginal inhabitants of these countries I have regarded with the commiseration their history inspires. Endowed with the faculties and the rights of men, breathing an ardent love of liberty and independence, and occupying a country which left them no desire but to be undisturbed, the stream of overflowing population from other regions directed itself on these shores; without power to divert or habits to contend against it, they have been overwhelmed by the current or driven before it; now reduced within limits too narrow for the hunter's state, humanity enjoins us to teach them agriculture and the domestic arts; to encourage them to that industry which alone can enable them to maintain their place in existence and to prepare them in time for that state of society which to bodily comforts adds the improvement of the mind and morals. We have therefore liberally furnished them with the implements of husbandry and household use; we have placed among them instructors in the arts of first necessity, and they are covered with the aegis of the law against aggressors from among ourselves.

But the endeavors to enlighten them on the fate which awaits their present course of life, to induce them to exercise their reason, follow its dictates, and change their pursuits with the change of circumstances have powerful obstacles to encounter; they are combated by the habits of their bodies, prejudices of their minds, ignorance, pride, and the influence of interested and crafty individuals among them who feel themselves something in the present order of things and fear to become nothing in any other. These persons inculcate a sanctimonious reverence for the customs of their ancestors; that whatsoever they did must be done through all time; that reason is a false guide, and to advance under its counsel in their physical, moral, or political condition is perilous innovation; that their duty is to remain as their Creator made them, ignorance being safety and knowledge full of danger; in short, my friends, among them also is seen the action and counteraction of good sense and of bigotry; they too have their antiphilosophists who find an interest in keeping things in their present state, who dread reformation, and exert all their faculties to maintain the ascendancy of habit over the duty of improving our reason and obeying its mandates.

In giving these outlines I do not mean, fellow-citizens, to arrogate to myself the merit of the measures. That is due, in the first place, to the reflecting character of our citizens at large, who, by the weight of public opinion, influence and strengthen the public measures. It is due to the sound discretion with which they select from among themselves those to whom they confide the legislative duties. It is due to the zeal and wisdom of the characters thus selected, who lay the foundations of public happiness in wholesome laws, the execution of which alone remains for others, and it is due to the able and faithful auxiliaries, whose patriotism has associated them with me in the executive functions.

During this course of administration, and in order to disturb it, the artillery of the press has been leveled against us, charged with whatsoever its licentiousness could devise or dare. These abuses of an institution so important to freedom and science are deeply to be regretted, inasmuch as they tend to lessen its usefulness and to sap its safety. They might, indeed, have been corrected by the wholesome punishments reserved to and provided by the laws of the several States against falsehood and defamation, but public duties more urgent press on the time of public servants, and the offenders have therefore been left to find their punishment in the public indignation.

Nor was it uninteresting to the world that an experiment should be fairly and fully made, whether freedom of discussion, unaided by power, is not sufficient for the propagation and protection of truth—whether a government conducting itself in the true spirit of its constitution, with zeal and purity, and doing no act which it would be unwilling the whole world should witness, can be written down by falsehood and defamation. The experiment has been tried; you have witnessed the scene; our fellow-citizens looked on, cool and collected; they saw the latent source from which these outrages proceeded; they gathered around their public functionaries, and when the Constitution called them to the decision by suffrage, they pronounced their verdict, honorable to those who had served them and consolatory to the friend of man who believes that he may be trusted with the control of his own affairs.

No inference is here intended that the laws provided by the States against false and defamatory publications should not be enforced; he who has time renders a service to public morals and public tranquillity in reforming these abuses by the salutary coercions of the law; but the experiment is noted to prove that, since truth and reason have maintained their ground against false opinions in league with false facts, the press, confined to truth, needs no other legal restraint; the public judgment will correct false reasoning and opinions on a full hearing of all parties; and no other definite line can be drawn between the inestimable liberty of the press and its demoralizing licentiousness. If there be still improprieties which this rule would not restrain, its supplement must be sought in the censorship of public opinion.

Contemplating the union of sentiment now manifested so generally as auguring harmony and happiness to our future course, I offer to our country sincere congratulations. With those, too, not yet rallied to the same point the disposition to do so is gaining strength; facts are piercing through the veil drawn over them, and our doubting brethren will at length see that the mass of their fellow-citizens with whom they can not yet resolve to act as to principles and measures, think as they think and desire what they desire; that our wish as well as theirs is that the public efforts may be directed honestly to the public good, that peace be cultivated, civil and religious liberty unassailed, law and order preserved, equality of rights maintained, and that state of property, equal or unequal, which results to every man from his own industry or that of his father's. When satisfied of these views it is not in human nature that they should not approve and support them. In the meantime let us cherish them with patient affection, let us do them justice, and more than justice, in all competitions of interest; and

we need not doubt that truth, reason, and their own interests will at length prevail, will gather them into the fold of their country, and will complete that entire union of opinion which gives to a nation the blessing of harmony and the benefit of all its strength.

I shall now enter on the duties to which my fellow-citizens have again called me, and shall proceed in the spirit of those principles which they have approved. I fear not that any motives of interest may lead me astray; I am sensible of no passion which could seduce me knowingly from the path of justice, but the weaknesses of human nature and the limits of my own understanding will produce errors of judgment sometimes injurious to your interests. I shall need, therefore, all the indulgence which I have heretofore experienced from my constituents; the want of it will certainly not lessen with increasing years. I shall need, too, the favor of that Being in whose hands we are, who led our fathers, as Israel of old, from their native land and planted them in a country flowing with all the necessaries and comforts of life; who has covered our infancy with His providence and our riper years with His wisdom and power, and to whose goodness I ask you to join in supplications with me that He will so enlighten the minds of your servants, guide their councils, and prosper their measures that whatsoever they do shall result in your good, and shall secure to you the peace, friendship, and approbation of all nations.

James Madison

First Inaugural Address

Saturday, March 4, 1809

Unwilling to depart from examples of the most revered authority, I avail myself of the occasion now presented to express the profound impression made on me by the call of my country to the station to the duties of which I am about to pledge myself by the most solemn of sanctions. So distinguished a mark of confidence, proceeding from the deliberate and tranquil suffrage of a free and virtuous nation, would under any circumstances have commanded my gratitude and devotion, as well as filled me with an awful sense of the trust to be assumed. Under the various circumstances which give peculiar solemnity to the existing period, I feel that both the honor and the responsibility allotted to me are inexpressibly enhanced.

The present situation of the world is indeed without a parallel, and that of our own country full of difficulties. The pressure of these, too, is the more severely felt because they have fallen upon us at a moment when the national prosperity being at a height not before attained, the contrast resulting from the change has been rendered the more striking. Under the benign influence of our republican institutions, and the maintenance of peace with all nations whilst so many of them were engaged in bloody and wasteful wars, the fruits of a just policy were enjoyed in an unrivaled growth of our faculties and resources. Proofs of this were seen in the improvements of agriculture, in the successful enterprises of commerce, in the progress of manufacturers and useful arts, in the increase of the public revenue and the use made of it in reducing the public debt, and in the valuable works and establishments everywhere multiplying over the face of our land.

It is a precious reflection that the transition from this prosperous condition of our country to the scene which has for some time been distressing us is not chargeable on any unwarrantable views, nor, as I trust, on any involuntary errors in the public councils. Indulging no passions which trespass on the

rights or the repose of other nations, it has been the true glory of the United States to cultivate peace by observing justice, and to entitle themselves to the respect of the nations at war by fulfilling their neutral obligations with the most scrupulous impartiality. If there be candor in the world, the truth of these assertions will not be questioned; posterity at least will do justice to them.

This unexceptionable course could not avail against the injustice and violence of the belligerent powers. In their rage against each other, or impelled by more direct motives, principles of retaliation have been introduced equally contrary to universal reason and acknowledged law. How long their arbitrary edicts will be continued in spite of the demonstrations that not even a pretext for them has been given by the United States, and of the fair and liberal attempt to induce a revocation of them, can not be anticipated. Assuring myself that under every vicissitude the determined spirit and united councils of the nation will be safeguards to its honor and its essential interests, I repair to the post assigned me with no other discouragement than what springs from my own inadequacy to its high duties. If I do not sink under the weight of this deep conviction it is because I find some support in a consciousness of the purposes and a confidence in the principles which I bring with me into this arduous service.

To cherish peace and friendly intercourse with all nations having correspondent dispositions; to maintain sincere neutrality toward belligerent nations; to prefer in all cases amicable discussion and reasonable accommodation of differences to a decision of them by an appeal to arms; to exclude foreign intrigues and foreign partialities, so degrading to all countries and so baneful to free ones; to foster a spirit of independence too just to invade the rights of others, too proud to surrender our own, too liberal to indulge unworthy prejudices ourselves and too elevated not to look down upon them in others; to hold the union of the

States as the basis of their peace and happiness; to support the Constitution, which is the cement of the Union, as well in its limitations as in its authorities; to respect the rights and authorities reserved to the States and to the people as equally incorporated with and essential to the success of the general system; to avoid the slightest interference with the right of conscience or the functions of religion, so wisely exempted from civil jurisdiction; to preserve in their full energy the other salutary provisions in behalf of private and personal rights, and of the freedom of the press; to observe economy in public expenditures; to liberate the public resources by an honorable discharge of the public debts; to keep within the requisite limits a standing military force, always remembering that an armed and trained militia is the firmest bulwark of republics—that without standing armies their liberty can never be in danger, nor with large ones safe; to promote by authorized means improvements friendly to agriculture, to manufactures, and to external as well as internal commerce; to favor in like manner the advancement of science and the diffusion of information as the best aliment to true liberty; to carry on the benevolent plans which have been so meritoriously applied to the conversion of our aboriginal neighbors from the degradation and wretchedness of savage life to a participation of the improvements of which the human mind and manners are susceptible in a civilized state—as far as

sentiments and intentions such as these can aid the fulfillment of my duty, they will be a resource which can not fail me.

It is my good fortune, moreover, to have the path in which I am to tread lighted by examples of illustrious services successfully rendered in the most trying difficulties by those who have marched before me. Of those of my immediate predecessor it might least become me here to speak. I may, however, be pardoned for not suppressing the sympathy with which my heart is full in the rich reward he enjoys in the benedictions of a beloved country, gratefully bestowed or exalted talents zealously devoted through a long career to the advancement of its highest interest and happiness.

But the source to which I look or the aids which alone can supply my deficiencies is in the well-tried intelligence and virtue of my fellow-citizens, and in the counsels of those representing them in the other departments associated in the care of the national interests. In these my confidence will under every difficulty be best placed, next to that which we have all been encouraged to feel in the guardianship and guidance of that Almighty Being whose power regulates the destiny of nations, whose blessings have been so conspicuously dispensed to this rising Republic, and to whom we are bound to address our devout gratitude for the past, as well as our fervent supplications and best hopes for the future.

Second Inaugural Address

Thursday, March 4, 1813

About to add the solemnity of an oath to the obligations imposed by a second call to the station in which my country heretofore placed me, I find in the presence of this respectable assembly an opportunity of publicly repeating my profound sense of so distinguished a confidence and of the responsibility united with it. The impressions on me are strengthened by such an evidence that my faithful endeavors to discharge my arduous duties have been favorably estimated, and by a consideration of the momentous period at which the trust has been renewed. From the weight and magnitude now belonging to it I should be compelled to shrink if I had less reliance on the support of an enlightened and generous people, and felt less deeply a conviction that war with a powerful nation, which forms so prominent a feature in our situation, is stamped with that justice which invites the smiles of Heaven on the means of conducting it to a successful termination.

May we not cherish this sentiment without presumption when we reflect on the characters by which this war is distinguished?

It was not declared on the part of the United States until it had been long made on them, in reality though not in name; until arguments and postulations had been exhausted; until a positive declaration had been received that the wrongs provoking it would not be discontinued; nor until this last appeal could no longer be delayed without breaking down the spirit of the nation, destroying all confidence in itself and in its political institutions, and either perpetuating a state of disgraceful suffering or regaining by more costly sacrifices and more severe struggles our lost rank and respect among independent powers.

On the issue of the war are staked our national sovereignty on the high seas and the security of an important class of citizens, whose occupations give the proper value to those of every other class. Not to contend for such a stake is to surrender our equality with other powers on the element common to all and to violate the sacred title which every member of the society has to its protection. I need not call into view the unlawfulness of the

practice by which our mariners are forced at the will of every cruising officer from their own vessels into foreign ones, nor paint the outrages inseparable from it. The proofs are in the records of each successive Administration of our Government, and the cruel sufferings of that portion of the American people have found their way to every bosom not dead to the sympathies of human nature.

As the war was just in its origin and necessary and noble in its objects, we can reflect with a proud satisfaction that in carrying it on no principle of justice or honor, no usage of civilized nations, no precept of courtesy or humanity, have been infringed. The war has been waged on our part with scrupulous regard to all these obligations, and in a spirit of liberality which was never surpassed.

How little has been the effect of this example on the conduct of the enemy!

They have retained as prisoners of war citizens of the United States not liable to be so considered under the usages of war.

They have refused to consider as prisoners of war, and threatened to punish as traitors and deserters, persons emigrating without restraint to the United States, incorporated by naturalization into our political family, and fighting under the authority of their adopted country in open and honorable war for the maintenance of its rights and safety. Such is the avowed purpose of a Government which is in the practice of naturalizing by thousands citizens of other countries, and not only of permitting but compelling them to fight its battles against their native country.

They have not, it is true, taken into their own hands the hatchet and the knife, devoted to indiscriminate massacre, but they have let loose the savages armed with these cruel instruments; have allured them into their service, and carried them to battle by their sides, eager to glut their savage thirst with the blood of the vanquished and to finish the work of torture and death on maimed and defenseless captives. And, what was never before seen, British commanders have extorted victory over the unconquerable valor of our troops by presenting to the sympathy of their chief captives awaiting massacre from their savage associates. And now we find them, in further contempt of the modes of honorable warfare, supplying the place of a conquering force by attempts to disorganize our political society, to dismember our confederated Republic. Happily, like others, these will recoil on the authors; but they mark the degenerate counsels from which they emanate, and if they did not belong to a sense of unexampled inconsistencies might excite the greater wonder as proceeding from a Government which founded the very war in which it has been so long engaged on a charge against the disorganizing and insurrectional policy of its adversary.

To render the justice of the war on our part the more conspicuous, the reluctance to commence it was followed by the earliest and strongest manifestations of a disposition to arrest its progress. The sword was scarcely out of the scabbard before the enemy was apprised of the reasonable terms on which it would be resheathed. Still more precise advances were repeated, and have been received in a spirit forbidding every reliance not placed on the military resources of the nation.

These resources are amply sufficient to bring the war to an honorable issue. Our nation is in number more than half that of the British Isles. It is composed of a brave, a free, a virtuous, and an intelligent people. Our country abounds in the necessaries, the arts, and the comforts of life. A general prosperity is visible in the public countenance. The means employed by the British cabinet to undermine it have recoiled on themselves; have given to our national faculties a more rapid development, and, draining or diverting the precious metals from British circulation and British vaults, have poured them into those of the United States. It is a propitious consideration that an unavoidable war should have found this seasonable facility for the contributions required to support it. When the public voice called for war, all knew, and still know, that without them it could not be carried on through the period which it might last, and the patriotism, the good sense, and the manly spirit of our fellow-citizens are pledges for the cheerfulness with which they will bear each his share of the common burden. To render the war short and its success sure, animated and systematic exertions alone are necessary, and the success of our arms now may long preserve our country from the necessity of another resort to them. Already have the gallant exploits of our naval heroes proved to the world our inherent capacity to maintain our rights on one element. If the reputation of our arms has been thrown under clouds on the other, presaging flashes of heroic enterprise assure us that nothing is wanting to correspondent triumphs there also but the discipline and habits which are in daily progress.

James Monroe

First Inaugural Address

Tuesday, March 4, 1817

I should be destitute of feeling if I was not deeply affected by the strong proof which my fellow-citizens have given me of their confidence in calling me to the high office whose functions I am about to assume. As the expression of their good opinion of my conduct in the public service, I derive from it a gratification which those who are conscious of having done all that they could to merit it can alone feel. My sensibility is increased by a just estimate of the importance of the trust and of the nature and extent of its duties, with the proper discharge of which the highest interests of a great and free people are intimately connected. Conscious of my own deficiency, I cannot enter on these duties without great anxiety for the result. From a just responsibility I will never shrink, calculating with confidence that in my best efforts to promote the public welfare my motives will always be duly appreciated and my conduct be viewed with that candor and indulgence which I have experienced in other stations.

In commencing the duties of the chief executive office it has been the practice of the distinguished men who have gone before me to explain the principles which would govern them in their respective Administrations. In following their venerated example my attention is naturally drawn to the great causes which have contributed in a principal degree to produce the present happy condition of the United States. They will best explain the nature of our duties and shed much light on the policy which ought to be pursued in future.

From the commencement of our Revolution to the present day almost forty years have elapsed, and from the establishment of this Constitution twenty-eight. Through this whole term the Government has been what may emphatically be called self-government. And what has been the effect? To whatever object we turn our attention, whether it relates to our foreign or domestic concerns, we find abundant cause to felicitate ourselves in the excellence of our institutions. During a period fraught with difficulties and marked by very extraordinary events the United States have flourished beyond example. Their citizens individually have been happy and the nation prosperous.

Under this Constitution our commerce has been wisely regulated with foreign nations and between the States; new States have been admitted into our Union; our territory has been enlarged by fair and honorable treaty, and with great advantage to the original States; the States, respectively protected by the National Government under a mild, parental system against foreign dangers, and enjoying within their separate spheres, by a wise partition of power, a just proportion of the sovereignty, have improved their police, extended their settlements, and attained a strength and maturity which are the best proofs of wholesome laws well administered. And if we look to the condition of individuals what a proud spectacle does it exhibit! On whom has oppression fallen in any quarter of our Union? Who has been deprived of any right of person or property? Who restrained from offering his vows in the mode which he prefers to the Divine Author of his being? It is well known that all these blessings have been enjoyed in their fullest extent; and I add with peculiar satisfaction that there has been no example of a capital punishment being inflicted on anyone for the crime of high treason.

Some who might admit the competency of our Government to these beneficent duties might doubt it in trials which put to the test its strength and efficiency as a member of the great community of nations. Here too experience has afforded us the most satisfactory proof in its favor. Just as this Constitution was put into action several of the principal States of Europe had become much agitated and some of them seriously convulsed. Destructive wars ensued, which have of late only been terminated. In the course of these conflicts the United States received great injury from several of the parties. It was their interest to stand aloof from the contest, to demand justice from the party committing the injury, and to cultivate by a fair and honorable conduct the friendship of all. War became at length inevitable, and the result has shown that our Government is equal to that, the greatest of trials, under the most unfavorable circumstances. Of the virtue of the people and of the heroic exploits of the Army, the Navy, and the militia I need not speak.

Such, then, is the happy Government under which we live—a Government adequate to every purpose for which the social compact is formed; a Government elective in all its branches, under which every citizen may by his merit obtain the highest trust recognized by the Constitution; which contains within it no cause of discord, none to put at variance one portion of the community with another; a Government which protects every citizen in the full enjoyment of his rights, and is able to protect the nation against injustice from foreign powers.

Other considerations of the highest importance admonish us to cherish our Union and to cling to the Government which supports it. Fortunate as we are in our political institutions, we have not been less so in other circumstances on which our prosperity and happiness essentially depend. Situated within the temperate zone, and extending through many degrees of latitude along the Atlantic, the United States enjoy all the varieties of climate, and every production incident to that portion of the globe. Penetrating internally to the Great Lakes and beyond the sources of the great rivers which communicate through our whole interior, no country was ever happier with respect to its domain. Blessed, too, with a fertile soil, our produce has always been very abundant, leaving, even in years the least favorable, a surplus for the wants of our fellow-men in other countries. Such is our peculiar felicity that there is not a part of our Union that is not particularly interested in preserving it. The great agricultural interest of the nation prospers under its protection. Local interests are not less fostered by it. Our fellow-citizens of the North engaged in navigation find great encouragement in being made the favored carriers of the vast productions of the other portions of the United States, while the inhabitants of these are amply recompensed, in their turn, by the nursery for seamen and naval force thus formed and reared up for the support of our common rights. Our manufactures find a generous encouragement by the policy which patronizes domestic industry, and the surplus of our produce a steady and profitable market by local wants in less–favored parts at home.

Such, then, being the highly favored condition of our country, it is the interest of every citizen to maintain it. What are the dangers which menace us? If any exist they ought to be ascertained and guarded against.

In explaining my sentiments on this subject it may be asked, What raised us to the present happy state? How did we accomplish the Revolution? How remedy the defects of the first instrument of our Union, by infusing into the National Government sufficient power for national purposes, without impairing the just rights of the States or affecting those of individuals? How sustain and pass with glory through the late war? The Government has been in the hands of the people. To the people, therefore, and to the faithful and able depositaries of their trust is the credit due. Had the people of the United States been educated in different principles, had they been less intelligent, less independent, or less virtuous, can it be believed that we should have maintained the same steady and consistent career or been blessed with the same success? While, then, the constituent body retains its present sound and healthful state everything will be safe. They will choose competent and faithful representatives for every department. It is only when the people become ignorant and corrupt, when they degenerate into a populace, that they are incapable of exercising the sovereignty. Usurpation is then an easy attainment, and an usurper soon found. The people themselves become the willing instruments of their own debasement and ruin. Let us, then, look to the great cause, and endeavor to preserve it in full force. Let us by all wise and constitutional measures promote intelligence among the people as the best means of preserving our liberties.

Dangers from abroad are not less deserving of attention. Experiencing the fortune of other nations, the United States may be again involved in war, and it may in that event be the object of the adverse party to overset our Government, to break our Union, and demolish us as a nation. Our distance from Europe and the just, moderate, and pacific policy of our Government may form some security against these dangers, but they ought to be anticipated and guarded against. Many of our citizens are engaged in commerce and navigation, and all of them are in a certain degree dependent on their prosperous state. Many are engaged in the fisheries. These interests are exposed to invasion in the wars between other powers, and we should disregard the faithful admonition of experience if we did not expect it. We must support our rights or lose our character, and with it, perhaps, our liberties. A people who fail to do it can scarcely be said to hold a place among independent nations. National honor is national property of the highest value. The sentiment in the mind of every citizen is national strength. It ought therefore to be cherished.

To secure us against these dangers our coast and inland frontiers should be fortified, our Army and Navy, regulated upon just principles as to the force of each, be kept in perfect order, and our militia placed on the best practicable footing. To put our extensive coast in such a state of defense as to secure our cities and interior from invasion will be attended with expense, but the work when finished will be permanent, and it is fair to presume that a single campaign of invasion by a naval force superior to our own, aided by a few thousand land troops, would expose us to greater expense, without taking into the estimate the loss of property and distress of our citizens, than would be sufficient for this great work. Our land and naval forces should be moderate, but adequate to the necessary purposes—the former to garrison and preserve our fortifications and to meet the first invasions of a foreign foe, and, while constituting the elements of a greater force, to preserve the science as well as all the necessary implements of war in a state to be brought into activity in the event of war; the latter, retained within the limits proper in a state of peace, might aid in maintaining the neutrality of the United States with dignity in the wars of other powers and in saving the property of their citizens from spoliation. In time of war, with the enlargement of which the great naval resources of the country render it susceptible, and which should be duly fostered in time of peace, it would contribute essentially, both as an auxiliary of defense and as a powerful engine of annoyance, to diminish the calamities of war and to bring the war to a speedy and honorable termination.

But it ought always to be held prominently in view that the safety of these States and of everything dear to a free people must depend in an eminent degree on the militia. Invasions may be made too formidable to be resisted by any land and naval force which it would comport either with the principles of our Government or the circumstances of the United States to maintain. In such cases recourse must be had to the great body of the people, and in a manner to produce the best effect. It is of the highest importance, therefore, that they be so organized and trained as to be prepared for any emergency. The arrangement should be such as to put at the command of the Government the ardent patriotism and youthful vigor of the country. If formed on equal and just principles, it can not be oppressive. It is the crisis which makes the pressure, and not the laws which provide a remedy for it. This arrangement should be formed, too, in time of peace, to be the better prepared for war. With such an organization of such a people the United States have nothing to dread from foreign invasion. At its approach an overwhelming force of gallant men might always be put in motion.

Other interests of high importance will claim attention, among which the improvement of our country by roads and canals, proceeding always with a constitutional sanction, holds a distinguished place. By thus facilitating the intercourse between the States we shall add much to the convenience and comfort of our fellow-citizens, much to the ornament of the country, and, what is of greater importance, we shall shorten distances, and, by making each part more accessible to and dependent on the other, we shall bind the Union more closely together. Nature has done so much for us by intersecting the country with so many great rivers, bays, and lakes, approaching from distant points so near to each other, that the inducement to complete the work seems to be peculiarly strong. A more interesting spectacle was perhaps never seen than is exhibited within the limits of the United States—a territory so vast and advantageously situated, containing objects so grand, so useful, so happily connected in all their parts!

Our manufacturers will likewise require the systematic and fostering care of the Government. Possessing as we do all the raw materials, the fruit of our own soil and industry, we ought not to depend in the degree we have done on supplies from other countries. While we are thus dependent the sudden event of war, unsought and unexpected, can not fail to plunge us into the most serious difficulties. It is important, too, that the capital which nourishes our manufacturers should be domestic, as its influence in that case instead of exhausting, as it may do in foreign hands, would be felt advantageously on agriculture and every other branch of industry. Equally important is it to provide at home a market for our raw materials, as by extending the competition it will enhance the price and protect the cultivator against the casualties incident to foreign markets.

With the Indian tribes it is our duty to cultivate friendly relations and to act with kindness and liberality in all our transactions. Equally proper is it to persevere in our efforts to extend to them the advantages of civilization.

The great amount of our revenue and the flourishing state of the Treasury are a full proof of the competency of the national resources for any emergency, as they are of the willingness of our fellow-citizens to bear the burdens which the public necessities require. The vast amount of vacant lands, the value of which daily augments, forms an additional resource of great extent and duration. These resources, besides accomplishing every other necessary purpose, put it completely in the power of the United States to discharge the national debt at an early period. Peace is the best time for improvement and preparation of every kind; it is in peace that our commerce flourishes most, that taxes are most easily paid, and that the revenue is most productive.

The Executive is charged officially in the Departments under it with the disbursement of the public money, and is responsible for the faithful application of it to the purposes for which it is raised. The Legislature is the watchful guardian over the public purse. It is its duty to see that the disbursement has been honestly made. To meet the requisite responsibility every facility should be afforded to the Executive to enable it to bring the public agents intrusted with the public money strictly and promptly to account. Nothing should be presumed against them; but if, with the requisite facilities, the public money is suffered to lie long and uselessly in their hands, they will not be the only defaulters, nor

will the demoralizing effect be confined to them. It will evince a relaxation and want of tone in the Administration which will be felt by the whole community. I shall do all I can to secure economy and fidelity in this important branch of the Administration, and I doubt not that the Legislature will perform its duty with equal zeal. A thorough examination should be regularly made, and I will promote it.

It is particularly gratifying to me to enter on the discharge of these duties at a time when the United States are blessed with peace. It is a state most consistent with their prosperity and happiness. It will be my sincere desire to preserve it, so far as depends on the Executive, on just principles with all nations, claiming nothing unreasonable of any and rendering to each what is its due.

Equally gratifying is it to witness the increased harmony of opinion which pervades our Union. Discord does not belong to our system. Union is recommended as well by the free and benign principles of our Government, extending its blessings to every individual, as by the other eminent advantages attending it. The American people have encountered together great dangers and sustained severe trials with success. They constitute one great family with a common interest. Experience has enlightened us on some questions of essential importance to the country. The progress has been slow, dictated by a just reflection and a faithful regard to every interest connected with it. To promote this harmony in accord with the principles of our republican Government and in a manner to give them the most complete effect, and to advance in all other respects the best interests of our Union, will be the object of my constant and zealous exertions.

Never did a government commence under auspices so favorable, nor ever was success so complete. If we look to the history of other nations, ancient or modern, we find no example of a growth so rapid, so gigantic, of a people so prosperous and happy. In contemplating what we have still to perform, the heart of every citizen must expand with joy when he reflects how near our Government has approached to perfection; that in respect to it we have no essential improvement to make; that the great object is to preserve it in the essential principles and features which characterize it, and that is to be done by preserving the virtue and enlightening the minds of the people; and as a security against foreign dangers to adopt such arrangements as are indispensable to the support of our independence, our rights and liberties. If we persevere in the career in which we have advanced so far and in the path already traced, we can not fail, under the favor of a gracious Providence, to attain the high destiny which seems to await us.

In the Administrations of the illustrious men who have preceded me in this high station, with some of whom I have been connected by the closest ties from early life, examples are presented which will always be found highly instructive and useful to their successors. From these I shall endeavor to derive all the advantages which they may afford. Of my immediate predecessor, under whom so important a portion of this great and successful experiment has been made, I shall be pardoned for expressing my earnest wishes that he may long enjoy in his retirement the affections of a grateful country, the best reward of exalted talents and the most faithful and meritorious service. Relying on the aid to be derived from the other departments of the Government, I enter on the trust to which I have been called by the suffrages of my fellow-citizens with my fervent prayers to the Almighty that He will be graciously pleased to continue to us that protection which He has already so conspicuously displayed in our favor.

Second Inaugural Address

Thursday, March 4, 1813

Fellow-Citizens:

I shall not attempt to describe the grateful emotions which the new and very distinguished proof of the confidence of my fellow-citizens, evinced by my reelection to this high trust, has excited in my bosom. The approbation which it announces of my conduct in the preceding term affords me a consolation which I shall profoundly feel through life. The general accord with which it has been expressed adds to the great and never-ceasing obligations which it imposes. To merit the continuance of this good opinion, and to carry it with me into my retirement as the solace of advancing years, will be the object of my most zealous and unceasing efforts.

Having no pretensions to the high and commanding claims of my predecessors, whose names are so much more conspicuously identified with our Revolution, and who contributed so preeminently to promote its success, I consider myself rather as the instrument than the cause of the union which has prevailed in the late election. In surmounting, in favor of my humble pretensions, the difficulties which so often produce division in like occurrences, it is obvious that other powerful causes, indicating the great strength and stability of our Union, have essentially contributed to draw you together. That these powerful causes exist, and that they are permanent, is my fixed opinion; that they may produce a like accord in all questions touching, however remotely, the liberty, prosperity, and happiness of our country will always be the object of my most fervent prayers to the Supreme Author of All Good.

In a government which is founded by the people, who possess exclusively the sovereignty, it seems proper that the person who may be placed by their suffrages in this high trust should declare on commencing its duties the principles on which he intends to conduct the Administration. If the person thus elected has served the preceding term, an opportunity is afforded him to review its principal occurrences and to give such further explanation respecting them as in his judgment may be useful to his constituents. The events of one year have influence on those of another, and, in like manner, of a preceding on the succeeding Administration. The movements of a great nation are connected in all their parts. If errors have been committed they ought to be corrected; if the policy is sound it ought to be supported. It is by a thorough knowledge of the whole subject that our fellow-citizens are enabled to judge correctly of the past and to give a proper direction to the future.

Just before the commencement of the last term the United States had concluded a war with a very powerful nation on conditions equal and honorable to both parties. The events of that war are too recent and too deeply impressed on the memory of all to require a development from me. Our commerce had been in a great measure driven from the sea, our Atlantic and inland frontiers were invaded in almost every part; the waste of life along our coast and on some parts of our inland frontiers, to the defense of which our gallant and patriotic citizens were called, was immense, in addition to which not less than $120,000,000 were added at its end to the public debt.

As soon as the war had terminated, the nation, admonished by its events, resolved to place itself in a situation which should be better calculated to prevent the recurrence of a like evil, and, in case it should recur, to mitigate its calamities. With this view, after reducing our land force to the basis of a peace establishment, which has been further modified since, provision was made for the construction of fortifications at proper points through the whole extent of our coast and such an augmentation of our naval force as should be well adapted to both purposes. The laws making this provision were passed in 1815 and 1816, and it has been since the constant effort of the Executive to carry them into effect.

The advantage of these fortifications and of an augmented naval force in the extent contemplated, in a point of economy, has been fully illustrated by a report of the Board of Engineers and Naval Commissioners lately communicated to Congress, by which it appears that in an invasion by 20,000 men, with a correspondent naval force, in a campaign of six months only, the whole expense of the construction of the works would be defrayed by the difference in the sum necessary to maintain the force which would be adequate to our defense with the aid of those works and that which would be incurred without them. The reason of this difference is obvious. If fortifications are judiciously placed on our great inlets, as distant from our cities as circumstances will permit, they will form the only points of attack, and the enemy will be detained there by a small regular force a sufficient time to enable our militia to collect and repair to that on which the attack is made. A force adequate to the enemy, collected at that single point, with suitable preparation for such others as might be menaced, is all that would be requisite. But if there were no fortifications, then the enemy might go where he pleased, and, changing his position and sailing from place to place, our force must be called out and spread in vast numbers along the whole coast and on both sides of every bay and river as high up in each as it might be navigable for ships of war. By these fortifications, supported by our Navy, to which they would afford like support, we should present to other powers an armed front from St. Croix to the Sabine, which would protect in the event of war our whole coast and interior from invasion; and even in the wars of other powers, in which we were neutral, they would be found eminently useful, as, by keeping their public ships at a distance from our cities, peace and order in them would be preserved and the Government be protected from insult.

It need scarcely be remarked that these measures have not been resorted to in a spirit of hostility to other powers. Such a disposition does not exist toward any power. Peace and good will have been, and will hereafter be, cultivated with all, and by the most faithful regard to justice. They have been dictated by a love of peace, of economy, and an earnest desire to save the lives of our fellow-citizens from that destruction and our country from that devastation which are inseparable from war when it finds us unprepared for it. It is believed, and experience has shown, that such a preparation is the best expedient that can be resorted to prevent war. I add with much pleasure that considerable progress has already been made in these measures of defense, and that they will be completed in a few years, considering the great extent and importance of the object, if the plan be zealously and steadily persevered in.

The conduct of the Government in what relates to foreign powers is always an object of the highest importance to the nation. Its agriculture, commerce, manufactures, fisheries, revenue, in short, its peace, may all be affected by it. Attention is therefore due to this subject.

At the period adverted to the powers of Europe, after having been engaged in long and destructive wars with each other, had concluded a peace, which happily still exists. Our peace with the power with whom we had been engaged had also been concluded.

The war between Spain and the colonies in South America, which had commenced many years before, was then the only conflict that remained unsettled. This being a contest between different parts of the same community, in which other powers had not interfered, was not affected by their accommodations.

This contest was considered at an early stage by my predecessor a civil war in which the parties were entitled to equal rights in our ports. This decision, the first made by any power, being formed on great consideration of the comparative strength and resources of the parties, the length of time, and successful opposition made by the colonies, and of all other circumstances on which it ought to depend, was in strict accord with the law of nations. Congress has invariably acted on this principle, having made no change in our relations with either party. Our attitude has therefore been that of neutrality between them, which has been maintained by the Government with the strictest impartiality. No aid has been afforded to either, nor has any privilege been enjoyed by the one which has not been equally open to the other party, and every exertion has been made in its power to enforce the execution of the laws prohibiting illegal equipments with equal rigor against both.

By this equality between the parties their public vessels have been received in our ports on the same footing; they have enjoyed an equal right to purchase and export arms, munitions of war, and every other supply, the exportation of all articles whatever being permitted under laws which were passed long before the commencement of the contest; our citizens have traded equally with both, and their commerce with each has been alike protected by the Government.

Respecting the attitude which it may be proper for the United States to maintain hereafter between the parties, I have no hesitation in stating it as my opinion that the neutrality heretofore observed should still be adhered to. From the change in the Government of Spain and the negotiation now depending, invited by the Cortes and accepted by the colonies, it may be presumed, that their differences will be settled on the terms proposed by the colonies. Should the war be continued, the United States, regarding its occurrences, will always have it in their power to adopt such measures respecting it as their honor and interest may require.

Shortly after the general peace a band of adventurers took advantage of this conflict and of the facility which it afforded to establish a system of buccaneering in the neighboring seas, to the great annoyance of the commerce of the United States, and, as was represented, of that of other powers. Of this spirit and of its injurious bearing on the United States strong proofs were afforded by the establishment at Amelia Island, and the purposes to which it was made instrumental by this band in 1817, and by the occurrences which took place in other parts of Florida in 1818, the details of which in both instances are too well known to require to be now recited. I am satisfied had a less decisive course been adopted that the worst consequences would have resulted from it. We have seen that these checks, decisive as they were, were not sufficient to crush that piratical spirit. Many culprits brought within our limits have been condemned to suffer death, the punishment due to that atrocious crime. The decisions of upright and enlightened tribunals fall equally on all whose crimes subject them, by a fair interpretation of the law, to its censure. It belongs to the Executive not to suffer the executions under these decisions to transcend the great purpose for which punishment is necessary. The full benefit of example being secured, policy as well as humanity equally forbids that they should be carried further. I have acted on this principle, pardoning those who appear to have been led astray by ignorance of the criminality of the acts they had committed, and suffering the law to take effect on those only in whose favor no extenuating circumstances could

be urged.

Great confidence is entertained that the late treaty with Spain, which has been ratified by both the parties, and the ratifications whereof have been exchanged, has placed the relations of the two countries on a basis of permanent friendship. The provision made by it for such of our citizens as have claims on Spain of the character described will, it is presumed, be very satisfactory to them, and the boundary which is established between the territories of the parties westward of the Mississippi, heretofore in dispute, has, it is thought, been settled on conditions just and advantageous to both. But to the acquisition of Florida too much importance can not be attached. It secures to the United States a territory important in itself, and whose importance is much increased by its bearing on many of the highest interests of the Union. It opens to several of the neighboring States a free passage to the ocean, through the Province ceded, by several rivers, having their sources high up within their limits. It secures us against all future annoyance from powerful Indian tribes. It gives us several excellent harbors in the Gulf of Mexico for ships of war of the largest size. It covers by its position in the Gulf the Mississippi and other great waters within our extended limits, and thereby enables the United States to afford complete protection to the vast and very valuable productions of our whole Western country, which find a market through those streams.

By a treaty with the British Government, bearing date on the 20th of October, 1818, the convention regulating the commerce between the United States and Great Britain, concluded on the 3d of July, 1815, which was about expiring, was revived and continued for the term of ten years from the time of its expiration. By that treaty, also, the differences which had arisen under the treaty of Ghent respecting the right claimed by the United States for their citizens to take and cure fish on the coast of His Britannic Majesty's dominions in America, with other differences on important interests, were adjusted to the satisfaction of both parties. No agreement has yet been entered into respecting the commerce between the United States and the British dominions in the West Indies and on this continent. The restraints imposed on that commerce by Great Britain, and reciprocated by the United States on a principle of defense, continue still in force.

The negotiation with France for the regulation of the commercial relations between the two countries, which in the course of the last summer had been commenced at Paris, has since been transferred to this city, and will be pursued on the part of the United States in the spirit of conciliation, and with an earnest desire that it may terminate in an arrangement satisfactory to both parties.

Our relations with the Barbary Powers are preserved in the same state and by the same means that were employed when I came into this office. As early as 1801 it was found necessary to send a squadron into the Mediterranean for the protection of our commerce, and no period has intervened, a short term excepted, when it was thought advisable to withdraw it. The great interests which the United States have in the Pacific, in commerce and in the fisheries, have also made it necessary to maintain a naval force there. In disposing of this force in both instances the most effectual measures in our power have been taken, without interfering with its other duties, for the suppression of the slave trade and of piracy in the neighboring seas.

The situation of the United States in regard to their resources, the extent of their revenue, and the facility with which it is raised affords a most gratifying spectacle. The payment of nearly $67,000,000 of the public debt, with the great progress made in measures of defense and in other improvements of various kinds since the late war, are conclusive proofs of this extraordinary prosperity, especially when it is recollected that these expenditures have been defrayed without a burthen on the people, the direct tax and excise having been repealed soon after the conclusion of the late war, and the revenue applied to these great objects having been raised in a manner not to be felt. Our great resources therefore remain untouched for any purpose which may affect the vital interests of the nation. For all such purposes they are inexhaustible. They are more especially to be found in the virtue, patriotism, and intelligence of our fellow-citizens, and in the devotion with which they would yield up by any just measure of taxation all their property in support of the rights and honor of their country.

Under the present depression of prices, affecting all the productions of the country and every branch of industry, proceeding from causes explained on a former occasion, the revenue has considerably diminished, the effect of which has been to compel Congress either to abandon these great measures of defense or to resort to loans or internal taxes to supply the deficiency. On the presumption that this depression and the deficiency in the revenue arising from it would be temporary, loans were authorized for the demands of the last and present year. Anxious to relieve my fellow-citizens in 1817 from every burthen which could be dispensed with, and the state of the Treasury permitting it, I recommended the repeal of the internal taxes, knowing that such relief was then peculiarly necessary in consequence of the great exertions made in the late war. I made that recommendation under a pledge that should the public exigencies require a recurrence to them at any time while I remained in this trust, I would with equal promptitude perform the duty which would then be alike incumbent on me. By the experiment now making it will be seen by the next session of Congress whether the revenue shall have been so augmented as to be adequate to all these necessary purposes. Should the deficiency still continue, and especially should it be probable that it would be permanent, the course to be pursued appears to me to be obvious. I am satisfied that under certain circumstances loans may be resorted to with great advantage. I am equally well satisfied, as a general rule, that the demands of the current year, especially in time of peace, should be provided for by the revenue of that year.

I have never dreaded, nor have I ever shunned, in any situation in which I have been placed making appeals to the virtue and patriotism of my fellow-citizens, well knowing that they could never be made in vain, especially in times of great emergency or for purposes of high national importance. Independently of the exigency of the case, many considerations of great weight urge a policy having in view a provision of revenue to meet to a certain extent the demands of the nation, without relying altogether on the precarious resource of foreign commerce. I am satisfied that internal duties and excises, with corresponding imposts on foreign articles of the same kind, would, without imposing any serious burdens on the people, enhance the price of produce, promote our manufactures, and augment the revenue, at the same time that they made it more secure and permanent.

The care of the Indian tribes within our limits has long been an essential part of our system, but, unfortunately, it has not been executed in a manner to accomplish all the objects intended by it. We have treated them as independent nations, without their having any substantial pretensions to that rank. The distinction has flattered their pride, retarded their improvement, and in many instances paved the way to their destruction. The progress of our settlements westward, supported as they are by a dense population, has constantly driven them back, with almost the total sacrifice of the lands which they have been compelled to abandon. They have claims on the magnanimity and, I may add,

on the justice of this nation which we must all feel. We should become their real benefactors; we should perform the office of their Great Father, the endearing title which they emphatically give to the Chief Magistrate of our Union. Their sovereignty over vast territories should cease, in lieu of which the right of soil should be secured to each individual and his posterity in competent portions; and for the territory thus ceded by each tribe some reasonable equivalent should be granted, to be vested in permanent funds for the support of civil government over them and for the education of their children, for their instruction in the arts of husbandry, and to provide sustenance for them until they could provide it for themselves. My earnest hope is that Congress will digest some plan, founded on these principles, with such improvements as their wisdom may suggest, and carry it into effect as soon as it may be practicable.

Europe is again unsettled and the prospect of war increasing. Should the flame light up in any quarter, how far it may extend it is impossible to foresee. It is our peculiar felicity to be altogether unconnected with the causes which produce this menacing aspect elsewhere. With every power we are in perfect amity, and it is our interest to remain so if it be practicable on just conditions. I see no reasonable cause to apprehend variance with any power, unless it proceed from a violation of our maritime rights. In these contests, should they occur, and to whatever extent they may be carried, we shall be neutral; but as a neutral power we have rights which it is our duty to maintain. For like injuries it will be incumbent on us to seek redress in a spirit of amity, in full confidence that, injuring none, none would knowingly injure us. For more imminent dangers we should be prepared, and it should always be recollected that such preparation adapted to the circumstances and sanctioned by the judgment and wishes of our constituents can not fail to have a good effect in averting dangers of every kind. We should recollect also that the season of peace is best adapted to these preparations.

If we turn our attention, fellow-citizens, more immediately to the internal concerns of our country, and more especially to those on which its future welfare depends, we have every reason to anticipate the happiest results. It is now rather more than forty-four years since we declared our independence, and thirty-seven since it was acknowledged. The talents and virtues which were displayed in that great struggle were a sure presage of all that has since followed. A people who were able to surmount in their infant state such great perils would be more competent as they rose into manhood to repel any which they might meet in their progress. Their physical strength would be more adequate to foreign danger, and the practice of self-government, aided by the light of experience, could not fail to produce an effect equally salutary on all those questions connected with the internal organization. These favorable anticipations have been realized.

In our whole system, national and State, we have shunned all the defects which unceasingly preyed on the vitals and destroyed the ancient Republics. In them there were distinct orders, a nobility and a people, or the people governed in one assembly. Thus, in the one instance there was a perpetual conflict between the orders in society for the ascendency, in which the victory of either terminated in the overthrow of the government and the ruin of the state; in the other, in which the people governed in a body, and whose dominions seldom exceeded the dimensions of a county in one of our States, a tumultuous and disorderly movement permitted only a transitory existence. In this great nation there is but one order, that of the people, whose power, by a peculiarly happy improvement of the representative principle, is transferred from them, without impairing in the slightest degree their sovereignty, to bodies of their own creation, and to persons elected by themselves, in the full extent necessary for all the purposes of free, enlightened and efficient government. The whole system is elective, the complete sovereignty being in the people, and every officer in every department deriving his authority from and being responsible to them for his conduct.

Our career has corresponded with this great outline. Perfection in our organization could not have been expected in the outset either in the National or State Governments or in tracing the line between their respective powers. But no serious conflict has arisen, nor any contest but such as are managed by argument and by a fair appeal to the good sense of the people, and many of the defects which experience had clearly demonstrated in both Governments have been remedied. By steadily pursuing this course in this spirit there is every reason to believe that our system will soon attain the highest degree of perfection of which human institutions are capable, and that the movement in all its branches will exhibit such a degree of order and harmony as to command the admiration and respect of the civilized world.

Our physical attainments have not been less eminent. Twenty-five years ago the river Mississippi was shut up and our Western brethren had no outlet for their commerce. What has been the progress since that time? The river has not only become the property of the United States from its source to the ocean, with all its tributary streams (with the exception of the upper part of the Red River only), but Louisiana, with a fair and liberal boundary on the western side and the Floridas on the eastern, have been ceded to us. The United States now enjoy the complete and uninterrupted sovereignty over the whole territory from St. Croix to the Sabine. New States, settled from among ourselves in this and in other parts, have been admitted into our Union in equal participation in the national sovereignty with the original States. Our population has augmented in an astonishing degree and extended in every direction. We now, fellow-citizens, comprise within our limits the dimensions and faculties of a great power under a Government possessing all the energies of any government ever known to the Old World, with an utter incapacity to oppress the people.

Entering with these views the office which I have just solemnly sworn to execute with fidelity and to the utmost of my ability, I derive great satisfaction from a knowledge that I shall be assisted in the several Departments by the very enlightened and upright citizens from whom I have received so much aid in the preceding term. With full confidence in the continuance of that candor and generous indulgence from my fellow-citizens at large which I have heretofore experienced, and with a firm reliance on the protection of Almighty God, I shall forthwith commence the duties of the high trust to which you have called me.

John Quincy Adams

Inaugural Address

Friday, March 4, 1825

In compliance with an usage coeval with the existence of our Federal Constitution, and sanctioned by the example of my predecessors in the career upon which I am about to enter, I appear, my fellow-citizens, in your presence and in that of Heaven to bind myself by the solemnities of religious obligation to the faithful performance of the duties allotted to me in the station to which I have been called.

In unfolding to my countrymen the principles by which I shall be governed in the fulfillment of those duties my first resort will be to that Constitution which I shall swear to the best of my ability to preserve, protect, and defend. That revered instrument enumerates the powers and prescribes the duties of the Executive Magistrate, and in its first words declares the purposes to which these and the whole action of the Government instituted by it should be invariably and sacredly devoted—to form a more perfect union, establish justice, insure domestic tranquility, provide for the common defense, promote the general welfare, and secure the blessings of liberty to the people of this Union in their successive generations. Since the adoption of this social compact one of these generations has passed away. It is the work of our forefathers. Administered by some of the most eminent men who contributed to its formation, through a most eventful period in the annals of the world, and through all the vicissitudes of peace and war incidental to the condition of associated man, it has not disappointed the hopes and aspirations of those illustrious benefactors of their age and nation. It has promoted the lasting welfare of that country so dear to us all; it has to an extent far beyond the ordinary lot of humanity secured the freedom and happiness of this people. We now receive it as a precious inheritance from those to whom we are indebted for its establishment, doubly bound by the examples which they have left us and by the blessings which we have enjoyed as the fruits of their labors to transmit the same unimpaired to the succeeding generation. In the compass of thirty-six years since this great national covenant was instituted a body of laws enacted under its authority and in conformity with its provisions has unfolded its powers and carried into practical operation its effective energies. Subordinate departments have distributed the executive functions in their various relations to foreign affairs, to the revenue and expenditures, and to the military force of the Union by land and sea. A coordinate department of the judiciary has expounded the Constitution and the laws, settling in harmonious coincidence with the legislative will numerous weighty questions of construction which the imperfection of human language had rendered unavoidable. The year of jubilee since the first formation of our Union has just elapsed; that of the declaration of our independence is at hand. The consummation of both was effected by this Constitution.

Since that period a population of four millions has multiplied to twelve. A territory bounded by the Mississippi has been extended from sea to sea. New States have been admitted to the Union in numbers nearly equal to those of the first Confederation. Treaties of peace, amity, and commerce have been concluded with the principal dominions of the earth. The people of other nations, inhabitants of regions acquired not by conquest, but by compact, have been united with us in the participation of our rights and duties, of our burdens and blessings. The forest has fallen by the ax of our woodsmen; the soil has been made to teem by the tillage of our farmers; our commerce has whitened every ocean. The dominion of man over physical nature has been extended by the invention of our artists. Liberty and law have marched hand in hand. All the purposes of human association have been accomplished as effectively as under any other government on the globe, and at a cost little exceeding in a whole generation the expenditure of other nations in a single year.

Such is the unexaggerated picture of our condition under a

Constitution founded upon the republican principle of equal rights. To admit that this picture has its shades is but to say that it is still the condition of men upon earth. From evil—physical, moral, and political—it is not our claim to be exempt. We have suffered sometimes by the visitation of Heaven through disease; often by the wrongs and injustice of other nations, even to the extremities of war; and, lastly, by dissensions among ourselves— dissensions perhaps inseparable from the enjoyment of freedom, but which have more than once appeared to threaten the dissolution of the Union, and with it the overthrow of all the enjoyments of our present lot and all our earthly hopes of the future. The causes of these dissensions have been various, founded upon differences of speculation in the theory of republican government; upon conflicting views of policy in our relations with foreign nations; upon jealousies of partial and sectional interests, aggravated by prejudices and prepossessions which strangers to each other are ever apt to entertain.

It is a source of gratification and of encouragement to me to observe that the great result of this experiment upon the theory of human rights has at the close of that generation by which it was formed been crowned with success equal to the most sanguine expectations of its founders. Union, justice, tranquility, the common defense, the general welfare, and the blessings of liberty—all have been promoted by the Government under which we have lived. Standing at this point of time, looking back to that generation which has gone by and forward to that which is advancing, we may at once indulge in grateful exultation and in cheering hope. From the experience of the past we derive instructive lessons for the future. Of the two great political parties which have divided the opinions and feelings of our country, the candid and the just will now admit that both have contributed splendid talents, spotless integrity, ardent patriotism, and disinterested sacrifices to the formation and administration of this Government, and that both have required a liberal indulgence for a portion of human infirmity and error. The revolutionary wars of Europe, commencing precisely at the moment when the Government of the United States first went into operation under this Constitution, excited a collision of sentiments and of sympathies which kindled all the passions and imbittered the conflict of parties till the nation was involved in war and the Union was shaken to its center. This time of trial embraced a period of five and twenty years, during which the policy of the Union in its relations with Europe constituted the principal basis of our political divisions and the most arduous part of the action of our Federal Government. With the catastrophe in which the wars of the French Revolution terminated, and our own subsequent peace with Great Britain, this baneful weed of party strife was uprooted. From that time no difference of principle, connected either with the theory of government or with our intercourse with foreign nations, has existed or been called forth in force sufficient to sustain a continued combination of parties or to give more than wholesome animation to public sentiment or legislative debate. Our political creed is, without a dissenting voice that can be heard, that the will of the people is the source and the happiness of the people the end of all legitimate government upon earth; that the best security for the beneficence and the best guaranty against the abuse of power consists in the freedom, the purity, and the frequency of popular elections; that the General Government of the Union and the separate governments of the States are all sovereignties of limited powers, fellow-servants of the same masters, uncontrolled within their respective spheres, uncontrollable by encroachments upon each other; that the firmest security of peace is the preparation during peace of the defenses of war; that a rigorous economy and accountability of public expenditures should guard against the aggravation and alleviate when possible the burden of taxation;

that the military should be kept in strict subordination to the civil power; that the freedom of the press and of religious opinion should be inviolate; that the policy of our country is peace and the ark of our salvation union are articles of faith upon which we are all now agreed. If there have been those who doubted whether a confederated representative democracy were a government competent to the wise and orderly management of the common concerns of a mighty nation, those doubts have been dispelled; if there have been projects of partial confederacies to be erected upon the ruins of the Union, they have been scattered to the winds; if there have been dangerous attachments to one foreign nation and antipathies against another, they have been extinguished. Ten years of peace, at home and abroad, have assuaged the animosities of political contention and blended into harmony the most discordant elements of public opinion. There still remains one effort of magnanimity, one sacrifice of prejudice and passion, to be made by the individuals throughout the nation who have heretofore followed the standards of political party. It is that of discarding every remnant of rancor against each other, of embracing as countrymen and friends, and of yielding to talents and virtue alone that confidence which in times of contention for principle was bestowed only upon those who bore the badge of party communion.

The collisions of party spirit which originate in speculative opinions or in different views of administrative policy are in their nature transitory. Those which are founded on geographical divisions, adverse interests of soil, climate, and modes of domestic life are more permanent, and therefore, perhaps, more dangerous. It is this which gives inestimable value to the character of our Government, at once federal and national. It holds out to us a perpetual admonition to preserve alike and with equal anxiety the rights of each individual State in its own government and the rights of the whole nation in that of the Union. Whatsoever is of domestic concernment, unconnected with the other members of the Union or with foreign lands, belongs exclusively to the administration of the State governments. Whatsoever directly involves the rights and interests of the federative fraternity or of foreign powers is of the resort of this General Government. The duties of both are obvious in the general principle, though sometimes perplexed with difficulties in the detail. To respect the rights of the State governments is the inviolable duty of that of the Union; the government of every State will feel its own obligation to respect and preserve the rights of the whole. The prejudices everywhere too commonly entertained against distant strangers are worn away, and the jealousies of jarring interests are allayed by the composition and functions of the great national councils annually assembled from all quarters of the Union at this place. Here the distinguished men from every section of our country, while meeting to deliberate upon the great interests of those by whom they are deputed, learn to estimate the talents and do justice to the virtues of each other. The harmony of the nation is promoted and the whole Union is knit together by the sentiments of mutual respect, the habits of social intercourse, and the ties of personal friendship formed between the representatives of its several parts in the performance of their service at this metropolis.

Passing from this general review of the purposes and injunctions of the Federal Constitution and their results as indicating the first traces of the path of duty in the discharge of my public trust, I turn to the Administration of my immediate predecessor as the second. It has passed away in a period of profound peace, how much to the satisfaction of our country and to the honor of our country's name is known to you all. The great features of its policy, in general concurrence with the will of the Legislature, have been to cherish peace while preparing for defensive war; to yield exact justice to other nations and maintain

of the rights of the several States and the integrity of the Union.

These great objects are necessarily connected, and can only be attained by an enlightened exercise of the powers of each within its appropriate sphere in conformity with the public will constitutionally expressed. To this end it becomes the duty of all to yield a ready and patriotic submission to the laws constitutionally enacted, and thereby promote and strengthen a proper confidence in those institutions of the several States and of the United States which the people themselves have ordained for their own government.

My experience in public concerns and the observation of a life somewhat advanced confirm the opinions long since imbibed by me, that the destruction of our State governments or the annihilation of their control over the local concerns of the people would lead directly to revolution and anarchy, and finally to despotism and military domination. In proportion, therefore, as the General Government encroaches upon the rights of the States, in the same proportion does it impair its own power and detract from its ability to fulfill the purposes of its creation. Solemnly impressed with these considerations, my countrymen will ever find me ready to exercise my constitutional powers in arresting measures which may directly or indirectly encroach upon the rights of the States or tend to consolidate all political power in the General Government. But of equal, and, indeed, of incalculable, importance is the union of these States, and the sacred duty of all to contribute to its preservation by a liberal support of the General Government in the exercise of its just powers. You have been wisely admonished to "accustom yourselves to think and speak of the Union as of the palladium of your political safety and prosperity, watching for its preservation with jealous anxiety, discountenancing whatever may suggest even a suspicion that it can in any event be abandoned, and indignantly frowning upon the first dawning of any attempt to alienate any portion of our country from the rest or to enfeeble the sacred ties which now link together the various parts." Without union our independence and liberty would never have been achieved; without union they never can be maintained. Divided into twenty-four, or even a smaller number, of separate communities, we shall see our internal trade burdened with numberless restraints and exactions; communication between distant points and sections obstructed or cut off; our sons made soldiers to deluge with blood the fields they now till in peace; the mass of our people borne down and impoverished by taxes to support armies and navies, and military leaders at the head of their victorious legions becoming our lawgivers and judges. The loss of liberty, of all good government, of peace, plenty, and happiness, must inevitably follow a dissolution of the Union. In supporting it, therefore, we support all that is dear to the freeman and the philanthropist.

The time at which I stand before you is full of interest. The eyes of all nations are fixed on our Republic. The event of the existing crisis will be decisive in the opinion of mankind of the practicability of our federal system of government. Great is the stake placed in our hands; great is the responsibility which must rest upon the people of the United States. Let us realize the importance of the attitude in which we stand before the world. Let us exercise forbearance and firmness. Let us extricate our country from the dangers which surround it and learn wisdom from the lessons they inculcate.

Deeply impressed with the truth of these observations, and under the obligation of that solemn oath which I am about to take, I shall continue to exert all my faculties to maintain the just powers of the Constitution and to transmit unimpaired to posterity the blessings of our Federal Union. At the same time, it will be my aim to inculcate by my official acts the necessity of exercising by the General Government those powers only that are clearly delegated; to encourage simplicity and economy in the expenditures of the Government; to raise no more money from the people than may be requisite for these objects, and in a manner that will best promote the interests of all classes of the community and of all portions of the Union. Constantly bearing in mind that in entering into society "individuals must give up a share of liberty to preserve the rest," it will be my desire so to discharge my duties as to foster with our brethren in all parts of the country a spirit of liberal concession and compromise, and, by reconciling our fellow-citizens to those partial sacrifices which they must unavoidably make for the preservation of a greater good, to recommend our invaluable Government and Union to the confidence and affections of the American people.

Finally, it is my most fervent prayer to that Almighty Being before whom I now stand, and who has kept us in His hands from the infancy of our Republic to the present day, that He will so overrule all my intentions and actions and inspire the hearts of my fellow-citizens that we may be preserved from dangers of all kinds and continue forever a united and happy people.

Martin Van Buren

Inaugural Address

Monday, March 4, 1837

Fellow-Citizens:

The practice of all my predecessors imposes on me an obligation I cheerfully fulfill—to accompany the first and solemn act of my public trust with an avowal of the principles that will guide me in performing it and an expression of my feelings on assuming a charge so responsible and vast. In imitating their example I tread in the footsteps of illustrious men, whose superiors it is our happiness to believe are not found on the executive calendar of any country. Among th em we recognize the earliest and firmest pillars of the Republic—those by whom our national independence was first declared, him who above all others contributed to establish it on the field of battle, and those whose expanded intellect and patriotis m constructed, improved, and perfected the inestimable institutions under which we live. If such men in the position I now occupy felt themselves overwhelmed by a sense of gratitude for this the highest of all marks of their country's confidence, and by a consciousness of their inability adequately to discharge the duties of an office so difficult and exalted, how much more must these considerations affect one who can rely on no such claims for favor or forbearance! Unlike all who have preceded me, the Re volution that gave us existence as one people was achieved at the period of my birth; and whilst I contemplate with grateful reverence that memorable event, I feel that I belong to a later age and that I may not expect my countrymen to weigh my actions wi th the same kind and partial hand.

So sensibly, fellow-citizens, do these circumstances press

themselves upon me that I should not dare to enter upon my path of duty did I not look for the generous aid of those who will be associated with me in the various and coordinate branches of the Government; did I not repose with unwavering reliance on the patriotism, the intelligence, and the kindness of a people who never yet deserted a public servant honestly laboring their cause; and, above all, did I not permit myself humbly to hope for the sustaining support of an ever-watchful and beneficent Providence.

To the confidence and consolation derived from these sources it would be ungrateful not to add those which spring from our present fortunate condition. Though not altogether exempt from embarrassments that disturb our tranquillity at home and threaten it abroad, yet in all the attributes of a great, happy, and flourishing people we stand without a parallel in the world. Abroad we enjoy the respect and, with scarcely an exception, the friendship of every nation; at home, while our Government quietly but efficiently performs the sole legitimate end of political institutions—in doing the greatest good to the greatest number—we present an aggregate of human prosperity surely not elsewhere to be found.

How imperious, then, is the obligation imposed upon every citizen, in his own sphere of action, whether limited or extended, to exert himself in perpetuating a condition of things so singularly happy! All the lessons of history and experience must be lost upon us if we are content to trust alone to the peculiar advantages we happen to possess. Position and climate and the bounteous resources that nature has scattered with so liberal a hand—even the diffused intelligence and elevated character of our people—will avail us nothing if we fail sacredly to uphold those political institutions that were wisely and deliberately formed with reference to every circumstance that could preserve or might endanger the blessings we enjoy. The thoughtful framers of our Constitution legislated for our country as they found it. Looking upon it with the eyes of statesmen and patriots, they saw all the sources of rapid and wonderful prosperity; but they saw also that various habits, opinions, and institutions peculiar to the various portions of so vast a region were deeply fixed. Distinct sovereignties were in actual existence, whose cordial union was essential to the welfare and happiness of all. Between many of them there was, at least to some extent, a real diversity of interests, liable to be exaggerated through sinister designs; they differed in size, in population, in wealth, and in actual and prospective resources and power; they varied in the character of their industry and staple productions, and [in some] existed domestic institutions which, unwisely disturbed, might endanger the harmony of the whole. Most carefully were all these circumstances weighed, and the foundations of the new Government laid upon principles of reciprocal concession and equitable compromise. The jealousies which the smaller States might entertain of the power of the rest were allayed by a rule of representation confessedly unequal at the time, and designed forever to remain so. A natural fear that the broad scope of general legislation might be urged and unwisely control particular interests was counteracted by limits strictly drawn around the action of the Federal authority, and to the people and the States was left unimpaired their sovereign power over the innumerable subjects embraced in the internal government of a just republic, excepting such only as necessarily appertain to the concerns of the whole confederacy or its intercourse as a united community with the other nations of the world.

This provident forecast has been verified by time. Half a century, teeming with extraordinary events, and elsewhere producing astonishing results, has passed along, but on our institutions it has left no injurious mark. From a small community we have risen to a people powerful in numbers and in strength; but with our increase has gone hand in hand the progress of just principles. The privileges, civil and religious, of the humblest individual are still sacredly protected at home, and while the valor and fortitude of our people have removed far from us the slightest apprehension of foreign power, they have not yet induced us in a single instance to forget what is right. Our commerce has been extended to the remotest nations; the value and even nature of our productions have been greatly changed; a wide difference has arisen in the relative wealth and resources of every portion of our country; yet the spirit of mutual regard and of faithful adherence to existing compacts has continued to prevail in our councils and never long been absent from our conduct. We have learned by experience a fruitful lesson—that an implicit and undeviating adherence to the principles on which we set out can carry us prosperously onward through all the conflicts of circumstances and vicissitudes inseparable from the lapse of years.

The success that has thus attended our great experiment is in itself a sufficient cause for gratitude, on account of the happiness it has actually conferred and the example it has unanswerably given. But to me, my fellow-citizens, looking forward to the far-distant future with ardent prayers and confiding hopes, this retrospect presents a ground for still deeper delight. It impresses on my mind a firm belief that the perpetuity of our institutions depends upon ourselves; that if we maintain the principles on which they were established they are destined to confer their benefits on countless generations yet to come, and that America will present to every friend of mankind the cheering proof that a popular government, wisely formed, is wanting in no element of endurance or strength. Fifty years ago its rapid failure was boldly predicted. Latent and uncontrollable causes of dissolution were supposed to exist even by the wise and good, and not only did unfriendly or speculative theorists anticipate for us the fate of past republics, but the fears of many an honest patriot overbalanced his sanguine hopes. Look back on these forebodings, not hastily but reluctantly made, and see how in every instance they have completely failed.

An imperfect experience during the struggles of the Revolution was supposed to warrant the belief that the people would not bear the taxation requisite to discharge an immense public debt already incurred and to pay the necessary expenses of the Government. The cost of two wars has been paid, not only without a murmur, but with unequaled alacrity. No one is now left to doubt that every burden will be cheerfully borne that may be necessary to sustain our civil institutions or guard our honor or welfare. Indeed, all experience has shown that the willingness of the people to contribute to these ends in cases of emergency has uniformly outrun the confidence of their representatives

In the early stages of the new Government, when all felt the imposing influence as they recognized the unequaled services of the first President, it was a common sentiment that the great weight of his character could alone bind the discordant materials of our Government together and save us from the violence of contending factions. Since his death nearly forty years are gone. Party exasperation has been often carried to its highest point; the virtue and fortitude of the people have sometimes been greatly tried; yet our system, purified and enhanced in value by all it has encountered, still preserves its spirit of free and fearless discussion, blended with unimpaired fraternal feeling.

The capacity of the people for self-government, and their willingness, from a high sense of duty and without those exhibitions of coercive power so generally employed in other countries, to submit to all needful restraints and exactions of municipal law, have also been favorably exemplified in the history of the American States. Occasionally, it is true, the ardor of public sentiment, outrunning the regular progress of the judicial tribunals or seeking to reach cases not denounced as c riminal by the existing law, has displayed itself in a manner calculated to give pain to the friends of free government and to encourage the hopes of those who wish for its overthrow. These occurrences, however, have been far less frequent in our country than in any other of equal population on the globe, and with the diffusion of intelligence it may well be hoped that they will constantly diminish in frequency and violence. The generous patriotism and sound common sense of the great mass of our fellow-ci tizens will assuredly in time produce this result; for as every assumption of illegal power not only wounds the majesty of the law, but furnishes a pretext for abridging the liberties of the people, the latter have the most direct and permanent interest i n preserving the landmarks of social order and maintaining on all occasions the inviolability of those constitutional and legal provisions which they themselves have made.

In a supposed unfitness of our institutions for those hostile emergencies which no country can always avoid their friends found a fruitful source of apprehension, their enemies of hope. While they foresaw less promptness of action than in governments differently formed, they overlooked the far more important consideration that with us war could never be the result of individual or irresponsible will, but must be a measure of redress for injuries sustained, voluntarily resorted to by th ose who were to bear the necessary sacrifice, who would consequently feel an individual interest in the contest, and whose energy would be commensurate with the difficulties to be encountered. Actual events have proved their error; the last war, far from impairing, gave new confidence to our Government, and amid recent apprehensions of a similar conflict we saw that the energies of our country would not be wanting in ample season to vindicate its rights. We may not possess, as we should not desire to poss ess, the extended and ever-ready military organization of other nations; we may occasionally suffer in the outset for the want of it; but among ourselves all doubt upon this great point has ceased, while a salutary experience will prevent a contrary opini on from inviting aggression from abroad.

Certain danger was foretold from the extension of our territory, the multiplication of States, and the increase of population. Our system was supposed to be adapted only to boundaries comparatively narrow. These have been widened beyon d conjecture; the members of our Confederacy are already doubled, and the numbers of our people are incredibly augmented. The alleged causes of danger have long surpassed anticipation, but none of the consequences have followed. The power and influence of the Republic have arisen to a height obvious to all mankind; respect for its authority was not more apparent at its ancient than it is at its present limits; new and inexhaustible sources of general prosperity have been opened; the effects of distance ha ve been averted by the inventive genius of our people, developed and fostered by the spirit of our institutions; and the enlarged variety and amount of interests, productions, and pursuits have strengthened the chain of mutual dependence and formed a circ le of mutual benefits too apparent ever to be overlooked.

In justly balancing the powers of the Federal and State authorities difficulties nearly insurmountable arose at the outset and subsequent collisions were deemed inevitable. Amid these it was scarcely believed possible that a scheme of government so complex in construction could remain uninjured. From time to time embarrassments have certainly occurred; but how just is the confidence of future safety imparted by the knowledge that each in succession has been happily removed! Overlooking partial and temporary evils as inseparable from the practical operation of all human institutions, and looking only to the general result, every patriot has reason to be satisfied. While the Federal Government has successfully performed its appropriate f unctions in relation to foreign affairs and concerns evidently national, that of every State has remarkably improved in protecting and developing local interests and individual welfare; and if the vibrations of authority have occasionally tended too much toward one or the other, it is unquestionably certain that the ultimate operation of the entire system has been to strengthen all the existing institutions and to elevate our whole country in prosperity and renown.

The last, perhaps the greatest, of the prominent sources of discord and disaster supposed to lurk in our political condition was the institution of domestic slavery. Our forefathers were deeply impressed with the delicacy of this subje ct, and they treated it with a forbearance so evidently wise that in spite of every sinister foreboding it never until the present period disturbed the tranquillity of our common country. Such a result is sufficient evidence of the justice and the patriot ism of their course; it is evidence not to be mistaken that an adherence to it can prevent all embarrassment from this as well as from every other anticipated cause of difficulty or danger. Have not recent events made it obvious to the slightest reflectio n that the least deviation from this spirit of forbearance is injurious to every interest, that of humanity included? Amidst the violence of excited passions this generous and fraternal feeling has been sometimes disregarded; and standing as I now do befo re my countrymen, in this high place of honor and of trust, I can not refrain from anxiously invoking my fellow-citizens never to be deaf to its dictates. Perceiving before my election the deep interest this subject was beginning to excite, I believed it a solemn duty fully to make known my sentiments in regard to it, and now, when every motive for misrepresentation has passed away, I trust that they will be candidly weighed and understood. At least they will be my standard of conduct in the path before m e. I then declared that if the desire of those of my countrymen who were favorable to my election was gratified "I must go into the Presidential chair the inflexible and uncompromising opponent of every attempt on the part of Congress to abolish slavery i n the District of Columbia against the wishes of the slaveholding States, and also with a determination equally decided to resist the slightest interference with it in the States where it exists." I submitted also to my fellow-citizens, with fullness and frankness, the reasons which led me to this determination. The result authorizes me to believe that they have been approved and are confided in by a majority of the people of the United States, including those whom they most immediately affect. It now onl y remains to add that no bill conflicting with these views can ever receive my constitutional sanction. These opinions have been adopted in the firm belief that they are in accordance with the spirit that actuated the venerated fathers of the Republic, an d that succeeding experience has proved them to be humane, patriotic, expedient, honorable, and just. If the agitation of this subject was intended to reach the stability of our institutions, enough has occurred to show that it has signally failed, and th at in this as in every other instance the apprehensions of the timid and the hopes of the wicked for the destruction of our Government are again destined to be disappointed. Here and there, indeed, scenes of dangerous excitement have occurred, terrifying instances of local violence have been witnessed, and a reckless disregard of the consequences of their conduct has exposed individuals to popular indignation; but neither masses of the people nor sections of the country have been swerved from their devoti on to the bond of union and the principles it has made sacred. It will be ever thus. Such attempts at dangerous agitation may periodically return, but with each the object will be better understood. That predominating affection for our political system wh ich prevails throughout our territorial limits, that calm and enlightened judgment which ultimately governs our people as one vast body, will always be at hand to resist and control every effort, foreign or domestic, which aims or would lead to overthrow our institutions.

What can be more gratifying than such a retrospect as this? We look back on obstacles avoided and dangers overcome, on expectations more than realized and prosperity perfectly secured. To the hopes of the hostile, the fears of the timi d, and the doubts of the anxious actual experience has given the conclusive reply. We have seen time gradually dispel every unfavorable foreboding and our Constitution surmount every adverse circumstance dreaded at the outset as beyond control. Present ex citement will at all times magnify present dangers, but true philosophy must teach us that none more threatening than the past can remain to be overcome; and we ought (for we have just reason) to entertain an abiding confidence in the stability of our ins titutions and an entire conviction that if administered in the true form, character, and spirit in which they were established they are abundantly adequate to preserve to us and our children the rich blessings already derived from them, to make our belove d land for a thousand generations that chosen spot where happiness springs from a perfect equality of political rights.

For myself, therefore, I desire to declare that the principle that will govern me in the high duty to which my country calls me is a strict adherence to the letter and spirit of the Constitution as it was designed by those who framed i t. Looking back to it as a sacred instrument carefully and not easily framed; remembering that it was throughout a work of concession and compromise; viewing it as limited to national objects; regarding it as leaving to the people and the States all power not explicitly parted with, I shall endeavor to preserve, protect, and defend it by anxiously referring to its provision for direction in every action. To matters of domestic concernment which it has intrusted to the Federal Government and to such as rel ate to our intercourse with foreign nations I shall zealously devote myself; beyond those limits I shall never pass.

To enter on this occasion into a further or more minute exposition of my views on the various questions of domestic policy would be as obtrusive as it is probably unexpected. Before the suffrages of my countrymen were conferred upon me I submitted to them, with great precision, my opinions on all the most prominent of these subjects. Those opinions I shall endeavor to carry out with my utmost ability.

Our course of foreign policy has been so uniform and

intelligible as to constitute a rule of Executive conduct which leaves little to my discretion, unless, indeed, I were willing to run counter to the lights of experience and the know n opinions of my constituents. We sedulously cultivate the friendship of all nations as the conditions most compatible with our welfare and the principles of our Government. We decline alliances as adverse to our peace. We desire commercial relations on e qual terms, being ever willing to give a fair equivalent for advantages received. We endeavor to conduct our intercourse with openness and sincerity, promptly avowing our objects and seeking to establish that mutual frankness which is as beneficial in the dealings of nations as of men. We have no disposition and we disclaim all right to meddle in disputes, whether internal or foreign, that may molest other countries, regarding them in their actual state as social communities, and preserving a strict neutr ality in all their controversies. Well knowing the tried valor of our people and our exhaustless resources, we neither anticipate nor fear any designed aggression; and in the consciousness of our own just conduct we feel a security that we shall never be called upon to exert our determination never to permit an invasion of our rights without punishment or redress.

In approaching, then, in the presence of my assembled countrymen, to make the solemn promise that yet remains, and to pledge myself that I will faithfully execute the office I am about to fill, I bring with me a settled purpose to main tain the institutions of my country, which I trust will atone for the errors I commit.

In receiving from the people the sacred trust twice confided to my illustrious predecessor, and which he has discharged so faithfully and so well, I know that I can not expect to perform the arduous task with equal ability and success. But united as I have been in his counsels, a daily witness of his exclusive and unsurpassed devotion to his country's welfare, agreeing with him in sentiments which his countrymen have warmly supported, and permitted to partake largely of his confidence, I may hope that somewhat of the same cheering approbation will be found to attend upon my path. For him I but express with my own the wishes of all, that he may yet long live to enjoy the brilliant evening of his well-spent life; and for myself, consciou s of but one desire, faithfully to serve my country, I throw myself without fear on its justice and its kindness. Beyond that I only look to the gracious protection of the Divine Being whose strengthening support I humbly solicit, and whom I fervently pra y to look down upon us all. May it be among the dispensations of His providence to bless our beloved country with honors and with length of days. May her ways be ways of pleasantness and all her paths be peace!

William Henry Harrison

Inaugural Address

Thursday, March 4, 1841

Called from a retirement which I had supposed was to continue for the residue of my life to fill the chief executive office of this great and free nation, I appear before you, fellow-citizens, to take the oaths which the Constitution prescribes as a necessary qualification for the performance of its duties; and in obedience to a custom coeval with our Government and what I believe to be your expectations I proceed to present to you a summary of the principles which will govern me in the discharge of the duties which I shall be called upon to perform.

It was the remark of a Roman consul in an early period of that celebrated Republic that a most striking contrast was observable in the conduct of candidates for offices of power and trust before and after obtaining them, they seldom carrying out in the latter case the pledges and promises made in the former. However much the world may have improved in many respects in the lapse of upward of two thousand years since the remark was made by the virtuous and indignant Roman, I fear that a strict examination of the annals of some of the modern elective governments would develop similar instances of violated confidence.

Although the fiat of the people has gone forth proclaiming me the Chief Magistrate of this glorious Union, nothing upon their part remaining to be done, it may be thought that a motive may exist to keep up the delusion under which they may be supposed to have acted in relation to my principles and opinions; and perhaps there may be some in this assembly who have come here either prepared to condemn those I shall now deliver, or, approving them, to doubt the sincerity with which they are now uttered. But the lapse of a few months will confirm or dispel their fears. The outline of principles to govern and measures to be adopted by an Administration not yet begun will soon be exchanged for immutable history, and I shall stand either exonerated by my countrymen or classed with the mass of those who promised that they might deceive and flattered with the intention to betray. However strong may be my present purpose to realize the expectations of a magnanimous and confiding people, I too well understand the dangerous temptations to which I shall be exposed from the magnitude of the power which it has been the pleasure of the people to commit to my hands not to place my chief confidence upon the aid of that Almighty Power which has hitherto protected me and enabled me to bring to favorable issues other important but still greatly inferior trusts heretofore confided to me by my country.

The broad foundation upon which our Constitution rests being the people—a breath of theirs having made, as a breath can unmake, change, or modify it—it can be assigned to none of the great divisions of government but to that of democracy. If such is its theory, those who are called upon to administer it must recognize as its leading principle the duty of shaping their measures so as to produce the greatest good to the greatest number. But with these broad admissions, if we would compare the sovereignty acknowledged to exist in the mass of our people with the power claimed by other sovereignties, even by those which have been considered most purely democratic, we shall find a most essential difference. All others lay claim to power limited only by their own will. The majority of our citizens, on the contrary, possess a sovereignty with an amount of power precisely equal to that which has been granted to them by the parties to the national compact, and nothing beyond. We admit of no government by divine right, believing that so far as power is concerned the Beneficent Creator has made no distinction amongst men; that all are upon an equality, and that the only legitimate right to govern is an express grant of power from the governed. The Constitution of the United States is the instrument containing this grant of power to the several departments composing the Government. On an examination of that instrument it will be found to contain declarations of power granted and of power withheld. The latter is also susceptible of division into power which the majority had the right to grant, but which they do not think proper to intrust to their agents, and that which they could not have granted, not being possessed by themselves. In other words, there are certain rights possessed by each individual American citizen which in his compact with the others he has never surrendered. Some of them, indeed, he is unable to surrender, being, in the language of our system, unalienable. The boasted privilege of a Roman citizen was to him a shield only against a petty provincial ruler, whilst the proud democrat of Athens would console himself under a sentence of death for a supposed violation of the national faith—which no one understood and which at times was the subject of the mockery of all—or the banishment from his home, his family, and his country with or without an alleged cause, that it was the act not of a single tyrant or hated aristocracy, but of his

assembled countrymen. Far different is the power of our sovereignty. It can interfere with no one's faith, prescribe forms of worship for no one's observance, inflict no punishment but after well-ascertained guilt, the result of investigation under rules prescribed by the Constitution itself. These precious privileges, and those scarcely less important of giving expression to his thoughts and opinions, either by writing or speaking, unrestrained but by the liability for injury to others, and that of a full participation in all the advantages which flow from the Government, the acknowledged property of all, the American citizen derives from no charter granted by his fellow-man. He claims them because he is himself a man, fashioned by the same Almighty hand as the rest of his species and entitled to a full share of the blessings with which He has endowed them. Notwithstanding the limited sovereignty possessed by the people of the United States and the restricted grant of power to the Government which they have adopted, enough has been given to accomplish all the objects for which it was created. It has been found powerful in war, and hitherto justice has been administered, and intimate union effected, domestic tranquillity preserved, and personal liberty secured to the citizen. As was to be expected, however, from the defect of language and the necessarily sententious manner in which the Constitution is written, disputes have arisen as to the amount of power which it has actually granted or was intended to grant.

This is more particularly the case in relation to that part of the instrument which treats of the legislative branch, and not only as regards the exercise of powers claimed under a general clause giving that body the authority to pass all laws necessary to carry into effect the specified powers, but in relation to the latter also. It is, however, consolatory to reflect that most of the instances of alleged departure from the letter or spirit of the Constitution have ultimately received the sanction of a majority of the people. And the fact that many of our statesmen most distinguished for talent and patriotism have been at one time or other of their political career on both sides of each of the most warmly disputed questions forces upon us the inference that the errors, if errors there were, are attributable to the intrinsic difficulty in many instances of ascertaining the intentions of the framers of the Constitution rather than the influence of any sinister or unpatriotic motive. But the great danger to our institutions does not appear to me to be in a usurpation by the Government of power not granted by the people, but by the accumulation in one of the departments of that which was assigned to others. Limited as are the powers which have been granted, still enough have been granted to constitute a despotism if concentrated in one of the departments. This danger is greatly heightened, as it has been always observable that men are less jealous of encroachments of one department upon another than upon their own reserved rights. When the Constitution of the United States first came from the hands of the Convention which formed it, many of the sternest republicans of the day were alarmed at the extent of the power which had been granted to the Federal Government, and more particularly of that portion which had been assigned to the executive branch. There were in it features which appeared not to be in harmony with their ideas of a simple representative democracy or republic, and knowing the tendency of power to increase itself, particularly when exercised by a single individual, predictions were made that at no very remote period the Government would terminate in virtual monarchy. It would not become me to say that the fears of these patriots have been already realized; but as I sincerely believe that the tendency of measures and of men's opinions for some years past has been in that direction, it is, I conceive, strictly proper that I should take this occasion to repeat the assurances I have heretofore given of my determination to arrest the progress of that tendency if it really exists and restore the Government to its pristine health and vigor, as far as this can be effected by any legitimate exercise of the power placed in my hands.

I proceed to state in as summary a manner as I can my opinion of the sources of the evils which have been so extensively complained of and the correctives which may be applied. Some of the former are unquestionably to be found in the defects of the Constitution; others, in my judgment, are attributable to a misconstruction of some of its provisions. Of the former is the eligibility of the same individual to a second term of the Presidency. The sagacious mind of Mr. Jefferson early saw and lamented this error, and attempts have been made, hitherto without success, to apply the amendatory power of the States to its correction. As, however, one mode of correction is in the power of every President, and consequently in mine, it would be useless, and perhaps invidious, to enumerate the evils of which, in the opinion of many of our fellow-citizens, this error of the sages who framed the Constitution may have been the source and the bitter fruits which we are still to gather from it if it continues to disfigure our system. It may be observed, however, as a general remark, that republics can commit no greater error than to adopt or continue any feature in their systems of government which may be calculated to create or increase the lover of power in the bosoms of those to whom necessity obliges them to commit the management of their affairs; and surely nothing is more likely to produce such a state of mind than the long continuance of an office of high trust. Nothing can be more corrupting, nothing more destructive of all those noble feelings which belong to the character of a devoted republican patriot. When this corrupting passion once takes possession of the human mind, like the love of gold it becomes insatiable. It is the never-dying worm in his bosom, grows with his growth and strengthens with the declining years of its victim. If this is true, it is the part of wisdom for a republic to limit the service of that officer at least to whom she has intrusted the management of her foreign relations, the execution of her laws, and the command of her armies and navies to a period so short as to prevent his forgetting that he is the accountable agent, not the principal; the servant, not the master. Until an amendment of the Constitution can be effected public opinion may secure the desired object. I give my aid to it by renewing the pledge heretofore given that under no circumstances will I consent to serve a second term.

But if there is danger to public liberty from the acknowledged defects of the Constitution in the want of limit to the continuance of the Executive power in the same hands, there is, I apprehend, not much less from a misconstruction of that instrument as it regards the powers actually given. I can not conceive that by a fair construction any or either of its provisions would be found to constitute the President a part of the legislative power. It can not be claimed from the power to recommend, since, although enjoined as a duty upon him, it is a privilege which he holds in common with every other citizen; and although there may be something more of confidence in the propriety of the measures recommended in the one case than in the other, in the obligations of ultimate decision there can be no difference. In the language of the Constitution, "all the legislative powers" which it grants "are vested in the Congress of the United States." It would be a solecism in language to say that any portion of these is not included in the whole.

It may be said, indeed, that the Constitution has given to the Executive the power to annul the acts of the legislative body by refusing to them his assent. So a similar power has necessarily resulted from that instrument to the judiciary, and yet the judiciary forms no part of the Legislature. There is, it is true, this

difference between these grants of power: The Executive can put his negative upon the acts of the Legislature for other cause than that of want of conformity to the Constitution, whilst the judiciary can only declare void those which violate that instrument. But the decision of the judiciary is final in such a case, whereas in every instance where the veto of the Executive is applied it may be overcome by a vote of two-thirds of both Houses of Congress. The negative upon the acts of the legislative by the executive authority, and that in the hands of one individual, would seem to be an incongruity in our system. Like some others of a similar character, however, it appears to be highly expedient, and if used only with the forbearance and in the spirit which was intended by its authors it may be productive of great good and be found one of the best safeguards to the Union. At the period of the formation of the Constitution the principle does not appear to have enjoyed much favor in the State governments. It existed but in two, and in one of these there was a plural executive. If we would search for the motives which operated upon the purely patriotic and enlightened assembly which framed the Constitution for the adoption of a provision so apparently repugnant to the leading democratic principle that the majority should govern, we must reject the idea that they anticipated from it any benefit to the ordinary course of legislation. They knew too well the high degree of intelligence which existed among the people and the enlightened character of the State legislatures not to have the fullest confidence that the two bodies elected by them would be worthy representatives of such constituents, and, of course, that they would require no aid in conceiving and maturing the measures which the circumstances of the country might require. And it is preposterous to suppose that a thought could for a moment have been entertained that the President, placed at the capital, in the center of the country, could better understand the wants and wishes of the people than their own immediate representatives, who spend a part of every year among them, living with them, often laboring with them, and bound to them by the triple tie of interest, duty, and affection. To assist or control Congress, then, in its ordinary legislation could not, I conceive, have been the motive for conferring the veto power on the President. This argument acquires additional force from the fact of its never having been thus used by the first six Presidents—and two of them were members of the Convention, one presiding over its deliberations and the other bearing a larger share in consummating the labors of that august body than any other person. But if bills were never returned to Congress by either of the Presidents above referred to upon the ground of their being inexpedient or not as well adapted as they might be to the wants of the people, the veto was applied upon that of want of conformity to the Constitution or because errors had been committed from a too hasty enactment.

There is another ground for the adoption of the veto principle, which had probably more influence in recommending it to the Convention than any other. I refer to the security which it gives to the just and equitable action of the Legislature upon all parts of the Union. It could not but have occurred to the Convention that in a country so extensive, embracing so great a variety of soil and climate, and consequently of products, and which from the same causes must ever exhibit a great difference in the amount of the population of its various sections, calling for a great diversity in the employments of the people, that the legislation of the majority might not always justly regard the rights and interests of the minority, and that acts of this character might be passed under an express grant by the words of the Constitution, and therefore not within the competency of the judiciary to declare void; that however enlightened and patriotic they might suppose from past experience the members of

Congress might be, and however largely partaking, in the general, of the liberal feelings of the people, it was impossible to expect that bodies so constituted should not sometimes be controlled by local interests and sectional feelings. It was proper, therefore, to provide some umpire from whose situation and mode of appointment more independence and freedom from such influences might be expected. Such a one was afforded by the executive department constituted by the Constitution. A person elected to that high office, having his constituents in every section, State, and subdivision of the Union, must consider himself bound by the most solemn sanctions to guard, protect, and defend the rights of all and of every portion, great or small, from the injustice and oppression of the rest. I consider the veto power, therefore, given by the Constitution to the Executive of the United States solely as a conservative power, to be used only first, to protect the Constitution from violation; secondly, the people from the effects of hasty legislation where their will has been probably disregarded or not well understood, and, thirdly, to prevent the effects of combinations violative of the rights of minorities. In reference to the second of these objects I may observe that I consider it the right and privilege of the people to decide disputed points of the Constitution arising from the general grant of power to Congress to carry into effect the powers expressly given; and I believe with Mr. Madison that "repeated recognitions under varied circumstances in acts of the legislative, executive, and judicial branches of the Government, accompanied by indications in different modes of the concurrence of the general will of the nation," as affording to the President sufficient authority for his considering such disputed points as settled.

Upward of half a century has elapsed since the adoption of the present form of government. It would be an object more highly desirable than the gratification of the curiosity of speculative statesmen if its precise situation could be ascertained, a fair exhibit made of the operations of each of its departments, of the powers which they respectively claim and exercise, of the collisions which have occurred between them or between the whole Government and those of the States or either of them. We could then compare our actual condition after fifty years' trial of our system with what it was in the commencement of its operations and ascertain whether the predictions of the patriots who opposed its adoption or the confident hopes of its advocates have been best realized. The great dread of the former seems to have been that the reserved powers of the States would be absorbed by those of the Federal Government and a consolidated power established, leaving to the States the shadow only of that independent action for which they had so zealously contended and on the preservation of which they relied as the last hope of liberty. Without denying that the result to which they looked with so much apprehension is in the way of being realized, it is obvious that they did not clearly see the mode of its accomplishment. The General Government has seized upon none of the reserved rights of the States. As far as any open warfare may have gone, the State authorities have amply maintained their rights. To a casual observer our system presents no appearance of discord between the different members which compose it. Even the addition of many new ones has produced no jarring. They move in their respective orbits in perfect harmony with the central head and with each other. But there is still an undercurrent at work by which, if not seasonably checked, the worst apprehensions of our antifederal patriots will be realized, and not only will the State authorities be overshadowed by the great increase of power in the executive department of the General Government, but the character of that Government, if not its designation, be essentially and radically changed. This state of things has been in part effected by causes inherent in the

Constitution and in part by the never-failing tendency of political power to increase itself. By making the President the sole distributer of all the patronage of the Government the framers of the Constitution do not appear to have anticipated at how short a period it would become a formidable instrument to control the free operations of the State governments. Of trifling importance at first, it had early in Mr. Jefferson's Administration become so powerful as to create great alarm in the mind of that patriot from the potent influence it might exert in controlling the freedom of the elective franchise. If such could have then been the effects of its influence, how much greater must be the danger at this time, quadrupled in amount as it certainly is and more completely under the control of the Executive will than their construction of their powers allowed or the forbearing characters of all the early Presidents permitted them to make. But it is not by the extent of its patronage alone that the executive department has become dangerous, but by the use which it appears may be made of the appointing power to bring under its control the whole revenues of the country. The Constitution has declared it to be the duty of the President to see that the laws are executed, and it makes him the Commander in Chief of the Armies and Navy of the United States. If the opinion of the most approved writers upon that species of mixed government which in modern Europe is termed monarchy in contradistinction to despotism is correct, there was wanting no other addition to the powers of our Chief Magistrate to stamp a monarchical character on our Government but the control of the public finances; and to me it appears strange indeed that anyone should doubt that the entire control which the President possesses over the officers who have the custody of the public money, by the power of removal with or without cause, does, for all mischievous purposes at least, virtually subject the treasure also to his disposal. The first Roman Emperor, in his attempt to seize the sacred treasure, silenced the opposition of the officer to whose charge it had been committed by a significant allusion to his sword. By a selection of political instruments for the care of the public money a reference to their commissions by a President would be quite as effectual an argument as that of Caesar to the Roman knight. I am not insensible of the great difficulty that exists in drawing a proper plan for the safe-keeping and disbursement of the public revenues, and I know the importance which has been attached by men of great abilities and patriotism to the divorce, as it is called, of the Treasury from the banking institutions. It is not the divorce which is complained of, but the unhallowed union of the Treasury with the executive department, which has created such extensive alarm. To this danger to our republican institutions and that created by the influence given to the Executive through the instrumentality of the Federal officers I propose to apply all the remedies which may be at my command. It was certainly a great error in the framers of the Constitution not to have made the officer at the head of the Treasury Department entirely independent of the Executive. He should at least have been removable only upon the demand of the popular branch of the Legislature. I have determined never to remove a Secretary of the Treasury without communicating all the circumstances attending such removal to both Houses of Congress.

The influence of the Executive in controlling the freedom of the elective franchise through the medium of the public officers can be effectually checked by renewing the prohibition published by Mr. Jefferson forbidding their interference in elections further than giving their own votes, and their own independence secured by an assurance of perfect immunity in exercising this sacred privilege of freemen under the dictates of their own unbiased judgments. Never with my consent shall an officer of the people, compensated for his services out of their pockets, become the pliant instrument of Executive will.

There is no part of the means placed in the hands of the Executive which might be used with greater effect for unhallowed purposes than the control of the public press. The maxim which our ancestors derived from the mother country that "the freedom of the press is the great bulwark of civil and religious liberty" is one of the most precious legacies which they have left us. We have learned, too, from our own as well as the experience of other countries, that golden shackles, by whomsoever or by whatever pretense imposed, are as fatal to it as the iron bonds of despotism. The presses in the necessary employment of the Government should never be used "to clear the guilty or to varnish crime." A decent and manly examination of the acts of the Government should be not only tolerated, but encouraged.

Upon another occasion I have given my opinion at some length upon the impropriety of Executive interference in the legislation of Congress—that the article in the Constitution making it the duty of the President to communicate information and authorizing him to recommend measures was not intended to make him the source in legislation, and, in particular, that he should never be looked to for schemes of finance. It would be very strange, indeed, that the Constitution should have strictly forbidden one branch of the Legislature from interfering in the origination of such bills and that it should be considered proper that an altogether different department of the Government should be permitted to do so. Some of our best political maxims and opinions have been drawn from our parent isle. There are others, however, which can not be introduced in our system without singular incongruity and the production of much mischief, and this I conceive to be one. No matter in which of the houses of Parliament a bill may originate nor by whom introduced—a minister or a member of the opposition—by the fiction of law, or rather of constitutional principle, the sovereign is supposed to have prepared it agreeably to his will and then submitted it to Parliament for their advice and consent. Now the very reverse is the case here, not only with regard to the principle, but the forms prescribed by the Constitution. The principle certainly assigns to the only body constituted by the Constitution (the legislative body) the power to make laws, and the forms even direct that the enactment should be ascribed to them. The Senate, in relation to revenue bills, have the right to propose amendments, and so has the Executive by the power given him to return them to the House of Representatives with his objections. It is in his power also to propose amendments in the existing revenue laws, suggested by his observations upon their defective or injurious operation. But the delicate duty of devising schemes of revenue should be left where the Constitution has placed it—with the immediate representatives of the people. For similar reasons the mode of keeping the public treasure should be prescribed by them, and the further removed it may be from the control of the Executive the more wholesome the arrangement and the more in accordance with republican principle.

Connected with this subject is the character of the currency. The idea of making it exclusively metallic, however well intended, appears to me to be fraught with more fatal consequences than any other scheme having no relation to the personal rights of the citizens that has ever been devised. If any single scheme could produce the effect of arresting at once that mutation of condition by which thousands of our most indigent fellow-citizens by their industry and enterprise are raised to the possession of wealth, that is the one. If there is one measure better calculated than another to produce that state of things so much deprecated by all true republicans, by which the rich are daily adding to their hoards and the poor sinking deeper into penury, it is an exclusive metallic currency. Or if there is a

process by which the character of the country for generosity and nobleness of feeling may be destroyed by the great increase and neck toleration of usury, it is an exclusive metallic currency.

Amongst the other duties of a delicate character which the President is called upon to perform is the supervision of the government of the Territories of the United States. Those of them which are destined to become members of our great political family are compensated by their rapid progress from infancy to manhood for the partial and temporary deprivation of their political rights. It is in this District only where American citizens are to be found who under a settled policy are deprived of many important political privileges without any inspiring hope as to the future. Their only consolation under circumstances of such deprivation is that of the devoted exterior guards of a camp—that their sufferings secure tranquillity and safety within. Are there any of their countrymen, who would subject them to greater sacrifices, to any other humiliations than those essentially necessary to the security of the object for which they were thus separated from their fellow-citizens? Are their rights alone not to be guaranteed by the application of those great principles upon which all our constitutions are founded? We are told by the greatest of British orators and statesmen that at the commencement of the War of the Revolution the most stupid men in England spoke of "their American subjects." Are there, indeed, citizens of any of our States who have dreamed of their subjects in the District of Columbia? Such dreams can never be realized by any agency of mine. The people of the District of Columbia are not the subjects of the people of the States, but free American citizens. Being in the latter condition when the Constitution was formed, no words used in that instrument could have been intended to deprive them of that character. If there is anything in the great principle of unalienable rights so emphatically insisted upon in our Declaration of Independence, they could neither make nor the United States accept a surrender of their liberties and become the subjects—in other words, the slaves—of their former fellow-citizens. If this be true—and it will scarcely be denied by anyone who has a correct idea of his own rights as an American citizen—the grant to Congress of exclusive jurisdiction in the District of Columbia can be interpreted, so far as respects the aggregate people of the United States, as meaning nothing more than to allow to Congress the controlling power necessary to afford a free and safe exercise of the functions assigned to the General Government by the Constitution. In all other respects the legislation of Congress should be adapted to their peculiar position and wants and be conformable with their deliberate opinions of their own interests.

I have spoken of the necessity of keeping the respective departments of the Government, as well as all the other authorities of our country, within their appropriate orbits. This is a matter of difficulty in some cases, as the powers which they respectively claim are often not defined by any distinct lines. Mischievous, however, in their tendencies as collisions of this kind may be, those which arise between the respective communities which for certain purposes compose one nation are much more so, for no such nation can long exist without the careful culture of those feelings of confidence and affection which are the effective bonds to union between free and confederated states. Strong as is the tie of interest, it has been often found ineffectual. Men blinded by their passions have been known to adopt measures for their country in direct opposition to all the suggestions of policy. The alternative, then, is to destroy or keep down a bad passion by creating and fostering a good one, and this seems to be the corner stone upon which our American political architects have reared the fabric of our Government. The cement which was to bind it and perpetuate its existence was the affectionate attachment between all its members. To insure the continuance of this feeling, produced at first by a community of dangers, of sufferings, and of interests, the advantages of each were made accessible to all. No participation in any good possessed by any member of our extensive Confederacy, except in domestic government, was withheld from the citizen of any other member. By a process attended with no difficulty, no delay, no expense but that of removal, the citizen of one might become the citizen of any other, and successively of the whole. The lines, too, separating powers to be exercised by the citizens of one State from those of another seem to be so distinctly drawn as to leave no room for misunderstanding. The citizens of each State unite in their persons all the privileges which that character confers and all that they may claim as citizens of the United States, but in no case can the same persons at the same time act as the citizen of two separate States, and he is therefore positively precluded from any interference with the reserved powers of any State but that of which he is for the time being a citizen. He may, indeed, offer to the citizens of other States his advice as to their management, and the form in which it is tendered is left to his own discretion and sense of propriety. It may be observed, however, that organized associations of citizens requiring compliance with their wishes too much resemble the recommendations of Athens to her allies, supported by an armed and powerful fleet. It was, indeed, to the ambition of the leading States of Greece to control the domestic concerns of the others that the destruction of that celebrated Confederacy, and subsequently of all its members, is mainly to be attributed, and it is owing to the absence of that spirit that the Helvetic Confederacy has for so many years been preserved. Never has there been seen in the institutions of the separate members of any confederacy more elements of discord. In the principles and forms of government and religion, as well as in the circumstances of the several Cantons, so marked a discrepancy was observable as to promise anything but harmony in their intercourse or permanency in their alliance, and yet for ages neither has been interrupted. Content with the positive benefits which their union produced, with the independence and safety from foreign aggression which it secured, these sagacious people respected the institutions of each other, however repugnant to their own principles and prejudices.

Our Confederacy, fellow-citizens, can only be preserved by the same forbearance. Our citizens must be content with the exercise of the powers with which the Constitution clothes them. The attempt of those of one State to control the domestic institutions of another can only result in feelings of distrust and jealousy, the certain harbingers of disunion, violence, and civil war, and the ultimate destruction of our free institutions. Our Confederacy is perfectly illustrated by the terms and principles governing a common copartnership. There is a fund of power to be exercised under the direction of the joint councils of the allied members, but that which has been reserved by the individual members is intangible by the common Government or the individual members composing it. To attempt it finds no support in the principles of our Constitution.

It should be our constant and earnest endeavor mutually to cultivate a spirit of concord and harmony among the various parts of our Confederacy. Experience has abundantly taught us that the agitation by citizens of one part of the Union of a subject not confided to the General Government, but exclusively under the guardianship of the local authorities, is productive of no other consequences than bitterness, alienation, discord, and injury to the very cause which is intended to be advanced. Of all the great interests which appertain to our country, that of union—cordial, confiding, fraternal union—is by far the most important, since it is the only true and sure guaranty of all others.

In consequence of the embarrassed state of business and the currency, some of the States may meet with difficulty in their financial concerns. However deeply we may regret anything imprudent or excessive in the engagements into which States have entered for purposes of their own, it does not become us to disparage the States governments, nor to discourage them from making proper efforts for their own relief. On the contrary, it is our duty to encourage them to the extent of our constitutional authority to apply their best means and cheerfully to make all necessary sacrifices and submit to all necessary burdens to fulfill their engagements and maintain their credit, for the character and credit of the several States form a part of the character and credit of the whole country. The resources of the country are abundant, the enterprise and activity of our people proverbial, and we may well hope that wise legislation and prudent administration by the respective governments, each acting within its own sphere, will restore former prosperity.

Unpleasant and even dangerous as collisions may sometimes be between the constituted authorities of the citizens of our country in relation to the lines which separate their respective jurisdictions, the results can be of no vital injury to our institutions if that ardent patriotism, that devoted attachment to liberty, that spirit of moderation and forbearance for which our countrymen were once distinguished, continue to be cherished. If this continues to be the ruling passion of our souls, the weaker feeling of the mistaken enthusiast will be corrected, the Utopian dreams of the scheming politician dissipated, and the complicated intrigues of the demagogue rendered harmless. The spirit of liberty is the sovereign balm for every injury which our institutions may receive. On the contrary, no care that can be used in the construction of our Government, no division of powers, no distribution of checks in its several departments, will prove effectual to keep us a free people if this spirit is suffered to decay; and decay it will without constant nurture. To the neglect of this duty the best historians agree in attributing the ruin of all the republics with whose existence and fall their writings have made us acquainted. The same causes will ever produce the same effects, and as long as the love of power is a dominant passion of the human bosom, and as long as the understandings of men can be warped and their affections changed by operations upon their passions and prejudices, so long will the liberties of a people depend on their own constant attention to its preservation. The danger to all well-established free governments arises from the unwillingness of the people to believe in its existence or from the influence of designing men diverting their attention from the quarter whence it approaches to a source from which it can never come. This is the old trick of those who would usurp the government of their country. In the name of democracy they speak, warning the people against the influence of wealth and the danger of aristocracy. History, ancient and modern, is full of such examples. Caesar became the master of the Roman people and the senate under the pretense of supporting the democratic claims of the former against the aristocracy of the latter; Cromwell, in the character of protector of the liberties of the people, became the dictator of England, and Bolivar possessed himself of unlimited power with the title of his country's liberator. There is, on the contrary, no instance on record of an extensive and well-established republic being changed into an aristocracy. The tendencies of all such governments in their decline is to monarchy, and the antagonist principle to liberty there is the spirit of faction—a spirit which assumes the character and in times of great excitement imposes itself upon the people as the genuine spirit of freedom, and, like the false Christs whose coming was foretold by the Savior, seeks to, and were it possible would, impose upon the true and most faithful disciples of liberty. It is in periods like this that it behooves the people to be most watchful of those to whom they have intrusted power. And although there is at times much difficulty in distinguishing the false from the true spirit, a calm and dispassionate investigation will detect the counterfeit, as well by the character of its operations as the results that are produced. The true spirit of liberty, although devoted, persevering, bold, and uncompromising in principle, that secured is mild and tolerant and scrupulous as to the means it employs, whilst the spirit of party, assuming to be that of liberty, is harsh, vindictive, and intolerant, and totally reckless as to the character of the allies which it brings to the aid of its cause. When the genuine spirit of liberty animates the body of a people to a thorough examination of their affairs, it leads to the excision of every excrescence which may have fastened itself upon any of the departments of the government, and restores the system to its pristine health and beauty. But the reign of an intolerant spirit of party amongst a free people seldom fails to result in a dangerous accession to the executive power introduced and established amidst unusual professions of devotion to democracy.

The foregoing remarks relate almost exclusively to matters connected with our domestic concerns. It may be proper, however, that I should give some indications to my fellow-citizens of my proposed course of conduct in the management of our foreign relations. I assure them, therefore, that it is my intention to use every means in my power to preserve the friendly intercourse which now so happily subsists with every foreign nation, and that although, of course, not well informed as to the state of pending negotiations with any of them, I see in the personal characters of the sovereigns, as well as in the mutual interests of our own and of the governments with which our relations are most intimate, a pleasing guaranty that the harmony so important to the interests of their subjects as well as of our citizens will not be interrupted by the advancement of any claim or pretension upon their part to which our honor would not permit us to yield. Long the defender of my country's rights in the field, I trust that my fellow-citizens will not see in my earnest desire to preserve peace with foreign powers any indication that their rights will ever be sacrificed or the honor of the nation tarnished by any admission on the part of their Chief Magistrate unworthy of their former glory. In our intercourse with our aboriginal neighbors the same liberality and justice which marked the course prescribed to me by two of my illustrious predecessors when acting under their direction in the discharge of the duties of superintendent and commissioner shall be strictly observed. I can conceive of no more sublime spectacle, none more likely to propitiate an impartial and common Creator, than a rigid adherence to the principles of justice on the part of a powerful nation in its transactions with a weaker and uncivilized people whom circumstances have placed at its disposal.

Before concluding, fellow-citizens, I must say something to you on the subject of the parties at this time existing in our country. To me it appears perfectly clear that the interest of that country requires that the violence of the spirit by which those parties are at this time governed must be greatly mitigated, if not entirely extinguished, or consequences will ensue which are appalling to be thought of.

If parties in a republic are necessary to secure a degree of vigilance sufficient to keep the public functionaries within the bounds of law and duty, at that point their usefulness ends. Beyond that they become destructive of public virtue, the parent of a spirit antagonist to that of liberty, and eventually its inevitable conqueror. We have examples of republics where the love of country and of liberty at one time were the dominant passions of the whole mass of citizens, and yet, with the continuance of the name and forms of free government, not a vestige of these qualities remaining in the bosoms of any one of its citizens. It was the beautiful remark of a distinguished English writer that "in the Roman senate Octavius had a party and Anthony a party, but the Commonwealth had none." Yet the senate continued to meet in the temple of liberty to talk of the sacredness and beauty of the Commonwealth and gaze at the statues of the elder Brutus and of the Curtii and Decii, and the people assembled in the forum, not, as in the days of Camillus and the Scipios, to cast their free votes for annual magistrates or pass upon the acts of the senate, but to receive from the hands of the leaders of the respective parties their share of the spoils and to shout for one or the other, as those collected in Gaul or Egypt and the lesser Asia would furnish the larger dividend. The spirit of liberty had fled, and, avoiding the abodes of civilized man, had sought protection in the wilds of Scythia or Scandinavia; and so under the operation of the same causes and influences it will fly from our Capitol and our forums. A calamity so awful, not only to our country, but to the world, must be deprecated by every patriot and every tendency to a state of things likely to produce it immediately checked. Such a tendency has existed—does exist. Always the friend of my countrymen, never their flatterer, it becomes my duty to say to them from this high place to which their partiality has exalted me that there exists in the land a spirit hostile to their best interests—hostile to liberty itself. It is a spirit contracted in its views, selfish in its objects. It looks to the aggrandizement of a few even to the destruction of the interests of the whole. The entire remedy is with the people. Something, however, may be effected by the means which they have placed in my hands. It is union that we want, not of a party for the sake of that party, but a union of the whole country for the sake of the whole country, for the defense of its interests and its honor against foreign aggression, for the defense of those principles for which our ancestors so gloriously contended. As far as it depends upon me it shall be accomplished. All the influence that I possess shall be exerted to prevent the formation at least of an Executive party in the halls of the legislative body. I wish for the support of no member of that body to any measure of mine that does not satisfy his judgment and his sense of duty to those from whom he holds his appointment, nor any confidence in advance from the people but that asked for by Mr. Jefferson, "to give firmness and effect to the legal administration of their affairs."

I deem the present occasion sufficiently important and solemn to justify me in expressing to my fellow-citizens a profound reverence for the Christian religion and a thorough conviction that sound morals, religious liberty, and a just sense of religious responsibility are essentially connected with all true and lasting happiness; and to that good Being who has blessed us by the gifts of civil and religious freedom, who watched over and prospered the labors of our fathers and has hitherto preserved to us institutions far exceeding in excellence those of any other people, let us unite in fervently commending every interest of our beloved country in all future time.

Fellow-citizens, being fully invested with that high office to which the partiality of my countrymen has called me, I now take an affectionate leave of you. You will bear with you to your homes the remembrance of the pledge I have this day given to discharge all the high duties of my exalted station according to the best of my ability, and I shall enter upon their performance with entire confidence in the support of a just and generous people.

James Knox Polk

Inaugural Address

Tuesday, March 4, 1845

Fellow-Citizens:

Without solicitation on my part, I have been chosen by the free and voluntary suffrages of my countrymen to the most honorable and most responsible office on earth. I am deeply impressed with gratitude for the confidence reposed in me. Honored with this distinguished consideration at an earlier period of life than any of my predecessors, I can not disguise the diffidence with which I am about to enter on the discharge of my official duties.

If the more aged and experienced men who have filled the office of President of the United States even in the infancy of the Republic distrusted their ability to discharge the duties of that exalted station, what ought not to be the apprehensions of one so much younger and less endowed now that our domain extends from ocean to ocean, that our people have so greatly increased in numbers, and at a time when so great diversity of opinion prevails in regard to the principles and policy which should characterize the administration of our Government? Well may the boldest fear and the wisest tremble when incurring responsibilities on which may depend our country's peace and prosperity, and in some degree the hopes and happiness of the whole human family.

In assuming responsibilities so vast I fervently invoke the aid of that Almighty Ruler of the Universe in whose hands are the destinies of nations and of men to guard this Heaven-favored land against the mischiefs which without His guidance might arise from an unwise public policy. With a firm reliance upon the wisdom of Omnipotence to sustain and direct me in the path of duty which I am appointed to pursue, I stand in the presence of this assembled multitude of my countrymen to take upon myself the solemn obligation "to the best of my ability to preserve, protect, and defend the Constitution of the United States."

A concise enumeration of the principles which will guide me in the administrative policy of the Government is not only in accordance with the examples set me by all my predecessors, but is eminently befitting the occasion.

The Constitution itself, plainly written as it is, the safeguard of our federative compact, the offspring of concession and compromise, binding together in the bonds of peace and union this great and increasing family of free and independent States, will be the chart by which I shall be directed.

It will be my first care to administer the Government in the true spirit of that instrument, and to assume no powers not expressly granted or clearly implied in its terms. The Government of the United States is one of delegated and limited powers, and it is by a strict adherence to the clearly granted powers and by abstaining from the exercise of doubtful or unauthorized implied powers that we have the only sure guaranty against the recurrence of those unfortunate collisions between the Federal and State authorities which have occasionally so much disturbed the harmony of our system and even threatened the perpetuity of our glorious Union.

"To the States, respectively, or to the people" have been reserved "the powers not delegated to the United States by the Constitution nor prohibited by it to the States." Each State is a complete sovereignty within the sphere of its reserved powers. The Government of the Union, acting within the sphere of its delegated authority, is also a complete sovereignty. While the General Government should abstain from the exercise of authority not clearly delegated to it, the States should be equally careful that in the maintenance of their rights they do not overstep the limits of powers reserved to them. One of the most distinguished of my predecessors attached deserved importance to "the support of the State governments in all their rights, as the most competent administration for our domestic concerns and the surest bulwark against antirepublican tendencies," and to the "preservation of the General Government in its whole constitutional vigor, as the sheet anchor of our peace at home and safety abroad."

To the Government of the United States has been intrusted the exclusive management of our foreign affairs. Beyond that it wields a few general enumerated powers. It does not force reform on the States. It leaves individuals, over whom it casts its protecting influence, entirely free to improve their own condition by the legitimate exercise of all their mental and physical powers. It is a common protector of each and all the States; of every man who lives upon our soil, whether of native or foreign birth; of every religious sect, in their worship of the Almighty according to the dictates of their own conscience; of every shade of opinion, and the most free inquiry; of every art, trade, and occupation consistent with the laws of the States. And we rejoice in the general happiness, prosperity, and advancement of our country, which have been the offspring of freedom, and not of power.

This most admirable and wisest system of well-regulated self-government among men ever devised by human minds has been tested by its successful operation for more than half a century, and if preserved from the usurpations of the Federal Government on the one hand and the exercise by the States of powers not reserved to them on the other, will, I fervently hope and believe, endure for ages to come and dispense the blessings of civil and religious liberty to distant generations. To effect objects so dear to every patriot I shall devote myself with anxious solicitude. It will be my desire to guard against that most fruitful source of danger to the harmonious action of our system which consists in substituting the mere discretion and caprice of the Executive or of majorities in the legislative department of the Government for powers which have been withheld from the Federal Government by the Constitution. By the theory of our Government majorities rule, but this right is not an arbitrary or unlimited one. It is a right to be exercised in subordination to the Constitution and in conformity to it. One great object of the Constitution was to restrain majorities from oppressing minorities or encroaching upon their just rights. Minorities have a right to appeal to the Constitution as a shield against such oppression.

That the blessings of liberty which our Constitution secures may be enjoyed alike by minorities and majorities, the Executive has been wisely invested with a qualified veto upon the acts of the Legislature. It is a negative power, and is conservative in its character. It arrests for the time hasty, inconsiderate, or unconstitutional legislation, invites reconsideration, and transfers questions at issue between the legislative and executive departments to the tribunal of the people. Like all other powers, it is subject to be abused. When judiciously and properly exercised, the Constitution itself may be saved from infraction and the rights of all preserved and protected.

The inestimable value of our Federal Union is felt and acknowledged by all. By this system of united and confederated States our people are permitted collectively and individually to seek their own happiness in their own way, and the consequences have been most auspicious. Since the Union was formed the number of the States has increased from thirteen to twenty-eight; two of these have taken their position as members of the Confederacy within the last week. Our population has increased from three to twenty millions. New communities and States are seeking protection under its aegis, and multitudes from the Old World are flocking to our shores to participate in its blessings. Beneath its benign sway peace and prosperity prevail. Freed from the burdens and miseries of war, our trade and intercourse have extended throughout the world. Mind, no longer tasked in devising means to accomplish or resist schemes of ambition, usurpation, or conquest, is devoting itself to man's true interests in developing his faculties and powers and the capacity of nature to minister to his enjoyments. Genius is free to announce its inventions and discoveries, and the hand is free to accomplish whatever the head conceives not incompatible with the rights of a fellow-being. All distinctions of birth or of rank have been abolished. All citizens, whether native or adopted, are placed upon terms of precise equality. All are entitled to equal rights and equal protection. No union exists between church and state, and perfect freedom of opinion is guaranteed to all sects and creeds.

These are some of the blessings secured to our happy land by our Federal Union. To perpetuate them it is our sacred duty to preserve it. Who shall assign limits to the achievements of free minds and free hands under the protection of this glorious Union? No treason to mankind since the organization of society would be equal in atrocity to that of him who would lift his hand to destroy it. He would overthrow the noblest structure of human wisdom, which protects himself and his fellow-man. He would stop the progress of free government and involve his country either in anarchy or despotism. He would extinguish the fire of liberty, which warms and animates the hearts of happy millions and invites all the nations of the earth to imitate our example. If he say that error and wrong are committed in the administration of the Government, let him remember that nothing human can be perfect, and that under no other system of government revealed by Heaven or devised by man has reason been allowed so free and broad a scope to combat error. Has the sword of despots proved to be a safer or surer instrument of reform in government than enlightened reason? Does he expect to find among the ruins of this Union a happier abode for our swarming millions than they now have under it? Every lover of his country must shudder at the thought of the possibility of its dissolution, and will be ready to adopt the patriotic sentiment, "Our Federal Union—it must be preserved." To preserve it the compromises which alone enabled our fathers to form a common constitution for the government and protection of so many States and distinct communities, of such diversified habits, interests, and domestic institutions, must be sacredly and religiously observed. Any attempt to disturb or destroy these compromises, being terms of the compact of union, can lead to none other than the most ruinous and disastrous consequences.

It is a source of deep regret that in some sections of our country misguided persons have occasionally indulged in schemes and agitations whose object is the destruction of domestic institutions existing in other sections—institutions which existed at the adoption of the Constitution and were recognized and protected by it. All must see that if it were possible for them to be successful in attaining their object the dissolution of the Union and the consequent destruction of our happy form of government must speedily follow.

I am happy to believe that at every period of our existence as a nation there has existed, and continues to exist, among the great mass of our people a devotion to the Union of the States which will shield and protect it against the moral treason of any who would seriously contemplate its destruction. To secure a continuance of that devotion the compromises of the Constitution must not only be preserved, but sectional jealousies and heartburnings must be discountenanced, and all should remember that they are members of the same political family, having a common destiny. To increase the attachment of our people to the Union, our laws should be just. Any policy which shall tend to favor monopolies or the peculiar interests of sections or classes must operate to the prejudice of the interest of their fellow-citizens, and should be avoided. If the compromises of the Constitution be preserved, if sectional jealousies and heartburnings be discountenanced, if our laws be just and the Government be practically administered strictly within the limits of power prescribed to it, we may discard all apprehensions for the safety of the Union.

With these views of the nature, character, and objects of the Government and the value of the Union, I shall steadily oppose the creation of those institutions and systems which in their nature tend to pervert it from its legitimate purposes and make it the instrument of sections, classes, and individuals. We need no national banks or other extraneous institutions planted around the Government to control or strengthen it in opposition to the will of its authors. Experience has taught us how unnecessary they are as auxiliaries of the public authorities—how impotent for good and how powerful for mischief.

Ours was intended to be a plain and frugal government, and I shall regard it to be my duty to recommend to Congress and, as far as the Executive is concerned, to enforce by all the means within my power the strictest economy in the expenditure of the public money which may be compatible with the public interests.

A national debt has become almost an institution of European monarchies. It is viewed in some of them as an essential prop to existing governments. Melancholy is the condition of that people whose government can be sustained only by a system which periodically transfers large amounts from the labor of the many to the coffers of the few. Such a system is incompatible with the ends for which our republican Government was instituted. Under a wise policy the debts contracted in our Revolution and during the War of 1812 have been happily extinguished. By a judicious application of the revenues not required for other necessary purposes, it is not doubted that the debt which has grown out of the circumstances of the last few years may be speedily paid off.

I congratulate my fellow-citizens on the entire restoration of the credit of the General Government of the Union and that of many of the States. Happy would it be for the indebted States if they were freed from their liabilities, many of which were incautiously contracted. Although the Government of the Union is neither in a legal nor a moral sense bound for the debts of the States, and it would be a violation of our compact of union to assume them, yet we can not but feel a deep interest in seeing all the States meet their public liabilities and pay off their just debts at the earliest practicable period. That they will do so as soon as it can be done without imposing too heavy burdens on their citizens there is no reason to doubt. The sound moral and honorable feeling of the people of the indebted States can not be questioned, and we are happy to perceive a settled disposition on their part, as their ability returns after a season of unexampled pecuniary embarrassment, to pay off all just demands and to acquiesce in any reasonable measures to accomplish that object.

One of the difficulties which we have had to encounter in the practical administration of the Government consists in the adjustment of our revenue laws and the levy of the taxes necessary for the support of Government. In the general proposition that no more money shall be collected than the necessities of an economical administration shall require all parties seem to acquiesce. Nor does there seem to be any material difference of opinion as to the absence of right in the Government to tax one section of country, or one class of citizens, or one occupation, for the mere profit of another. "Justice and sound policy forbid the Federal Government to foster one branch of industry to the detriment of another, or to cherish the interests of one portion to the injury of another portion of our common country." I have heretofore declared to my fellow-citizens that "in my judgment it is the duty of the Government to extend, as far as it may be practicable to do so, by its revenue laws and all other means within its power, fair and just protection to all of the great interests of the whole Union, embracing agriculture, manufactures, the mechanic arts, commerce, and navigation." I have also declared my opinion to be "in favor of a tariff for revenue," and that "in adjusting the details of such a tariff I have sanctioned such moderate discriminating duties as would produce the amount of revenue needed and at the same time afford reasonable incidental protection to our home industry," and that I was "opposed to a tariff for protection merely, and not for revenue."

The power "to lay and collect taxes, duties, imposts, and excises" was an indispensable one to be conferred on the Federal Government, which without it would possess no means of providing for its own support. In executing this power by levying a tariff of duties for the support of Government, the raising of revenue should be the object and protection the incident. To reverse this principle and make protection the object and revenue the incident would be to inflict manifest injustice upon all other than the protected interests. In levying duties for revenue it is doubtless proper to make such discriminations within the revenue principle as will afford incidental protection to our home interests. Within the revenue limit there is a discretion to discriminate; beyond that limit the rightful exercise of the power is not conceded. The incidental protection afforded to our home interests by discriminations within the revenue range it is believed will be ample. In making discriminations all our home interests should as far as practicable be equally protected. The largest portion of our people are agriculturists. Others are employed in manufactures, commerce, navigation, and the mechanic arts. They are all engaged in their respective pursuits and their joint labors constitute the national or home industry. To tax one branch of this home industry for the benefit of another would be unjust. No one of these interests can rightfully claim an advantage over the others, or to be enriched by impoverishing the others. All are equally entitled to the fostering care and protection of the Government. In exercising a sound discretion in levying discriminating duties within the limit prescribed, care should be taken that it be done in a manner not to benefit the wealthy few at the expense of the toiling millions by taxing lowest the luxuries of life, or articles of superior quality and high price, which can only be consumed by the wealthy, and highest the necessaries of life, or articles of coarse quality and low price, which the poor and great mass of our people must consume. The burdens of government should as far as practicable be distributed justly and equally among all classes of our population. These general views, long entertained on this subject, I have deemed it proper to reiterate. It is a subject upon which conflicting interests of sections and occupations are supposed to exist, and a spirit of mutual concession and compromise in adjusting its details should be cherished by every part of our widespread country as the only means of preserving harmony and a cheerful acquiescence of all

in the operation of our revenue laws. Our patriotic citizens in every part of the Union will readily submit to the payment of such taxes as shall be needed for the support of their Government, whether in peace or in war, if they are so levied as to distribute the burdens as equally as possible among them.

The Republic of Texas has made known her desire to come into our Union, to form a part of our Confederacy and enjoy with us the blessings of liberty secured and guaranteed by our Constitution. Texas was once a part of our country—was unwisely ceded away to a foreign power—is now independent, and possesses an undoubted right to dispose of a part or the whole of her territory and to merge her sovereignty as a separate and independent state in ours. I congratulate my country that by an act of the late Congress of the United States the assent of this Government has been given to the reunion, and it only remains for the two countries to agree upon the terms to consummate an object so important to both.

I regard the question of annexation as belonging exclusively to the United States and Texas. They are independent powers competent to contract, and foreign nations have no right to interfere with them or to take exceptions to their reunion. Foreign powers do not seem to appreciate the true character of our Government. Our Union is a confederation of independent States, whose policy is peace with each other and all the world. To enlarge its limits is to extend the dominions of peace over additional territories and increasing millions. The world has nothing to fear from military ambition in our Government. While the Chief Magistrate and the popular branch of Congress are elected for short terms by the suffrages of those millions who must in their own persons bear all the burdens and miseries of war, our Government can not be otherwise than pacific. Foreign powers should therefore look on the annexation of Texas to the United States not as the conquest of a nation seeking to extend her dominions by arms and violence, but as the peaceful acquisition of a territory once her own, by adding another member to our confederation, with the consent of that member, thereby diminishing the chances of war and opening to them new and ever-increasing markets for their products.

To Texas the reunion is important, because the strong protecting arm of our Government would be extended over her, and the vast resources of her fertile soil and genial climate would be speedily developed, while the safety of New Orleans and of our whole southwestern frontier against hostile aggression, as well as the interests of the whole Union, would be promoted by it.

In the earlier stages of our national existence the opinion prevailed with some that our system of confederated States could not operate successfully over an extended territory, and serious objections have at different times been made to the enlargement of our boundaries. These objections were earnestly urged when we acquired Louisiana. Experience has shown that they were not well founded. The title of numerous Indian tribes to vast tracts of country has been extinguished; new States have been admitted into the Union; new Territories have been created and our jurisdiction and laws extended over them. As our population has expanded, the Union has been cemented and strengthened. As our boundaries have been enlarged and our agricultural population has been spread over a large surface, our federative system has acquired additional strength and security. It may well be doubted whether it would not be in greater danger of overthrow if our present population were confined to the comparatively narrow limits of the original thirteen States than it is now that they are sparsely settled over a more expanded territory. It is confidently believed that our system may be safely extended to the utmost bounds of our territorial limits, and that as it shall be extended the bonds of our Union, so far from being weakened, will become stronger.

None can fail to see the danger to our safety and future peace if Texas remains an independent state or becomes an ally or dependency of some foreign nation more powerful than herself. Is there one among our citizens who would not prefer perpetual peace with Texas to occasional wars, which so often occur between bordering independent nations? Is there one who would not prefer free intercourse with her to high duties on all our products and manufactures which enter her ports or cross her frontiers? Is there one who would not prefer an unrestricted communication with her citizens to the frontier obstructions which must occur if she remains out of the Union? Whatever is good or evil in the local institutions of Texas will remain her own whether annexed to the United States or not. None of the present States will be responsible for them any more than they are for the local institutions of each other. They have confederated together for certain specified objects. Upon the same principle that they would refuse to form a perpetual union with Texas because of her local institutions our forefathers would have been prevented from forming our present Union. Perceiving no valid objection to the measure and many reasons for its adoption vitally affecting the peace, the safety, and the prosperity of both countries, I shall on the broad principle which formed the basis and produced the adoption of our Constitution, and not in any narrow spirit of sectional policy, endeavor by all constitutional, honorable, and appropriate means to consummate the expressed will of the people and Government of the United States by the reannexation of Texas to our Union at the earliest practicable period.

Nor will it become in a less degree my duty to assert and maintain by all constitutional means the right of the United States to that portion of our territory which lies beyond the Rocky Mountains. Our title to the country of the Oregon is "clear and unquestionable," and already are our people preparing to perfect that title by occupying it with their wives and children. But eighty years ago our population was confined on the west by the ridge of the Alleghanies. Within that period—within the lifetime, I might say, of some of my hearers—our people, increasing to many millions, have filled the eastern valley of the Mississippi, adventurously ascended the Missouri to its headsprings, and are already engaged in establishing the blessings of self-government in valleys of which the rivers flow to the Pacific. The world beholds the peaceful triumphs of the industry of our emigrants. To us belongs the duty of protecting them adequately wherever they may be upon our soil. The jurisdiction of our laws and the benefits of our republican institutions should be extended over them in the distant regions which they have selected for their homes. The increasing facilities of intercourse will easily bring the States, of which the formation in that part of our territory can not be long delayed, within the sphere of our federative Union. In the meantime every obligation imposed by treaty or conventional stipulations should be sacredly respected.

In the management of our foreign relations it will be my aim to observe a careful respect for the rights of other nations, while our own will be the subject of constant watchfulness. Equal and exact justice should characterize all our intercourse with foreign countries. All alliances having a tendency to jeopard the welfare and honor of our country or sacrifice any one of the national interests will be studiously avoided, and yet no opportunity will be lost to cultivate a favorable understanding with foreign governments by which our navigation and commerce may be extended and the ample products of our fertile soil, as well as the manufactures of our skillful artisans, find a ready market and remunerating prices in foreign countries.

In taking "care that the laws be faithfully executed," a strict performance of duty will be exacted from all public officers. From those officers, especially, who are charged with the collection and disbursement of the public revenue will prompt and rigid accountability be required. Any culpable failure or delay on their part to account for the moneys intrusted to them at the times and in the manner required by law will in every instance terminate the official connection of such defaulting officer with the Government.

Although in our country the Chief Magistrate must almost of necessity be chosen by a party and stand pledged to its principles and measures, yet in his official action he should not be the President of a part only, but of the whole people of the United States. While he executes the laws with an impartial hand, shrinks from no proper responsibility, and faithfully carries out in the executive department of the Government the principles and policy of those who have chosen him, he should not be unmindful that our fellow-citizens who have differed with him in opinion are entitled to the full and free exercise of their opinions and judgments, and that the rights of all are entitled to respect and regard.

Confidently relying upon the aid and assistance of the coordinate departments of the Government in conducting our public affairs, I enter upon the discharge of the high duties which have been assigned me by the people, again humbly supplicating that Divine Being who has watched over and protected our beloved country from its infancy to the present hour to continue His gracious benedictions upon us, that we may continue to be a prosperous and happy people.

Zachary Taylor

Inaugural Address

Monday, March 5, 1849

Elected by the American people to the highest office known to our laws, I appear here to take the oath prescribed by the Constitution, and, in compliance with a time-honored custom, to address those who are now assembled.

The confidence and respect shown by my countrymen in calling me to be the Chief Magistrate of a Republic holding a high rank among the nations of the earth have inspired me with feelings of the most profound gratitude; but when I reflect that the acceptance of the office which their partiality has bestowed imposes the discharge of the most arduous duties and involves the weightiest obligations, I am conscious that the position which I have been called to fill, though sufficient to satisfy the loftiest ambition, is surrounded by fearful responsibilities. Happily, however, in the performance of my new duties I shall not be without able cooperation. The legislative and judicial branches of the Government present prominent examples of distinguished civil attainments and matured experience, and it shall be my endeavor to call to my assistance in the Executive Departments individuals whose talents, integrity, and purity of character will furnish ample guaranties for the faithful and honorable performance of the trusts to be committed to their charge. With such aids and an honest purpose to do whatever is right, I hope to execute diligently, impartially, and for the best interests of the country the manifold duties devolved upon me.

In the discharge of these duties my guide will be the Constitution, which I this day swear to "preserve, protect, and defend." For the interpretation of that instrument I shall look to the decisions of the judicial tribunals established by its authority and to the practice of the Government under the earlier Presidents, who had so large a share in its formation. To the example of those illustrious patriots I shall always defer with reverence, and especially to his example who was by so many titles "the Father of his Country."

To command the Army and Navy of the United States; with the advice and consent of the Senate, to make treaties and to appoint ambassadors and other officers; to give to Congress information of the state of the Union and recommend such measures as he shall judge to be necessary; and to take care that the laws shall be faithfully executed—these are the most important functions intrusted to the President by the Constitution, and it may be expected that I shall briefly indicate the principles which will control me in their execution.

Chosen by the body of the people under the assurance that my Administration would be devoted to the welfare of the whole country, and not to the support of any particular section or merely local interest, I this day renew the declarations I have heretofore made and proclaim my fixed determination to maintain to the extent of my ability the Government in its original purity and to adopt as the basis of my public policy those great republican doctrines which constitute the strength of our national existence.

In reference to the Army and Navy, lately employed with so much distinction on active service, care shall be taken to insure the highest condition of efficiency, and in furtherance of that object the military and naval schools, sustained by the liberality of Congress, shall receive the special attention of the Executive.

As American freemen we can not but sympathize in all efforts to extend the blessings of civil and political liberty, but at the same time we are warned by the admonitions of history and the voice of our own beloved Washington to abstain from entangling alliances with foreign nations. In all disputes between conflicting governments it is our interest not less than our duty to remain strictly neutral, while our geographical position, the genius of our institutions and our people, the advancing spirit of civilization, and, above all, the dictates of religion direct us to the cultivation of peaceful and friendly relations with all other powers. It is to be hoped that no international question can now arise which a government confident in its own strength and resolved to protect its own just rights may not settle by wise negotiation; and it eminently becomes a government like our own, founded on the morality and intelligence of its citizens and upheld by their affections, to exhaust every resort of honorable diplomacy before appealing to arms. In the conduct of our foreign relations I shall conform to these views, as I believe them essential to the best interests and the true honor of the country.

The appointing power vested in the President imposes delicate and onerous duties. So far as it is possible to be informed, I shall make honesty, capacity, and fidelity indispensable prerequisites to the bestowal of office, and the absence of either of these qualities shall be deemed sufficient cause for removal.

It shall be my study to recommend such constitutional measures to Congress as may be necessary and proper to secure encouragement and protection to the great interests of agriculture, commerce, and manufactures, to improve our rivers and harbors, to provide for the speedy extinguishment of the public debt, to enforce a strict accountability on the part of all officers of the Government and the utmost economy in all public expenditures; but it is for the wisdom of Congress itself, in which all legislative powers are vested by the Constitution, to regulate these and other matters of domestic policy. I shall look with confidence to the enlightened patriotism of that body to adopt such measures of conciliation as may harmonize conflicting interests and tend to perpetuate that Union which should be the paramount object of our hopes and affections. In any action calculated to promote an object so near the heart of everyone who truly loves his country I will zealously unite with the coordinate branches of the Government.

In conclusion I congratulate you, my fellow-citizens, upon the high state of prosperity to which the goodness of Divine Providence has conducted our common country. Let us invoke a continuance of the same protecting care which has led us from small beginnings to the eminence we this day occupy, and let us seek to deserve that continuance by prudence and moderation in our councils, by well-directed attempts to assuage the bitterness which too often marks unavoidable differences of opinion, by the promulgation and practice of just and liberal principles, and by an enlarged patriotism, which shall acknowledge no limits but those of our own widespread Republic.

Franklin Pierce

Inaugural Address

Friday, March 4, 1853

My Countrymen:

IT a relief to feel that no heart but my own can know the personal regret and bitter sorrow over which I have been borne to a position so suitable for others rather than desirable for myself.

The circumstances under which I have been called for a limited period to preside over the destinies of the Republic fill me with a profound sense of responsibility, but with nothing like shrinking apprehension. I repair to the post assigned me not as to one sought, but in obedience to the unsolicited expression of your will, answerable only for a fearless, faithful, and diligent exercise of my best powers. I ought to be, and am, truly grateful for the rare manifestation of the nation's confidence; but this, so far from lightening my obligations, only adds to their weight. You have summoned me in my weakness; you must sustain me by your strength. When looking for the fulfillment of reasonable requirements, you will not be unmindful of the great changes which have occurred, even within the last quarter of a century, and the consequent augmentation and complexity of duties imposed in the administration both of your home and foreign affairs.

Whether the elements of inherent force in the Republic have kept pace with its unparalleled progression in territory, population, and wealth has been the subject of earnest thought and discussion on both sides of the ocean. Less than sixty-four years ago the Father of his Country made "the" then "recent accession of the important State of North Carolina to the Constitution of the United States" one of the subjects of his special congratulation. At that moment, however, when the agitation consequent upon the Revolutionary struggle had hardly subsided, when we were just emerging from the weakness and embarrassments of the Confederation, there was an evident consciousness of vigor equal to the great mission so wisely and bravely fulfilled by our fathers. It was not a presumptuous assurance, but a calm faith, springing from a clear view of the sources of power in a government constituted like ours. It is no paradox to say that although comparatively weak the new-born nation was intrinsically strong. Inconsiderable in population and apparent resources, it was upheld by a broad and intelligent comprehension of rights and an all-pervading purpose to maintain them, stronger than armaments. It came from the furnace of the Revolution, tempered to the necessities of the times. The thoughts of the men of that day were as practical as their sentiments were patriotic. They wasted no portion of their energies upon idle and delusive speculations, but with a firm and fearless step advanced beyond the governmental landmarks which had hitherto circumscribed the limits of human freedom and planted their standard, where it has stood against dangers which have threatened from abroad, and internal agitation, which has at times fearfully menaced at home. They proved themselves equal to the solution of the great problem, to understand which their minds had been illuminated by the dawning lights of the Revolution. The object sought was not a thing dreamed of; it was a thing realized. They had exhibited only the power to achieve, but, what all history affirms to be so much more unusual, the capacity to maintain. The oppressed throughout the world from that day to the present have turned their eyes hitherward, not to find those lights extinguished or to fear lest they should wane, but to be constantly cheered by their steady and increasing radiance.

In this our country has, in my judgment, thus far fulfilled its highest duty to suffering humanity. It has spoken and will continue to speak, not only by its words, but by its acts, the language of sympathy, encouragement, and hope to those who earnestly listen to tones which pronounce for the largest rational liberty. But after all, the most animating encouragement and potent appeal for freedom will be its own history—its trials and its triumphs. Preeminently, the power of our advocacy reposes in our example; but no example, be it remembered, can be powerful for lasting good, whatever apparent advantages may be gained, which is not based upon eternal principles of right and justice. Our fathers decided for themselves, both upon the hour to declare and the hour to strike. They were their own judges of the circumstances under which it became them to pledge to each other "their lives, their fortunes, and their sacred honor" for the acquisition of the priceless inheritance transmitted to us. The energy with which that great conflict was opened and, under the guidance of a manifest and beneficent Providence the uncomplaining endurance with which it was prosecuted to its consummation were only surpassed by the wisdom and patriotic spirit of concession which characterized all the counsels of the early fathers.

One of the most impressive evidences of that wisdom is to be found in the fact that the actual working of our system has dispelled a degree of solicitude which at the outset disturbed bold hearts and far-reaching intellects. The apprehension of dangers from extended territory, multiplied States, accumulated wealth, and augmented population has proved to be unfounded. The stars upon your banner have become nearly threefold their original number; your densely populated possessions skirt the shores of the two great oceans; and yet this vast increase of people and territory has not only shown itself compatible with the harmonious action of the States and Federal Government in their respective constitutional spheres, but has afforded an additional guaranty of the strength and integrity of both.

With an experience thus suggestive and cheering, the policy of my Administration will not be controlled by any timid forebodings of evil from expansion. Indeed, it is not to be disguised that our attitude as a nation and our position on the globe render the acquisition of certain possessions not within our jurisdiction eminently important for our protection, if not in the future essential for the preservation of the rights of commerce and the peace of the world. Should they be obtained, it will be through no grasping spirit, but with a view to obvious national interest and security, and in a manner entirely consistent with the strictest observance of national faith. We have nothing in our history or position to invite aggression; we have everything to beckon us to the cultivation of relations of peace and amity with all nations. Purposes, therefore, at once just and pacific will be significantly marked in the conduct of our foreign affairs. I intend that my Administration shall leave no blot upon our fair record, and trust I may safely give the assurance that no act within the legitimate scope of my constitutional control will be tolerated on the part of any portion of our citizens which can not challenge a ready justification before the tribunal of the civilized world. An Administration would be unworthy of confidence at home or respect abroad should it cease to be influenced by the conviction that no apparent advantage can be purchased at a price so dear as that of national wrong or dishonor. It is not your privilege as a nation to speak of a distant past. The striking incidents of your history, replete with instruction and furnishing abundant grounds for hopeful confidence, are comprised in a period comparatively brief. But if your past is limited, your future is boundless. Its obligations throng the unexplored pathway of advancement, and will be limitless as duration. Hence a sound and comprehensive policy should embrace not less the distant future than the urgent present.

The great objects of our pursuit as a people are best to be attained by peace, and are entirely consistent with the tranquillity and interests of the rest of mankind. With the neighboring nations upon our continent we should cultivate kindly and fraternal relations. We can desire nothing in regard to them so much as to see them consolidate their strength and pursue the paths of prosperity and happiness. If in the course of their growth we should open new channels of trade and create additional facilities for friendly intercourse, the benefits realized will be equal and mutual. Of the complicated European systems of national polity we have heretofore been independent. From their wars, their tumults, and anxieties we have been, happily, almost entirely exempt. Whilst these are confined to the nations which gave them existence, and within their legitimate jurisdiction, they can not affect us except as they appeal to our sympathies in the cause of human freedom and universal advancement. But the vast interests of commerce are common to all mankind, and the advantages of trade and international intercourse must always present a noble field for the moral influence of a great people.

With these views firmly and honestly carried out, we have a right to expect, and shall under all circumstances require, prompt reciprocity. The rights which belong to us as a nation are not alone to be regarded, but those which pertain to every citizen in his individual capacity, at home and abroad, must be sacredly maintained. So long as he can discern every star in its place upon that ensign, without wealth to purchase for him preferment or title to secure for him place, it will be his privilege, and must be his acknowledged right, to stand unabashed even in the presence of princes, with a proud consciousness that he is himself one of a nation of sovereigns and that he can not in legitimate pursuit wander so far from home that the agent whom he shall leave behind in the place which I now occupy will not see that no rude hand of power or tyrannical passion is laid upon him with impunity. He must realize that upon every sea and on every soil where our enterprise may rightfully seek the protection of our flag American citizenship is an inviolable panoply for the security of American rights. And in this connection it can hardly be necessary to reaffirm a principle which should now be regarded as fundamental. The rights, security, and repose of this Confederacy reject the idea of interference or colonization on this side of the ocean by any foreign power beyond present jurisdiction as utterly inadmissible.

The opportunities of observation furnished by my brief experience as a soldier confirmed in my own mind the opinion, entertained and acted upon by others from the formation of the Government, that the maintenance of large standing armies in our country would be not only dangerous, but unnecessary. They also illustrated the importance—I might well say the absolute necessity—of the military science and practical skill furnished in such an eminent degree by the institution which has made your Army what it is, under the discipline and instruction of officers not more distinguished for their solid attainments, gallantry, and devotion to the public service than for unobtrusive bearing and high moral tone. The Army as organized must be the nucleus around which in every time of need the strength of your military power, the sure bulwark of your defense—a national militia— may be readily formed into a well-disciplined and efficient organization. And the skill and self-devotion of the Navy assure you that you may take the performance of the past as a pledge for the future, and may confidently expect that the flag which has waved its untarnished folds over every sea will still float in undiminished honor. But these, like many other subjects, will be appropriately brought at a future time to the attention of the coordinate branches of the Government, to which I shall always look with profound respect and with trustful confidence that they will accord to me the aid and support which I shall so much need and which their experience and wisdom will readily suggest.

In the administration of domestic affairs you expect a devoted integrity in the public service and an observance of rigid economy in all departments, so marked as never justly to be questioned. If this reasonable expectation be not realized, I frankly confess that one of your leading hopes is doomed to disappointment, and that my efforts in a very important particular must result in a humiliating failure. Offices can be properly regarded only in the light of aids for the accomplishment of these objects, and as occupancy can confer no prerogative nor importunate desire for preferment any claim, the public interest imperatively demands that they be considered with sole reference to the duties to be performed. Good citizens may well claim the protection of good laws and the benign influence of good government, but a claim for office is what the people of a republic should never recognize. No reasonable man of any party will expect the Administration to be so regardless of its responsibility and of the obvious elements of success as to retain persons known to be under the influence of political hostility and partisan prejudice in positions which will require not only severe labor, but cordial cooperation. Having no implied engagements to ratify, no rewards to bestow, no resentments to remember, and no personal wishes to consult in selections for official station, I shall fulfill this difficult and delicate trust, admitting no motive as worthy either of my character or position which does not contemplate an efficient discharge of duty and the best interests of my country. I acknowledge my obligations to the masses of my

countrymen, and to them alone. Higher objects than personal aggrandizement gave direction and energy to their exertions in the late canvass, and they shall not be disappointed. They require at my hands diligence, integrity, and capacity wherever there are duties to be performed. Without these qualities in their public servants, more stringent laws for the prevention or punishment of fraud, negligence, and peculation will be vain. With them they will be unnecessary.

But these are not the only points to which you look for vigilant watchfulness. The dangers of a concentration of all power in the general government of a confederacy so vast as ours are too obvious to be disregarded. You have a right, therefore, to expect your agents in every department to regard strictly the limits imposed upon them by the Constitution of the United States. The great scheme of our constitutional liberty rests upon a proper distribution of power between the State and Federal authorities, and experience has shown that the harmony and happiness of our people must depend upon a just discrimination between the separate rights and responsibilities of the States and your common rights and obligations under the General Government; and here, in my opinion, are the considerations which should form the true basis of future concord in regard to the questions which have most seriously disturbed public tranquillity. If the Federal Government will confine itself to the exercise of powers clearly granted by the Constitution, it can hardly happen that its action upon any question should endanger the institutions of the States or interfere with their right to manage matters strictly domestic according to the will of their own people.

In expressing briefly my views upon an important subject rich has recently agitated the nation to almost a fearful degree, I am moved by no other impulse than a most earnest desire for the perpetuation of that Union which has made us what we are, showering upon us blessings and conferring a power and influence which our fathers could hardly have anticipated, even with their most sanguine hopes directed to a far-off future. The sentiments I now announce were not unknown before the expression of the voice which called me here. My own position upon this subject was clear and unequivocal, upon the record of my words and my acts, and it is only recurred to at this time because silence might perhaps be misconstrued. With the Union my best and dearest earthly hopes are entwined. Without it what are we individually or collectively? What becomes of the noblest field ever opened for the advancement of our race in religion, in government, in the arts, and in all that dignifies and adorns mankind? From that radiant constellation which both illumines our own way and points out to struggling nations their course, let but a single star be lost, and, if these be not utter darkness, the luster of the whole is dimmed. Do my countrymen need any assurance that such a catastrophe is not to overtake them while I possess the power to stay it? It is with me an earnest and vital belief that as the Union has been the source, under Providence, of our prosperity to this time, so it is the surest pledge of a continuance of the blessings we have enjoyed, and which we are sacredly bound to transmit undiminished to our children. The field of calm and free discussion in our country is open, and will always be so, but never has been and never can be traversed for good in a spirit of sectionalism and uncharitableness. The founders of the Republic dealt with things as they were presented to them, in a spirit of self-sacrificing patriotism, and, as time has proved, with a comprehensive wisdom which it will always be safe for us to consult. Every measure tending to strengthen the fraternal feelings of all the members of our Union has had my heartfelt approbation. To every theory of society or government, whether the offspring of feverish ambition or of morbid enthusiasm, calculated to dissolve the bonds of law and affection which unite us, I shall interpose a ready and stern resistance. I believe that involuntary servitude, as it exists in different States of this Confederacy, is recognized by the Constitution. I believe that it stands like any other admitted right, and that the States where it exists are entitled to efficient remedies to enforce the constitutional provisions. I hold that the laws of 1850, commonly called the "compromise measures," are strictly constitutional and to be unhesitatingly carried into effect. I believe that the constituted authorities of this Republic are bound to regard the rights of the South in this respect as they would view any other legal and constitutional right, and that the laws to enforce them should be respected and obeyed, not with a reluctance encouraged by abstract opinions as to their propriety in a different state of society, but cheerfully and according to the decisions of the tribunal to which their exposition belongs. Such have been, and are, my convictions, and upon them I shall act. I fervently hope that the question is at rest, and that no sectional or ambitious or fanatical excitement may again threaten the durability of our institutions or obscure the light of our prosperity.

But let not the foundation of our hope rest upon man's wisdom. It will not be sufficient that sectional prejudices find no place in the public deliberations. It will not be sufficient that the rash counsels of human passion are rejected. It must be felt that there is no national security but in the nation's humble, acknowledged dependence upon God and His overruling providence.

We have been carried in safety through a perilous crisis. Wise counsels, like those which gave us the Constitution, prevailed to uphold it. Let the period be remembered as an admonition, and not as an encouragement, in any section of the Union, to make experiments where experiments are fraught with such fearful hazard. Let it be impressed upon all hearts that, beautiful as our fabric is, no earthly power or wisdom could ever reunite its broken fragments. Standing, as I do, almost within view of the green slopes of Monticello, and, as it were, within reach of the tomb of Washington, with all the cherished memories of the past gathering around me like so many eloquent voices of exhortation from heaven, I can express no better hope for my country than that the kind Providence which smiled upon our fathers may enable their children to preserve the blessings they have inherited.

James Buchanan

Inaugural Address

Wednesday, March 4, 1857

Fellow-Citizens:

I APPEAR before you this day to take the solemn oath "that I will faithfully execute the office of President of the United States and will to the best of my ability preserve, protect, and defend the Constitution of the United States."

In entering upon this great office I must humbly invoke the God of our fathers for wisdom and firmness to execute its high and responsible duties in such a manner as to restore harmony and ancient friendship among the people of the several States and to preserve our free institutions throughout many generations. Convinced that I owe my election to the inherent love for the Constitution and the Union which still animates the hearts of the American people, let me earnestly ask their powerful support in sustaining all just measures calculated to perpetuate these, the richest political blessings which Heaven has ever bestowed upon any nation. Having determined not to become a candidate for reelection, I shall have no motive to influence my conduct in administering the Government except the desire ably and faithfully to serve my country and to live in grateful memory of my countrymen.

We have recently passed through a Presidential contest in which the passions of our fellow-citizens were excited to the highest degree by questions of deep and vital importance; but when the people proclaimed their will the tempest at once subsided and all was calm.

The voice of the majority, speaking in the manner prescribed by the Constitution, was heard, and instant submission followed. Our own country could alone have exhibited so grand and striking a spectacle of the capacity of man for self-government.

What a happy conception, then, was it for Congress to apply this simple rule, that the will of the majority shall govern, to the settlement of the question of domestic slavery in the Territories. Congress is neither "to legislate slavery into any Territory or State nor to exclude it therefrom, but to leave the people thereof perfectly free to form and regulate their domestic institutions in their own way, subject only to the Constitution of the United States."

As a natural consequence, Congress has also prescribed that when the Territory of Kansas shall be admitted as a State it "shall be received into the Union with or without slavery, as their constitution may prescribe at the time of their admission."

A difference of opinion has arisen in regard to the point of time when the people of a Territory shall decide this question for themselves.

This is, happily, a matter of but little practical importance. Besides, it is a judicial question, which legitimately belongs to the Supreme Court of the United States, before whom it is now pending, and will, it is understood, be speedily and finally settled. To their decision, in common with all good citizens, I shall cheerfully submit, whatever this may be, though it has ever been my individual opinion that under the Nebraska-Kansas act the appropriate period will be when the number of actual residents in the Territory shall justify the formation of a constitution with a view to its admission as a State into the Union. But be this as it may, it is the imperative and indispensable duty of the Government of the United States to secure to every resident inhabitant the free and independent expression of his opinion by his vote. This sacred right of each individual must be preserved. That being accomplished, nothing can be fairer than to leave the people of a Territory free from all foreign interference to decide their own destiny for themselves, subject only to the Constitution of the United States.

The whole Territorial question being thus settled upon the principle of popular sovereignty—a principle as ancient as free government itself—everything of a practical nature has been decided. No other question remains for adjustment, because all agree that under the Constitution slavery in the States is beyond the reach of any human power except that of the respective States themselves wherein it exists. May we not, then, hope that the long agitation on this subject is approaching its end, and that the geographical parties to which it has given birth, so much dreaded by the Father of his Country, will speedily become extinct? Most happy will it be for the country when the public mind shall be diverted from this question to others of more pressing and practical importance. Throughout the whole progress of this agitation, which has scarcely known any intermission for more than twenty years, whilst it has been productive of no positive good to any human being it has been the prolific source of great evils to the master, to the slave, and to the whole country. It has alienated and estranged the people of the sister States from each other, and has even seriously endangered the very existence of the Union. Nor has the danger yet entirely ceased. Under our system there is a remedy for all mere political evils in the sound sense and sober judgment of the people. Time is a great corrective. Political subjects which but a few years ago excited and exasperated the public mind have passed away and are now nearly forgotten. But this question of domestic slavery is of far graver importance than any mere political question, because should the agitation continue it may eventually endanger the personal safety of a large portion of our countrymen where the institution exists. In that event no form of government, however admirable in itself and however productive of material benefits, can compensate for the loss of peace and domestic security around the family altar. Let every Union-loving man, therefore, exert his best influence to suppress this agitation, which since the recent legislation of Congress is without any legitimate object.

It is an evil omen of the times that men have undertaken to calculate the mere material value of the Union. Reasoned estimates have been presented of the pecuniary profits and local advantages which would result to different States and sections from its dissolution and of the comparative injuries which such an event would inflict on other States and sections. Even descending to this low and narrow view of the mighty question, all such calculations are at fault. The bare reference to a single consideration will be conclusive on this point. We at present enjoy a free trade throughout our extensive and expanding country such as the world has never witnessed. This trade is conducted on railroads and canals, on noble rivers and arms of the sea, which bind together the North and the South, the East and the West, of our Confederacy. Annihilate this trade, arrest its free progress by the geographical lines of jealous and hostile States, and you destroy the prosperity and onward march of the whole and every part and involve all in one common ruin. But such considerations, important as they are in themselves, sink into insignificance when we reflect on the terrific evils which would result from disunion to every portion of the Confederacy—to the North, not more than to the South, to the East not more than to the West. These I shall not attempt to portray, because I feel an humble confidence that the kind Providence which inspired our fathers with wisdom to frame the most perfect form of government and union ever devised by man will not suffer it to perish until it shall have been peacefully instrumental by its example in the extension of civil and religious liberty throughout the world.

Next in importance to the maintenance of the Constitution and the Union is the duty of preserving the Government free from the taint or even the suspicion of corruption. Public virtue is the vital spirit of republics, and history proves that when this has decayed and the love of money has usurped its place, although the forms of free government may remain for a season, the substance has departed forever.

Our present financial condition is without a parallel in history. No nation has ever before been embarrassed from too large a surplus in its treasury. This almost necessarily gives birth to extravagant legislation. It produces wild schemes of expenditure and begets a race of speculators and jobbers, whose

ingenuity is exerted in contriving and promoting expedients to obtain public money. The purity of official agents, whether rightfully or wrongfully, is suspected, and the character of the government suffers in the estimation of the people. This is in itself a very great evil.

The natural mode of relief from this embarrassment is to appropriate the surplus in the Treasury to great national objects for which a clear warrant can be found in the Constitution. Among these I might mention the extinguishment of the public debt, a reasonable increase of the Navy, which is at present inadequate to the protection of our vast tonnage afloat, now greater than that of any other nation, as well as to the defense of our extended seacoast.

It is beyond all question the true principle that no more revenue ought to be collected from the people than the amount necessary to defray the expenses of a wise, economical, and efficient administration of the Government. To reach this point it was necessary to resort to a modification of the tariff, and this has, I trust, been accomplished in such a manner as to do as little injury as may have been practicable to our domestic manufactures, especially those necessary for the defense of the country. Any discrimination against a particular branch for the purpose of benefiting favored corporations, individuals, or interests would have been unjust to the rest of the community and inconsistent with that spirit of fairness and equality which ought to govern in the adjustment of a revenue tariff.

But the squandering of the public money sinks into comparative insignificance as a temptation to corruption when compared with the squandering of the public lands.

No nation in the tide of time has ever been blessed with so rich and noble an inheritance as we enjoy in the public lands. In administering this important trust, whilst it may be wise to grant portions of them for the improvement of the remainder, yet we should never forget that it is our cardinal policy to reserve these lands, as much as may be, for actual settlers, and this at moderate prices. We shall thus not only best promote the prosperity of the new States and Territories, by furnishing them a hardy and independent race of honest and industrious citizens, but shall secure homes for our children and our children's children, as well as for those exiles from foreign shores who may seek in this country to improve their condition and to enjoy the blessings of civil and religious liberty. Such emigrants have done much to promote the growth and prosperity of the country. They have proved faithful both in peace and in war. After becoming citizens they are entitled, under the Constitution and laws, to be placed on a perfect equality with native-born citizens, and in this character they should ever be kindly recognized.

The Federal Constitution is a grant from the States to Congress of certain specific powers, and the question whether this grant should be liberally or strictly construed has more or less divided political parties from the beginning. Without entering into the argument, I desire to state at the commencement of my Administration that long experience and observation have convinced me that a strict construction of the powers of the Government is the only true, as well as the only safe, theory of the Constitution. Whenever in our past history doubtful powers have been exercised by Congress, these have never failed to produce injurious and unhappy consequences. Many such instances might be adduced if this were the proper occasion. Neither is it necessary for the public service to strain the language of the Constitution, because all the great and useful powers required for a successful administration of the Government, both in peace and in war, have been granted, either in express terms or by the plainest implication.

Whilst deeply convinced of these truths, I yet consider it

clear that under the war-making power Congress may appropriate money toward the construction of a military road when this is absolutely necessary for the defense of any State or Territory of the Union against foreign invasion. Under the Constitution Congress has power "to declare war," "to raise and support armies," "to provide and maintain a navy," and to call forth the militia to "repel invasions." Thus endowed, in an ample manner, with the war-making power, the corresponding duty is required that "the United States shall protect each of them [the States] against invasion." Now, how is it possible to afford this protection to California and our Pacific possessions except by means of a military road through the Territories of the United States, over which men and munitions of war may be speedily transported from the Atlantic States to meet and to repel the invader? In the event of a war with a naval power much stronger than our own we should then have no other available access to the Pacific Coast, because such a power would instantly close the route across the isthmus of Central America. It is impossible to conceive that whilst the Constitution has expressly required Congress to defend all the States it should yet deny to them, by any fair construction, the only possible means by which one of these States can be defended. Besides, the Government, ever since its origin, has been in the constant practice of constructing military roads. It might also be wise to consider whether the love for the Union which now animates our fellow-citizens on the Pacific Coast may not be impaired by our neglect or refusal to provide for them, in their remote and isolated condition, the only means by which the power of the States on this side of the Rocky Mountains can reach them in sufficient time to "protect" them "against invasion." I forbear for the present from expressing an opinion as to the wisest and most economical mode in which the Government can lend its aid in accomplishing this great and necessary work. I believe that many of the difficulties in the way, which now appear formidable, will in a great degree vanish as soon as the nearest and best route shall have been satisfactorily ascertained.

It may be proper that on this occasion I should make some brief remarks in regard to our rights and duties as a member of the great family of nations. In our intercourse with them there are some plain principles, approved by our own experience, from which we should never depart. We ought to cultivate peace, commerce, and friendship with all nations, and this not merely as the best means of promoting our own material interests, but in a spirit of Christian benevolence toward our fellow-men, wherever their lot may be cast. Our diplomacy should be direct and frank, neither seeking to obtain more nor accepting less than is our due. We ought to cherish a sacred regard for the independence of all nations, and never attempt to interfere in the domestic concerns of any unless this shall be imperatively required by the great law of self-preservation. To avoid entangling alliances has been a maxim of our policy ever since the days of Washington, and its wisdom's no one will attempt to dispute. In short, we ought to do justice in a kindly spirit to all nations and require justice from them in return.

It is our glory that whilst other nations have extended their dominions by the sword we have never acquired any territory except by fair purchase or, as in the case of Texas, by the voluntary determination of a brave, kindred, and independent people to blend their destinies with our own. Even our acquisitions from Mexico form no exception. Unwilling to take advantage of the fortune of war against a sister republic, we purchased these possessions under the treaty of peace for a sum which was considered at the time a fair equivalent. Our past history forbids that we shall in the future acquire territory unless this be sanctioned by the laws of justice and honor. Acting on this principle, no nation will have a right to interfere or to complain if in the progress of events we shall still further extend our possessions. Hitherto in all our acquisitions the people, under the protection of the American flag, have enjoyed civil and religious liberty, as well as equal and just laws, and have been contented, prosperous, and happy. Their trade with the rest of the world has rapidly increased, and thus every commercial nation has shared largely in their successful progress.

I shall now proceed to take the oath prescribed by the Constitution, whilst humbly invoking the blessing of Divine Providence on this great people.

Abraham Lincoln

First Inaugural Address

Monday, March 4, 1861

Fellow-Citizens of the United States:

In compliance with a custom as old as the Government itself, I appear before you to address you briefly and to take in your presence the oath prescribed by the Constitution of the United States to be taken by the President "before he enters on the execution of this office."

I do not consider it necessary at present for me to discuss those matters of administration about which there is no special anxiety or excitement.

Apprehension seems to exist among the people of the Southern States that by the accession of a Republican Administration their property and their peace and personal security are to be endangered. There has never been any reasonable cause for such apprehension. Indeed, the most ample evidence to the contrary has all the while existed and been open to their inspection. It is found in nearly all the published speeches of him who now addresses you. I do but quote from one of those speeches when I declare that—

I have no purpose, directly or indirectly, to interfere with the institution of slavery in the States where it exists. I believe I have no lawful right to do so, and I have no inclination to do so.

Those who nominated and elected me did so with full knowledge that I had made this and many similar declarations and had never recanted them; and more than this, they placed in the platform for my acceptance, and as a law to themselves and to me, the clear and emphatic resolution which I now read:

Resolved, That the maintenance inviolate of the rights of the States, and especially the right of each State to order and control its own domestic institutions according to its own judgment exclusively, is essential to that balance of power on which the perfection and endurance of our political fabric depend; and we denounce the lawless invasion by armed force of the soil of any State or Territory, no matter what pretext, as among the gravest of crimes.

I now reiterate these sentiments, and in doing so I only press upon the public attention the most conclusive evidence of which the case is susceptible that the property, peace, and security of no section are to be in any wise endangered by the now incoming Administration. I add, too, that all the protection which, consistently with the Constitution and the laws, can be given will be cheerfully given to all the States when lawfully demanded, for whatever cause—as cheerfully to one section as to another. There is much controversy about the delivering up of fugitives from service or labor. The clause I now read is as plainly written in the Constitution as any other of its provisions:

No person held to service or labor in one State, under the laws thereof, escaping into another, shall in consequence of any law or regulation therein be discharged from such service or labor, but shall be delivered up on claim of the party to whom such service or labor may be due.

It is scarcely questioned that this provision was intended by those who made it for the reclaiming of what we call fugitive slaves; and the intention of the lawgiver is the law. All members of Congress swear their support to the whole Constitution—to this provision as much as to any other. To the proposition, then, that slaves whose cases come within the terms of this clause "shall be delivered up" their oaths are unanimous. Now, if they would make the effort in good temper, could they not with nearly equal unanimity frame and pass a law by means of which to keep good that unanimous oath?

There is some difference of opinion whether this clause should be enforced by national or by State authority, but surely that difference is not a very material one. If the slave is to be surrendered, it can be of but little consequence to him or to others by which authority it is done. And should anyone in any case be content that his oath shall go unkept on a merely unsubstantial controversy as to how it shall be kept?

Again: In any law upon this subject ought not all the safeguards of liberty known in civilized and humane jurisprudence to be introduced, so that a free man be not in any case surrendered as a slave? And might it not be well at the same time to provide by law for the enforcement of that clause in the Constitution which guarantees that "the citizens of each State shall be entitled to all privileges and immunities of citizens in the several States"?

I take the official oath to-day with no mental reservations and with no purpose to construe the Constitution or laws by any hypercritical rules; and while I do not choose now to specify particular acts of Congress as proper to be enforced, I do suggest that it will be much safer for all, both in official and private stations, to conform to and abide by all those acts which stand unrepealed than to violate any of them trusting to find impunity in having them held to be unconstitutional.

It is seventy-two years since the first inauguration of a President under our National Constitution. During that period fifteen different and greatly distinguished citizens have in succession administered the executive branch of the Government. They have conducted it through many perils, and generally with great success. Yet, with all this scope of precedent, I now enter upon the same task for the brief constitutional term of four years under great and peculiar difficulty. A disruption of the Federal Union, heretofore only menaced, is now formidably attempted.

I hold that in contemplation of universal law and of the Constitution the Union of these States is perpetual. Perpetuity is implied, if not expressed, in the fundamental law of all national governments. It is safe to assert that no government proper ever had a provision in its organic law for its own termination. Continue to execute all the express provisions of our National Constitution, and the Union will endure forever, it being impossible to destroy it except by some action not provided for in the instrument itself.

Again: If the United States be not a government proper, but an association of States in the nature of contract merely, can it, as a contract, be peaceably unmade by less than all the parties who made it? One party to a contract may violate it—break it, so to speak—but does it not require all to lawfully rescind it?

Descending from these general principles, we find the proposition that in legal contemplation the Union is perpetual confirmed by the history of the Union itself. The Union is much older than the Constitution. It was formed, in fact, by the Articles of Association in 1774. It was matured and continued by the Declaration of Independence in 1776. It was further matured, and the faith of all the then thirteen States expressly plighted and engaged that it should be perpetual, by the Articles of Confederation in 1778. And finally, in 1787, one of the declared objects for ordaining and establishing the Constitution was "to form a more perfect Union."

But if destruction of the Union by one or by a part only of the States be lawfully possible, the Union is less perfect than before the Constitution, having lost the vital element of perpetuity.

It follows from these views that no State upon its own mere motion can lawfully get out of the Union; that resolves and ordinances to that effect are legally void, and that acts of violence within any State or States against the authority of the United States are insurrectionary or revolutionary, according to circumstances.

I therefore consider that in view of the Constitution and the laws the Union is unbroken, and to the extent of my ability, I shall take care, as the Constitution itself expressly enjoins upon me, that the laws of the Union be faithfully executed in all the States. Doing this I deem to be only a simple duty on my part, and I shall perform it so far as practicable unless my rightful masters, the American people, shall withhold the requisite means or in some authoritative manner direct the contrary. I trust this will not be regarded as a menace, but only as the declared purpose of the Union that it will constitutionally defend and maintain itself.

In doing this there needs to be no bloodshed or violence, and there shall be none unless it be forced upon the national authority. The power confided to me will be used to hold, occupy, and possess the property and places belonging to the Government and to collect the duties and imposts; but beyond what may be necessary for these objects, there will be no invasion, no using of force against or among the people anywhere. Where hostility to the United States in any interior locality shall be so great and universal as to prevent competent resident citizens from holding the Federal offices, there will be no attempt to force obnoxious strangers among the people for that object. While the strict legal right may exist in the Government to enforce the exercise of these offices, the attempt to do so would be so irritating and so nearly impracticable withal that I deem it better to forego for the time the uses of such offices.

The mails, unless repelled, will continue to be furnished in all parts of the Union. So far as possible the people everywhere shall have that sense of perfect security which is most favorable to calm thought and reflection. The course here indicated will be followed unless current events and experience shall show a modification or change to be proper, and in every case and exigency my best discretion will be exercised, according to circumstances actually existing and with a view and a hope of a peaceful solution of the national troubles and the restoration of fraternal sympathies and affections.

That there are persons in one section or another who seek to destroy the Union at all events and are glad of any pretext to do it

I will neither affirm nor deny; but if there be such, I need address no word to them. To those, however, who really love the Union may I not speak?

Before entering upon so grave a matter as the destruction of our national fabric, with all its benefits, its memories, and its hopes, would it not be wise to ascertain precisely why we do it? Will you hazard so desperate a step while there is any possibility that any portion of the ills you fly from have no real existence? Will you, while the certain ills you fly to are greater than all the real ones you fly from, will you risk the commission of so fearful a mistake?

All profess to be content in the Union if all constitutional rights can be maintained. Is it true, then, that any right plainly written in the Constitution has been denied? I think not. Happily, the human mind is so constituted that no party can reach to the audacity of doing this. Think, if you can, of a single instance in which a plainly written provision of the Constitution has ever been denied. If by the mere force of numbers a majority should deprive a minority of any clearly written constitutional right, it might in a moral point of view justify revolution; certainly would if such right were a vital one. But such is not our case. All the vital rights of minorities and of individuals are so plainly assured to them by affirmations and negations, guaranties and prohibitions, in the Constitution that controversies never arise concerning them. But no organic law can ever be framed with a provision specifically applicable to every question which may occur in practical administration. No foresight can anticipate nor any document of reasonable length contain express provisions for all possible questions. Shall fugitives from labor be surrendered by national or by State authority? The Constitution does not expressly say. May Congress prohibit slavery in the Territories? The Constitution does not expressly say. Must Congress protect slavery in the Territories? The Constitution does not expressly say.

From questions of this class spring all our constitutional controversies, and we divide upon them into majorities and minorities. If the minority will not acquiesce, the majority must, or the Government must cease. There is no other alternative, for continuing the Government is acquiescence on one side or the other. If a minority in such case will secede rather than acquiesce, they make a precedent which in turn will divide and ruin them, for a minority of their own will secede from them whenever a majority refuses to be controlled by such minority. For instance, why may not any portion of a new confederacy a year or two hence arbitrarily secede again, precisely as portions of the present Union now claim to secede from it? All who cherish disunion sentiments are now being educated to the exact temper of doing this.

Is there such perfect identity of interests among the States to compose a new union as to produce harmony only and prevent renewed secession?

Plainly the central idea of secession is the essence of anarchy. A majority held in restraint by constitutional checks and limitations, and always changing easily with deliberate changes of popular opinions and sentiments, is the only true sovereign of a free people. Whoever rejects it does of necessity fly to anarchy or to despotism. Unanimity is impossible. The rule of a minority, as a permanent arrangement, is wholly inadmissible; so that, rejecting the majority principle, anarchy or despotism in some form is all that is left.

I do not forget the position assumed by some that constitutional questions are to be decided by the Supreme Court, nor do I deny that such decisions must be binding in any case upon the parties to a suit as to the object of that suit, while they are also entitled to very high respect and consideration in all parallel cases by all other departments of the Government. And while it is obviously possible that such decision may be erroneous in any given case, still the evil effect following it, being limited to that particular case, with the chance that it may be overruled and never become a precedent for other cases, can better be borne than could the evils of a different practice. At the same time, the candid citizen must confess that if the policy of the Government upon vital questions affecting the whole people is to be irrevocably fixed by decisions of the Supreme Court, the instant they are made in ordinary litigation between parties in personal actions the people will have ceased to be their own rulers, having to that extent practically resigned their Government into the hands of that eminent tribunal. Nor is there in this view any assault upon the court or the judges. It is a duty from which they may not shrink to decide cases properly brought before them, and it is no fault of theirs if others seek to turn their decisions to political purposes.

One section of our country believes slavery is right and ought to be extended, while the other believes it is wrong and ought not to be extended. This is the only substantial dispute. The fugitive-slave clause of the Constitution and the law for the suppression of the foreign slave trade are each as well enforced, perhaps, as any law can ever be in a community where the moral sense of the people imperfectly supports the law itself. The great body of the people abide by the dry legal obligation in both cases, and a few break over in each. This, I think, can not be perfectly cured, and it would be worse in both cases after the separation of the sections than before. The foreign slave trade, now imperfectly suppressed, would be ultimately revived without restriction in one section, while fugitive slaves, now only partially surrendered, would not be surrendered at all by the other.

Physically speaking, we can not separate. We can not remove our respective sections from each other nor build an impassable wall between them. A husband and wife may be divorced and go out of the presence and beyond the reach of each other, but the different parts of our country can not do this. They can not but remain face to face, and intercourse, either amicable or hostile, must continue between them. Is it possible, then, to make that intercourse more advantageous or more satisfactory after separation than before? Can aliens make treaties easier than friends can make laws? Can treaties be more faithfully enforced between aliens than laws can among friends? Suppose you go to war, you can not fight always; and when, after much loss on both sides and no gain on either, you cease fighting, the identical old questions, as to terms of intercourse, are again upon you.

This country, with its institutions, belongs to the people who inhabit it. Whenever they shall grow weary of the existing Government, they can exercise their constitutional right of amending it or their revolutionary right to dismember or overthrow it. I can not be ignorant of the fact that many worthy and patriotic citizens are desirous of having the National Constitution amended. While I make no recommendation of amendments, I fully recognize the rightful authority of the people over the whole subject, to be exercised in either of the modes prescribed in the instrument itself; and I should, under existing circumstances, favor rather than oppose a fair opportunity being afforded the people to act upon it. I will venture to add that to me the convention mode seems preferable, in that it allows amendments to originate with the people themselves, instead of only permitting them to take or reject propositions originated by others, not especially chosen for the purpose, and which might not be precisely such as they would wish to either accept or refuse. I understand a proposed amendment to the Constitution— which amendment, however, I have not seen—has passed Congress, to the effect that the Federal Government shall never interfere with the domestic institutions of the States, including that of persons held to service. To avoid misconstruction of what I have said, I depart from my purpose not to speak of particular amendments so far as to say that, holding such a provision to now be implied constitutional law, I have no objection to its being made express and irrevocable.

The Chief Magistrate derives all his authority from the people, and they have referred none upon him to fix terms for the separation of the States. The people themselves can do this if also they choose, but the Executive as such has nothing to do with it. His duty is to administer the present Government as it came to his hands and to transmit it unimpaired by him to his successor.

Why should there not be a patient confidence in the ultimate justice of the people? Is there any better or equal hope in the world? In our present differences, is either party without faith of being in the right? If the Almighty Ruler of Nations, with His eternal truth and justice, be on your side of the North, or on yours of the South, that truth and that justice will surely prevail by the judgment of this great tribunal of the American people. By the frame of the Government under which we live this same people have wisely given their public servants but little power for mischief, and have with equal wisdom provided for the return of that little to their own hands at very short intervals. While the people retain their virtue and vigilance no Administration by any extreme of wickedness or folly can very seriously injure the Government in the short space of four years.

My countrymen, one and all, think calmly and well upon this whole subject. Nothing valuable can be lost by taking time. If there be an object to hurry any of you in hot haste to a step which you would never take deliberately, that object will be frustrated by taking time; but no good object can be frustrated by it. Such of you as are now dissatisfied still have the old Constitution unimpaired, and, on the sensitive point, the laws of your own framing under it; while the new Administration will have no immediate power, if it would, to change either. If it were admitted that you who are dissatisfied hold the right side in the dispute, there still is no single good reason for precipitate action. Intelligence, patriotism, Christianity, and a firm reliance on Him who has never yet forsaken this favored land are still competent to adjust in the best way all our present difficulty.

In your hands, my dissatisfied fellow-countrymen, and not in mine, is the momentous issue of civil war. The Government will not assail you. You can have no conflict without being yourselves the aggressors. You have no oath registered in heaven to destroy the Government, while I shall have the most solemn one to "preserve, protect, and defend it."

I am loath to close. We are not enemies, but friends. We must not be enemies. Though passion may have strained it must not break our bonds of affection. The mystic chords of memory, stretching from every battlefield and patriot grave to every living heart and hearthstone all over this broad land, will yet swell the chorus of the Union, when again touched, as surely they will be, by the better angels of our nature.

Second Inaugural Address

Saturday, March 4, 1865

Fellow-Countrymen:

At this second appearing to take the oath of the Presidential office there is less occasion for an extended address than there was at the first. Then a statement somewhat in detail of a course to be pursued seemed fitting and proper. Now, at the expiration of four years, during which public declarations have been constantly called forth on every point and phase of the great contest which still absorbs the attention and engrosses the energies of the nation, little that is new could be presented. The progress of our arms, upon which all else chiefly depends, is as well known to the public as to myself, and it is, I trust, reasonably satisfactory and encouraging to all. With high hope for the future, no prediction in regard to it is ventured.

On the occasion corresponding to this four years ago all thoughts were anxiously directed to an impending civil war. All dreaded it, all sought to avert it. While the inaugural address was being delivered from this place, devoted altogether to saving the Union without war, urgent agents were in the city seeking to destroy it without war—seeking to dissolve the Union and divide effects by negotiation. Both parties deprecated war, but one of them would make war rather than let the nation survive, and the other would accept war rather than let it perish, and the war came.

One-eighth of the whole population were colored slaves, not distributed generally over the Union, but localized in the southern part of it. These slaves constituted a peculiar and powerful interest. All knew that this interest was somehow the cause of the war. To strengthen, perpetuate, and extend this interest was the object for which the insurgents would rend the Union even by war, while the Government claimed no right to do more than to restrict the territorial enlargement of it. Neither party expected for the war the magnitude or the duration which it has already attained. Neither anticipated that the cause of the conflict might cease with or even before the conflict itself should cease. Each looked for an easier triumph, and a result less fundamental and astounding. Both read the same Bible and pray to the same God, and each invokes His aid against the other. It may seem strange that any men should dare to ask a just God's assistance in wringing their bread from the sweat of other men's faces, but let us judge not, that we be not judged. The prayers of both could not be answered. That of neither has been answered fully. The Almighty has His own purposes. "Woe unto the world because of offenses; for it must needs be that offenses come, but woe to that man by whom the offense cometh." If we shall suppose that American slavery is one of those offenses which, in the providence of God, must needs come, but which, having continued through His appointed time, He now wills to remove, and that He gives to both North and South this terrible war as the woe due to those by whom the offense came, shall we discern therein any departure from those divine attributes which the believers in a living God always ascribe to Him? Fondly do we hope, fervently do we pray, that this mighty scourge of war may speedily pass away. Yet, if God wills that it continue until all the wealth piled by the bondsman's two hundred and fifty years of unrequited toil shall be sunk, and until every drop of blood drawn with the lash shall be paid by another drawn with the sword, as was said three thousand years ago, so still it must be said "the judgments of the Lord are true and righteous altogether."

With malice toward none, with charity for all, with firmness in the right as God gives us to see the right, let us strive on to finish the work we are in, to bind up the nation's wounds, to care for him who shall have borne the battle and for his widow and his orphan, to do all which may achieve and cherish a just and lasting peace among ourselves and with all nations.

Ulysses S. Grant

First Inaugural Address

Thursday, March 4, 1869

Citizens of the United States:

Your suffrages having elected me to the office of President of the United States, I have, in conformity to the Constitution of our country, taken the oath of office prescribed therein. I have taken this oath without mental reservation and with the determination to do to the best of my ability all that is required of me. The responsibilities of the position I feel, but accept them without fear. The office has come to me unsought; I commence its duties untrammeled. I bring to it a conscious desire and determination to fill it to the best of my ability to the satisfaction of the people.

On all leading questions agitating the public mind I will always express my views to Congress and urge them according to my judgment, and when I think it advisable will exercise the constitutional privilege of interposing a veto to defeat measures which I oppose; but all laws will be faithfully executed, whether they meet my approval or not.

I shall on all subjects have a policy to recommend, but none to enforce against the will of the people. Laws are to govern all alike—those opposed as well as those who favor them. I know no method to secure the repeal of bad or obnoxious laws so effective as their stringent execution.

The country having just emerged from a great rebellion, many questions will come before it for settlement in the next four years which preceding Administrations have never had to deal with. In meeting these it is desirable that they should be approached calmly, without prejudice, hate, or sectional pride, remembering that the greatest good to the greatest number is the object to be attained.

This requires security of person, property, and free religious and political opinion in every part of our common country, without regard to local prejudice. All laws to secure these ends will receive my best efforts for their enforcement

A great debt has been contracted in securing to us and our posterity the Union. The payment of this, principal and interest, as well as the return to a specie basis as soon as it can be accomplished without material detriment to the debtor class or to the country at large, must be provided for. To protect the national honor, every dollar of Government indebtedness should be paid in gold, unless otherwise expressly stipulated in the contract. Let it be understood that no repudiator of one farthing of our public debt will be trusted in public place, and it will go far toward strengthening a credit which ought to be the best in the world, and will ultimately enable us to replace the debt with bonds bearing less interest than we now pay. To this should be added a faithful collection of the revenue, a strict accountability to the Treasury for every dollar collected, and the greatest practicable retrenchment in expenditure in every department of Government.

When we compare the paying capacity of the country now, with the ten States in poverty from the effects of war, but soon to emerge, I trust, into greater prosperity than ever before, with its paying capacity twenty-five years ago, and calculate what it probably will be twenty-five years hence, who can doubt the feasibility of paying every dollar then with more ease than we now pay for useless luxuries? Why, it looks as though Providence had bestowed upon us a strong box in the precious metals locked up in the sterile mountains of the far West, and which we are now forging the key to unlock, to meet the very contingency that is now upon us.

Ultimately it may be necessary to insure the facilities to reach these riches and it may be necessary also that the General Government should give its aid to secure this access; but that should only be when a dollar of obligation to pay secures precisely the same sort of dollar to use now, and not before. Whilst the question of specie payments is in abeyance the prudent business man is careful about contracting debts payable in the distant future. The nation should follow the same rule. A prostrate commerce is to be rebuilt and all industries encouraged.

The young men of the country—those who from their age must be its rulers twenty-five years hence—have a peculiar interest in maintaining the national honor. A moment's reflection as to what will be our commanding influence among the nations of the earth in their day, if they are only true to themselves, should inspire them with national pride. All divisions— geographical, political, and religious—can join in this common sentiment. How the public debt is to be paid or specie payments resumed is not so important as that a plan should be adopted and acquiesced in. A united determination to do is worth more than divided counsels upon the method of doing. Legislation upon this subject may not be necessary now, or even advisable, but it will be when the civil law is more fully restored in all parts of the country and trade resumes its wonted channels.

It will be my endeavor to execute all laws in good faith, to collect all revenues assessed, and to have them properly accounted for and economically disbursed. I will to the best of my ability appoint to office those only who will carry out this design.

In regard to foreign policy, I would deal with nations as equitable law requires individuals to deal with each other, and I would protect the law-abiding citizen, whether of native or foreign birth, wherever his rights are jeopardized or the flag of our country floats. I would respect the rights of all nations, demanding equal respect for our own. If others depart from this rule in their dealings with us, we may be compelled to follow their precedent.

The proper treatment of the original occupants of this land— the Indians one deserving of careful study. I will favor any course toward them which tends to their civilization and ultimate citizenship.

The question of suffrage is one which is likely to agitate the public so long as a portion of the citizens of the nation are excluded from its privileges in any State. It seems to me very desirable that this question should be settled now, and I entertain the hope and express the desire that it may be by the ratification of the fifteenth article of amendment to the Constitution.

In conclusion I ask patient forbearance one toward another throughout the land, and a determined effort on the part of every citizen to do his share toward cementing a happy union; and I ask the prayers of the nation to Almighty God in behalf of this consummation.

Second Inaugural Address

Tuesday, March 4, 1873

Fellow-Citizens:

Under Providence I have been called a second time to act as Executive over this great nation. It has been my endeavor in the past to maintain all the laws, and, so far as lay in my power, to act for the best interests of the whole people. My best efforts will be given in the same direction in the future, aided, I trust, by my four years' experience in the office.

When my first term of the office of Chief Executive began, the country had not recovered from the effects of a great internal revolution, and three of the former States of the Union had not been restored to their Federal relations.

It seemed to me wise that no new questions should be raised so long as that condition of affairs existed. Therefore the past four years, so far as I could control events, have been consumed in the effort to restore harmony, public credit, commerce, and all the arts of peace and progress. It is my firm conviction that the civilized world is tending toward republicanism, or government by the people through their chosen representatives, and that our own great Republic is destined to be the guiding star to all others.

Under our Republic we support an army less than that of any European power of any standing and a navy less than that of either of at least five of them. There could be no extension of territory on the continent which would call for an increase of this force, but rather might such extension enable us to diminish it.

The theory of government changes with general progress. Now that the telegraph is made available for communicating thought, together with rapid transit by steam, all parts of a continent are made contiguous for all purposes of government, and communication between the extreme limits of the country made easier than it was throughout the old thirteen States at the beginning of our national existence.

The effects of the late civil strife have been to free the slave and make him a citizen. Yet he is not possessed of the civil rights which citizenship should carry with it. This is wrong, and should be corrected. To this correction I stand committed, so far as Executive influence can avail.

Social equality is not a subject to be legislated upon, nor shall I ask that anything be done to advance the social status of the colored man, except to give him a fair chance to develop what there is good in him, give him access to the schools, and when he travels let him feel assured that his conduct will regulate the treatment and fare he will receive.

The States lately at war with the General Government are now happily rehabilitated, and no Executive control is exercised in any one of them that would not be exercised in any other State under like circumstances.

In the first year of the past Administration the proposition came up for the admission of Santo Domingo as a Territory of the Union. It was not a question of my seeking, but was a proposition from the people of Santo Domingo, and which I entertained. I believe now, as I did then, that it was for the best interest of this country, for the people of Santo Domingo, and all concerned that the proposition should be received favorably. It was, however, rejected constitutionally, and therefore the subject was never brought up again by me.

In future, while I hold my present office, the subject of acquisition of territory must have the support of the people before I will recommend any proposition looking to such acquisition. I say here, however, that I do not share in the apprehension held by many as to the danger of governments becoming weakened and destroyed by reason of their extension of territory. Commerce, education, and rapid transit of thought and matter by telegraph and steam have changed all this. Rather do I believe that our Great Maker is preparing the world, in His own good time, to become one nation, speaking one language, and when armies and navies will be no longer required.

My efforts in the future will be directed to the restoration of good feeling between the different sections of our common country; to the restoration of our currency to a fixed value as compared with the world's standard of values—gold—and, if possible, to a par with it; to the construction of cheap routes of transit throughout the land, to the end that the products of all may find a market and leave a living remuneration to the producer; to the maintenance of friendly relations with all our neighbors and with distant nations; to the reestablishment of our commerce and share in the carrying trade upon the ocean; to the encouragement of such manufacturing industries as can be economically pursued in this country, to the end that the exports of home products and industries may pay for our imports—the only sure method of returning to and permanently maintaining a specie basis; to the elevation of labor; and, by a humane course, to bring the aborigines of the country under the benign influences of education and civilization. It is either this or war of extermination: Wars of extermination, engaged in by people pursuing commerce and all industrial pursuits, are expensive even against the weakest people, and are demoralizing and wicked. Our superiority of strength and advantages of civilization should make us lenient toward the Indian. The wrong inflicted upon him should be taken into account and the balance placed to his credit. The moral view of the question should be considered and the question asked, Can not the Indian be made a useful and productive member of society by proper teaching and treatment? If the effort is made in good faith, we will stand better before the civilized nations of the earth and in our own consciences for having made it.

All these things are not to be accomplished by one individual, but they will receive my support and such recommendations to Congress as will in my judgment best serve to carry them into effect. I beg your support and encouragement.

It has been, and is, my earnest desire to correct abuses that have grown up in the civil service of the country. To secure this reformation rules regulating methods of appointment and promotions were established and have been tried. My efforts for such reformation shall be continued to the best of my judgment. The spirit of the rules adopted will be maintained.

I acknowledge before this assemblage, representing, as it does, every section of our country, the obligation I am under to my countrymen for the great honor they have conferred on me by returning me to the highest office within their gift, and the further obligation resting on me to render to them the best services within my power. This I promise, looking forward with the greatest anxiety to the day when I shall be released from responsibilities that at times are almost overwhelming, and from which I have scarcely had a respite since the eventful firing upon Fort Sumter, in April, 1861, to the present day. My services were then tendered and accepted under the first call for troops growing out of that event.

I did not ask for place or position, and was entirely without influence or the acquaintance of persons of influence, but was resolved to perform my part in a struggle threatening the very existence of the nation. I performed a conscientious duty, without asking promotion or command, and without a revengeful feeling toward any section or individual.

Notwithstanding this, throughout the war, and from my candidacy for my present office in 1868 to the close of the last Presidential campaign, I have been the subject of abuse and slander scarcely ever equaled in political history, which to-day I feel that I can afford to disregard in view of your verdict, which I gratefully accept as my vindication.

Rutherford B. Hayes

Inaugural Address

Monday, March 5, 1877

Fellow-Citizens:

We have assembled to repeat the public ceremonial, begun by Washington, observed by all my predecessors, and now a time-honored custom, which marks the commencement of a new term of the Presidential office. Called to the duties of this great trust, I proceed, in compliance with usage, to announce some of the leading principles, on the subjects that now chiefly engage the public attention, by which it is my desire to be guided in the discharge of those duties. I shall not undertake to lay down irrevocably principles or measures of administration, but rather to speak of the motives which should animate us, and to suggest certain important ends to be attained in accordance with our institutions and essential to the welfare of our country.

At the outset of the discussions which preceded the recent Presidential election it seemed to me fitting that I should fully make known my sentiments in regard to several of the important questions which then appeared to demand the consideration of the country. Following the example, and in part adopting the language, of one of my predecessors, I wish now, when every motive for misrepresentation has passed away, to repeat what was said before the election, trusting that my countrymen will candidly weigh and understand it, and that they will feel assured that the sentiments declared in accepting the nomination for the Presidency will be the standard of my conduct in the path before me, charged, as I now am, with the grave and difficult task of carrying them out in the practical administration of the Government so far as depends, under the Constitution and laws on the Chief Executive of the nation.

The permanent pacification of the country upon such principles and by such measures as will secure the complete protection of all its citizens in the free enjoyment of all their constitutional rights is now the one subject in our public affairs which all thoughtful and patriotic citizens regard as of supreme importance.

Many of the calamitous efforts of the tremendous revolution which has passed over the Southern States still remain. The immeasurable benefits which will surely follow, sooner or later, the hearty and generous acceptance of the legitimate results of that revolution have not yet been realized. Difficult and embarrassing questions meet us at the threshold of this subject. The people of those States are still impoverished, and the inestimable blessing of wise, honest, and peaceful local self-government is not fully enjoyed. Whatever difference of opinion may exist as to the cause of this condition of things, the fact is clear that in the progress of events the time has come when such government is the imperative necessity required by all the varied interests, public and private, of those States. But it must not be forgotten that only a local government which recognizes and maintains inviolate the rights of all is a true self-government.

With respect to the two distinct races whose peculiar relations to each other have brought upon us the deplorable complications and perplexities which exist in those States, it must be a government which guards the interests of both races carefully and equally. It must be a government which submits loyally and heartily to the Constitution and the laws—the laws of the nation and the laws of the States themselves—accepting and obeying faithfully the whole Constitution as it is.

Resting upon this sure and substantial foundation, the superstructure of beneficent local governments can be built up, and not otherwise. In furtherance of such obedience to the letter and the spirit of the Constitution, and in behalf of all that its attainment implies, all so-called party interests lose their apparent importance, and party lines may well be permitted to fade into insignificance. The question we have to consider for the immediate welfare of those States of the Union is the question of government or no government; of social order and all the peaceful industries and the happiness that belongs to it, or a return to barbarism. It is a question in which every citizen of the nation is deeply interested, and with respect to which we ought not to be, in a partisan sense, either Republicans or Democrats, but fellow-citizens and fellowmen, to whom the interests of a common country and a common humanity are dear.

The sweeping revolution of the entire labor system of a large portion of our country and the advance of 4,000,000 people from a condition of servitude to that of citizenship, upon an equal footing with their former masters, could not occur without presenting problems of the gravest moment, to be dealt with by the emancipated race, by their former masters, and by the General Government, the author of the act of emancipation. That it was a wise, just, and providential act, fraught with good for all concerned, is not generally conceded throughout the country. That a moral obligation rests upon the National Government to employ its constitutional power and influence to establish the rights of the people it has emancipated, and to protect them in the enjoyment of those rights when they are infringed or assailed, is also generally admitted.

The evils which afflict the Southern States can only be removed or remedied by the united and harmonious efforts of both races, actuated by motives of mutual sympathy and regard; and while in duty bound and fully determined to protect the rights of all by every constitutional means at the disposal of my Administration, I am sincerely anxious to use every legitimate influence in favor of honest and efficient local self-government as the true resource of those States for the promotion of the contentment and prosperity of their citizens. In the effort I shall make to accomplish this purpose I ask the cordial cooperation of all who cherish an interest in the welfare of the country, trusting that party ties and the prejudice of race will be freely surrendered in behalf of the great purpose to be accomplished. In the important work of restoring the South it is not the political situation alone that merits attention. The material development of that section of the country has been arrested by the social and political revolution through which it has passed, and now needs and deserves the considerate care of the National Government within the just limits prescribed by the Constitution and wise public economy.

But at the basis of all prosperity, for that as well as for every other part of the country, lies the improvement of the intellectual and moral condition of the people. Universal suffrage should rest upon universal education. To this end, liberal and permanent provision should be made for the support of free schools by the State governments, and, if need be, supplemented by legitimate aid from national authority.

Let me assure my countrymen of the Southern States that it is my earnest desire to regard and promote their truest interest—the interests of the white and of the colored people both and equally—and to put forth my best efforts in behalf of a civil policy which will forever wipe out in our political affairs the color line and the distinction between North and South, to the end that we may have not merely a united North or a united South, but a united country.

I ask the attention of the public to the paramount necessity of reform in our civil service—a reform not merely as to certain abuses and practices of so-called official patronage which have come to have the sanction of usage in the several Departments of our Government, but a change in the system of appointment itself; a reform that shall be thorough, radical, and complete; a return to the principles and practices of the founders of the Government. They neither expected nor desired from public officers any partisan service. They meant that public officers should owe their whole service to the Government and to the people. They meant that the officer should be secure in his tenure as long as his personal character remained untarnished and the performance of his duties satisfactory. They held that appointments to office were not to be made nor expected merely as rewards for partisan services, nor merely on the nomination of members of Congress, as being entitled in any respect to the control of such appointments.

The fact that both the great political parties of the country, in declaring their principles prior to the election, gave a prominent place to the subject of reform of our civil service, recognizing and strongly urging its necessity, in terms almost identical in their specific import with those I have here employed, must be accepted as a conclusive argument in behalf of these measures. It must be regarded as the expression of the united voice and will of the whole country upon this subject, and both political parties are virtually pledged to give it their unreserved support.

The President of the United States of necessity owes his election to office to the suffrage and zealous labors of a political party, the members of which cherish with ardor and regard as of essential importance the principles of their party organization; but he should strive to be always mindful of the fact that he serves his party best who serves the country best.

In furtherance of the reform we seek, and in other important respects a change of great importance, I recommend an amendment to the Constitution prescribing a term of six years for the Presidential office and forbidding a reelection.

With respect to the financial condition of the country, I shall not attempt an extended history of the embarrassment and prostration which we have suffered during the past three years. The depression in all our varied commercial and manufacturing interests throughout the country, which began in September, 1873, still continues. It is very gratifying, however, to be able to say that there are indications all around us of a coming change to prosperous times.

Upon the currency question, intimately connected, as it is, with this topic, I may be permitted to repeat here the statement made in my letter of acceptance, that in my judgment the feeling of uncertainty inseparable from an irredeemable paper currency, with its fluctuation of values, is one of the greatest obstacles to a return to prosperous times. The only safe paper currency is one which rests upon a coin basis and is at all times and promptly convertible into coin.

I adhere to the views heretofore expressed by me in favor of Congressional legislation in behalf of an early resumption of specie payments, and I am satisfied not only that this is wise, but that the interests, as well as the public sentiment, of the country imperatively demand it.

Passing from these remarks upon the condition of our own country to consider our relations with other lands, we are reminded by the international complications abroad, threatening the peace of Europe, that our traditional rule of noninterference in the affairs of foreign nations has proved of great value in past times and ought to be strictly observed.

The policy inaugurated by my honored predecessor, President Grant, of submitting to arbitration grave questions in dispute between ourselves and foreign powers points to a new, and incomparably the best, instrumentality for the preservation of peace, and will, as I believe, become a beneficent example of the course to be pursued in similar emergencies by other nations.

If, unhappily, questions of difference should at any time during the period of my Administration arise between the United States and any foreign government, it will certainly be my disposition and my hope to aid in their settlement in the same peaceful and honorable way, thus securing to our country the great blessings of peace and mutual good offices with all the nations of the world.

Fellow-citizens, we have reached the close of a political contest marked by the excitement which usually attends the contests between great political parties whose members espouse and advocate with earnest faith their respective creeds. The circumstances were, perhaps, in no respect extraordinary save in the closeness and the consequent uncertainty of the result.

For the first time in the history of the country it has been deemed best, in view of the peculiar circumstances of the case, that the objections and questions in dispute with reference to the counting of the electoral votes should be referred to the decision of a tribunal appointed for this purpose.

That tribunal—established by law for this sole purpose; its members, all of them, men of long-established reputation for integrity and intelligence, and, with the exception of those who are also members of the supreme judiciary, chosen equally from both political parties; its deliberations enlightened by the research and the arguments of able counsel—was entitled to the fullest confidence of the American people. Its decisions have been patiently waited for, and accepted as legally conclusive by the general judgment of the public. For the present, opinion will widely vary as to the wisdom of the several conclusions announced by that tribunal. This is to be anticipated in every instance where matters of dispute are made the subject of arbitration under the forms of law. Human judgment is never unerring, and is rarely regarded as otherwise than wrong by the unsuccessful party in the contest.

The fact that two great political parties have in this way settled a dispute in regard to which good men differ as to the facts and the law no less than as to the proper course to be pursued in solving the question in controversy is an occasion for general rejoicing.

Upon one point there is entire unanimity in public sentiment—that conflicting claims to the Presidency must be amicably and peaceably adjusted, and that when so adjusted the general acquiescence of the nation ought surely to follow.

It has been reserved for a government of the people, where

the right of suffrage is universal, to give to the world the first example in history of a great nation, in the midst of the struggle of opposing parties for power, hushing its party tumults to yield the issue of the contest to adjustment according to the forms of law.

Looking for the guidance of that Divine Hand by which the destinies of nations and individuals are shaped, I call upon you, Senators, Representatives, judges, fellow-citizens, here and everywhere, to unite with me in an earnest effort to secure to our country the blessings, not only of material prosperity, but of justice, peace, and union—a union depending not upon the constraint of force, but upon the loving devotion of a free people; "and that all things may be so ordered and settled upon the best and surest foundations that peace and happiness, truth and justice, religion and piety, may be established among us for all generations."

James A. Garfield

Inaugural Address

Friday, March 4, 1881

Fellow-Citizens:

WE stand to-day upon an eminence which overlooks a hundred years of national life—a century crowded with perils, but crowned with the triumphs of liberty and law. Before continuing the onward march let us pause on this height for a moment to strengthen our faith and renew our hope by a glance at the pathway along which our people have traveled.

It is now three days more than a hundred years since the adoption of the first written constitution of the United States—the Articles of Confederation and Perpetual Union. The new Republic was then beset with danger on every hand. It had not conquered a place in the family of nations. The decisive battle of the war for independence, whose centennial anniversary will soon be gratefully celebrated at Yorktown, had not yet been fought. The colonists were struggling not only against the armies of a great nation, but against the settled opinions of mankind; for the world did not then believe that the supreme authority of government could be safely intrusted to the guardianship of the people themselves.

We can not overestimate the fervent love of liberty, the intelligent courage, and the sum of common sense with which our fathers made the great experiment of self-government. When they found, after a short trial, that the confederacy of States, was too weak to meet the necessities of a vigorous and expanding republic, they boldly set it aside, and in its stead established a National Union, founded directly upon the will of the people, endowed with full power of self-preservation and ample authority for the accomplishment of its great object.

Under this Constitution the boundaries of freedom have been enlarged, the foundations of order and peace have been strengthened, and the growth of our people in all the better elements of national life has indicated the wisdom of the founders and given new hope to their descendants. Under this Constitution our people long ago made themselves safe against danger from without and secured for their mariners and flag equality of rights on all the seas. Under this Constitution twenty-five States have been added to the Union, with constitutions and laws, framed and enforced by their own citizens, to secure the manifold blessings of local self-government.

The jurisdiction of this Constitution now covers an area fifty times greater than that of the original thirteen States and a population twenty times greater than that of 1780.

The supreme trial of the Constitution came at last under the tremendous pressure of civil war. We ourselves are witnesses that the Union emerged from the blood and fire of that conflict purified and made stronger for all the beneficent purposes of good government.

And now, at the close of this first century of growth, with the inspirations of its history in their hearts, our people have lately reviewed the condition of the nation, passed judgment upon the conduct and opinions of political parties, and have registered their will concerning the future administration of the Government. To interpret and to execute that will in accordance with the Constitution is the paramount duty of the Executive.

Even from this brief review it is manifest that the nation is resolutely facing to the front, resolved to employ its best energies in developing the great possibilities of the future. Sacredly preserving whatever has been gained to liberty and good government during the century, our people are determined to leave behind them all those bitter controversies concerning things which have been irrevocably settled, and the further discussion of which can only stir up strife and delay the onward march.

The supremacy of the nation and its laws should be no longer a subject of debate. That discussion, which for half a century threatened the existence of the Union, was closed at last in the high court of war by a decree from which there is no appeal—that the Constitution and the laws made in pursuance thereof are and shall continue to be the supreme law of the land, binding alike upon the States and the people. This decree does not disturb the autonomy of the States nor interfere with any of their necessary rights of local self-government, but it does fix and establish the permanent supremacy of the Union.

The will of the nation, speaking with the voice of battle and through the amended Constitution, has fulfilled the great promise of 1776 by proclaiming "liberty throughout the land to all the inhabitants thereof."

The elevation of the negro race from slavery to the full rights of citizenship is the most important political change we have known since the adoption of the Constitution of 1787. NO thoughtful man can fail to appreciate its beneficent effect upon our institutions and people. It has freed us from the perpetual danger of war and dissolution. It has added immensely to the moral and industrial forces of our people. It has liberated the master as well as the slave from a relation which wronged and enfeebled both. It has surrendered to their own guardianship the manhood of more than 5,000,000 people, and has opened to each one of them a career of freedom and usefulness. It has given new inspiration to the power of self-help in both races by making labor more honorable to the one and more necessary to the other. The influence of this force will grow greater and bear richer fruit with the coming years.

No doubt this great change has caused serious disturbance to our Southern communities. This is to be deplored, though it was perhaps unavoidable. But those who resisted the change should remember that under our institutions there was no middle ground for the negro race between slavery and equal citizenship. There can be no permanent disfranchised peasantry in the United States. Freedom can never yield its fullness of blessings so long as the law or its administration places the smallest obstacle in the pathway of any virtuous citizen.

The emancipated race has already made remarkable progress. With unquestioning devotion to the Union, with a patience and gentleness not born of fear, they have "followed the light as God gave them to see the light." They are rapidly laying the material foundations of self-support, widening their circle of intelligence, and beginning to enjoy the blessings that gather around the homes of the industrious poor. They deserve the generous encouragement of all good men. So far as my authority can lawfully extend they shall enjoy the full and equal protection of the Constitution and the laws.

The free enjoyment of equal suffrage is still in question, and a frank statement of the issue may aid its solution. It is alleged that in many communities negro citizens are practically denied the freedom of the ballot. In so far as the truth of this allegation is admitted, it is answered that in many places honest local government is impossible if the mass of uneducated negroes are allowed to vote. These are grave allegations. So far as the latter is true, it is the only palliation that can be offered for opposing the freedom of the ballot. Bad local government is certainly a great evil, which ought to be prevented; but to violate the freedom and sanctities of the suffrage is more than an evil. It is a crime which, if persisted in, will destroy the Government itself. Suicide is not a remedy. If in other lands it be high treason to compass the death of the king, it shall be counted no less a crime here to strangle our sovereign power and stifle its voice.

It has been said that unsettled questions have no pity for the repose of nations. It should be said with the utmost emphasis that this question of the suffrage will never give repose or safety to the States or to the nation until each, within its own jurisdiction, makes and keeps the ballot free and pure by the strong sanctions of the law.

But the danger which arises from ignorance in the voter can not be denied. It covers a field far wider than that of negro suffrage and the present condition of the race. It is a danger that lurks and hides in the sources and fountains of power in every state. We have no standard by which to measure the disaster that may be brought upon us by ignorance and vice in the citizens when joined to corruption and fraud in the suffrage.

The voters of the Union, who make and unmake constitutions, and upon whose will hang the destinies of our governments, can transmit their supreme authority to no successors save the coming generation of voters, who are the sole heirs of sovereign power. If that generation comes to its inheritance blinded by ignorance and corrupted by vice, the fall of the Republic will be certain and remediless.

The census has already sounded the alarm in the appalling figures which mark how dangerously high the tide of illiteracy has risen among our voters and their children.

To the South this question is of supreme importance. But the responsibility for the existence of slavery did not rest upon the South alone. The nation itself is responsible for the extension of the suffrage, and is under special obligations to aid in removing the illiteracy which it has added to the voting population. For the North and South alike there is but one remedy. All the constitutional power of the nation and of the States and all the volunteer forces of the people should be surrendered to meet this danger by the savory influence of universal education.

It is the high privilege and sacred duty of those now living to educate their successors and fit them, by intelligence and virtue, for the inheritance which awaits them.

In this beneficent work sections and races should be forgotten and partisanship should be unknown. Let our people find a new meaning in the divine oracle which declares that "a little child shall lead them," for our own little children will soon control the destinies of the Republic.

My countrymen, we do not now differ in our judgment concerning the controversies of past generations, and fifty years hence our children will not be divided in their opinions concerning our controversies. They will surely bless their fathers and their fathers' God that the Union was preserved, that slavery was overthrown, and that both races were made equal before the law. We may hasten or we may retard, but we can not prevent, the final reconciliation. Is it not possible for us now to make a truce with time by anticipating and accepting its inevitable verdict?

Enterprises of the highest importance to our moral and material well-being unite us and offer ample employment of our best powers. Let all our people, leaving behind them the battlefields of dead issues, move forward and in their strength of liberty and the restored Union win the grander victories of peace.

The prosperity which now prevails is without parallel in our history. Fruitful seasons have done much to secure it, but they have not done all. The preservation of the public credit and the resumption of specie payments, so successfully attained by the Administration of my predecessors, have enabled our people to secure the blessings which the seasons brought.

By the experience of commercial nations in all ages it has been found that gold and silver afford the only safe foundation for a monetary system. Confusion has recently been created by variations in the relative value of the two metals, but I confidently believe that arrangements can be made between the leading commercial nations which will secure the general use of both metals. Congress should provide that the compulsory coinage of silver now required by law may not disturb our monetary system by driving either metal out of circulation. If possible, such an adjustment should be made that the purchasing power of every coined dollar will be exactly equal to its debt-paying power in all the markets of the world.

The chief duty of the National Government in connection with the currency of the country is to coin money and declare its value. Grave doubts have been entertained whether Congress is authorized by the Constitution to make any form of paper money legal tender. The present issue of United States notes has been sustained by the necessities of war; but such paper should depend for its value and currency upon its convenience in use and its prompt redemption in coin at the will of the holder, and not upon its compulsory circulation. These notes are not money, but promises to pay money. If the holders demand it, the promise should be kept.

The refunding of the national debt at a lower rate of interest should be accomplished without compelling the withdrawal of the national-bank notes, and thus disturbing the business of the country.

I venture to refer to the position I have occupied on financial questions during a long service in Congress, and to say that time and experience have strengthened the opinions I have so often expressed on these subjects.

The finances of the Government shall suffer no detriment which it may be possible for my Administration to prevent.

The interests of agriculture deserve more attention from the Government than they have yet received. The farms of the United States afford homes and employment for more than one-half our people, and furnish much the largest part of all our exports. As the Government lights our coasts for the protection of mariners and the benefit of commerce, so it should give to the tillers of the soil the best lights of practical science and experience.

Our manufacturers are rapidly making us industrially independent, and are opening to capital and labor new and profitable fields of employment. Their steady and healthy growth should still be matured. Our facilities for transportation should be promoted by the continued improvement of our harbors and great interior waterways and by the increase of our tonnage on the ocean.

The development of the world's commerce has led to an urgent demand for shortening the great sea voyage around Cape Horn by constructing ship canals or railways across the isthmus which unites the continents. Various plans to this end have been suggested and will need consideration, but none of them has been sufficiently matured to warrant the United States in extending pecuniary aid. The subject, however, is one which will immediately engage the attention of the Government with a view to a thorough protection to American interests. We will urge no narrow policy nor seek peculiar or exclusive privileges in any commercial route; but, in the language of my predecessor, I believe it to be the right "and duty of the United States to assert and maintain such supervision and authority over any interoceanic canal across the isthmus that connects North and South America as will protect our national interest."

The Constitution guarantees absolute religious freedom. Congress is prohibited from making any law respecting an establishment of religion or prohibiting the free exercise thereof. The Territories of the United States are subject to the direct legislative authority of Congress, and hence the General Government is responsible for any violation of the Constitution in any of them. It is therefore a reproach to the Government that in the most populous of the Territories the constitutional guaranty is not enjoyed by the people and the authority of Congress is set at naught. The Mormon Church not only offends the moral sense of manhood by sanctioning polygamy, but prevents the administration of justice through ordinary instrumentalities of law.

In my judgment it is the duty of Congress, while respecting to the uttermost the conscientious convictions and religious scruples of every citizen, to prohibit within its jurisdiction all criminal practices, especially of that class which destroy the family relations and endanger social order. Nor can any ecclesiastical organization be safely permitted to usurp in the smallest degree the functions and powers of the National Government.

The civil service can never be placed on a satisfactory basis until it is regulated by law. For the good of the service itself, for the protection of those who are intrusted with the appointing power against the waste of time and obstruction to the public business caused by the inordinate pressure for place, and for the protection of incumbents against intrigue and wrong, I shall at the proper time ask Congress to fix the tenure of the minor offices of the several Executive Departments and prescribe the grounds upon which removals shall be made during the terms for which incumbents have been appointed.

Finally, acting always within the authority and limitations of the Constitution, invading neither the rights of the States nor the reserved rights of the people, it will be the purpose of my Administration to maintain the authority of the nation in all places within its jurisdiction; to enforce obedience to all the laws of the Union in the interests of the people; to demand rigid economy in all the expenditures of the Government, and to require the honest and faithful service of all executive officers, remembering that the offices were created, not for the benefit of incumbents or their supporters, but for the service of the Government.

And now, fellow-citizens, I am about to assume the great trust which you have committed to my hands. I appeal to you for that earnest and thoughtful support which makes this Government in fact, as it is in law, a government of the people.

I shall greatly rely upon the wisdom and patriotism of Congress and of those who may share with me the responsibilities and duties of administration, and, above all, upon our efforts to promote the welfare of this great people and their Government I reverently invoke the support and blessings of Almighty God.

Grover Cleveland

First Inaugural Address

Wednesday, March 4, 1885

Fellow-Citizens:

In the presence of this vast assemblage of my countrymen I am about to supplement and seal by the oath which I shall take the manifestation of the will of a great and free people. In the exercise of their power and right of self-government they have committed to one of their fellow-citizens a supreme and sacred trust, and he here consecrates himself to their service.

This impressive ceremony adds little to the solemn sense of responsibility with which I contemplate the duty I owe to all the people of the land. Nothing can relieve me from anxiety lest by any act of mine their interests may suffer, and nothing is needed to strengthen my resolution to engage every faculty and effort in the promotion of their welfare.

Amid the din of party strife the people's choice was made, but its attendant circumstances have demonstrated anew the strength and safety of a government by the people. In each succeeding year it more clearly appears that our democratic principle needs no apology, and that in its fearless and faithful application is to be found the surest guaranty of good government.

But the best results in the operation of a government wherein every citizen has a share largely depend upon a proper limitation of purely partisan zeal and effort and a correct appreciation of the time when the heat of the partisan should be merged in the patriotism of the citizen.

To-day the executive branch of the Government is transferred to new keeping. But this is still the Government of all the people, and it should be none the less an object of their affectionate solicitude. At this hour the animosities of political strife, the bitterness of partisan defeat, and the exultation of partisan triumph should be supplanted by an ungrudging acquiescence in the popular will and a sober, conscientious concern for the general weal. Moreover, if from this hour we cheerfully and honestly abandon all sectional prejudice and distrust, and determine, with manly confidence in one another, to work out harmoniously the achievements of our national destiny, we shall deserve to realize all the benefits which our happy form of government can bestow.

On this auspicious occasion we may well renew the pledge of our devotion to the Constitution, which, launched by the founders of the Republic and consecrated by their prayers and patriotic devotion, has for almost a century borne the hopes and the aspirations of a great people through prosperity and peace and through the shock of foreign conflicts and the perils of domestic strife and vicissitudes.

By the Father of his Country our Constitution was commended for adoption as "the result of a spirit of amity and mutual concession." In that same spirit it should be administered, in order to promote the lasting welfare of the country and to secure the full measure of its priceless benefits to us and to those who will succeed to the blessings of our national life. The large variety of diverse and competing interests subject to Federal control, persistently seeking the recognition of their claims, need give us no fear that "the greatest good to the greatest number" will fail to be accomplished if in the halls of national legislation that spirit of amity and mutual concession shall prevail in which the Constitution had its birth. If this involves the surrender or postponement of private interests and the abandonment of local advantages, compensation will be found in the assurance that the common interest is subserved and the general welfare advanced.

In the discharge of my official duty I shall endeavor to be guided by a just and unstrained construction of the Constitution, a careful observance of the distinction between the powers granted to the Federal Government and those reserved to the States or to the people, and by a cautious appreciation of those functions which by the Constitution and laws have been especially assigned to the executive branch of the Government.

But he who takes the oath today to preserve, protect, and defend the Constitution of the United States only assumes the solemn obligation which every patriotic citizen—on the farm, in the workshop, in the busy marts of trade, and everywhere— should share with him. The Constitution which prescribes his oath, my countrymen, is yours; the Government you have chosen him to administer for a time is yours; the suffrage which executes the will of freemen is yours; the laws and the entire scheme of our civil rule, from the town meeting to the State capitals and the national capital, is yours. Your every voter, as surely as your Chief Magistrate, under the same high sanction, though in a different sphere, exercises a public trust. Nor is this all. Every citizen owes to the country a vigilant watch and close scrutiny of its public servants and a fair and reasonable estimate of their fidelity and usefulness. Thus is the people's will impressed upon the whole framework of our civil polity—municipal, State, and Federal; and this is the price of our liberty and the inspiration of our faith in the Republic.

It is the duty of those serving the people in public place to closely limit public expenditures to the actual needs of the Government economically administered, because this bounds the right of the Government to exact tribute from the earnings of labor or the property of the citizen, and because public extravagance begets extravagance among the people. We should never be ashamed of the simplicity and prudential economies which are best suited to the operation of a republican form of government and most compatible with the mission of the American people. Those who are selected for a limited time to manage public affairs are still of the people, and may do much by their example to encourage, consistently with the dignity of their official functions, that plain way of life which among their fellow-citizens aids integrity and promotes thrift and prosperity.

The genius of our institutions, the needs of our people in their home life, and the attention which is demanded for the settlement and development of the resources of our vast territory dictate the scrupulous avoidance of any departure from that foreign policy commended by the history, the traditions, and the prosperity of our Republic. It is the policy of independence, favored by our position and defended by our known love of justice and by our power. It is the policy of peace suitable to our interests. It is the policy of neutrality, rejecting any share in foreign broils and ambitions upon other continents and repelling their intrusion here. It is the policy of Monroe and of Washington and Jefferson—"Peace, commerce, and honest friendship with all nations; entangling alliance with none."

A due regard for the interests and prosperity of all the people demands that our finances shall be established upon such a sound and sensible basis as shall secure the safety and confidence of business interests and make the wage of labor sure and steady, and that our system of revenue shall be so adjusted as to relieve the people of unnecessary taxation, having a due regard to the interests of capital invested and workingmen employed in American industries, and preventing the accumulation of a surplus in the Treasury to tempt extravagance and waste.

Care for the property of the nation and for the needs of future settlers requires that the public domain should be protected from purloining schemes and unlawful occupation.

The conscience of the people demands that the Indians within our boundaries shall be fairly and honestly treated as wards of the Government and their education and civilization promoted with a view to their ultimate citizenship, and that polygamy in the Territories, destructive of the family relation and offensive to the moral sense of the civilized world, shall be repressed.

The laws should be rigidly enforced which prohibit the immigration of a servile class to compete with American labor, with no intention of acquiring citizenship, and bringing with them and retaining habits and customs repugnant to our civilization.

The people demand reform in the administration of the Government and the application of business principles to public affairs. As a means to this end, civil-service reform should be in good faith enforced. Our citizens have the right to protection from the incompetency of public employees who hold their places solely as the reward of partisan service, and from the corrupting influence of those who promise and the vicious methods of those who expect such rewards; and those who worthily seek public employment have the right to insist that merit and competency shall be recognized instead of party subserviency or the surrender of honest political belief.

In the administration of a government pledged to do equal and exact justice to all men there should be no pretext for anxiety touching the protection of the freedmen in their rights or their security in the enjoyment of their privileges under the Constitution and its amendments. All discussion as to their fitness for the place accorded to them as American citizens is idle and unprofitable except as it suggests the necessity for their improvement. The fact that they are citizens entitles them to all the rights due to that relation and charges them with all its duties, obligations, and responsibilities.

These topics and the constant and ever-varying wants of an active and enterprising population may well receive the attention and the patriotic endeavor of all who make and execute the Federal law. Our duties are practical and call for industrious application, an intelligent perception of the claims of public office, and, above all, a firm determination, by united action, to secure to all the people of the land the full benefits of the best form of government ever vouchsafed to man. And let us not trust to human effort alone, but humbly acknowledging the power and goodness of Almighty God, who presides over the destiny of nations, and who has at all times been revealed in our country's history, let us invoke His aid and His blessings upon our labors.

Second Inaugural Address

Saturday, March 4, 1893

My Fellow-Citizens:

In obedience of the mandate of my countrymen I am about to dedicate myself to their service under the sanction of a solemn oath. Deeply moved by the expression of confidence and personal attachment which has called me to this service, I am sure my gratitude can make no better return than the pledge I now give before God and these witnesses of unreserved and complete devotion to the interests and welfare of those who have honored me.

I deem it fitting on this occasion, while indicating the opinion I hold concerning public questions of present importance, to also briefly refer to the existence of certain conditions and tendencies among our people which seem to menace the integrity and usefulness of their Government.

While every American citizen must contemplate with the utmost pride and enthusiasm the growth and expansion of our country, the sufficiency of our institutions to stand against the rudest shocks of violence, the wonderful thrift and enterprise of our people, and the demonstrated superiority of our free government, it behooves us to constantly watch for every symptom of insidious infirmity that threatens our national vigor.

The strong man who in the confidence of sturdy health courts the sternest activities of life and rejoices in the hardihood of constant labor may still have lurking near his vitals the unheeded disease that dooms him to sudden collapse.

It can not be doubted that our stupendous achievements as a people and our country's robust strength have given rise to heedlessness of those laws governing our national health which we can no more evade than human life can escape the laws of God and nature.

Manifestly nothing is more vital to our supremacy as a nation and to the beneficent purposes of our Government than a sound and stable currency. Its exposure to degradation should at once arouse to activity the most enlightened statesmanship, and the danger of depreciation in the purchasing power of the wages paid to toil should furnish the strongest incentive to prompt and conservative precaution.

In dealing with our present embarrassing situation as related to this subject we will be wise if we temper our confidence and faith in our national strength and resources with the frank concession that even these will not permit us to defy with impunity the inexorable laws of finance and trade. At the same time, in our efforts to adjust differences of opinion we should be free from intolerance or passion, and our judgments should be unmoved by alluring phrases and unvexed by selfish interests.

I am confident that such an approach to the subject will result in prudent and effective remedial legislation. In the meantime, so far as the executive branch of the Government can intervene, none of the powers with which it is invested will be withheld when their exercise is deemed necessary to maintain our national credit or avert financial disaster.

Closely related to the exaggerated confidence in our country's greatness which tends to a disregard of the rules of national safety, another danger confronts us not less serious. I refer to the prevalence of a popular disposition to expect from the operation of the Government especial and direct individual advantages.

The verdict of our voters which condemned the injustice of maintaining protection for protection's sake enjoins upon the people's servants the duty of exposing and destroying the brood of kindred evils which are the unwholesome progeny of paternalism. This is the bane of republican institutions and the constant peril of our government by the people. It degrades to the purposes of wily craft the plan of rule our fathers established and bequeathed to us as an object of our love and veneration. It perverts the patriotic sentiments of our countrymen and tempts them to pitiful calculation of the sordid gain to be derived from their Government's maintenance. It undermines the self-reliance of our people and substitutes in its place dependence upon governmental favoritism. It stifles the spirit of true Americanism and stupefies every ennobling trait of American citizenship.

The lessons of paternalism ought to be unlearned and the better lesson taught that while the people should patriotically and cheerfully support their Government its functions do not include the support of the people.

The acceptance of this principle leads to a refusal of bounties and subsidies, which burden the labor and thrift of a portion of our citizens to aid ill-advised or languishing enterprises in which they have no concern. It leads also to a challenge of wild and reckless pension expenditure, which overleaps the bounds of grateful recognition of patriotic service and prostitutes to vicious uses the people's prompt and generous impulse to aid those disabled in their country's defense.

Every thoughtful American must realize the importance of checking at its beginning any tendency in public or private station to regard frugality and economy as virtues which we may safely outgrow. The toleration of this idea results in the waste of the people's money by their chosen servants and encourages prodigality and extravagance in the home life of our countrymen.

Under our scheme of government the waste of public money is a crime against the citizen, and the contempt of our people for economy and frugality in their personal affairs deplorably saps the strength and sturdiness of our national character.

It is a plain dictate of honesty and good government that public expenditures should be limited by public necessity, and that this should be measured by the rules of strict economy; and it is equally clear that frugality among the people is the best guaranty of a contented and strong support of free institutions.

One mode of the misappropriation of public funds is avoided when appointments to office, instead of being the rewards of partisan activity, are awarded to those whose efficiency promises a fair return of work for the compensation paid to them. To secure the fitness and competency of appointees to office and remove from political action the demoralizing madness for spoils, civil-service reform has found a place in our public policy and laws. The benefits already gained through this instrumentality and the further usefulness it promises entitle it to the hearty support and encouragement of all who desire to see our public service well performed or who hope for the elevation of political sentiment and the purification of political methods.

The existence of immense aggregations of kindred enterprises and combinations of business interests formed for the purpose of limiting production and fixing prices is inconsistent with the fair field which ought to be open to every independent activity. Legitimate strife in business should not be superseded by an enforced concession to the demands of combinations that have the power to destroy, nor should the people to be served lose the benefit of cheapness which usually results from wholesome competition. These aggregations and combinations frequently constitute conspiracies against the interests of the people, and in all their phases they are unnatural and opposed to our American sense of fairness. To the extent that they can be reached and restrained by Federal power the General Government should relieve our citizens from their interference and exactions.

Loyalty to the principles upon which our Government rests positively demands that the equality before the law which it guarantees to every citizen should be justly and in good faith conceded in all parts of the land. The enjoyment of this right follows the badge of citizenship wherever found, and, unimpaired by race or color, it appeals for recognition to American manliness and fairness.

Our relations with the Indians located within our border impose upon us responsibilities we can not escape. Humanity and consistency require us to treat them with forbearance and in our dealings with them to honestly and considerately regard their rights and interests. Every effort should be made to lead them, through the paths of civilization and education, to self-supporting and independent citizenship. In the meantime, as the nation's wards, they should be promptly defended against the cupidity of designing men and shielded from every influence or temptation that retards their advancement.

The people of the United States have decreed that on this day the control of their Government in its legislative and executive branches shall be given to a political party pledged in the most positive terms to the accomplishment of tariff reform. They have thus determined in favor of a more just and equitable system of Federal taxation. The agents they have chosen to carry out their purposes are bound by their promises not less than by the command of their masters to devote themselves unremittingly to this service.

While there should be no surrender of principle, our task must be undertaken wisely and without heedless vindictiveness. Our mission is not punishment, but the rectification of wrong. If in lifting burdens from the daily life of our people we reduce inordinate and unequal advantages too long enjoyed, this is but a necessary incident of our return to right and justice. If we exact from unwilling minds acquiescence in the theory of an honest distribution of the fund of the governmental beneficence treasured up for all, we but insist upon a principle which underlies our free institutions. When we tear aside the delusions and misconceptions which have blinded our countrymen to their condition under vicious tariff laws, we but show them how far they have been led away from the paths of contentment and prosperity. When we proclaim that the necessity for revenue to support the Government furnishes the only justification for taxing the people, we announce a truth so plain that its denial would seem to indicate the extent to which judgment may be influenced by familiarity with perversions of the taxing power. And when we seek to reinstate the self-confidence and business enterprise of our citizens by discrediting an abject dependence upon governmental favor, we strive to stimulate those elements of American character which support the hope of American achievement.

Anxiety for the redemption of the pledges which my party has made and solicitude for the complete justification of the trust the people have reposed in us constrain me to remind those with whom I am to cooperate that we can succeed in doing the work which has been especially set before us only by the most sincere, harmonious, and disinterested effort. Even if insuperable obstacles and opposition prevent the consummation of our task, we shall hardly be excused; and if failure can be traced to our fault or neglect we may be sure the people will hold us to a swift and exacting accountability.

The oath I now take to preserve, protect, and defend the Constitution of the United States not only impressively defines the great responsibility I assume, but suggests obedience to constitutional commands as the rule by which my official conduct must be guided. I shall to the best of my ability and within my sphere of duty preserve the Constitution by loyally protecting every grant of Federal power it contains, by defending all its restraints when attacked by impatience and restlessness, and by enforcing its limitations and reservations in favor of the States and the people.

Fully impressed with the gravity of the duties that confront me and mindful of my weakness, I should be appalled if it were my lot to bear unaided the responsibilities which await me. I am, however, saved from discouragement when I remember that I shall have the support and the counsel and cooperation of wise and patriotic men who will stand at my side in Cabinet places or will represent the people in their legislative halls.

I find also much comfort in remembering that my countrymen are just and generous and in the assurance that they will not condemn those who by sincere devotion to their service deserve their forbearance and approval.

Above all, I know there is a Supreme Being who rules the affairs of men and whose goodness and mercy have always followed the American people, and I know He will not turn from us now if we humbly and reverently seek His powerful aid.

Benjamin Harrison

Inaugural Address

Monday, March 4, 1889

Fellow-Citizens:

There is no constitutional or legal requirement that the President shall take the oath of office in the presence of the people, but there is so manifest an appropriateness in the public induction to office of the chief executive officer of the nation that from the beginning of the Government the people, to whose service the official oath consecrates the officer, have been called to witness the solemn ceremonial. The oath taken in the presence of the people becomes a mutual covenant. The officer covenants to serve the whole body of the people by a faithful execution of the laws, so that they may be the unfailing defense and security of those who respect and observe them, and that neither wealth, station, nor the power of combinations shall be able to evade their just penalties or to wrest them from a beneficent public purpose to serve the ends of cruelty or selfishness.

My promise is spoken; yours unspoken, but not the less real and solemn. The people of every State have here their representatives. Surely I do not misinterpret the spirit of the occasion when I assume that the whole body of the people covenant with me and with each other to-day to support and defend the Constitution and the Union of the States, to yield willing obedience to all the laws and each to every other citizen his equal civil and political rights. Entering thus solemnly into covenant with each other, we may reverently invoke and confidently expect the favor and help of Almighty God—that He will give to me wisdom, strength, and fidelity, and to our people a spirit of fraternity and a love of righteousness and peace.

This occasion derives peculiar interest from the fact that the Presidential term which begins this day is the twenty-sixth under our Constitution. The first inauguration of President Washington took place in New York, where Congress was then sitting, on the 30th day of April, 1789, having been deferred by reason of delays attending the organization of the Congress and the canvass of the electoral vote. Our people have already worthily observed the centennials of the Declaration of Independence, of the battle of Yorktown, and of the adoption of the Constitution, and will shortly celebrate in New York the institution of the second great department of our constitutional scheme of government. When the centennial of the institution of the judicial department, by the organization of the Supreme Court, shall have been suitably observed, as I trust it will be, our nation will have fully entered its second century.

I will not attempt to note the marvelous and in great part happy contrasts between our country as it steps over the threshold into its second century of organized existence under the Constitution and that weak but wisely ordered young nation that looked undauntedly down the first century, when all its years stretched out before it.

Our people will not fail at this time to recall the incidents which accompanied the institution of government under the Constitution, or to find inspiration and guidance in the teachings and example of Washington and his great associates, and hope and courage in the contrast which thirty-eight populous and prosperous States offer to the thirteen States, weak in everything except courage and the love of liberty, that then fringed our Atlantic seaboard.

The Territory of Dakota has now a population greater than any of the original States (except Virginia) and greater than the aggregate of five of the smaller States in 1790. The center of population when our national capital was located was east of Baltimore, and it was argued by many well-informed persons that it would move eastward rather than westward; yet in 1880 it was found to be near Cincinnati, and the new census about to be taken will show another stride to the westward. That which was the body has come to be only the rich fringe of the nation's robe. But our growth has not been limited to territory, population and aggregate wealth, marvelous as it has been in each of those directions. The masses of our people are better fed, clothed, and housed than their fathers were. The facilities for popular education have been vastly enlarged and more generally diffused.

The virtues of courage and patriotism have given recent proof of their continued presence and increasing power in the hearts and over the lives of our people. The influences of religion have been multiplied and strengthened. The sweet offices of charity have greatly increased. The virtue of temperance is held in higher estimation. We have not attained an ideal condition. Not all of our people are happy and prosperous; not all of them are virtuous and law-abiding. But on the whole the opportunities offered to the individual to secure the comforts of life are better than are found elsewhere and largely better than they were here one hundred years ago.

The surrender of a large measure of sovereignty to the General Government, effected by the adoption of the Constitution, was not accomplished until the suggestions of reason were strongly reenforced by the more imperative voice of experience. The divergent interests of peace speedily demanded a "more perfect union." The merchant, the shipmaster, and the manufacturer discovered and disclosed to our statesmen and to the people that commercial emancipation must be added to the political freedom which had been so bravely won. The commercial policy of the mother country had not relaxed any of its hard and oppressive features. To hold in check the development of our commercial marine, to prevent or retard the establishment and growth of manufactures in the States, and so to secure the American market for their shops and the carrying trade for their ships, was the policy of European statesmen, and was pursued with the most selfish vigor.

Petitions poured in upon Congress urging the imposition of discriminating duties that should encourage the production of needed things at home. The patriotism of the people, which no longer found afield of exercise in war, was energetically directed to the duty of equipping the young Republic for the defense of its independence by making its people self-dependent. Societies for the promotion of home manufactures and for encouraging the use of domestics in the dress of the people were organized in many of the States. The revival at the end of the century of the same patriotic interest in the preservation and development of domestic industries and the defense of our working people against injurious foreign competition is an incident worthy of attention. It is not a departure but a return that we have witnessed. The protective policy had then its opponents. The argument was made, as now, that its benefits inured to particular classes or sections.

If the question became in any sense or at any time sectional, it was only because slavery existed in some of the States. But for this there was no reason why the cotton-producing States should not have led or walked abreast with the New England States in the production of cotton fabrics. There was this reason only why the States that divide with Pennsylvania the mineral treasures of the great southeastern and central mountain ranges should have been so tardy in bringing to the smelting furnace and to the mill the coal and iron from their near opposing hillsides. Mill fires were lighted at the funeral pile of slavery. The emancipation proclamation was heard in the depths of the earth as well as in the sky; men were made free, and material things became our better servants.

The sectional element has happily been eliminated from the tariff discussion. We have no longer States that are necessarily only planting States. None are excluded from achieving that diversification of pursuits among the people which brings wealth and contentment. The cotton plantation will not be less valuable when the product is spun in the country town by operatives whose necessities call for diversified crops and create a home demand for garden and agricultural products. Every new mine, furnace, and factory is an extension of the productive capacity of the State more real and valuable than added territory.

Shall the prejudices and paralysis of slavery continue to hang upon the skirts of progress? How long will those who rejoice that slavery no longer exists cherish or tolerate the incapacities it put upon their communities? I look hopefully to the continuance of our protective system and to the consequent development of manufacturing and mining enterprises in the States hitherto wholly given to agriculture as a potent influence in the perfect unification of our people. The men who have invested their capital in these enterprises, the farmers who have felt the benefit of their neighborhood, and the men who work in shop or field will not fail to find and to defend a community of interest.

Is it not quite possible that the farmers and the promoters of the great mining and manufacturing enterprises which have recently been established in the South may yet find that the free ballot of the workingman, without distinction of race, is needed for their defense as well as for his own? I do not doubt that if those men in the South who now accept the tariff views of Clay and the constitutional expositions of Webster would courageously avow and defend their real convictions they would not find it difficult, by friendly instruction and cooperation, to make the black man their efficient and safe ally, not only in establishing correct principles in our national administration, but in preserving for their local communities the benefits of social order and economical and honest government. At least until the good offices of kindness and education have been fairly tried the contrary conclusion can not be plausibly urged.

I have altogether rejected the suggestion of a special Executive policy for any section of our country. It is the duty of the Executive to administer and enforce in the methods and by the instrumentalities pointed out and provided by the Constitution all the laws enacted by Congress. These laws are general and their administration should be uniform and equal. As a citizen may not elect what laws he will obey, neither may the Executive eject which he will enforce. The duty to obey and to execute embraces the Constitution in its entirety and the whole code of laws enacted under it. The evil example of permitting individuals, corporations, or communities to nullify the laws because they cross some selfish or local interest or prejudices is full of danger, not only to the nation at large, but much more to those who use this pernicious expedient to escape their just obligations or to obtain an unjust advantage over others. They will presently themselves be compelled to appeal to the law for protection, and those who would use the law as a defense must not deny that use of it to others.

If our great corporations would more scrupulously observe their legal limitations and duties, they would have less cause to complain of the unlawful limitations of their rights or of violent interference with their operations. The community that by concert, open or secret, among its citizens denies to a portion of its members their plain rights under the law has severed the only safe bond of social order and prosperity. The evil works from a bad center both ways. It demoralizes those who practice it and destroys the faith of those who suffer by it in the efficiency of the law as a safe protector. The man in whose breast that faith has been darkened is naturally the subject of dangerous and uncanny suggestions. Those who use unlawful methods, if moved by no higher motive than the selfishness that prompted them, may well stop and inquire what is to be the end of this.

An unlawful expedient can not become a permanent condition of government. If the educated and influential classes in a community either practice or connive at the systematic violation of laws that seem to them to cross their convenience, what can they expect when the lesson that convenience or a supposed class interest is a sufficient cause for lawlessness has been well learned by the ignorant classes? A community where law is the rule of conduct and where courts, not mobs, execute its penalties is the only attractive field for business investments and honest labor.

Our naturalization laws should be so amended as to make the inquiry into the character and good disposition of persons applying for citizenship more careful and searching. Our existing laws have been in their administration an unimpressive and often an unintelligible form. We accept the man as a citizen without any knowledge of his fitness, and he assumes the duties of citizenship without any knowledge as to what they are. The privileges of American citizenship are so great and its duties so grave that we may well insist upon a good knowledge of every person applying for citizenship and a good knowledge by him of our institutions. We should not cease to be hospitable to immigration, but we should cease to be careless as to the character of it. There are men of all races, even the best, whose coming is necessarily a burden upon our public revenues or a threat to social order. These should be identified and excluded.

We have happily maintained a policy of avoiding all interference with European affairs. We have been only interested spectators of their contentions in diplomacy and in war, ready to use our friendly offices to promote peace, but never obtruding our

advice and never attempting unfairly to coin the distresses of other powers into commercial advantage to ourselves. We have a just right to expect that our European policy will be the American policy of European courts.

It is so manifestly incompatible with those precautions for our peace and safety which all the great powers habitually observe and enforce in matters affecting them that a shorter waterway between our eastern and western seaboards should be dominated by any European Government that we may confidently expect that such a purpose will not be entertained by any friendly power.

We shall in the future, as in the past, use every endeavor to maintain and enlarge our friendly relations with all the great powers, but they will not expect us to look kindly upon any project that would leave us subject to the dangers of a hostile observation or environment. We have not sought to dominate or to absorb any of our weaker neighbors, but rather to aid and encourage them to establish free and stable governments resting upon the consent of their own people. We have a clear right to expect, therefore, that no European Government will seek to establish colonial dependencies upon the territory of these independent American States. That which a sense of justice restrains us from seeking they may be reasonably expected willingly to forego.

It must not be assumed, however, that our interests are so exclusively American that our entire inattention to any events that may transpire elsewhere can be taken for granted. Our citizens domiciled for purposes of trade in all countries and in many of the islands of the sea demand and will have our adequate care in their personal and commercial rights. The necessities of our Navy require convenient coaling stations and dock and harbor privileges. These and other trading privileges we will feel free to obtain only by means that do not in any degree partake of coercion, however feeble the government from which we ask such concessions. But having fairly obtained them by methods and for purposes entirely consistent with the most friendly disposition toward all other powers, our consent will be necessary to any modification or impairment of the concession.

We shall neither fail to respect the flag of any friendly nation or the just rights of its citizens, nor to exact the like treatment for our own. Calmness, justice, and consideration should characterize our diplomacy. The offices of an intelligent diplomacy or of friendly arbitration in proper cases should be adequate to the peaceful adjustment of all international difficulties. By such methods we will make our contribution to the world's peace, which no nation values more highly, and avoid the opprobrium which must fall upon the nation that ruthlessly breaks it.

The duty devolved by law upon the President to nominate and, by and with the advice and consent of the Senate, to appoint all public officers whose appointment is not otherwise provided for in the Constitution or by act of Congress has become very burdensome and its wise and efficient discharge full of difficulty. The civil list is so large that a personal knowledge of any large number of the applicants is impossible. The President must rely upon the representations of others, and these are often made inconsiderately and without any just sense of responsibility. I have a right, I think, to insist that those who volunteer or are invited to give advice as to appointments shall exercise consideration and fidelity. A high sense of duty and an ambition to improve the service should characterize all public officers.

There are many ways in which the convenience and comfort of those who have business with our public offices may be promoted by a thoughtful and obliging officer, and I shall expect those whom I may appoint to justify their selection by a conspicuous efficiency in the discharge of their duties. Honorable party service will certainly not be esteemed by me a disqualification for public office, but it will in no case be allowed to serve as a shield of official negligence, incompetency, or delinquency. It is entirely creditable to seek public office by proper methods and with proper motives, and all applicants will be treated with consideration; but I shall need, and the heads of Departments will need, time for inquiry and deliberation. Persistent importunity will not, therefore, be the best support of an application for office. Heads of Departments, bureaus, and all other public officers having any duty connected therewith will be expected to enforce the civil-service law fully and without evasion. Beyond this obvious duty I hope to do something more to advance the reform of the civil service. The ideal, or even my own ideal, I shall probably not attain. Retrospect will be a safer basis of judgment than promises. We shall not, however, I am sure, be able to put our civil service upon a nonpartisan basis until we have secured an incumbency that fair-minded men of the opposition will approve for impartiality and integrity. As the number of such in the civil list is increased removals from office will diminish.

While a Treasury surplus is not the greatest evil, it is a serious evil. Our revenue should be ample to meet the ordinary annual demands upon our Treasury, with a sufficient margin for those extraordinary but scarcely less imperative demands which arise now and then. Expenditure should always be made with economy and only upon public necessity. Wastefulness, profligacy, or favoritism in public expenditures is criminal. But there is nothing in the condition of our country or of our people to suggest that anything presently necessary to the public prosperity, security, or honor should be unduly postponed.

It will be the duty of Congress wisely to forecast and estimate these extraordinary demands, and, having added them to our ordinary expenditures, to so adjust our revenue laws that no considerable annual surplus will remain. We will fortunately be able to apply to the redemption of the public debt any small and unforeseen excess of revenue. This is better than to reduce our income below our necessary expenditures, with the resulting choice between another change of our revenue laws and an increase of the public debt. It is quite possible, I am sure, to effect the necessary reduction in our revenues without breaking down our protective tariff or seriously injuring any domestic industry.

The construction of a sufficient number of modern war ships and of their necessary armament should progress as rapidly as is consistent with care and perfection in plans and workmanship. The spirit, courage, and skill of our naval officers and seamen have many times in our history given to weak ships and inefficient guns a rating greatly beyond that of the naval list. That they will again do so upon occasion I do not doubt; but they ought not, by premeditation or neglect, to be left to the risks and exigencies of an unequal combat. We should encourage the establishment of American steamship lines. The exchanges of commerce demand stated, reliable, and rapid means of communication, and until these are provided the development of our trade with the States lying south of us is impossible.

Our pension laws should give more adequate and discriminating relief to the Union soldiers and sailors and to their widows and orphans. Such occasions as this should remind us that we owe everything to their valor and sacrifice.

It is a subject of congratulation that there is a near prospect of the admission into the Union of the Dakotas and Montana and Washington Territories. This act of justice has been unreasonably delayed in the case of some of them. The people who have settled these Territories are intelligent, enterprising, and patriotic, and the accession these new States will add strength to the nation. It is due to the settlers in the Territories who have availed themselves of the invitations of our land laws to make homes upon the public domain that their titles should be speedily adjusted and their honest entries confirmed by patent.

It is very gratifying to observe the general interest now being manifested in the reform of our election laws. Those who have been for years calling attention to the pressing necessity of throwing about the ballot box and about the elector further safeguards, in order that our elections might not only be free and pure, but might clearly appear to be so, will welcome the accession of any who did not so soon discover the need of reform. The National Congress has not as yet taken control of elections in that case over which the Constitution gives it jurisdiction, but has accepted and adopted the election laws of the several States, provided penalties for their violation and a method of supervision. Only the inefficiency of the State laws or an unfair partisan administration of them could suggest a departure from this policy.

It was clearly, however, in the contemplation of the framers of the Constitution that such an exigency might arise, and provision was wisely made for it. The freedom of the ballot is a condition of our national life, and no power vested in Congress or in the Executive to secure or perpetuate it should remain unused upon occasion. The people of all the Congressional districts have an equal interest that the election in each shall truly express the views and wishes of a majority of the qualified electors residing within it. The results of such elections are not local, and the insistence of electors residing in other districts that they shall be pure and free does not savor at all of impertinence.

If in any of the States the public security is thought to be threatened by ignorance among the electors, the obvious remedy is education. The sympathy and help of our people will not be withheld from any community struggling with special embarrassments or difficulties connected with the suffrage if the remedies proposed proceed upon lawful lines and are promoted by just and honorable methods. How shall those who practice election frauds recover that respect for the sanctity of the ballot which is the first condition and obligation of good citizenship? The man who has come to regard the ballot box as a juggler's hat has renounced his allegiance.

Let us exalt patriotism and moderate our party contentions. Let those who would die for the flag on the field of battle give a better proof of their patriotism and a higher glory to their country by promoting fraternity and justice. A party success that is achieved by unfair methods or by practices that partake of revolution is hurtful and evanescent even from a party standpoint. We should hold our differing opinions in mutual respect, and, having submitted them to the arbitrament of the ballot, should accept an adverse judgment with the same respect that we would have demanded of our opponents if the decision had been in our favor.

No other people have a government more worthy of their respect and love or a land so magnificent in extent, so pleasant to look upon, and so full of generous suggestion to enterprise and labor. God has placed upon our head a diadem and has laid at our feet power and wealth beyond definition or calculation. But we must not forget that we take these gifts upon the condition that justice and mercy shall hold the reins of power and that the upward avenues of hope shall be free to all the people.

I do not mistrust the future. Dangers have been in frequent ambush along our path, but we have uncovered and vanquished them all. Passion has swept some of our communities, but only to give us a new demonstration that the great body of our people are stable, patriotic, and law-abiding. No political party can long pursue advantage at the expense of public honor or by rude and indecent methods without protest and fatal disaffection in its own body. The peaceful agencies of commerce are more fully revealing the necessary unity of all our communities, and the increasing intercourse of our people is promoting mutual respect. We shall find unalloyed pleasure in the revelation which our next census will make of the swift development of the great resources of some of the States. Each State will bring its generous contribution to the great aggregate of the nation's increase. And when the harvests from the fields, the cattle from the hills, and the ores of the earth shall have been weighed, counted, and valued, we will turn from them all to crown with the highest honor the State that has most promoted education, virtue, justice, and patriotism among its people.

William McKinley

First Inaugural Address

Thursday, March 4, 1897

Fellow-Citizens:

In obedience to the will of the people, and in their presence, by the authority vested in me by this oath, I assume the arduous and responsible duties of President of the United States, relying upon the support of my countrymen and invoking the guidance of Almighty God. Our faith teaches that there is no safer reliance than upon the God of our fathers, who has so singularly favored the American people in every national trial, and who will not forsake us so long as we obey His commandments and walk humbly in His footsteps.

The responsibilities of the high trust to which I have been called—always of grave importance—are augmented by the prevailing business conditions entailing idleness upon willing labor and loss to useful enterprises. The country is suffering from industrial disturbances from which speedy relief must be had. Our financial system needs some revision; our money is all good now, but its value must not further be threatened. It should all be put upon an enduring basis, not subject to easy attack, nor its stability to doubt or dispute. Our currency should continue under the supervision of the Government. The several forms of our paper money offer, in my judgment, a constant embarrassment to the Government and a safe balance in the Treasury. Therefore I believe it necessary to devise a system which, without diminishing the circulating medium or offering a premium for its contraction, will present a remedy for those arrangements which, temporary in their nature, might well in the years of our prosperity have been displaced by wiser provisions. With adequate revenue secured, but not until then, we can enter upon such changes in our fiscal laws as will, while insuring safety and volume to our money, no longer impose upon the Government the necessity of maintaining so large a gold reserve, with its attendant and inevitable temptations to speculation. Most of our financial laws are the outgrowth of experience and trial, and should not be amended without investigation and demonstration of the wisdom of the proposed changes. We must be both "sure we are right" and "make haste slowly." If, therefore, Congress, in its wisdom, shall deem it expedient to create a commission to take under early consideration the revision of our coinage, banking and currency laws, and give them that exhaustive, careful and dispassionate examination that their importance demands, I shall cordially concur in such action. If such power is vested in the President, it is my purpose to appoint a commission of prominent, well-informed citizens of different parties, who will command public confidence, both on account of their ability and special fitness for the work. Business experience and public training may thus be combined, and the patriotic zeal of the friends of the country be so directed that such a report will be made as to receive the support of all parties, and our finances cease to be the subject of mere partisan contention. The experiment is, at all events, worth a trial, and, in my opinion, it can but prove beneficial to the entire country.

The question of international bimetallism will have early and earnest attention. It will be my constant endeavor to secure it by co-operation with the other great commercial powers of the world. Until that condition is realized when the parity between our gold and silver money springs from and is supported by the relative value of the two metals, the value of the silver already coined and of that which may hereafter be coined, must be kept constantly at par with gold by every resource at our command. The credit of the Government, the integrity of its currency, and the inviolability of its obligations must be preserved. This was the commanding verdict of the people, and it will not be unheeded.

Economy is demanded in every branch of the Government at all times, but especially in periods, like the present, of depression in business and distress among the people. The severest economy must be observed in all public expenditures, and extravagance stopped wherever it is found, and prevented wherever in the future it may be developed. If the revenues are to remain as now, the only relief that can come must be from decreased expenditures. But the present must not become the permanent condition of the Government. It has been our uniform practice to retire, not increase our outstanding obligations, and this policy must again be resumed and vigorously enforced. Our revenues should always be large enough to meet with ease and promptness not only our current needs and the principal and interest of the public debt, but to make proper and liberal provision for that most deserving body of public creditors, the soldiers and sailors and the widows and orphans who are the pensioners of the United States.

The Government should not be permitted to run behind or increase its debt in times like the present. Suitably to provide against this is the mandate of duty—the certain and easy remedy for most of our financial difficulties. A deficiency is inevitable so long as the expenditures of the Government exceed its receipts. It can only be met by loans or an increased revenue. While a large annual surplus of revenue may invite waste and extravagance, inadequate revenue creates distrust and undermines public and private credit. Neither should be encouraged. Between more loans and more revenue there ought to be but one opinion. We should have more revenue, and that without delay, hindrance, or postponement. A surplus in the Treasury created by loans is not a permanent or safe reliance. It will suffice while it lasts, but it can not last long while the outlays of the Government are greater than its receipts, as has been the case during the past two years. Nor must it be forgotten that however much such loans may temporarily relieve the situation, the Government is still indebted for the amount of the surplus thus accrued, which it must ultimately pay, while its ability to pay is not strengthened, but weakened by a continued deficit. Loans are imperative in great emergencies to preserve the Government or its credit, but a failure to supply needed revenue in time of peace for the maintenance of either has no justification.

The best way for the Government to maintain its credit is to pay as it goes—not by resorting to loans, but by keeping out of debt—through an adequate income secured by a system of taxation, external or internal, or both. It is the settled policy of the Government, pursued from the beginning and practiced by all parties and Administrations, to raise the bulk of our revenue from taxes upon foreign productions entering the United States for sale and consumption, and avoiding, for the most part, every form of direct taxation, except in time of war. The country is clearly opposed to any needless additions to the subject of internal taxation, and is committed by its latest popular utterance to the system of tariff taxation. There can be no misunderstanding, either, about the principle upon which this tariff taxation shall be levied. Nothing has ever been made plainer at a general election than that the controlling principle in the raising of revenue from duties on imports is zealous care for American interests and American labor. The people have declared that such legislation should be had as will give ample protection and encouragement to the industries and the development of our country. It is, therefore, earnestly hoped and expected that Congress will, at the earliest practicable moment, enact revenue legislation that shall be fair, reasonable, conservative, and just, and which, while supplying sufficient revenue for public purposes, will still be signally beneficial and helpful to every section and every enterprise of the people. To this policy we are all, of whatever party, firmly bound by the voice of the people—a power vastly more potential than the expression of any political platform. The paramount duty of Congress is to stop deficiencies by the restoration of that protective legislation which has always been the firmest prop of the Treasury. The passage of such a law or laws would strengthen the credit of the Government both at home and abroad, and go far toward stopping the drain upon the gold reserve held for the redemption of our currency, which has been heavy and well-nigh constant for several years.

In the revision of the tariff especial attention should be given to the re-enactment and extension of the reciprocity principle of the law of 1890, under which so great a stimulus was given to our foreign trade in new and advantageous markets for our surplus agricultural and manufactured products. The brief trial given this legislation amply justifies a further experiment and additional discretionary power in the making of commercial treaties, the end in view always to be the opening up of new markets for the products of our country, by granting concessions to the products of other lands that we need and cannot produce ourselves, and which do not involve any loss of labor to our own people, but tend to increase their employment.

The depression of the past four years has fallen with especial severity upon the great body of toilers of the country, and upon none more than the holders of small farms. Agriculture has languished and labor suffered. The revival of manufacturing will be a relief to both. No portion of our population is more devoted to the institution of free government nor more loyal in their support, while none bears more cheerfully or fully its proper share in the maintenance of the Government or is better entitled to its wise and liberal care and protection. Legislation helpful to producers is beneficial to all. The depressed condition of industry on the farm and in the mine and factory has lessened the ability of the people to meet the demands upon them, and they rightfully expect that not only a system of revenue shall be established that will secure the largest income with the least burden, but that every means will be taken to decrease, rather than increase, our public expenditures. Business conditions are not the most promising. It will take time to restore the prosperity of former years. If we cannot promptly attain it, we can resolutely turn our faces in that direction and aid its return by friendly legislation. However troublesome the situation may appear, Congress will not, I am sure, be found lacking in disposition or ability to relieve it as far as legislation can do so. The restoration of confidence and the revival of business, which men of all parties so much desire, depend more largely upon the prompt, energetic, and intelligent action of Congress than upon any other single agency affecting the situation.

It is inspiring, too, to remember that no great emergency in the one hundred and eight years of our eventful national life has ever arisen that has not been met with wisdom and courage by the American people, with fidelity to their best interests and highest destiny, and to the honor of the American name. These years of glorious history have exalted mankind and advanced the cause of freedom throughout the world, and immeasurably strengthened the precious free institutions which we enjoy. The people love and will sustain these institutions. The great essential to our happiness and prosperity is that we adhere to the principles upon which the Government was established and insist upon their faithful observance. Equality of rights must prevail, and our laws be always and everywhere respected and obeyed. We may have failed in the discharge of our full duty as citizens of the great Republic, but it is consoling and encouraging to realize that free speech, a free press, free thought, free schools, the free and unmolested right of religious liberty and worship, and free and fair elections are dearer and more universally enjoyed to-day than ever before. These guaranties must be sacredly preserved and wisely strengthened. The constituted authorities must be cheerfully and vigorously upheld. Lynchings must not be tolerated in a great and civilized country like the United States; courts, not mobs, must execute the penalties of the law. The preservation of public order, the right of discussion, the integrity of courts, and the orderly administration of justice must continue forever the rock of safety upon which our Government securely rests.

One of the lessons taught by the late election, which all can rejoice in, is that the citizens of the United States are both law-respecting and law-abiding people, not easily swerved from the path of patriotism and honor. This is in entire accord with the genius of our institutions, and but emphasizes the advantages of inculcating even a greater love for law and order in the future. Immunity should be granted to none who violate the laws, whether individuals, corporations, or communities; and as the Constitution imposes upon the President the duty of both its own execution, and of the statutes enacted in pursuance of its provisions, I shall endeavor carefully to carry them into effect. The declaration of the party now restored to power has been in the past that of "opposition to all combinations of capital organized in trusts, or otherwise, to control arbitrarily the condition of trade among our citizens," and it has supported "such legislation as will prevent the execution of all schemes to oppress the people by undue charges on their supplies, or by unjust rates for the transportation of their products to the market." This purpose will be steadily pursued, both by the enforcement of the laws now in existence and the recommendation and support of such new statutes as may be necessary to carry it into effect.

Our naturalization and immigration laws should be further improved to the constant promotion of a safer, a better, and a higher citizenship. A grave peril to the Republic would be a citizenship too ignorant to understand or too vicious to appreciate the great value and beneficence of our institutions and laws, and against all who come here to make war upon them our gates must be promptly and tightly closed. Nor must we be unmindful of the need of improvement among our own citizens, but with the zeal of our forefathers encourage the spread of knowledge and free education. Illiteracy must be banished from the land if we shall attain that high destiny as the foremost of the enlightened nations of the world which, under Providence, we ought to achieve.

Reforms in the civil service must go on; but the changes should be real and genuine, not perfunctory, or prompted by a zeal in behalf of any party simply because it happens to be in power. As a member of Congress I voted and spoke in favor of the present law, and I shall attempt its enforcement in the spirit in which it was enacted. The purpose in view was to secure the most efficient service of the best men who would accept appointment under the Government, retaining faithful and devoted public servants in office, but shielding none, under the authority of any rule or custom, who are inefficient, incompetent, or unworthy. The best interests of the country demand this, and the people heartily approve the law wherever and whenever it has been thus administered.

Congress should give prompt attention to the restoration of our American merchant marine, once the pride of the seas in all the great ocean highways of commerce. To my mind, few more important subjects so imperatively demand its intelligent consideration. The United States has progressed with marvelous rapidity in every field of enterprise and endeavor until we have become foremost in nearly all the great lines of inland trade, commerce, and industry. Yet, while this is true, our American merchant marine has been steadily declining until it is now lower, both in the percentage of tonnage and the number of vessels employed, than it was prior to the Civil War. Commendable progress has been made of late years in the upbuilding of the American Navy, but we must supplement these efforts by providing as a proper consort for it a merchant marine amply sufficient for our own carrying trade to foreign countries. The question is one that appeals both to our business necessities and the patriotic aspirations of a great people.

It has been the policy of the United States since the foundation of the Government to cultivate relations of peace and amity with all the nations of the world, and this accords with my conception of our duty now. We have cherished the policy of non-interference with affairs of foreign governments wisely inaugurated by Washington, keeping ourselves free from entanglement, either as allies or foes, content to leave undisturbed with them the settlement of their own domestic concerns. It will be our aim to pursue a firm and dignified foreign policy, which shall be just, impartial, ever watchful of our national honor, and always insisting upon the enforcement of the lawful rights of American citizens everywhere. Our diplomacy should seek nothing more and accept nothing less than is due us. We want no wars of conquest; we must avoid the temptation of territorial aggression. War should never be entered upon until every agency of peace has failed; peace is preferable to war in almost every contingency. Arbitration is the true method of settlement of international as well as local or individual differences. It was recognized as the best means of adjustment of differences between employers and employees by the Forty-ninth Congress, in 1886, and its application was extended to our diplomatic relations by the unanimous concurrence of the Senate and House of the Fifty-first Congress in 1890. The latter resolution was accepted as the basis of negotiations with us by the British House of Commons in 1893, and upon our invitation a treaty of arbitration between the United States and Great Britain was signed at Washington and transmitted to the Senate for its ratification in January last. Since this treaty is clearly the result of our own initiative; since it has been recognized as the leading feature of our foreign policy throughout our entire national history—the adjustment of difficulties by judicial methods rather than force of arms—and since it presents to the world the glorious example of reason and peace, not passion and war,

controlling the relations between two of the greatest nations in the world, an example certain to be followed by others, I respectfully urge the early action of the Senate thereon, not merely as a matter of policy, but as a duty to mankind. The importance and moral influence of the ratification of such a treaty can hardly be overestimated in the cause of advancing civilization. It may well engage the best thought of the statesmen and people of every country, and I cannot but consider it fortunate that it was reserved to the United States to have the leadership in so grand a work.

It has been the uniform practice of each President to avoid, as far as possible, the convening of Congress in extraordinary session. It is an example which, under ordinary circumstances and in the absence of a public necessity, is to be commended. But a failure to convene the representatives of the people in Congress in extra session when it involves neglect of a public duty places the responsibility of such neglect upon the Executive himself. The condition of the public Treasury, as has been indicated, demands the immediate consideration of Congress. It alone has the power to provide revenues for the Government. Not to convene it under such circumstances I can view in no other sense than the neglect of a plain duty. I do not sympathize with the sentiment that Congress in session is dangerous to our general business interests. Its members are the agents of the people, and their presence at the seat of Government in the execution of the sovereign will should not operate as an injury, but a benefit. There could be no better time to put the Government upon a sound financial and economic basis than now. The people have only recently voted that this should be done, and nothing is more binding upon the agents of their will than the obligation of immediate action. It has always seemed to me that the postponement of the meeting of Congress until more than a year after it has been chosen deprived Congress too often of the inspiration of the popular will and the country of the corresponding benefits. It is evident, therefore, that to postpone action in the presence of so great a necessity would be unwise on the part of the Executive because unjust to the interests of the people. Our action now will be freer from mere partisan consideration than if the question of tariff revision was postponed until the regular session of Congress. We are nearly two years from a Congressional election, and politics cannot so greatly distract us as if such contest was immediately pending. We can approach the problem calmly and patriotically, without fearing its effect upon an early election.

Our fellow-citizens who may disagree with us upon the character of this legislation prefer to have the question settled now, even against their preconceived views, and perhaps settled so reasonably, as I trust and believe it will be, as to insure great permanence, than to have further uncertainty menacing the vast and varied business interests of the United States. Again, whatever action Congress may take will be given a fair opportunity for trial before the people are called to pass judgment upon it, and this I consider a great essential to the rightful and lasting settlement of the question. In view of these considerations, I shall deem it my duty as President to convene Congress in extraordinary session on Monday, the 15th day of March, 1897.

In conclusion, I congratulate the country upon the fraternal spirit of the people and the manifestations of good will everywhere so apparent. The recent election not only most fortunately demonstrated the obliteration of sectional or geographical lines, but to some extent also the prejudices which for years have distracted our councils and marred our true greatness as a nation. The triumph of the people, whose verdict is carried into effect today, is not the triumph of one section, nor wholly of one party, but of all sections and all the people. The North and the South no longer divide on the old lines, but upon principles and policies; and in this fact surely every lover of the country can find cause for true felicitation. Let us rejoice in and cultivate this spirit; it is ennobling and will be both a gain and a blessing to our beloved country. It will be my constant aim to do nothing, and permit nothing to be done, that will arrest or disturb this growing sentiment of unity and cooperation, this revival of esteem and affiliation which now animates so many thousands in both the old antagonistic sections, but I shall cheerfully do everything possible to promote and increase it.

Let me again repeat the words of the oath administered by the Chief Justice which, in their respective spheres, so far as applicable, I would have all my countrymen observe: "I will faithfully execute the office of President of the United States, and will, to the best of my ability, preserve, protect, and defend the Constitution of the United States." This is the obligation I have reverently taken before the Lord Most High. To keep it will be my single purpose, my constant prayer; and I shall confidently rely upon the forbearance and assistance of all the people in the discharge of my solemn responsibilities.

Second Inaugural Address

Monday, March 4, 1901

My Fellow-Citizens:

When we assembled here on the 4th of March, 1897, there was great anxiety with regard to our currency and credit. None exists now. Then our Treasury receipts were inadequate to meet the current obligations of the Government. Now they are sufficient for all public needs, and we have a surplus instead of a deficit. Then I felt constrained to convene the Congress in extraordinary session to devise revenues to pay the ordinary expenses of the Government. Now I have the satisfaction to announce that the Congress just closed has reduced taxation in the sum of $41,000,000. Then there was deep solicitude because of the long depression in our manufacturing, mining, agricultural, and mercantile industries and the consequent distress of our laboring population. Now every avenue of production is crowded with activity, labor is well employed, and American products find good markets at home and abroad.

Our diversified productions, however, are increasing in such unprecedented volume as to admonish us of the necessity of still further enlarging our foreign markets by broader commercial relations. For this purpose reciprocal trade arrangements with other nations should in liberal spirit be carefully cultivated and promoted.

The national verdict of 1896 has for the most part been executed. Whatever remains unfulfilled is a continuing obligation resting with undiminished force upon the Executive and the Congress. But fortunate as our condition is, its permanence can only be assured by sound business methods and strict economy in national administration and legislation. We should not permit our great prosperity to lead us to reckless ventures in business or profligacy in public expenditures. While the Congress determines the objects and the sum of appropriations, the officials of the executive departments are responsible for honest and faithful disbursement, and it should be their constant care to avoid waste and extravagance.

Honesty, capacity, and industry are nowhere more indispensable than in public employment. These should be fundamental requisites to original appointment and the surest guaranties against removal.

Four years ago we stood on the brink of war without the people knowing it and without any preparation or effort at preparation for the impending peril. I did all that in honor could be done to avert the war, but without avail. It became inevitable; and the Congress at its first regular session, without party division, provided money in anticipation of the crisis and in preparation to meet it. It came. The result was signally favorable to American arms and in the highest degree honorable to the Government. It imposed upon us obligations from which we cannot escape and from which it would be dishonorable to seek escape. We are now at peace with the world, and it is my fervent prayer that if differences arise between us and other powers they may be settled by peaceful arbitration and that hereafter we may be spared the horrors of war.

Intrusted by the people for a second time with the office of President, I enter upon its administration appreciating the great responsibilities which attach to this renewed honor and commission, promising unreserved devotion on my part to their faithful discharge and reverently invoking for my guidance the direction and favor of Almighty God. I should shrink from the duties this day assumed if I did not feel that in their performance I should have the co-operation of the wise and patriotic men of all parties. It encourages me for the great task which I now undertake to believe that those who voluntarily committed to me the trust imposed upon the Chief Executive of the Republic will give me generous support in my duties to "preserve, protect, and defend, the Constitution of the United States" and to "care that the laws be faithfully executed." The national purpose is indicated through a national election. It is the constitutional method of ascertaining the public will. When once it is registered it is a law to us all, and faithful observance should follow its decrees.

Strong hearts and helpful hands are needed, and, fortunately, we have them in every part of our beloved country. We are reunited. Sectionalism has disappeared. Division on public questions can no longer be traced by the war maps of 1861. These old differences less and less disturb the judgment. Existing problems demand the thought and quicken the conscience of the country, and the responsibility for their presence, as well as for their righteous settlement, rests upon us all—no more upon me than upon you. There are some national questions in the solution of which patriotism should exclude partisanship. Magnifying their difficulties will not take them off our hands nor facilitate their adjustment. Distrust of the capacity, integrity, and high purposes of the American people will not be an inspiring theme for future political contests. Dark pictures and gloomy forebodings are worse than useless. These only becloud, they do not help to point the way of safety and honor. "Hope maketh not ashamed." The prophets of evil were not the builders of the Republic, nor in its crises since have they saved or served it. The faith of the fathers was a mighty force in its creation, and the faith of their descendants has wrought its progress and furnished its defenders. They are obstructionists who despair, and who would destroy confidence in the ability of our people to solve wisely and for civilization the mighty problems resting upon them. The American people, intrenched in freedom at home, take their love for it with them wherever they go, and they reject as mistaken and unworthy the doctrine that we lose our own liberties by securing the enduring foundations of liberty to others. Our institutions will not deteriorate by extension, and our sense of justice will not abate under tropic suns in distant seas. As heretofore, so hereafter will the nation demonstrate its fitness to administer any new estate which events devolve upon it, and in the fear of God will "take occasion by the hand and make the bounds of freedom wider yet." If there are those among us who would make our way more difficult, we must not be disheartened, but the more earnestly dedicate ourselves to the task upon which we have rightly entered. The path of progress is seldom smooth. New things are often found hard to do. Our fathers found them so. We find them so. They are inconvenient. They cost us something. But are we not made better for the effort and sacrifice, and are not those we serve lifted up and blessed?

We will be consoled, too, with the fact that opposition has confronted every onward movement of the Republic from its opening hour until now, but without success. The Republic has marched on and on, and its step has exalted freedom and humanity. We are undergoing the same ordeal as did our predecessors nearly a century ago. We are following the course they blazed. They triumphed. Will their successors falter and plead organic impotency in the nation? Surely after 125 years of achievement for mankind we will not now surrender our equality with other powers on matters fundamental and essential to nationality. With no such purpose was the nation created. In no such spirit has it developed its full and independent sovereignty. We adhere to the principle of equality among ourselves, and by no act of ours will we assign to ourselves a subordinate rank in the family of nations.

My fellow-citizens, the public events of the past four years have gone into history. They are too near to justify recital. Some of them were unforeseen; many of them momentous and far-reaching in their consequences to ourselves and our relations with the rest of the world. The part which the United States bore so honorably in the thrilling scenes in China, while new to American life, has been in harmony with its true spirit and best traditions, and in dealing with the results its policy will be that of moderation and fairness.

We face at this moment a most important question that of the future relations of the United States and Cuba. With our near neighbors we must remain close friends. The declaration of the purposes of this Government in the resolution of April 20, 1898, must be made good. Ever since the evacuation of the island by the army of Spain, the Executive, with all practicable speed, has been assisting its people in the successive steps necessary to the establishment of a free and independent government prepared to assume and perform the obligations of international law which now rest upon the United States under the treaty of Paris. The convention elected by the people to frame a constitution is approaching the completion of its labors. The transfer of American control to the new government is of such great importance, involving an obligation resulting from our intervention and the treaty of peace, that I am glad to be advised by the recent act of Congress of the policy which the legislative branch of the Government deems essential to the best interests of Cuba and the United States. The principles which led to our intervention require that the fundamental law upon which the new government rests should be adapted to secure a government capable of performing the duties and discharging the functions of a separate nation, of observing its international obligations of protecting life and property, insuring order, safety, and liberty, and conforming to the established and historical policy of the United States in its relation to Cuba.

The peace which we are pledged to leave to the Cuban people must carry with it the guaranties of permanence. We became sponsors for the pacification of the island, and we remain accountable to the Cubans, no less than to our own country and people, for the reconstruction of Cuba as a free commonwealth on abiding foundations of right, justice, liberty, and assured order. Our enfranchisement of the people will not be completed until free Cuba shall "be a reality, not a name; a perfect entity, not a hasty experiment bearing within itself the elements of failure."

While the treaty of peace with Spain was ratified on the 6th of February, 1899, and ratifications were exchanged nearly two years ago, the Congress has indicated no form of government for the Philippine Islands. It has, however, provided an army to enable the Executive to suppress insurrection, restore peace, give security to the inhabitants, and establish the authority of the United States throughout the archipelago. It has authorized the organization of native troops as auxiliary to the regular force. It has been advised from time to time of the acts of the military and naval officers in the islands, of my action in appointing civil commissions, of the instructions with which they were charged, of their duties and powers, of their recommendations, and of their several acts under executive commission, together with the very complete general information they have submitted. These reports fully set forth the conditions, past and present, in the islands, and the instructions clearly show the principles which will guide the Executive until the Congress shall, as it is required to do by the treaty, determine "the civil rights and political status of the native inhabitants." The Congress having added the sanction of its authority to the powers already possessed and exercised by the Executive under the Constitution, thereby leaving with the Executive the responsibility for the government of the Philippines, I shall continue the efforts already begun until order shall be restored throughout the islands, and as fast as conditions permit will establish local governments, in the formation of which the full co-operation of the people has been already invited, and when established will encourage the people to administer them. The settled purpose, long ago proclaimed, to afford the inhabitants of the islands self-government as fast as they were ready for it will be pursued with earnestness and fidelity. Already something has been accomplished in this direction. The Government's representatives, civil and military, are doing faithful and noble work in their mission of emancipation and merit the approval and support of their countrymen. The most liberal terms of amnesty have already been communicated to the insurgents, and the way is still open for those who have raised their arms against the Government for honorable submission to its authority. Our countrymen should not be deceived. We are not waging war against the inhabitants of the Philippine Islands. A portion of them are making war against the United States. By far the greater part of the inhabitants recognize American sovereignty and welcome it as a guaranty of order and of security for life, property, liberty, freedom of conscience, and the pursuit of happiness. To them full protection will be given. They shall not be abandoned. We will not leave the destiny of the loyal millions the islands to the disloyal thousands who are in rebellion against the United States. Order under civil institutions will come as soon as those who now break the peace shall keep it. Force will not be needed or used when those who make war against us shall make it no more. May it end without further bloodshed, and there be ushered in the reign of peace to be made permanent by a government of liberty under law!

Theodore Roosevelt

Inaugural Address

Saturday, March 4, 1905

MY fellow-citizens, no people on earth have more cause to be thankful than ours, and this is said reverently, in no spirit of boastfulness in our own strength, but with gratitude to the Giver of Good who has blessed us with the conditions which have enabled us to achieve so large a measure of well-being and of happiness. To us as a people it has been granted to lay the foundations of our national life in a new continent. We are the heirs of the ages, and yet we have had to pay few of the penalties which in old countries are exacted by the dead hand of a bygone civilization. We have not been obliged to fight for our existence against any alien race; and yet our life has called for the vigor and effort without which the manlier and hardier virtues wither away. Under such conditions it would be our own fault if we failed; and the success which we have had in the past, the success which we confidently believe the future will bring, should cause in us no feeling of vainglory, but rather a deep and abiding realization of all which life has offered us; a full acknowledgment of the responsibility which is ours; and a fixed determination to show that under a free government a mighty people can thrive best, alike as regards the things of the body and the things of the soul.

Much has been given us, and much will rightfully be expected from us. We have duties to others and duties to ourselves; and we can shirk neither. We have become a great nation, forced by the fact of its greatness into relations with the other nations of the earth, and we must behave as beseems a people with such responsibilities. Toward all other nations, large and small, our attitude must be one of cordial and sincere friendship. We must show not only in our words, but in our deeds, that we are earnestly desirous of securing their good will by acting toward them in a spirit of just and generous recognition of all their rights. But justice and generosity in a nation, as in an individual, count most when shown not by the weak but by the strong. While ever careful to refrain from wrongdoing others, we must be no less insistent that we are not wronged ourselves. We wish peace, but we wish the peace of justice, the peace of righteousness. We wish it because we think it is right and not because we are afraid. No weak nation that acts manfully and justly should ever have cause to fear us, and no strong power should ever be able to single us out as a subject for insolent aggression.

Our relations with the other powers of the world are important; but still more important are our relations among ourselves. Such growth in wealth, in population, and in power as this nation has seen during the century and a quarter of its national life is inevitably accompanied by a like growth in the problems which are ever before every nation that rises to greatness. Power invariably means both responsibility and danger. Our forefathers faced certain perils which we have outgrown. We now face other perils, the very existence of which it was impossible that they should foresee. Modern life is both complex and intense, and the tremendous changes wrought by the extraordinary industrial development of the last half century are felt in every fiber of our social and political being. Never before have men tried so vast and formidable an experiment as that of administering the affairs of a continent under the forms of a Democratic republic. The conditions which have told for our marvelous material well-being, which have developed to a very high degree our energy, self-reliance, and individual initiative, have also brought the care and anxiety inseparable from the accumulation of great wealth in industrial centers. Upon the success of our experiment much depends, not only as regards our own welfare, but as regards the welfare of mankind. If we fail, the cause of free self-government throughout the world will rock to its foundations, and therefore our responsibility is heavy, to ourselves, to the world as it is to-day, and to the generations yet unborn. There is no good reason why we should fear the future, but there is every reason why we should face it seriously, neither hiding from ourselves the gravity of the problems before us nor fearing to approach these problems with the unbending, unflinching purpose to solve them aright.

Yet, after all, though the problems are new, though the tasks set before us differ from the tasks set before our fathers who founded and preserved this Republic, the spirit in which these tasks must be undertaken and these problems faced, if our duty is to be well done, remains essentially unchanged. We know that self-government is difficult. We know that no people needs such high traits of character as that people which seeks to govern its affairs aright through the freely expressed will of the freemen who compose it. But we have faith that we shall not prove false to the memories of the men of the mighty past. They did their work, they left us the splendid heritage we now enjoy. We in our turn have an assured confidence that we shall be able to leave this heritage unwasted and enlarged to our children and our children's children. To do so we must show, not merely in great crises, but in the everyday affairs of life, the qualities of practical intelligence, of courage, of hardihood, and endurance, and above all the power of devotion to a lofty ideal, which made great the men who founded this Republic in the days of Washington, which made great the men who preserved this Republic in the days of Abraham Lincoln.

William Howard Taft

Inaugural Address

Thursday, March 4, 1909

My Fellow-Citizens:

ANYONE who has taken the oath I have just taken must feel a heavy weight of responsibility. If not, he has no conception of the powers and duties of the office upon which he is about to enter, or he is lacking in a proper sense of the obligation which the oath imposes.

The office of an inaugural address is to give a summary outline of the main policies of the new administration, so far as they can be anticipated. I have had the honor to be one of the advisers of my distinguished predecessor, and, as such, to hold up his hands in the reforms he has initiated. I should be untrue to myself, to my promises, and to the declarations of the party platform upon which I was elected to office, if I did not make the maintenance and enforcement of those reforms a most important feature of my administration. They were directed to the suppression of the lawlessness and abuses of power of the great combinations of capital invested in railroads and in industrial enterprises carrying on interstate commerce. The steps which my predecessor took and the legislation passed on his recommendation have accomplished much, have caused a general halt in the vicious policies which created popular alarm, and have brought about in the business affected a much higher regard for existing law.

To render the reforms lasting, however, and to secure at the same time freedom from alarm on the part of those pursuing proper and progressive business methods, further legislative and executive action are needed. Relief of the railroads from certain restrictions of the antitrust law have been urged by my predecessor and will be urged by me. On the other hand, the administration is pledged to legislation looking to a proper federal supervision and restriction to prevent excessive issues of bonds and stock by companies owning and operating interstate commerce railroads.

Then, too, a reorganization of the Department of Justice, of the Bureau of Corporations in the Department of Commerce and Labor, and of the Interstate Commerce Commission, looking to effective cooperation of these agencies, is needed to secure a more rapid and certain enforcement of the laws affecting interstate railroads and industrial combinations.

I hope to be able to submit at the first regular session of the incoming Congress, in December next, definite suggestions in respect to the needed amendments to the antitrust and the interstate commerce law and the changes required in the executive departments concerned in their enforcement.

It is believed that with the changes to be recommended American business can be assured of that measure of stability and certainty in respect to those things that may be done and those that are prohibited which is essential to the life and growth of all business. Such a plan must include the right of the people to avail themselves of those methods of combining capital and effort deemed necessary to reach the highest degree of economic efficiency, at the same time differentiating between combinations based upon legitimate economic reasons and those formed with the intent of creating monopolies and artificially controlling prices.

The work of formulating into practical shape such changes is creative word of the highest order, and requires all the deliberation possible in the interval. I believe that the amendments to be proposed are just as necessary in the protection of legitimate business as in the clinching of the reforms which properly bear the name of my predecessor.

A matter of most pressing importance is the revision of the tariff. In accordance with the promises of the platform upon which I was elected, I shall call Congress into extra session to meet on the 15th day of March, in order that consideration may be at once given to a bill revising the Dingley Act. This should secure an adequate revenue and adjust the duties in such a manner as to afford to labor and to all industries in this country, whether of the farm, mine or factory, protection by tariff equal to the difference between the cost of production abroad and the cost of production here, and have a provision which shall put into force, upon executive determination of certain facts, a higher or maximum tariff against those countries whose trade policy toward us equitably requires such discrimination. It is thought that there has been such a change in conditions since the enactment of the Dingley Act, drafted on a similarly protective principle, that the measure of the tariff above stated will permit the reduction of rates in certain schedules and will require the advancement of few, if any.

The proposal to revise the tariff made in such an authoritative way as to lead the business community to count upon it necessarily halts all those branches of business directly affected; and as these are most important, it disturbs the whole business of the country. It is imperatively necessary, therefore, that a tariff bill be drawn in good faith in accordance with promises made before the election by the party in power, and as promptly passed as due consideration will permit. It is not that the tariff is more important in the long run than the perfecting of the reforms in respect to antitrust legislation and interstate commerce regulation, but the need for action when the revision of the tariff has been determined upon is more immediate to avoid embarrassment of business. To secure the needed speed in the passage of the tariff bill, it would seem wise to attempt no other legislation at the extra session. I venture this as a suggestion only, for the course to be taken by Congress, upon the call of the Executive, is wholly within its discretion.

In the mailing of a tariff bill the prime motive is taxation and the securing thereby of a revenue. Due largely to the business depression which followed the financial panic of 1907, the revenue from customs and other sources has decreased to such an extent that the expenditures for the current fiscal year will exceed the receipts by $100,000,000. It is imperative that such a deficit shall not continue, and the framers of the tariff bill must, of course, have in mind the total revenues likely to be produced by it and so arrange the duties as to secure an adequate income. Should it be impossible to do so by import duties, new kinds of taxation must be adopted, and among these I recommend a graduated inheritance tax as correct in principle and as certain and easy of collection.

The obligation on the part of those responsible for the expenditures made to carry on the Government, to be as economical as possible, and to make the burden of taxation as light as possible, is plain, and should be affirmed in every declaration of government policy. This is especially true when we are face to face with a heavy deficit. But when the desire to win the popular approval leads to the cutting off of expenditures really needed to make the Government effective and to enable it to accomplish its proper objects, the result is as much to be condemned as the waste of government funds in unnecessary expenditure. The scope of a modern government in what it can and ought to accomplish for its people has been widened far beyond the principles laid down by the old "laissez faire" school of political writers, and this widening has met popular approval.

In the Department of Agriculture the use of scientific experiments on a large scale and the spread of information derived from them for the improvement of general agriculture must go on.

The importance of supervising business of great railways and industrial combinations and the necessary investigation and prosecution of unlawful business methods are another necessary tax upon Government which did not exist half a century ago.

The putting into force of laws which shall secure the conservation of our resources, so far as they may be within the jurisdiction of the Federal Government, including the most important work of saving and restoring our forests and the great improvement of waterways, are all proper government functions which must involve large expenditure if properly performed. While some of them, like the reclamation of arid lands, are made to pay for themselves, others are of such an indirect benefit that this cannot be expected of them. A permanent improvement, like the Panama Canal, should be treated as a distinct enterprise, and should be paid for by the proceeds of bonds, the issue of which will distribute its cost between the present and future generations in accordance with the benefits derived. It may well be submitted to the serious consideration of Congress whether the deepening and control of the channel of a great river system, like that of the Ohio or of the Mississippi, when definite and practical plans for the enterprise have been approved and determined upon, should not be provided for in the same way.

Then, too, there are expenditures of Government absolutely necessary if our country is to maintain its proper place among the nations of the world, and is to exercise its proper influence in defense of its own trade interests in the maintenance of traditional American policy against the colonization of European monarchies in this hemisphere, and in the promotion of peace and international morality. I refer to the cost of maintaining a proper army, a proper navy, and suitable fortifications upon the mainland of the United States and in its dependencies.

We should have an army so organized and so officered as to be capable in time of emergency, in cooperation with the national militia and under the provisions of a proper national volunteer law, rapidly to expand into a force sufficient to resist all probable invasion from abroad and to furnish a respectable expeditionary force if necessary in the maintenance of our traditional American policy which bears the name of President Monroe.

Our fortifications are yet in a state of only partial completeness, and the number of men to man them is insufficient. In a few years however, the usual annual appropriations for our coast defenses, both on the mainland and in the dependencies, will make them sufficient to resist all direct attack, and by that time we may hope that the men to man them will be provided as a necessary adjunct. The distance of our shores from Europe and Asia of course reduces the necessity for maintaining under arms a great army, but it does not take away the requirement of mere prudence—that we should have an army sufficiently large and so constituted as to form a nucleus out of which a suitable force can quickly grow.

What has been said of the army may be affirmed in even a more emphatic way of the navy. A modern navy can not be improvised. It must be built and in existence when the emergency arises which calls for its use and operation. My distinguished predecessor has in many speeches and messages set out with great force and striking language the necessity for maintaining a strong navy commensurate with the coast line, the governmental resources, and the foreign trade of our Nation; and I wish to reiterate all the reasons which he has presented in favor of the policy of maintaining a strong navy as the best conservator of our peace with other nations, and the best means of securing respect for the assertion of our rights, the defense of our interests, and the exercise of our influence in international matters.

Our international policy is always to promote peace. We shall enter into any war with a full consciousness of the awful consequences that it always entails, whether successful or not, and we, of course, shall make every effort consistent with national honor and the highest national interest to avoid a resort to arms. We favor every instrumentality, like that of the Hague Tribunal and arbitration treaties made with a view to its use in all international controversies, in order to maintain peace and to avoid war. But we should be blind to existing conditions and should allow ourselves to become foolish idealists if we did not realize that, with all the nations of the world armed and prepared for war, we must be ourselves in a similar condition, in order to prevent other nations from taking advantage of us and of our inability to defend our interests and assert our rights with a strong hand.

In the international controversies that are likely to arise in the Orient growing out of the question of the open door and other issues the United States can maintain her interests intact and can secure respect for her just demands. She will not be able to do so, however, if it is understood that she never intends to back up her assertion of right and her defense of her interest by anything but mere verbal protest and diplomatic note. For these reasons the expenses of the army and navy and of coast defenses should always be considered as something which the Government must pay for, and they should not be cut off through a false consideration of economy. Our Government is able to afford a suitable army and a suitable navy. It may maintain them without the slightest danger to the Republic or the cause of free institutions, and fear of additional taxation ought not to change a proper policy in this regard.

The policy of the United States in the Spanish war and since has given it a position of influence among the nations that it never had before, and should be constantly exerted to securing to its bona fide citizens, whether native or naturalized, respect for them as such in foreign countries. We should make every effort to prevent humiliating and degrading prohibition against any of our citizens wishing temporarily to sojourn in foreign countries because of race or religion.

The admission of Asiatic immigrants who cannot be amalgamated with our population has been made the subject either of prohibitory clauses in our treaties and statutes or of strict administrative regulation secured by diplomatic negotiation. I sincerely hope that we may continue to minimize the evils likely to arise from such immigration without unnecessary friction and by mutual concessions between self-respecting governments. Meantime we must take every precaution to prevent, or failing that, to punish outbursts of race feeling among our people against foreigners of whatever nationality who have by our grant a treaty right to pursue lawful business here and to be protected against lawless assault or injury.

This leads me to point out a serious defect in the present federal jurisdiction, which ought to be remedied at once. Having assured to other countries by treaty the protection of our laws for such of their subjects or citizens as we permit to come within our jurisdiction, we now leave to a state or a city, not under the control of the Federal Government, the duty of performing our international obligations in this respect. By proper legislation we may, and ought to, place in the hands of the Federal Executive the means of enforcing the treaty rights of such aliens in the courts of the Federal Government. It puts our Government in a pusillanimous position to make definite engagements to protect aliens and then to excuse the failure to perform those engagements by an explanation that the duty to keep them is in States or cities, not within our control. If we would promise we must put ourselves in a position to perform our promise. We cannot permit the possible failure of justice, due to local prejudice in any State or municipal government, to expose us to the risk of a war which might be avoided if federal jurisdiction was asserted by suitable legislation by Congress and carried out by proper proceedings instituted by the Executive in the courts of the National Government.

One of the reforms to be carried out during the incoming administration is a change of our monetary and banking laws, so as to secure greater elasticity in the forms of currency available for trade and to prevent the limitations of law from operating to increase the embarrassment of a financial panic. The monetary commission, lately appointed, is giving full consideration to existing conditions and to all proposed remedies, and will doubtless suggest one that will meet the requirements of business and of public interest.

We may hope that the report will embody neither the narrow dew of those who believe that the sole purpose of the new system should be to secure a large return on banking capital or of those who would have greater expansion of currency with little regard to provisions for its immediate redemption or ultimate security. There is no subject of economic discussion so intricate and so likely to evoke differing views and dogmatic statements as this one. The commission, in studying the general influence of currency on business and of business on currency, have wisely extended their investigations in European banking and monetary methods. The information that they have derived from such experts as they have found abroad will undoubtedly be found helpful in the solution of the difficult problem they have in hand.

The incoming Congress should promptly fulfill the promise of the Republican platform and pass a proper postal savings bank bill. It will not be unwise or excessive paternalism. The promise to repay by the Government will furnish an inducement to savings deposits which private enterprise can not supply and at such a low rate of interest as not to withdraw custom from existing banks. It will substantially increase the funds available for investment as capital in useful enterprises. It will furnish absolute security which makes the proposed scheme of government guaranty of deposits so alluring, without its pernicious results.

I sincerely hope that the incoming Congress will be alive, as it should be, to the importance of our foreign trade and of encouraging it in every way feasible. The possibility of increasing this trade in the Orient, in the Philippines, and in South America are known to everyone who has given the matter attention. The direct effect of free trade between this country and the Philippines will be marked upon our sales of cottons, agricultural machinery, and other manufactures. The necessity of the establishment of direct lines of steamers between North and South America has been brought to the attention of Congress by my predecessor and by Mr. Root before and after his noteworthy visit to that continent, and I sincerely hope that Congress may be induced to see the wisdom of a tentative effort to establish such lines by the use of mail subsidies.

The importance of the part which the Departments of

Agriculture and of Commerce and Labor may play in ridding the markets of Europe of prohibitions and discriminations against the importation of our products is fully understood, and it is hoped that the use of the maximum and minimum feature of our tariff law to be soon passed will be effective to remove many of those restrictions.

The Panama Canal will have a most important bearing upon the trade between the eastern and far western sections of our country, and will greatly increase the facilities for transportation between the eastern and the western seaboard, and may possibly revolutionize the transcontinental rates with respect to bulky merchandise. It will also have a most beneficial effect to increase the trade between the eastern seaboard of the United States and the western coast of South America, and, indeed, with some of the important ports on the east coast of South America reached by rail from the west coast.

The work on the canal is making most satisfactory progress. The type of the canal as a lock canal was fixed by Congress after a full consideration of the conflicting reports of the majority and minority of the consulting board, and after the recommendation of the War Department and the Executive upon those reports. Recent suggestion that something had occurred on the Isthmus to make the lock type of the canal less feasible than it was supposed to be when the reports were made and the policy determined on led to a visit to the Isthmus of a board of competent engineers to examine the Gatun dam and locks, which are the key of the lock type. The report of that board shows nothing has occurred in the nature of newly revealed evidence which should change the views once formed in the original discussion. The construction will go on under a most effective organization controlled by Colonel Goethals and his fellow army engineers associated with him, and will certainly be completed early in the next administration, if not before.

Some type of canal must be constructed. The lock type has been selected. We are all in favor of having it built as promptly as possible. We must not now, therefore, keep up a fire in the rear of the agents whom we have authorized to do our work on the Isthmus. We must hold up their hands, and speaking for the incoming administration I wish to say that I propose to devote all the energy possible and under my control to pushing of this work on the plans which have been adopted, and to stand behind the men who are doing faithful, hard work to bring about the early completion of this, the greatest constructive enterprise of modern times.

The governments of our dependencies in Porto Rico and the Philippines are progressing as favorably as could be desired. The prosperity of Porto Rico continues unabated. The business conditions in the Philippines are not all that we could wish them to be, but with the passage of the new tariff bill permitting free trade between the United States and the archipelago, with such limitations on sugar and tobacco as shall prevent injury to domestic interests in those products, we can count on an improvement in business conditions in the Philippines and the development of a mutually profitable trade between this country and the islands. Meantime our Government in each dependency is upholding the traditions of civil liberty and increasing popular control which might be expected under American auspices. The work which we are doing there redounds to our credit as a nation.

I look forward with hope to increasing the already good feeling between the South and the other sections of the country. My chief purpose is not to effect a change in the electoral vote of the Southern States. That is a secondary consideration. What I look forward to is an increase in the tolerance of political views of all kinds and their advocacy throughout the South, and the existence of a respectable political opposition in every State; even more than this, to an increased feeling on the part of all the people in the South that this Government is their Government, and that its officers in their states are their officers.0

The consideration of this question can not, however, be complete and full without reference to the negro race, its progress and its present condition. The thirteenth amendment secured them freedom; the fourteenth amendment due process of law, protection of property, and the pursuit of happiness; and the fifteenth amendment attempted to secure the negro against any deprivation of the privilege to vote because he was a negro. The thirteenth and fourteenth amendments have been generally enforced and have secured the objects for which they are intended. While the fifteenth amendment has not been generally observed in the past, it ought to be observed, and the tendency of Southern legislation today is toward the enactment of electoral qualifications which shall square with that amendment. Of course, the mere adoption of a constitutional law is only one step in the right direction. It must be fairly and justly enforced as well. In time both will come. Hence it is clear to all that the domination of an ignorant, irresponsible element can be prevented by constitutional laws which shall exclude from voting both negroes and whites not having education or other qualifications thought to be necessary for a proper electorate. The danger of the control of an ignorant electorate has therefore passed. With this change, the interest which many of the Southern white citizens take in the welfare of the negroes has increased. The colored men must base their hope on the results of their own industry, self-restraint, thrift, and business success, as well as upon the aid and comfort and sympathy which they may receive from their white neighbors of the South.

There was a time when Northerners who sympathized with the negro in his necessary struggle for better conditions sought to give him the suffrage as a protection to enforce its exercise against the prevailing sentiment of the South. The movement proved to be a failure. What remains is the fifteenth amendment to the Constitution and the right to have statutes of States specifying qualifications for electors subjected to the test of compliance with that amendment. This is a great protection to the negro. It never will be repealed, and it never ought to be repealed. If it had not passed, it might be difficult now to adopt it; but with it in our fundamental law, the policy of Southern legislation must and will tend to obey it, and so long as the statutes of the States meet the test of this amendment and are not otherwise in conflict with the Constitution and laws of the United States, it is not the disposition or within the province of the Federal Government to interfere with the regulation by Southern States of their domestic affairs. There is in the South a stronger feeling than ever among the intelligent well-to-do, and influential element in favor of the industrial education of the negro and the encouragement of the race to make themselves useful members of the community. The progress which the negro has made in the last fifty years, from slavery, when its statistics are reviewed, is marvelous, and it furnishes every reason to hope that in the next twenty-five years a still greater improvement in his condition as a productive member of society, on the farm, and in the shop, and in other occupations may come.

The negroes are now Americans. Their ancestors came here years ago against their will, and this is their only country and their only flag. They have shown themselves anxious to live for it and to die for it. Encountering the race feeling against them, subjected at times to cruel injustice growing out of it, they may well have our profound sympathy and aid in the struggle they are making. We are charged with the sacred duty of making their path as smooth and easy as we can. Any recognition of their distinguished men, any appointment to office from among their number, is properly taken as an encouragement and an appreciation of their progress, and this just policy should be pursued when suitable occasion offers.

But it may well admit of doubt whether, in the case of any race, an appointment of one of their number to a local office in a community in which the race feeling is so widespread and acute as to interfere with the ease and facility with which the local government business can be done by the appointee is of sufficient benefit by way of encouragement to the race to outweigh the recurrence and increase of race feeling which such an appointment is likely to engender. Therefore the Executive, in recognizing the negro race by appointments, must exercise a careful discretion not thereby to do it more harm than good. On the other hand, we must be careful not to encourage the mere pretense of race feeling manufactured in the interest of individual political ambition.

Personally, I have not the slightest race prejudice or feeling, and recognition of its existence only awakens in my heart a deeper sympathy for those who have to bear it or suffer from it, and I question the wisdom of a policy which is likely to increase it. Meantime, if nothing is done to prevent it, a better feeling between the negroes and the whites in the South will continue to grow, and more and more of the white people will come to realize that the future of the South is to be much benefited by the industrial and intellectual progress of the negro. The exercise of political franchises by those of this race who are intelligent and well to do will be acquiesced in, and the right to vote will be withheld only from the ignorant and irresponsible of both races.

There is one other matter to which I shall refer. It was made the subject of great controversy during the election and calls for at least a passing reference now. My distinguished predecessor has given much attention to the cause of labor, with whose struggle for better things he has shown the sincerest sympathy. At his instance Congress has passed the bill fixing the liability of interstate carriers to their employees for injury sustained in the course of employment, abolishing the rule of fellow-servant and the common-law rule as to contributory negligence, and substituting therefor the so-called rule of "comparative negligence." It has also passed a law fixing the compensation of government employees for injuries sustained in the employ of the Government through the negligence of the superior. It has also passed a model child-labor law for the District of Columbia. In previous administrations an arbitration law for interstate commerce railroads and their employees, and laws for the application of safety devices to save the lives and limbs of employees of interstate railroads had been passed. Additional legislation of this kind was passed by the outgoing Congress.

I wish to say that insofar as I can I hope to promote the enactment of further legislation of this character. I am strongly convinced that the Government should make itself as responsible to employees injured in its employ as an interstate-railway corporation is made responsible by federal law to its employees; and I shall be glad, whenever any additional reasonable safety device can be invented to reduce the loss of life and limb among railway employees, to urge Congress to require its adoption by interstate railways.

Another labor question has arisen which has awakened the most excited discussion. That is in respect to the power of the federal courts to issue injunctions in industrial disputes. As to that, my convictions are fixed. Take away from the courts, if it could be taken away, the power to issue injunctions in labor disputes, and it would create a privileged class among the laborers and save the lawless among their number from a most needful remedy available to all men for the protection of their business against lawless invasion. The proposition that business is not a property or pecuniary right which can be protected by equitable injunction is utterly without foundation in precedent or reason. The proposition is usually linked with one to make the secondary boycott lawful. Such a proposition is at variance with the American instinct, and will find no support, in my judgment, when submitted to the American people. The secondary boycott is an instrument of tyranny, and ought not to be made legitimate.

The issue of a temporary restraining order without notice has in several instances been abused by its inconsiderate exercise, and to remedy this the platform upon which I was elected recommends the formulation in a statute of the conditions under which such a temporary restraining order ought to issue. A statute can and ought to be framed to embody the best modern practice, and can bring the subject so closely to the attention of the court as to make abuses of the process unlikely in the future. The American people, if I understand them, insist that the authority of the courts shall be sustained, and are opposed to any change in the procedure by which the powers of a court may be weakened and the fearless and effective administration of justice be interfered with.

Having thus reviewed the questions likely to recur during my administration, and having expressed in a summary way the position which I expect to take in recommendations to Congress and in my conduct as an Executive, I invoke the considerate sympathy and support of my fellow-citizens and the aid of the Almighty God in the discharge of my responsible duties.

Woodrow Wilson

First Inaugural Address

Tuesday, March 4, 1913

THERE has been a change of government. It began two years ago, when the House of Representatives became Democratic by a decisive majority. It has now been completed. The Senate about to assemble will also be Democratic. The offices of President and Vice-President have been put into the hands of Democrats. What does the change mean? That is the question that is uppermost in our minds to-day. That is the question I am going to try to answer, in order, if I may, to interpret the occasion.

It means much more than the mere success of a party. The success of a party means little except when the Nation is using that party for a large and definite purpose. No one can mistake the purpose for which the Nation now seeks to use the Democratic Party. It seeks to use it to interpret a change in its own plans and point of view. Some old things with which we had grown familiar, and which had begun to creep into the very habit of our thought and of our lives, have altered their aspect as we have latterly looked critically upon them, with fresh, awakened eyes; have dropped their disguises and shown themselves alien and sinister. Some new things, as we look frankly upon them, willing to comprehend their real character, have come to assume the aspect of things long believed in and familiar, stuff of our own convictions. We have been refreshed by a new insight into our own life.

We see that in many things that life is very great. It is incomparably great in its material aspects, in its body of wealth, in the diversity and sweep of its energy, in the industries which have been conceived and built up by the genius of individual men and the limitless enterprise of groups of men. It is great, also, very great, in its moral force. Nowhere else in the world have noble men and women exhibited in more striking forms the beauty and the energy of sympathy and helpfulness and counsel in their efforts to rectify wrong, alleviate suffering, and set the weak in the way of strength and hope. We have built up, moreover, a great system of government, which has stood through a long age in many respects a model for those who seek to set liberty upon foundations that will endure against fortuitous change, against storm and accident. Our life contains every great thing, and contains it in rich abundance.

But the evil has come with the good, and much fine gold has been corroded. With riches has come inexcusable waste. We have squandered a great part of what we might have used, and have not stopped to conserve the exceeding bounty of nature, without which our genius for enterprise would have been worthless and impotent, scorning to be careful, shamefully prodigal as well as admirably efficient. We have been proud of our industrial achievements, but we have not hitherto stopped thoughtfully enough to count the human cost, the cost of lives snuffed out, of energies overtaxed and broken, the fearful physical and spiritual cost to the men and women and children upon whom the dead weight and burden of it all has fallen pitilessly the years through. The groans and agony of it all had not yet reached our ears, the solemn, moving undertone of our life, coming up out of the mines and factories, and out of every home where the struggle had its intimate and familiar seat. With the great Government went many deep secret things which we too long delayed to look into and scrutinize with candid, fearless eyes. The great Government we loved has too often been made use of for private and selfish purposes, and those who used it had forgotten the people.

At last a vision has been vouchsafed us of our life as a whole. We see the bad with the good, the debased and decadent with the sound and vital. With this vision we approach new affairs. Our duty is to cleanse, to reconsider, to restore, to correct the evil without impairing the good, to purify and humanize every process of our common life without weakening or sentimentalizing it. There has been something crude and heartless and unfeeling in our haste to succeed and be great. Our thought has been "Let every man look out for himself, let every generation look out for itself," while we reared giant machinery which made it impossible that any but those who stood at the levers of control should have a chance to look out for themselves. We had not forgotten our morals. We remembered well enough that we had set up a policy which was meant to serve the humblest as well as the most powerful, with an eye single to the standards of justice and fair play, and remembered it with pride. But we were very heedless and in a hurry to be great.

We have come now to the sober second thought. The scales of heedlessness have fallen from our eyes. We have made up our minds to square every process of our national life again with the standards we so proudly set up at the beginning and have always carried at our hearts. Our work is a work of restoration.

We have itemized with some degree of particularity the things that ought to be altered and here are some of the chief items: A tariff which cuts us off from our proper part in the commerce of the world, violates the just principles of taxation, and makes the Government a facile instrument in the hand of private interests; a banking and currency system based upon the necessity of the Government to sell its bonds fifty years ago and perfectly adapted to concentrating cash and restricting credits; an industrial system which, take it on all its sides, financial as well as administrative, holds capital in leading strings, restricts the liberties and limits the opportunities of labor, and exploits without renewing or conserving the natural resources of the country; a body of agricultural activities never yet given the efficiency of great business undertakings or served as it should be through the instrumentality of science taken directly to the farm, or afforded the facilities of credit best suited to its practical needs; watercourses undeveloped, waste places unreclaimed, forests untended, fast disappearing without plan or prospect of renewal, unregarded waste heaps at every mine. We have studied as perhaps no other nation has the most effective means of production, but we have not studied cost or economy as we should either as organizers of industry, as statesmen, or as individuals.

Nor have we studied and perfected the means by which government may be put at the service of humanity, in safeguarding the health of the Nation, the health of its men and its women and its children, as well as their rights in the struggle for existence. This is no sentimental duty. The firm basis of government is justice, not pity. These are matters of justice. There can be no equality or opportunity, the first essential of justice in the body politic, if men and women and children be not shielded in their lives, their very vitality, from the consequences of great industrial and social processes which they can not alter, control, or singly cope with. Society must see to it that it does not itself crush or weaken or damage its own constituent parts. The first duty of law is to keep sound the society it serves. Sanitary laws, pure food laws, and laws determining conditions of labor which individuals are powerless to determine for themselves are intimate parts of the very business of justice and legal efficiency.

These are some of the things we ought to do, and not leave the others undone, the old-fashioned, never-to-be-neglected,

fundamental safeguarding of property and of individual right. This is the high enterprise of the new day: To lift everything that concerns our life as a Nation to the light that shines from the hearthfire of every man's conscience and vision of the right. It is inconceivable that we should do this as partisans; it is inconceivable we should do it in ignorance of the facts as they are or in blind haste. We shall restore, not destroy. We shall deal with our economic system as it is and as it may be modified, not as it might be if we had a clean sheet of paper to write upon; and step by step we shall make it what it should be, in the spirit of those who question their own wisdom and seek counsel and knowledge, not shallow self-satisfaction or the excitement of excursions whither they can not tell. Justice, and only justice, shall always be our motto.

And yet it will be no cool process of mere science. The Nation has been deeply stirred, stirred by a solemn passion, stirred by the knowledge of wrong, of ideals lost, of government too often debauched and made an instrument of evil. The feelings with which we face this new age of right and opportunity sweep across our heartstrings like some air out of God's own presence, where justice and mercy are reconciled and the judge and the brother are one. We know our task to be no mere task of politics but a task which shall search us through and through, whether we be able to understand our time and the need of our people, whether we be indeed their spokesmen and interpreters, whether we have the pure heart to comprehend and the rectified will to choose our high course of action.

This is not a day of triumph; it is a day of dedication. Here muster, not the forces of party, but the forces of humanity. Men's hearts wait upon us; men's lives hang in the balance; men's hopes call upon us to say what we will do. Who shall live up to the great trust? Who dares fail to try? I summon all honest men, all patriotic, all forward-looking men, to my side. God helping me, I will not fail them, if they will but counsel and sustain me!

Second Inaugural Address

Monday, March 5, 1917

My Fellow Citizens:

THE four years which have elapsed since last I stood in this place have been crowded with counsel and action of the most vital interest and consequence. Perhaps no equal period in our history has been so fruitful of important reforms in our economic and industrial life or so full of significant changes in the spirit and purpose of our political action. We have sought very thoughtfully to set our house in order, correct the grosser errors and abuses of our industrial life, liberate and quicken the processes of our national genius and energy, and lift our politics to a broader view of the people's essential interests.

It is a record of singular variety and singular distinction. But I shall not attempt to review it. It speaks for itself and will be of increasing influence as the years go by. This is not the time for retrospect. It is time rather to speak our thoughts and purposes concerning the present and the immediate future.

Although we have centered counsel and action with such unusual concentration and success upon the great problems of domestic legislation to which we addressed ourselves four years ago, other matters have more and more forced themselves upon our attention—matters lying outside our own life as a nation and over which we had no control, but which, despite our wish to keep free of them, have drawn us more and more irresistibly into their own current and influence.

It has been impossible to avoid them. They have affected the life of the whole world. They have shaken men everywhere with a passion and an apprehension they never knew before. It has been hard to preserve calm counsel while the thought of our own people swayed this way and that under their influence. We are a composite and cosmopolitan people. We are of the blood of all the nations that are at war. The currents of our thoughts as well as the currents of our trade run quick at all seasons back and forth between us and them. The war inevitably set its mark from the first alike upon our minds, our industries, our commerce, our politics and our social action. To be indifferent to it, or independent of it, was out of the question.

And yet all the while we have been conscious that we were not part of it. In that consciousness, despite many divisions, we have drawn closer together. We have been deeply wronged upon the seas, but we have not wished to wrong or injure in return; have retained throughout the consciousness of standing in some sort apart, intent upon an interest that transcended the immediate issues of the war itself.

As some of the injuries done us have become intolerable we have still been clear that we wished nothing for ourselves that we were not ready to demand for all mankind—fair dealing, justice, the freedom to live and to be at ease against organized wrong.

It is in this spirit and with this thought that we have grown more and more aware, more and more certain that the part we

materially and spiritually, body and soul, to national defense. I can vision the ideal republic, where every man and woman is called under the flag for assignment to duty for whatever service, military or civic, the individual is best fitted; where we may call to universal service every plant, agency, or facility, all in the sublime sacrifice for country, and not one penny of war profit shall inure to the benefit of private individual, corporation, or combination, but all above the normal shall flow into the defense chest of the Nation. There is something inherently wrong, something out of accord with the ideals of representative democracy, when one portion of our citizenship turns its activities to private gain amid defensive war while another is fighting, sacrificing, or dying for national preservation.

Out of such universal service will come a new unity of spirit and purpose, a new confidence and consecration, which would make our defense impregnable, our triumph assured. Then we should have little or no disorganization of our economic, industrial, and commercial systems at home, no staggering war debts, no swollen fortunes to flout the sacrifices of our soldiers, no excuse for sedition, no pitiable slackerism, no outrage of treason. Envy and jealousy would have no soil for their menacing development, and revolution would be without the passion which engenders it.

A regret for the mistakes of yesterday must not, however, blind us to the tasks of today. War never left such an aftermath. There has been staggering loss of life and measureless wastage of materials. Nations are still groping for return to stable ways. Discouraging indebtedness confronts us like all the war-torn nations, and these obligations must be provided for. No civilization can survive repudiation.

We can reduce the abnormal expenditures, and we will. We can strike at war taxation, and we must. We must face the grim necessity, with full knowledge that the task is to be solved, and we must proceed with a full realization that no statute enacted by man can repeal the inexorable laws of nature. Our most dangerous tendency is to expect too much of government, and at the same time do for it too little. We contemplate the immediate task of putting our public household in order. We need a rigid and yet sane economy, combined with fiscal justice, and it must be attended by individual prudence and thrift, which are so essential to this trying hour and reassuring for the future.

The business world reflects the disturbance of war's reaction. Herein flows the lifeblood of material existence. The economic mechanism is intricate and its parts interdependent, and has suffered the shocks and jars incident to abnormal demands, credit inflations, and price upheavals. The normal balances have been impaired, the channels of distribution have been clogged, the relations of labor and management have been strained. We must seek the readjustment with care and courage. Our people must give and take. Prices must reflect the receding fever of war activities. Perhaps we never shall know the old levels of wages again, because war invariably readjusts compensations, and the necessaries of life will show their inseparable relationship, but we must strive for normalcy to reach stability. All the penalties will not be light, nor evenly distributed. There is no way of making them so. There is no instant step from disorder to order. We must face a condition of grim reality, charge off our losses and start afresh. It is the oldest lesson of civilization. I would like government to do all it can to mitigate; then, in understanding, in mutuality of interest, in concern for the common good, our tasks will be solved. No altered system will work a miracle. Any wild experiment will only add to the confusion. Our best assurance lies in efficient administration of our proven system.

The forward course of the business cycle is unmistakable. Peoples are turning from destruction to production. Industry has sensed the changed order and our own people are turning to resume their normal, onward way. The call is for productive America to go on. I know that Congress and the Administration will favor every wise Government policy to aid the resumption and encourage continued progress.

I speak for administrative efficiency, for lightened tax burdens, for sound commercial practices, for adequate credit facilities, for sympathetic concern for all agricultural problems, for the omission of unnecessary interference of Government with business, for an end to Government's experiment in business, and for more efficient business in Government administration. With all of this must attend a mindfulness of the human side of all activities, so that social, industrial, and economic justice will be squared with the purposes of a righteous people.

With the nation-wide induction of womanhood into our political life, we may count upon her intuitions, her refinements, her intelligence, and her influence to exalt the social order. We count upon her exercise of the full privileges and the performance of the duties of citizenship to speed the attainment of the highest state.

I wish for an America no less alert in guarding against dangers from within than it is watchful against enemies from without. Our fundamental law recognizes no class, no group, no section; there must be none in legislation or administration. The supreme inspiration is the common weal. Humanity hungers for international peace, and we crave it with all mankind. My most reverent prayer for America is for industrial peace, with its rewards, widely and generally distributed, amid the inspirations of equal opportunity. No one justly may deny the equality of opportunity which made us what we are. We have mistaken unpreparedness to embrace it to be a challenge of the reality, and due concern for making all citizens fit for participation will give added strength of citizenship and magnify our achievement.

If revolution insists upon overturning established order, let other peoples make the tragic experiment. There is no place for it in America. When World War threatened civilization we pledged our resources and our lives to its preservation, and when revolution threatens we unfurl the flag of law and order and renew our consecration. Ours is a constitutional freedom where the popular will is the law supreme and minorities are sacredly protected. Our revisions, reformations, and evolutions reflect a deliberate judgment and an orderly progress, and we mean to cure our ills, but never destroy or permit destruction by force.

I had rather submit our industrial controversies to the conference table in advance than to a settlement table after conflict and suffering. The earth is thirsting for the cup of good will, understanding is its fountain source. I would like to acclaim an era of good feeling amid dependable prosperity and all the blessings which attend.

It has been proved again and again that we cannot, while throwing our markets open to the world, maintain American standards of living and opportunity, and hold our industrial eminence in such unequal competition. There is a luring fallacy in the theory of banished barriers of trade, but preserved American standards require our higher production costs to be reflected in our tariffs on imports. Today, as never before, when peoples are seeking trade restoration and expansion, we must adjust our tariffs to the new order. We seek participation in the world's exchanges, because therein lies our way to widened influence and the triumphs of peace. We know full well we cannot sell where we do not buy, and we cannot sell successfully where we do not carry. Opportunity is calling not alone for the restoration, but for a new era in production, transportation and trade. We shall answer it best by meeting the demand of a surpassing home market, by promoting self-reliance in production, and by bidding enterprise, genius, and efficiency to carry our cargoes in American bottoms to the marts of the world.

We would not have an America living within and for herself alone, but we would have her self-reliant, independent, and ever nobler, stronger, and richer. Believing in our higher standards, reared through constitutional liberty and maintained opportunity, we invite the world to the same heights. But pride in things wrought is no reflex of a completed task. Common welfare is the goal of our national endeavor. Wealth is not inimical to welfare; it ought to be its friendliest agency. There never can be equality of rewards or possessions so long as the human plan contains varied talents and differing degrees of industry and thrift, but ours ought to be a country free from the great blotches of distressed poverty. We ought to find a way to guard against the perils and penalties of unemployment. We want an America of homes, illumined with hope and happiness, where mothers, freed from the necessity for long hours of toil beyond their own doors, may preside as befits the hearthstone of American citizenship. We want the cradle of American childhood rocked under conditions so wholesome and so hopeful that no blight may touch it in its development, and we want to provide that no selfish interest, no material necessity, no lack of opportunity shall prevent the gaining of that education so essential to best citizenship.

There is no short cut to the making of these ideals into glad realities. The world has witnessed again and again the futility and the mischief of ill-considered remedies for social and economic disorders. But we are mindful today as never before of the friction of modern industrialism, and we must learn its causes and reduce its evil consequences by sober and tested methods. Where genius has made for great possibilities, justice and happiness must be reflected in a greater common welfare.

Service is the supreme commitment of life. I would rejoice to acclaim the era of the Golden Rule and crown it with the autocracy of service. I pledge an administration wherein all the agencies of Government are called to serve, and ever promote an understanding of Government purely as an expression of the popular will.

One cannot stand in this presence and be unmindful of the tremendous responsibility. The world upheaval has added heavily to our tasks. But with the realization comes the surge of high resolve, and there is reassurance in belief in the God-given destiny of our Republic. If I felt that there is to be sole responsibility in the Executive for the America of tomorrow I should shrink from the burden. But here are a hundred millions, with common concern and shared responsibility, answerable to God and country. The Republic summons them to their duty, and I invite co-operation.

I accept my part with single-mindedness of purpose and humility of spirit, and implore the favor and guidance of God in His Heaven. With these I am unafraid, and confidently face the future.

I have taken the solemn oath of office on that passage of Holy Writ wherein it is asked: "What doth the Lord require of thee but to do justly, and to love mercy, and to walk humbly with thy God?" This I plight to God and country.

Calvin Coolidge

Inaugural Address

Wednesday, March 4, 1925

My Countrymen:

NO one can contemplate current conditions without finding much that is satisfying and still more that is encouraging. Our own country is leading the world in the general readjustment to the results of the great conflict. Many of its burdens will bear heavily upon us for years, and the secondary and indirect effects we must expect to experience for some time. But we are beginning to comprehend more definitely what course should be pursued, what remedies ought to be applied, what actions should be taken for our deliverance, and are clearly manifesting a determined will faithfully and conscientiously to adopt these methods of relief. Already we have sufficiently rearranged our domestic affairs so that confidence has returned, business has revived, and we appear to be entering an era of prosperity which is gradually reaching into every part of the Nation. Realizing that we can not live unto ourselves alone, we have contributed of our resources and our counsel to the relief of the suffering and the settlement of the disputes among the European nations. Because of what America is and what America has done, a firmer courage, a higher hope, inspires the heart of all humanity.

These results have not occurred by mere chance. They have been secured by a constant and enlightened effort marked by many sacrifices and extending over many generations. We can not continue these brilliant successes in the future, unless we continue to learn from the past. It is necessary to keep the former experiences of our country both at home and abroad continually before us, if we are to have any science of government. If we wish to erect new structures, we must have a definite knowledge of the old foundations. We must realize that human nature is about the most constant thing in the universe and that the essentials of human relationship do not change. We must frequently take our bearings from these fixed stars of our political firmament if we expect to hold a true course. If we examine carefully what we have done, we can determine the more accurately what we can do.

We stand at the opening of the one hundred and fiftieth year since our national consciousness first asserted itself by unmistakable action with an array of force. The old sentiment of detached and dependent colonies disappeared in the new sentiment of a united and independent Nation. Men began to discard the narrow confines of a local charter for the broader opportunities of a national constitution. Under the eternal urge of freedom we became an independent Nation. A little less than 50 years later that freedom and independence were reasserted in the face of all the world, and guarded, supported, and secured by the Monroe doctrine. The narrow fringe of States along the Atlantic seaboard advanced its frontiers across the hills and plains of an intervening continent until it passed down the golden slope to the Pacific. We made freedom a birthright. We extended our domain over distant islands in order to safeguard our own interests and accepted the consequent obligation to bestow justice and liberty upon less favored peoples. In the defense of our own ideals and in the general cause of liberty we entered the Great War. When victory had been fully secured, we withdrew to our own shores unrecompensed save in the consciousness of duty done.

Throughout all these experiences we have enlarged our freedom, we have strengthened our independence. We have been, and propose to be, more and more American. We believe that we can best serve our own country and most successfully discharge our obligations to humanity by continuing to be openly and candidly, intensely and scrupulously, American. If we have any heritage, it has been that. If we have any destiny, we have found it in that direction.

But if we wish to continue to be distinctively American, we must continue to make that term comprehensive enough to embrace the legitimate desires of a civilized and enlightened people determined in all their relations to pursue a conscientious and religious life. We can not permit ourselves to be narrowed and dwarfed by slogans and phrases. It is not the adjective, but the substantive, which is of real importance. It is not the name of the action, but the result of the action, which is the chief concern. It will be well not to be too much disturbed by the thought of either isolation or entanglement of pacifists and militarists. The physical configuration of the earth has separated us from all of the Old World, but the common brotherhood of man, the highest law of all our being, has united us by inseparable bonds with all humanity. Our country represents nothing but peaceful intentions toward all the earth, but it ought not to fail to maintain such a military force as comports with the dignity and security of a great people. It ought to be a balanced force, intensely modern, capable of defense by sea and land, beneath the surface and in the air. But it should be so conducted that all the world may see in it, not a menace, but an instrument of security and peace.

This Nation believes thoroughly in an honorable peace under which the rights of its citizens are to be everywhere protected. It has never found that the necessary enjoyment of such a peace could be maintained only by a great and threatening array of arms. In common with other nations, it is now more determined than ever to promote peace through friendliness and good will, through mutual understandings and mutual forbearance. We have never practiced the policy of competitive armaments. We have recently committed ourselves by covenants with the other great nations to a limitation of our sea power. As one result of this, our Navy ranks larger, in comparison, than it ever did before. Removing the burden of expense and jealousy, which must always accrue from a keen rivalry, is one of the most effective methods of diminishing that unreasonable hysteria and misunderstanding which are the most potent means of fomenting war. This policy represents a new departure in the world. It is a thought, an ideal, which has led to an entirely new line of action. It will not be easy to maintain. Some never moved from their old positions, some are constantly slipping back to the old ways of thought and the old action of seizing a musket and relying on force. America has taken the lead in this new direction, and that lead America must continue to hold. If we expect others to rely on our fairness and justice we must show that we rely on their fairness and justice.

If we are to judge by past experience, there is much to be hoped for in international relations from frequent conferences and consultations. We have before us the beneficial results of the Washington conference and the various consultations recently held upon European affairs, some of which were in response to our suggestions and in some of which we were active participants. Even the failures can not but be accounted useful and an immeasurable advance over threatened or actual warfare. I am strongly in favor of continuation of this policy, whenever conditions are such that there is even a promise that practical and favorable results might be secured.

In conformity with the principle that a display of reason rather than a threat of force should be the determining factor in the intercourse among nations, we have long advocated the peaceful settlement of disputes by methods of arbitration and

have negotiated many treaties to secure that result. The same considerations should lead to our adherence to the Permanent Court of International Justice. Where great principles are involved, where great movements are under way which promise much for the welfare of humanity by reason of the very fact that many other nations have given such movements their actual support, we ought not to withhold our own sanction because of any small and inessential difference, but only upon the ground of the most important and compelling fundamental reasons. We can not barter away our independence or our sovereignty, but we ought to engage in no refinements of logic, no sophistries, and no subterfuges, to argue away the undoubted duty of this country by reason of the might of its numbers, the power of its resources, and its position of leadership in the world, actively and comprehensively to signify its approval and to bear its full share of the responsibility of a candid and disinterested attempt at the establishment of a tribunal for the administration of even-handed justice between nation and nation. The weight of our enormous influence must be cast upon the side of a reign not of force but of law and trial, not by battle but by reason.

We have never any wish to interfere in the political conditions of any other countries. Especially are we determined not to become implicated in the political controversies of the Old World. With a great deal of hesitation, we have responded to appeals for help to maintain order, protect life and property, and establish responsible government in some of the small countries of the Western Hemisphere. Our private citizens have advanced large sums of money to assist in the necessary financing and relief of the Old World. We have not failed, nor shall we fail to respond, whenever necessary to mitigate human suffering and assist in the rehabilitation of distressed nations. These, too, are requirements which must be met by reason of our vast powers and the place we hold in the world.

Some of the best thought of mankind has long been seeking for a formula for permanent peace. Undoubtedly the clarification of the principles of international law would be helpful, and the efforts of scholars to prepare such a work for adoption by the various nations should have our sympathy and support. Much may be hoped for from the earnest studies of those who advocate the outlawing of aggressive war. But all these plans and preparations, these treaties and covenants, will not of themselves be adequate. One of the greatest dangers to peace lies in the economic pressure to which people find themselves subjected. One of the most practical things to be done in the world is to seek arrangements under which such pressure may be removed, so that opportunity may be renewed and hope may be revived. There must be some assurance that effort and endeavor will be followed by success and prosperity. In the making and financing of such adjustments there is not only an opportunity, but a real duty, for America to respond with her counsel and her resources. Conditions must be provided under which people can make a living and work out of their difficulties. But there is another element, more important than all, without which there can not be the slightest hope of a permanent peace. That element lies in the heart of humanity. Unless the desire for peace be cherished there, unless this fundamental and only natural source of brotherly love be cultivated to its highest degree, all artificial efforts will be in vain. Peace will come when there is realization that only under a reign of law, based on righteousness and supported by the religious conviction of the brotherhood of man, can there be any hope of a complete and satisfying life. Parchment will fail, the sword will fail, it is only the spiritual nature of man that can be triumphant.

It seems altogether probable that we can contribute most to these important objects by maintaining our position of political detachment and independence. We are not identified with any Old

World interests. This position should be made more and more clear in our relations with all foreign countries. We are at peace with all of them. Our program is never to oppress, but always to assist. But while we do justice to others, we must require that justice be done to us. With us a treaty of peace means peace, and a treaty of amity means amity. We have made great contributions to the settlement of contentious differences in both Europe and Asia. But there is a very definite point beyond which we can not go. We can only help those who help themselves. Mindful of these limitations, the one great duty that stands out requires us to use our enormous powers to trim the balance of the world.

While we can look with a great deal of pleasure upon what we have done abroad, we must remember that our continued success in that direction depends upon what we do at home. Since its very outset, it has been found necessary to conduct our Government by means of political parties. That system would not have survived from generation to generation if it had not been fundamentally sound and provided the best instrumentalities for the most complete expression of the popular will. It is not necessary to claim that it has always worked perfectly. It is enough to know that nothing better has been devised. No one would deny that there should be full and free expression and an opportunity for independence of action within the party. There is no salvation in a narrow and bigoted partisanship. But if there is to be responsible party government, the party label must be something more than a mere device for securing office. Unless those who are elected under the same party designation are willing to assume sufficient responsibility and exhibit sufficient loyalty and coherence, so that they can cooperate with each other in the support of the broad general principles, of the party platform, the election is merely a mockery, no decision is made at the polls, and there is no representation of the popular will. Common honesty and good faith with the people who support a party at the polls require that party, when it enters office, to assume the control of that portion of the Government to which it has been elected. Any other course is bad faith and a violation of the party pledges.

When the country has bestowed its confidence upon a party by making it a majority in the Congress, it has a right to expect such unity of action as will make the party majority an effective instrument of government. This Administration has come into power with a very clear and definite mandate from the people. The expression of the popular will in favor of maintaining our constitutional guarantees was overwhelming and decisive. There was a manifestation of such faith in the integrity of the courts that we can consider that issue rejected for some time to come. Likewise, the policy of public ownership of railroads and certain electric utilities met with unmistakable defeat. The people declared that they wanted their rights to have not a political but a judicial determination, and their independence and freedom continued and supported by having the ownership and control of their property, not in the Government, but in their own hands. As they always do when they have a fair chance, the people demonstrated that they are sound and are determined to have a sound government.

When we turn from what was rejected to inquire what was accepted, the policy that stands out with the greatest clearness is that of economy in public expenditure with reduction and reform of taxation. The principle involved in this effort is that of conservation. The resources of this country are almost beyond computation. No mind can comprehend them. But the cost of our combined governments is likewise almost beyond definition. Not only those who are now making their tax returns, but those who meet the enhanced cost of existence in their monthly bills, know by hard experience what this great burden is and what it does. No matter what others may want, these people want a drastic economy. They are opposed to waste. They know that extravagance lengthens the hours and diminishes the rewards of their labor. I favor the policy of economy, not because I wish to save money, but because I wish to save people. The men and women of this country who toil are the ones who bear the cost of the Government. Every dollar that we carelessly waste means that their life will be so much the more meager. Every dollar that we prudently save means that their life will be so much the more abundant. Economy is idealism in its most practical form.

If extravagance were not reflected in taxation, and through taxation both directly and indirectly injuriously affecting the people, it would not be of so much consequence. The wisest and soundest method of solving our tax problem is through economy. Fortunately, of all the great nations this country is best in a position to adopt that simple remedy. We do not any longer need wartime revenues. The collection of any taxes which are not absolutely required, which do not beyond reasonable doubt contribute to the public welfare, is only a species of legalized larceny. Under this republic the rewards of industry belong to those who earn them. The only constitutional tax is the tax which ministers to public necessity. The property of the country belongs to the people of the country. Their title is absolute. They do not support any privileged class; they do not need to maintain great military forces; they ought not to be burdened with a great array of public employees. They are not required to make any contribution to Government expenditures except that which they voluntarily assess upon themselves through the action of their own representatives. Whenever taxes become burdensome a remedy can be applied by the people; but if they do not act for themselves, no one can be very successful in acting for them.

The time is arriving when we can have further tax reduction, when, unless we wish to hamper the people in their right to earn a living, we must have tax reform. The method of raising revenue ought not to impede the transaction of business; it ought to encourage it. I am opposed to extremely high rates, because they produce little or no revenue, because they are bad for the country, and, finally, because they are wrong. We can not finance the country, we can not improve social conditions, through any system of injustice, even if we attempt to inflict it upon the rich. Those who suffer the most harm will be the poor. This country believes in prosperity. It is absurd to suppose that it is envious of those who are already prosperous. The wise and correct course to follow in taxation and all other economic legislation is not to destroy those who have already secured success but to create conditions under which every one will have a better chance to be successful. The verdict of the country has been given on this question. That verdict stands. We shall do well to heed it.

These questions involve moral issues. We need not concern ourselves much about the rights of property if we will faithfully observe the rights of persons. Under our institutions their rights are supreme. It is not property but the right to hold property, both great and small, which our Constitution guarantees. All owners of property are charged with a service. These rights and duties have been revealed, through the conscience of society, to have a divine sanction. The very stability of our society rests upon production and conservation. For individuals or for governments to waste and squander their resources is to deny these rights and disregard these obligations. The result of economic dissipation to a nation is always moral decay.

These policies of better international understandings, greater economy, and lower taxes have contributed largely to peaceful and prosperous industrial relations. Under the helpful influences of restrictive immigration and a protective tariff, employment is plentiful, the rate of pay is high, and wage earners are in a state of contentment seldom before seen. Our transportation systems have been gradually recovering and have been able to meet all the requirements of the service. Agriculture has been very slow in reviving, but the price of cereals at last indicates that the day of its deliverance is at hand.

We are not without our problems, but our most important problem is not to secure new advantages but to maintain those which we already possess. Our system of government made up of three separate and independent departments, our divided sovereignty composed of Nation and State, the matchless wisdom that is enshrined in our Constitution, all these need constant effort and tireless vigilance for their protection and support.

In a republic the first rule for the guidance of the citizen is obedience to law. Under a despotism the law may be imposed upon the subject. He has no voice in its making, no influence in its administration, it does not represent him. Under a free government the citizen makes his own laws, chooses his own administrators, which do represent him. Those who want their rights respected under the Constitution and the law ought to set the example themselves of observing the Constitution and the law. While there may be those of high intelligence who violate the law at times, the barbarian and the defective always violate it. Those who disregard the rules of society are not exhibiting a superior intelligence, are not promoting freedom and independence, are not following the path of civilization, but are displaying the traits of ignorance, of servitude, of savagery, and treading the way that leads back to the jungle.

The essence of a republic is representative government. Our Congress represents the people and the States. In all legislative affairs it is the natural collaborator with the President. In spite of all the criticism which often falls to its lot, I do not hesitate to say that there is no more independent and effective legislative body in the world. It is, and should be, jealous of its prerogative. I welcome its cooperation, and expect to share with it not only the responsibility, but the credit, for our common effort to secure beneficial legislation.

These are some of the principles which America represents. We have not by any means put them fully into practice, but we have strongly signified our belief in them. The encouraging feature of our country is not that it has reached its destination, but that it has overwhelmingly expressed its determination to proceed in the right direction. It is true that we could, with profit, be less sectional and more national in our thought. It would be well if we could replace much that is only a false and ignorant prejudice with a true and enlightened pride of race. But the last election showed that appeals to class and nationality had little effect. We were all found loyal to a common citizenship. The fundamental precept of liberty is toleration. We can not permit any inquisition either within or without the law or apply any religious test to the holding of office. The mind of America must be forever free.

It is in such contemplations, my fellow countrymen, which are not exhaustive but only representative, that I find ample warrant for satisfaction and encouragement. We should not let the much that is to do obscure the much which has been done. The past and present show faith and hope and courage fully justified. Here stands our country, an example of tranquillity at home, a patron of tranquillity abroad. Here stands its Government, aware of its might but obedient to its conscience. Here it will continue to stand, seeking peace and prosperity, solicitous for the welfare of the wage earner, promoting enterprise, developing waterways and natural resources, attentive to the intuitive counsel of womanhood, encouraging education, desiring the advancement of religion, supporting the cause of justice and honor among the nations. America seeks no earthly empire built on blood and force. No ambition, no temptation, lures her to thought of foreign dominions. The legions which she sends forth are armed, not with the sword, but with the cross. The higher state to which she seeks the allegiance of all mankind is not of human, but of divine origin. She cherishes no purpose save to merit the favor of Almighty God.My Countrymen:

Herbert Hoover

Inaugural Address

Monday, March 4, 1929

My Countrymen:

THIS occasion is not alone the administration of the most sacred oath which can be assumed by an American citizen. It is a dedication and consecration under God to the highest office in service of our people. I assume this trust in the humility of knowledge that only through the guidance of Almighty Providence can I hope to discharge its ever-increasing burdens.

It is in keeping with tradition throughout our history that I should express simply and directly the opinions which I hold concerning some of the matters of present importance.

Our Progress

If we survey the situation of our Nation both at home and abroad, we find many satisfactions; we find some causes for concern. We have emerged from the losses of the Great War and the reconstruction following it with increased virility and strength. From this strength we have contributed to the recovery and progress of the world. What America has done has given renewed hope and courage to all who have faith in government by the people. In the large view, we have reached a higher degree of comfort and security than ever existed before in the history of the world. Through liberation from widespread poverty we have reached a higher degree of individual freedom than ever before. The devotion to and concern for our institutions are deep and sincere. We are steadily building a new race—a new civilization great in its own attainments. The influence and high purposes of our Nation are respected among the peoples of the world. We aspire to distinction in the world, but to a distinction based upon confidence in our sense of justice as well as our accomplishments within our own borders and in our own lives. For wise guidance in this great period of recovery the Nation is deeply indebted to Calvin Coolidge.

But all this majestic advance should not obscure the constant dangers from which self-government must be safeguarded. The strong man must at all times be alert to the attack of insidious disease.

The Failure of Our System of Criminal Justice

The most malign of all these dangers today is disregard and disobedience of law. Crime is increasing. Confidence in rigid and speedy justice is decreasing. I am not prepared to believe that this indicates any decay in the moral fiber of the American people. I am not prepared to believe that it indicates an impotence of the Federal Government to enforce its laws.

It is only in part due to the additional burdens imposed upon our judicial system by the eighteenth amendment. The problem is much wider than that. Many influences had increasingly complicated and weakened our law enforcement organization long before the adoption of the eighteenth amendment.

To reestablish the vigor and effectiveness of law enforcement we must critically consider the entire Federal machinery of justice, the redistribution of its functions, the simplification of its procedure, the provision of additional special tribunals, the better selection of juries, and the more effective organization of our agencies of investigation and prosecution that justice may be sure and that it may be swift. While the authority of the Federal Government extends to but part of our vast system of national, State, and local justice, yet the standards which the Federal Government establishes have the most profound influence upon the whole structure.

We are fortunate in the ability and integrity of our Federal judges and attorneys. But the system which these officers are called upon to administer is in many respects ill adapted to present-day conditions. Its intricate and involved rules of procedure have become the refuge of both big and little criminals. There is a belief abroad that by invoking technicalities, subterfuge, and delay, the ends of justice may be thwarted by those who can pay the cost.

Reform, reorganization and strengthening of our whole judicial and enforcement system, both in civil and criminal sides, have been advocated for years by statesmen, judges, and bar associations. First steps toward that end should not longer be delayed. Rigid and expeditious justice is the first safeguard of freedom, the basis of all ordered liberty, the vital force of progress. It must not come to be in our Republic that it can be defeated by the indifference of the citizen, by exploitation of the delays and entanglements of the law, or by combinations of criminals. Justice must not fail because the agencies of enforcement are either delinquent or inefficiently organized. To consider these evils, to find their remedy, is the most sore necessity of our times.

Enforcement of the Eighteenth Amendment

Of the undoubted abuses which have grown up under the eighteenth amendment, part are due to the causes I have just mentioned; but part are due to the failure of some States to accept their share of responsibility for concurrent enforcement and to the failure of many State and local officials to accept the obligation under their oath of office zealously to enforce the laws. With the failures from these many causes has come a dangerous expansion in the criminal elements who have found enlarged opportunities in dealing in illegal liquor.

But a large responsibility rests directly upon our citizens. There would be little traffic in illegal liquor if only criminals patronized it. We must awake to the fact that this patronage from large numbers of law-abiding citizens is supplying the rewards and stimulating crime.

I have been selected by you to execute and enforce the laws of the country. I propose to do so to the extent of my own abilities, but the measure of success that the Government shall attain will depend upon the moral support which you, as citizens, extend. The duty of citizens to support the laws of the land is coequal with the duty of their Government to enforce the laws which exist. No greater national service can be given by men and women of good will—who, I know, are not unmindful of the responsibilities of citizenship—than that they should, by their example, assist in stamping out crime and outlawry by refusing participation in and condemning all transactions with illegal liquor. Our whole system of self-government will crumble either if officials elect what laws they will enforce or citizens elect what laws they will support. The worst evil of disregard for some law is that it destroys respect for all law. For our citizens to patronize the violation of a particular law on the ground that they are opposed to it is destructive of the very basis of all that protection of life, of homes and property which they rightly claim under other laws. If citizens do not like a law, their duty as honest men and women is to discourage its violation; their right is openly to work for its repeal.

To those of criminal mind there can be no appeal but vigorous enforcement of the law. Fortunately they are but a small percentage of our people. Their activities must be stopped.

A National Investigation

I propose to appoint a national commission for a searching investigation of the whole structure of our Federal system of jurisprudence, to include the method of enforcement of the eighteenth amendment and the causes of abuse under it. Its purpose will be to make such recommendations for reorganization of the administration of Federal laws and court procedure as may be found desirable. In the meantime it is essential that a large part of the enforcement activities be transferred from the Treasury Department to the Department of Justice as a beginning of more effective organization.

The Relation of Government to Business

The election has again confirmed the determination of the American people that regulation of private enterprise and not Government ownership or operation is the course rightly to be pursued in our relation to business. In recent years we have established a differentiation in the whole method of business regulation between the industries which produce and distribute commodities on the one hand and public utilities on the other. In the former, our laws insist upon effective competition; in the latter, because we substantially confer a monopoly by limiting competition, we must regulate their services and rates. The rigid enforcement of the laws applicable to both groups is the very base of equal opportunity and freedom from domination for all our people, and it is just as essential for the stability and prosperity of business itself as for the protection of the public at large. Such regulation should be extended by the Federal Government within the limitations of the Constitution and only when the individual States are without power to protect their citizens through their own authority. On the other hand, we should be fearless when the authority rests only in the Federal Government.

Cooperation by the Government

The larger purpose of our economic thought should be to establish more firmly stability and security of business and employment and thereby remove poverty still further from our borders. Our people have in recent years developed a new-found capacity for cooperation among themselves to effect high purposes in public welfare. It is an advance toward the highest conception of self-government. Self-government does not and should not imply the use of political agencies alone. Progress is born of cooperation in the community—not from governmental restraints. The Government should assist and encourage these movements of collective self-help by itself cooperating with them. Business has by cooperation made great progress in the advancement of service, in stability, in regularity of employment and in the correction of its own abuses. Such progress, however, can continue only so long as business manifests its respect for law.

There is an equally important field of cooperation by the Federal Government with the multitude of agencies, State, municipal and private, in the systematic development of those processes which directly affect public health, recreation, education, and the home. We have need further to perfect the means by which Government can be adapted to human service.

Education

Although education is primarily a responsibility of the States and local communities, and rightly so, yet the Nation as a whole is vitally concerned in its development everywhere to the highest standards and to complete universality. Self-government can succeed only through an instructed electorate. Our objective is not simply to overcome illiteracy. The Nation has marched far beyond that. The more complex the problems of the Nation become, the greater is the need for more and more advanced instruction. Moreover, as our numbers increase and as our life expands with science and invention, we must discover more and more leaders for every walk of life. We can not hope to succeed in directing this increasingly complex civilization unless we can draw all the talent of leadership from the whole people. One civilization after another has been wrecked upon the attempt to secure sufficient leadership from a single group or class. If we would prevent the growth of class distinctions and would constantly refresh our leadership with the ideals of our people, we must draw constantly from the general mass. The full opportunity for every boy and girl to rise through the selective processes of education can alone secure to us this leadership.

Public Health

In public health the discoveries of science have opened a new era. Many sections of our country and many groups of our citizens suffer from diseases the eradication of which are mere matters of administration and moderate expenditure. Public health service should be as fully organized and as universally incorporated into our governmental system as is public education. The returns are a thousand fold in economic benefits, and infinitely more in reduction of suffering and promotion of human happiness.

World Peace

The United States fully accepts the profound truth that our own progress, prosperity, and peace are interlocked with the progress, prosperity, and peace of all humanity. The whole world is at peace. The dangers to a continuation of this peace to-day are largely the fear and suspicion which still haunt the world. No suspicion or fear can be rightly directed toward our country.

Those who have a true understanding of America know that we have no desire for territorial expansion, for economic or other domination of other peoples. Such purposes are repugnant to our ideals of human freedom. Our form of government is ill adapted to the responsibilities which inevitably follow permanent limitation of the independence of other peoples. Superficial observers seem to find no destiny for our abounding increase in population, in wealth and power except that of imperialism. They fail to see that the American people are engrossed in the building for themselves of a new economic system, a new social system, a new political system all of which are characterized by aspirations of freedom of opportunity and thereby are the negation of imperialism. They fail to realize that because of our abounding prosperity our youth are pressing more and more into our institutions of learning; that our people are seeking a larger vision through art, literature, science, and travel; that they are moving toward stronger moral and spiritual life—that from these things

our sympathies are broadening beyond the bounds of our Nation and race toward their true expression in a real brotherhood of man. They fail to see that the idealism of America will lead it to no narrow or selfish channel, but inspire it to do its full share as a nation toward the advancement of civilization. It will do that not by mere declaration but by taking a practical part in supporting all useful international undertakings. We not only desire peace with the world, but to see peace maintained throughout the world. We wish to advance the reign of justice and reason toward the extinction of force.

The recent treaty for the renunciation of war as an instrument of national policy sets an advanced standard in our conception of the relations of nations. Its acceptance should pave the way to greater limitation of armament, the offer of which we sincerely extend to the world. But its full realization also implies a greater and greater perfection in the instrumentalities for pacific settlement of controversies between nations. In the creation and use of these instrumentalities we should support every sound method of conciliation, arbitration, and judicial settlement. American statesmen were among the first to propose and they have constantly urged upon the world, the establishment of a tribunal for the settlement of controversies of a justiciable character. The Permanent Court of International Justice in its major purpose is thus peculiarly identified with American ideals and with American statesmanship. No more potent instrumentality for this purpose has ever been conceived and no other is practicable of establishment. The reservations placed upon our adherence should not be misinterpreted. The United States seeks by these reservations no special privilege or advantage but only to clarify our relation to advisory opinions and other matters which are subsidiary to the major purpose of the court. The way should, and I believe will, be found by which we may take our proper place in a movement so fundamental to the progress of peace.

Our people have determined that we should make no political engagements such as membership in the League of Nations, which may commit us in advance as a nation to become involved in the settlements of controversies between other countries. They adhere to the belief that the independence of America from such obligations increases its ability and availability for service in all fields of human progress.

I have lately returned from a journey among our sister Republics of the Western Hemisphere. I have received unbounded hospitality and courtesy as their expression of friendliness to our country. We are held by particular bonds of sympathy and common interest with them. They are each of them building a racial character and a culture which is an impressive contribution to human progress. We wish only for the maintenance of their independence, the growth of their stability, and their prosperity. While we have had wars in the Western Hemisphere, yet on the whole the record is in encouraging contrast with that of other parts of the world. Fortunately the New World is largely free from the inheritances of fear and distrust which have so troubled the Old World. We should keep it so.

It is impossible, my countrymen, to speak of peace without profound emotion. In thousands of homes in America, in millions of homes around the world, there are vacant chairs. It would be a shameful confession of our unworthiness if it should develop that we have abandoned the hope for which all these men died. Surely civilization is old enough, surely mankind is mature enough so that we ought in our own lifetime to find a way to permanent peace. Abroad, to west and east, are nations whose sons mingled their blood with the blood of our sons on the battlefields. Most of these nations have contributed to our race, to our culture, our knowledge, and our progress. From one of them we derive our very language and from many of them much of the genius of our institutions. Their desire for peace is as deep and sincere as our own.

Peace can be contributed to by respect for our ability in defense. Peace can be promoted by the limitation of arms and by the creation of the instrumentalities for peaceful settlement of controversies. But it will become a reality only through self-restraint and active effort in friendliness and helpfulness. I covet for this administration a record of having further contributed to advance the cause of peace.

Party Responsibilities

In our form of democracy the expression of the popular will can be effected only through the instrumentality of political parties. We maintain party government not to promote intolerant partisanship but because opportunity must be given for expression of the popular will, and organization provided for the execution of its mandates and for accountability of government to the people. It follows that the government both in the executive and the legislative branches must carry out in good faith the platforms upon which the party was entrusted with power. But the government is that of the whole people; the party is the instrument through which policies are determined and men chosen to bring them into being. The animosities of elections should have no place in our Government, for government must concern itself alone with the common weal.

Special Session of the Congress

Action upon some of the proposals upon which the Republican Party was returned to power, particularly further agricultural relief and limited changes in the tariff, cannot in justice to our farmers, our labor, and our manufacturers be postponed. I shall therefore request a special session of Congress for the consideration of these two questions. I shall deal with each of them upon the assembly of the Congress.

Other Mandates from the Election

It appears to me that the more important further mandates from the recent election were the maintenance of the integrity of the Constitution; the vigorous enforcement of the laws; the continuance of economy in public expenditure; the continued regulation of business to prevent domination in the community; the denial of ownership or operation of business by the Government in competition with its citizens; the avoidance of policies which would involve us in the controversies of foreign nations; the more effective reorganization of the departments of the Federal Government; the expansion of public works; and the promotion of welfare activities affecting education and the home.

These were the more tangible determinations of the election, but beyond them was the confidence and belief of the people that we would not neglect the support of the embedded ideals and aspirations of America. These ideals and aspirations are the touchstones upon which the day-to-day administration and legislative acts of government must be tested. More than this, the Government must, so far as lies within its proper powers, give leadership to the realization of these ideals and to the fruition of these aspirations. No one can adequately reduce these things of the spirit to phrases or to a catalogue of definitions. We do know what the attainments of these ideals should be: The preservation of self-government and its full foundations in local government; the perfection of justice whether in economic or in social fields; the maintenance of ordered liberty; the denial of domination by any group or class; the building up and preservation of equality of opportunity; the stimulation of initiative and individuality; absolute integrity in public affairs; the choice of officials for fitness to office; the direction of economic progress toward prosperity for the further lessening of poverty; the freedom of public opinion; the sustaining of education and of the advancement of knowledge; the growth of religious spirit and the tolerance of all faiths; the strengthening of the home; the advancement of peace.

There is no short road to the realization of these aspirations. Ours is a progressive people, but with a determination that progress must be based upon the foundation of experience. Ill-considered remedies for our faults bring only penalties after them. But if we hold the faith of the men in our mighty past who created these ideals, we shall leave them heightened and strengthened for our children.

Conclusion

This is not the time and place for extended discussion. The questions before our country are problems of progress to higher standards; they are not the problems of degeneration. They demand thought and they serve to quicken the conscience and enlist our sense of responsibility for their settlement. And that responsibility rests upon you, my countrymen, as much as upon those of us who have been selected for office.

Ours is a land rich in resources; stimulating in its glorious beauty; filled with millions of happy homes; blessed with comfort and opportunity. In no nation are the institutions of progress more advanced. In no nation are the fruits of accomplishment more secure. In no nation is the government more worthy of respect. No country is more loved by its people. I have an abiding faith in their capacity, integrity and high purpose. I have no fears for the future of our country. It is bright with hope.

In the presence of my countrymen, mindful of the solemnity of this occasion, knowing what the task means and the responsibility which it involves, I beg your tolerance, your aid, and your cooperation. I ask the help of Almighty God in this service to my country to which you have called me.

Franklin D. Roosevelt

First Inaugural Address

Saturday, March 4, 1933

I AM certain that my fellow Americans expect that on my induction into the Presidency I will address them with a candor and a decision which the present situation of our Nation impels. This is preeminently the time to speak the truth, the whole truth, frankly and boldly. Nor need we shrink from honestly facing conditions in our country today. This great Nation will endure as it has endured, will revive and will prosper. So, first of all, let me assert my firm belief that the only thing we have to fear is fear itself—nameless, unreasoning, unjustified terror which paralyzes needed efforts to convert retreat into advance. In every dark hour of our national life a leadership of frankness and vigor has met with that understanding and support of the people themselves which is essential to victory. I am convinced that you will again give that support to leadership in these critical days.

In such a spirit on my part and on yours we face our common difficulties. They concern, thank God, only material things. Values have shrunken to fantastic levels; taxes have risen; our ability to pay has fallen; government of all kinds is faced by serious curtailment of income; the means of exchange are frozen in the currents of trade; the withered leaves of industrial enterprise lie on every side; farmers find no markets for their produce; the savings of many years in thousands of families are gone.

More important, a host of unemployed citizens face the grim problem of existence, and an equally great number toil with little return. Only a foolish optimist can deny the dark realities of the moment.

Yet our distress comes from no failure of substance. We are stricken by no plague of locusts. Compared with the perils which our forefathers conquered because they believed and were not afraid, we have still much to be thankful for. Nature still offers her bounty and human efforts have multiplied it. Plenty is at our doorstep, but a generous use of it languishes in the very sight of the supply. Primarily this is because the rulers of the exchange of mankind's goods have failed, through their own stubbornness and their own incompetence, have admitted their failure, and abdicated. Practices of the unscrupulous money changers stand indicted in the court of public opinion, rejected by the hearts and minds of men.

True they have tried, but their efforts have been cast in the pattern of an outworn tradition. Faced by failure of credit they have proposed only the lending of more money. Stripped of the lure of profit by which to induce our people to follow their false leadership, they have resorted to exhortations, pleading tearfully for restored confidence. They know only the rules of a generation of self-seekers. They have no vision, and when there is no vision the people perish.

The money changers have fled from their high seats in the temple of our civilization. We may now restore that temple to the ancient truths. The measure of the restoration lies in the extent to which we apply social values more noble than mere monetary profit.

Happiness lies not in the mere possession of money; it lies in the joy of achievement, in the thrill of creative effort. The joy and moral stimulation of work no longer must be forgotten in the mad chase of evanescent profits. These dark days will be worth all they cost us if they teach us that our true destiny is not to be ministered unto but to minister to ourselves and to our fellow men.

Recognition of the falsity of material wealth as the standard of success goes hand in hand with the abandonment of the false belief that public office and high political position are to be valued only by the standards of pride of place and personal profit; and there must be an end to a conduct in banking and in business which too often has given to a sacred trust the likeness of callous and selfish wrongdoing. Small wonder that confidence languishes, for it thrives only on honesty, on honor, on the sacredness of obligations, on faithful protection, on unselfish performance; without them it cannot live.

Restoration calls, however, not for changes in ethics alone. This Nation asks for action, and action now.

Our greatest primary task is to put people to work. This is no unsolvable problem if we face it wisely and courageously. It can be accomplished in part by direct recruiting by the Government itself, treating the task as we would treat the emergency of a war, but at the same time, through this employment, accomplishing greatly needed projects to stimulate and reorganize the use of our natural resources.

Hand in hand with this we must frankly recognize the overbalance of population in our industrial centers and, by engaging on a national scale in a redistribution, endeavor to provide a better use of the land for those best fitted for the land. The task can be helped by definite efforts to raise the values of agricultural products and with this the power to purchase the output of our cities. It can be helped by preventing realistically the tragedy of the growing loss through foreclosure of our small homes and our farms. It can be helped by insistence that the Federal, State, and local governments act forthwith on the demand that their cost be drastically reduced. It can be helped by the unifying of relief activities which today are often scattered, uneconomical, and unequal. It can be helped by national planning for and supervision of all forms of transportation and of communications and other utilities which have a definitely public character. There are many ways in which it can be helped, but it can never be helped merely by talking about it. We must act and act quickly.

Finally, in our progress toward a resumption of work we require two safeguards against a return of the evils of the old order; there must be a strict supervision of all banking and credits and investments; there must be an end to speculation with other people's money, and there must be provision for an adequate but sound currency.

There are the lines of attack. I shall presently urge upon a new Congress in special session detailed measures for their fulfillment, and I shall seek the immediate assistance of the several States.

Through this program of action we address ourselves to putting our own national house in order and making income balance outgo. Our international trade relations, though vastly important, are in point of time and necessity secondary to the establishment of a sound national economy. I favor as a practical policy the putting of first things first. I shall spare no effort to restore world trade by international economic readjustment, but the emergency at home cannot wait on that accomplishment.

The basic thought that guides these specific means of national recovery is not narrowly nationalistic. It is the insistence, as a first consideration, upon the interdependence of the various elements in all parts of the United States—a recognition of the old and permanently important manifestation of the American spirit of the pioneer. It is the way to recovery. It is the immediate way. It is the strongest assurance that the recovery will endure.

In the field of world policy I would dedicate this Nation to the policy of the good neighbor—the neighbor who resolutely respects himself and, because he does so, respects the rights of others—the neighbor who respects his obligations and respects the sanctity of his agreements in and with a world of neighbors.

If I read the temper of our people correctly, we now realize as we have never realized before our interdependence on each other; that we can not merely take but we must give as well; that if we are to go forward, we must move as a trained and loyal army willing to sacrifice for the good of a common discipline, because without such discipline no progress is made, no leadership becomes effective. We are, I know, ready and willing to submit our lives and property to such discipline, because it makes possible a leadership which aims at a larger good. This I propose to offer, pledging that the larger purposes will bind upon us all as a sacred obligation with a unity of duty hitherto evoked only in time of armed strife.

With this pledge taken, I assume unhesitatingly the leadership of this great army of our people dedicated to a disciplined attack upon our common problems.

Action in this image and to this end is feasible under the form of government which we have inherited from our ancestors. Our Constitution is so simple and practical that it is possible always to meet extraordinary needs by changes in emphasis and arrangement without loss of essential form. That is why our constitutional system has proved itself the most superbly enduring political mechanism the modern world has produced. It has met every stress of vast expansion of territory, of foreign wars, of bitter internal strife, of world relations.

It is to be hoped that the normal balance of executive and legislative authority may be wholly adequate to meet the unprecedented task before us. But it may be that an unprecedented demand and need for undelayed action may call for temporary departure from that normal balance of public procedure.

I am prepared under my constitutional duty to recommend the measures that a stricken nation in the midst of a stricken world may require. These measures, or such other measures as the Congress may build out of its experience and wisdom, I shall seek, within my constitutional authority, to bring to speedy adoption.

But in the event that the Congress shall fail to take one of these two courses, and in the event that the national emergency is still critical, I shall not evade the clear course of duty that will then confront me. I shall ask the Congress for the one remaining instrument to meet the crisis—broad Executive power to wage a war against the emergency, as great as the power that would be given to me if we were in fact invaded by a foreign foe.

For the trust reposed in me I will return the courage and the devotion that befit the time. I can do no less.

We face the arduous days that lie before us in the warm courage of the national unity; with the clear consciousness of seeking old and precious moral values; with the clean satisfaction that comes from the stern performance of duty by old and young alike. We aim at the assurance of a rounded and permanent national life.

We do not distrust the future of essential democracy. The people of the United States have not failed. In their need they have registered a mandate that they want direct, vigorous action. They have asked for discipline and direction under leadership. They have made me the present instrument of their wishes. In the spirit of the gift I take it.

In this dedication of a Nation we humbly ask the blessing of God. May He protect each and every one of us. May He guide me in the days.

Second Inaugural Address

Wednesday, January 20, 1937

WHEN four years ago we met to inaugurate a President, the Republic, single-minded in anxiety, stood in spirit here. We dedicated ourselves to the fulfillment of a vision—to speed the time when there would be for all the people that security and peace essential to the pursuit of happiness. We of the Republic pledged ourselves to drive from the temple of our ancient faith those who had profaned it; to end by action, tireless and unafraid, the stagnation and despair of that day. We did those first things first.

Our covenant with ourselves did not stop there. Instinctively we recognized a deeper need—the need to find through government the instrument of our united purpose to solve for the individual the ever-rising problems of a complex civilization. Repeated attempts at their solution without the aid of government had left us baffled and bewildered. For, without that aid, we had been unable to create those moral controls over the services of science which are necessary to make science a useful servant instead of a ruthless master of mankind. To do this we knew that we must find practical controls over blind economic forces and blindly selfish men.

We of the Republic sensed the truth that democratic government has innate capacity to protect its people against disasters once considered inevitable, to solve problems once considered unsolvable. We would not admit that we could not find a way to master economic epidemics just as, after centuries of fatalistic suffering, we had found a way to master epidemics of disease. We refused to leave the problems of our common welfare to be solved by the winds of chance and the hurricanes of disaster.

In this we Americans were discovering no wholly new truth; we were writing a new chapter in our book of self-government.

This year marks the one hundred and fiftieth anniversary of the Constitutional Convention which made us a nation. At that Convention our forefathers found the way out of the chaos which followed the Revolutionary War; they created a strong government with powers of united action sufficient then and now to solve problems utterly beyond individual or local solution. A century and a half ago they established the Federal Government in order to promote the general welfare and secure the blessings of liberty to the American people.

Today we invoke those same powers of government to achieve the same objectives.

Four years of new experience have not belied our historic instinct. They hold out the clear hope that government within communities, government within the separate States, and government of the United States can do the things the times require, without yielding its democracy. Our tasks in the last four years did not force democracy to take a holiday.

Nearly all of us recognize that as intricacies of human relationships increase, so power to govern them also must increase—power to stop evil; power to do good. The essential democracy of our Nation and the safety of our people depend not upon the absence of power, but upon lodging it with those whom the people can change or continue at stated intervals through an honest and free system of elections. The Constitution of 1787 did not make our democracy impotent.

In fact, in these last four years, we have made the exercise of all power more democratic; for we have begun to bring private autocratic powers into their proper subordination to the public's government. The legend that they were invincible—above and beyond the processes of a democracy—has been shattered. They have been challenged and beaten.

Our progress out of the depression is obvious. But that is not all that you and I mean by the new order of things. Our pledge was not merely to do a patchwork job with secondhand materials. By using the new materials of social justice we have undertaken to erect on the old foundations a more enduring structure for the better use of future generations.

In that purpose we have been helped by achievements of mind and spirit. Old truths have been relearned; untruths have been unlearned. We have always known that heedless self-interest was bad morals; we know now that it is bad economics. Out of the collapse of a prosperity whose builders boasted their practicality has come the conviction that in the long run economic morality pays. We are beginning to wipe out the line that divides the practical from the ideal; and in so doing we are fashioning an instrument of unimagined power for the establishment of a morally better world.

This new understanding undermines the old admiration of worldly success as such. We are beginning to abandon our tolerance of the abuse of power by those who betray for profit the elementary decencies of life.

In this process evil things formerly accepted will not be so easily condoned. Hard-headedness will not so easily excuse hardheartedness. We are moving toward an era of good feeling. But we realize that there can be no era of good feeling save among men of good will.

For these reasons I am justified in believing that the greatest change we have witnessed has been the change in the moral climate of America.

Among men of good will, science and democracy together offer an ever-richer life and ever-larger satisfaction to the individual. With this change in our moral climate and our rediscovered ability to improve our economic order, we have set our feet upon the road of enduring progress.

Shall we pause now and turn our back upon the road that lies ahead? Shall we call this the promised land? Or, shall we continue on our way? For "each age is a dream that is dying, or one that is coming to birth."

Many voices are heard as we face a great decision. Comfort says, "Tarry a while." Opportunism says, "This is a good spot." Timidity asks, "How difficult is the road ahead?"

True, we have come far from the days of stagnation and despair. Vitality has been preserved. Courage and confidence have been restored. Mental and moral horizons have been extended.

But our present gains were won under the pressure of more than ordinary circumstances. Advance became imperative under the goad of fear and suffering. The times were on the side of progress.

To hold to progress today, however, is more difficult. Dulled conscience, irresponsibility, and ruthless self-interest already reappear. Such symptoms of prosperity may become portents of

disaster! Prosperity already tests the persistence of our progressive purpose.

Let us ask again: Have we reached the goal of our vision of that fourth day of March 1933? Have we found our happy valley?

I see a great nation, upon a great continent, blessed with a great wealth of natural resources. Its hundred and thirty million people are at peace among themselves; they are making their country a good neighbor among the nations. I see a United States which can demonstrate that, under democratic methods of government, national wealth can be translated into a spreading volume of human comforts hitherto unknown, and the lowest standard of living can be raised far above the level of mere subsistence.

But here is the challenge to our democracy: In this nation I see tens of millions of its citizens—a substantial part of its whole population—who at this very moment are denied the greater part of what the very lowest standards of today call the necessities of life.

I see millions of families trying to live on incomes so meager that the pall of family disaster hangs over them day by day.

I see millions whose daily lives in city and on farm continue under conditions labeled indecent by a so-called polite society half a century ago.

I see millions denied education, recreation, and the opportunity to better their lot and the lot of their children.

I see millions lacking the means to buy the products of farm and factory and by their poverty denying work and productiveness to many other millions.

I see one-third of a nation ill-housed, ill-clad, ill-nourished.

It is not in despair that I paint you that picture. I paint it for you in hope—because the Nation, seeing and understanding the injustice in it, proposes to paint it out. We are determined to make every American citizen the subject of his country's interest and concern; and we will never regard any faithful law-abiding group within our borders as superfluous. The test of our progress is not whether we add more to the abundance of those who have much; it is whether we provide enough for those who have too little.

If I know aught of the spirit and purpose of our Nation, we will not listen to Comfort, Opportunism, and Timidity. We will carry on.

Overwhelmingly, we of the Republic are men and women of good will; men and women who have more than warm hearts of dedication; men and women who have cool heads and willing hands of practical purpose as well. They will insist that every agency of popular government use effective instruments to carry out their will.

Government is competent when all who compose it work as trustees for the whole people. It can make constant progress when it keeps abreast of all the facts. It can obtain justified support and legitimate criticism when the people receive true information of all that government does.

If I know aught of the will of our people, they will demand that these conditions of effective government shall be created and maintained. They will demand a nation uncorrupted by cancers of injustice and, therefore, strong among the nations in its example of the will to peace.

Today we reconsecrate our country to long-cherished ideals in a suddenly changed civilization. In every land there are always at work forces that drive men apart and forces that draw men together. In our personal ambitions we are individualists. But in our seeking for economic and political progress as a nation, we all go up, or else we all go down, as one people.

To maintain a democracy of effort requires a vast amount of patience in dealing with differing methods, a vast amount of humility. But out of the confusion of many voices rises an understanding of dominant public need. Then political leadership can voice common ideals, and aid in their realization.

In taking again the oath of office as President of the United States, I assume the solemn obligation of leading the American people forward along the road over which they have chosen to advance.

While this duty rests upon me I shall do my utmost to speak their purpose and to do their will, seeking Divine guidance to help us each and every one to give light to them that sit in darkness and to guide our feet into the way of peace.

Third Inaugural Address

Monday, January 20, 1941

ON each national day of inauguration since 1789, the people have renewed their sense of dedication to the United States.

In Washington's day the task of the people was to create and weld together a nation.

In Lincoln's day the task of the people was to preserve that Nation from disruption from within.

In this day the task of the people is to save that Nation and its institutions from disruption from without.

To us there has come a time, in the midst of swift happenings, to pause for a moment and take stock—to recall what our place in history has been, and to rediscover what we are and what we may be. If we do not, we risk the real peril of inaction.

Lives of nations are determined not by the count of years, but by the lifetime of the human spirit. The life of a man is three-score years and ten: a little more, a little less. The life of a nation is the fullness of the measure of its will to live.

There are men who doubt this. There are men who believe that democracy, as a form of Government and a frame of life, is limited or measured by a kind of mystical and artificial fate that, for some unexplained reason, tyranny and slavery have become the surging wave of the future—and that freedom is an ebbing tide.

But we Americans know that this is not true.

Eight years ago, when the life of this Republic seemed frozen by a fatalistic terror, we proved that this is not true. We were in the midst of shock—but we acted. We acted quickly, boldly, decisively.

These later years have been living years—fruitful years for the people of this democracy. For they have brought to us greater security and, I hope, a better understanding that life's ideals are to be measured in other than material things.

Most vital to our present and our future is this experience of a democracy which successfully survived crisis at home; put away many evil things; built new structures on enduring lines; and, through it all, maintained the fact of its democracy.

For action has been taken within the three-way framework of the Constitution of the United States. The coordinate branches of the Government continue freely to function. The Bill of Rights remains inviolate. The freedom of elections is wholly maintained. Prophets of the downfall of American democracy have seen their dire predictions come to naught.

Democracy is not dying.

We know it because we have seen it revive—and grow.

We know it cannot die—because it is built on the unhampered initiative of individual men and women joined together in a common enterprise—an enterprise undertaken and carried through by the free expression of a free majority.

We know it because democracy alone, of all forms of government, enlists the full force of men's enlightened will.

We know it because democracy alone has constructed an unlimited civilization capable of infinite progress in the improvement of human life.

We know it because, if we look below the surface, we sense it still spreading on every continent—for it is the most humane, the most advanced, and in the end the most unconquerable of all forms of human society.

A nation, like a person, has a body—a body that must be fed and clothed and housed, invigorated and rested, in a manner that measures up to the objectives of our time.

A nation, like a person, has a mind—a mind that must be kept informed and alert, that must know itself, that understands the hopes and the needs of its neighbors—all the other nations that live within the narrowing circle of the world.

And a nation, like a person, has something deeper, something more permanent, something larger than the sum of all its parts. It is that something which matters most to its future—which calls forth the most sacred guarding of its present.

It is a thing for which we find it difficult—even impossible—to hit upon a single, simple word.

And yet we all understand what it is—the spirit—the faith of America. It is the product of centuries. It was born in the multitudes of those who came from many lands—some of high degree, but mostly plain people, who sought here, early and late, to find freedom more freely.

The democratic aspiration is no mere recent phase in human history. It is human history. It permeated the ancient life of early peoples. It blazed anew in the middle ages. It was written in Magna Charta.

In the Americas its impact has been irresistible. America has been the New World in all tongues, to all peoples, not because this continent was a new-found land, but because all those who came here believed they could create upon this continent a new life—a life that should be new in freedom.

Its vitality was written into our own Mayflower Compact, into the Declaration of Independence, into the Constitution of the United States, into the Gettysburg Address.

Those who first came here to carry out the longings of their spirit, and the millions who followed, and the stock that sprang from them—all have moved forward constantly and consistently toward an ideal which in itself has gained stature and clarity with each generation.

The hopes of the Republic cannot forever tolerate either undeserved poverty or self-serving wealth.

We know that we still have far to go; that we must more greatly build the security and the opportunity and the knowledge of every citizen, in the measure justified by the resources and the capacity of the land.

But it is not enough to achieve these purposes alone. It is not enough to clothe and feed the body of this Nation, and instruct and inform its mind. For there is also the spirit. And of the three, the greatest is the spirit.

Without the body and the mind, as all men know, the Nation could not live.

But if the spirit of America were killed, even though the Nation's body and mind, constricted in an alien world, lived on, the America we know would have perished.

That spirit—that faith—speaks to us in our daily lives in ways often unnoticed, because they seem so obvious. It speaks to us here in the Capital of the Nation. It speaks to us through the processes of governing in the sovereignties of 48 States. It speaks to us in our counties, in our cities, in our towns, and in our

overwhelming force, the armed attack might never occur.

I hope soon to send to the Senate a treaty respecting the North Atlantic security plan.

In addition, we will provide military advice and equipment to free nations which will cooperate with us in the maintenance of peace and security.

Fourth, we must embark on a bold new program for making the benefits of our scientific advances and industrial progress available for the improvement and growth of underdeveloped areas.

More than half the people of the world are living in conditions approaching misery. Their food is inadequate. They are victims of disease. Their economic life is primitive and stagnant. Their poverty is a handicap and a threat both to them and to more prosperous areas.

For the first time in history, humanity possesses the knowledge and the skill to relieve the suffering of these people.

The United States is pre-eminent among nations in the development of industrial and scientific techniques. The material resources which we can afford to use for the assistance of other peoples are limited. But our imponderable resources in technical knowledge are constantly growing and are inexhaustible.

I believe that we should make available to peace-loving peoples the benefits of our store of technical knowledge in order to help them realize their aspirations for a better life. And, in cooperation with other nations, we should foster capital investment in areas needing development.

Our aim should be to help the free peoples of the world, through their own efforts, to produce more food, more clothing, more materials for housing, and more mechanical power to lighten their burdens.

We invite other countries to pool their technological resources in this undertaking. Their contributions will be warmly welcomed. This should be a cooperative enterprise in which all nations work together through the United Nations and its specialized agencies wherever practicable. It must be a worldwide effort for the achievement of peace, plenty, and freedom.

With the cooperation of business, private capital, agriculture, and labor in this country, this program can greatly increase the industrial activity in other nations and can raise substantially their standards of living.

Such new economic developments must be devised and controlled to benefit the peoples of the areas in which they are established. Guarantees to the investor must be balanced by guarantees in the interest of the people whose resources and whose labor go into these developments.

The old imperialism—exploitation for foreign profit—has no place in our plans. What we envisage is a program of development based on the concepts of democratic fair-dealing.

All countries, including our own, will greatly benefit from a constructive program for the better use of the world's human and natural resources. Experience shows that our commerce with other countries expands as they progress industrially and economically.

Greater production is the key to prosperity and peace. And the key to greater production is a wider and more vigorous application of modern scientific and technical knowledge.

Only by helping the least fortunate of its members to help themselves can the human family achieve the decent, satisfying life that is the right of all people.

Democracy alone can supply the vitalizing force to stir the peoples of the world into triumphant action, not only against their human oppressors, but also against their ancient enemies— hunger, misery, and despair.

On the basis of these four major courses of action we hope to help create the conditions that will lead eventually to personal freedom and happiness for all mankind.

If we are to be successful in carrying out these policies, it is clear that we must have continued prosperity in this country and we must keep ourselves strong.

Slowly but surely we are weaving a world fabric of international security and growing prosperity.

We are aided by all who wish to live in freedom from fear— even by those who live today in fear under their own governments.

We are aided by all who want relief from the lies of propaganda—who desire truth and sincerity.

We are aided by all who desire self-government and a voice in deciding their own affairs.

We are aided by all who long for economic security—for the security and abundance that men in free societies can enjoy.

We are aided by all who desire freedom of speech, freedom of religion, and freedom to live their own lives for useful ends.

Our allies are the millions who hunger and thirst after righteousness.

In due time, as our stability becomes manifest, as more and more nations come to know the benefits of democracy and to participate in growing abundance, I believe that those countries which now oppose us will abandon their delusions and join with the free nations of the world in a just settlement of international differences.

Events have brought our American democracy to new influence and new responsibilities. They will test our courage, our devotion to duty, and our concept of liberty.

But I say to all men, what we have achieved in liberty, we will surpass in greater liberty.

Steadfast in our faith in the Almighty, we will advance toward a world where man's freedom is secure.

To that end we will devote our strength, our resources, and our firmness of resolve. With God's help, the future of mankind will be assured in a world of justice, harmony, and peace.

Dwight D. Eisenhower

First Inaugural Address

Tuesday, January 20, 1953

MY friends, before I begin the expression of those thoughts that I deem appropriate to this moment, would you permit me the privilege of uttering a little private prayer of my own. And I ask that you bow your heads:

Almighty God, as we stand here at this moment my future associates in the executive branch of government join me in beseeching that Thou will make full and complete our dedication to the service of the people in this throng, and their fellow citizens everywhere.

Give us, we pray, the power to discern clearly right from wrong, and allow all our words and actions to be governed thereby, and by the laws of this land. Especially we pray that our concern shall be for all the people regardless of station, race, or calling.

May cooperation be permitted and be the mutual aim of those who, under the concepts of our Constitution, hold to differing political faiths; so that all may work for the good of our beloved country and Thy glory. Amen.

My fellow citizens:

The world and we have passed the midway point of a century of continuing challenge. We sense with all our faculties that forces of good and evil are massed and armed and opposed as rarely before in history.

This fact defines the meaning of this day. We are summoned by this honored and historic ceremony to witness more than the act of one citizen swearing his oath of service, in the presence of God. We are called as a people to give testimony in the sight of the world to our faith that the future shall belong to the free.

Since this century's beginning, a time of tempest has seemed to come upon the continents of the earth. Masses of Asia have awakened to strike off shackles of the past. Great nations of Europe have fought their bloodiest wars. Thrones have toppled and their vast empires have disappeared. New nations have been born.

For our own country, it has been a time of recurring trial. We have grown in power and in responsibility. We have passed through the anxieties of depression and of war to a summit unmatched in man's history. Seeking to secure peace in the world, we have had to fight through the forests of the Argonne, to the shores of Iwo Jima, and to the cold mountains of Korea.

In the swift rush of great events, we find ourselves groping to know the full sense and meaning of these times in which we live. In our quest of understanding, we beseech God's guidance. We summon all our knowledge of the past and we scan all signs of the future. We bring all our wit and all our will to meet the question:

How far have we come in man's long pilgrimage from darkness toward light? Are we nearing the light—a day of freedom and of peace for all mankind? Or are the shadows of another night closing in upon us?

Great as are the preoccupations absorbing us at home, concerned as we are with matters that deeply affect our livelihood today and our vision of the future, each of these domestic problems is dwarfed by, and often even created by, this question that involves all humankind.

This trial comes at a moment when man's power to achieve good or to inflict evil surpasses the brightest hopes and the sharpest fears of all ages. We can turn rivers in their courses, level mountains to the plains. Oceans and land and sky are avenues for our colossal commerce. Disease diminishes and life lengthens.

Yet the promise of this life is imperiled by the very genius that has made it possible. Nations amass wealth. Labor sweats to create—and turns out devices to level not only mountains but also cities. Science seems ready to confer upon us, as its final gift, the power to erase human life from this planet.

At such a time in history, we who are free must proclaim anew our faith. This faith is the abiding creed of our fathers. It is our faith in the deathless dignity of man, governed by eternal moral and natural laws.

This faith defines our full view of life. It establishes, beyond debate, those gifts of the Creator that are man's inalienable rights, and that make all men equal in His sight.

In the light of this equality, we know that the virtues most cherished by free people—love of truth, pride of work, devotion to country—all are treasures equally precious in the lives of the most humble and of the most exalted. The men who mine coal and fire furnaces and balance ledgers and turn lathes and pick cotton and heal the sick and plant corn—all serve as proudly, and as profitably, for America as the statesmen who draft treaties and the legislators who enact laws.

This faith rules our whole way of life. It decrees that we, the people, elect leaders not to rule but to serve. It asserts that we have the right to choice of our own work and to the reward of our own toil. It inspires the initiative that makes our productivity the wonder of the world. And it warns that any man who seeks to deny equality among all his brothers betrays the spirit of the free and invites the mockery of the tyrant.

It is because we, all of us, hold to these principles that the political changes accomplished this day do not imply turbulence, upheaval or disorder. Rather this change expresses a purpose of strengthening our dedication and devotion to the precepts of our founding documents, a conscious renewal of faith in our country and in the watchfulness of a Divine Providence.

The enemies of this faith know no god but force, no devotion but its use. They tutor men in treason. They feed upon the hunger of others. Whatever defies them, they torture, especially the truth.

Here, then, is joined no argument between slightly differing philosophies. This conflict strikes directly at the faith of our fathers and the lives of our sons. No principle or treasure that we hold, from the spiritual knowledge of our free schools and churches to the creative magic of free labor and capital, nothing lies safely beyond the reach of this struggle.

Freedom is pitted against slavery; lightness against the dark.

The faith we hold belongs not to us alone but to the free of all the world. This common bond binds the grower of rice in Burma and the planter of wheat in Iowa, the shepherd in southern Italy and the mountaineer in the Andes. It confers a common dignity upon the French soldier who dies in Indo-China, the British soldier killed in Malaya, the American life given in Korea.

We know, beyond this, that we are linked to all free peoples not merely by a noble idea but by a simple need. No free people can for long cling to any privilege or enjoy any safety in economic solitude. For all our own material might, even we need markets in the world for the surpluses of our farms and our factories. Equally, we need for these same farms and factories vital materials and products of distant lands. This basic law of interdependence, so manifest in the commerce of peace, applies with thousand-fold intensity in the event of war.

So we are persuaded by necessity and by belief that the strength of all free peoples lies in unity; their danger, in discord.

To produce this unity, to meet the challenge of our time, destiny has laid upon our country the responsibility of the free world's leadership.

So it is proper that we assure our friends once again that, in the discharge of this responsibility, we Americans know and we observe the difference between world leadership and imperialism; between firmness and truculence; between a thoughtfully calculated goal and spasmodic reaction to the stimulus of emergencies.

We wish our friends the world over to know this above all: we face the threat—not with dread and confusion—but with confidence and conviction.

We feel this moral strength because we know that we are not helpless prisoners of history. We are free men. We shall remain free, never to be proven guilty of the one capital offense against freedom, a lack of stanch faith.

In pleading our just cause before the bar of history and in pressing our labor for world peace, we shall be guided by certain fixed principles.

These principles are:

(1) Abhorring war as a chosen way to balk the purposes of those who threaten us, we hold it to be the first task of

statesmanship to develop the strength that will deter the forces of aggression and promote the conditions of peace. For, as it must be the supreme purpose of all free men, so it must be the dedication of their leaders, to save humanity from preying upon itself.

In the light of this principle, we stand ready to engage with any and all others in joint effort to remove the causes of mutual fear and distrust among nations, so as to make possible drastic reduction of armaments. The sole requisites for undertaking such effort are that—in their purpose—they be aimed logically and honestly toward secure peace for all; and that—in their result— they provide methods by which every participating nation will prove good faith in carrying out its pledge.

(2) Realizing that common sense and common decency alike dictate the futility of appeasement, we shall never try to placate an aggressor by the false and wicked bargain of trading honor for security. Americans, indeed all free men, remember that in the final choice a soldier's pack is not so heavy a burden as a prisoner's chains.

(3) Knowing that only a United States that is strong and immensely productive can help defend freedom in our world, we view our Nation's strength and security as a trust upon which rests the hope of free men everywhere. It is the firm duty of each of our free citizens and of every free citizen everywhere to place the cause of his country before the comfort, the convenience of himself.

(4) Honoring the identity and the special heritage of each nation in the world, we shall never use our strength to try to impress upon another people our own cherished political and economic institutions.

(5) Assessing realistically the needs and capacities of proven friends of freedom, we shall strive to help them to achieve their own security and well-being. Likewise, we shall count upon them to assume, within the limits of their resources, their full and just burdens in the common defense of freedom.

(6) Recognizing economic health as an indispensable basis of military strength and the free world's peace, we shall strive to foster everywhere, and to practice ourselves, policies that encourage productivity and profitable trade. For the impoverishment of any single people in the world means danger to the well-being of all other peoples.

(7) Appreciating that economic need, military security and political wisdom combine to suggest regional groupings of free peoples, we hope, within the framework of the United Nations, to help strengthen such special bonds the world over. The nature of these ties must vary with the different problems of different areas.

In the Western Hemisphere, we enthusiastically join with all our neighbors in the work of perfecting a community of fraternal trust and common purpose.

In Europe, we ask that enlightened and inspired leaders of the Western nations strive with renewed vigor to make the unity of their peoples a reality. Only as free Europe unitedly marshals its strength can it effectively safeguard, even with our help, its

spiritual and cultural heritage.

(8) Conceiving the defense of freedom, like freedom itself, to be one and indivisible, we hold all continents and peoples in equal regard and honor. We reject any insinuation that one race or another, one people or another, is in any sense inferior or expendable.

(9) Respecting the United Nations as the living sign of all people's hope for peace, we shall strive to make it not merely an eloquent symbol but an effective force. And in our quest for an honorable peace, we shall neither compromise, nor tire, nor ever cease.

By these rules of conduct, we hope to be known to all peoples.

By their observance, an earth of peace may become not a vision but a fact.

This hope—this supreme aspiration—must rule the way we live.

We must be ready to dare all for our country. For history does not long entrust the care of freedom to the weak or the timid. We must acquire proficiency in defense and display stamina in purpose.

We must be willing, individually and as a Nation, to accept whatever sacrifices may be required of us. A people that values its privileges above its principles soon loses both.

These basic precepts are not lofty abstractions, far removed from matters of daily living. They are laws of spiritual strength that generate and define our material strength. Patriotism means equipped forces and a prepared citizenry. Moral stamina means more energy and more productivity, on the farm and in the factory. Love of liberty means the guarding of every resource that makes freedom possible—from the sanctity of our families and the wealth of our soil to the genius of our scientists.

And so each citizen plays an indispensable role. The productivity of our heads, our hands, and our hearts is the source of all the strength we can command, for both the enrichment of our lives and the winning of the peace.

No person, no home, no community can be beyond the reach of this call. We are summoned to act in wisdom and in conscience, to work with industry, to teach with persuasion, to preach with conviction, to weigh our every deed with care and with compassion. For this truth must be clear before us: whatever America hopes to bring to pass in the world must first come to pass in the heart of America.

The peace we seek, then, is nothing less than the practice and fulfillment of our whole faith among ourselves and in our dealings with others. This signifies more than the stilling of guns, easing the sorrow of war. More than escape from death, it is a way of life. More than a haven for the weary, it is a hope for the brave.

This is the hope that beckons us onward in this century of trial. This is the work that awaits us all, to be done with bravery, with charity, and with prayer to Almighty God.

Second Inaugural Address

Monday, January 21, 1957

THE PRICE OF PEACE

Mr. Chairman, Mr. Vice President, Mr. Chief Justice, Mr. Speaker, members of my family and friends, my countrymen, and the friends of my country, wherever they may be, we meet again, as upon a like moment four years ago, and again you have witnessed my solemn oath of service to you.

I, too, am a witness, today testifying in your name to the principles and purposes to which we, as a people, are pledged.

Before all else, we seek, upon our common labor as a nation, the blessings of Almighty God. And the hopes in our hearts fashion the deepest prayers of our whole people.

May we pursue the right—without self-righteousness.

May we know unity—without conformity.

May we grow in strength—without pride in self.

May we, in our dealings with all peoples of the earth, ever speak truth and serve justice.

And so shall America—in the sight of all men of good will—prove true to the honorable purposes that bind and rule us as a people in all this time of trial through which we pass.

We live in a land of plenty, but rarely has this earth known such peril as today.

In our nation work and wealth abound. Our population grows. Commerce crowds our rivers and rails, our skies, harbors, and highways. Our soil is fertile, our agriculture productive. The air rings with the song of our industry—rolling mills and blast furnaces, dynamos, dams, and assembly lines—the chorus of America the bountiful.

This is our home—yet this is not the whole of our world. For our world is where our full destiny lies—with men, of all people, and all nations, who are or would be free. And for them—and so for us—this is no time of ease or of rest.

In too much of the earth there is want, discord, danger. New forces and new nations stir and strive across the earth, with power to bring, by their fate, great good or great evil to the free world's future. From the deserts of North Africa to the islands of the South Pacific one third of all mankind has entered upon an historic struggle for a new freedom; freedom from grinding poverty. Across all continents, nearly a billion people seek, sometimes almost in desperation, for the skills and knowledge and assistance by which they may satisfy from their own resources, the material wants common to all mankind.

No nation, however old or great, escapes this tempest of change and turmoil. Some, impoverished by the recent World War, seek to restore their means of livelihood. In the heart of Europe, Germany still stands tragically divided. So is the whole continent divided. And so, too, is all the world.

The divisive force is International Communism and the power that it controls.

The designs of that power, dark in purpose, are clear in practice. It strives to seal forever the fate of those it has enslaved. It strives to break the ties that unite the free. And it strives to capture—to exploit for its own greater power—all forces of change in the world, especially the needs of the hungry and the hopes of the oppressed.

Yet the world of International Communism has itself been shaken by a fierce and mighty force: the readiness of men who love freedom to pledge their lives to that love. Through the night of their bondage, the unconquerable will of heroes has struck with the swift, sharp thrust of lightning. Budapest is no longer merely the name of a city; henceforth it is a new and shining symbol of man's yearning to be free.

Thus across all the globe there harshly blow the winds of change. And, we—though fortunate be our lot—know that we can never turn our backs to them.

We look upon this shaken earth, and we declare our firm and fixed purpose—the building of a peace with justice in a world where moral law prevails.

The building of such a peace is a bold and solemn purpose. To proclaim it is easy. To serve it will be hard. And to attain it, we must be aware of its full meaning—and ready to pay its full price.

We know clearly what we seek, and why.

We seek peace, knowing that peace is the climate of freedom. And now, as in no other age, we seek it because we have been warned, by the power of modern weapons, that peace may be the only climate possible for human life itself.

Yet this peace we seek cannot be born of fear alone: it must be rooted in the lives of nations. There must be justice, sensed and shared by all peoples, for, without justice the world can know only a tense and unstable truce. There must be law, steadily invoked and respected by all nations, for without law, the world promises only such meager justice as the pity of the strong upon the weak. But the law of which we speak, comprehending the values of freedom, affirms the equality of all nations, great and small.

Splendid as can be the blessings of such a peace, high will be its cost: in toil patiently sustained, in help honorably given, in sacrifice calmly borne.

We are called to meet the price of this peace.

To counter the threat of those who seek to rule by force, we must pay the costs of our own needed military strength, and help to build the security of others.

We must use our skills and knowledge and, at times, our substance, to help others rise from misery, however far the scene of suffering may be from our shores. For wherever in the world a people knows desperate want, there must appear at least the spark of hope, the hope of progress—or there will surely rise at last the flames of conflict.

We recognize and accept our own deep involvement in the destiny of men everywhere. We are accordingly pledged to honor, and to strive to fortify, the authority of the United Nations. For in that body rests the best hope of our age for the assertion of that law by which all nations may live in dignity.

And, beyond this general resolve, we are called to act a responsible role in the world's great concerns or conflicts—whether they touch upon the affairs of a vast region, the fate of an island in the Pacific, or the use of a canal in the Middle East. Only in respecting the hopes and cultures of others will we practice the equality of all nations. Only as we show willingness and wisdom in giving counsel—in receiving counsel—and in sharing burdens, will we wisely perform the work of peace.

For one truth must rule all we think and all we do. No people can live to itself alone. The unity of all who dwell in freedom is their only sure defense. The economic need of all nations—in mutual dependence—makes isolation an impossibility; not even America's prosperity could long survive if other nations did not also prosper. No nation can longer be a fortress, lone and strong and safe. And any people, seeking such shelter for themselves, can now build only their own prison.

Our pledge to these principles is constant, because we believe in their rightness.

We do not fear this world of change. America is no stranger to much of its spirit. Everywhere we see the seeds of the same growth that America itself has known. The American experiment has, for generations, fired the passion and the courage of millions elsewhere seeking freedom, equality, and opportunity. And the American story of material progress has helped excite the longing of all needy peoples for some satisfaction of their human wants. These hopes that we have helped to inspire, we can help to fulfill.

In this confidence, we speak plainly to all peoples.

We cherish our friendship with all nations that are or would be free. We respect, no less, their independence. And when, in time of want or peril, they ask our help, they may honorably receive it; for we no more seek to buy their sovereignty than we would sell our own. Sovereignty is never bartered among freemen.

We honor the aspirations of those nations which, now captive, long for freedom. We seek neither their military alliance nor any artificial imitation of our society. And they can know the warmth of the welcome that awaits them when, as must be, they join again the ranks of freedom.

We honor, no less in this divided world than in a less tormented time, the people of Russia. We do not dread, rather do we welcome, their progress in education and industry. We wish them success in their demands for more intellectual freedom, greater security before their own laws, fuller enjoyment of the rewards of their own toil. For as such things come to pass, the more certain will be the coming of that day when our peoples may freely meet in friendship.

So we voice our hope and our belief that we can help to heal this divided world. Thus may the nations cease to live in trembling before the menace of force. Thus may the weight of fear and the weight of arms be taken from the burdened shoulders of mankind.

This, nothing less, is the labor to which we are called and our strength dedicated.

And so the prayer of our people carries far beyond our own frontiers, to the wide world of our duty and our destiny.

May the light of freedom, coming to all darkened lands, flame brightly—until at last the darkness is no more.

May the turbulence of our age yield to a true time of peace, when men and nations shall share a life that honors the dignity of each, the brotherhood of all.

John F. Kennedy

Inaugural Address

Friday, January 20, 1961

Vice President Johnson, Mr. Speaker, Mr. Chief Justice, President Eisenhower, Vice President Nixon, President Truman, reverend clergy, fellow citizens, we observe today not a victory of party, but a celebration of freedom—symbolizing an end, as well as a beginning—signifying renewal, as well as change. For I have sworn before you and Almighty God the same solemn oath our forebears prescribed nearly a century and three quarters ago.

The world is very different now. For man holds in his mortal hands the power to abolish all forms of human poverty and all forms of human life. And yet the same revolutionary beliefs for which our forebears fought are still at issue around the globe— the belief that the rights of man come not from the generosity of the state, but from the hand of God.

We dare not forget today that we are the heirs of that first revolution. Let the word go forth from this time and place, to friend and foe alike, that the torch has been passed to a new generation of Americans—born in this century, tempered by war, disciplined by a hard and bitter peace, proud of our ancient heritage—and unwilling to witness or permit the slow undoing of those human rights to which this Nation has always been committed, and to which we are committed today at home and around the world.

Let every nation know, whether it wishes us well or ill, that we shall pay any price, bear any burden, meet any hardship, support any friend, oppose any foe, in order to assure the survival and the success of liberty.

This much we pledge—and more.

To those old allies whose cultural and spiritual origins we share, we pledge the loyalty of faithful friends. United, there is little we cannot do in a host of cooperative ventures. Divided, there is little we can do—for we dare not meet a powerful challenge at odds and split asunder.

To those new States whom we welcome to the ranks of the free, we pledge our word that one form of colonial control shall not have passed away merely to be replaced by a far more iron tyranny. We shall not always expect to find them supporting our view. But we shall always hope to find them strongly supporting their own freedom—and to remember that, in the past, those who foolishly sought power by riding the back of the tiger ended up inside.

To those peoples in the huts and villages across the globe struggling to break the bonds of mass misery, we pledge our best efforts to help them help themselves, for whatever period is required—not because the Communists may be doing it, not because we seek their votes, but because it is right. If a free society cannot help the many who are poor, it cannot save the few who are rich.

To our sister republics south of our border, we offer a special pledge—to convert our good words into good deeds—in a new alliance for progress—to assist free men and free governments in casting off the chains of poverty. But this peaceful revolution of hope cannot become the prey of hostile powers. Let all our neighbors know that we shall join with them to oppose aggression or subversion anywhere in the Americas. And let every other power know that this Hemisphere intends to remain the master of its own house.

To that world assembly of sovereign states, the United Nations, our last best hope in an age where the instruments of war have far outpaced the instruments of peace, we renew our pledge of support—to prevent it from becoming merely a forum for invective—to strengthen its shield of the new and the weak— and to enlarge the area in which its writ may run.

Finally, to those nations who would make themselves our adversary, we offer not a pledge but a request: that both sides begin anew the quest for peace, before the dark powers of destruction unleashed by science engulf all humanity in planned or accidental self-destruction.

We dare not tempt them with weakness. For only when our arms are sufficient beyond doubt can we be certain beyond doubt that they will never be employed.

But neither can two great and powerful groups of nations take comfort from our present course—both sides overburdened by the cost of modern weapons, both rightly alarmed by the steady spread of the deadly atom, yet both racing to alter that uncertain balance of terror that stays the hand of mankind's final war.

So let us begin anew—remembering on both sides that civility is not a sign of weakness, and sincerity is always subject to proof. Let us never negotiate out of fear. But let us never fear to negotiate.

Let both sides explore what problems unite us instead of belaboring those problems which divide us.

Let both sides, for the first time, formulate serious and precise proposals for the inspection and control of arms—and bring the absolute power to destroy other nations under the absolute control of all nations.

Let both sides seek to invoke the wonders of science instead of its terrors. Together let us explore the stars, conquer the deserts, eradicate disease, tap the ocean depths, and encourage the arts and commerce.

Let both sides unite to heed in all corners of the earth the command of Isaiah—to "undo the heavy burdens ... and to let the oppressed go free."

And if a beachhead of cooperation may push back the jungle of suspicion, let both sides join in creating a new endeavor, not a new balance of power, but a new world of law, where the strong are just and the weak secure and the peace preserved.

All this will not be finished in the first 100 days. Nor will it be finished in the first 1,000 days, nor in the life of this Administration, nor even perhaps in our lifetime on this planet. But let us begin.

In your hands, my fellow citizens, more than in mine, will rest the final success or failure of our course. Since this country was founded, each generation of Americans has been summoned to give testimony to its national loyalty. The graves of young Americans who answered the call to service surround the globe.

Now the trumpet summons us again—not as a call to bear arms, though arms we need; not as a call to battle, though embattled we are—but a call to bear the burden of a long twilight struggle, year in and year out, "rejoicing in hope, patient in tribulation"—a struggle against the common enemies of man: tyranny, poverty, disease, and war itself.

Can we forge against these enemies a grand and global alliance, North and South, East and West, that can assure a more fruitful life for all mankind? Will you join in that historic effort?

In the long history of the world, only a few generations have been granted the role of defending freedom in its hour of maximum danger. I do not shrink from this responsibility—I welcome it. I do not believe that any of us would exchange places with any other people or any other generation. The energy, the faith, the devotion which we bring to this endeavor will light our country and all who serve it—and the glow from that fire can truly light the world.

And so, my fellow Americans: ask not what your country can do for you—ask what you can do for your country.

My fellow citizens of the world: ask not what America will do for you, but what together we can do for the freedom of man.

Finally, whether you are citizens of America or citizens of the world, ask of us the same high standards of strength and sacrifice which we ask of you. With a good conscience our only sure reward, with history the final judge of our deeds, let us go forth to lead the land we love, asking His blessing and His help, but knowing that here on earth God's work must truly be our own.

Lyndon Baines Johnson

Inaugural Address

Wednesday, January 20, 1965

My fellow countrymen, on this occasion, the oath I have taken before you and before God is not mine alone, but ours together. We are one nation and one people. Our fate as a nation and our future as a people rest not upon one citizen, but upon all citizens.

This is the majesty and the meaning of this moment.

For every generation, there is a destiny. For some, history decides. For this generation, the choice must be our own.

Even now, a rocket moves toward Mars. It reminds us that the world will not be the same for our children, or even for ourselves in a short span of years. The next man to stand here will look out on a scene different from our own, because ours is a time of change—rapid and fantastic change bearing the secrets of nature, multiplying the nations, placing in uncertain hands new weapons for mastery and destruction, shaking old values, and uprooting old ways.

Our destiny in the midst of change will rest on the unchanged character of our people, and on their faith.

THE AMERICAN COVENANT

They came here—the exile and the stranger, brave but frightened—to find a place where a man could be his own man. They made a covenant with this land. Conceived in justice, written in liberty, bound in union, it was meant one day to inspire the hopes of all mankind; and it binds us still. If we keep its terms, we shall flourish.

JUSTICE AND CHANGE

First, justice was the promise that all who made the journey would share in the fruits of the land.

In a land of great wealth, families must not live in hopeless poverty. In a land rich in harvest, children just must not go hungry. In a land of healing miracles, neighbors must not suffer and die unattended. In a great land of learning and scholars, young people must be taught to read and write.

For the more than 30 years that I have served this Nation, I have believed that this injustice to our people, this waste of our resources, was our real enemy. For 30 years or more, with the resources I have had, I have vigilantly fought against it. I have learned, and I know, that it will not surrender easily.

But change has given us new weapons. Before this generation of Americans is finished, this enemy will not only retreat—it will be conquered.

Justice requires us to remember that when any citizen denies his fellow, saying, "His color is not mine," or "His beliefs are strange and different," in that moment he betrays America, though his forebears created this Nation.

LIBERTY AND CHANGE

Liberty was the second article of our covenant. It was self-government. It was our Bill of Rights. But it was more. America would be a place where each man could be proud to be himself: stretching his talents, rejoicing in his work, important in the life of his neighbors and his nation.

This has become more difficult in a world where change and growth seem to tower beyond the control and even the judgment of men. We must work to provide the knowledge and the surroundings which can enlarge the possibilities of every citizen.

The American covenant called on us to help show the way for the liberation of man. And that is today our goal. Thus, if as a nation there is much outside our control, as a people no stranger is outside our hope.

Change has brought new meaning to that old mission. We can never again stand aside, prideful in isolation. Terrific dangers and troubles that we once called "foreign" now constantly live among us. If American lives must end, and American treasure be spilled, in countries we barely know, that is the price that change has demanded of conviction and of our enduring covenant.

Think of our world as it looks from the rocket that is heading toward Mars. It is like a child's globe, hanging in space, the continents stuck to its side like colored maps. We are all fellow passengers on a dot of earth. And each of us, in the span of time, has really only a moment among our companions.

How incredible it is that in this fragile existence, we should hate and destroy one another. There are possibilities enough for all who will abandon mastery over others to pursue mastery over nature. There is world enough for all to seek their happiness in their own way.

Our Nation's course is abundantly clear. We aspire to nothing that belongs to others. We seek no dominion over our fellow man, but man's dominion over tyranny and misery.

But more is required. Men want to be a part of a common enterprise—a cause greater than themselves. Each of us must find a way to advance the purpose of the Nation, thus finding new purpose for ourselves. Without this, we shall become a nation of strangers.

UNION AND CHANGE

The third article was union. To those who were small and few against the wilderness, the success of liberty demanded the strength of union. Two centuries of change have made this true again.

No longer need capitalist and worker, farmer and clerk, city and countryside, struggle to divide our bounty. By working shoulder to shoulder, together we can increase the bounty of all. We have discovered that every child who learns, every man who finds work, every sick body that is made whole—like a candle added to an altar—brightens the hope of all the faithful.

So let us reject any among us who seek to reopen old wounds and to rekindle old hatreds. They stand in the way of a seeking nation.

Let us now join reason to faith and action to experience, to transform our unity of interest into a unity of purpose. For the hour and the day and the time are here to achieve progress without strife, to achieve change without hatred—not without difference of opinion, but without the deep and abiding divisions which scar the union for generations.

THE AMERICAN BELIEF

Under this covenant of justice, liberty, and union we have become a nation—prosperous, great, and mighty. And we have kept our freedom. But we have no promise from God that our greatness will endure. We have been allowed by Him to seek greatness with the sweat of our hands and the strength of our spirit.

I do not believe that the Great Society is the ordered, changeless, and sterile battalion of the ants. It is the excitement of becoming—always becoming, trying, probing, falling, resting, and trying again—but always trying and always gaining.

In each generation, with toil and tears, we have had to earn our heritage again.

If we fail now, we shall have forgotten in abundance what we learned in hardship: that democracy rests on faith, that freedom asks more than it gives, and that the judgment of God is harshest on those who are most favored.

If we succeed, it will not be because of what we have, but it will be because of what we are; not because of what we own, but, rather because of what we believe.

For we are a nation of believers. Underneath the clamor of building and the rush of our day's pursuits, we are believers in justice and liberty and union, and in our own Union. We believe that every man must someday be free. And we believe in ourselves.

Our enemies have always made the same mistake. In my lifetime—in depression and in war—they have awaited our defeat. Each time, from the secret places of the American heart, came forth the faith they could not see or that they could not even imagine. It brought us victory. And it will again.

For this is what America is all about. It is the uncrossed desert and the unclimbed ridge. It is the star that is not reached and the harvest sleeping in the unplowed ground. Is our world gone? We say "Farewell." Is a new world coming? We welcome it—and we will bend it to the hopes of man.

To these trusted public servants and to my family and those close friends of mine who have followed me down a long, winding road, and to all the people of this Union and the world, I will repeat today what I said on that sorrowful day in November 1963: "I will lead and I will do the best I can."

But you must look within your own hearts to the old promises and to the old dream. They will lead you best of all.

For myself, I ask only, in the words of an ancient leader: "Give me now wisdom and knowledge, that I may go out and come in before this people: for who can judge this thy people, that is so great?"

Richard Milhous Nixon

First Inaugural Address

Monday, January 20, 1969

Senator Dirksen, Mr. Chief Justice, Mr. Vice President, President Johnson, Vice President Humphrey, my fellow Americans—and my fellow citizens of the world community:

I ask you to share with me today the majesty of this moment. In the orderly transfer of power, we celebrate the unity that keeps us free.

Each moment in history is a fleeting time, precious and unique. But some stand out as moments of beginning, in which courses are set that shape decades or centuries.

This can be such a moment.

Forces now are converging that make possible, for the first time, the hope that many of man's deepest aspirations can at last be realized. The spiraling pace of change allows us to contemplate, within our own lifetime, advances that once would have taken centuries.

In throwing wide the horizons of space, we have discovered new horizons on earth.

For the first time, because the people of the world want peace, and the leaders of the world are afraid of war, the times are on the side of peace.

Eight years from now America will celebrate its 200th anniversary as a nation. Within the lifetime of most people now living, mankind will celebrate that great new year which comes only once in a thousand years—the beginning of the third millennium.

What kind of nation we will be, what kind of world we will live in, whether we shape the future in the image of our hopes, is ours to determine by our actions and our choices.

The greatest honor history can bestow is the title of peacemaker. This honor now beckons America—the chance to help lead the world at last out of the valley of turmoil, and onto that high ground of peace that man has dreamed of since the dawn of civilization.

If we succeed, generations to come will say of us now living that we mastered our moment, that we helped make the world safe for mankind.

This is our summons to greatness.

I believe the American people are ready to answer this call.

The second third of this century has been a time of proud achievement. We have made enormous strides in science and industry and agriculture. We have shared our wealth more broadly than ever. We have learned at last to manage a modern economy to assure its continued growth. We have given freedom new reach, and we have begun to make its promise real for black as well as for white. We see the hope of tomorrow in the youth of today. I know America's youth. I believe in them. We can be proud that they are better educated, more committed, more passionately driven by conscience than any generation in our history.

No people has ever been so close to the achievement of a just and abundant society, or so possessed of the will to achieve it. Because our strengths are so great, we can afford to appraise our weaknesses with candor and to approach them with hope.

Standing in this same place a third of a century ago, Franklin Delano Roosevelt addressed a Nation ravaged by depression and gripped in fear. He could say in surveying the Nation's troubles: "They concern, thank God, only material things."

Our crisis today is the reverse. We have found ourselves rich in goods, but ragged in spirit; reaching with magnificent precision for the moon, but falling into raucous discord on earth.

We are caught in war, wanting peace. We are torn by division, wanting unity. We see around us empty lives, wanting fulfillment. We see tasks that need doing, waiting for hands to do them.

To a crisis of the spirit, we need an answer of the spirit.

To find that answer, we need only look within ourselves.

When we listen to "the better angels of our nature," we find that they celebrate the simple things, the basic things—such as goodness, decency, love, kindness.

Greatness comes in simple trappings. The simple things are the ones most needed today if we are to surmount what divides us, and cement what unites us. To lower our voices would be a simple thing.

In these difficult years, America has suffered from a fever of words; from inflated rhetoric that promises more than it can deliver; from angry rhetoric that fans discontents into hatreds; from bombastic rhetoric that postures instead of persuading.

We cannot learn from one another until we stop shouting at one another—until we speak quietly enough so that our words can be heard as well as our voices.

For its part, government will listen. We will strive to listen in new ways—to the voices of quiet anguish, the voices that speak without words, the voices of the heart—to the injured voices, the anxious voices, the voices that have despaired of being heard. Those who have been left out, we will try to bring in. Those left behind, we will help to catch up.

For all of our people, we will set as our goal the decent order that makes progress possible and our lives secure. As we reach toward our hopes, our task is to build on what has gone before—not turning away from the old, but turning toward the new.

In this past third of a century, government has passed more laws, spent more money, initiated more programs, than in all our previous history.

In pursuing our goals of full employment, better housing, excellence in education; in rebuilding our cities and improving our rural areas; in protecting our environment and enhancing the quality of life—in all these and more, we will and must press urgently forward.

We shall plan now for the day when our wealth can be transferred from the destruction of war abroad to the urgent needs of our people at home.

The American dream does not come to those who fall asleep. But we are approaching the limits of what government alone can do. Our greatest need now is to reach beyond government, and to enlist the legions of the concerned and the committed.

What has to be done, has to be done by government and people together or it will not be done at all. The lesson of past agony is that without the people we can do nothing; with the people we can do everything.

To match the magnitude of our tasks, we need the energies of our people—enlisted not only in grand enterprises, but more importantly in those small, splendid efforts that make headlines in the neighborhood newspaper instead of the national journal.

With these, we can build a great cathedral of the spirit—each of us raising it one stone at a time, as he reaches out to his neighbor, helping, caring, doing.

I do not offer a life of uninspiring ease. I do not call for a life of grim sacrifice. I ask you to join in a high adventure—one as rich as humanity itself, and as exciting as the times we live in.

The essence of freedom is that each of us shares in the shaping of his own destiny.

Until he has been part of a cause larger than himself, no man is truly whole. The way to fulfillment is in the use of our talents; we achieve nobility in the spirit that inspires that use.

As we measure what can be done, we shall promise only what we know we can produce, but as we chart our goals we shall be lifted by our dreams. No man can be fully free while his neighbor is not. To go forward at all is to go forward together.

This means black and white together, as one nation, not two. The laws have caught up with our conscience. What remains is to give life to what is in the law: to ensure at last that as all are born equal in dignity before God, all are born equal in dignity before man. As we learn to go forward together at home, let us also seek to go forward together with all mankind.

Let us take as our goal: where peace is unknown, make it welcome; where peace is fragile, make it strong; where peace is temporary, make it permanent.

After a period of confrontation, we are entering an era of negotiation. Let all nations know that during this administration our lines of communication will be open.

We seek an open world—open to ideas, open to the exchange of goods and people—a world in which no people, great or small, will live in angry isolation. We cannot expect to make everyone our friend, but we can try to make no one our enemy.

Those who would be our adversaries, we invite to a peaceful competition—not in conquering territory or extending dominion, but in enriching the life of man.

As we explore the reaches of space, let us go to the new worlds together—not as new worlds to be conquered, but as a new adventure to be shared.

With those who are willing to join, let us cooperate to reduce the burden of arms, to strengthen the structure of peace, to lift up the poor and the hungry.

But to all those who would be tempted by weakness, let us leave no doubt that we will be as strong as we need to be for as long as we need to be. Over the past twenty years, since I first came to this Capital as a freshman Congressman, I have visited most of the nations of the world.

I have come to know the leaders of the world, and the great forces, the hatreds, the fears that divide the world. I know that peace does not come through wishing for it—that there is no substitute for days and even years of patient and prolonged diplomacy. I also know the people of the world. I have seen the hunger of a homeless child, the pain of a man wounded in battle, the grief of a mother who has lost her son. I know these have no ideology, no race.

I know America. I know the heart of America is good.

I speak from my own heart, and the heart of my country, the deep concern we have for those who suffer, and those who sorrow.

I have taken an oath today in the presence of God and my countrymen to uphold and defend the Constitution of the United States. To that oath I now add this sacred commitment: I shall consecrate my office, my energies, and all the wisdom I can summon, to the cause of peace among nations. Let this message be heard by strong and weak alike:

The peace we seek to win is not victory over any other people, but the peace that comes "with healing in its wings"; with compassion for those who have suffered; with understanding for those who have opposed us; with the opportunity for all the peoples of this earth to choose their own destiny. Only a few short weeks ago, we shared the glory of man's first sight of the world as God sees it, as a single sphere reflecting light in the darkness.

As the Apollo astronauts flew over the moon's gray surface on Christmas Eve, they spoke to us of the beauty of earth—and in that voice so clear across the lunar distance, we heard them invoke God's blessing on its goodness.

In that moment, their view from the moon moved poet Archibald MacLeish to write:

"To see the earth as it truly is, small and blue and beautiful in that eternal silence where it floats, is to see ourselves as riders on the earth together, brothers on that bright loveliness in the eternal cold—brothers who know now they are truly brothers."

In that moment of surpassing technological triumph, men turned their thoughts toward home and humanity—seeing in that far perspective that man's destiny on earth is not divisible; telling us that however far we reach into the cosmos, our destiny lies not in the stars but on Earth itself, in our own hands, in our own hearts.

We have endured a long night of the American spirit. But as our eyes catch the dimness of the first rays of dawn, let us not curse the remaining dark. Let us gather the light.

Our destiny offers, not the cup of despair, but the chalice of opportunity. So let us seize it, not in fear, but in gladness—and, "riders on the earth together," let us go forward, firm in our faith, steadfast in our purpose, cautious of the dangers; but sustained by our confidence in the will of God and the promise of man.

Second Inaugural Address

Saturday, January 20, 1973

Mr. Vice President, Mr. Speaker, Mr. Chief Justice, Senator Cook, Mrs. Eisenhower, and my fellow citizens of this great and good country we share together:

When we met here four years ago, America was bleak in spirit, depressed by the prospect of seemingly endless war abroad and of destructive conflict at home.

As we meet here today, we stand on the threshold of a new era of peace in the world.

The central question before us is: How shall we use that peace? Let us resolve that this era we are about to enter will not be what other postwar periods have so often been: a time of retreat and isolation that leads to stagnation at home and invites new danger abroad.

Let us resolve that this will be what it can become: a time of great responsibilities greatly borne, in which we renew the spirit and the promise of America as we enter our third century as a nation.

This past year saw far-reaching results from our new policies for peace. By continuing to revitalize our traditional friendships, and by our missions to Peking and to Moscow, we were able to establish the base for a new and more durable pattern of relationships among the nations of the world. Because of America's bold initiatives, 1972 will be long remembered as the year of the greatest progress since the end of World War II toward a lasting peace in the world.

The peace we seek in the world is not the flimsy peace which is merely an interlude between wars, but a peace which can endure for generations to come.

It is important that we understand both the necessity and the limitations of America's role in maintaining that peace. Unless we in America work to preserve the peace, there will be no peace. Unless we in America work to preserve freedom, there will be no freedom.

But let us clearly understand the new nature of America's role, as a result of the new policies we have adopted over these past four years.

We shall respect our treaty commitments. We shall support vigorously the principle that no country has the right to impose its will or rule on another by force. We shall continue, in this era of negotiation, to work for the limitation of nuclear arms, and to reduce the danger of confrontation between the great powers.

We shall do our share in defending peace and freedom in the world. But we shall expect others to do their share.

The time has passed when America will make every other nation's conflict our own, or make every other nation's future our responsibility, or presume to tell the people of other nations how to manage their own affairs.

Just as we respect the right of each nation to determine its own future, we also recognize the responsibility of each nation to secure its own future.

Just as America's role is indispensable in preserving the world's peace, so is each nation's role indispensable in preserving its own peace.

Together with the rest of the world, let us resolve to move forward from the beginnings we have made. Let us continue to bring down the walls of hostility which have divided the world for too long, and to build in their place bridges of understanding—so that despite profound differences between systems of government, the people of the world can be friends.

Let us build a structure of peace in the world in which the weak are as safe as the strong—in which each respects the right of the other to live by a different system—in which those who would influence others will do so by the strength of their ideas, and not by the force of their arms.

Let us accept that high responsibility not as a burden, but gladly—gladly because the chance to build such a peace is the noblest endeavor in which a nation can engage; gladly, also, because only if we act greatly in meeting our responsibilities abroad will we remain a great Nation, and only if we remain a great Nation will we act greatly in meeting our challenges at home.

We have the chance today to do more than ever before in our history to make life better in America—to ensure better education, better health, better housing, better transportation, a cleaner environment—to restore respect for law, to make our communities more livable—and to insure the God-given right of every American to full and equal opportunity.

Because the range of our needs is so great—because the reach of our opportunities is so great—let us be bold in our determination to meet those needs in new ways.

Just as building a structure of peace abroad has required turning away from old policies that failed, so building a new era of progress at home requires turning away from old policies that have failed.

Abroad, the shift from old policies to new has not been a retreat from our responsibilities, but a better way to peace.

And at home, the shift from old policies to new will not be a retreat from our responsibilities, but a better way to progress.

Abroad and at home, the key to those new responsibilities lies in the placing and the division of responsibility. We have lived too long with the consequences of attempting to gather all power and responsibility in Washington.

Abroad and at home, the time has come to turn away from the condescending policies of paternalism—of "Washington knows best."

A person can be expected to act responsibly only if he has responsibility. This is human nature. So let us encourage individuals at home and nations abroad to do more for themselves, to decide more for themselves. Let us locate responsibility in more places. Let us measure what we will do for others by what they will do for themselves.

That is why today I offer no promise of a purely governmental solution for every problem. We have lived too long with that false promise. In trusting too much in government, we have asked of it more than it can deliver. This leads only to inflated expectations, to reduced individual effort, and to a disappointment and frustration that erode confidence both in what government can do and in what people can do.

Government must learn to take less from people so that people can do more for themselves.

Let us remember that America was built not by government, but by people—not by welfare, but by work—not by shirking responsibility, but by seeking responsibility.

In our own lives, let each of us ask—not just what will government do for me, but what can I do for myself?

In the challenges we face together, let each of us ask—not just how can government help, but how can I help?

Your National Government has a great and vital role to play. And I pledge to you that where this Government should act, we will act boldly and we will lead boldly. But just as important is the role that each and every one of us must play, as an individual and as a member of his own community.

From this day forward, let each of us make a solemn commitment in his own heart: to bear his responsibility, to do his part, to live his ideals—so that together, we can see the dawn of a new age of progress for America, and together, as we celebrate our 200th anniversary as a nation, we can do so proud in the fulfillment of our promise to ourselves and to the world.

As America's longest and most difficult war comes to an end, let us again learn to debate our differences with civility and decency. And let each of us reach out for that one precious quality government cannot provide—a new level of respect for the rights and feelings of one another, a new level of respect for the individual human dignity which is the cherished birthright of every American.

Above all else, the time has come for us to renew our faith in ourselves and in America.

In recent years, that faith has been challenged.

Our children have been taught to be ashamed of their country, ashamed of their parents, ashamed of America's record at home and of its role in the world.

At every turn, we have been beset by those who find everything wrong with America and little that is right. But I am confident that this will not be the judgment of history on these remarkable times in which we are privileged to live.

America's record in this century has been unparalleled in the world's history for its responsibility, for its generosity, for its creativity and for its progress.

Let us be proud that our system has produced and provided more freedom and more abundance, more widely shared, than any other system in the history of the world.

Let us be proud that in each of the four wars in which we have been engaged in this century, including the one we are now bringing to an end, we have fought not for our selfish advantage, but to help others resist aggression.

Let us be proud that by our bold, new initiatives, and by our steadfastness for peace with honor, we have made a break-through toward creating in the world what the world has not known before—a structure of peace that can last, not merely for our time, but for generations to come.

We are embarking here today on an era that presents challenges great as those any nation, or any generation, has ever faced.

We shall answer to God, to history, and to our conscience for the way in which we use these years.

As I stand in this place, so hallowed by history, I think of others who have stood here before me. I think of the dreams they had for America, and I think of how each recognized that he needed help far beyond himself in order to make those dreams come true.

Today, I ask your prayers that in the years ahead I may have God's help in making decisions that are right for America, and I pray for your help so that together we may be worthy of our challenge.

Let us pledge together to make these next four years the best four years in America's history, so that on its 200th birthday America will be as young and as vital as when it began, and as bright a beacon of hope for all the world.

Let us go forward from here confident in hope, strong in our faith in one another, sustained by our faith in God who created us, and striving always to serve His purpose.

Jimmy Carter

Inaugural Address

Thursday, January 20, 1977

FOR myself and for our Nation, I want to thank my predecessor for all he has done to heal our land.

In this outward and physical ceremony we attest once again to the inner and spiritual strength of our Nation. As my high school teacher, Miss Julia Coleman, used to say: "We must adjust to changing times and still hold to unchanging principles."

Here before me is the Bible used in the inauguration of our first President, in 1789, and I have just taken the oath of office on the Bible my mother gave me a few years ago, opened to a timeless admonition from the ancient prophet Micah:

"He hath showed thee, O man, what is good; and what doth the Lord require of thee, but to do justly, and to love mercy, and to walk humbly with thy God." (Micah 6:8)

This inauguration ceremony marks a new beginning, a new dedication within our Government, and a new spirit among us all. A President may sense and proclaim that new spirit, but only a people can provide it.

Two centuries ago our Nation's birth was a milestone in the long quest for freedom, but the bold and brilliant dream which excited the founders of this Nation still awaits its consummation. I have no new dream to set forth today, but rather urge a fresh faith in the old dream.

Ours was the first society openly to define itself in terms of both spirituality and of human liberty. It is that unique self-definition which has given us an exceptional appeal, but it also imposes on us a special obligation, to take on those moral duties which, when assumed, seem invariably to be in our own best interests.

You have given me a great responsibility—to stay close to you, to be worthy of you, and to exemplify what you are. Let us create together a new national spirit of unity and trust. Your strength can compensate for my weakness, and your wisdom can help to minimize my mistakes.

Let us learn together and laugh together and work together and pray together, confident that in the end we will triumph together in the right.

The American dream endures. We must once again have full faith in our country—and in one another. I believe America can be better. We can be even stronger than before.

Let our recent mistakes bring a resurgent commitment to the basic principles of our Nation, for we know that if we despise our own government we have no future. We recall in special times when we have stood briefly, but magnificently, united. In those times no prize was beyond our grasp.

But we cannot dwell upon remembered glory. We cannot afford to drift. We reject the prospect of failure or mediocrity or an inferior quality of life for any person. Our Government must at the same time be both competent and compassionate.

We have already found a high degree of personal liberty, and we are now struggling to enhance equality of opportunity. Our commitment to human rights must be absolute, our laws fair, our natural beauty preserved; the powerful must not persecute the weak, and human dignity must be enhanced. We have learned that "more" is not necessarily "better," that even our great Nation has its recognized limits, and that we can neither answer all questions nor solve all problems. We cannot afford to do everything, nor can we afford to lack boldness as we meet the future. So, together, in a spirit of individual sacrifice for the common good, we must simply do our best.

Our Nation can be strong abroad only if it is strong at home. And we know that the best way to enhance freedom in other lands is to demonstrate here that our democratic system is worthy of emulation.

To be true to ourselves, we must be true to others. We will not behave in foreign places so as to violate our rules and standards here at home, for we know that the trust which our Nation earns is essential to our strength.

The world itself is now dominated by a new spirit. Peoples more numerous and more politically aware are craving and now demanding their place in the sun—not just for the benefit of their own physical condition, but for basic human rights.

The passion for freedom is on the rise. Tapping this new spirit, there can be no nobler nor more ambitious task for America to undertake on this day of a new beginning than to help shape a just and peaceful world that is truly humane.

We are a strong nation, and we will maintain strength so sufficient that it need not be proven in combat—a quiet strength based not merely on the size of an arsenal, but on the nobility of ideas.

We will be ever vigilant and never vulnerable, and we will fight our wars against poverty, ignorance, and injustice—for those are the enemies against which our forces can be honorably marshaled.

We are a purely idealistic Nation, but let no one confuse our idealism with weakness.

Because we are free we can never be indifferent to the fate of freedom elsewhere. Our moral sense dictates a clearcut preference for these societies which share with us an abiding respect for individual human rights. We do not seek to intimidate, but it is clear that a world which others can dominate with impunity would be inhospitable to decency and a threat to the well-being of all people.

The world is still engaged in a massive armaments race designed to ensure continuing equivalent strength among potential adversaries. We pledge perseverance and wisdom in our efforts to limit the world's armaments to those necessary for each nation's own domestic safety. And we will move this year a step toward ultimate goal—the elimination of all nuclear weapons from this Earth. We urge all other people to join us, for success can mean life instead of death.

Within us, the people of the United States, there is evident a serious and purposeful rekindling of confidence. And I join in the hope that when my time as your President has ended, people might say this about our Nation:

– that we had remembered the words of Micah and renewed our search for humility, mercy, and justice;

– that we had torn down the barriers that separated those of different race and region and religion, and where there had been mistrust, built unity, with a respect for diversity;

– that we had found productive work for those able to perform it;

– that we had strengthened the American family, which is the basis of our society;

– that we had ensured respect for the law, and equal treatment under the law, for the weak and the powerful, for the rich and the poor;

– and that we had enabled our people to be proud of their own Government once again.

I would hope that the nations of the world might say that we had built a lasting peace, built not on weapons of war but on international policies which reflect our own most precious values.

These are not just my goals, and they will not be my accomplishments, but the affirmation of our Nation's continuing moral strength and our belief in an undiminished, ever-expanding American dream.

Ronald Reagan

First Inaugural Address

Tuesday, January 20, 1981

Senator Hatfield, Mr. Chief Justice, Mr. President, Vice President Bush, Vice President Mondale, Senator Baker, Speaker O'Neill, Reverend Moomaw, and my fellow citizens:

To a few of us here today, this is a solemn and most momentous occasion; and yet, in the history of our Nation, it is a commonplace occurrence. The orderly transfer of authority as called for in the Constitution routinely takes place as it has for almost two centuries and few of us stop to think how unique we really are. In the eyes of many in the world, this every-4-year ceremony we accept as normal is nothing less than a miracle.

Mr. President, I want our fellow citizens to know how much you did to carry on this tradition. By your gracious cooperation in the transition process, you have shown a watching world that we are a united people pledged to maintaining a political system which guarantees individual liberty to a greater degree than any other, and I thank you and your people for all your help in maintaining the continuity which is the bulwark of our Republic.

The business of our nation goes forward. These United States are confronted with an economic affliction of great proportions. We suffer from the longest and one of the worst sustained inflations in our national history. It distorts our economic decisions, penalizes thrift, and crushes the struggling young and the fixed-income elderly alike. It threatens to shatter the lives of millions of our people.

Idle industries have cast workers into unemployment, causing human misery and personal indignity. Those who do work are denied a fair return for their labor by a tax system which penalizes successful achievement and keeps us from maintaining full productivity.

But great as our tax burden is, it has not kept pace with public spending. For decades, we have piled deficit upon deficit, mortgaging our future and our children's future for the temporary convenience of the present. To continue this long trend is to guarantee tremendous social, cultural, political, and economic upheavals.

You and I, as individuals, can, by borrowing, live beyond our means, but for only a limited period of time. Why, then, should we think that collectively, as a nation, we are not bound by that same limitation?

We must act today in order to preserve tomorrow. And let there be no misunderstanding—we are going to begin to act, beginning today.

The economic ills we suffer have come upon us over several decades. They will not go away in days, weeks, or months, but they will go away. They will go away because we, as Americans, have the capacity now, as we have had in the past, to do whatever needs to be done to preserve this last and greatest bastion of freedom.

In this present crisis, government is not the solution to our problem.

From time to time, we have been tempted to believe that society has become too complex to be managed by self-rule, that government by an elite group is superior to government for, by, and of the people. But if no one among us is capable of governing himself, then who among us has the capacity to govern someone else? All of us together, in and out of government, must bear the burden. The solutions we seek must be equitable, with no one group singled out to pay a higher price.

We hear much of special interest groups. Our concern must be for a special interest group that has been too long neglected. It knows no sectional boundaries or ethnic and racial divisions, and it crosses political party lines. It is made up of men and women who raise our food, patrol our streets, man our mines and our factories, teach our children, keep our homes, and heal us when we are sick—professionals, industrialists, shopkeepers, clerks, cabbies, and truckdrivers. They are, in short, "We the people," this breed called Americans.

Well, this administration's objective will be a healthy, vigorous, growing economy that provides equal opportunity for all Americans, with no barriers born of bigotry or discrimination. Putting America back to work means putting all Americans back to work. Ending inflation means freeing all Americans from the terror of runaway living costs. All must share in the productive work of this "new beginning" and all must share in the bounty of a revived economy. With the idealism and fair play which are the core of our system and our strength, we can have a strong and prosperous America at peace with itself and the world.

So, as we begin, let us take inventory. We are a nation that has a government—not the other way around. And this makes us special among the nations of the Earth. Our Government has no power except that granted it by the people. It is time to check and reverse the growth of government which shows signs of having grown beyond the consent of the governed.

It is my intention to curb the size and influence of the Federal establishment and to demand recognition of the distinction between the powers granted to the Federal Government and those reserved to the States or to the people. All of us need to be reminded that the Federal Government did not create the States; the States created the Federal Government.

Now, so there will be no misunderstanding, it is not my intention to do away with government. It is, rather, to make it work—work with us, not over us; to stand by our side, not ride on our back. Government can and must provide opportunity, not smother it; foster productivity, not stifle it.

If we look to the answer as to why, for so many years, we achieved so much, prospered as no other people on Earth, it was because here, in this land, we unleashed the energy and individual genius of man to a greater extent than has ever been done before. Freedom and the dignity of the individual have been more available and assured here than in any other place on Earth. The price for this freedom at times has been high, but we have never been unwilling to pay that price.

It is no coincidence that our present troubles parallel and are proportionate to the intervention and intrusion in our lives that result from unnecessary and excessive growth of government. It is time for us to realize that we are too great a nation to limit ourselves to small dreams. We are not, as some would have us believe, doomed to an inevitable decline. I do not believe in a fate that will fall on us no matter what we do. I do believe in a fate that will fall on us if we do nothing. So, with all the creative energy at our command, let us begin an era of national renewal. Let us renew our determination, our courage, and our strength. And let us renew our faith and our hope.

We have every right to dream heroic dreams. Those who say that we are in a time when there are no heroes just don't know where to look. You can see heroes every day going in and out of factory gates. Others, a handful in number, produce enough food to feed all of us and then the world beyond. You meet heroes across a counter—and they are on both sides of that counter. There are entrepreneurs with faith in themselves and faith in an idea who create new jobs, new wealth and opportunity. They are individuals and families whose taxes support the Government and whose voluntary gifts support church, charity, culture, art, and education. Their patriotism is quiet but deep. Their values sustain our national life.

I have used the words "they" and "their" in speaking of these heroes. I could say "you" and "your" because I am addressing the heroes of whom I speak—you, the citizens of this blessed land. Your dreams, your hopes, your goals are going to be the dreams, the hopes, and the goals of this administration, so help me God.

We shall reflect the compassion that is so much a part of your makeup. How can we love our country and not love our countrymen, and loving them, reach out a hand when they fall, heal them when they are sick, and provide opportunities to make them self-sufficient so they will be equal in fact and not just in theory?

Can we solve the problems confronting us? Well, the answer is an unequivocal and emphatic "yes." To paraphrase Winston Churchill, I did not take the oath I have just taken with the intention of presiding over the dissolution of the world's strongest economy.

In the days ahead I will propose removing the roadblocks that have slowed our economy and reduced productivity. Steps will be taken aimed at restoring the balance between the various levels of government. Progress may be slow—measured in inches and feet, not miles—but we will progress. Is it time to reawaken this industrial giant, to get government back within its means, and to lighten our punitive tax burden. And these will be our first priorities, and on these principles, there will be no compromise.

On the eve of our struggle for independence a man who might have been one of the greatest among the Founding Fathers, Dr. Joseph Warren, President of the Massachusetts Congress, said to his fellow Americans, "Our country is in danger, but not to be despaired of.... On you depend the fortunes of America. You are to decide the important questions upon which rests the happiness and the liberty of millions yet unborn. Act worthy of yourselves."

Well, I believe we, the Americans of today, are ready to act worthy of ourselves, ready to do what must be done to ensure happiness and liberty for ourselves, our children and our children's children.

And as we renew ourselves here in our own land, we will be seen as having greater strength throughout the world. We will again be the exemplar of freedom and a beacon of hope for those who do not now have freedom.

To those neighbors and allies who share our freedom, we will strengthen our historic ties and assure them of our support and firm commitment. We will match loyalty with loyalty. We will strive for mutually beneficial relations. We will not use our friendship to impose on their sovereignty, for our own sovereignty is not for sale.

As for the enemies of freedom, those who are potential adversaries, they will be reminded that peace is the highest aspiration of the American people. We will negotiate for it, sacrifice for it; we will not surrender for it—now or ever.

Our forbearance should never be misunderstood. Our reluctance for conflict should not be misjudged as a failure of will. When action is required to preserve our national security, we will act. We will maintain sufficient strength to prevail if need be, knowing that if we do so we have the best chance of never having to use that strength.

Above all, we must realize that no arsenal, or no weapon in the arsenals of the world, is so formidable as the will and moral courage of free men and women. It is a weapon our adversaries in today's world do not have. It is a weapon that we as Americans do have. Let that be understood by those who practice terrorism and prey upon their neighbors.

I am told that tens of thousands of prayer meetings are being held on this day, and for that I am deeply grateful. We are a nation under God, and I believe God intended for us to be free. It would be fitting and good, I think, if on each Inauguration Day in future years it should be declared a day of prayer.

This is the first time in history that this ceremony has been held, as you have been told, on this West Front of the Capitol. Standing here, one faces a magnificent vista, opening up on this city's special beauty and history. At the end of this open mall are those shrines to the giants on whose shoulders we stand.

Directly in front of me, the monument to a monumental man: George Washington, Father of our country. A man of humility who came to greatness reluctantly. He led America out of revolutionary victory into infant nationhood. Off to one side, the stately memorial to Thomas Jefferson. The Declaration of Independence flames with his eloquence.

And then beyond the Reflecting Pool the dignified columns of the Lincoln Memorial. Whoever would understand in his heart the meaning of America will find it in the life of Abraham Lincoln.

Beyond those monuments to heroism is the Potomac River, and on the far shore the sloping hills of Arlington National Cemetery with its row on row of simple white markers bearing crosses or Stars of David. They add up to only a tiny fraction of the price that has been paid for our freedom.

Each one of those markers is a monument to the kinds of hero I spoke of earlier. Their lives ended in places called Belleau Wood, The Argonne, Omaha Beach, Salerno and halfway around the world on Guadalcanal, Tarawa, Pork Chop Hill, the Chosin Reservoir, and in a hundred rice paddies and jungles of a place called Vietnam.

Under one such marker lies a young man—Martin Treptow—who left his job in a small town barber shop in 1917 to go to France with the famed Rainbow Division. There, on the western front, he was killed trying to carry a message between battalions under heavy artillery fire.

We are told that on his body was found a diary. On the flyleaf under the heading, "My Pledge," he had written these words: "America must win this war. Therefore, I will work, I will save, I will sacrifice, I will endure, I will fight cheerfully and do my utmost, as if the issue of the whole struggle depended on me alone."

The crisis we are facing today does not require of us the kind of sacrifice that Martin Treptow and so many thousands of others were called upon to make. It does require, however, our best effort, and our willingness to believe in ourselves and to believe in our capacity to perform great deeds; to believe that together, with God's help, we can and will resolve the problems which now confront us.

And, after all, why shouldn't we believe that? We are Americans. God bless you, and thank you.

Second Inaugural Address

Saturday, January 20, 1973

Senator Mathias, Chief Justice Burger, Vice President Bush, Speaker O'Neill, Senator Dole, Reverend Clergy, members of my family and friends, and my fellow citizens:

This day has been made brighter with the presence here of one who, for a time, has been absent—Senator John Stennis.

God bless you and welcome back.

There is, however, one who is not with us today: Representative Gillis Long of Louisiana left us last night. I wonder if we could all join in a moment of silent prayer. (Moment of silent prayer.) Amen.

There are no words adequate to express my thanks for the great honor that you have bestowed on me. I will do my utmost to be deserving of your trust.

This is, as Senator Mathias told us, the 50th time that we the people have celebrated this historic occasion. When the first President, George Washington, placed his hand upon the Bible, he stood less than a single day's journey by horseback from raw, untamed wilderness. There were 4 million Americans in a union of 13 States. Today we are 60 times as many in a union of 50 States. We have lighted the world with our inventions, gone to the aid of mankind wherever in the world there was a cry for help, journeyed to the Moon and safely returned. So much has changed. And yet we stand together as we did two centuries ago.

When I took this oath four years ago, I did so in a time of economic stress. Voices were raised saying we had to look to our past for the greatness and glory. But we, the present-day Americans, are not given to looking backward. In this blessed land, there is always a better tomorrow.

Four years ago, I spoke to you of a new beginning and we have accomplished that. But in another sense, our new beginning is a continuation of that beginning created two centuries ago when, for the first time in history, government, the people said, was not our master, it is our servant; its only power that which we the people allow it to have.

That system has never failed us, but, for a time, we failed the system. We asked things of government that government was not equipped to give. We yielded authority to the National Government that properly belonged to States or to local governments or to the people themselves. We allowed taxes and inflation to rob us of our earnings and savings and watched the great industrial machine that had made us the most productive people on Earth slow down and the number of unemployed increase.

By 1980, we knew it was time to renew our faith, to strive with all our strength toward the ultimate in individual freedom consistent with an orderly society.

We believed then and now there are no limits to growth and human progress when men and women are free to follow their dreams.

And we were right to believe that. Tax rates have been reduced, inflation cut dramatically, and more people are employed than ever before in our history.

We are creating a nation once again vibrant, robust, and alive. But there are many mountains yet to climb. We will not rest until every American enjoys the fullness of freedom, dignity, and opportunity as our birthright. It is our birthright as citizens of this great Republic, and we'll meet this challenge.

These will be years when Americans have restored their confidence and tradition of progress; when our values of faith, family, work, and neighborhood were restated for a modern age; when our economy was finally freed from government's grip; when we made sincere efforts at meaningful arms reduction, rebuilding our defenses, our economy, and developing new technologies, and helped preserve peace in a troubled world; when Americans courageously supported the struggle for liberty, self-government, and free enterprise throughout the world, and turned the tide of history away from totalitarian darkness and into the warm sunlight of human freedom.

My fellow citizens, our Nation is poised for greatness. We must do what we know is right and do it with all our might. Let history say of us, "These were golden years—when the American Revolution was reborn, when freedom gained new life, when America reached for her best."

Our two-party system has served us well over the years, but never better than in those times of great challenge when we came together not as Democrats or Republicans, but as Americans united in a common cause.

Two of our Founding Fathers, a Boston lawyer named Adams and a Virginia planter named Jefferson, members of that remarkable group who met in Independence Hall and dared to think they could start the world over again, left us an important lesson. They had become political rivals in the Presidential election of 1800. Then years later, when both were retired, and age had softened their anger, they began to speak to each other again through letters. A bond was reestablished between those two who had helped create this government of ours.

In 1826, the 50th anniversary of the Declaration of Independence, they both died. They died on the same day, within a few hours of each other, and that day was the Fourth of July.

In one of those letters exchanged in the sunset of their lives, Jefferson wrote: "It carries me back to the times when, beset with difficulties and dangers, we were fellow laborers in the same cause, struggling for what is most valuable to man, his right to self-government. Laboring always at the same oar, with some wave ever ahead threatening to overwhelm us, and yet passing harmless ... we rode through the storm with heart and hand."

Well, with heart and hand, let us stand as one today: One people under God determined that our future shall be worthy of our past. As we do, we must not repeat the well-intentioned errors of our past. We must never again abuse the trust of working men and women, by sending their earnings on a futile chase after the spiraling demands of a bloated Federal Establishment. You elected us in 1980 to end this prescription for disaster, and I don't believe you reelected us in 1984 to reverse course.

At the heart of our efforts is one idea vindicated by 25 straight months of economic growth: Freedom and incentives unleash the drive and entrepreneurial genius that are the core of human progress. We have begun to increase the rewards for work, savings, and investment; reduce the increase in the cost and size of government and its interference in people's lives.

We must simplify our tax system, make it more fair, and bring the rates down for all who work and earn. We must think anew and move with a new boldness, so every American who seeks work can find work; so the least among us shall have an equal chance to achieve the greatest things—to be heroes who heal our sick, feed the hungry, protect peace among nations, and leave this world a better place.

The time has come for a new American emancipation—a great national drive to tear down economic barriers and liberate the spirit of enterprise in the most distressed areas of our country. My friends, together we can do this, and do it we must, so help me God.

From new freedom will spring new opportunities for growth, a more productive, fulfilled and united people, and a stronger America— an America that will lead the technological revolution, and also open its mind and heart and soul to the treasures of literature, music, and poetry, and the values of faith, courage, and love.

A dynamic economy, with more citizens working and paying taxes, will be our strongest tool to bring down budget deficits. But an almost unbroken 50 years of deficit spending has finally brought us to a time of reckoning. We have come to a turning point, a moment for hard decisions. I have asked the Cabinet and my staff a question, and now I put the same question to all of you: If not us, who? And if not now, when? It must be done by all of us going forward with a program aimed at reaching a balanced budget. We can then begin reducing the national debt.

I will shortly submit a budget to the Congress aimed at freezing government program spending for the next year. Beyond that, we must take further steps to permanently control Government's power to tax and spend. We must act now to protect future generations from Government's desire to spend its citizens' money and tax them into servitude when the bills come due. Let us make it unconstitutional for the Federal Government to spend more than the Federal Government takes in.

We have already started returning to the people and to State and local governments responsibilities better handled by them. Now, there is a place for the Federal Government in matters of social compassion. But our fundamental goals must be to reduce dependency and upgrade the dignity of those who are infirm or disadvantaged. And here a growing economy and support from family and community offer our best chance for a society where compassion is a way of life, where the old and infirm are cared for, the young and, yes, the unborn protected, and the unfortunate looked after and made self-sufficient.

And there is another area where the Federal Government can play a part. As an older American, I remember a time when people of different race, creed, or ethnic origin in our land found hatred and prejudice installed in social custom and, yes, in law. There is no story more heartening in our history than the progress that we have made toward the "brotherhood of man" that God intended for us. Let us resolve there will be no turning back or hesitation on the road to an America rich in dignity and abundant with opportunity for all our citizens.

Let us resolve that we the people will build an American opportunity society in which all of us—white and black, rich and poor, young and old—will go forward together arm in arm. Again, let us remember that though our heritage is one of blood lines from every corner of the Earth, we are all Americans pledged to carry on this last, best hope of man on Earth.

I have spoken of our domestic goals and the limitations which we should put on our National Government. Now let me turn to a task which is the primary responsibility of National Government—the safety and security of our people.

Today, we utter no prayer more fervently than the ancient prayer for peace on Earth. Yet history has shown that peace will not come, nor will our freedom be preserved, by good will alone. There are those in the world who scorn our vision of human dignity and freedom. One nation, the Soviet Union, has conducted the greatest military buildup in the history of man, building arsenals of awesome offensive weapons.

We have made progress in restoring our defense capability. But much remains to be done. There must be no wavering by us, nor any doubts by others, that America will meet her responsibilities to remain free, secure, and at peace.

There is only one way safely and legitimately to reduce the cost of national security, and that is to reduce the need for it. And this we are trying to do in negotiations with the Soviet Union. We are not just discussing limits on a further increase of nuclear weapons. We seek, instead, to reduce their number. We seek the total elimination one day of nuclear weapons from the face of the Earth.

Now, for decades, we and the Soviets have lived under the threat of mutual assured destruction; if either resorted to the use of nuclear weapons, the other could retaliate and destroy the one who had started it. Is there either logic or morality in believing that if one side threatens to kill tens of millions of our people, our only recourse is to threaten killing tens of millions of theirs?

I have approved a research program to find, if we can, a security shield that would destroy nuclear missiles before they reach their target. It wouldn't kill people, it would destroy weapons. It wouldn't militarize space, it would help demilitarize the arsenals of Earth. It would render nuclear weapons obsolete. We will meet with the Soviets, hoping that we can agree on a way to rid the world of the threat of nuclear destruction.

We strive for peace and security, heartened by the changes all around us. Since the turn of the century, the number of democracies in the world has grown fourfold. Human freedom is on the march, and nowhere more so than our own hemisphere. Freedom is one of the deepest and noblest aspirations of the human spirit. People, worldwide, hunger for the right of self-determination, for those inalienable rights that make for human dignity and progress.

America must remain freedom's staunchest friend, for freedom is our best ally. And it is the world's only hope, to conquer poverty and preserve peace. Every blow we inflict against poverty will be a blow against its dark allies of oppression and war. Every victory for human freedom will be a victory for world peace. So we go forward today, a nation still mighty in its youth and powerful in its purpose. With our alliances strengthened, with our economy leading the world to a new age of economic expansion, we look forward to a world rich in possibilities. And all this because we have worked and acted together, not as members of political parties, but as Americans.

My friends, we live in a world that is lit by lightning. So much is changing and will change, but so much endures, and transcends time.

History is a ribbon, always unfurling; history is a journey. And as we continue our journey, we think of those who traveled before us. We stand together again at the steps of this symbol of our democracy—or we would have been standing at the steps if it hadn't gotten so cold. Now we are standing inside this symbol of our democracy. Now we hear again the echoes of our past: a general falls to his knees in the hard snow of Valley Forge; a lonely President paces the darkened halls, and ponders his struggle to preserve the Union; the men of the Alamo call out encouragement to each other; a settler pushes west and sings a song, and the song echoes out forever and fills the unknowing air.

It is the American sound. It is hopeful, big-hearted, idealistic, daring, decent, and fair. That's our heritage; that is our song. We sing it still. For all our problems, our differences, we are together as of old, as we raise our voices to the God who is the Author of this most tender music. And may He continue to hold us close as we fill the world with our sound—sound in unity, affection, and love—one people under God, dedicated to the dream of freedom that He has placed in the human heart, called upon now to pass that dream on to a waiting and hopeful world.

God bless you and may God bless America.

George Bush

Inaugural Address

Friday, January 20, 1989

Mr. Chief Justice, Mr. President, Vice President Quayle, Senator Mitchell, Speaker Wright, Senator Dole, Congressman Michel, and fellow citizens, neighbors, and friends:

There is a man here who has earned a lasting place in our hearts and in our history. President Reagan, on behalf of our Nation, I thank you for the wonderful things that you have done for America.

I have just repeated word for word the oath taken by George Washington 200 years ago, and the Bible on which I placed my hand is the Bible on which he placed his. It is right that the memory of Washington be with us today, not only because this is our Bicentennial Inauguration, but because Washington remains the Father of our Country. And he would, I think, be gladdened by this day; for today is the concrete expression of a stunning fact: our continuity these 200 years since our government began.

We meet on democracy's front porch, a good place to talk as neighbors and as friends. For this is a day when our nation is made whole, when our differences, for a moment, are suspended.

And my first act as President is a prayer. I ask you to bow your heads:

Heavenly Father, we bow our heads and thank You for Your love. Accept our thanks for the peace that yields this day and the shared faith that makes its continuance likely. Make us strong to do Your work, willing to heed and hear Your will, and write on our hearts these words: "Use power to help people." For we are given power not to advance our own purposes, nor to make a great show in the world, nor a name. There is but one just use of power, and it is to serve people. Help us to remember it, Lord. Amen.

I come before you and assume the Presidency at a moment rich with promise. We live in a peaceful, prosperous time, but we can make it better. For a new breeze is blowing, and a world refreshed by freedom seems reborn; for in man's heart, if not in fact, the day of the dictator is over. The totalitarian era is passing, its old ideas blown away like leaves from an ancient, lifeless tree. A new breeze is blowing, and a nation refreshed by freedom stands ready to push on. There is new ground to be broken, and new action to be taken. There are times when the future seems thick as a fog; you sit and wait, hoping the mists will lift and reveal the right path. But this is a time when the future seems a door you can walk right through into a room called tomorrow.

Great nations of the world are moving toward democracy through the door to freedom. Men and women of the world move toward free markets through the door to prosperity. The people of the world agitate for free expression and free thought through the door to the moral and intellectual satisfactions that only liberty allows.

We know what works: Freedom works. We know what's right: Freedom is right. We know how to secure a more just and prosperous life for man on Earth: through free markets, free speech, free elections, and the exercise of free will unhampered by the state.

For the first time in this century, for the first time in perhaps all history, man does not have to invent a system by which to live. We don't have to talk late into the night about which form of government is better. We don't have to wrest justice from the kings. We only have to summon it from within ourselves. We must act on what we know. I take as my guide the hope of a saint: In crucial things, unity; in important things, diversity; in all things, generosity.

America today is a proud, free nation, decent and civil, a place we cannot help but love. We know in our hearts, not loudly and proudly, but as a simple fact, that this country has meaning beyond what we see, and that our strength is a force for good. But have we changed as a nation even in our time? Are we enthralled with material things, less appreciative of the nobility of work and sacrifice?

My friends, we are not the sum of our possessions. They are not the measure of our lives. In our hearts we know what matters. We cannot hope only to leave our children a bigger car, a bigger bank account. We must hope to give them a sense of what it means to be a loyal friend, a loving parent, a citizen who leaves his home, his neighborhood and town better than he found it. What do we want the men and women who work with us to say when we are no longer there? That we were more driven to succeed than anyone around us? Or that we stopped to ask if a sick child had gotten better, and stayed a moment there to trade a word of friendship?

No President, no government, can teach us to remember what is best in what we are. But if the man you have chosen to lead this government can help make a difference; if he can celebrate the quieter, deeper successes that are made not of gold and silk, but of better hearts and finer souls; if he can do these things, then he must.

America is never wholly herself unless she is engaged in high moral principle. We as a people have such a purpose today. It is to make kinder the face of the Nation and gentler the face of the world. My friends, we have work to do. There are the homeless, lost and roaming. There are the children who have nothing, no love, no normalcy. There are those who cannot free themselves of enslavement to whatever addiction—drugs, welfare, the demoralization that rules the slums. There is crime to be conquered, the rough crime of the streets. There are young women to be helped who are about to become mothers of children they can't care for and might not love. They need our care, our guidance, and our education, though we bless them for choosing life.

The old solution, the old way, was to think that public money alone could end these problems. But we have learned that is not so. And in any case, our funds are low. We have a deficit to bring down. We have more will than wallet; but will is what we need. We will make the hard choices, looking at what we have and perhaps allocating it differently, making our decisions based on honest need and prudent safety. And then we will do the wisest thing of all: We will turn to the only resource we have that in times of need always grows—the goodness and the courage of the American people.

I am speaking of a new engagement in the lives of others, a new activism, hands-on and involved, that gets the job done. We must bring in the generations, harnessing the unused talent of the elderly and the unfocused energy of the young. For not only leadership is passed from generation to generation, but so is stewardship. And the generation born after the Second World War has come of age.

I have spoken of a thousand points of light, of all the community organizations that are spread like stars throughout the Nation, doing good. We will work hand in hand, encouraging, sometimes leading, sometimes being led, rewarding. We will work on this in the White House, in the Cabinet agencies. I will go to the people and the programs that are the brighter points of light, and I will ask every member of my government to become involved. The old ideas are new again because they are not old, they are timeless: duty, sacrifice, commitment, and a patriotism that finds its expression in taking part and pitching in.

We need a new engagement, too, between the Executive and the Congress. The challenges before us will be thrashed out with the House and the Senate. We must bring the Federal budget into balance. And we must ensure that America stands before the world united, strong, at peace, and fiscally sound. But, of course, things may be difficult. We need compromise; we have had dissension. We need harmony; we have had a chorus of discordant voices.

For Congress, too, has changed in our time. There has grown a certain divisiveness. We have seen the hard looks and heard the statements in which not each other's ideas are challenged, but each other's motives. And our great parties have too often been far apart and untrusting of each other. It has been this way since Vietnam. That war cleaves us still. But, friends, that war began in earnest a quarter of a century ago; and surely the statute of limitations has been reached. This is a fact: The final lesson of Vietnam is that no great nation can long

afford to be sundered by a memory. A new breeze is blowing, and the old bipartisanship must be made new again.

To my friends—and yes, I do mean friends—in the loyal opposition—and yes, I mean loyal: I put out my hand. I am putting out my hand to you, Mr. Speaker. I am putting out my hand to you, Mr. Majority Leader. For this is the thing: This is the age of the offered hand. We can't turn back clocks, and I don't want to. But when our fathers were young, Mr. Speaker, our differences ended at the water's edge. And we don't wish to turn back time, but when our mothers were young, Mr. Majority Leader, the Congress and the Executive were capable of working together to produce a budget on which this nation could live. Let us negotiate soon and hard. But in the end, let us produce. The American people await action. They didn't send us here to bicker. They ask us to rise above the merely partisan. "In crucial things, unity"—and this, my friends, is crucial.

To the world, too, we offer new engagement and a renewed vow: We will stay strong to protect the peace. The "offered hand" is a reluctant fist; but once made, strong, and can be used with great effect. There are today Americans who are held against their will in foreign lands, and Americans who are unaccounted for. Assistance can be shown here, and will be long remembered. Good will begets good will. Good faith can be a spiral that endlessly moves on.

Great nations like great men must keep their word. When America says something, America means it, whether a treaty or an agreement or a vow made on marble steps. We will always try to speak clearly, for candor is a compliment, but subtlety, too, is good and has its place. While keeping our alliances and friendships around the world strong, ever strong, we will continue the new closeness with the Soviet Union, consistent both with our security and with progress. One might say that our new relationship in part reflects the triumph of hope and strength over experience. But hope is good, and so are strength and vigilance.

Here today are tens of thousands of our citizens who feel the understandable satisfaction of those who have taken part in democracy and seen their hopes fulfilled. But my thoughts have been turning the past few days to those who would be watching at home, to an older fellow who will throw a salute by himself when the flag goes by, and the women who will tell her sons the words of the battle hymns. I don't mean this to be sentimental. I mean that on days like this, we remember that we are all part of a continuum, inescapably connected by the ties that bind.

Our children are watching in schools throughout our great land. And to them I say, thank you for watching democracy's big day. For democracy belongs to us all, and freedom is like a beautiful kite that can go higher and higher with the breeze. And to all I say: No matter what your circumstances or where you are, you are part of this day, you are part of the life of our great nation.

A President is neither prince nor pope, and I don't seek a window on men's souls. In fact, I yearn for a greater tolerance, an easy-goingness about each other's attitudes and way of life.

There are few clear areas in which we as a society must rise up united and express our intolerance. The most obvious now is drugs. And when that first cocaine was smuggled in on a ship, it may as well have been a deadly bacteria, so much has it hurt the body, the soul of our country. And there is much to be done and to be said, but take my word for it: This scourge will stop.

And so, there is much to do; and tomorrow the work begins. I do not mistrust the future; I do not fear what is ahead. For our problems are large, but our heart is larger. Our challenges are great, but our will is greater.

And if our flaws are endless, God's love is truly boundless. Some see leadership as high drama, and the sound of trumpets calling, and sometimes it is that. But I see history as a book with many pages, and each day we fill a page with acts of hopefulness and meaning. The new breeze blows, a page turns, the story unfolds. And so today a chapter begins, a small and stately story of unity, diversity, and generosity— shared, and written, together.

Thank you. God bless you and God bless the United States of America.

Bill Clinton

First Inaugural Address

Wednesday, January 21, 1993

My fellow citizens:

Today we celebrate the mystery of American renewal. This ceremony is held in the depth of winter. But, by the words we speak and the faces we show the world, we force the spring.

A spring reborn in the world's oldest democracy, that brings forth the vision and courage to reinvent America. When our founders boldly declared America's independence to the world and our purposes to the Almighty, they knew that America, to endure, would have to change.

Not change for change's sake, but change to preserve America's ideals—life, liberty, the pursuit of happiness. Though we march to the music of our time, our mission is timeless.

Each generation of Americans must define what it means to be an American. On behalf of our nation, I salute my predecessor, President Bush, for his half-century of service to America. And I thank the millions of men and women whose steadfastness and sacrifice triumphed over Depression, fascism and Communism.

Today, a generation raised in the shadows of the Cold War assumes new responsibilities in a world warmed by the sunshine of freedom but threatened still by ancient hatreds and new plagues.

Raised in unrivaled prosperity, we inherit an economy that is still the world's strongest, but is weakened by business failures, stagnant wages, increasing inequality, and deep divisions among our people. When George Washington first took the oath I have just sworn to uphold, news traveled slowly across the land by horseback and across the ocean by boat. Now, the sights and sounds of this ceremony are broadcast instantaneously to billions around the world.

Communications and commerce are global; investment is mobile; technology is almost magical; and ambition for a better life is now universal. We earn our livelihood in peaceful competition with people all across the earth. Profound and powerful forces are shaking and remaking our world, and the urgent question of our time is whether we can make change our friend and not our enemy.

This new world has already enriched the lives of millions of Americans who are able to compete and win in it. But when most people are working harder for less; when others cannot work at all; when the cost of health care devastates families and threatens to bankrupt many of our enterprises, great and small; when fear of crime robs law-abiding citizens of their freedom; and when millions of poor children cannot even imagine the lives we are calling them to lead—we have not made change our friend. We know we have to face hard truths and take strong steps. But we have not done so. Instead, we have drifted, and that drifting has eroded our resources, fractured our economy, and shaken our confidence.

Though our challenges are fearsome, so are our strengths. And Americans have ever been a restless, questing, hopeful people. We must bring to our task today the vision and will of those who came before us.

From our revolution, the Civil War, to the Great Depression to the civil rights movement, our people have always mustered the determination to construct from these crises the pillars of our history.

Thomas Jefferson believed that to preserve the very foundations of our nation, we would need dramatic change from time to time. Well, my fellow citizens, this is our time. Let us embrace it. Our democracy must be not only the envy of the world but the engine of our own renewal. There is nothing wrong with America that cannot be cured by what is right with America.

And so today, we pledge an end to the era of deadlock and drift—a new season of American renewal has begun.

To renew America, we must be bold.

We must do what no generation has had to do before. We must invest more in our own people, in their jobs, in their future, and at the same time cut our massive debt. And we must do so in a world in which we must compete for every opportunity.

It will not be easy; it will require sacrifice. But it can be done, and done fairly, not choosing sacrifice for its own sake, but for our own sake. We must provide for our nation the way a family provides for its children.

Our Founders saw themselves in the light of posterity. We can do no less. Anyone who has ever watched a child's eyes wander into sleep knows what posterity is. Posterity is the world to come—the world for whom we hold our ideals, from whom we have borrowed our planet, and to whom we bear sacred responsibility.

We must do what America does best: offer more opportunity to all and demand responsibility from all.

It is time to break the bad habit of expecting something for nothing, from our government or from each other. Let us all take more responsibility, not only for ourselves and our families but for our communities and our country.

To renew America, we must revitalize our democracy. This beautiful capital, like every capital since the dawn of civilization, is often a place of intrigue and calculation. Powerful people maneuver for position and worry endlessly about who is in and who is out, who is up and who is down, forgetting those people whose toil and sweat sends us here and pays our way.

Americans deserve better, and in this city today, there are people who want to do better. And so I say to all of us here, let us resolve to reform our politics, so that power and privilege no longer shout down the voice of the people. Let us put aside personal advantage so that we can feel the pain and see the promise of America.

Let us resolve to make our government a place for what Franklin Roosevelt called "bold, persistent experimentation," a government for our tomorrows, not our yesterdays. Let us give this capital back to the people to whom it belongs.

To renew America, we must meet challenges abroad as well at home. There is no longer division between what is foreign and what is domestic—the world economy, the world environment, the world AIDS crisis, the world arms race—they affect us all.

Today, as an old order passes, the new world is more free but less stable. Communism's collapse has called forth old animosities and new dangers. Clearly America must continue to lead the world we did so much to make. While America rebuilds at home, we will not shrink from the challenges, nor fail to seize the opportunities, of this new world. Together with our friends and allies, we will work to shape change, lest it engulf us.

When our vital interests are challenged, or the will and conscience of the international community is defied, we will act—with peaceful diplomacy when ever possible, with force when necessary. The brave Americans serving our nation today in the Persian Gulf, in Somalia, and wherever else they stand are testament to our resolve. But our greatest strength is the power of our ideas, which are still new in many lands. Across the world, we see them embraced—and we rejoice. Our hopes, our hearts, our hands, are with those on every continent who are building democracy and freedom. Their cause is America's cause.

The American people have summoned the change we celebrate today. You have raised your voices in an unmistakable chorus. You have cast your votes in historic numbers. And you have changed the face of Congress, the presidency and the political process itself. Yes, you, my fellow Americans have forced the spring. Now, we must do the work the season demands.

To that work I now turn, with all the authority of my office. I ask the Congress to join with me. But no president, no Congress, no government, can undertake this mission alone. My fellow Americans, you, too, must play your part in our renewal. I challenge a new generation of young Americans to a season of service—to act on your idealism by helping troubled children, keeping company with those in need, reconnecting our torn communities. There is so much to be done—enough indeed for millions of others who are still young in spirit to give of themselves in service, too.

In serving, we recognize a simple but powerful truth—we need each other. And we must care for one another. Today, we do more than celebrate America; we rededicate ourselves to the very idea of America.

An idea born in revolution and renewed through 2 centuries of challenge. An idea tempered by the knowledge that, but for fate, we—the fortunate and the unfortunate—might have been each other. An idea ennobled by the faith that our nation can summon from its myriad diversity the deepest measure of unity. An idea infused with the conviction that America's long heroic journey must go forever upward.

And so, my fellow Americans, at the edge of the 21st century, let us begin with energy and hope, with faith and discipline, and let us work until our work is done. The scripture says, "And let us not be weary in well-doing, for in due season, we shall reap, if we faint not."

From this joyful mountaintop of celebration, we hear a call to service in the valley. We have heard the trumpets. We have changed the guard. And now, each in our way, and with God's help, we must answer the call.

Thank you and God bless you all.

Second Inaugural Address

January 20, 1997

My fellow citizens:

At this last presidential inauguration of the 20th century, let us lift our eyes toward the challenges that await us in the next century. It is our great good fortune that time and chance have put us not only at the edge of a new century, in a new millennium, but on the edge of a bright new prospect in human affairs—a moment that will define our course, and our character, for decades to come. We must keep our old democracy forever young. Guided by the ancient vision of a promised land, let us set our sights upon a land of new promise.

The promise of America was born in the 18th century out of the bold conviction that we are all created equal. It was extended and preserved in the 19th century, when our nation spread across the continent, saved the union, and abolished the awful scourge of slavery.

Then, in turmoil and triumph, that promise exploded onto the world stage to make this the American Century. And what a century it has been. America became the world's mightiest industrial power; saved the world from tyranny in two world wars and a long cold war; and time and again, reached out across the globe to millions who, like us, longed for the blessings of liberty.

Along the way, Americans produced a great middle class and security in old age; built unrivaled centers of learning and opened public schools to all; split the atom and explored the heavens; invented the computer and the microchip; and deepened the wellspring of justice by making a revolution in civil rights for African Americans and all minorities, and extending the circle of citizenship, opportunity and dignity to women.

Now, for the third time, a new century is upon us, and another time to choose. We began the 19th century with a choice, to spread our nation from coast to coast. We began the 20th century with a choice, to harness the Industrial Revolution to our values of free enterprise, conservation, and human decency. Those choices made all the difference. At the dawn of the 21st century a free people must now choose to shape the forces of the Information Age and the global society, to unleash the limitless potential of all our people, and, yes, to form a more perfect union.

When last we gathered, our march to this new future seemed less certain than it does today. We vowed then to set a clear course to renew our nation.

In these four years, we have been touched by tragedy, exhilarated by challenge, strengthened by achievement. America stands alone as the world's indispensable nation. Once again, our economy is the strongest on Earth. Once again, we are building stronger families, thriving communities, better educational opportunities, a cleaner environment. Problems that once seemed destined to deepen now bend to our efforts: our streets are safer and record numbers of our fellow citizens have moved from welfare to work.

And once again, we have resolved for our time a great debate over the role of government. Today we can declare: Government is not the problem, and government is not the solution. We—the American people—we are the solution. Our founders understood that well and gave us a democracy strong enough to endure for centuries, flexible enough to face our common challenges and advance our common dreams in each new day.

As times change, so government must change. We need a new government for a new century—humble enough not to try to solve all our problems for us, but strong enough to give us the tools to solve our problems for ourselves; a government that is smaller, lives within its means, and does more with less. Yet where it can stand up for our values and interests in the world, and where it can give Americans the power to make a real difference in their everyday lives, government should do more, not less. The preeminent mission of our new government is to give all Americans an opportunity—not a guarantee, but a real opportunity—to build better lives.

Beyond that, my fellow citizens, the future is up to us. Our founders taught us that the preservation of our liberty and our union depends upon responsible citizenship. And we need a new sense of responsibility for a new century. There is work to do, work that government alone cannot do: teaching children to read; hiring people off welfare rolls; coming out from behind locked doors and shuttered windows to help reclaim our streets from drugs and gangs and crime; taking time out of our own lives to serve others.

Each and every one of us, in our own way, must assume personal responsibility—not only for ourselves and our families, but for our neighbors and our nation. Our greatest responsibility is to embrace a new spirit of community for a new century. For any one of us to succeed, we must succeed as one America.

The challenge of our past remains the challenge of our future—will we be one nation, one people, with one common destiny, or not? Will we all come together, or come apart?

The divide of race has been America's constant curse. And each new wave of immigrants gives new targets to old prejudices. Prejudice and contempt, cloaked in the pretense of religious or political conviction are no different. These forces have nearly destroyed our nation in the past. They plague us still. They fuel the fanaticism of terror. And they torment the lives of millions in fractured nations all around the world.

These obsessions cripple both those who hate and, of course, those who are hated, robbing both of what they might become. We cannot, we will not, succumb to the dark impulses that lurk in the far regions of the soul everywhere. We shall overcome them. And we shall replace them with the generous spirit of a people who feel at home with one another.

Our rich texture of racial, religious and political diversity will be a Godsend in the 21st century. Great rewards will come to those who can live together, learn together, work together, forge new ties that bind together. As this new era approaches we can already see its broad outlines. Ten years ago, the Internet was the mystical province of physicists; today, it is a commonplace encyclopedia for millions of schoolchildren. Scientists now are decoding the blueprint of human life. Cures for our most feared illnesses seem close at hand.

The world is no longer divided into two hostile camps. Instead, now we are building bonds with nations that once were our adversaries. Growing connections of commerce and culture give us a chance to lift the fortunes and spirits of people the world over. And for the very first time in all of history, more people on this planet live under democracy than dictatorship.

My fellow Americans, as we look back at this remarkable century, we may ask, can we hope not just to follow, but even to surpass the achievements of the 20th century in America and to avoid the awful bloodshed that stained its legacy? To that question, every American here and every American in our land today must answer a resounding "Yes." This is the heart of our task. With a new vision of government, a new sense of responsibility, a new spirit of community, we will sustain America's journey. The promise we sought in a new land we will find again in a land of new promise.

In this new land, education will be every citizen's most prized possession. Our schools will have the highest standards in the world, igniting the spark of possibility in the eyes of every girl and every boy. And the doors of higher education will be open to all. The knowledge and power of the Information Age will be within reach not just of the few, but of every classroom, every library, every child. Parents and children will have time not only to work, but to read and play together. And the plans they make at their kitchen table will be those of a better home, a better job, the certain chance to go to college.

Our streets will echo again with the laughter of our children, because no one will try to shoot them or sell them drugs anymore. Everyone who can work, will work, with today's permanent under class part of tomorrow's growing middle class. New miracles of medicine at last will reach not only those who can claim care now, but the children and hardworking families too long denied. We will stand mighty for peace and freedom, and maintain a strong defense against terror and destruction. Our children will sleep free from the threat of nuclear, chemical or biological weapons. Ports and airports, farms and factories will thrive with trade and innovation and ideas. And the world's greatest democracy will lead a whole world of democracies.

Our land of new promise will be a nation that meets its obligations—a nation that balances its budget, but never loses the balance of its values. A nation where our grandparents have secure retirement and health care, and their grandchildren know we have made the reforms necessary to sustain those benefits for their time. A nation that fortifies the world's most productive economy even as it protects the great natural bounty of our water, air, and majestic land.

And in this land of new promise, we will have reformed our politics so that the voice of the people will always speak louder than the din of narrow interests—regaining the participation and deserving the trust of all Americans.

Fellow citizens, let us build that America, a nation ever moving forward toward realizing the full potential of all its citizens. Prosperity and power—yes, they are important, and we must maintain them. But let us never forget: The greatest progress we have made, and the greatest progress we have yet to make, is in the human heart. In the end, all the world's wealth and a thousand armies are no match for the strength and decency of the human spirit.

Thirty-four years ago, the man whose life we celebrate today spoke to us down there, at the other end of this Mall, in words that moved the conscience of a nation. Like a prophet of old, he told of his dream that one day America would rise up and treat all its citizens as equals before the law and in the heart. Martin Luther King's dream was the American Dream. His quest is our quest: the ceaseless striving to live out our true creed. Our history has been built on such dreams and labors. And by our dreams and labors we will redeem the promise of America in the 21st century.

To that effort I pledge all my strength and every power of my office. I ask the members of Congress here to join in that pledge. The American people returned to office a President of one party and a Congress of another. Surely, they did not do this to advance the politics of petty bickering and extreme partisanship they plainly deplore. No, they call on us instead to be repairers of the breach, and to move on with America's mission. America demands and deserves big things from us—and nothing big ever came from being small. Let us remember the timeless wisdom of Cardinal Bernardin, when facing the end of his own life. He said: "It is wrong to waste the precious gift of time, on acrimony and division."

Fellow citizens, we must not waste the precious gift of this time. For all of us are on that same journey of our lives, and our journey, too, will come to an end. But the journey of our America must go on. And so, my fellow Americans, we must be strong, for there is much to dare. The demands of our time are great and they are different. Let us meet them with faith and courage, with patience and a grateful and happy heart. Let us shape the hope of this day into the noblest chapter in our history. Yes, let us build our bridge. A bridge wide enough and strong enough for every American to cross over to a blessed land of new promise.

May those generations whose faces we cannot yet see, whose names we may never know, say of us here that we led our beloved land into a new century with the American Dream alive for all her children; with the American promise of a more perfect union a reality for all her people; with America's bright flame of freedom spreading throughout all the world.

From the height of this place and the summit of this century, let us go forth. May God strengthen our hands for the good work ahead—and always, always bless our America.

George W. Bush

Inaugural Address

Saturday, January 20, 2001

President Clinton, distinguished guests and my fellow citizens, the peaceful transfer of authority is rare in history, yet common in our country. With a simple oath, we affirm old traditions and make new beginnings.

As I begin, I thank President Clinton for his service to our nation. And I thank Vice President Gore for a contest conducted with spirit and ended with grace.

I am honored and humbled to stand here, where so many of America's leaders have come before me, and so many will follow. We have a place, all of us, in a long story—a story we continue, but whose end we will not see. It is the story of a new world that became a friend and liberator of the old, a story of a slave-holding society that became a servant of freedom, the story of a power that went into the world to protect but not possess, to defend but not to conquer.

It is the American story—a story of flawed and fallible people, united across the generations by grand and enduring ideals.

The grandest of these ideals is an unfolding American promise that everyone belongs, that everyone deserves a chance, that no insignificant person was ever born.

Americans are called to enact this promise in our lives and in our laws. And though our nation has sometimes halted, and sometimes delayed, we must follow no other course.

Through much of the last century, America's faith in freedom and democracy was a rock in a raging sea. Now it is a seed upon the wind, taking root in many nations.

Our democratic faith is more than the creed of our country, it is the inborn hope of our humanity, an ideal we carry but do not own, a trust we bear and pass along. And even after nearly 225 years, we have a long way yet to travel.

While many of our citizens prosper, others doubt the promise, even the justice, of our own country. The ambitions of some Americans are limited by failing schools and hidden prejudice and the circumstances of their birth. And sometimes our differences run so deep, it seems we share a continent, but not a country.

We do not accept this, and we will not allow it. Our unity, our union, is the serious work of leaders and citizens in every generation. And this is my solemn pledge: I will work to build a single nation of justice and opportunity.

I know this is in our reach because we are guided by a power larger than ourselves who creates us equal in His image.

And we are confident in principles that unite and lead us onward. America has never been united by blood or birth or soil. We are bound by ideals that move us beyond our backgrounds, lift us above our interests and teach us what it means to be citizens. Every child must be taught these principles. Every citizen must uphold them. And every immigrant, by embracing these ideals, makes our country more, not less, American.

Today, we affirm a new commitment to live out our nation's promise through civility, courage, compassion and character.

America, at its best, matches a commitment to principle with a concern for civility. A civil society demands from each of us good will and respect, fair dealing and forgiveness.

Some seem to believe that our politics can afford to be petty because, in a time of peace, the stakes of our debates appear small.

But the stakes for America are never small. If our country does not lead the cause of freedom, it will not be led. If we do not turn the hearts of children toward knowledge and character, we will lose their gifts and undermine their idealism. If we permit our economy to drift and decline, the vulnerable will suffer most.

We must live up to the calling we share. Civility is not a tactic or a sentiment. It is the determined choice of trust over cynicism, of community over chaos. And this commitment, if we keep it, is a way to shared accomplishment. America, at its best, is also courageous.

Our national courage has been clear in times of depression and war, when defending common dangers defined our common good. Now we must choose if the example of our fathers and mothers will inspire us or condemn us. We must show courage in a time of blessing by confronting problems instead of passing them on to future generations.

Together, we will reclaim America's schools, before ignorance and apathy claim more young lives.

We will reform Social Security and Medicare, sparing our children from struggles we have the power to prevent. And we will reduce taxes, to recover the momentum of our economy and reward the effort and enterprise of working Americans.

We will build our defenses beyond challenge, lest weakness invite challenge.

We will confront weapons of mass destruction, so that a new century is spared new horrors.

The enemies of liberty and our country should make no mistake: America remains engaged in the world by history and by choice, shaping a balance of power that favors freedom. We will defend our allies and our interests. We will show purpose without arrogance. We will meet aggression and bad faith with resolve and strength. And to all nations, we will speak for the values that gave our nation birth.

America, at its best, is compassionate. In the quiet of American conscience, we know that deep, persistent poverty is unworthy of our nation's promise.

And whatever our views of its cause, we can agree that children at risk are not at fault. Abandonment and abuse are not acts of God, they are failures of love.

And the proliferation of prisons, however necessary, is no substitute for hope and order in our souls.

Where there is suffering, there is duty. Americans in need are not strangers, they are citizens, not problems, but priorities. And all of us are diminished when any are hopeless.

Government has great responsibilities for public safety and public health, for civil rights and common schools. Yet compassion is the work of a nation, not just a government.

And some needs and hurts are so deep they will only respond to a mentor's touch or a pastor's prayer. Church and charity, synagogue and mosque lend our communities their humanity, and they will have an honored place in our plans and in our laws.

Many in our country do not know the pain of poverty, but we can listen to those who do.

And I can pledge our nation to a goal: When we see that wounded traveler on the road to Jericho, we will not pass to the other side.

America, at its best, is a place where personal responsibility is valued and expected.

Encouraging responsibility is not a search for scapegoats, it is a call to conscience. And though it requires sacrifice, it brings a deeper fulfillment. We find the fullness of life not only in options, but in commitments. And we find that children and community are the commitments that set us free.

Our public interest depends on private character, on civic duty and family bonds and basic fairness, on uncounted, unhonored acts of decency which give direction to our freedom.

Sometimes in life we are called to do great things. But as a saint of our times has said, every day we are called to do small things with great love. The most important tasks of a democracy are done by everyone.

I will live and lead by these principles: to advance my convictions with civility, to pursue the public interest with courage, to speak for greater justice and compassion, to call for responsibility and try to live it as well.

In all these ways, I will bring the values of our history to the care of our times.

What you do is as important as anything government does. I ask you to seek a common good beyond your comfort; to defend needed reforms against easy attacks; to serve your nation, beginning with your neighbor. I ask you to be citizens: citizens, not spectators; citizens, not subjects; responsible citizens, building communities of service and a nation of character.

Americans are generous and strong and decent, not because we believe in ourselves, but because we hold beliefs beyond ourselves. When this spirit of citizenship is missing, no government program can replace it. When this spirit is present, no wrong can stand against it.

After the Declaration of Independence was signed, Virginia statesman John Page wrote to Thomas Jefferson: "We know the race is not to the swift nor the battle to the strong. Do you not think an angel rides in the whirlwind and directs this storm?"

Much time has passed since Jefferson arrived for his inauguration. The years and changes accumulate. But the themes of this day he would know: our nation's grand story of courage and its simple dream of dignity.

We are not this story's author, who fills time and eternity with his purpose. Yet his purpose is achieved in our duty, and our duty is fulfilled in service to one another.

Never tiring, never yielding, never finishing, we renew that purpose today, to make our country more just and generous, to affirm the dignity of our lives and every life.

This work continues. This story goes on. And an angel still rides in the whirlwind and directs this storm.

God bless you all, and God bless America.

INDEX

Index